Tax Reform in Developing Countries

Tax Reform in Developing Countries

·········

Malcolm Gillis, Editor

·········

Fiscal Reform in the Developing World

Duke University Press   Durham and London

1989

© 1989 Duke University Press
All rights reserved
Printed in the United States of America
on acid-free paper ∞
Library of Congress Cataloging-in-Publication Data
Tax reform in developing countries / edited
by Malcolm Gillis.
p. cm.
Based on papers presented at a conference held in Washington in
Apr. 1988.
Includes bibliographies and index.
ISBN 0-8223-0874-6. — ISBN 0-8223-0898-3 (pbk.)
1. Taxation—Developing countries—Congresses. I. Gillis,
Malcolm.
HJ2351.7.L47   1989
336.2'05'091724—dc19   88-36859 CIP

For Eva May and Douglas

Contents

·······

Acknowledgments

....

The book, and the conference upon which it was essentially based, is a product of the Center for International Development Research (CIDR) of the Institute of Policy Sciences at Duke University. Several staff members and graduate students associated with CIDR and the Graduate School have played instrumental roles in transforming conference papers into the book chapters contained herein. They include Janet Syme, Tom Campbell, Leej Copperfield, Catherine Johnson, and Ginger Brent. In addition, a group of hardworking, efficient staff within CIDR managed logistics and word processing in order to complete the volume ahead of schedule: Steve Ganote, Monica Mapp, Joyce Persaud, Brent Fogt, and Tanya Hinesley.

Research for this volume, as well as the April 1988 conference where results were presented, was financed by the United States Agency for International Development (USAID), under grant number PDC-0085-GSS-6048-00.

·······

Introduction

·······

Malcolm Gillis

I. Tax Reform: Worldwide Phenomenon?

In introducing a recent Brookings study of tax reform in eleven industrial nations in the eighties, a noted tax analyst concluded: "In judging
by this sample of countries, the tax reform movement is almost universal. Many reforms have already been put into place, and others are being
phased in over a period of years. By the end of the 1980s the developed
world will have lower individual and corporate tax rates and fewer tax
preferences, particularly incentives for investment, than at the beginning of the decade."[1]

Although the focus of the present volume is that of the entire postwar period, rather than the present decade alone, the studies included
herein, taken together with those of the Brookings book, support an
even broader generalization than that presented in quotes above: the
tax reform movement is pervasive not only among developed nations,
but also among the over 100 nations that are conventionally classified
as "developing." Moreover, this volume indicates that the pace of tax
reform among developing countries has been accelerating since the
mid-1970s, and for many of the same reasons as offered in the introduction and overview papers of the Brookings study: the almost universal
recognition of the distortions and inequities created by high tax rates,
years of inflation, and ineffective tax preferences.[2] Finally, the thrust of
tax reform programs in developing nations in the past decade and a half
has been notably, almost remarkably, similar to that found in developed
nations in the 1980s. The present worldwide wave of tax reform has
been not only to "level the playing field" in income taxation through
base broadening and rate flattening both in industrial[3] and developing

nations, but in developing nations it has also involved a shift toward more comprehensive, simpler, internal indirect taxes levied at rates much more uniform than were common even a decade ago.

Much of the stimulus for worldwide episodes of tax reform, particularly those of more recent vintage, has been attributed to a response to the 1986 U.S. reform.[4] The U.S. example has been a noticeable factor in motivating income tax reform in developing nations as well, particularly since the 1986 reductions in U.S. corporate tax rates have caused some developing nations to reexamine the creditability of their income taxes against those of the U.S. Otherwise, "demonstration effects" of the U.S. 1986 reform for developing countries do not appear all that strong, particularly since base broadening and rate flattening were major features in both income and sales tax reforms in many LDCs prior to 1986. This was as true for experiences studied in detail in this volume, such as Chile and Uruguay (Harberger, chapter 2), Colombia (McLure, chapter 3), Indonesia (Gillis, chapter 4), Jamaica (Bahl, chapter 5), as for another diverse set of nations cited herein, including India, Pakistan, Bolivia, Thailand, Nicaragua, and Turkey (Gillis, chapter 14).

For the bulk of those developing countries that have enacted or attempted major tax reforms in the past decade and a half, reform was animated not so much by political ideology or by examples elsewhere, but by realization of the glaring inequities and inefficiencies that have resulted from decades of efforts to impose high tax rates on constricted tax bases under complex legislation in the presence of weak tax administration (Bird, chapter 9). Under such circumstances, the redistributive, developmental, and revenue goals of tax policy in LDCs proved impossible to attain. Simply put, the tax systems of most LDCs were, more often than not, designed to conform to conditions prevailing in very few of them. Tax simplification, which under present technology *requires* base broadening and rate flattening, has therefore been an unavoidable feature of successful tax reforms.

II. Genesis of the Present Volume

This book has its origins in conversations between the editor and Neal Riden of USAID in Washington in the fall of 1985, at a time when the results of several recent and/or pending tax reforms in North America, Europe, Asia, and Latin America were very much in doubt. In reviewing nascent reform activity in several South and Southeast Asian nations and in the Caribbean, Riden and the editor began to cast about for compendia containing illustrative lessons from the postwar experience with tax reform in LDCs.

This experience was known to be most variegated, and possibly rich. Between themselves, the two identified perhaps twenty examples of what this book has called *comprehensive* tax reform (Gillis, chapter 1), and dozens of episodes of significant *partial* reforms. Moreover, many of the economists, lawyers, and government officials who had helped to instigate or at least facilitate many of those reforms were still involved to one degree or another in the design and/or implementation of tax reform around the world. This group included the four American "deans" of tax reform—John Due, Arnold Harberger, Richard Musgrave, and Carl Shoup—as well as a number of somewhat younger economists and lawyers in universities, governments, and international organizations, including Roy Bahl, Richard Bird, Milka Casanegra, Sijbren Cnossen, Robert Conrad, Glenn Jenkins, Hiroshi Kaneko, Charles McLure, Guillermo Perry, and Miguel Urrutia.

Riden and the editor were surprised and somewhat chagrined to learn that not only had none of these individuals, jointly or separately, mounted an effort to consolidate and crystallize the lessons that might be drawn from postwar experience with tax reform across LDCs, none had any immediate plans to do so. Both from the editor's own experience in Bolivia, Colombia, Ghana, and Indonesia, and from Riden's long background in USAID, it was clear that a compendium of such lessons would be of potentially great utility to the growing numbers of LDCs that, for reasons discussed in chapter 1, might be contemplating tax reform in the 1980s and 1990s. This seemed particularly so given that a sizeable share of the energies expended in preparing for tax reform was typically, in our experience, devoted to the search (usually unsystematic) for structural and administrative innovations in taxation that worked well elsewhere, and an equally serious search to uncover examples of measures that proved unworkable in other LDCs, the better to avoid repeating these mistakes.

Accordingly, plans were drawn up for a major research project, financed by U.S. Agency for International Development (USAID), and administered through the Center for International Development Research of the Institute for Policy Sciences at Duke University. The project was designed to focus on lessons from postwar experience from tax reform in LDCs. As many of the experienced tax reform hands cited above as proved available, as well as relative newcomers to the field, would be called upon to distill their experiences into lessons that would be readily accessible and readily understandable for LDC tax authorities about to embark on programs of tax reform. One innovation of the project was the commissioning of papers by two political scientists to help illuminate the political dimensions of tax reform commonly overlooked by economists. Papers resulting from this process would be presented at a major conference involving not only the authors but also other practitioners who were initially unavailable for the undertaking of specific studies, officials of international organizations, and many representatives from countries affected by the reforms under review.

The studies would be confined to developing countries, with one important exception: the Japanese reform of 1949–50. The Japanese reform was included for two reasons. First, the Shoup Mission to Japan in those years was the first postwar example of a comprehensive tax reform program. Second, the Japanese experience was viewed as relevant for LDCs because Japan was at the time a war-torn nation under reconstruction, facing in 1949 many of the same types of tax reform issues as now encountered by such middle- and higher-income LDCs as Taiwan, Korea, Argentina, Colombia, and Chile. Indeed, many of the roots of the very recent controversy over tax reform in Japan may be traced to problems identified by the Shoup Mission in 1949 and 1950. This is true not only for those aspects of the Shoup recommendations that were accepted and enacted into law (and were still the basis of the Japanese income tax system in 1987) but several elements of the Shoup proposals that were ultimately rejected. Most prominent of the latter was the 1949 Shoup recommendation for a value-added tax. Although enacted into law, the tax was never implemented. A proposed value-added tax, this time to apply nationally, was again rejected in 1987, and for many of the same reasons as in 1950. Still, even after nearly four decades, the value-added tax remains a live, if contentious, fiscal issue in Japan.

In the end, more than a dozen papers were presented and critiqued at a conference organized by the editor and Mary Altomare, Executive Administrator of CIDR, held in Washington in late April. Tax reform experiences of eleven nations were discussed in some detail. These included Chile, Uruguay, and Mexico (chapter 2), Colombia (chapter 3), Indonesia (chapter 4), Jamaica (chapter 5), Japan (chapter 6), Sri Lanka (chapter 7), and Venezuela, Brazil, and Liberia (chapter 8). Appropriate lessons were drawn not only from these episodes but also from about two dozen other cases about which conference participants had some degree of special knowledge. In addition, five of the papers dealt with what might be called "generic," or crosscutting, issues commonly encountered in developing country tax reform efforts. Chapter 9, for example, deals with the much acknowledged but nevertheless often slighted administrative dimensions of tax reform. Chapter 10 draws major lessons for LDCs of U.S. tax reform in the eighties. Chapter 11 shows how new approaches in developing and applying simple general equilibrium models can help facilitate tax and other policy reforms in LDCs, primarily by helping to insure that the right questions get asked. Chapters 12 and 13, written by two political scientists, cover issues ordinarily neglected by economists and lawyers involved in tax reform (particularly the former): political constraints upon and political opportunities in tax reform.

The final chapter presents the editor's conception of what might be called the lessons that may be drawn from the rich worldwide experience with tax reform in LDCs over the postwar period, particularly the past decade and a half. These lessons were distilled not only from the papers presented at the conference, but from observations supplied in formal comments on each paper as well as those provided by general conference participants (Appendix 1 at the end of the book contains a list of all speakers and commentators for the conference). The spirited discussions that followed each paper resulted not only in significant changes in the final chapter, but in the tone if not the conclusions of the other thirteen chapters.

Notes

1 Joseph A. Pechman, "Introduction," in Joseph A. Pechman, ed., *World Tax Reform: A Progress Report* (Washington, The Brookings Institution, 1988), p. 13.
2 Pechman, "Introduction," p. 1.
3 Cf. Sijbren Cnossen, "Overview," in Pechman, ed., p. 263.
4 Cf. Charles E. McLure, chapter 10, this volume; Pechman, "Introduction"; John Bossons, "Comment," in Pechman, ed., p. 69; Adalbert Uelner and Thomas Menck, "Germany," in Pechman, ed., p. 120; Flip de Kam, "Comment," in Pechman, ed., p. 180; Leif Muten, "Comment," in Pechman, ed., p. 213.

1

....

Toward a Taxonomy for Tax Reform

....

Malcolm Gillis

I. Introduction

There have been perhaps one hundred identifiable attempts at major tax reform in developing nations since 1945. Many nations have made repeated attempts at tax reform in the postwar era; virtually no country has retained tax systems resembling those in place in the late 1940s. In 1987 alone, major reform efforts were under way in several countries, including Kenya, Malawi, Pakistan, and Thailand. This volume examines this rich worldwide experience in search of lessons of possible value to governments for which tax reform may become advisable or inevitable in the years to come.

While no less controversial a topic now than 40 years ago, tax reform has in the last decade become a matter of urgency in many developing countries (LDCs) in Asia, Africa, and Latin America, particularly since the latitude for other alternatives for public sector finance has shrunk. Inflation and borrowing appear much less viable as methods of resource mobilization than before 1980. Although the pace of inflation has accelerated, not declined, in many LDCs in the past decade, the corrosive effects of inflation upon growth, development, and income distribution are now more widely recognized than ever before. In the wake of the continuing international debt crisis, the flow of new resources from external borrowing has slowed to a trickle; the arrested development of money and capital markets in most developing countries precludes heavy reliance on domestic borrowing for orderly finance of government activity.

Governments in the 1980s have therefore increasingly looked to the tax system, not only for incremental finance but to help supplant resources formerly raised through inflation and/or borrowing. But few tax systems in place have proven capable of bearing the additional strain made all the more insupportable by debt service obligations that in many cases account for one-third or more of current government spending.

Growing imbalance between fiscal receipts and fiscal revenues has been the result in dozens of countries. Governments that have been unwilling or unable to reduce spending have, given the unavailability of debt service relief, either attempted major changes in taxation to restore orderly mobilization of resources, or by default have increasingly resorted to the disorderly process of inflationary finance.

A. An Outline of the Attributes of Reform

Few postwar tax-reform programs in LDCs have fulfilled the expectations of their architects. Several ambitious attempts were total failures. A small number have encountered limited short-run success, only to falter later; still fewer have been relatively successful over longer periods of time. Generalizing from the rich postwar reform experience in LDCs is extremely difficult both because many such efforts have not been well documented, and because there have been so many different kinds of tax reforms that the phrase has come to mean both everything and nothing about changes in tax policy during economic development.

Many lessons that may be learned from the variegated history of tax-reform undertakings in developing countries have been obscured precisely because "tax reform" can have so many meanings. Successful distillation of the lessons of experience from tax reforms in LDCs requires development of a serviceable *taxonomy* of tax reform. This chapter presents such a taxonomy. It has been developed primarily, but not exclusively, from examination of the tax-reform experiences included in this volume. But the discussion has also been informed by review of reform episodes in several other nations, including Ghana, Bolivia, Korea, Thailand, Pakistan, India, and Argentina. Absent such a taxonomy, generalizations about the aims and results of tax reform across countries involve comparisons not of apples with apples, nor even apples with pears, but rather apples with azaleas.

Close review of the experience of more than twenty-five reform initiatives since 1945 suggests that at least six general attributes may be utilized to classify tax-reform programs into categories that may facilitate systematic comparison of tax-reform efforts, including their outcomes. These attributes are:

(1) Breadth of Reform. A tax reform may focus on the entire *tax system,* including institutions for tax administration and compliance, or may be concerned only with changes in *tax structure.*

(2) Scope of Reform. Tax reform may be *comprehensive,* in the sense that it is intended to encompass most of the important revenue sources, or it may be *partial,* wherein reform efforts are confined to one or two significant components of the tax system.

(3) Revenue Goals. Tax reforms may be designed to increase tax reve-nues as a percent of GNP, in which case they are intended to be *revenue enhancing.* In some cases, however, tax-reform programs merely seek to replace the revenues the tax system would have generated absent reform. This is called *revenue neutral reform.* Examples of tax reforms designed to *reduce* overall *tax revenues* may exist, but documented examples appear unavailable.

(4) Equity Goals. Virtually all LDC tax-reform initiatives have been designed with specific equity objectives in mind, where tax equity is understood to involve both vertical and horizontal dimensions.

Vertical equity in taxation is typically taken to mean that people with unequal income (or consumption or wealth) should be treated unequally; those with higher incomes (consumption, wealth) should then ordinarily pay commensurately higher taxes. Horizontal equity is much easier to define than to measure. Horizontal equity in taxation is generally taken to require that equals (people in like circumstances) should be treated equally. Thus, according to this criterion, households with similar income and family circumstances should pay roughly equal taxes.

Policymakers have often sought tax reform that could enhance verti-cal equity through reduction of after-tax income inequality. Such reforms are here called *redistributive* in nature. On the other hand, reform programs have been implemented whose intent was to leave the distribution of income essentially unchanged. This is known as *distri-butionally neutral* reform. Both redistributive and distributionally neu-tral tax reform ordinarily seek also to rectify horizontal inequities. But for reasons developed below, the taxonomy does not include a separate category relating to horizontal equity.

(5) Resource Allocation Goals. In recent years there have been several instances where reforms have sought to reduce the scope for tax-induced barriers to more efficient resource allocation in LDCs. Such tax-reform programs may be labeled as *economically neutral.* On the other hand, governments have on occasion sought to use the tax system to influence the flow of resources to particular economic sectors or activities of priority to governments. Tax reforms so oriented are here called *interventionist* reforms.

(6) Timing of Reform. Some tax reforms have been designed to have all tax policy changes enacted at one time. These are examples of *contemporaneous* reforms. Other reforms have been implemented in separate, successive steps, and may be called *phased* reforms. Finally, there are a few examples of *successive* reforms, wherein essentially unrelated tax policy changes are enacted over a several-year period.

B. Using the Taxonomy

The six attributes outlined above provide a basis for classifying tax-reform programs according to their principal earmarks. The taxonomy must, however, be used with some care, not only because it is far from airtight, but also because not all reform programs can be adequately characterized by the six principal attributes used here.

(1) Breadth of Reform. Evidence cited later in this chapter and throughout this volume suggests that a necessary, but hardly sufficient, condition for successful tax reform in LDCs is that the reform program must result in fundamental changes in *tax systems.* A tax system has two principal, interdependent elements: the *tax structure,* and the mosaic of mechanisms and institutions governing *tax administration* and *tax compliance.* Most of the early postwar reforms focused primarily upon alterations in the tax structure alone, ordinarily a sufficient condition for failure of comprehensive if not partial reforms (see below). The tax structure consists of the configurations of tax bases and tax rates provided in legislation and/or decrees. Although it is sometimes obscured by layer upon layer of provisions enacted piecemeal over several decades, the tax structure is the most visible component of the tax system. Mechanisms and institutions of tax administration and compliance, however, include both readily observable as well as veiled elements often overlooked in diagnoses of fiscal ills. These include the procedural and legal frameworks governing assessment, collection, audit, sanctions,

appeals, and record keeping as well as the state of information technology, the reward structure facing the civil service, disclosure requirements for firms, and accounting conventions used by them.

(2) Scope of Reform. The normal state of tax systems thus defined is that of flux, not stasis. Modifications made on a more or less continuous basis, whether in underlying laws or in administrative rules and procedures, are best described as *tax adjustments* rather than reform. Changes in the tax system qualify as *tax reform* only when they involve discontinuity and significantly alter the trajectory of the system. Tax reform may embrace all or only a few major tax sources (income taxes, sales taxes, property taxes, import duties, etc.). When these changes include most or all important tax sources, they may be labeled *comprehensive* tax reform. Where reforms are undertaken only for one or two tax sources affecting less than, say, one-third of collections, they may be labeled *partial*.

(3) Revenue Goals. Partial as well as comprehensive tax-reform initiatives are often undertaken for *revenue enhancement*. But as subsequent chapters show, a significant number of reforms have been designed under the constraint that tax reform should *not* result, overall, in significant changes in the share of taxes in GNP, at least in the short term. These are examples of *revenue neutral* tax reform, wherein the time horizon for revenue neutrality is usually greater than one or two years.

(4) Equity Goals. Revenue neutral tax reform is not necessarily *distributionally neutral*, nor *economically neutral* tax reform.[1] Distributionally neutral tax reform is contrasted with *redistributive* tax reform that seeks significant alterations in vertical equity. Reforms geared to the former but not the latter objective are intended to preserve the preexistent pattern of aggregate tax liabilities across income brackets; the mix of these liabilities, however, may change drastically—as in, for example, replacement of wealth taxes by income taxes. Some tax reforms are explicitly distributionally neutral in terms of vertical equity, so as not to trigger distributional battles over the passage of the tax reform. Redistributive tax reform, it will be shown, may aim either at *"leveling down"* or *"leveling up"* in the income distribution, or both.

Improvement of horizontal equity is a common and often implicitly stated goal of tax reform. But care must be taken to avoid directly carrying over to LDCs, without substantial modification, concepts of horizontal (and vertical) equity initially developed to apply to conditions prevailing in high-income industrial countries. McLure (chapter 10) provides no fewer than four reasons why this is so. Tax reformers around the world have been mindful of the corrosive effects on taxpayer compliance of the existence of, or even the perception of, long-standing horizontal inequities. Horizontal equity in taxation, however, has proven much easier to describe than to secure, especially when, as in most LDCs, deficiencies in tax administration lead to horizontal inequities even when structures have been designed to minimize them. Indeed, tax evasion in LDCs may rival or surpass poor tax structure as a source of inequities. Still, since there do not seem to be any positive economic or political gains from reforms that deliberately seek to worsen horizontal equity, it is reasonable to assume that enhancement of, or at least maintenance of, horizontal equity (however defined) is an objective common to all reforms. That being the case, the taxonomy developed here need not include horizontal equity as a separate attribute for classifying reform programs.

(5) Resource Allocation GoalsReforms that are intended to be either revenue neutral or distributionally neutral may or may not also have economic neutrality as an objective. But reforms geared both to revenue and distributional neutrality typically have economic neutrality as an overriding goal. As discussed at greater length below, an economically "neutral" tax structure is not necessarily an "optimal" tax structure, nor even an "efficient" one. Rather, a neutral tax system is one that raises the desired amount of revenue in such a way as to leave economic decisions unaffected, except by the effects of taxes in reducing real income and wealth. Absent radical improvements in the effectiveness of tax administration, greater neutrality in taxation is generally thought to require a shift toward more uniformity in rates and greater consistency in definition of the tax base. And we will see (chapters 10 and 14) that attempts to purge the tax system of apparent horizontal inequities may be more important in reducing distortions in resource allocation than in improving horizontal equity.

Whereas the goals of revenue neutrality and distributional neutrality imply maintenance of the status quo in collections and income distribution respectively, pursuit of economic neutrality generally involves deliberate departures from the status quo, in that fewer and less severe tax-induced distortions are sought relative to those prior to reform. Economically neutral tax reform lies at one end of a continuum having *interventionist* tax reform at the other end. In the latter, deliberate attempts are made to use the tax system to guide private decision making to ends sought by the government. Early postwar tax reforms were closer to the interventionist end of the continuum than have been most reforms implemented or proposed after 1975.

(6) Timing of Reform. Finally, tax reforms differ with regard to phasing of implementation. This may be critical for the success of comprehensive reform efforts, for reasons offered below, but is largely irrelevant for partial reforms. Most commonly, governments have announced and attempted to implement all reform provisions at once. This can be called *contemporaneous* tax reform, even when transition rules delay full applicability of changes until subsequent years. Tax-reform measures announced and implemented in distinct stages, as integral parts of a larger design, are examples of *phased* tax reform. Finally, reform enacted serially on a tax-by-tax basis, with little more than incidental reference to a larger design, may be called *successive* tax reform.

It is readily apparent, therefore, that "tax reform" has many meanings. The taxonomy presented here refers only to differences in policymakers' *intentions* for tax reform, not to the extent to which these intentions are fulfilled in any given reform episode. Even so, the taxonomy yields more than two hundred different configurations of tax reform even without distinguishing between redistributive reforms that attempt to "level up" or "level down." That is to say, policymakers face at least six sets of alternatives in framing tax reform. To recapitulate, these are:

(a) reform of tax structures, or tax administration, or reform of tax systems (both structural and administrative reform)
   (b) comprehensive or partial reform
   (c) revenue-enhancing, revenue neutral, or revenue-decreasing reform
   (d) distributionally neutral or redistributive tax reform
   (e) economically neutral or interventionist reform
   (f) contemporaneous, phased, or successive reform

There are two choices in all but (a), (c), and (f), which contain three each, so the number of apparent combinations is $2^3 \times 3^3 = 216$, where all options are open. However, not all options are open in all cases. For example, a country constrained to seek revenue enhancement to meet a crisis in debt service would, at the very most, contemplate seventy-two different paths to tax reform ($2^3 \times 1^1 \times 3^2$). And as a practical matter, even fewer options are open in most cases, so that feasible paths to tax reform may number less than 10.

II. Sources of Lessons of Tax Reform

At least two dozen comprehensive tax-reform proposals have been proposed for developing countries from 1945 through 1987, several of which have been enacted in whole or in part. Examples of successful and unsuccessful partial tax reforms over the same period number in the dozens.

A. Comprehensive vs. Partial Reform

The first truly comprehensive postwar tax reform anywhere was that in occupied Japan in 1949–50,[2] at a time when that war-torn nation was then a rebuilding, if not a developing, country. Over the next three and a half decades, full-blown sets of proposals for reform of all major taxes were fashioned for Venezuela[3] in 1958–59, Colombia in 1968,[4] 1974, and 1986, and Liberia[5] in 1969. Chile[6] enacted major reforms in income, sales, and trade taxes in 1974–75, featuring both a value-added tax and a uniform import tariff applicable to all but autos. The Chilean episodes were notable also in that they involved the first attempt among LDCs to achieve full integration of the personal and corporation income tax (since discarded in favor of partial integration). A major comprehensive reform effort in Bolivia was aborted[7] in 1976–77. More recently, comprehensive reforms were proposed and enacted in Indonesia (1983–84),[8] Jamaica (1985–87)[9], and Bolivia (1986) and proposed for Pakistan (1986–87).[10]

Particularly notable among the dozens of partial reforms were the Kaldor-inspired innovations in India (1956)[11] and Sri Lanka (1959),[12] Brazil (1965),[13] and three cases in Uruguay (1967, 1968, and 1974–75).[14] Both the India and Sri Lanka episodes mark important milestones in tax reform: they were the first attempts to introduce a direct tax on expenditures as part of an interlocking set of taxes on income, wealth, and expenditures, intended to be more or less self-enforcing. Significant though these efforts were, they nevertheless qualify as examples of partial reform, because in both instances the expenditure tax was not a major source of revenue since it applied only to a very small proportion of the population.[15] Both expenditure taxes were short-lived. The tax was twice enacted and twice repealed in India; it was first enacted in

1960 in Sri Lanka, was abandoned after five years of unsatisfactory performance, and then tried again in 1976, but again discarded as unworkable.[16]

Two of the partial reforms in Brazil and Uruguay in the late 1960s are especially noteworthy chapters in the history of value-added taxation. Brazil and Uruguay were not only the first among developing nations to adopt a value-added tax extending through the retail level; they also preceded France and the rest of the European Community (EC) in implementing this now most common form of sales tax. (The tax was enacted for Japanese prefectures in 1950 but was never put into operation.) Indeed, adoption of the retail-type value-added tax (VAT) constituted important examples of partial tax reform in twenty other developing nations over the period 1970–86.[17] It is of considerable significance that virtually every developing country that has enacted sales tax reform since 1965 has chosen one or the other of the two most common forms of VAT: the retail type now used in virtually all Western European nations, or the manufacturer's VAT, enacted in Colombia in 1966, Indonesia in 1984, and proposed for Pakistan in 1987.[18] Among the forty-odd countries that have used the VAT, only Vietnam (then South Vietnam) has repealed it and this was during wartime (1971). Experience over the past two decades, then, suggests very strongly that insofar as tax reform is concerned, the VAT is the wave of the present, and possibly the future.[19]

Uruguay was also the scene of two other significant partial reforms.[20] The first, in 1967, resulted in the creation of the first operational presumptive income tax on agriculture at the national level. This tax was initially viewed as a model for similar levies in other LDCs, but has proved wanting where it has been tried. And, as discussed below, the presumptive tax in Uruguay today deviates sharply in structure and operation from that originally enacted. Uruguay was also the first—and, other than Bolivia (1986), apparently the only—country to abolish an operating personal income tax (1974). This was apparently a radical measure, but it should be noted that the personal income tax first came into existence in Uruguay only in the early 1960s, and never raised significant amounts of revenue prior to its abolition.

B. Tax Structures vs. Tax Systems

Until the late 1970s, both comprehensive and partial tax-reform initiatives (with the exception of Japan) tended strongly to focus upon tax structures rather than the broader tax system. This was clearly true for the comprehensive reform proposals for Colombia in 1968 (but not in a subsequent partial reform of the Colombian VAT in 1984), the abortive reform efforts in Ghana (1969–71), the partial reforms in India and Sri Lanka in the late 1950s, and for Brazil in 1965. In several other reform programs prior to 1980, broader tax system issues extending through tax administration and compliance were also addressed, but administrative aspects of tax reform were still peripheral, not central, to the proposals. These included Peru in 1968, Liberia (1969), and Bolivia (1976–77). In still other cases, including the Venezuelan reform proposals of 1958–59,[21] and the ongoing Korean tax reforms adopted almost every year between 1960 and 1976, much more substantial stress was placed on administrative aspects of tax reform.[22]

Also, the pathbreaking Japanese reform packages of 1949–50 went well beyond examination of structural issues in tax reform to detailed consideration of several key issues in tax administration and compliance. The blue-return system of business taxation devised by the Shoup team was an innovation in tax administration that has survived in Japan for nearly 40 years.[23] But it was not until the mid-1980s that comprehensive tax-reform programs again began to involve strong emphasis upon wider tax systems, as opposed to simply tax structures.

Finally, a sizable share of the preparations for the very recent Indonesian and Jamaican reforms was channeled into efforts intended to ameliorate vexing problems in tax administration and compliance, including computerization of the tax information system and major changes in taxpaying procedures. The Pakistan reform proposal of 1986–87 was notable in the sense that it involved strong emphasis upon administrative-compliance issues, with much less attention to serious problems in the underlying tax structure.

C. Revenue-Enhancing vs. Revenue Neutral Reform

In the dozens of attempts at partial or comprehensive reform the significance of revenue motives has been, in most instances, shrouded by the passage of time. It has generally been assumed that in most settings the prime impetus for tax reform has been the need for immediate revenue enhancement to surmount fiscal crisis. But postwar history provides a large number of examples of tax-reform programs that were intended to be more or less revenue neutral, in the short to medium term.

Immediate revenue enhancement was clearly not a major reason for mounting national tax-reform initiatives in occupied Japan[24] (where significant national government budget surpluses were expected in 1951), Brazil in 1965,[25] Liberia in 1969,[26] Bolivia in 1976–77,[27] or Colombia in 1986. The Jamaican reform program of 1986–87 was geared essentially toward revenue neutrality for income tax reform, but the still-pending VAT was expected to raise somewhat more revenue than the taxes it is to replace. The comprehensive Indonesian reform of 1983–84 was not initially conceived of as essential for averting short-term fiscal crisis or for expanding the share of overall tax revenues in GDP over the longer term. Nevertheless, preparation for reform began in early 1981 with the realization that the high oil prices of 1979–80 were not likely to continue, and that non-oil taxes would sooner or later have to be called upon to provide a much larger amount of revenues than could be expected without fundamental tax reform.[28] The Indonesian reform, then, was intended to be more or less revenue neutral over the short run, but like the Venezuelan reform proposal of 1959[29] was also expected to render the system capable of substantial revenue enhancement should the need arise over the longer term. In the event, tax reform as enacted proved strongly revenue-enhancing after oil prices collapsed in 1983–86: non-oil taxes rose from little more than 6 percent of GDP in 1980 to just above 9 percent in 1986. As in many other reform episodes, the value-added tax was primarily responsible for the sharp growth in revenues.

In other notable cases, immediate revenue enhancement was a prime motive for tax reform. In some cases the drive for revenue enhancement was impelled by acute fiscal crisis. This was true for the Colombian partial reform in 1965–66,[30] the short-lived Peruvian reform of 1968,[31] as well as the Bolivian tax changes enacted in 1986 as part of the draconian measures required to check hyperinflation. Also, the Colombian comprehensive reform of 1974, as well as the partial reforms of 1982, 1984, and 1985, was essentially a response to economic emergencies including the outgrowth of a crisis in debt service in the latter two years.[32] Fiscal crisis, however, has been by no means the only reason why governments have sought short-term revenue-enhancing reform in the tax system. The Venezuelan proposals of 1958–59 contemplated immediate revenue enhancement in order to increase government spending on education and health. And the Colombian proposals of 1968–70 sought revenue enhancement primarily to help finance new expenditure programs for primary and secondary education.[33]

D. Distributionally Neutral or Redistributive Tax Reform

Developing country tax reform programs in the first half of the postwar period were generally characterized by a much stronger emphasis on the need for income redistribution than has been the case since then. Preoccupation with enhancing progressivity of the tax system was in keeping with received wisdom of the day.[34] By the mid-1970s, however, the available evidence, both empirical and anecdotal, provided scant grounds for optimism that the tax side of the budget in developing countries could be used efficaciously to secure significant income redistribution from rich to poor households. This is particularly true because the preferred instrument for redistribution—the personal income tax —typically accounts for only about 2 percent of GDP in developing countries, with three-fourths of this coming not from capital income, but from wages and salaries.[35] Subsequently, attention shifted to the redistributive potential of the expenditure side,[36] as tax reformers increasingly pursued the more modest redistributional objective of preventing tax reform from making the poor "worse off."[37]

Indeed, most examples of avowedly redistributive tax reform programs were crafted prior to 1970. The most ardent arguments for redistribution through taxation were contained in the Kaldor proposals for expenditure taxes in India and Sri Lanka.[38] The comprehensive Venezuelan[39] and Colombian[40] (1968) proposals and, to a lesser extent, the Liberian package of 1969,[41] placed relatively heavy stress upon income redistribution through tax reform, primarily through reliance upon progressive rates of income tax that were high by standards prevailing in the late 1980s. Examples of successful income redistribution through tax reform are in any case rare, although the first two years of the Colombian 1974 reforms (based in part on the 1968 proposals) did achieve temporarily some measure of redistribution. Within two years, however, administrative and procedural provisions critical for success of the reform were gutted by subsequent legislation and undermined by both adverse Supreme Court decisions and taxpayer realization that penalties for evasion had no teeth.[42]

Except perhaps for the Chilean reform of 1974, none of the tax reform programs enacted or proposed in LDCs in the 1970s and 1980s were intended to be as distributionally neutral as the 1984 and 1986 U.S. reform proposals,[43] but few placed great emphasis on the use of tax reform as a means of redistributing income from rich to poor. The Bolivian proposals of 1976–77, for example, stressed the need for directing *increases* in income toward the lower end of the income scale, rather than on redistributing existing income through taxes and fiscal transfers.[44] And in the Final Report of the National Tax Reform Commission of Pakistan in 1987, it is noted that "realistic appraisal suggests that the cause of the poor can be served only to a marginal extent through tax policy measures."[45] The comprehensive reforms implemented in Indonesia (1983–85) and Jamaica (1985–86) embodied expectations that a rising share of tax liabilities would be paid by the highest quintile over the medium to long term, but neither reform was driven primarily by redistributional considerations. Indeed, the essence of both reforms was drastic simplification in both tax laws and tax procedures, achieved not only by purposeful shifts toward more uniform tax rates and abolition of egregious tax preferences, but also, in the case of income taxes, sizable reductions in tax rates made possible by base broadening. Clearly in the Indonesian case, emphasis was laid upon reduction, if not removal, of tax burdens on the poorest 40 percent, coupled with measures to narrow both the incentive and the scope for evasion of tax by the richest 20 percent. Consequently, the base of the uniform rate manufacturers VAT does not include spending on unprocessed food, expenditures upon which account for more than half of spending by the poorest 40 percent. And because the exemption structure of the income tax excludes the poorest 80 percent from the tax net, the reformed Indonesian income tax with a maximum tax rate of 35 percent would have a progressive impact by its very presence,[46] even if it were, as in Jamaica, imposed at a single, uniform rate.

Finally, in Colombia (1986) and in the more recent partial income tax reforms in India (1974, 1975, 1984), the top marginal rates of income tax were reduced notably in each case. These adjustments were motivated not by distributional goals, but by considerations both of tax administration/compliance and of economic growth.[47]

E. Economically Neutral vs. Interventionist Reform

With few notable exceptions, including the Japanese reforms of 1949–50, the evolution of tax systems until the late 1960s was marked by growing reliance upon tax provisions designed to guide private firms and individuals toward (or away from) investments and activities favored (disfavored) by government. These interventionist goals required a degree of fine-tuning of tax structures inconsistent with present realities of tax administration and tax compliance in virtually all developing, if not developed, nations.

Arguably, it was not coincidental that the most extensive use of special tax incentives to promote growth and development occurred in the period and in the countries when and where the least attention tended to be paid to issues in tax administration and tax compliance. Nations that relied particularly heavily upon tax incentive regimes through the 1960s and 1970s and into the 1980s included Bolivia,[48] Brazil,[49] Colombia,[50] Ghana, Indonesia, Liberia, Pakistan,[51] Sri Lanka,[52] Jamaica,[53] Venezuela, and Turkey. Incentives were used for many purposes: to promote investment in priority industries, to encourage location of firms in so-called backward regions, to foster exports, to use public accountants, to encourage domestic processing of raw materials, to promote embryonic domestic stock markets, to purchase insurance, to promote development of tourism, and of course to attract foreign investment.

Governments have in most cases proved extremely reluctant to forgo this type of fiscal fine-tuning even when presented with evidence of its corrosive effects on both revenues and tax administration. Still, a number of earlier reform programs, including those in Colombia (1968–70), Liberia (1969), and Ghana (1969–71), sought to curtail availability of incentive programs—but to little avail. The Colombian reform as enacted in 1974, however, essentially eliminated most income tax incentives.

Later reform efforts in the 1970s and 1980s reflected greater emphasis on neutrality and greater skepticism of the efficacy of differential tax incentives, particularly income tax holidays. The Bolivian proposals of 1976–77 called for a marked shift away from incentives providing tax relief through income tax exemptions and tax rate reductions toward investment grants, tax credits, and expensing of capital assets.[54] The Indonesian reforms of 1983–84 went much further. All special tax incentive provisions were abolished at one time, thereby making it possible to lower income tax rates sharply for both firms and individuals. Finally, the Bolivian reforms of 1986 and the Jamaican reforms of 1986–87 were as strongly addressed toward "getting prices right" as any tax reform through 1987. The 1986 Bolivian reform not only provided for a uniform rate VAT with no exemptions, but replaced personal income taxes with a 10 percent levy on incomes, from which the VAT is deductible. The Jamaican reform abolished 16 separate special purpose tax credits in the personal income tax and curtailed company tax incentives for both agricultural and industrial firms.[55]

F. Contemporaneous vs. Phased and Successive Reform

As noted earlier, these time-related distinctions are relevant largely for comprehensive tax-reform programs. Examples of differences in the execution of implementation of comprehensive tax reforms are, however, not numerous, largely because not all such reform programs discussed to this point were accepted by governments; some never reached the stage of draft legislation (Venezuela, 1959; Ghana, 1969–70; Liberia, 1969; Bolivia, 1976–77). A few reform packages were distilled into draft laws and then put aside (Colombia, 1968), to be revived thereafter — sometimes as long as half a decade later.

In almost all instances, governments that have sought comprehensive tax reform have intended that it also be contemporaneous. This was clearly the case in Japan (1949–50), Colombia (1974), Chile (1974–75), Indonesia (1983–84), and Bolivia (1986),[56] but not Jamaica (1985–86). But some essentially contemporaneous reforms have involved some phasing of key provisions. This was so for the Indonesian reform, wherein new income and sales tax laws were both enacted in 1983, to take effect in 1984, while final property tax reform legislation was delayed until 1986 and implemented only in 1987. In addition, the implementation date for sales tax reform, scheduled initially for 1984, was delayed until 1985 to allow greater administrative preparations for reform.

Recent Jamaican reforms furnish a good example of phased reform. A new, vastly simplified personal income tax was introduced in 1986; corporate tax reform was implemented a year later. A new VAT (including some large retailers) was scheduled for introduction in 1987 or 1988, but at this writing has been delayed indefinitely.

Finally, the Korean experience from 1960 through 1975 and that of Sri Lanka from 1977 through 1988[57] provide the best examples of successive tax reform. In Korea, major alterations in tax structure and tax administration took place virtually every year after 1960. Still, not all Korean tax reform could be characterized as successive: tax structures were drastically overhauled in 1967, 1971, and 1976.[58]

The apparent preference for contemporaneous reform in comprehensive tax reform programs may be due to two principal factors. First, both phased and successive reform may involve greater risk of adverse revenue consequences in the short term. A comprehensive reform may feature, for example, greater reliance on one major tax source (sales taxes) and lesser reliance on another (income taxes). Therefore, even for reforms intended overall to be revenue neutral, and particularly for those designed to be revenue-enhancing, all major elements may need to be implemented simultaneously to avoid revenue dislocation that might jeopardize the entire reform package. Second, tax reform inevitably involves winners and losers, particularly when, as in Uruguay in 1975, over one hundred separate taxes were affected.[59] Those interest groups perceiving themselves as "losers" from one element of a reform package may be "winners" from implementation of another component. If so, contemporaneous reform may decrease the intensity of their opposition against the offending reform provisions. This is because with a phased, not to mention a successive type of reform, taxpayers can never be certain that the elements favorable to them will be actually implemented. Moreover, attempts to implement tax reform on a tax-by-tax basis, or even a few at a time, allow each affected interest group to mobilize its spokesmen and allies for endless pleading and debate. Frontal assault on many taxes at once, as in Uruguay (1975),[60] Indonesia (1983–84), Chile (1974–75), Bolivia (1986), and Colombia (1974) has often proved critical in neutralizing the pleadings of interest groups benefiting most from the fiscal status quo.

On the other hand, contemporaneous reforms have the disadvantage that they allow, relative to phased reforms, less time for the tax administration to absorb changes in tax laws and administrative procedures.

III. Concluding Comments

The taxonomy of tax reform offered in the foregoing sections differs in several significant ways from the taxonomy the author had in mind in 1986 in the early phases of planning for this volume. Discussions with authors in varying stages of drafts of individual chapters indicated that many, but not all, aspects of the initial taxonomy stood up well to the findings flowing from individual country studies. These aspects included the taxonomic emphasis upon differences between reform of *tax structures* and reform of *tax systems*, the utility of differentiation between *comprehensive* and *partial* reform efforts, and the use of a separate category to characterize the revenue goals of tax reform.

But as drafts of the various papers prepared for this volume began to arrive, and particularly during spirited conference discussion of all papers in April 1988, it became apparent that qualifications were in order for some of the elements of the taxonomy. First, and perhaps most significantly, it became evident that there were many examples of reforms that were intended to be revenue neutral in the short to medium term, but which were expected to be *revenue-enhancing* in the longer term.

Second, the original taxonomy contained no reference to *economically neutral* reforms, not because economic neutrality was viewed as irrelevant, but because governments from 1950–75 rarely accorded this goal nearly as much status as those pertaining to revenues and income redistribution. But it became evident from perusal of some of the studies of tax-reform episodes in the 1980s, as for example in Bolivia, Indonesia, and Jamaica, that in many countries greater neutrality in resource allocation had become perhaps as significant a goal of tax reform as income redistribution was two or three decades ago.

Finally, it became obvious that any serviceable taxonomy required explicit distinctions regarding the timing of reform. Contrary to the author's expectation, *comprehensive* tax reform programs are rarely *contemporaneous*, insofar as timing of implementation is concerned. Thus there is a need to distinguish more clearly between *contemporaneous*, *phased*, and *successive* reform.

Chapters 2 through 8 contain eleven separate country studies that formed the basis not only for the final development of the taxonomy of chapter 1, but for the lessons drawn in chapter 14. Chapters 9 through 11 present significant tax reform issues of a generic, or cross-cutting, nature. Chapters 12 and 13 may be seen as results of a long-overdue attempt to induce economists, who have long dominated published discussion of tax reform involving LDCs, to recognize and come to terms with the political content of their handiwork.

Notes

The author acknowledges with thanks helpful comments on earlier drafts by Bill Ascher, Roy Bahl, Harley Hinrichs, Anne Krueger, Charles McLure, Zmarak Shalizi, Carl Shoup, Wayne Thirsk, and Ed Tower.

1 For a characterization of revenue, distributional, and economic goals in recent U.S. tax reform, see McLure, chapter 10 in this volume, and McLure and Zodrow (1987).
2 See Shoup (1949).
3 Shoup (1959).
4 Musgrave and Gillis (1971).
5 Shoup (1970).
6 Harberger, chapter 2 in this volume.
7 Musgrave et al. (1981).
8 Gillis (1985).

9   Bahl, chapter 5 in this volume.

10   National Tax Reform Commission (1986).

11   Kaldor (1956).

12   *Report of the Taxation Inquiry Commission* (Colombo, 1968).

13   Shoup (1965).

14   Harberger, chapter 2 in this volume.

15   Shoup (1970), p. 155.

16   Jenkins, chapter 7 in this volume.

17   Casanegra (1986).

18   Aside from Brazil and Uruguay, twenty nations reformed sales taxes by switching from cruder forms of sales tax (including manufacturers sales taxes, multiple-stage cascade taxes, and excise-like systems) to value-added taxes extending through the retail stage. These include Ecuador (1970); Bolivia (1973); Chile, Costa Rica, and Argentina (1975); Honduras (1976); Korea and Panama (1977); Mexico (1980); Peru, Nicaragua, and Haiti (1982); Guatemala (1983); Colombia, Dominican Republic, and Madagascar (1984); Turkey (1985); Niger, Portugal, and Taiwan (1986). (Gillis, Shoup, Sicat, forthcoming).

19   Further, in virtually all nations using the VAT, the tax has been of the consumption rather than the "income" type, has been collected using the tax credit mechanism, and has been imposed on the destination principle. Only Colombia and Argentina fully utilize the "income" form of VAT, wherein taxes collected on purchases of capital equipment cannot be credited from taxes due on sales, although both Turkey and Finland allow less than full credit for taxes paid on capital goods. (Gillis, Shoup, Sicat, forthcoming).

20   Harberger, chapter 2 in this volume.

21   About two-fifths of the income tax section of the Venezuelan report of 1959 was given over to administration of the tax (Shoup, 1959).

22   One authoritative source maintains that "institutional reform in both the content and the administration of the tax laws took place in almost every year after 1960" (Bahl, Kim, and Park [1986] p. 45).

23   Shoup, chapter 6 in this volume.

24   Ibid. More precisely, revenue enhancement was not a major goal for tax reform at the *national* level in occupied Japan. However, the prefectures were chronically revenue short, and the abortive prefectural VAT was developed to bolster their revenues.

25   Shoup, chapter 8 in this volume.

26   Shoup (1970).

27   Musgrave et al. (1981).

28   Total tax revenues as a percentage of GDP in Indonesia were 25 percent of GDP in 1981, but non-oil taxes were less than 7 percent. Inasmuch as government expenditures were nearly 25 percent of GDP, any significant weakening in oil prices from the early 1981 peak of $40 per barrel would create major demands on non-oil taxes, even if government spending were reduced by as much as one third.

29   Shoup (1959) and Shoup, chapter 8 in this volume. As in Indonesia a quarter century later, a major goal of the Venezuela reform proposal was to enable the tax system to *be ready* to raise substantially greater revenues from non-oil tax sources once oil revenues began to decline.

30   Bird (1970).

31 Ascher, chapter 12 in this volume.
32 Perry and Cárdenas (1986), pp. 43, 283.
33 Musgrave and Gillis (1971), pp. 18–20.
34 For example, see Kaldor (1963).
35 Tanzi and Casanegra (1987), p. 3.
36 See Gillis et al., *Economics of Development,* 2nd edition (1987) and references cited therein.
37 Bird and DeWulf (1975).
38 Kaldor (1963); Kaldor (1956).
39 Shoup (1959), pp. 60–65.
40 Musgrave and Gillis (1971).
41 Shoup (1970).
42 Gillis and McLure (1978).
43 Distributional neutrality in the U.S. proposals is discussed in McLure and Zodrow (1987).
44 Musgrave et al. (1981), p. 115.
45 National Tax Reform Commission, chapter 1, p. 16.
46 Gillis, introduction to this volume.
47 Bird, chapter 9 in this volume.
48 Gillis et al. (1978), Musgrave et al. (1981).
49 The early history of Brazilian tax incentives is addressed in Hirschman (1963).
50 Musgrave and Gillis (1971).
51 National Tax Reform Commission (1986).
52 Jenkins, chapter 7 in this volume.
53 Bahl (1987).
54 Musgrave et al. (1981), pp. 461–65.
55 Bahl (1987), pp. 11–12.
56 American Chamber of Commerce of Bolivia (1986).
57 Jenkins, chapter 7 in this volume.
58 Bahl et al. (1986).
59 Harberger, chapter 2 in this volume.
60 Ibid.

References

American Chamber of Commerce of Bolivia (1986), "Tax Reform Law: An Explanation of Its Contents," May.

Bahl, Roy (1987), "Tax Reform in Jamaica: Executive Summary" (Syracuse University, Draft, Sept.)

———, Chuk Nyo Kim, and Chong Kee Park, *Public Finances During the Korean Modernization Process* (Cambridge, Mass.: Harvard University Council on East Asian Studies, 1986).

Bird, Richard M. (1970), *Taxation and Development: Lessons From the Colombian Experience* (Cambridge, Mass.: Harvard University Press).

——— (1974), *Taxing Agricultural Land in Developing Countries* (Cambridge, Mass.: Harvard University Press).

————, and Luc Henry DeWulf (1975), "Taxation and Income Distribution in Latin America: A Critical View of Empirical Studies," International Monetary Fund, Staff Papers 20 (Nov.):639–82.

Casanegra, Milka (1986), "Problems of Administering a Value-Added Tax in Developing Countries: An Overview," forthcoming in Malcolm Gillis, Gerardo Sicat and Carl Shoup, editors, *The Value-Added Tax in Developing Countries*.

Gillis, Malcolm (1985), "Micro and Macroeconomics of Tax Reform: Indonesia," *Journal of Development Economics* 19, p. 221–54.

———— (1986), "Worldwide Experience in Sales Taxation: Lessons for North America," *Policy Sciences* 19, 125–42.

————, and Charles E. McLure Jr. (1978) "Taxation and Income Distribution: The Colombian Tax Reform of 1974," *Journal of Development Economics* 5, 233–50.

————, Carl Shoup, and Gerardo Sicat, ed., *The Value-Added Tax in Developing Countries* (forthcoming).

———— et al. (1978), *Taxation and Mining: Non-Fuel Minerals in Bolivia and Other Countries* (Cambridge, Mass.: Ballinger Press).

Idem (1987), *Economics of Development*, 2nd edition (New York: Norton).

Hirschman, Albert O. (1963), *Journeys Toward Progress* (New York: Norton).

Kaldor, Nicholas (1956), *Indian Tax Reform* (New Delhi).

———— (1963), "Will the Under-Developed Countries Ever Learn to Tax?" *Foreign Affairs* Vol. 41, No. 2, January.

McLure, Charles E. Jr., and George R. Zodrow (1987), "Treasury I and the Tax Reform Act of 1986: The Economics and Politics of Tax Reform" *The Journal of Economic Perspectives*, Vol. 1, No. 1 (Summer), p. 37–58.

Musgrave, Richard, and Malcolm Gillis (1971), *Fiscal Reform For Colombia* (Cambridge, International Tax Program).

Musgrave, Richard et al. (1981), *Fiscal Reform in Bolivia* (Cambridge, International Tax Program).

National Tax Reform Commission of Pakistan, *Final Report* (1986), Islamabad, December 31, 1986.

Perry, Guillermo and Mauricio Cárdenas (1986), *Diez Años de Reformas Tributarias en Colombia* (Bogotá, FEDESARROLLO).

Shoup, Carl S., et al. (1949), *Report on Japanese Taxation by the Shoup Mission* (Tokyo, Supreme Commander of the Allied Forces). Four volumes.

Shoup, Carl S. (1959), *The Fiscal System of Venezuela* (Baltimore: Johns Hopkins University Press).

———— (1965), *The Tax System of Brazil* (Rio de Janeiro: Fundacao Getulio Vargas).

———— (1969), *Public Finance* (Chicago: Aldine Publishing).

———— (1970), *The Tax System of Liberia* (New York: Columbia University Press).

Tanzi, Vito, and Milka Casanegra (1987), "Presumptive Income Taxation: Administrative, Efficacy and Equity Aspects," (Washington: International Monetary Fund, Working Papers WP/87/54).

2

Lessons of Tax Reform from the Experiences of Uruguay, Indonesia, and Chile

·······

Arnold C. Harberger

I. Introduction

This has been a difficult paper to write. Its original aim was to take its readers behind the veil of appearances and give them a taste of what it is really like to be "on the inside" of a process of tax reform. As I went around and interviewed participants, I thought stories would appear that would surprise readers, give them new insights into and understanding of what tax reform is all about. Maybe even it could serve to sharpen the perceptions of those who would engineer new reforms (perhaps in other countries), alerting them to dangers otherwise unseen, calling their attention to critical details that might easily be overlooked, and stamping in their minds the key requirements of a successful strategy.

The actual result was far from what I anticipated. To be sure, a few vignettes were generated, a few perhaps surprising anecdotes. But the bulk of the message was almost the opposite of what I had planned. Taking readers to the inside of the process of tax reform was not going to open their eyes to new marvels, nor strike them with lightning bolts of new wisdom. Instead it was going to pound home incessantly the importance of things we knew about all along: (a) clarity of conception in designing a reform, (b) professional-level attention to detail in converting that conception into laws, regulations, and procedures, and (c) administrative machinery for implementing the reform efficiently, fairly, and above all for the long run. These lessons, on the whole, were not exciting—more like "how to be a good public accountant" than "how to be a star in the movies or in the opera or on the football field."

Studying the history of tax reform in these three countries also reinforced my longstanding belief in the importance of appropriate timing. I do not mean timing in a very refined sense—it is not the day nor the month nor the season that matters, maybe not even the specific year. But there are times when the public at large, and/or the legislative assemblies, and/or even the government authorities (e.g., the president and the cabinet) themselves are more likely—and other times when they are less likely—to be receptive to the idea of tax reform. It is important for those who engineer a reform to be sensitive to this general receptivity, so as not to cast their seeds on barren ground (cf. ch. 1, ch. 4, this volume).

Sometimes the term "opportunity" fits better than "receptivity." This is particularly true when the existing system has generally broken down, betraying its own bankruptcy and at the same time yielding almost an open field to those who create its replacement. Opportunity may also come as a by-product of some external crisis that calls for the generation of substantial new revenues in a relatively short period of time. In either type of opportunity, there is a void that somehow is going to be filled—at worst by the inflation tax or by ill-conceived measures spawned by demagogy.

When opportunity strikes, the need is for someone to be ready with a well-conceived professional solution. Rarely will a solution drawn intact from the professional literature do the trick—careful tailoring will be needed to adapt it to local conditions and to the specific nature of the crisis. This task can be hard enough, even when the country's policy professionals have done a lot of prior work and are in that sense quite prepared to meet the crisis. If they are unprepared or simply not alert to the emerging situation, the opportunity represented by the crisis is likely to pass, with the void being filled by somebody else, and with the country's economy for years to come paying the cost of an inferior solution.

II. Uruguay

The main thrust of my story is well represented by Uruguay's case. I was somewhat familiar with the situation because I had served as a consultant on several occasions over a period of about three years in the mid-1970s. Unfortunately (in a sense) my consulting missions always entailed intensive work on one or two topics: for example, the social opportunity cost of capital, the role of fiscal factors in Uruguay's inflation, and the treatment of the financial sector under the value-added tax. My appreciation of the broad outlines of the country's tax system came, as it were, by osmosis—by contact with tax officials and other professionals, by references and summaries found in the general economic and tax literature, etc. From these contacts and sources I was impressed by two particular vignettes. First was the fact that in their tax reform effort of 1974 and 1975 the Uruguayan authorities had abolished the personal income tax. This came as a shock and a surprise; I really did not know what to think. Was I in favor of such a drastic measure or against it? What were the pros and the cons? Without knowing where I myself stood on the matter, the one thing I felt surest about was my admiration for the political courage it surely took to engineer such a drastic move.

The second item that impressed me was a presumptive tax on agricultural income based on the potential productivity of the soil. As originally described to me, this tax on potential income was an economist's dream tax. For each of some fifteen regions of the country, the land was divided into four or five quality groups. In each region-quality category, the most likely cropping pattern was adduced. Each pattern was described by a set of outputs per hectare, together with the inputs that "normally" would be applied to achieve those outputs. Inputs (F_j) and outputs (X_i) were then priced (at average prices w_j and p_i) for each year, and imputed income ($EX_iP_i-EF_jw_j$) was then computed as the base on which the tax was levied. When a relevant output price went up the tax would automatically increase; when an input price rose the tax would fall. But when the farmer leveled his land, introduced new varieties, applied fertilizer more scientifically, undertook fencing and drainage works, etc., the tax did not change a bit. Each farmer was the sole beneficiary of such advances and improvements.

It is easy, I think, for readers to imagine how impressed I was by the daring (if not audacity) revealed by the income-tax abolition, and by the professional refinement epitomized by this presumptive tax. Time and again I urged that these experiences be studied in depth, so as to reveal their secrets and their lessons. So, needless to say, when I agreed to write this paper for this conference, a deeper look into both these experiences came high on my agenda. So I went to Uruguay, I inquired, I looked, I studied, and I came away disheartened. In each case the truth belied the image. The search led to the conclusion that there were no secrets to be treasured and no major insights for future tax reforms.

In the case of the income tax, its abolition came only twelve years after its introduction. The tax had never really taken root, no effective enforcement machinery had ever been developed, and no important revenue had ever been generated (receipts never reached as high as one percent of GDP). Moreover, the tax that was abolished was really only the tip of the iceberg. It stood within a system of category taxation as the specific component striking (at progressive rates) the comprehensive income of individuals. After its abolition, the following taxes remain today:

a. A tax on the income from industry and commerce (30 percent maximum rate)
b. Taxes on agricultural income, either actual or imputed (30 percent maximum rate)
c. Social security contributions (employers' contribution of 12 percent plus employees' contribution of 13 percent)
d. Value-added tax (20 percent rate, subtraction method)
e. Selective excise taxes, mainly for fuels, tobacco products, alcoholic beverages, and electricity

In the case of the taxes on agriculture, my disillusionment came from another angle. The much-vaunted presumptive tax, far from calibrating cropping patterns to the region and quality of the soil, as its underlying concept would have dictated, imputed income on the assumption that everybody produced just two products—meat and wool. Soil quality came into play by classifying different region/soil groups as having land that was a specified fraction or multiple of the national average land quality.

Uruguay's concentration on the production of meat and wool is high enough that one cannot condemn the presumptive tax procedure as outright absurdity. Yet the blanket imputation of taxable income on the basis of cattle and sheep raising must have raised the hackles of truck farmers, orchard owners, poultry raisers, and the like. They did indeed complain, with the result that today all taxpayers with net receipts above a critical amount must pay a regular agricultural income tax, the impuesto de la renta agricultura (IRA), on their actual net income. Smaller agricultural enterprises now can opt for the IRA system or for a new system which in 1979 replaced the earlier presumptive system. The 1979 tax did not change the imputation significantly, however. Today the standard hectare's production pattern is still based on cattle and sheep raising, with any given hectare's imputed income being a fraction or multiple (depending on soil quality) of that of a standard or average hectare.

The virtues of the Uruguayan tax system are thus not to be found in either of the two aspects that so intrigued me and other professional observers. What, then, were the merits of the Uruguayan tax reform? Without any doubt the answer is tax simplification. In July of 1974, when Alejandro Vegh Villegas assumed the post of finance minister, Uruguay was plagued with a myriad of little taxes. These had been imposed to begin with in response to pressure groups (on the whole very small ones with tightly defined special interests), and as ad hoc levies to garner new sources of revenue to finance new expenditures as they were approved.

The Vegh Villegas tax simplification effort centered largely on a computerized system, identifying each tax separately together with its recent revenue history. The procedure by which taxes were then eliminated was extraordinarily simple and clear. After the taxes had been ranked in descending order of their revenue yields, those at the bottom of the computerized list were repealed en masse. In the first step, the budget law of 1975 eliminated about fifty taxes; then in a second step in late 1975 another eighty or so fell under the ax. The keys to the success of this procedure were its "objectivity" and "automaticity." If the taxes had been taken one by one or just a few at a time, endless pleading and debate would have ensued as each affected interest group mobilized its spokesmen and its allies. The frontal assault on many tiny taxes all at once gave the advantage to the fiscal authorities. The automaticity helped too, in that it was hard for opponents to question the broad principle of eliminating dozens upon dozens of tiny "nuisance" taxes. Whatever merit could be claimed by its supporters for any one such tax, it was certainly not its contribution to the fiscal till.

A second major element of simplification was the elimination of the stamp tax (impuesto de sellos). This tax had tentacles reaching into all sorts of activities and transactions—it struck bills, loan receipts, checks, virtually any document that had a legal status that might be subject to a complaint or lawsuit. The stamp tax spawned compliance and efficiency costs in all directions and was loathed by the business and commercial community. At the time of its elimination the stamp tax was the most important single revenue source in the entire system.

The third important tax that was eliminated was a sales tax striking gross receipts (entradas brutas). It functioned as a cascade tax, generating layer upon layer of distortions as goods passed through different productive stages.

Finally, there was a single stage tax on final sales.

All the above taxes were eliminated and folded into the evolving value-added tax, which quickly became the major revenue raiser of the system.

A final key feature of Uruguay's tax reform of the mid-seventies was the elimination of export taxes (*retenciónes*) on beef and wool. These taxes had been significant revenue sources but their most important effect was to deter international trade. Partly as a consequence, Uruguay's exports jumped from an average of about $200 million in 1968–72 to over $600 million in 1977–78 and over a billion dollars in 1980–82. In terms of the generalized purchasing power of the dollar over tradable goods, Uruguay's exports were $500–600 million (1980 dollars) in 1968–72, about $900 million (1980 dollars) in 1977–78, and over a billion such dollars in 1980–83.[1] Further discussion of these trade tax changes, along with the substantial liberalization of import restrictions that occurred in the late 1970s and early 1980s, is set to one side as being beyond my self-imposed limits as to the scope of the present paper.

III. Indonesia

The outstanding feature of the Indonesian tax reform of 1983 was the degree of care that went into its preparation. It surely has few equals in this regard, one of them being the work of the Canadian Royal Commission on Taxation in the late 1960s. The preparation in the Indonesian case worked on three levels—professional-technical, political, and administrative.

The cornerstone of the Indonesian tax reform effort was a contractual arrangement with the Harvard Institute for International Development (HIID), led by Professor Malcolm Gillis. Under this arrangement more than two dozen experts from six countries undertook basic studies of the existing Indonesian system and the potential for reform. The study period extended over more than two years and covered nearly every aspect of the tax system and its potential reform. Tariffs and other trade taxes were perhaps the most important (but quite conscious) omission (see chapter 4). Working side by side with the foreign experts were Indonesian cadres, many of whom in the process became local experts on the particular areas in which they worked.

The political side of the story was represented by two features of the Indonesia effort. First, the entire operation was placed under a steering committee of senior government officials, drawn from all parts of the

Finance Ministry. This committee took part in all decisions that dealt with key policy matters. It is important to realize that in the Indonesian context the high-level bureaucracy is probably the most important focus of political forces and pressures. It is the members of this bureaucracy who receive the complaints and the self-serving proposals of a myriad of interest groups. It is they who come to sense what is politically trivial at one extreme, politically untouchable at another. Their presence throughout the reform operation thus helped on the one hand to guarantee that the initiatives taken would not be totally out of line with Indonesian political reality, and on the other to ensure that the final product would stand a reasonable chance of approval and implementation.

The second political feature of the reform enterprise was its emphasis on carrying its recommendations all the way to the point of draft legislation. A team of lawyers from Indonesia and abroad started work at about the midpoint of the project's term, and by the end was engaged in an all-out effort to transform the team's technical papers and proposals into draft laws.

On the administrative side one had not only the counterpart cadres of Indonesian officials who worked with foreign experts, but also a program (at first within the HIID project, later continued on its own) for training abroad new cadres of officials. In addition the project included technical studies of administrative issues, and it produced as one of its important outputs a new computerized taxpayer-identification system that was to prove a great boon to the implementation of the reformed tax system.

Tax simplification

Simplification is the term that most aptly covers the many aspects of the Indonesian reform effort. It is no surprise that the cornerstone of this effort, on the side of indirect taxes, was the conversion from an old and poorly administered turnover tax (which in addition had a very low yield) to a modern value-added tax. The notion of simplification even explains why the value-added tax was confined to manufacturers (including imports, mining, and construction). To extend it either back to the agricultural stage or forward to the wholesale and retail stage would require huge administrative effort with little prospective increment in yield. The absence of agriculture from the system had the added consequence that unprocessed food products reached the consumer without any tax being paid (except that embodied in purchased inputs into farm operations). This carried political benefits since such items bulk large in the consumption baskets of the lower income strata in Indonesia.

The second great simplification in the Indonesian reform was the elimination of a plethora of tax incentives. Incentives covered a Pandora's box of activities—cooperatives, public accountants, natural resource exploration, technology transfer, regional investments, exports, so-called priority sectors, etc. Tax holidays and tax credits (both notoriously non-neutral in their impact on projects of different gestation periods and time profiles) were among the principal instruments by which incentives were granted. The new Indonesian law swept away the old incentive schemes, putting in their place a 35 percent tax rate (as compared with the previous rate of 45 percent).

Simplification on the personal income tax side came through broadening the base and reducing the rate structure, with the maximum marginal rate falling from 50 to 35 percent. The income tax replaced a total of four different taxes, perhaps best described as a crude sort of category income tax system. Simplification in the detail of the tax took the form of eliminating fringe benefits from income subject to personal tax, but at the same time eliminating their deductibility by businesses. Similarly, depreciation accounting for tax purposes was greatly simplified by using declining-balance depreciation covering four major categories, and withholding was generalized to cover payments of dividends, interest, and rents, as well as wages and salaries.

The final key element of simplification was the taxpayer-identification system itself. This system creates the possibility of cross-checking of returns by different firms, and between the income tax and the VAT (value-added tax). In addition it makes much more feasible the depersonalization of tax administration, selecting returns for audit on the basis of objective criteria and minimizing the possibility of collusion between taxpayers and officials.

IV. Chile

Of the countries considered here, Chile had the deepest and most *comprehensive* tax reform process. This is partly due to the circumstances created by the military coup of 1973 which ousted the government of Salvador Allende. In the opinion of many observers (myself included) the coup would never have taken place had it not been for the virtual breakdown of the economic system. Inflation came to exceed 400 percent a year (even 1000 percent if monthly rates are put on a yearly basis); production in virtually all areas was stagnant or falling; trade was grossly distorted by restrictions and by a Byzantine multiple-exchange-rate system.

These circumstances created a whole array of opportunities for policy reform. Fortunately, technicians were present who had thought at length about a number of the areas of opportunity. In relatively short order most price controls were released and the dozen or more multiple exchange rates were reduced to a single official rate plus a not very distant unofficial parallel market rate. Early tax reforms (in 1974 and 1975) included the introduction of a value-added tax, the reform of the personal income tax, the integration (for Chilean taxpayers) of the corporation and personal income taxes, and the indexation of the tax system. In addition to these measures a massive trade liberalization effort was set in motion in 1974, which culminated in a 10 percent uniform import tariff by 1979. (Today the uniform rate is 15 percent.)

The fiscal deficit, which was vast at the beginning of this process, was brought under control in the late 1970s. This was the key to the gradual reduction of the inflation rate (of the GDP deflator) from over 600 percent in 1974 to less than 15 percent in 1981. It also created the fiscal circumstances for one of the crowning achievements of Chilean policy in these years: the complete revamping of the social security system, turning it from a deficit-ridden, pay-as-you-go scheme into an essentially privatized system wherein each individual has a personal vested retirement account that can be moved from one fund to the other.

Indirect Taxes

Like Uruguay, Chile in the early 1970s had a plethora of small indirect taxes and a cascade-style sales tax. These were all abolished when the value-added tax was introduced in 1975.

Transition problems dominated the discussion at the time. As a first step to the introduction of the value-added tax, the sales tax was modified so as to eliminate the discrimination in rates between imported goods (12 percent) and domestic sales (8 percent). Once this had been done, the stage was set for the introduction of the value-added tax. One issue that came up concerned transition credits (i.e., whether the tax on inputs purchased under the turnover tax scheme could be deducted from a firm's liability under the value-added tax). The decision here was to give no transition credits to anybody. Firms received credit for inputs purchased on or after January 1, 1975, when the VAT became effective. All 1974 purchases were treated under the old system.

Other transition aspects had to do with coverage. Agriculture was initially left out of the VAT system, as were all hydrocarbons, electricity, water, and gas. Many services were also initially not taxed. In 1976, however, a major consolidation move was made, incorporating agriculture, fuels, public utilities, and most of the services omitted previously.

Indexation

The indexation of the Chilean tax system is built around the concept of the *Unidad Tributaria* (UT). Income for tax purposes is measured monthly in these units. Withholding on wages and salaries had always taken place contemporaneously, and under the Allende government the sums withheld were required to be remitted each month to the Treasury. Now business firms were also required to pay each month on their own estimated income. One way to visualize the UT system is as a monthly readjustment of all income tax brackets in accordance with a price index; thus, the same real wage or other income would lead to the same real tax, regardless of when it was received.

The accounting problems of business were handled deftly in the Chilean income tax law. Three simple rules are all it takes to handle the potentially highly complex problems associated with the presence, side-by-side, of real and nominal assets and real and nominal liabilities. The rules are:

(i) all real or indexed assets are written up by the relevant inflation percentages, and the amount that is written up is introduced as a profit item on the profit and loss statement

(ii) all real or indexed liabilities (including capital and surplus) are written up by the inflation percentage and that amount is introduced as a loss item on the profit and loss statement

(iii) depreciation is taken on the written-up value of depreciable assets

It is one of the miniature marvels of our era that such a simple system of inflation accounting was found. The key to its simplicity lies in recognizing that correcting for inflation entails correcting for just one price index movement in each period. In this sense inflation accounting is at the opposite extreme from replacement cost depreciation, which follows the price of each individual asset class.

Perhaps the most important attribute of Chile's indexation of the tax system was its effect on arrears. Whereas previously, as in many other inflationary countries, it was a genuine advantage for the taxpayer to postpone payments as long as possible, now any delays were automatically indexed and were subject in addition to interest and (where applicable) penalties. One cannot exaggerate the importance of indexation in making possible the increase in real receipts which in turn was the key element in the gradual reduction of the rate of inflation itself in the late 1970s and early 1980s.

Integration

The story of integration of corporate and personal income taxation in Chile is a curious blend of advance and retreat. Without a doubt the boldest step came first. Modeling their system after that recommended by the Royal Commission on Taxation in Canada (the so-called Carter Commission), the Chileans initially implemented a full imputation to each resident shareholder of the corporate income corresponding to his shares. This income was declared as personal income by him, regardless of whether it was retained in the corporation or paid out as dividends. The taxes paid at the corporate level on these shares were treated in the same way as the taxes withheld on wage and salary payments. At tax time the individual could claim full credit for the taxes paid on his account.

I do not have a clear sense of the reason why a step backward from full integration was taken in 1985. At this time Chile reverted to what I conceive of as essentially a European system of integration based on dividends alone. That is to say, the system became in effect one of simple withholding on dividend income, with dividends being grossed up by individuals as they declared their personal income subject to tax.

The present system, indeed, has two separate tax operations at the corporate level. One is a 10 percent tax on enterprise income, which is not integrated in any way with the personal income tax. The second is the withholding of an amount equal to four-fifths of the dividends actually paid out. It is this amount which individuals have to add to their dividend receipts as they declare their income. At the same time the withheld amount is in the end taken by individuals against the tax that is due.

In the shift from the earlier (full-integration) to the present (dividend-withholding) system, a certain conceptual elegance was lost. I infer that the move was taken mainly for administrative convenience and was perhaps rendered less controversial by the fact that the enterprise tax itself was at this time only 10 percent.

Social Security

Americans familiar with the system of Individual Retirement Accounts (IRAS) will have no trouble understanding the new Chilean social security system. As far as I can see, the two systems are virtually identical, the major difference being that the Chilean system places greater restriction on the entities (called AFPS, or administrators of pension funds) that handle the retirement accounts. This is perhaps reasonable in that the contribution to one or another such fund of an amount equal to 10 percent of one's income (up to a certain limit) is mandatory, and in addition the State introduces a sort of safety net in the event that a private AFP portfolio falls short of providing a certain minimum rate of return.[2] Rate of return has not, however, been a problem to date. From their inception in July of 1981 up to November of 1987 the pension funds have yielded an average cumulative real rate of return of 14.4 percent. The separate cumulative real rates of the twelve funds now in operation ranged from a low of 13.1 percent to a high of 15.2 percent. Another testimony to the success of Chile's new social security system is the fact that in the period indicated above, total investment assets of close to $3 billion (or about 15 percent of 1987's GNP) have been accumulated.

Obviously, a contributory pension scheme is in itself not a difficult thing to establish (insurance and annuity companies do it every day). The problem in the Chilean case was in the disastrous financial state and general disorganization of the previous system. Under that system different categories of employees had different retirement funds. There was one for public-salaried workers, another for private-salaried workers, and yet another for blue-collar workers. Separate funds existed for certain industry groups: one for bank employees, one for racetrack workers (!), etc. Most of these funds had started out on a sound actuarial basis, but had deteriorated into pay-as-you-go systems by the 1950s and 1960s. Successive Chilean governments had wrestled with the problem of social security reform, but all such schemes had foundered due to inadequate fiscal resources.

The key, therefore, to the success with which the AFP system was implanted in Chile thus lies fundamentally in the capacity of the government to handle the problem of transition. For the transition, everyone was given the option of staying with the old system or of entering the new. For those who chose to join the new system, the government assumed a liability (given to the new AFP in the form of an indexed "recognition bond") approximately equal to the capital value of the individual's own past contributions to the old system. Since on the whole the participants in the old system could not expect ultimate benefits equal to the capital value of their past contributions, this itself provided the incentive to join the new system.

Thus it is no surprise that more than two-thirds of the labor force chose to join the new system right away. The armed forces, which enjoyed a pension scheme based on 50 percent of their actual salaries, were simply left out of the new system (as a price for its adoption, as it were). Also left out were those whose retirement under the old system was less than five years away.

The seeds of the new system were due to Miguel Kast, a rising planning-office official who later became, in sequence, minister of planning and minister of labor. Other key figures in the process were Herman Buchi, Martin Costabal, Maria Teresa Infante, Luis Larrain, José Piñera, and Alfonso Serrano. This small group of technical people formed the nucleus in which the idea of the social security reform incubated and from which it was ultimately spawned. The road was difficult because initially the top government leaders (all military men) were not enthusiastic. An important early convert among them was Fernando Matthei, whose prime consideration was that "my dignity does not accept that my children should have to pay for my pension." Ultimately, at the highest levels of government, this was the argument that determined the demise of the pay-as-you-go system.

Administration

Economists have for too long tended to overlook the importance of administration in any successful tax performance (see chapter 9, this volume). In my mind there is little doubt that something close to half the total credit for Chile's accomplishments has to be assigned to the administrative side in reform of the *tax system*. What began as an antiquated internal revenue service, badly conceived, inefficient, and with overtones of corruption, was in a relatively short time converted into a service that ranks very high by international standards.

The old system had many weaknesses. Its information system was terrible; even the old returns of a given taxpayer were not at the disposal of inspectors; inspectors were assigned to given areas and tasks and remained with them for long periods of time (augmenting the possibilities of conspiracy with taxpayers).

The new system tried to improve on each of these lines. First, the link between inspectors and sectors was broken. Each day or week, inspectors would be assigned to new, very specific tasks. In the beginning these consisted mainly simply of getting additional information from given taxpayers and bringing it to a central office.

Much effort went into the development of an information system. Data were gathered on all types of ratios: What should wages be relative to sales in the bakery? What should inputs be relative to outputs in a textile mill? What should profits be relative to sales in a pharmacy? Several pages of summary relations of this type were developed, and returns that deviated significantly from the guideline rates were closely scrutinized. Value-added-tax and income-tax supervision were done simultaneously for business firms.

For individuals, the internal revenue service got records of purchases of most high-cost items. Those who bought cars and houses were asked to show where the money came from. Firms were required to list payments to individuals in accordance with their taxpayer number. Farmers' production mix was identified by aerial surveys that distinguished between fourteen different crops. Also, trucks were inspected on major highways in farming regions.

On the whole, the inspectors were relegated to the task of bringing in answers to specific questions. Many older employees were retired, and after a few years the system was largely staffed by new, mostly younger people who had been especially trained within the system.

This reform did not require great increases in budget, simply because of the huge amount of waste that had characterized the old administrative system. In the end many unnecessary bureaucratic operations were abandoned, staff in many sections was reduced, and employees that remained received significant increases in their real salaries.

The final and most important aspect of administrative reform in Chile was the cultivation of a clear sense that the law was being enforced evenhandedly. The use of objective criteria (ratios, etc.) to decide whom to audit was an important step in this direction. But perhaps most significant of all were cases of VIPs who were not able to use their influence to escape the tax net. One such case concerned the mayor of a town who was also the owner of a drugstore. Tax discipline called for the drugstore to be closed, but how could that be done if the mayor was still running his town? The solution: the drugstore was closed and the mayor was fired from his (appointive) job.

The most celebrated case concerned the president's brother, who owned a discotheque. When his data called for his being given a summons, the case went to the head of the Internal Revenue Service (Felipe Lamarca). He in turn called the president, who said that the same law and procedures should apply to his brother as to anyone else. Lamarca avers that in six years (1978–84) as director of internal revenue, neither the president of the republic nor any cabinet minister ever interfered with his pursuit of an evenhanded tax administration (*ley pareja*).

The simplification of the law is recognized by the Chilean administrators as an important factor in their own success. The introduction of the value-added tax not only helped because it replaced scores of little excises, it also proved a boon in the administration of personal and corporation income taxes. The new income tax law was also easier to administer than the old.

Collection procedures were also improved. Whereas previously an income tax declaration could be forwarded intact, with the treasury cashier tearing up his copy and keeping the money (or splitting it with the taxpayer), now the money has stayed with the declaration all through the procedure. Most payments are now made directly to banks, which serve as collection agents and credit the government's account directly. (Banks do not charge directly for this service because they get the use of the "flat" for a few days.)

V. Conclusions

The country reviews in the preceding sections reflect what I meant in saying that tax reform had more in common with learning to be a public accountant than with becoming a movie star. Solid preparation, with due attention to local institutions and political realities, was a big lesson from Indonesia; the importance of effective administration was a key lesson from Chile. Simplification was the watchword of all three reforms. This was in each case represented by a modern value-added tax taking over from a preexistent, old-fashioned turnover tax. In addition the simplification extended to an integration of income tax and value-added tax administration and (at least in Indonesia and Chile) the substantial computerization and depersonalization of administrative procedures. The only truly dramatic reform that is covered here is the new Chilean social security system, and even that is perhaps only dramatic because of the degree to which such systems all around the world have deteriorated to a pay-as-you-go basis (or even to chronic deficits that have to be financed from general revenue). Once it is recalled that most social security systems started out on something like an actuarial basis, the only truly novel attribute of the Chilean system becomes its use of private AFPS for its administration.

Seeking an analogy with which to wrap up the main messages of this paper, I can come up with nothing better than the old-fashioned version of marriage. The idea is that the partners spend a long time (while still single) learning the skills they will need in their future roles. This corresponds to the need for serious investment in study and research and preparation of a tax reform. Then, once married, they have to work continually to overcome the frictions and crises of conjugal life. This corresponds to the need to build robust systems of administration, capable of minimizing the number of problems and at the same time of surmounting those that do emerge. Finally, there is the sense of seizing opportunities, of knowing the right moment to act. On the Victorian marriage scene, this meant a sense of alertness, by bride and swain alike, to recognize and seize the critical moment when the "right person" came along. This too has its counterpart in tax reform, as testified by the tome upon tome of tax studies and commission reports that end up on library shelves and in archives, without the slightest step of implementation. Opportunity presented itself in all three cases, less so initially in Indonesia (where the foresight of future problems was the stimulus to the HIID project), but even there in the final analysis, as falling oil revenues perforce dictated some sort of tax policy move.

A high level of professionalism reflected throughout the three stages of preparation, adoption, and implementation is the final key to the success of these three tax reform efforts.

Notes

Principal Persons Consulted. A. Uruguay: Jorge Caumont, Ministry of Planning; Mario Soto, tax consultant; Carlos Steneri, Ministry of Planning; Alejandro Vegh Villegas, former minister of finance; Luis Viana, Central Bank of Uruguay. B. Indonesia: Malcolm Gillis, Duke University; Glenn P. Jenkins, HIID (Harvard University). C. Chile: Eduardo Aninat, Aninat & Mendez; Jorge Carias, former minister of finance; Hernan Cheyre, University of Chile; Martin Costabal, former budget director; Felipe Lamarca, former director of internal revenue; Juan Carlos Mendez, former budget director. D. General: Vito Tanzi, International Monetary Fund.

1 These figures show the dollar value of Uruguay's exports as given in International Finance Statistics, deflated by the SDR-WPI, a dollar price index on the wholesale price levels of France, Germany, Japan, the United Kingdom, and the United States, with weights equal to those used since January 1981 in calculating Special Treasury Rights at the International Monetary Fund.

2   Actually, each AFP must generate an average yield on its portfolio which is at least half the average yield of all the AFPs taken together. The AFPs are required to build a reserve against such shortfalls by setting aside specified amounts whenever they earn more than the average yield. When a fund has a prolonged shortfall in its rate of return and cannot cover it out of its capital and reserves, the government provides the funds to bring the rate of return up to the required minimum, but the AFP must then be dissolved and its assets transferred to such other AFPs as its participants choose.

Selected Bibliography

Cheyre, Hernan, "Reformas Tributarias, 1974–88," *Estudios Públicos*, no. 21 (Summer 1986), pp. 141–83.

Connoly, Michael, and John McDermott, ed., *The Economics of the Caribbean Basin* (New York: Praeger, 1985), pp. 1–11.

Gillis, Malcolm, "Micro- and Macroeconomics of Tax Reform," *Journal of Development Economics* 19 (1985), pp. 221–54.

Tanzi, Vito, "A Review of Major Tax Policy Missions in Developing Countries," in *The Relevance of Public Finance for Policy-Making, Proceedings of the 42nd Congress of the International Institute of Public Finance,* Madrid, 1985, pp. 225–36.

———, "Tax System and Policy Objectives in Developing Countries: General Principles and Diagnostic Test," *Tax Administration Review* 3 (January, 1987), pp. 23–34.

3
·······

Analysis and Reform of the
Colombian Tax System
·······

Charles E. McLure, Jr.

I. Introduction

The tax system of Colombia has been under almost constant study and
revision for at least the past twenty-five years.[1] As a result, Colombian
experience provides a fascinating story of the interplay of tax advice
and policy reform.

During the early 1960s a *Fiscal Survey of Colombia* (1965, hereafter
the Taylor Report, after Professor Milton Taylor, its mission chief) was
prepared as part of the joint program of the Organization of American
States and the Inter-American Development Bank. This led to several
important administrative innovations, but few concrete reforms of substance. Perhaps as important in its impact on policy was the small volume prepared by Professor Richard Bird (1970) on the basis of his experience as a resident adviser to the government of Colombia on tax and
fiscal policy during the two-year period 1964–66.

In 1968 Professor Richard Musgrave was asked by President Carlos
Lleras Restrepo to assemble a commission of Colombian and foreign
experts to appraise the tax system and make recommendations for
reform. The result, *Fiscal Reform for Colombia: Final Report and Staff
Papers of the Colombian Commission on Tax Reform* (Musgrave and
Gillis, 1971, hereafter the Musgrave Report), which has become a classic in the field of tax reform in developing countries, significantly
shaped the 1974 tax reform (and subsequent reforms) discussed below.

In late 1974 Colombia undertook a major reform of its tax system,
drawing heavily on the recommendations of the Musgrave Commission. A consultants' report for the World Bank, translated into Spanish
and published as *La Reforma Tributaria de 1974* (Gillis and McLure,

1977) provided an early appraisal of these reforms and suggested further improvements in the tax system. A subsequent World Bank Report which received some circulation in English in Colombia (McLure, 1982) analyzed further reforms that followed during the intervening period, as well as examining the 1974 reforms in greater depth.

Finally, in December 1986 the government of Colombia passed a major reform package that greatly simplified the income tax, lowered income tax rates, and provided further adjustments for inflation in the measurement of income from business and capital. The 1986 act contained an important provision that grants the government broad powers to alter the system of inflation adjustment during the two years following enactment. To assist the government in determining how best to use those powers, a comprehensive report on the taxation of income from business and capital (McLure, Mutti, Thuronyi, and Zodrow, forthcoming) has been prepared.

This survey of tax reform in Colombia examines both the recent history of tax reform initiatives and the major tax reform studies that have influenced the course of such reforms. It concludes that the tax system of Colombia has been improved markedly, if not steadily, by the efforts of the past quarter century. Significant credit for this improvement can probably be traced to the influence of the tax reform studies cited above. But the role of Colombian experts should not be understated; both the 1974 and 1986 reforms were formulated by local experts, with little or no outside advice. In many of the remaining areas where reform is still needed the problem is not that experts have not shown clearly the necessity and benefits of reform; it is, rather, that those with political influence—the wealthy (especially those involved in agriculture), politicians, and the military—continue to enjoy privileged tax status despite the inequities and inefficiencies inherent in such treatment.

The organizational plan followed in presenting this material is essentially chronological. Section II describes the salient features of the Colombian tax system as the Taylor Mission found it in the early 1960s. Sections III and IV indicate the reforms recommended by the Taylor and Musgrave Missions, respectively. Many of the provisions extant in 1960 and the Taylor and Musgrave proposals for dealing with them have cast long shadows, some extending even to the present; they are described in considerable detail in order to provide a benchmark for the appraisal of the tax reform that has followed. (Where provisions of early law are no longer applicable, or were modified relatively early in the period, such provisions are not described in great detail. By comparison, provisions that remain in effect or that were reformed only recently are treated in greater detail.)

Section V describes the fundamental reforms of 1974. Section VI describes the changes in the tax law that occurred between the major reforms of 1974 and 1986, and Section VII describes the 1986 reforms. The final section provides an appraisal of the past quarter century of analysis and reform of the tax system of Colombia.

Primary focus in this discussion is on structural features of the so-called income and complementary taxes. Only secondary attention is focused on domestic indirect taxes levied by the national government, especially the national sales tax. Little attention is devoted to either the politics of tax reform or the importance of macroeconomic conditions, including the need for more or less revenue, in shaping the timing and substance of reform. Many other important fiscal or quasi-fiscal issues, including some in the realm of income taxation, are also ignored. These include:

import duties and related policies such as quantitative restrictions, import licensing, and advance deposits
the special tax treatment accorded both foreign investment and natural resource industries
the domestic pricing of petroleum products
the use of differential exchange rates and other devices to tax exports of coffee
the taxation of quasi-governmental autonomous agencies
subnational taxes, including property taxes
intergovernmental fiscal relations, including earmarking of revenues and the use of valorization to finance local public services.[2]

One of the trends that can be discerned in both tax-reform studies and legislation in Colombia is increasing appreciation for the importance of tax administration and the role simplification can play in facilitating administration. Another is greater pragmatism—an increased realization that "things ain't always what they seem." That is, there is greater awareness that what matters for the equity and neutrality of a tax system is not merely what appears on paper in the tax law. Rather, it is important to understand what will result once the taxpayer makes his decisions, particularly if the taxpayer is well advised and perhaps relatively unafraid of the consequences of being found in violation of the law—a law known not to be well enforced.

II. Colombian Taxes in the 1960s

A. Income and Complementary Taxes

1. Income Tax. Colombia adopted a schedular tax on income in 1918 before switching to a tax on global income in 1927. Further reforms during the next three decades resulted in an income tax that was progressive and productive, as income tax revenues grew from 3 percent of total tax revenues and barely 0.3 percent of GDP at the beginning of the period to well over one-half of tax revenues and roughly 4 percent of GDP at the end.[3]

Space does not permit a detailed survey of developments of the Colombian tax system before the early 1960s. Yet several features of this development must be noted because they, too, have cast long shadows. First, the modernization and strengthening of the income tax in order to increase the progressivity of the Colombian tax system occurred during two periods of left-of-center government: under the Liberal party during the Great Depression years of 1931–36 and under the rule of military dictator Rojas Pinilla in 1953. Second, this thrust of tax policy was reversed in the 1960 reforms, which, following the advice of the UN Economic Commission for Latin America (ECLA), lowered tax rates and introduced a far-reaching system of tax incentives.[4] This pattern of reform and counterreform has been a continuing phenomenon in Colombia.

At the time of the Taylor Mission, just after a major reform in 1960, Colombia's system of "income and complementary taxes" consisted of the basic income tax, a net wealth tax, and an excess profits tax. In addition, there were five other taxes on income and wealth, each on a base that was generally different from that for the basic income and net wealth taxes.[5]

In principle, the base of the Colombian income tax in the early 1960s was quite broad in that it included all "enrichment"; thus it included imputed income from owner-occupied housing as well as corporate dividends and shares in the earnings of limited liability companies and partnerships. In fact, a wide array of income was tax-exempt for both individuals and juridical persons (legal entities).

For individual taxpayers exempt income included interest on governmental securities, social security benefits, "thirteenth month" service bonuses commonly paid in the private sector and corresponding Christmas bonuses in the public sector, vacation pay, compulsory severance pay equal to one month's salary for each year of service, family subsidies, maternity benefits, death and burial benefits, workmen's compensation, sick pay, income of the Catholic clergy, winnings from gambling, limited amounts of both interest and dividends, and allowances that essentially constituted salary but were ostensibly paid for travel and expenses of representation.[6] Finally, it was possible for high-income taxpayers largely to evade the individual income tax on dividends and interest on bearer securities, since a withholding tax of only 12 percent was levied on such income.[7]

Capital gains have been generally taxable only since 1960. Ten percent of such gains were exempt for each year the asset in question had been held. In addition, gains on securities and other personal property were exempt from tax except when realized in the normal course of business.

In addition to personal exemptions for the taxpayer, spouse, and other dependents, there was a complex system of personal deductions for expenditures on medical, educational, and other professional services; these deductions depended on the income and number of children of the taxpayer. To achieve equity between homeowners and renters the exclusion of a limited amount of imputed income of the former was matched by a small deduction for residential rent. Moreover, a deduction was allowed for all interest expense, for real estate taxes, and for contributions to social security and pension plans.[8]

Income of individuals was taxed under a graduated schedule consisting of 56 rates, ranging from 0.50 percent to 51 percent. Married persons were required to file separate returns, but within limits could split earned income in order to mitigate the effects of rate progression.[9]

Straight-line depreciation was allowed, based on useful lives of twenty years for real property, five years for airplanes and motor vehicles, and ten years for all other personal property. There was no provision for inflation-adjustment of depreciation allowances, but deductions were allowed for additions to a tax-free reserve for the replacement of industrial machinery and equipment acquired before June 1, 1957, to compensate for the effect of a large 1957 devaluation of the peso.[10]

As in many developing countries (and consistent with the conventional wisdom in development economics of the day, as indicated by the ECLA recommendations underlying the 1960 reforms), the Colombian tax system of the 1960s was used to subsidize investment in a wide range of activities that were deemed to make an important contribution to economic development or to be worthy of public support for some other reason, as well as to encourage saving. Thus tax incentives were provided for

> a long list of governmental and quasi-governmental financial, developmental, industrial and other enterprises. In addition, income tax exemptions, limitations, or reductions are granted as an incentive to oil companies, certain mining companies, large-scale agricultural improvements, cattle-raisers, rural real estate subdivisions, Colombian airlines, certain investment companies, public utility companies, tourist hotels, certain basic industries, manufacturers using products of the *Paz del Rio* steel plant, and to exporters of products other than coffee, petroleum, bananas, hides, and precious metals. (*Fiscal Survey* [1965], p. 33)

Incentives were also provided for investments in agriculture, accruals of an economic development reserve, and reserves for replacement of industrial machinery and equipment.[11]

Juridical persons were subject to graduated rates. Corporate rates (on *sociedades anónimas*), which applied to all foreign entities, were 12, 24, and 36 percent. By comparison, the rates applied to limited liability companies (*sociedades de responsabilidad limitada*), the business form used for many of the most important Colombian business ventures, were only 4, 8, and 12 percent, and the income of partnerships was taxed at rates of 3 and 6 percent.[12] Whereas the income of proprietorships was taxed only in the hands of the owner under the individual tax, that of juridical persons was taxed directly to the firm in question. The entire net income of limited liability companies (like that of partnerships) was taxed to the partners, whether or not distributed; by comparison, only dividends were taxed to owners of corporate shares.[13]

The tax system of Colombia suffered from many administrative problems in 1960. Most notably, there was almost no withholding, even on wages and salaries.

In certain respects administrative problems could be traced to procedural laws that impeded effective tax administration. To the extent this was true, the problems went beyond what is found in most developing countries; more important, such problems could be remedied, at least in principle. For example, a rule which required the filing of returns on which only exempt income was reported, though explicitly exempt, increased the number of exempt returns filed; while intended as an administrative safeguard, this requirement clogged the administrative machinery.[14]

A much more serious problem involved the interplay of an overly short statute of limitations (two years), a system of penalties and interest that encouraged false and delinquent returns, and an overburdened tax administration. In extreme cases taxpayers could avoid taxation completely by deliberately reporting false information and waiting for the statute of limitations to preclude correction by the fiscal authorities.[15]

2. *Net Wealth Tax.* Since 1935 Colombia has imposed a tax on net wealth (*impuesto complementario de patrimonio*), apparently to increase the tax burden related to income from capital and to induce more productive use of land. The tax also offsets to some extent the ability of high-income taxpayers to evade and avoid the income tax. Beginning in 1960 corporations and similar entities were exempted from payment of the tax. Taxable wealth was that held in Colombia, net of indebtedness (whether to local or foreign creditors). For this purpose, assets were generally valued at cost, less depreciation where applicable. Assessed values derived from property tax assessments were used for real estate, livestock was valued at its current value, and securities were valued at their stock exchange value or other current value.

As under the income tax, there were a large number of exemptions; for the most part these exemptions paralleled those under the income tax. Among exemptions of special interest, either because they were subsequently eliminated or because they have been perennially resistant to reform, are those for securities of governmental agencies, property incapable of producing income, livestock kept for breeding purposes, certain agricultural investments, assets of Colombian airlines, assets of public utility companies, investments in tourist hotels, investments in motor vehicle assembly or manufacturing plants, investments in securities of the *Paz del Rio* steel plant, and (until 1969) investments in certain basic industries and in certain iron and steel fabricators.[16]

3. *Excess-Profits Tax.* Beginning in 1935 Colombia imposed an excess-profits tax. Partnerships were exempt from this tax, which was applied instead to the partners. The calculation of excess profits—the excess over 12 percent of net wealth when the latter is in excess of a specified figure—was based on measures of profits and of net wealth that differed from the corresponding definitions under the income and net wealth taxes. A conceptually correct and important difference was the exclusion of income from personal services from the measure of profits for

this purpose. Because the excess profits tax was repealed in 1974, these adjustments are not described in detail.[17]

B. Internal Indirect Taxes

In the early 1960s the national government of Colombia employed only a quite rudimentary system of internal indirect taxes. Such taxes accounted for less than 10 percent of total national tax revenues in all but one year of the decade ending in 1961. There was no broad-based tax on consumption, such as a value-added tax or a retail-sales tax. Thus more than half of revenues of the national government from indirect taxes were derived from stamp taxes and sales of stamped paper. Only taxes on distilled liquors also yielded as much as 10 percent of revenues from internal indirect taxes.[18]

III. The Taylor Mission Proposals

A. Income and Complementary Taxes

The Taylor Mission gave the following glowing endorsement to the income and complementary taxes being levied by Colombia in the early 1960s: "The trinity of an income tax, excess profits tax, and net wealth tax represents a development that is essentially ingenious, progressive, and enlightened—both in terms of the goals of tax policy and administration." Though the Mission made technical proposals for the improvement of the first two members of the trinity, it noted that "the general pattern should be retained." By comparison, it recommended the repeal of the five surtaxes on income and wealth, characterizing them as nuisance taxes whose primary reason for existence was earmarking of revenues—a practice it described as indefensible.[19]

For the most part the recommendations of the Taylor Mission for the reform of the taxation of income were consistent with the conventional wisdom of the day. The Taylor proposals included suggestions that (a) most forms of exempt income should be subject to tax, (b) the itemized deductions for nonbusiness interest expense and property taxes and for contributions to social security and pensions should be eliminated, (c) the special personal exemptions for medical, educational, and other professional expenditures should be repealed or limited and made available on equal terms to all taxpayers, (d) the partial exemption for income from owner-occupied housing should be removed, (e) all realized capital gains should be taxed in full as ordinary income without regard to the holding period, and (f) the issuance of bearer shares should be prohibited or made unattractive by the imposition of a higher withholding tax. In addition, the Taylor Mission noted that both the bottom marginal rate of 0.5 percent and the top rate of 51 percent were too low and that there were far too many rate brackets.[20] It thus proposed that the top marginal rate be raised to 62 percent.[21] A more controversial proposal was the elimination of the option to split earned income.

The Taylor Mission produced an impressive analysis of the distortions and inequities that flow from the disparate treatment of individuals, corporations, limited liability companies, and partnerships. But having noted particularly the case for integration of the corporate (or company) and individual income taxes, it concluded that "a policy of integrating corporate and personal income taxes does not appear to be warranted at this time."[22] This apparent inconsistency may have reflected political realism as much as schizophrenic economic reasoning; since the double taxation of dividends had only been introduced in 1953 as part of the reforms of Rojas Pinilla, it may have been unrealistic to expect it to be eliminated so soon. Instead, the Mission's policy recommendations for the taxation of corporations focused heavily on the interplay between the income tax, two of the supplementary taxes on income (which it proposed to eliminate), and the excess-profits tax (which it advocated retaining with modifications). It favored an upward adjustment of the tax rates on limited liability companies, which it acknowledged were used "as a tax avoidance device."[23] It is unclear whether the Mission gave any consideration to the possibility of using the combination of limited liability companies and fragmentation of businesses to reduce taxes on the capital and business income of a family.

Beyond this, the Taylor Mission proposed more generous depreciation allowances as a means of spurring investment and economic development and compensating roughly for inflation. It rejected the need for "replacement cost depreciation" because the inflation rate was not sufficiently high to justify its introduction.[24] Moreover, it decried the structure of the provision intended to compensate for the 1957 devaluation. The Taylor Mission favored introduction of carry-forward of losses; it rejected carry-back, in part because of the administrative problem that would be created by opening past returns.

While favoring such general incentives for investment as accelerated depreciation and the elimination of impediments to development such as the inability to carry losses forward and the discriminatory tax treatment of corporations, the Taylor Mission did not condone the proliferation of incentives for special purposes, especially since those in the government who were responsible for administration of the incentives apparently had no clear idea how effective such incentives were in increasing investment or employment. The Mission did not, however, appear to believe that incentives based on careful appraisal of the potential to make contributions in these areas would be inappropriate.[25]

The Taylor Mission devoted particular attention to the agricultural sector because of both the potential revenue being lost and the role it saw for tax policy in stimulating efficient use of rural resources. Its most important proposal was for a presumptive calculation of income from agriculture equal to 10 percent of the assessed value of agricultural property. This innovation would prevent artificial losses in agriculture from being used to offset income from other sources, in addition to causing agriculture to make a positive contribution to the tax base. In order to make the presumptive income tax effective, as well as to improve the taxation of rural property, the Mission urged that the cadastral survey then underway should be given high priority.[26]

Perhaps as important as these proposals for structural tax reform were the administrative proposals advanced by the Taylor Mission. These included withholding for wages, salaries, interest, and dividends, the requirement for advance payments of taxes based on estimated liabilities, self-assessment, extension of the statute of limitations, and rigorous application of penalties.[27]

B. Internal Indirect Taxes

The Taylor Mission's recommendations in the area of national internal indirect taxes seem rather modest by today's standards, though at the time they represented an important break with prior policy. They included elimination of all stamp taxes levied only for revenue reasons, rationalization of other stamp taxes, and introduction of "a broad system of excises on semi-luxury and luxury goods." Especially important was the insistence that excises should be levied on domestically produced products, in order to prevent (or reverse) tax-induced incentives for uneconomical import substitution. In addition, it is worth noting that the system of excises was favored over the type of sales tax that had been legislated in 1963 because of the regressivity of the latter.[28]

IV. The Musgrave Commission's Proposals

At the time Richard Musgrave submitted the final report of his commission in February 1969 the tax system of Colombia was not much changed from that analyzed by the Taylor Mission a few years earlier, except for the introduction of withholding and estimated payments—an improvement of major importance. Essentially the same types of income were exempt, the same tax incentives existed, income was measured in much the same way, roughly the same special personal exemptions and itemized deductions were allowed, and the rate structure was basically the same as earlier.[29] For the most part the Taylor and Musgrave recommendations for income tax reform were broadly consistent. Thus it will be convenient to focus primarily on important instances in which the recommendations of the two missions differed.

A. Income and Complementary Taxes[30]

The Musgrave Commission did not share the enthusiasm of the Taylor Mission for the trinity of income, net wealth, and excess-profits taxes. While it said that "the Colombian income tax is a relatively well-developed and sophisticated statute in comparison with others in Latin America,"[31] and that "the net wealth tax fulfills a valuable role in the Colombian tax structure,"[32] it had little good to say about the excess-profits tax and recommended that it be abolished.[33] The Musgrave Commission shared the Taylor Mission's view that the supplemental taxes on income and wealth and the practice of earmarking revenues should be abolished.[34]

Noting the basic inconsistency between both exempting social security benefits from tax and allowing tax deductions (for the employer) and exemptions (for the employee) for contributions, the Musgrave Commission recommended that such benefits be made taxable.[35] It recommended continuation of a limited exemption for interest and dividends.[36] It also favored continuing the special exemptions for medical and educational expenses and making them more generally available, but eliminating the exemption for other payments to professionals.[37] Some forms of exempt income and the special exemptions would be made subject to a vanishing formula in order to limit the benefits of such provisions; that is, the exempt or deductible amount would decline as income rose above a specific amount. By comparison, it was suggested that a deduction should be allowed for charitable contributions in excess of 3 percent of income, without vanishing (but subject to a limit of 30 percent of income).[38]

In order to simplify administration, the Musgrave Commission also proposed introduction of a standard deduction equal to 5 percent of income, subject to a fixed peso limit.[39] In contrast to the Taylor Mission's condemnation of income splitting, the Musgrave Commission thought the provision of limited ability to split earned income to be a reasonable compromise between basing taxation entirely on the income of individuals and complete income splitting.[40] Like the Taylor Mission, the Musgrave Commission believed that the number of tax rates should be reduced and that personal exemptions and bracket limits should not be adjusted for inflation. It argued that "provision for automatic adjustment tends to remove resistance to inflation and to institutionalize a high inflation rate. These effects are detrimental to sound economic development."[41] It proposed raising the top individual tax rate from 52 percent to 55 percent.[42]

The Musgrave Mission offered two alternatives for the taxation of capital gains. Under one, the basis used for calculating gains would be adjusted for inflation, and gains would be taxed as ordinary income. Under the other, no inflation adjustment would be allowed, but the rate applied to gains would be five percentage points below that otherwise applicable. To qualify for capital gains treatment an asset would be subject to a two-year holding period. In either event gains on assets held for more than five years would be subject to averaging. The 10 percent per year exclusion based on the length of holding period would be eliminated. Coverage would be extended to essentially all assets; gains on sale of the principal residence of the taxpayer would be partially exempt, subject to the vanishing provision mentioned above. In order to prevent "lock-in" of appreciated assets, gains would be constructively realized at the time of death.[43]

Noting the difficulty of a solution to the problem of taxing income from owner-occupied housing that simultaneously achieves the economic goals of tax policy and is administratively feasible, the Musgrave Commission offered two alternatives without choosing between them: (a) taxation of the imputed income from owner-occupied housing, with full deduction of mortgage interest and property taxes and no special deduction for renters, and (b) omitting imputed income, disallowing deductions for mortgage interest and property taxes, and retaining a limited deduction for renters.

The Musgrave Commission noted that the introduction of withholding in 1967, which included a system of current payment for the self-employed, was an important advance. It repeated the call for heavier penalties for tax evasion and added a suggestion for the development of a master tax roll. It also added suggestions for improved taxation of the "hard-to-tax" groups such as small traders, independent professionals, and agriculture.[44]

Like the Taylor Mission, the Musgrave Commission devoted particular scrutiny to the agricultural sector and also proposed introduction of a presumptive measure of income based on assets invested in agriculture. It also proposed that agricultural losses should not be allowed to offset income from other sources.[45]

Integration of the taxes on businesses and on individuals was rejected by the Musgrave Commission, as it had been by the Taylor Mission. Instead, the Commission proposed that the income of corporations and limited-liability companies be subject to a unified system of taxation consisting of taxation at the entity level and taxation at the individual shareholder level only on income that is distributed. Partnerships would be taxed at the entity level at a substantially lower rate, and subject to certain conditions limited-liability companies would be given the option of being taxed like partnerships; the partners' shares in partnership profits would also be subject to individual taxation, whether distributed or not. Only limited relief would be available for small businesses through a preferential rate for small corporations and limited-liability companies; continuation of the existing system of highly graduated rates for such organizations was rejected.

The Musgrave Commission considered two types of integration schemes: a dividends-paid credit at the entity level and a dividend-received credit for shareholders. Among the reasons given for rejection were revenue loss, the possibility of shifting of the tax to consumers or wage-earners, the strong Colombian tradition of taxing income from capital more heavily than labor income, the increase in progressivity that results from an unintegrated system, the risk of inducing increased distribution and thus reduced private saving, and the practical difficulties of integration.[46]

Like the Taylor Mission, the Musgrave Commission did not favor allowing depreciation to be placed on a replacement cost basis; nor did it favor introducing general revaluation of assets to correct balance sheets for inflation. Instead, it followed the Taylor approach of suggesting more liberal depreciation allowances. The reasons the Musgrave Commission rejected inflation adjustment for depreciation allowances included the observation that "a general revaluation of assets is extremely difficult to apply, and one may doubt the equity of providing for a depreciation adjustment without considering other items in the balance sheet (such as a reduction in the real value of debt liability) and without applying similar adjustments to taxpayers who do not have depreciable assets."[47]

The Musgrave recommendations for liberalizing depreciation allowances included replacement of the system of straight-line depreciation based on three asset classes with a nine-class system that allowed double declining balance depreciation for assets with useful lives of at least five years. In addition, salvage value would be eliminated, and it was suggested that consideration might be given to permitting increased depreciation allowances for assets used in multiple shift operations.[48] Only new assets would be eligible for most of these changes.

Like the Taylor Mission, the Musgrave Commission found the incentive programs existing in the late 1960s to be "costly, inequitable, and ineffective." Since some of these (those for "basic industries," those for industries complementary with the *Paz del Rio* steel plant, and the special deduction for a reserve for development investments) were scheduled to expire at the end of 1969, it was simply suggested that they not be renewed. The Commission urged that direct grants, rather than tax incentives, be used in the future if incentives were thought necessary for the implementation of development policy. But if tax incentives were to be used, it suggested guidelines for incentives in three areas: raising the general level of investment, encouraging particular industries, and stimulating development of backwards regions.[49]

The Musgrave Commission recommended that the net wealth tax should be strengthened by eliminating exemptions for assets that are incapable of producing income, for assets located abroad, and for many assets benefiting from specific exemptions, including those yielding tax-exempt income and those in industries accorded tax-preferred status because of their presumed importance for development. The Commission also argued that debts should be deductible only if incurred in relation to or secured by taxable assets. In order to prevent abuse by nonprofit organizations, it was proposed that such organizations should be taxable on their business assets.[50]

The Musgrave Commission repeated (in some cases with modification of approach or details) several other recommendations of the Taylor Mission. These included five-year carryover of losses (and unused depreciation allowances), limitations on deductible salaries (to prevent nondeductible dividends from being paid as deductible salaries), and increased withholding on interest and dividends on bearer bonds and shares. In addition the Musgrave Commission added a recommendation that nonprofit organizations be taxed on any business earnings (but not on interest and dividends received from firms in the for-profit sector).[51]

B. Internal Indirect Taxes

Colombia introduced a national sales tax on January 1, 1965.[52] This was a single-stage manufacturers' tax levied at rates of 3 to 10 percent on "finished" domestic goods and imports. To prevent double taxation of value added, tax was not to be charged on a transaction upon receipt of certification from the buyer that the goods involved would undergo further processing. This system inevitably led to instances of both double taxation and evasion, and in June 1966 it was converted to a crude credit-type value added tax (VAT), but one that extended only through the manufacturing level and allowed no credit for tax paid on capital goods.[53]

Despite explicit recognition of the disadvantages of a manufacturers' level sales tax, the Musgrave Commission offered no recommendations for fundamental changes in the newly enacted sales tax. It did, however, suggest that it might be necessary in the long run to move toward a retail sales tax, perhaps of the "ring" type then being used in several Central American countries.[54] Though recognizing that adoption of a retail sales tax might require elimination of capital goods from the tax base, the Commission did not include a suggestion for such a change in the tax base for revenue and administrative reasons. Beyond that, the Musgrave Commission repeated the call of the Taylor Mission for reduced reliance on stamp taxes and increased taxation of luxury consumption.[55]

V. The 1974 Reforms

Though the Report of the Musgrave Commission had little immediate impact, its long-term effect was considerable. During the last four months of 1974 the government of newly elected president Alfonso López Michelson employed emergency powers provided by the constitution of Colombia to introduce a far-ranging reform package that included changes in the income and sales taxes, taxes and subsidies on international trade, and the tax treatment of governmental agencies. These reforms bore the distinct stamp of the Musgrave recommendations, which had been considered further and refined by local experts during the intervening half-decade.[56] Besides rationalizing many aspects of the income and net wealth taxes, the 1974 reforms eliminated the tax on excess profits, added a calculation of presumptive income based on net wealth, and further improved the system of internal indirect taxes.

A. Income and Complementary Taxes

1. Income Tax. The 1974 reforms eliminated many exemptions and other forms of preferential treatment for nonlabor income; these included the exclusion of interest on public debt, exemptions for automobile producers and private electrical companies, and deductions for reserves for investment. Exemptions or incentives were left intact for a few sectors (e.g., airlines, publishing, and reforestation) and for various activities in selected regions (primarily "frontier" and other less developed ones). State enterprises, other than those supplying public services, were initially subject to tax, although this reform was eventually repealed. Unfortunately the government was prohibited by the economic emergency provisions of the constitution under which it acted from also eliminating the equally egregious exemptions for labor income.[57]

In 1973 the special personal exemptions for medical and educational expenses, expenditures on other professional services, and rental payments had been made to vanish as income rose above various figures (not the same for all of the allowances), as suggested by the Musgrave Commission. This resulted in an unacceptable complication of tax filing, and the 1974 reforms converted the special deductions, the deduction for charitable contributions, the exemptions for interest and dividends, and the personal exemptions to tax credits. Moreover, a "standard credit" analogous to the more commonly employed standard deduction was provided.[58]

The 1974 reforms introduced a novel approach to the taxation of capital gains and other "occasional gains" (*ganancias ocasionales*). Receipts subject to this new regime included net capital gains on assets held for more than two years, as well as receipts from gambling, 80 percent of inheritances and gifts, the excess over 8 percent per annum of nominal interest on indexed savings accounts issued by financial institutions to fund residential mortgage lending (hereafter called by their Colombian acronym UPACS), and various other lump-sum payments and prizes. Twenty percent of occasional gains were added to ordinary income; the marginal tax rate to be applied to all occasional gains realized during the year was the marginal rate applicable to this sum under the regular income tax schedule, minus 10 percentage points.[59]

Realized gains on all assets were made subject to this tax; however, the reduction of gains by ten percent per year for each year of ownership was continued for owner-occupied residences. The new law did not provide for constructive realization of gains at death or upon transfer by gift.[60]

The 1974 law gave the taxpayer the option of annually adjusting asset values for inflation (up to 8 percent per year) occurring after enactment of the new law (as well as a one-time revaluation of assets to market values at the end of 1974). Any revaluations of assets had to be employed in calculating net wealth for purposes of the net wealth tax and the presumptive income tax (to be described below), as well as in the calculation of capital gains. Adjustments not made currently could not be made subsequently. Moreover, this revaluation of assets was not allowed to affect the basis of future depreciation deductions.[61]

The structure of taxation applied to business income represented partial movement toward the structure recommended by the Musgrave Commission. Graduated rates were replaced with flat-rate taxes. But the taxation of corporations and limited liability companies was not unified. Instead, the income of corporations was taxed at 40 percent and that of limited liability companies and partnerships at a rate of 20 percent. As before, shareholders in corporations paid tax only on dividends, whereas owners of limited liability companies and partnerships were required to pay tax currently on the share of the profits of the company imputed to them.

The depreciation rules contained in the 1974 reforms followed closely the recommendations of the Musgrave Commission: elimination of the 10 percent salvage value rule, availability of the double declining balance method for assets with useful lives of more than five years, and the increase of regular depreciation allowances by 25 percent for each extra shift. Asset lives were to be specified by regulation. As noted above, the basis of depreciable assets could not be revalued to reflect domestic inflation for purposes of calculating depreciation allowances. But depreciable basis could be adjusted for increases in the peso value of debt incurred to finance acquisition of such assets that is either denominated in foreign currencies or represented by securities of constant purchasing power.

The 1974 reforms also included the five-year carry-forward of losses suggested by the Musgrave Commission. In an apparent attempt to induce greater disclosure of financial information by limited liability companies, loss carry-forward was made available only to juridical entities subject to the supervision of the Superintendent of Corporations. Juridical entities were allowed to offset agricultural losses against income from any source; by comparison, agricultural losses of individuals could be offset only against agricultural income. If the presumptive income of a corporation exceeded its income as regularly determined, any loss carried over had to be used to offset this excess.

As initially promulgated, the 1974 reforms contained important procedural and administrative provisions that would have increased the ability of the tax administration to prevent the type of willful evasion that had concerned the Taylor Mission.[62] Unfortunately, the Counsel of State declared these procedural provisions to be outside the scope of reforms allowable under the emergency powers, and therefore unconstitutional. As a result, many of the administrative "teeth" of the 1974 reform were effectively extracted.

2. *Net Wealth Tax.* The 1974 reforms of the net wealth tax adopted many of the reforms recommended by the Musgrave Commission, and indeed went beyond them in some ways. Among the most important exemptions ended by the reform were those for mortgages and securities issued by governmental and quasi-governmental agencies after September 30, 1974, investments in nonprofit enterprises, assets yielding exempt income, investments in activities previously deemed to deserve exemptions as being especially important for the economic development of the country, assets not capable of producing income, limited amounts invested in stocks of Colombian corporations or in savings accounts, books and works of art, and personal effects.[63]

3. *Presumptive Income Tax.* In 1973 Colombia introduced a presumptive income tax on the agricultural sector, following the recommendations of the Taylor and Musgrave Missions. Because the problem of tax evasion was thought to be troublesome outside of agriculture, and to avoid having a schedular tax that applied only to one sector, the 1974 reforms extended the concept of presumptive income to the economy as a whole. Under this important new addition to the fiscal arsenal of Colombia—arguably the most important of the 1974 reforms—income (whether from labor or capital) was presumed to be no less than 8 percent of net wealth, defined generally in the same way as for the net wealth tax.[64] In addition, any increase in net wealth from year to year that could not be explained to result from exempt

income or income that had been taxed would be subject to tax as current income.

B. Internal Indirect Taxes

The 1974 reforms continued the movement of the national sales tax toward a full-fledged value-added tax, by eliminating the possibility of buying otherwise taxed items on an exempt basis simply by certifying to the seller that they were to be processed further; under the new law the tax credit (invoice) system was extended to all such transactions. This created administrative headaches because of the many claims for refunds that had to be processed.[65]

In order to reduce the regressivity of the VAT at the upper end of the income scale, the law expanded the base of the tax, especially by applying it to many services, including parking lots, insurance, international air fares, photographic developing and photocopying, telegraphic and telephone services, and fees of social clubs. For the same reason the degree of progressivity of the rate schedule applied to various goods, ranging from "wage" goods (6 percent) to luxuries (35 percent), was increased. The 1974 reforms also provided more widespread exemptions, for example, for almost all food and for selected agricultural machinery. For the most part these changes were consistent with the recommendations of the Musgrave Commission.

As under prior law, no credit was allowed on capital goods, in part to compensate for underpricing of capital resulting from various nontax policies, including an undervalued exchange rate. On the other hand, the law contained anomalous provision that exempted imports of capital goods destined for "basic" industries. The combination of these policies placed domestic producers of capital goods at a competitive disadvantage relative to foreign producers of imported capital goods.[66]

VI. The 1974–86 Period

The period from 1974 to 1986 can perhaps best be characterized as one of continued tinkering with the tax system of Colombia. Though some of the changes clearly represented improvements, some of the more important ones lacked justification in sound public policy; they represented retrogression, having been made in large part in response to the pleadings of politically powerful economic groups. Indeed, the 1977 and 1979 laws have been characterized as "counter-reforms."[67] Among the noteworthy changes were the virtual elimination of the tax on imputed income from owner-occupied housing and the introduction of several provisions intended to stimulate investment in publicly traded corporations. Moreover, many of the provisions identified by the Taylor and Musgrave Missions (and by subsequent analysts) as being inappropriate (especially exemptions of certain types of labor income) survived. Finally, weaknesses of administration persisted, since little was done to eliminate them, and stymied efforts to improve implementation. As a result, the equity, neutrality, and revenue potential of the system suffered.[68] The following are among the most important of these reforms and deforms.[69]

Since 1979, values fixed in nominal (monetary) terms, including personal allowances and bracket limits, have been fully indexed for inflation, following a period of partial indexing from 1975 to 1978. Beginning in 1983, 60 percent of the monetary correction for UPACS (40 percent in the case of other indexed debt) was exempt from tax. Withholding on interest payments was raised to 6 percent of the nominal amount.

In 1976 depreciation was liberalized by providing that flexible rates of the taxpayer's choosing could be used for all personal property (that is, all depreciable assets except real estate), as long as no more than 40 percent of the cost of an asset was deducted in one year. With the 25 percent augmentation for extra shifts, as much as 50 or 60 percent of cost could thus be written off in the year of acquisition in some cases; in any case such assets could be fully depreciated in three years.

In a world of stable prices this change would clearly be inappropriate; since such highly accelerated depreciation would not be required for the accurate measurement of income, it would reduce both the equity and the neutrality of the tax system. Given that Colombia experiences a substantial amount of inflation and yet allows no adjustment of depreciation allowances for price increases, the acceleration of depreciation allowances can be cast in a more favorable light. At an inflation rate of 25 percent the real present value of the depreciation allowances provided as an option in the 1976 legislation is roughly equal to that of indexed economic depreciation.[70] But at any other inflation rate these allowances are either too generous or not generous enough; moreover, they automatically produce an understatement of the depreciable asset component of the net wealth tax base. Thus they are likely to be a poor substitute for explicit inflation adjustment of depreciation allowances.

Law 20 of 1979 reintroduced substantial holes in the measurement of taxable income, partially reversing the progress that had been made in 1974. It effectively exempted income from cattle raising from income tax (by exempting income from the sale of calves in the year of their birth and artificially restating the cost basis of cattle sold during a given year to the value at the end of the previous year) and arbitrarily reduced the value of breeding stock and dairy cattle for net wealth and presumptive income tax purposes by 50 percent.[71]

For the complex calculation of tax on occasional gains of individuals provided by the 1974 reforms, Law 20 substituted a provision that such income should be taxed at one half the average rate applied to ordinary income, but no less than 10 percent. For high-income taxpayers, this represented a substantial reduction in the rate applied to capital gains. The same law provided that no tax would be due on capital gains on fixed assets if 80 percent or more of the gain (plus the original inflation-adjusted cost of the asset) were invested in specified assets. Since there was no requirement that the qualifying investment had to be held for any particular length of time, this provision served as a vehicle for the effective exemption of capital gains and for the evasion of tax on other income that could be converted to capital gains.[72]

Contrary to the case in the counterreforms of 1977 and 1979, the tax laws passed in 1983 largely continued the thrust of the 1974 reforms, especially in the area of the presumptive income tax. A series of incentives of questionable merit was, however, also introduced.[73]

In Law 9 of 1983 a tax credit of 10 percent of dividends received was provided as a means of reducing double taxation of dividends. More generous credits were provided for dividends by "open" corporations and for small amounts of dividends, and other incentives were also given in the effort to widen ownership of corporations.

The same law instituted a measure of presumptive income equal to 2 percent of gross receipts to supplement the measure based on net wealth. This reform was aimed specifically at the commerce and service sectors; the former were thought to evade the wealth-based presumptive tax by systematically understating inventories. In addition, it extended the presumptive income tax to limited liability companies.

Law 14 of 1983 provided for the automatic adjustment of cadastral values for inflation; this reform has the potential of improving the measurement of the value of real estate and is important for both the net wealth tax and the calculation of presumptive income. But, in a major reversal of tax reform, the value of rural real estate for purpose of the presumptive income tax was limited to 75 percent of its cadastral value. In addition, several more unjustified exemptions and deductions were granted the agricultural sector. On the other hand, a rule was introduced prohibiting the use of losses from any activity to offset labor income.

Several times during the period measures were taken to reduce the number of taxpayers required to file income and net wealth tax returns. Returns were not required if 80 percent of income was from labor subject to withholding, if the remaining 20 percent was also subject to withholding, if the taxpayer was not an owner of shares in a limited liability company (ownership of corporate shares was allowed), if net wealth fell below a certain level, and if the taxpayer was not liable for sales tax. For such taxpayers withholding fully discharged income tax liability, there was no liability for net wealth tax, and tax on sales of assets was withheld by the notary.

In 1983 the value-added tax was extended to the retail level, with a "simplified system" being made available to small retailers in the effort to ease compliance costs and administrative burden. Additional services (e.g., hotels, computing services, maintenance, and rental of goods and fixtures) were brought within the scope of the tax. Moreover, because of the difficulties of dealing with differential rates at the retail level, there was some unification of rates; this led to an increase in the rate of (noncreditable) tax applied to domestically produced capital goods. Imported capital goods used in basic industries continued to be exempt from tax. In 1984 exemptions for agricultural machinery, transportation equipment, and certain other goods were eliminated.[74]

VII. The 1986 Reforms

In 1986 the government of Colombia undertook another major reform of the income tax. The avowed purpose of these reforms was equity, economic neutrality, and simplification.[75]

These reforms contained several distinct and important components.[76] While some of these changes continued in the tradition of the Musgrave proposals, others seem to have been influenced more by the thinking that lay behind the U.S. tax reform of 1986.[77] Moreover, the 1986 reforms exhibited a heavy—and healthy—dose of pragmatism.

The government attempted yet another assault on the citadel of tax preferences. It was successful in eliminating the exemptions for severance pay and pensions (but only for those in excess of rather high floors), for the thirteenth-month and Christmas bonuses, for many travel and representation allowances of public and private employees, and for vacation pay.[78] The exemptions for severance pay and pensions below monthly ceilings, representation allowances for high-level government officials, judges, and teachers, and income of the military in excess of the basic amount were retained.[79] The 1986 reforms eliminated the tax exemption for reinvested capital gains contained in Law 20 of 1979.[80] It left some sectors favored; these include cattle raising, forestry, commercial airlines, and navigation. Only 60 percent of the cadastral value of real estate is to be included in the calculation of net wealth.[81]

The 1986 reform reduced tax rates dramatically. The top tax rate applied to individual income was reduced from 49 percent to 30 percent; the same rate is applied to the income of corporations and limited liability companies. At the same time the application of a preferential tax rate to occasional gains was eliminated.[82] Though the same rate schedule is applied to occasional gains as to ordinary income, it is applied separately to the two types of income, instead of to the aggregate of ordinary income and occasional gains.

Withholding taxes were made final taxes for a large portion of the taxpaying population. Filing may not be necessary, and is not allowed, depending inter alia on the size and composition of income (at least 80 percent from wages and salaries), the application of withholding to all income, and the size of net wealth.[83] The benefits of income splitting were abolished; thus the Colombian income tax is now based entirely on the income of individuals rather than on that of married couples. Credits for personal exemptions and special credits for rent and expenses of health and education have also been abolished. These changes make much more accurate withholding possible, and the three tables required previously were replaced with a single table.[84]

The provisions for taxing the imputed income from owner-occupied homes and allowing a limited credit for residential rent were eliminated.[85] Though mortgage interest remains deductible, deductions are subject to annual limits.[86]

Deductions for joint expenses of earning both taxable and exempt income are allowed in the proportion of taxable to total income. Moreover, no deduction is allowed for payments to nontaxable organizations related to the taxpayer.[87] Expense deductions of independent professionals were limited to 50 percent of income in an effort to curtail a major source of abuse and further the achievement of "rough justice."[88]

Taxation of decentralized agencies of the government, mixed enterprises (those with a combination of public and private ownership), and business enterprises and financial income of nonprofit organizations was increased in order to achieve parity with the for-profit private sector.[89]

The 1986 reforms unified the taxation of corporations and limited liability companies by taxing both at a rate of 30 percent. It "integrated" the taxation of companies and individuals by exempting corporate dividends and participation in profits of limited liability companies from tax at the individual shareholder/owner level.[90] Consistent with this treatment, losses, exempt income, and tax credits of companies cannot be used to offset income of their owners.[91] To prevent the provision of relief from double taxation of dividends where no double taxation exists, tax-free distributions are limited to seven-thirds of the amount of tax paid by the entity.[92] To be consistent, shares of corporations and limited liability corporations were excluded from the figure for net wealth used in the calculation of presumptive income.[93]

Inflation adjustment was extended to all interest income and expense. (Inflation adjustment will be fully effective only after a ten-year transition period, except in the case of interest income of individuals, for which full inflation adjustment was allowed beginning in 1986.)[94] The values of capital assets are to be adjusted for inflation for the purpose of calculating gains on dispositions.[95] Indexation was not applied to depreciable assets or to inventories. (Last-in, first-out inventory accounting is allowed, however.) The government was also granted power to make potentially far-reaching changes in the part of the law dealing with inflation adjustment during the two years following enactment.[96]

VIII. Appraisal

Tax policy in Colombia has generally improved over the past quarter century, though not without important episodes of retrogression or "counterreform." To a large degree the basic improvements made early in the period reviewed here reflect the recommendations of highly visible foreign tax missions, especially the Musgrave Commission (and, to a lesser degree, the Taylor Mission). Interestingly enough, many of these reforms undid mischief advocated by earlier foreign missions, especially the interventionist incentive policies proposed by ECLA.[97] But as a cadre of local experts trained in policy analysis and experienced in tax administration has emerged, the recommendations of foreigners have been modified and extended in important ways by Colombian nationals, especially in the 1974 reforms.

More recently reforms have been essentially "homegrown," the products of local expertise, with only minimal foreign input; this is especially true of the 1986 reforms. As this has occurred, foreign influences of a different sort can be discerned. These include greater attention to the policy goals that underlay the 1984 proposals for tax reform offered by the U.S. Treasury Department: economic neutrality, equity, simplicity, and lower rates.

It seems reasonable to say that throughout the period Colombian tax reform has to a remarkable extent been aiming at the target of an ideal tax system specified by the conventional wisdom imported from more advanced countries. One of the reasons reform proposals have changed over time and that reforms recently implemented often reverse reforms undertaken earlier is that the conventional wisdom has not remained static. Of course, the pattern of reform and counterreform seen over the last half century has also often reflected the ebb and flow of political power of interest groups.

A. Patterns of Change

It is useful to examine briefly the changes that have been made in various aspects of the tax system of Colombia since the early 1960s. Space does not, however, allow adequate discussion and appraisal of the many reforms that have occurred over the past quarter century.[98]

Exemptions and incentives have been substantially curtailed. As a result most elements of the inequitable and distortionary interventionist policies incorporated in the 1960 reforms have been eliminated. Even so, progress has not been uninterrupted, and egregious gaps remain in the income tax base. Exemptions for labor income include many fringe benefits provided by employers, income of the military, and representation allowances of high-level government officials. Income from agriculture, especially cattle raising, and forestry are among the sectors still benefiting from the most outrageously favorable tax treatment.

The taxation of housing has undergone an interesting evolution in Colombia. Twenty-five years ago imputed income from owner-occupied housing in excess of a specified figure was taxed, as the normative theory of tax policy says is proper; to be consistent there was a limited deduction for residential rent, and the deduction of mortgage interest was allowed. By 1986 it was realized that the taxation of imputed income could not be enforced effectively, so this provision and the limited credit for residential rent were repealed. Though mortgage interest continues to be deductible, the deduction is limited. This seems to be a movement in the right direction, given administrative realities in Colombia, especially if the interest deduction can be reduced further.

Simplification has been furthered by the recent changes that eliminate the requirement to file income and net-wealth tax returns for many whose income is primarily from labor and subject to withholding. Elimination of the taxation of imputed income on owner-occupied housing, income splitting, personal exemptions, and special exemptions, while otherwise questionable on policy grounds, facilitates this important reform. On balance the "rough justice" that these reforms make possible is preferable to the attempt to implement the more sophisticated and complex provisions of prior law; the latter approach may have been preferable from a theoretical standpoint, but often it could not actually be achieved.

Rate reduction of the type seen in 1986 (a top individual rate of 30 percent, to be applied to income of companies as well) is quite remarkable, considering the recommendations of the Taylor and Musgrave missions to raise the top individual rate to 62 percent or to 55 percent, respectively. This is one aspect of reform that appears to show the effect of U.S. thinking on the matter in the 1980s. Of course, alternative explanations can also be given, such as a resurgence of the political power of the right in Colombia and response to the same influences that led to rate reduction in developed countries, including the United Kingdom.

The unification and integration of the taxation of companies and their owners contained in the 1986 reforms is at the same time consistent and inconsistent with the recommendations of the Musgrave Commission. There is little doubt that the unification of rates, one of the recommendations of the Musgrave Commission, is appropriate; given the economic importance of limited liability companies, unification was necessary to achieve equity and neutrality with corporations. Responding to fears of decapitalization of the Colombian economy, the government chose to exclude dividends from the taxable income of individual shareholders. This "rough justice" form of integration also seems appropriate for Colombia, despite its variance from standard practice and advice; given administrative realities it would have made little sense to attempt one of the approaches that are correct conceptually but much more demanding of scarce resources for compliance and administration. By comparison, the Musgrave Commission thought integration to be unnecessary.

Depreciation allowances are much faster than would be justified in a world of no inflation or in an indexed income tax system. By coincidence, at recent inflation rates the present pattern of depreciation allowances is roughly equivalent in real present value to indexed economic depreciation. Yet acceleration of allowances is a poor substitute for explicit inflation adjustment of asset values, both because the rate of inflation may change and because it produces an understated measure of the net wealth tax base.

Inflation adjustment has become increasingly sophisticated. The 1986 provisions for adjustment of interest income and expense and of the basis used in calculating capital gains constitutes a major improvement in the tax system of Colombia. It would be appropriate to extend inflation adjustment to depreciable assets and to inventories, while adopting more realistic (longer) useful lives.[99] Of course, if that is done, the inflation-adjusted values of assets should be used for purposes of calculating net wealth and presumptive income.

Presumptive income taxation is an important and useful addition to the fiscal arsenal of Colombia. It could be improved, however, by comparing presumptive income (based on net wealth) only to nonlabor income in the calculation of total income. Moreover, the limitation of the value of real estate to only 75 percent of its cadastral value should be eliminated. Finally, the use of receipts to calculate presumptive income does not make economic sense.

The excess-profits tax was appropriately eliminated. Similarly, it was proper to abolish the supplementary taxes that were levied on income and wealth at the beginning of the period under examination.

Tax administration has not been improved as much as might be desired. However, recent changes in the tax law that relieve large numbers of taxpayers subject to withholding of the obligation of filing returns should assist in freeing up administrative resources for more productive tasks. This trend of tailoring the tax system to the capabilities of the tax administration is a healthy development as long as revenue, equity, and neutrality are not needlessly sacrificed.[100]

Sales tax reform has improved greatly the implementation of this relatively recent addition to the Colombian tax system. In particular, conversion to a more-or-less standard credit method VAT improves the administration of the tax. It appears that extension of the tax to the retail level may have been premature, especially since the simplified system for small retailers does not provide appreciable administrative benefits.[101] Continuation of the practice of allowing no credit for capital goods is also highly questionable; it is reasonable only if it is thought that the price of capital remains artificially low. Important progress has been made in reducing the reliance on stamp taxes, but more remains to be done in this area.

B. A Final Observation

During the remainder of 1988 the government of Colombia will presumably be considering ways to improve the system of inflation adjustment, as provided by the 1986 statute. Among obvious issues to be discussed are the indexing of depreciable assets and inventories.[102] Any changes made for the income tax should also carry over into the measurement of net wealth and the calculation of presumptive income.

Because of the complexities involved in inflation adjustment, not to mention timing issues that arise under the income tax, even in a world without inflation, another question naturally arises. That is whether Colombia should switch to a system of direct taxation based on consumption, rather than income. Under such a system expensing would be allowed for all business purchases, neither interest expense nor dividends would be deductible, and neither interest nor dividends would be taxable.[103]

The movement to such a system would actually be relatively small, given the changes already under way as a result of the 1986 act. Depreciation is so accelerated for some assets that movement to expensing would involve little change. Dividends are already exempt and nondeductible. Following the ten-year transition period provided by the 1986 act, the majority of interest will also be exempt and nondeductible.[104]

Adopting a system of this type would greatly simplify compliance and administration of the "income" tax, since no inflation adjustment is required and timing issues (such as depreciation) do not arise. Adopting such a tax would, however, raise important issues of equity, taxation of foreign capital, and transition.[105] Moreover, a consumption-based direct tax would not dovetail with the net-wealth tax in the way that the income tax does. Finally, no matter what further reforms are undertaken, it is important to focus on tax administration, for a tax system cannot be truly satisfactory if it is not administered effectively.

Notes

The author has benefited from valuable comments on an earlier draft of this paper from Richard Bird, Wayne Thirsk, and George Zodrow. The views expressed here are, however, solely his own.

1   Moreover, the history of analysis and reform has been well documented. For analyses of the Colombian tax system by external advisers and consultants, see *Fiscal Survey of Colombia* (1965), Bird (1970), Musgrave and Gillis (1971), Gillis and McLure (1977), McLure (1982), Thirsk (1988), and McLure, Mutti, Thuronyi, and Zodrow (forthcoming). Of course, there have also been numerous studies by Colom-

bian authors of particular reform issues; for example, Carrizosa (1986) deals with taxation and the revitalization of Colombian capital markets. For a thorough review and analysis of tax policy in Colombia, especially during the period from the fundamental reforms of 1974 until 1985, as well as a brief overview of pre-1974 tax policy and an extensive list of references on tax reform in Colombia, see Perry and Cárdenas (1986). (It is worth noting that Perry, as director general of internal taxes, was intimately involved in the formulation of the 1974 reforms.) Hernández (1987) reproduces many of the documents explaining the rationale for the 1986 reforms. Rojas (1983) describes several aspects of the tax reforms of 1960, 1967, 1974, and 1982–83. This last source, which Richard Bird brought to the attention of the author only after the paper was essentially in final form, has not been consulted adequately.

2   Many of these topics have, however, been the subject of analyses by tax reform groups. See, for example, *Fiscal Survey* (1965), chapters 7 (urban real property), 8 (revenues from foreign commerce), 9 (tariffs and development), 10 (internal indirect taxes of subnational governments), and 12 (autonomous agencies); Bird (1970), chapter 5 (local government finance); Musgrave and Gillis (1971), pp. 648–69 (municipal indirect taxes), pp. 692–719 (automotive tax reform, including the pricing of petroleum products), and pp. 723–805 (subnational taxes and intergovernmental relations); Gillis and McLure (1977), chapter 5 (taxes and subsidies on the external sector); Ascher (1988—political economy of reform); and Perry and Cárdenas (1986), chapters 4–6 (macroeconomic conditions and revenues) and 13–15 (political economy of reform). Intergovernmental relations in Colombia have been the subject of a special commission; see Bird (1984), which also discusses earmarking of revenues as well as other issues. Subnational taxation has been the subject of considerable reform during the 1980s.

3   See Perry and Cárdenas (1986), pp. 15–21, especially pp. 16, 19–20, *Fiscal Survey* (1965), pp. 26–27, and Hernández (1987), pp. 1–8. *Fiscal Survey* (1965), p. 26 notes that Colombia's history of income taxation dates from 1821, when it became the first nation in the Western Hemisphere to impose such a tax, a schedular levy.

4   See Perry and Cárdenas (1986), pp. 15–18, Bird (1970), pp. 191–203, and Rojas (1983), pp. 40–41. Thirsk (1988) provides an excellent summary of the history of tax reform in Colombia, especially that during the last quarter century.

5   This discussion draws heavily on *Fiscal Survey* (1965), pp. 26–27.

6   *Fiscal Survey* (1965), pp. 30, 68–69. Neither *Fiscal Survey* (1965) nor Musgrave and Gillis (1971) mentions the allowances for travel and representation, perhaps through oversight.

7   *Fiscal Survey* (1965), p. 35.

8   Ibid., pp. 65–68.

9   Ibid., pp. 27–32.

10   Ibid., pp. 82–83. The law provided for the use of declining balance methods of depreciation, but since the factor to be applied to the declining balance could be no greater than 100 percent, this alternative would not be attractive. Bird (1970), p. 253 notes that machinery used more than ten hours per day could legally be depreciated more rapidly than under a 10-year straight-line schedule, but the provision was apparently never put into practice.

11   Ibid., p. 33, 87–90.

12   See *Fiscal Survey* (1965), pp. 27–30, which also describes the characteristics of these

organizational forms as well as those of several economically less important ones.

13   Ibid., p. 55.

14   Ibid., p. 63.

15   Ibid., pp. 97−98.

16   Ibid., pp. 37−40.

17   See, however, *Fiscal Survey* (1965), pp. 35−37.

18   Ibid., pp. 210−11. Figures on revenue patterns during that period may be distorted by the high yield of taxes on foreign commerce, since those years were characterized by high imports; see Bird (1970), pp. 3−7.

19   Ibid., p. 54.

20   Ibid., pp. 60−61. It might be noted that the Taylor Mission also thought that the personal exemptions then being allowed were too high, but did not propose reducing them since their real value was being eroded by inflation.

21   Ibid., p. 98.

22   Ibid., pp. 54−58 and pp. 244−68; the quotation is from p. 58.

23   Ibid., pp. 70−77.

24   The consumer price index for Bogotá had risen by 76.4 percent during the period 1954−55 to 1962, or at an annual rate of about 8 percent. The official exchange rate of pesos for U.S. dollars had changed from 2.51 in 1952−56 to 9.09 in 1962. *Fiscal Survey* (1965), pp. 82−85 and 263−67. The discussion of inflation adjustment is quite inadequate in several respects, though not atypical for its day; in particular, it fails to distinguish between basing depreciation on replacement costs and allowing price-level adjustments of the historical-cost basis of depreciable assets.

25   *Fiscal Survey* (1965), pp. 21, 90−91. For a more complete discussion that reaches much the same conclusions, but is more skeptical about the usefulness of special incentives, see Bird (1970), pp. 132−46.

26   *Fiscal Survey* (1965), chapter 6, especially pp. 121−25 and 129−33. Bird (1970), p. 89, and Perry and Junguito (1978), p. 33, note that proposals for the presumptive taxation of income from agriculture had been made several times before the Taylor Report. Hirschman (1963), pp. 116−41, describes the early history of proposals to use tax policy to improve the productivity of Colombian agriculture.

27   *Fiscal Survey* (1965), pp. 96−98.

28   *Fiscal Survey* (1965), p. 217, 220. Bird (1970), pp. 112−14, also favors increased use of selective excises rather than a broad-based sales tax, but for administrative reasons. He also favors a wholesale level tax over a manufacturers' tax.

29   One important change had been made. The form of the subsidy for nontraditional exports had been changed in 1967 from an income tax exemption (with export profits presumed to be 40 percent of the value of exports) to a system of negotiable and tax-exempt tax-credit certificates based on the value of exports. Although the credit was equal to 15 percent of exports, it could not be utilized to pay taxes until one year after issue. Bird (1970), p. 143, notes that at the end of 1967 the certificates were trading at a discount of 30 percent, and thus were worth about 10 percent of exports.

30   References provided in the footnotes to this section relate primarily to the final report of the Musgrave Commission in Part I of Musgrave and Gillis (1971). Important background for the recommendations reported here is contained in the staff papers, which also appear in Musgrave and Gillis (1971). On the income tax, see especially White and Quale (1971) and Slitor (1971).

31   Musgrave and Gillis (1971), p. 35.

32   Ibid., p. 98.

33   "The excess profits tax is a major contributor to the high and erratic marginal rate structure. It . . . has no place in a peacetime economy . . . . Even inflation at continuous moderate rates inevitably warps the significance and intertaxpayer comparability of historic investment costs (by which net wealth is largely measured for Colombian excess profits purposes) . . . . Any function the excess profits tax may have served in the past is now outweighed by its evident inequities, distortions, incentives to waste 'cheap tax pesos,' and disincentives to growth and efficiency." Musgrave and Gillis (1971), p. 77. For another negative appraisal of the excess-profits tax, see Bird (1970), pp. 83–84.

34   For a more thorough analysis of earmarking, see Bird (1984).

35   Musgrave and Gillis (1971), pp. 38–40.

36   Ibid., pp. 41–42.

37   Ibid., pp. 43–44.

38   Ibid., pp. 44–45. The Taylor report makes no mention of the deduction for contributions; this was presumably an oversight.

39   Ibid., pp. 44–45.

40   Ibid., pp. 50–51.

41   Ibid., pp. 51–53.

42   Ibid., p. 62.

43   Ibid., pp. 46–50.

44   Ibid., pp. 63–69. For further discussions of the taxation of "hard-to-tax" sectors in Colombia, see also Bird (1970), pp. 96–102.

45   Musgrave and Gillis (1971), pp. 66–67.

46   Ibid., pp. 78–81. Of course, the heavier taxation of capital may be more apparent than real.

47   Ibid., p. 82. It also offered the counsel that "the proper solution for Colombia lies in a well-designed stabilization policy." While one can hardly disagree with the accuracy of this statement, one can question the propriety of deliberately choosing not to modify the tax system in order to avoid the inequities and distortions that otherwise result in a world in which this prescription is not followed.

48   Bird (1970), pp. 85–86 favors similar provisions.

49   Among these guidelines were: relatively greater emphasis on increasing saving than on increasing investment, avoidance of interference with decisions on factor proportions, general availability of credits with less administrative discretion, and carry-forward of unused credits (Musgrave and Gillis [1971], pp. 91–94). The Musgrave Commission also discussed trade-related incentives; these are not reviewed here, as they are beyond the scope of this paper. But see Musgrave and Gillis (1971), pp. 94–96.

50   Musgrave and Gillis (1971), pp. 98–105.

51   Ibid., pp. 84–89.

52   Though the tax was established in 1963, it was not actually applied until 1965.

53   See Gillis (1971), pp. 594–97 for a description of the early evolution of the sales tax. Perry (forthcoming) provides greater detail on the development of the tax (especially on post-1968 developments), including efforts to free business inputs from tax, and describes both economic and administrative difficulties with the tax.

54 See Due (1972) for a description of ring systems of sales taxation.

55 Musgrave and Gillis (1971), pp. 115–19.

56 Perry and Cárdenas (1986), p. 12, indicates that these reforms were prepared by a team that was 100 percent Colombian. See also Gillis and McLure (1977), chapter I. (Page numbers are to the version of this report published in Spanish. Chapter numbers correspond to section numbers in the xeroxed English version.)

57 Perry and Cárdenas (1986), pp. 24–25, 32, and 267, and Gillis and McLure (1977), chap. II. For full details of the 1974 reforms, see *Impuesto sobre la Renta en Colombia* (1984). The 1977 reforms allowed certain state enterprises, including Ecopetrol, to deduct their gross investments from the amount of their tax liability; see Perry and Cárdenas (1986), p. 41.

58 Perry and Cárdenas (1986), pp. 23–25; Gillis and McLure (1977), chapter II.

59 Perry and Cárdenas (1986), pp. 25–26.

60 Gillis and McLure (1977), chapter II.

61 Perry and Cárdenas (1986), pp. 26–27.

62 Gillis and McLure (1977), chapter III, pp. 103–4, provide examples of how taxpayers could benefit from intentional "errors" and delays.

63 Ibid., chapter II, pp. 68–69.

64 Perry and Cárdenas (1986), pp. 27–28; Perry and Junguito (1978), pp. 34–36.

65 Perry (forthcoming). Under prior law no tax would have been collected on inputs to zero-rated sales or exports. Under the credit system, tax would be collected on all purchases; this could necessitate refunds in the above cases.

66 Gillis and McLure (1977), chapter IV and Perry (forthcoming). Bird (1970), pp. 119–21 argues in favor of taxing capital goods, but notes that discrimination against imported capital goods might be appropriate.

67 Perry and Cárdenas (1986), pp. 11, 41–42.

68 Ibid., pp. 41–43; McLure (1982), pp. 1–2.

69 For further details of law and analysis, see *Impuesto sobre la Renta en Colombia* (1984) and McLure (1982).

70 See McLure, Mutti, Thuronyi, and Zodrow (forthcoming), chapter 4.

71 This restored loopholes that had existed twenty years earlier and were only closed in 1974; see *Fiscal Survey* (1965), p. 123, and Perry and Cárdenas (1986), p. 25, where this system is called "peculiar," and p. 42.

72 Perry and Cárdenas (1986), pp. 42–43; McLure (1982).

73 For a description and appraisal of these laws, see Perry and Cárdenas (1986), pp. 43–50.

74 Perry (forthcoming).

75 See Colombia, Ministerio de Hacienda y Crédito Público, *Exposición de Motivos* (1986).

76 *Nueva Reforma Tributaria* (1987) is a particularly useful compilation of Law 75 of 1986. Besides containing the text of the law and regulations issued through February 26, 1987, it includes provision-by-provision explanations taken from the government's *Exposición de Motivos*, as well as the text of provisions of prior law repealed by Law 75.

77 See the emphasis on equity, neutrality, simplicity, and lower rates in *Exposición de Motivos* (1986). The reforms of the taxation of income from business and capital reflect the influence of such writings as Carrizosa (1986). The influence of U.S. tax

reform can be seen clearly in Article 44 of the 1986 tax reform act, which gives the government authority to change tax rates applied to the income of foreign taxpayers if such changes should be deemed appropriate in the light of changes being made in the tax laws of countries of origin of capital invested in Colombia; of course, the United States is the country that has made the most dramatic changes in its income tax, as well as being the most important source of foreign investment in Colombia.

78   *Nueva Reforma Tributaria*, Law 75 of 1986, Article 108, repealing Article 72 of decree 2053 of 1974.

79   Ibid., Article 35.

80   Ibid., Article 108, repealing Article 10 of Law 20 of 1979.

81   Ibid., Article 73.

82   Ibid., Article 4.

83   Ibid., Article 63.

84   Ibid., Article 82 and Article 108, repealing Article 85 of Decree 2053 of 1974 and Article 2 of Law 20 of 1979. It is worth noting that this approach is consistent with the approach advocated almost twenty years ago in Bird (1970), pp. 61, 62–63: "Given the limits of administrative capacity in Colombia, however, some sacrifice will have to be made with regard to fair treatment of different taxpayers in order to make a current-payment system workable . . . . Adoption of a full-fledged current-payment and withholding system would require substantial simplification of the rate and base of the Colombian income tax in order to be feasible."

85   Ibid., Article 108, repealing Article 70 of decree 2053 of 1974 and Article 2 of Law 20 of 1979.

86   Ibid., Article 40.

87   Ibid., Article 43.

88   Ibid., Article 36.

89   Ibid., Articles 31–33.

90   Ibid., Article 21.

91   Ibid., Articles 24 and 84.

92   Ibid., Article 22.

93   Ibid., Article 48.

94   Ibid., Articles 27–30.

95   Ibid., Article 64.

96   McLure, Mutti, Thuronyi, and Zodrow (forthcoming) was prepared for the government of Colombia as background for possible changes in the law. The full contents of this report could not be made public at the time.

97   Bird (1970), p. 203, offered the following similar assessment almost twenty years ago: "Colombia thus has a long tradition of foreign tax missions, as well as a surprisingly good record of listening to them, not always with desirable results." Thirsk (1988) also notes the importance of "the prevailing intellectual climate," as well as the "clout of special interests," in shaping the tax laws of Colombia.

98   See, however, Perry and Cárdenas (1986), Gillis and McLure (1977), McLure (1982), Thirsk (1988), and McLure, Mutti, Thuronyi, and Zodrow (forthcoming). Since nothing has been said thus far about the role of macroeconomic conditions and revenue needs in influencing the timing and nature of reform, it may be well to note as background to the discussion that follows the conclusion of Perry and Cárdenas

(1986), p. 81, that most reforms that increased revenues (except those of 1953 and 1974) occurred when external crises reduced revenues and made it difficult to finance government expenditures and that those that reduced revenues occurred during periods of fiscal plenty. By comparison, the 1986 reforms were motivated by concerns for equity, neutrality, and simplicity and were intended to be revenue neutral. Thirsk (1988) draws important lessons from the Colombian experience in the following areas: the role of fiscal crisis, the power of ideas, the clout of special interests, the importance of macroeconomic performance for the perceived success of reform, the interrelations between tax instruments, and the conflict between equity and simplicity.

99   There is, of course, some risk that inflation will be worse if the tax system allows inflation adjustment than if it does not. Even so, the inequities and distortions that result from the failure to allow inflation adjustment seem to outweigh this risk.

100   This development reminds one of the following advice of Bird (1970), p. 201: "One improvement would be to recognize explicitly the need for crude, arbitrary solutions in many instances and to attempt to be consistent in applying them rather than assuming that a perfect law can be perfectly administered .... A less-than-ideal tax designed for a poor administration may work better—its effects may be more in line with those desired—than a 'good' tax badly administered."

101   Perry (forthcoming) indicates that the problems of administering the tax at the retail level were "so severe as to cast serious doubts about the presumed 'superiority' of the VAT that extends all the way to the retail level, in a country like Colombia."

102   See the statement by Pardo (1987), pp. 30–31, to this effect.

103   See McLure, Mutti, Thuronyi, and Zodrow (forthcoming) or Zodrow and McLure (1988) for an argument that this approach to the treatment of debt and interest is far superior to the consumption-based alternative that taxes cash flows, including proceeds of borrowing and interest income (and allows deductions for lending and interest expense).

104   If the nominal interest rate is 25 percent and the inflation rate is 20 percent, 80 percent of interest income and expense would be disregarded for tax purposes.

105   See Zodrow and McLure (1988) for a discussion of some of these issues.

References

Ascher, William, "Risk, Politics, and Tax Reform: Lessons from Some Latin American Experiences, presented at a Duke University Conference on 'Lessons from Fundamental Tax Reform in Developing Countries,'" Washington, April 22–23, 1988.

Bird, Richard M., *Taxation and Development: Lessons from the Colombian Experience* (Cambridge, Mass.: Harvard University Press, 1970).

———, *Intergovernmental Finance in Colombia* (Cambridge, Mass.: Harvard University International Tax Program, 1984).

Carrizosa S., Mauricio, *Hacia la Recuperación del Mercado de Capitales en Colombia* (Bogotá: Bolsa de Bogotá, 1986).

Due, John F., "Alternative Forms of Sales Taxation in Developing Countries," *Journal of Development Studies*, Vol. 8 (January 1972), pp. 260–76.

Fiscal Survey of Colombia (Baltimore: Johns Hopkins University Press, 1965).

Gillis, Malcolm, "Sales Tax Reform," in Musgrave and Gillis, *Fiscal Reform*, pp. 593–647.

Gillis, Malcolm, and Charles E. McLure, Jr., *La Reforma Tributaria Colombiana de 1974* (Bogotá: Banco Popular, 1977).

Hernández V., Rafael, *Reforma Tributaria de Barco: Un Paso Hacia el Futuro* (Bogotá: Compañía Editorial Integrada, 1987).

Hirschman, Albert O., *Journeys Toward Progress: Studies of Economic Policymaking in Latin America* (New York: Twentieth Century Fund, 1963).

Impuesto sobre la Renta en Colombia: Compilación Cronológica de Normas Vigentes del Impuesto sobre la Renta, Complementarios, y Procedimiento (Bogotá: Ministerio de Hacienda y Crédito Público, 1984).

Low M., Enrique, and Jorge Gomez R., *Política Fiscal* (Bogotá: Universidad Externado de Colombia, 1986).

McLure, Charles E., Jr., "Income and Complementary Taxes," xeroxed, 1982.

———, "Lessons for LDCs of U.S. Income Tax Reform," this volume.

———, "Tax Reform in an Inflationary Environment: the Case of Colombia," xeroxed, 1988.

McLure, Charles E., Jr., Jack Mutti, Victor Thuronyi, and George Zodrow, *The Taxation of Income from Business and Capital in Colombia* (Durham, N.C.: Duke University Press forthcoming).

Musgrave, Richard A., and Malcolm Gillis, *Fiscal Reform for Colombia: The Final Report and Staff Papers of the Colombian Commission on Tax Reform* (Cambridge, Mass.: Harvard University International Tax Program, 1971).

Nueva Reforma Tributaria, Segunda Edición (Bogotá: Cámara de Comercio de Bogotá, 1987).

Pardo R., Santiago, "Fundamentos, Objectivos e Instrumentos de la Reforma: Alcance de las Facultades Extraordinarios Otorgadas al Ejecutivo," in *Nueva Reforma Tributaria*, Segunda Edición (Bogotá: Cámara de Comercio de Bogotá, 1987), pp. 21–31.

Perry, Guillermo, "Development of the Value Added Tax in Colombia," in Malcolm Gillis, Gerardo Sicat, and Carl Shoup, editors, *Value Added Taxation in Developing Countries* (forthcoming, The World Bank).

Perry, R., Guillermo, and Cárdenas S., Mauricio, *Diez Años de Reformas Tributarios en Colombia* (Bogotá: FEDESARROLLO, 1986).

Perry, Guillermo, and Junguito, Roberto, "Evaluación del Régimen de la Renta Presuntiva Mínima en Colombia," *Coyuntura Económica*, vol. 8, no. 3 (October 1978), pp. 33–50.

Rojas H., Fernando, *La Reforma Tributaria 1982–83* (Bogotá: Asociación Nacional de Instituciones Financieras, 1983).

Slitor, Richard, "Reform of the Business Tax Structure: Analysis of Problems and Alternative Remedial Proposals," in Musgrave and Gillis, *Fiscal Reform*, pp. 463–529.

Thirsk, Wayne, "The 1986 Tax Reform in Colombia," World Bank Development Research Department Paper, March 1987.

———, "Some Lessons from the Colombian Experience," Provisional Papers in Public Economics, World Bank, Washington, April 8, 1988.

White, Melvin, and Andrew C. Quale, Jr., "The Colombian Individual Income Tax: Rates, Exemptions, Deductions, and Administrative Aspects," in Musgrave and Gillis, *Fiscal Reform*, pp. 301–30.

Zodrow, George R., and Charles E. McLure, Jr., "Alternative Methods of Implementing Direct Consumption Taxes in Developing Countries," xeroxed, 1988.

4

Comprehensive Tax Reform: The Indonesian Experience, 1981–1988

....

Malcolm Gillis

I. Introduction

(A) Barriers to Tax Reform

Indonesia enacted major tax reform in the mid-1980s. The new system represents a sharp departure from tax policies followed since independence in 1945. This chapter explains why tax reform was so long in coming in this country, what it sought to achieve, the extent to which objectives were fulfilled, and why. The chapter also draws important lessons from this experience, lessons that may or may not prove useful in other settings.

This tax reform is best understood against the broader backdrop of overall economic policymaking following the economic and social upheavals of the mid-1960s that led to virtual national collapse in 1966. Indonesian economic history since that time is laden with notable examples of fundamental policy reforms affecting such key "macro prices" as exchange rates, interest rates, domestic oil prices, and prices of agricultural staples, especially rice (Gillis, 1984). To illustrate: two major and largely successful reforms in policies affecting credit and growth of liquid assets were enacted over the period 1967–83. Further, there were five devaluations, of which at least four were successful by almost any measure (Gillis and Dapice, 1986). Also, successive reforms in agricultural price and subsidy policies over the fifteen years prior to 1983 had, by 1979, yielded generally positive results both for production of staples and rural income growth (Collier et al., 1982).

Policy reform in these critical areas from 1966–83 played a significant role in improving living standards in this, the fifth most populous country in the world after the United States. Over that period, real GDP more than doubled (Gillis, 1984), so that by 1983, income per capita, at $560, was high enough to place Indonesia among those nations classified by the World Bank as lower-middle income developing countries (World Bank, 1985, *World Development Report*).

The tax system, however, remained essentially untouched by any significant reform initiatives throughout the 1970s and early 1980s, in spite of widely acknowledged defects in tax structure and tax administration. Many of the most serious defects in tax structure stemmed from the fact that income, sales, and property taxes were all based on outdated tax legislation left as one of the dubious legacies of the last few decades of three centuries of Dutch colonial administration.

To be sure, changes were introduced in the system after independence in 1945, but most of these resulted from generally unsuccessful efforts to fine-tune the tax system to achieve such nonrevenue goals as regional development, income redistribution, and industrial growth. By 1981, the tax system had, as a result of decades of such manipulation, become a complex maze of virtually unenforceable, if not unintelligible, amendments, decrees, and regulations. Because it was both outdated and unusually complex, the generally applicable tax system was unproductive of revenue, a source of substantial economic waste, and essentially inequitable in every important sense. Given the glaring weaknesses in the tax system through the early 1980s, the nation was able to avoid massive budget deficits only because of rapid growth in taxes on foreign oil companies (table 4.1, column 2). These taxes were collected on the basis of special, much simpler, tax provisions contained in the oil agreements themselves.

Inattention to the need for tax reform, in the face of such obvious problems, was due to at least four factors. First, low-income groups were generally unaware of the costs imposed upon them by a system of indirect taxes that was almost wholly hidden from ultimate consumers. Second, few higher-income persons could have been dissatisfied with a system that extracted so little from them: personal income taxes were little more than 1 percent of GDP; virtually all corporation tax collections came from larger state-owned enterprises and foreign firms, and in any case amounted to less than one and one-half percent of GDP. Moreover, penalties for tax evasion, when imposed at all, were so light as to be virtually nonexistent. Third, the tax administration was by and large quite comfortable with the system, particularly since it demanded little effort from them. Also, the extreme complexity of the system meant that very few outside the tax administration knew exactly which tax laws and regulations applied in any given case: the scope for corruption in tax administration was therefore very wide.

The three foregoing factors, however, were relatively unimportant impediments to tax reform compared to the fourth: the massive inflow of government receipts from oil, and later liquified natural gas (LNG), from 1973–81. The implications of these natural-resource revenues in stifling tax reform are most apparent when comparing trends in non-oil taxation and government spending. Table 4.1 portrays the evolution of the tax ratio (ratio of taxes to GDP) in Indonesia over the twenty-year period beginning in 1967. In interpreting this table, it is essential to know that the tax system had virtually vanished in the years of extreme economic instability of 1963–66 that culminated in hyperinflation in 1966–67. The revenue capacity of the system recovered steadily but slowly, weakened both by growing complexity and erosion in standards of conduct in tax administration. The tax ratio reached 10.3 percent in 1970 and 13 percent in 1972, the year before the first oil boom. For the period 1972–76, the tax ratio for Indonesia averaged 16 percent, just about matching the average for all LDCs over the same period (Gillis et al., 1987). However, in Indonesia's case, more than half of government revenues then came from the enclave oil sector (including LNG). Dependency upon oil revenues became even more pronounced after the onset of the second oil boom in late 1978: for the next four years, oil and LNG revenues accounted for more than two-thirds of total domestic tax revenue (see table 4.1).

The successive explosions in oil revenues in 1973–75 and 1979–81 not only precluded any serious tax reform initiatives, but also allowed a palpable slackening in the efforts of the tax administration to collect domestic non-oil taxes. By that year, the ratio of non-oil taxes to GDP had slipped to 6.1 percent, the lowest since the early years of economic rehabilitation in 1967–68, and easily among the lowest in the world.

(B) Planning for Tax Reform

The minister of finance, supported by influential colleagues in the Planning Agency, decided early in January 1981 to initiate preparations for fundamental tax reform, for implementation sometime before the middle of the decade. This decision was made at a time when most institutions, particularly the World Bank, were projecting continued strength in world oil markets through the decade (World Bank, 1981).

Over the next six months, decisions were reached on virtually all

Table 4.1   Indonesia: Domestic Tax Revenues as a Percentage of GDP, 1967−86

Year	(1) Non-oil domestic tax receipts as a percentage of GDP[a]	(2) Total tax receipts on oil and LNG exports as a percentage of GDP	(3) Total domestic tax receipts as a percentage of GDP (1) + (2)
1967	6.2	0.9	7.1
1968	6.0	1.2	7.2
1969	7.3	1.7	9.0
1970	8.3	2.0	10.3
1971	8.7	3.0	11.6
1972	8.7	4.3	13.0
1973	9.2	5.1	14.3
1974	7.4	9.0	16.4
1975	7.9	9.8	17.7
1976	8.4	10.4	18.8
1977	8.4	10.2	18.6
1978	8.8	10.2	19.0
1979	7.9	13.7	21.6
1980	7.2	15.8	23.0
1981	6.1	15.0	21.1
1982	6.8	12.2	19.0
1983	6.7	14.1	20.8
1984	6.1	14.6	20.7
1985	8.0	11.8	19.8
1986	9.1	5.2	14.3
1987 (est.)	8.4[b]	7.1[b]	15.5[b]

a. Non-oil tax revenue includes surpluses from *domestic* oil operations in 1986 and 1987: 1986 = 977 billion rupiah, 1987 = 114 billion rupiah.
b. Estimated.
Source: 1967−79, Gillis (1984) table 3; 1980−87, Dep. Keuangan.

questions of strategy and tactics to be employed in securing reform. Most of these decisions were taken after a brief review of the tax reform experiences of such diverse nations as Japan, Indonesia, Bolivia, Colombia, and Ghana (Gillis, 1985), to draw lessons that might be drawn for Indonesia's benefit.

The first decision was to provide for ample time for preparation of policy options and for drafting of actual reform legislation. A lengthy period would in fact be required for several reasons, not least of which was the need to compile reliable evidence on the impact of the existing tax system upon resource allocation, income distribution, and economic growth. In the end it was this evidence that strongly conditioned

Table 4.2   Indonesia: Pre- and Post-Tax Reform Government Spending, Revenue, and Deficits

Year	(1) Government spending as a percentage of GDP[a]	(2) Total domestic tax receipts as a percentage of GDP[b]	(3) Total foreign grants as a percentage of GDP[c]	(4) Budget deficit as a percentage of GDP (1)−(2 + 3)	(5) Project aid as a percentage of GDP[e]
1971	14.8	11.6	0.3	−3.4	−3.0
1981	23.8	21.1	0.2	−2.5	2.9
1982	22.9	19.0	0.1	−3.8	3.1
1983	24.8	20.8	0.1	−3.9	5.3
1984	22.1	20.7	0.1	−1.3	3.9
1985	23.7	19.8	0.1	−3.8	3.6
1986	20.9	14.3	0.2	−6.4	3.3
1987[d]	17.1	15.1	0.2	−1.8	n.a.

Sources: (a) IBRD and IBRD, GDP figures; (b) Ministry of Finance; (c) IMF; (d) projection, based on assumption of real growth in GDP of 3.2 percent and domestic inflation of 8.0 percent, so that 1987 GDP is RP. 119,618 million; (e) IBRD (1987), table 5.2.

the reform package in the direction of greater economic neutrality (see below). The decision to prepare actual draft legislation was a direct consequence of the author's own experiences in tax reform in Colombia. There, a drafting team was able to detect inconsistencies in policy decisions in time to send them back to decisionmakers for resolution before final drafts were prepared. As it turned out in Indonesia, substantial time and energy were in fact consumed in the process of converting tax policy decisions into actual draft legislation.

The second decision was strongly shaped by the first. In contrast to tax reform initiatives mounted in many other LDCs, the Indonesian effort would focus upon the entire *tax system*, including not only the tax structure but also the complex of mechanisms and institutions governing tax administration and compliance (see chapter 1).

The third decision was that the reform would be *comprehensive* in nature: it was intended to affect most important revenue sources, including foreign oil companies. The reform therefore embraced all income, sales, and property taxes. The only tax sources left out of the scope of the reform program were taxes on foreign trade, primarily import duties. At the time, such taxes accounted for only one twelfth of total central government revenues. Policymakers did not, in 1981, wish to complicate the issue of tax reform by getting into issues of tariff policy, regarded as a troublesome matter for reform of trade, not tax policy. Policymakers judged that in the Indonesian context at least, reform of trade and tariff policies involved even greater bureaucratic and political difficulties than tax reform.[1] Nevertheless, significant liberalizations of trade policy were carried out in 1986 and 1987, but the changes were not nearly as fundamental as those made in the tax system.

The fourth decision related to the taxation of foreign oil companies. In particular, steps were to be taken to avoid disturbing the status quo in oil taxation, so as to avoid a repetition of the acrimonious exchanges between the companies and the government in 1976, when the latter undertook the renegotiation of production-sharing contract arrangements in oil in order to increase taxes due to Indonesia (Gillis, 1980, p. 6). In response to this 1976 initiative, most of the companies undertook sharp cutbacks in exploration in the three subsequent years. The government did not wish another such confrontation. Accordingly, it was decided that oil companies with production-sharing contracts signed *before* the effective date of the reform would be entitled to retain the tax treatment specified in those contracts. For contracts signed after the effective date of the tax reform, the new tax law would apply, but companies were to be assured that *total* tax obligations to Indonesia (given prices and given production volumes), would not be materially changed by tax reform. Thus, any increase in income tax obligations arising from reform would be compensated for by reduction in royalties or other levels; any decrease in income tax rates on oil companies would be made up by other levies upon them.

The fifth decision was that, to the extent possible, the reform would be *contemporaneous* in nature. It was intended that the entire set of reform proposals would be presented at one time, as a package, not as a separable set of initiatives to be proposed and implemented over several years. Moreover, it was decided that effective dates for new sales, income, and property taxes would be as close together as possible. The basis for these timing decisions was a purely political judgment that a series of reform initiatives spread over time would stand a poorer chance of acceptance than one large reform package. This judgment proved to be only partly correct. Although income and sales tax reform were announced together, implementation of the latter was ultimately delayed for fifteen months, and property tax reform was postponed for two years (until 1986).

A sixth decision had to do with the extent of foreign involvement in the reform program. Participation by bilateral and multilateral foreign-aid donors was ruled out, even to the extent of not seeking their help in defraying any of the costs of preparing for reform. Use of expatriate technical assistance, however, was endorsed, given a critical shortage of Indonesians trained in fiscal economics, international tax law, tax accounting, and computer science. Accordingly, the author was requested to organize a team of expatriates with such skills to direct research into topics considered critical for tax reform, and to prepare a draft reform package for consideration by the minister.

It was also decided that the group of foreign specialists would maintain a low profile, in sharp contrast to several previous tax missions organized for several other LDCs. In the end, twenty-eight expatriates from seven countries were involved over the next three years, only one of which resided in Indonesia for longer than four months at a time (Gillis, 1986).

The final decision was that the Ministry of Finance would make substantial investments not only in the training of a new generation of tax officials to operate the new tax system over the remainder of the century but in a new, computerized tax information system. In accordance with the training objectives, a program was established wherein dozens of Ministry of Finance officials were to be sent abroad for advanced training not only in tax administration (primarily in the Netherlands) but in economics, computer science, and accounting (primarily in the United States). As of January 1988, the pipeline of new trainees remained nearly full, while over three dozen earlier trainees had already returned to take up new positions in the tax administration. The first step taken to establish the new computerized information system was the earmarking of funds for hardware.

(C) Objectives

Characterization of objectives sought for any particular set of policy reforms is fraught with problems. To begin with, decisionmakers do not always clearly articulate, at the outset, any or all objectives to be sought from a given policy change. Rather, a clear expression of goals often emerges only toward the middle or even the end of deliberations over reform. In addition, objectives often change over the course of investigation and discussion of reform programs: options that initially appeared feasible may be ruled out by the accumulation of evidence as to their likely effects, and vice versa. Further, characterization of objectives for any given policy reform is often done after the fact, and the interpretation of the relative importance of different objectives may be unduly colored by the self-interest and/or other limitations of the observer responsible for the interpretation.

Attempts at characterization of the objectives of the 1983–84 Indonesian tax reform doubtless suffer from all of these problems. Nevertheless, scrutiny of this particular reform episode does suggest that four principal objectives were uppermost in the minds of decisionmakers when preparations for tax reform began in early 1981. These goals come under four general headings: revenue, income distribution, economic efficiency, and tax administration and compliance.

1. Revenues: From Revenue Neutrality to Revenue Enhancement. By 1981, tax revenues from oil and LNG amounted to 15 percent of GDP, compared to only 3 percent just ten years earlier. Rapid growth in these revenues fueled marked expansion in government spending across all sectors from 1971 to 1981, particularly in new programs in primary education, rural development, and in large new infrastructure projects in electric power, steel, mining, and transportation. Moreover, civil servants' salaries were raised sharply as well. As a result, government spending as a percent of GDP rose from only 14.8 percent in 1971 to 23.8 percent in 1981 (see table 4.2).

The time was propitious for initiation of preparations for major tax reform, independent of short- and medium-term prospects for world oil prices. On the one hand, the government was spending nearly one quarter of GDP, and financing only one quarter of that spending with non-oil taxes (see tables 4.1 and 4.2). Thus, the economy was highly vulnerable to any downturn in oil prices over the next few years, particularly inasmuch as Indonesian oil production had already begun to decline in the late 1970s. It was therefore clear that revenue-enhancing reform of non-oil would be essential in the event of near-term softening in world oil markets, because it was not expected that sharp reductions in government spending could be quickly enacted (Gillis, 1985, p. 226).

On the other hand, a scenario involving rising real prices in world oil markets, regarded as likely by some institutions as late as April 1981 (World Bank, 1981), was also seen as conducive to fundamental tax reform with or without higher tax revenues. In the first instance, revenue-enhancing tax reform would allow the government to expand important, and previously underfunded, programs in health, education, and rural development (all intensive in nontraded goods) without running undue risks of contracting a severe case of so-called "Dutch Disease" (Gillis, 1985), as actually befell Nigeria and other LDC oil exporters in the early 1980s. Tax revenues from the enclave oil sector could not, in the absence of substantial liberalization of imports, be used to finance domestic social programs without fueling more inflation than was deemed acceptable at the time. And the prospects for any significant liberalization of Indonesian trade were not bright in the early eighties (Gillis and Dapice, 1986). In the second instance, continued strength in world oil markets would mean that tax reform with any base-broadening at all, would, at the low ratios of non-oil taxes to GDP characteristic of Indonesia in the 1970s, mean lower tax rates, and therefore better chances for a politically acceptable tax reform supportive of economic neutrality.

In the end, the decision to move ahead on reform was made in early 1981, prior to the emergence of evidence of any clear downward trends in world oil prices. Immediate revenue enhancement was not the objective; no fiscal crises loomed at the time. Rather, plans were for implementation of a more or less revenue-neutral reform package for the near term, with broader tax bases and lower tax rates. The base-broadening measures were nevertheless expected to render the tax system capable of quick and substantial revenue improvements through relatively small rate increases, should the need arise in the future. Therefore, it was expected that the reform would prepare the tax system to respond to possible future fiscal crises that would surely result from any significant weakening in the world oil market. This future arrived rather more quickly than expected. By the time the reform package was submitted to parliament in late 1983, it was evident that some combination of drastic cutbacks in spending and sharply revenue-enhancing tax reform would be required to forestall a series of budget deficits that threatened to be upwards of 10 percent of GDP.

Matters worsened steadily over the next three years. By mid-1986, world oil prices had dropped to levels viewed as unthinkable five years earlier: average export prices, at only about $13.00 per barrel, were one third the peak price in 1981. With government oil revenues critically dependent on oil prices, tax collections from the oil/LNG sector quickly sank to just over 5 percent of GDP (table 4.1), or one third that of 1981. Expenditure cutbacks and tax reform contributed, in virtually equal measure, to the shrinkage of the potential budget deficit; the spending ratio fell by 3 percent of GDP and the tax ratio rose by 3 percent of GDP.

By 1987, austerity measures had reduced projected government spending from one quarter to little more than 17 percent of GDP, while the tax reform, in combination with mild recovery in oil prices, pushed the overall tax ratio to just above 15 percent. These developments, together with relatively small foreign aid grants, reduced the projected budget deficit to a manageable 1.8 percent of GDP (see table 4.2).

By early 1988, Indonesia had, virtually alone among large oil-exporting LDCs, managed to restructure economic policies to cope with a new phase of substantially lower oil prices, now over half a decade in length. Moreover, this was done while domestic inflation was held in check throughout; inflation exceeded 10 percent only in 1983, and even then was limited to 12 percent. Further, while growth slowed markedly, the economy continued to grow throughout the period following the end of the second oil boom in 1982, a year when real GDP declined. Since then, and until 1986, real GDP growth averaged just under 3.2 percent per year, or about double the rate for all lower middle income LDCs over the same period (World Bank, *World Development Report*, 1987, table 4.2).

The tax reform was but one of several policy measures that, at least until 1988, allowed Indonesia to deal with the post-1981 collapse in oil markets with limited inflationary consequences and continued, if slowed, economic growth. The contribution made by the tax reform to this outcome extends well beyond that made by the apparent revenue results: in relatively short order, a 50 percent increase in the ratio of non-oil taxes to GDP was attained (see table 4.1). A non-negligible share of the contribution of tax reform to continued growth, it may be argued, came in the form of reduced costs of administration and compliance and the lower efficiency costs associated with the much greater simplicity in tax laws and uniformity in tax rates brought by the reform.

2. *Distribution Neutrality and Absolute Impoverishment.* Since 1966, Indonesian economic policymakers have been less concerned with rectifying problems of relative impoverishment (uneven distribution of income across income classes) than with alleviating absolute impoverishment: raising levels of living of the poorest 40 percent of society. There have been at least two reasons for the past emphasis on reducing absolute rather than relative impoverishment.

First, in the half decade or so after the national economic collapse in 1965 – 66, maldistribution of income was not perceived as a significant problem, because the poverty of those years was widely shared by groups across society. The precarious existence of millions of rural households, especially in Java, was seen as the most urgent social *and* economic problem; the imperative of alleviating absolute impoverishment therefore dominated all equity objectives. In turn, programs and policies intended to promote rural development were believed to be the most effective measures for reducing rural poverty. Subsidies and transfers from the central government budget were viewed as appropriate tools for securing this objective. Budget subsidies for fertilizer and kerosene, both intended largely to help low income rural households, grew rapidly from 1967 through 1981. Together these subsidies were equivalent to upwards of 7 percent of government tax revenues by the late 1970s (Gillis, 1980, pp. 51–54). Central government transfers to county and village governments rose steadily as well. Further, a very sharp expansion in primary education programs after 1973, particularly in rural areas, had the effect of doubling the percentage of the age cohort 5–12 attending school by 1980. Certainly in the minds of policymakers, expansion of primary education was regarded as a critical step for reducing absolute impoverishment in the long term, especially among rural households. These measures met with some success, even by the standards of many critics of post-1966 economic policy (Collier et al., 1982).

But while the budget was deemed important as a tool for rectifying problems of income distribution, emphasis was almost wholly on the expenditure side, not the tax side. Although it was expected that the tax system could provide for growing revenues for finance of programs designed to deal with poverty, particularly rural poverty, tax instruments were not regarded per se as useful in reducing relative impoverishment through leveling down of high incomes. Pessimism over the role of taxation in income redistribution stemmed primarily from widespread recognition of very serious and long-standing weaknesses in tax administration. Moreover, empirical studies conducted under the research program for the tax reform indicated that decades of emphasis upon redistributive tax policies had accomplished little in the way of income redistribution in Indonesia. For example, the effective rate of income tax for the top 5 percent of the income distribution was only 4 percent in 1981, although nominal tax rates applicable to income in this group were 50 percent (Gillis, 1985).

Ineffectuality of the tax system in promoting redistribution was also a consequence of defects in the tax structure. Income, sales, and property taxes prevailing before the 1983 reform were riddled with exclusions and exemptions. Although proponents of many of these provisions had actually sought to justify them on grounds of reducing income inequality, the effects were generally otherwise. Items excluded or favored under the income tax were received overwhelmingly by the wealthiest one fifth of the income distribution: housing and auto allowances, free use of vacation homes, physicians' fees interest income, and salaries of civil servants.

The failure of progressive rates of income and sales taxes in securing significant income redistribution was apparent from an incidence study carried out in 1982–83 for the reform program. Although this study, like all incidence studies everywhere, suffers from significant methodological and data limitations, it is nevertheless the most comprehensive ever undertaken for Indonesia. Results indicated that the poorest third of the population paid 5 percent of their income in taxes, a share not much below that of all higher income groups up to the richest decile. And even in the richest decile, taxes were only 9 percent of income except for the top quarter of this group (the top 2 percent of the income distribution) for whom the effective tax rate was estimated at 13.6 percent. And it is to be noted that this figure for the topmost 2 percent was largely a consequence of the assumption that the *entire* burden of both personal income taxes *and* export taxes was borne by this most affluent group (Gillis, 1985).

In view of Indonesian fiscal experience since 1966, and in light of such conclusions on fiscal incidence as were available, policymakers came to view the appropriate income distribution goal for tax reform as that of insuring that changes in taxation would not make the poor worse off, primarily by placing low-income households outside the tax net, to the extent possible. The tax side of the budget, then, was not to be used as an active tool for redressing problems of relative impoverishment. Nevertheless, decisionmakers and their advisers believed, in the end, that the tax reform as enacted would result in marked increases in the share of taxes paid by the upper two deciles, if for no other reason than the reduction of evasion and avoidance expected from base-broadening and drastic simplification of the system. Moreover, the architects of reform believed that the sharp reduction in income-tax rates that became a prominent feature of the reform package would have a progressive impact, because of two factors. First, the rate reductions were made possible by elimination of exemptions that primarily benefited upper income groups. Second, because the reform excluded the poorest 85 percent of households from the income tax base, the new income tax would have been progressive, *even* if it had been imposed at a flat rate of 30 percent (as originally proposed).

3. Economic Neutrality. Indonesian tax policy in the three decades prior to 1984 was purposefully nonneutral in orientation. The tax system was viewed not only as a means of raising revenues, but as a useful tool for guiding private consumption, investment, and employment decisions to ends sought by the state. Tax exemptions and differentiation of tax rates were the preferred techniques for securing desired nonneutralities. Favored activities or pursuits were provided tax incentives, primarily in the form of reduced, often zero, rates. Disfavored activities and products were ineligible for such incentives, or in some cases subjected to special rates of tax higher than those generally applicable to taxable undertakings.

By 1981, thirty years of active pursuit of nonneutralities in taxation had yielded a tax system so interlaced with complex tax incentive arrangements as to be almost inadministrable. Some tax preferences were similar in structure to incentive schemes commonly used in other countries; some were peculiar to Indonesia. The former included tax incentives to promote foreign investment, to encourage domestic investment in specified activities, and to attract both foreign and domestic investment to so-called "backward" regions. With these "common" incentives solidly in place by 1970, it was but a short step to further proliferation of tax incentives over the next decade. These ranged from the unusual to the truly bizarre: tax incentives to encourage development of a national stock market, to purchase life insurance, to encourage construction of bowling alleys, to finance tournament travel of chess players, and to promote use of public accountants.

By 1981, it had become clear to many within the government that whatever useful social purposes served by the system of tax incentives —and there is scant evidence that useful purposes were in fact served —the attendant costs had become unacceptably high. These costs were measured not only in terms of tax revenues thereby forgone, but in terms of the administrative difficulties involved in operating a system overloaded with complexity (Gillis, 1985, pp. 245–49).

By 1982, decisionmakers were in any case already predisposed to discard as unworkable most of the elaborate system of tax preferences that had evolved over the previous two decades. By 1983, this predisposition had changed to a strong preference for economic neutrality in the tax structure, owing to results of several studies of tax incentives undertaken for the reform. These studies indicated the wastes and complexities of not only the more bizarre types of tax preferences (the incentive to "go public" and thereby promote a premature stock market, the incentive for using public accountants) but the most hallowed incentive of all: tax holidays for promotion of foreign investment (Gillis, 1986).

Accordingly, economic neutrality came to be a central emphasis of the reform package as presented to the parliament in late 1983. Stress on neutrality was most evident in the shift toward more uniformity in tax rates, the complete abandonment of tax incentives and the broadening of the tax base. In turn, these measures made possible the general lowering of income- and sales-tax rates, further advancing the goal of neutrality and the reduction of economic waste.[2]

4. Administration and Compliance. The impetus for tax reform in Indonesia did not originate within the tax administration itself. On the contrary: in early 1981 there was initially no significant support for reform among any of the senior officials responsible for assessment and collection of taxes. Heavy inflows of oil tax revenues from 1973–81 meant minimal pressure for better tax collection performance; tax administrators had little reason for undertaking changes of any kind since large numbers of them had come to enjoy financial prosperity well beyond that supportable by official salaries for civil servants. Except for the most senior officials, installed in mid-1981, the tax administration remained ambivalent if not hostile to the reform program right up to the time it was implemented.

Nevertheless, the relevant decisionmakers in the Ministry of Finance and in the rest of the cabinet were acutely conscious of extremely serious shortcomings in the machinery for assessing and collecting taxes. They therefore decided that a major objective of the reform would be that of improving the administration of taxation and facilitating taxpayer compliance and in the process, curbing needless costs of collection and payment and reducing the scope for corruption. The means adopted for achieving this objective were threefold:

(a) drastic simplification of tax laws
(b) establishment of a new, computerized tax information system
(c) reform of tax procedures (rules and regulations governing filing, penalties, assessments, etc.), with stress on the need for depersonalization of tax administration

Simplification would have been a significant emphasis of the 1983 reforms even in the absence of any explicit decision to seek fundamental improvements in tax administration and compliance. The decision to deemphasize the role of the tax system in income redistribution, as well as the shift toward greater economic neutrality in taxation would by themselves have required reduced complexity in tax laws and regulations. But in addition, simplification was seen as a *sine qua non* for major improvements in tax administration. It was expected that simplification would reduce the scope for corruption, since complexities and ambiguities in tax law were used by tax collectors and taxpayers alike to cloak their transgressions. Simplification was also expected to foster improved taxpayer compliance by increasing certainty in tax collections.

Finally, simplification of income- and sales-tax law was required in order to make tractable the task of revamping and modernization of the tax information system. Efforts to computerize some of the operations of the Ministry of Finance extended all the way back to 1971. All those initiatives were stillborn, however, partly because they were seen as threatening to some groups within the tax administration and partly for a purely mechanical reason. Some upper-level officials of the tax administration had long opposed installation of computerized systems on grounds that the system would likely be under the control of other agencies within the Ministry, e.g., the office of automatic data processing, rather than the tax department. Further, the cash registers used to record taxpayer payments at local treasury offices around the nation had space for only nine digits, an insufficient number to allow utilization of a workable system of taxpayer identification numbers. This mundane problem was solved by a fortuitous 1981 decision—unrelated to the tax reform initiative—by the Budget Bureau of the Finance Ministry. This bureau decided to purchase new electronic cash registers capable of handling sixteen digits, more than enough to accommodate a usable taxpayer identification number. It was at this point, and over the objections of most senior officials of the tax administration, that the final decision was taken to make substantial investments in hardware, software, and foreign expertise in the construction of a new computerized tax information system that would ultimately allow not only vastly improved master tax files, but also speedier and more systematic monitoring of collection performance.

Reform of taxpaying procedures was not viewed as a critical need in the initial stages of preparation for this tax reform. But as the architects of the reform came to understand the importance of procedural reform, this too became an important priority. Tax procedures include provisions specifying how taxpayers shall comply with their tax obligations as well as the administrative structure governing the execution of responsibilities of tax officials. Specific examples of tax procedures include those governing assessment and refund of taxes, timing of payments, filing of returns, collections of arrears, objections, appeals, fines, and penalties.

These procedures varied from tax to tax, and many had gone unrevised for decades. Further, the levels for many fines and penalties had been set in the 1950s and 1960s, so that inflation had eroded any deterrent effect they once may have had (example: six months in jail, or a fine of 1,000 rupiahs or U.S. 75 cents at 1986 exchange rates). Other penalties were set at such unrealistically high levels as to be unenforceable. It soon became clear that a completely new law, consolidating all procedures for all taxes, would be required as an essential complement to new laws to govern income and sales tax structure. Two themes were to shape this new law on procedures: simplification, as also planned for the tax structure, and depersonalization of tax administration. Depersonalization in the first instance involved a general reduction in discretionary authority in the hands of tax officials. It also involved a reduction in the frequency of direct contacts between taxpayers and tax officials. Instead, greater reliance would be placed on withholding methods and electronic data processing of taxpayer information sent to district offices. Finally, depersonalization required a shift from the decades-old tradition of official assessment of tax liabilities to self-assessments by taxpayers. The move toward self-assessment was also supportive of other aims of procedural reform. With self-assessment, the number of direct contacts between taxpayers and officials—and therefore the number of opportunities for collusion—is less. Also, the shift toward self-assessment reduced the routine workload on tax officials, allowing for more and better audits of cases promising high revenue payoffs.

II. Elements of Tax Reform

(A) Overview: The Old System and the Reformed System

The essence of the old tax system was that of extreme complexity stemming from decades of attempts to manipulate tax rates and tax bases to achieve nonrevenue goals. Framers of the reform did not abjure nonrevenue goals such as income distribution and economic efficiency. Rather, the new system reflected the view that these goals are best furthered by a tax system oriented primarily toward raising of revenues. Accordingly, the tax reform involved heavy stress upon simplification both of tax structure and tax administration. Simplification in structure required extensive broadening of the base of both income and consumption taxes, with reliance upon much greater uniformity of tax rates than had prevailed at any previous period in modern Indonesian history.

The centerpiece of the reform, certainly from the point of tax revenue implications, was the replacement of an outdated sales tax, riddled with exemptions and complicated by use of multiple rates, by a crude form of value-added tax (VAT). The VAT is one of the simplest ever adopted anywhere in the world. It is imposed at a flat rate of 10 percent on all taxable transactions. Because this particular tax is at present a manufacturer's-importer type of VAT, the base excludes all retailers and most wholesalers while embracing all imports. Moreover, as originally adopted, there were no exemptions by product category.

Neutrality objectives dominated income-tax reform proposals. Economic neutrality goals were to be furthered not only through very significant base-broadening and a shift toward generally lower and more uniform tax rates, but by the dismantling of all tax-incentive programs. And in the short run, income-tax changes were expected to be revenue-neutral at worst, or mildly revenue-enhancing at best. The income-tax proposals were designed to be distributionally neutral only in the sense that income-tax reform did not seek to achieve much in the way of "leveling-down" of higher incomes (see chapter 1). Rather, the focus was upon "leveling-up," through income tax exemption of all but the uppermost levels of the income distribution. To illustrate: prior to the reform, a worker with a spouse and three children was liable for income tax once his income exceeded approximately U.S. $1,000. The reform, by raising sharply the level of personal exemptions, meant that this same worker could earn almost U.S. $3,000 before becoming liable for income tax.

Administrative neutrality as well as revenue objectives were emphasized in property tax reform: A new land and buildings tax replaced seven different land-tax ordinances, including a misnamed "tax on wealth." The property tax, like the income and sales taxes, is collected and administered by the central government, but the bulk of property tax revenues are assigned to subnational governments.

(B) Internal Indirect Taxes

Prior to the tax reform the internal indirect tax system consisted of three principal elements: a sales tax of the turnover type extending

Table 4.3   Indonesia: Tax Structure, Pre- and Post-Reform

	1983		
	Billions rupiah	Percentage of total tax revenue	Percentage of GDP
I. Internal indirect taxes	1,670	10.9	2.3
A. Sales taxes	830	5.4	1.1
B. Excises	775	5.1	1.1
C. Stamp duties and other	65	0.4	0.1
II. Taxes on foreign trade	661	4.3	0.9
A. Import duties	557	3.6	0.8
B. Export duties	104	0.7	0.1
III. Income taxes	12,331	80.5	16.7
A. On oil/LNG firms	10,398	67.9	14.1
B. Non-oil income taxes[a]	1,785	11.7	2.4
C. Interest, dividends, and royalty tax	148	0.9	0.2
IV. Property taxes	132	0.9	0.2
V. "Non-tax" revenue[b]	520	3.4	0.7
Total revenue	15,314	100.00	20.8
Non-oil revenue (omits III-A)	(4,916)	32.19	(6.7)

[a]For non-oil income taxes, the share for corporate income taxes in 1986 GDP was 1.4 percent. The share of individual income taxes was less than half as high, at only 0.6 percent of GDP.

through the manufacturing stage, sumptuary excise taxes on tobacco, beer, sugar, and spirits, and assorted stamp duties. Together, these taxes accounted for about 11 percent of total tax revenues, or about 2.3 percent of GDP (see table 4.3).

Basic decisions about indirect tax reform were made by July of 1981. The excise system, the fourth largest source of revenue, was working reasonably well; accordingly, a decision was made to leave these levies unchanged. Stamp taxes, insignificant revenue sources in any case, were to be abolished except for a small number that were easily enforced. The principal focus of indirect tax reform was to be upon the sales tax.

The antiquated turnover tax utilized in Indonesia had been discarded by virtually all countries well before 1980. The inherent defects of this form of sales tax (Due, 1957) were compounded in Indonesia by an extreme degree of rate differentiation, involving eight tax rates ranging from 1 percent to 20 percent. Largely because of a complicated exemption structure, the tax was also unproductive of revenue. In other LDCs,

Billions rupiah	1986	
	Percentage of total tax revenue	Percentage of GDP
4,129	27.0	3.9
2,942	19.2	2.8
991	6.5	0.9
196	1.3	0.2
885	5.8	0.8
820	5.4	0.7
65	0.4	0.1
8,019	52.4	7.5
5,559	36.4	5.2
2,189	14.3	2.0
271	1.8	0.3
238	1.6	0.2
2,022	13.2	1.9
15,293	100.0	14.3
(9,734)	(67.3)	(9.1)

[b]Primarily dividends from government-owned enterprises for 1983. Figure for 1986 includes temporary windfall from surplus on domestic oil operations.
Source: Department of Finance, Government of Indonesia.

sales taxes typically account for 20–25 percent of revenue (Ahmad and Stern, 1987) and 4 percent to 5 percent of GDP (Tait, Gratz, and Eichengreen, 1987). But in Indonesia, the sales tax accounted for only 5 percent of total tax collections and about 1 percent of GDP.

Policymakers quickly settled upon a reform option involving a crude form of VAT having most but not all of the significant features of VATs used in Europe. The principal departure from the European model was that the Indonesian tax was initially confined to the manufacturer-importer level, in contrast to European VATs (and those of nearly twenty LDCs) which extend all the way through the retail level. This was done because of the severe administrative difficulties that would have been involved in bringing hundreds of thousands of wholesale and retail firms within the scope of the VAT. The new sales-tax law, however, allows extension of the VAT to the wholesale and retail levels whenever the tax authorities deem it administratively feasible, but almost certainly not before the year 2000.

At the time of its enactment, the structure of the Indonesian VAT was the simplest of any such tax in operation anywhere in the world. The VAT adopted by Bolivia in May 1986, however, appears almost as simple (American Chamber of Commerce, 1986). The Indonesian tax, like that of Bolivia, is imposed at a uniform rate of 10 percent on all taxable goods, whether imported or of domestic origin. VAT is assessed on imports in the customs house on the tariff-inclusive value of imports. All imports were initially subject to tax, but by 1988, a limited number of capital good imports and raw materials used in large projects had been awarded deferral of and/or partial relief from VAT liability: VAT on these items may be postponed until a later date, typically when the project commences operation. In other cases, VAT liability is "suspended" on imports.[3] And in a limited number of cases, the VAT on the delivery and/or importation of certain taxable goods is borne by the government; as a practical matter such goods are exempt.[4]

The Indonesian VAT, like those used in the European community, is imposed on the destination principle, employs the tax credit method of collection, and is intended to be a levy on consumption. Because the implications of each of these features are discussed at length in other sources (Conrad and Gillis, 1984; Conrad, 1986; Gillis, 1985) the present chapter provides only a brief discussion of their significance.

Destination-principle taxes are intended to free exports from indirect tax burden, while fully taxing all imports in the country where they are consumed. A tax-credit type of VAT may be collected without having to directly compute a firm's value-added. A taxable firm merely applies the VAT tax rate to all its sales, to find tentative taxes due in any given period, say one month. The firm then subtracts (credits) taxes it had paid on its purchases against tentative taxes due on sales. The difference is the amount owed by the firm to the government. Finally, a consumption-type VAT is one under which VAT paid by a firm on its purchases of capital equipment is treated exactly like VAT paid on raw materials and fuel: all such VAT taxes may be credited against VAT due on sales. In this way, the VAT base may be confined to consumption. If, on the other hand, taxes paid on capital equipment were not creditable, the base of the VAT would be gross income, not consumption (Shoup, 1969).

Finally, the Indonesian VAT as adopted in 1983 differed from all others utilized by other countries (except Bolivia) through 1987 in one very important respect: except for small firms, the VAT law allows neither exemptions nor zero-rating of any manufactured products consumed domestically.[5] (Since 1985, some activities have, however, managed to secure limited relief from the VAT.) The general unavailability of exemptions may, at first glance, make the Indonesian VAT appear quite regressive. It is important to note, however, that the base of a manufacturer's tax such as that used in Indonesia does not extend to such items as unprocessed food or other staples that do not go through a manufacturing stage. Since such items are outside the tax base, and inasmuch as up to half of the consumption of the poorest 60 percent of households has been in the form of unprocessed food, then the application of a uniform tax rate involves little risk that the VAT, as now constituted, involves significant burdens for the poor, as long as agricultural producers do not make use of significant amounts of taxable inputs other than fertilizer (the sale of which is highly subsidized through the budget).[6]

The VAT as described in the foregoing paragraphs contains few of the features that have bedeviled sales tax administration elsewhere. The same uniform tax rate applies to all taxable commodities. Moreover, the 1984 sales tax law prohibits use of differentiated rates, but does allow the government to move the uniform rate (initially 10 percent) to as high as 15 percent or as low as 5 percent, depending on revenue needs. Both the absence of exemptions by product category and the reliance on a uniform rate were intended to eliminate uncertainty as to what is taxable under the VAT and at what rate.

The prospects for successful operation of the new VAT were aided immensely by the fact that nearly two thirds of the base of the tax passes through three bottlenecks that are easily accessible to the government, and therefore the tax administration: the customs house, sales of refined petroleum products by PERTAMINA (the state oil enterprise)[7] and sales of the 200-odd government-owned enterprises that are now taxable under the new tax law. Given these bottlenecks, the tax administration is in a position to collect more than half the potential VAT revenues with minimal expenditure of administrative resources, thereby enabling enforcement efforts to be focused on the remaining, less accessible portions of the tax base.

Administrative feasibility was a critically important consideration in adoption of this simple tax since it was intended that the VAT furnish at least 60 percent of any incremental revenues expected from tax reform. But policy makers recognized that whatever the administrative, revenue, and neutrality arguments in favor of an indirect tax imposed at a flat rate with virtually no exemptions, the political acceptability of such a tax would be limited; belief in the efficacy of rate differentiation in taxation was simply too widespread to ignore.

Accordingly, in order to improve the political acceptability of the reform package a special, separately administered "luxury" sales tax was proposed and enacted. This tax is applied to sales of a very limited number of income-elastic products at rates of 10 and 20 percent. Taxable products include stereo sound systems, autos, firearms, aircraft, cameras, and yachts. These items are also subject to the ordinary VAT as well, so that "luxury" items carry an indirect tax burden two to three times higher than "nonluxuries." Altogether, the items subjected to the special higher rates of luxury tax constitute much too small a proportion of total consumption to generate substantial tax revenues, and account for too low a share of the spending of the rich, to achieve much income redistribution. The interaction of the luxury tax with the VAT has also led to some inequities and administrative problems (Gillis, 1988). Nevertheless, the luxury tax has thus far served to protect the integrity of the uniform rate VAT, and for that reason its political role in the success of the reform has been much larger than its limited revenue significance.

(C) Income Taxes

Prior to the reform, the Indonesian income tax structure consisted of two separate taxes on individuals and firms. The tax on individuals, called the *Pajak Pendapatan* (PPD) was imposed at steeply progressive rates beginning at 5 percent and rising to 50 percent, on a base riddled with exemptions and exclusions.[8] The tax on business firms, the *Pajak Perseroan* (PPS) was also applied at graduated rates of 20 percent, 30 percent, and 45 percent. A special income-tax regime applied to the operations of foreign oil companies. Methods for determination of tax liabilities of oil companies were spelled out in contracts between them and the government oil company. The essence of taxes on oil companies was that all levies combined were intended to capture 85 percent of their *net* income (after deduction of all allowable costs). As noted, companies with contracts signed before January 1, 1984, continued to be subject to tax provisions in force before that date.

Non-oil income taxes were not major sources of total revenue prior to 1985; they were but 2.4 percent of GDP in 1983. Personal income tax revenues by themselves were less than one half of one percent of GDP (see table 4.3).

Poor revenue performance of these income taxes was attributable partly to structural defects and partly to administrative shortcomings.

The PPD left large chunks of individual income untaxed or lightly taxed, including virtually all fringe benefits, interest, capital gains, and pensions, all of which flowed primarily to the top half of the income distribution. Income from cooperatives, however, was also exempt, benefiting some low-income families. The most anomalous of exemptions was that for income of civil servants. Thus tax collectors themselves were not subject to income taxes. Deductions as well as exemptions tended to favor the relatively wealthy: interest expenses were deductible even though interest income was untaxed; deductions were also allowed for life-insurance premiums and pension contributions, even though insurance proceeds and pensions were untaxed.

The base of the business income tax (PPS) had been similarly eroded over the years. The most significant factor in the narrowing of the base of the PPS, however, was the availability of very generous tax incentives for private firms, both foreign and domestic. Largely because of the presence of these preferences, private sector firms typically were responsible for less than one third of total business income tax collections over the period 1970–80; the twenty-five largest government-owned firms (excluding the state oil enterprise, PERTAMINA) were the source of nearly two thirds of company tax collections. The incentive programs suffered from several serious defects, all of which have been examined in some detail elsewhere (Gillis, 1985, pp. 246–48). They were expensive in terms of revenue, biased in favor of capital intensive investment, and discriminatory against smaller firms. They also gave rise to intractable problems in tax administration. Finally, they were generally ineffective in achieving their central objective of attracting beneficial investments to Indonesia in general and to so-called backward regions within the country.

Notwithstanding these serious difficulties, the political leadership generally viewed the incentive programs as having been successful. It was reasoned that since generous tax preferences had been available in Indonesia since 1967, and since the period 1967–81 had been a period of rapid growth and development, then tax incentives must have contributed to this prosperity. Although this claim was not supported by any reliable evidence, it was clear by 1983 that abandoning the incentives would be politically difficult. But any worthwhile reform would require first and foremost substantial broadening of the income tax base, and significant base-broadening could not occur unless income-tax rates could be reduced at the same time. And there was no possibility that income tax rates could be sharply reduced as long as tax incentives were widely available.

The constricting effects of the incentives on the tax base become clear from research studies done in 1982–83. Inspection of the tax records of 900 larger foreign and domestic firms indicated that only about 12 percent of the foreign firms and 8 percent of domestic firms paid the maximum 45 percent rate of income tax (Gillis, 1985). This information on the revenue forgone and other evidence on the inefficacy of tax incentives in Indonesia led policymakers to the conclusion that income tax reform would be futile as long as the incentives remained. While the reform that was taking shape contained important innovations in the taxation of fringe benefits, the treatment of depreciation, and the taxation of pension funds and insurance, it was doubtful that these measures could be implemented. Their adoption depended on lower tax rates, impossible if tax incentives were maintained.

At this critical point (June and July 1983), proponents of reform settled on an approach for securing acceptance of fundamental alterations in income taxation. This approach was employed in lobbying both the chief executive and the parliament on behalf of tax reform. Since tax incentives were widely perceived as having been useful, it was unwise to argue against the use of incentives per se. Rather, the lobbying effort would have to be couched in terms of *replacing* the existing incentive program with *another*, more effective one. Therefore, the proponents of reform took the position that the most effective program of income tax incentives would be that of *generally lower* tax rates for all activities *in place of* the *differential* incentives offered from 1967–83.

However, the effort to abolish differential incentives ran some significant political risk. Embedded within the tax legislation were some near-sacred incentives for constituencies of some political importance to any government in Indonesia. The success of the initiative depended upon the elimination of *all* differential tax incentives. Retention of any incentive would severely weaken the case for refusing others. Among the apparently untouchable incentives were those for cooperatives.[9] Moreover, the minister for cooperatives was an influential and persuasive person with clear access to the president. If he were to successfully argue that cooperatives should continue to benefit from favorable tax treatment, other pressure groups seeking tax incentives could point to the incentive for cooperatives as an exception that should be available to them also.

In view of these considerations, the architects of reform placed a high premium on securing the support of the minister of cooperatives for abolition of all special tax incentives. This support was in fact granted after the minister was convinced that as a practical matter, even without special tax incentives, taxes on members' income from bona fide cooperatives would be low or nil if, as planned under the reform, tax exempt income for typical households was increased by nearly three-fold, through sharp increases in personal exemptions.

Having secured the support of the president and the rest of the cabinet, the policymakers then took the entire set of tax proposals to the legislature. Within a few weeks, agreement was secured from key legislative committees and the reform package was adopted nearly as initially proposed, with two significant exceptions discussed below.

Emerging from this process was a single income tax called the *Pajak Penghasilan* (PPH). The new law applies to the income of all business firms and individuals, thereby ending one of the most serious shortcomings of the old income tax structure, where different tax laws applied to individuals and firms respectively. This feature had led to substantial inequities between different forms of business organization (corporations, partnerships, etc.). Under the new law, deductions available to firms are also available to individuals; only individuals, however, can claim personal exemptions. Foreign oil companies with contracts signed after January 1, 1984, are now subject to the PPH on operations governed by such contracts.

Although the reform was planned with two income tax rates in mind (15 percent and 30 percent), the process of political compromise yielded in the end a three-tier rate structure of 14 percent, 25 percent, and 35 percent.[10] As a result, Indonesian tax rates on personal income became the lowest in Southeast Asia, and among these nations only Thailand had a tax rate on business income as low as that of Indonesia. However, foreign firms remitting dividends to the home office abroad are subject to a 20 percent tax on the amounts remitted, so that the effective tax rate for repatriated income is 48 percent.[11]

Quite apart from ending tax incentives for business firms, the new law ends the favored treatment of several types of income and deductions formerly available to individuals. Long-term capital gains were, for administrative reasons, made taxable for the first time,[12] as were fringe benefits to employees, civil servants' salaries, and pension income. Other income items formerly lightly taxed were subjected to full taxation. These included rental income, honoraria, and leave and educational allowances. Inasmuch as virtually all these income items are concentrated in the upper tenth of the income distribution, these changes introduced greater progressivity into the tax law.

One of the most controversial aspects of the reform was the tax treatment of interest on bank deposits. Interest was fully exempt from taxation under the old income-tax structure. Policymakers recognized that exemption of interest was inadvisable on several counts, as long as interest costs continued to be allowed as a deduction. Under such circumstances, exemption of interest provides great scope for tax evasion, is costly in terms of tax revenue, complicates the administration of income taxes, is inimical to healthy financial development, and favors high-income families over families with low income (Gillis, 1985). The draft income-tax law as presented to the legislature therefore provided for full taxation of interest income. Strong pressure from financial and industrial circles, however, resulted in a compromise wherein interest remained taxable in principle, but would continue to be exempt, by regulation, until further notice. This was a serious omission from the point of view of supporters of reform, but it was the only significant setback prior to enactment of the new law.

(D) Property Taxes

Although most of the key decisions on property tax reform were made before 1984, enactment of new legislation for property taxes was postponed until 1986 to allow the government to concentrate implementation efforts upon the rest of the reform package.

Property taxation in Indonesia dates back to the very early stages of Dutch colonialization in the 1600s (Kelley, 1987, p. 8). Historically, the most important property tax has been the Contribution for Regional Development (*Iuran Pembangunan Daerah*, or IPEDA) which applied to both rural and urban properties. The nominal tax base of the IPEDA was the annual rental value (yield) of land. The basic rate for IPEDA was 0.5 percent of yield, but in practice, different rates applied to different types of land.[13] Exemptions riddled the system,[14] and property valuations were seriously out of date. As a result, the IPEDA was not a significant source of revenue in the two decades prior to 1986. By 1983, the tax accounted for less than 1 percent of total tax revenue and only 0.2 percent of GDP (see table 4.3).

Midway through preparations for tax reform in 1983, decisionmakers decided to collapse all property and wealth taxes into one single levy with a vastly simplified IPEDA at the core. This decision was reflected in the new Land and Building Tax (*Pajak Bumi Dan Bangungan*, or PBB) enacted in 1986. This tax replaced not only the IPEDA, but also a widely evaded central government Net Wealth Tax, a substantial "Household" tax, and four other land-based taxes. The principles of uniformity, simplicity, and generality governing income and sales tax reform were carried through also to property tax reform.

Under the new tax, only one rate applies to all types of property. The tax base was switched from the annual rental value to capital market value of land and buildings, where capital market value is to be derived from arms-length transactions.[15] Further, urban land used for residential purposes was treated identically with that used for commercial purposes. The discretionary authority for the granting of property tax exemptions was severely curtailed as a result of the 1986 reform. Exemptions are generally restricted to land owned by nonprofit organizations, protected forests, national parks, traditional grazing land, diplomatic offices, international offices, and graveyards. In addition, temporary exemptions are available for land affected by natural disasters.

The approach to income distribution issues in property-tax reform was identical to that followed in income- and sales-tax reform: emphasis was upon rectifying absolute rather than relative impoverishment. For that reason, all buildings were granted an exemption of Rupiah 2 million (U.S. $1,600 at 1986 exchange rates). As a result, virtually all rural housing and a large share of low-income housing lies outside the tax base, enabling the tax administration to focus its efforts on higher-valued properties (Kelley, 1987, p. 13).

III. Outcomes

By early 1988, the new income-tax system had been in place for four years, the new value-added tax for nearly three, and the new property tax for one year. There has been sufficient experience with the first two taxes, but not the latter, to provide some basis for limited extrapolations for the future. There is enough early evidence of the impact of reform upon revenues, economic stability, and tax administration to allow some tentative generalizations. But several more years will be required before informed judgments can be made about the income distribution and resource allocation implications of the 1983 reforms.

(A) Revenues

Evidence to date suggests that in revenue terms, the reform has been successful beyond expectations. The ratio of non-oil taxes to GDP in 1986 exceeded 9 percent for only the second time in Indonesian history, and was fully 50 percent greater than in 1984 (table 4.1). This occurred in spite of a sluggish economy: with stagnant export income, rates of economic growth since 1981 have been less than half that of the 1970s. As has been common in many other tax reform programs in other LDCs since 1970 (Gillis, chapter 14, this volume), the VAT was the principal source of incremental revenue. Table 4.3 shows that in only the second year of the existence of the VAT, nominal revenues from this source were 3.5 times the turnover tax it replaced and fully one-third greater than the revenues accruing from non-oil income taxes. Moreover, the share of the VAT in GDP (at 2.8 percent) was 2.5 times that of the old turnover tax.

The revenue performance of the VAT is all the more unusual given the low rate of the tax relative to similar taxes elsewhere. Most of the 20-odd LDCs using the *retail* VAT use a standard rate of between 10 and 15 percent, and in those countries the share of VAT collections in GDP has typically been between 2 percent and 4 percent (Ahmad and Stern, 1987, p. 61). The Indonesian VAT, however, is a manufacturer's VAT imposed at a rate of 10 percent. The retail equivalent of this rate is about 5 or 6 percent, since a manufacturer-level tax does not generally include wholesale and retail distribution margins. Even so, the share of the Indonesian VAT in GDP is just about as high as in those countries imposing higher (retail equivalent) rates. The simplicity and uniformity of the Indonesian VAT may indeed account for much of its strong revenue performance relative to value-added taxes used in other LDCs.

The new income tax was not expected to generate sizable new revenues in the short term, partly because firms that had received tax incentives prior to 1984 still retained their privileges and partly because of long lead times expected for any significant strengthening of income tax administration. Even by 1986 and 1987 many firms were still in their tax-holiday periods. In any case the share of non-oil income taxes in GDP actually declined from 1983 through 1986.

(B) Economic Stability

In retrospect, the tax reform could not have come at a more propitious time. With another precipitous decline in oil prices in 1986–87, the absence of reform would have required even steeper cuts in government spending beyond the draconian measures implemented in those years, or (as noted in section I) would have resulted in substantially larger deficits than actually occurred.

We have seen that the early revenue success of the tax reform was due almost wholly to indirect tax reform, and in particular the VAT. The contribution of the VAT to revenues was, however, not the only way it affected stability. The VAT was implemented with almost negligible effects on the price level, contrary to the predictions of many business-men as well as economists who claimed that introduction of the VAT would result in an acceleration of *inflation*. In this respect, the Indo-nesian experience with the adoption of the VAT was not inconsistent with that of nearly three dozen other countries for which studies of price effects of the VAT have been made (Tait, 1986).

The introduction of the VAT in Indonesia not only had no impact on *inflation* (unsurprising to any macroeconomist), but the implementa-tion of the tax had no noticeable effects on the *price level*. The intro-duction of the VAT in April 1985 coincided with a decline in consumer price indices in April and May. Moreover, domestic inflation for the next twelve months was well below that for the previous year.

Decisionmakers had announced with some confidence in January and February of 1985 that the price level, not to mention the inflationary impact, of the switch to the VAT would be nil. Their confidence was due to two factors. First was their recognition of the fact that the VAT was to be substituted for a turnover tax that itself may have involved some price-level effects. Second, economic decisionmakers were well aware that the rate of monetary expansion in the first quarter of 1985 had decelerated; they knew from long experience that domestically gener-ated inflation arises from monetary expansion, not tax adjustments.

(C) Tax Administration

It may be argued that the administration of taxes has improved since enactment of fundamental tax reform. This is true in the sense that with the introduction of the VAT, tax evasion has likely declined. Much of the revenue gains from the VAT are attributable to structural and procedural simplification and to the fact that sales tax reform was designed to take advantage of such "tax handles" as the domestic sales of the state oil monopoly, the customs house, and the larger government-owned manufacturing enterprises. It is difficult to misapply a uniform rate VAT to these easily accessible collection points. There has been, however, little evidence of improvement in administrative *practices* in the tax department. And although the newly installed computerized tax information system will ultimately enable significant gains in col-lection and enforcement, its potential had barely begun to be exploited by 1987. The system is still unfamiliar to most officials, and its imple-mentation has been plagued by coordination problems as well as some residual resistance from within the tax administration.[16]

Consequently, the revenue potential of the VAT was placed in jeopardy in the first few months of its existence by administrative slippages and oversights. Although all taxable firms were required to register for the tax prior to April 1, 1985, only 25,000 had done so by that date. Concerted efforts were undertaken to rectify the problem, and by September 1985, 51,000 taxable firms had registered, about the number anticipated. But only 36 percent of registered firms were by then complying with the monthly filing requirement for the VAT, and no audits of any VAT taxpayers, even the largest thousand firms, had begun by 1986 and 1987. But by mid-1987, some progress was notable. By that time, the number of firms registered for VAT had increased by almost 50 percent over 1985, to 74,634. Moreover, plans were announced for expansion of VAT audits, to enable collections to increase by at least 20 percent for the year.

Performance in income tax administration in the first three years of the reform was rather less promising, in spite of a much publicized "tax amnesty" designed to induce habitual tax evaders to enter the tax rolls. Under the amnesty, inspired partly by glowing reports on amnesties offered in Massachusetts in the early 1980s, evaders were forgiven for past transgressions, provided they adhered to the law in the future.[17] Even so, non-oil income tax collections were running at only 40 percent of forecast amounts by late 1985. By mid-1986, it was clear that not only was the amnesty a failure, but also that problems in income tax administration had begun to threaten the revenue objectives of reform, and at the very least had eroded seriously the credibility of the income-tax portion of the reform.

The Ministry of Finance decided to reverse these trends by creating, in June 1986, a special independent "strike force" of auditors, consisting largely of recent returnees from the overseas training program mounted as part of preparations for reform in 1981. Reporting directly to the director-general of taxes, the group consisted of 30 persons headed by a veteran official of proven capability.[18]

The results of the activities of this elite group clearly demonstrated not only the presence of great "slack" in tax administration, but also the tremendous potential returns available from investments in targeted audits. Two dozen companies reporting zero or negative tax liability for 1985 were audited by this group between June 1986 and June 1987, at a cost of just under U.S. $200,000 (Rp. 250 million). As a result, these firms were assessed U.S. $68 million (Rp. 87 billion), in taxes, fines, and penalties (another U.S. $5.9 million was still being disputed in 1988). The strike force, therefore, yielded a direct return that was 340 times the investment. Indirect returns, in the form of improved compliance from other firms not yet audited, are unknowable but were surely substantial.[19]

IV. Lessons

Some fairly clear lessons can be drawn from the Indonesian experience with tax reform in the middle 1980s. It is not, however, obvious that all of these lessons have much relevance for other times or other countries, or even, for that matter, Indonesia in the 1990s.

The first and perhaps most important of these lessons applies to economic policies generally. The Indonesian experience with tax reform —indeed virtually all economic policy reforms in that country—attests to the critical importance of continuity, commitment, and competence among top economic decisionmakers. The reform was conceived and nurtured by the then minister of finance and implemented by him and three other current and former ministers (including a newly appointed minister of finance in 1983). All served as persuasive champions of the reform package before the president, the legislature, and the public. All had served more or less continuously as officials in charge of economic policy since 1967: between these four people was a remarkable total of three-quarters of a century's experience as ministers of the government. All four continued to serve in the government through mid-March of 1988, two as cabinet members.

The track record of this economic team is a long one; it is widely recognized as a very good one. Perhaps one reason their record was good was precisely because it was long, in more than one sense. More by experience than by training, this unusual group of officials developed a long-term perspective on economic policy that is rare enough among economists and rarer still among policymakers. In times of prosperity and abundant financial resources, their influence waned, along with the need for hard policy choices for which the economic team was noted. Consequently, economic policies in the first and second oil booms, in 1973–75 and 1979–82 respectively, bear the stamp of other government officials having much shorter policy horizons. Such interludes were utilized by the economic team to plan alternative policies for coping with future rounds of economic adversity. The team was therefore prepared to respond to economic crises after 1982 not only with policies for short-term management, but also with a series of policy reforms focused upon restructuring of the economy in the medium to long term.[20]

The Indonesian experience, then, suggests that competence and continuity in economic policymaking are critical for success in policy reform in general and tax reform in particular. The usefulness of this lesson for other countries is not so apparent. Although many countries may be blessed with an ample supply of competent economic analysts available for cabinet positions, not many (including, perhaps, the Indonesia of the future) can count on them staying in office long enough to duplicate the achievements of the Indonesian economic team of the past two decades.

The second lesson, not unrelated to the first, attests to the importance of distinguishing between tax reform initiatives that are politically impossible and those that are merely politically difficult (see Harberger, chapter 2), and then identifying approaches for surmounting such difficulties without expending energies on overcoming the impossible. Sensible tax reform of course requires avoiding measures that seek to attain the politically impossible, however advisable these may be on economic, administrative, or equity grounds. In Indonesia these would have included a shift to a direct consumption tax, the abolition of deductibility of interest in tandem with the exclusion of interest income from the tax base (Gillis, 1985), and incarceration of tax evaders. Many other measures were widely alleged to be politically impossible but in fact turned out to only be politically difficult, to one degree or another. Income tax incentives were alleged to be politically untouchable, as well as tax preferences for cooperatives and tax exemption of income of civil servants. In the end, incentives were abolished, preferences ended for cooperatives, and civil servants' income became taxable. In each case, the architects of reform invested considerable time and energy in overcoming political objections to each measure.

The third lesson that may be drawn from the Indonesian experience is that at least in developing-country tax-reform programs where revenue objectives are important, relatively heavier stress should be placed on changes in indirect rather than direct taxes. Certainly the Indonesian reform would already be marked as something of a failure but for the revenue success of the VAT. This is not to argue against pursuit of fundamental income tax reform. It is to stress the inherently limited revenue potential of income tax reform, particularly personal income tax reform in most LDCs. This limitation stems both from administrative

complexities in income taxation and from the relatively small proportion of the population with incomes high enough to be taxed.

A fourth lesson furnished by the Indonesian experience is the importance of designing tax reform to enable the tax system to do that for
which it is best suited (the raising of revenues) rather than to seek goals
for which it is ill-suited. Much of the revenue success of the reform, at
least in its first three years, has been due to the fact that the reform
program was not overloaded with nonrevenue objectives, including
explicit tax measures to redress income maldistribution or foster economic growth and stability. However, the revenue success of the reform
has nonetheless contributed to both economic stability and the allevia-
tion of poverty.

Astute fiscal specialists (Shoup, 1969; Bird, 1988) have long stressed
the revenue payoffs possible from investment in tax administration. A
fifth lesson from the Indonesian experience is that such investments
really can be made to pay very high returns. One dramatic example was
the investment of U.S. $200,000 in the operations of a special strike
force in tax audit in 1986–87, an investment that brought a direct
return of 340 times the initial outlay. Indeed, in the first year alone, this
experiment yielded enough additional revenue to cover the costs of two
other major investments in tax administration as well: the overseas
training of about seventy-five young tax officials from 1981–88, and the
entire cost of all hardware and software used to date in the new computerized tax-information system erected for the tax reform.

A sixth lesson is that successful reform can be critically dependent
upon the follow-up to reform. This was clearly the case in Indonesia
where the tax administration itself was, except at the highest levels,
less than fully supportive of reform. Policymakers found it essential to
closely monitor not only the initial implementation of reform by the
tax administration, but to apply continual pressure for improved performance in tax collections throughout the first three years after it was
put into place.

A seventh lesson from the Indonesian reform merely confirms lessons available from experience elsewhere: adoption of a VAT by a country need not, and likely will not, have any significant impact upon that
country's price level, and almost certainly will not lead to greater
inflation.

The final lesson available from the Indonesian reform is that good
economics does matter in debates over the shape of tax reform. To illustrate, Indonesian tax incentives were abolished not on grounds of

abstract arguments but because the reform program made available empirical evidence clearly indicating the economic wastes and revenue losses associated with the incentives. The importance of ending tax incentives in the success of the reform cannot be overstated. Further, a flat-rate VAT was adopted because it could be shown that even a relatively low rate of VAT could become a "money machine," provided a uniform rate is used for all taxable goods, and provided the tax was collected on petroleum products and on imports.

Notes

1 Indeed, radical measures proved unavoidable in the area of customs administration. In April 1985, the government placed the sensitive task of certifying import values and tariff rates in the hands of a private Swiss surveying firm; most customs officials were sent home. This was done to reduce import bottlenecks arising both from excessively complex import procedures and corruption in the customs service.

2 The architects of the Indonesian tax reform believed that, certainly in the Indonesian context, a shift toward more uniform taxation was tantamount to a shift toward more "efficient" taxation. But "uniformity" was never confused with "optimality."

3 As in the Benelux countries, VAT liability may be deferred for machinery imported for projects with long gestation periods. The Indonesian system allows deferral for one to five years, or until the project begins commercial operation. In addition, raw materials and equipment imported for use in export manufacture may qualify for "suspension" of VAT, which for all practical purposes amounts to exemption. All departures from universal application of the VAT to products are summarized in Directorate for Indirect Taxes, Department of Finance, "Special Provisions Regarding Value-Added Tax" (Jakarta, May 19, 1987).

4 These modifications were all adopted in 1986. Goods eligible for this treatment include low-cost housing, goods for the armed forces, cattle and poultry feed, and water.

5 Cattle and poultry feed are not subject to VAT but, strictly speaking, are not exempt as such (see footnote 3). Although there are no exemptions by product category, VAT is not collected on the sales of "small" enterprises (firms with an annual turnover of less than U.S. $5,000 or total capital level less than U.S. $8,000).

6 Where agricultural firms do make significant use of inputs and machinery taxable under the VAT, they may actually seek to register for VAT, in order to credit taxes paid on their purchases against taxes due on sales.

7 The decision to include refined petroleum products in the VAT base was made at some political costs, as gasoline, kerosene, and similar products were never subject to the old turnover tax. But once that decision was made, it was apparent that with a uniform rate, and virtually no exemptions, the VAT would be among the simplest and most collectible of any tax ever implemented anywhere.

8 The PPD rate was 5 percent on taxable incomes equivalent to U.S. $188 (1986), and reached 50 percent on taxable income in excess of U.S. $14,030 (U.S. $1 = 1,282

Rupiah in 1986). For the PPS, the 20 percent rate applied to annual profits below U.S. $19,500 (1986). The highest rate of 45 percent was imposed on all profits in excess of U.S. $39,000.

9 Cooperatives were, under the old law, fully exempt from income tax for their first five years of operation, and nominally subject only to a 20 percent tax rate after the exemption period. As a practical matter, however, few if any cooperatives paid any significant income taxes.

10 The rate structure is as follows (Rupiahs converted to dollars at 1986 exchange rates): for taxable income of $0–7,794, 15 percent; $7,795–38,971, 25 percent; $38,972 and above, 35 percent.

11 The 20 percent withholding tax can be lowered by tax treaty.

12 No one expected the taxation of capital gains to result in significant revenue during this century. Rather, gains were made taxable only to protect the rest of the income tax, in order to prevent taxpayers from converting ordinary income into capital gains that formerly went untaxed.

13 Rural nonforest land and estates were subject to progressive rates. Taxes on forest land were assessed at 20 percent of logging royalties. Special negotiated rates also applied to mining lands. For urban land, a 50 percent exemption applied to residential property.

14 The tax administration enjoyed wide latitude in granting exemptions by land use, by size of property, by ownership, and by value (Kelley, 1987).

15 To reduce transitional problems, the assessment ratio for 1986 was set at 20 percent of capital value, to be raised in steps, eventually to 100 percent.

16 In the early stages of VAT registration in 1984–85, district offices ignored central directives on registration procedures and failed to forward applications for becoming a VAT taxpayer to the computer sections of district tax offices, thereby reducing the utility of the master file system for the 90 percent of VAT taxpayers who registered prior to correction of this problem.

17 The amnesty came in the form of a presidential decree issued in April 1984. It provided forgiveness on tax matters for all infractions prior to 1984, provided amnesty seekers came forward before 1985. When only a relatively small number of persons requested amnesty, the deadline was later extended to mid-1985.

18 Members of the strike force received an additional salary of about $400 per month (1986 dollars).

19 Prospects for future specialized strike forces in tax administration are uncertain. Some members, including the head of the group, were subjected to clearly false libelous accusations, presumably from interests harmed by the undertaking.

20 A series of five major policy adjustments was carried out by the economic team in 1983 alone, only two of which can be characterized as examples of short-term crisis management policies. These two were a freeze on government consumption in January and the cancellation and/or postponement in May of billions of dollars worth of large-scale governmental projects of a highly capital-intensive nature. The other reforms were focused primarily on longer-term structural adjustments. The first was a reversal in domestic energy policies in January 1983, involving a drastic reduction in subsidies to domestic energy consumption. The second was a major devaluation in March. The third was adoption of fundamental financial reform in June, involving liberalization of interest rate policies.

References

Ahmad, Ethisham, and Nicholas Stern (1987), *Report on Tax Reform in Pakistan*, November, unpublished (Table 3.16).

American Chamber of Commerce in Bolivia (1986), *Tax Reform Law: An Explanation of its Contents* (La Paz).

Bird, Richard, chapter 9, this volume.

Collier, William, et al. (January, 1982), "Rural Development in Java. *Bulletin of Indonesian Economic Studies* 16, pp. 84–100.

Conrad, Robert (1986), "Essays on the Indonesian Tax Reform," *CPD Discussion Paper No. 1986-8* (February), World Bank.

Conrad, Robert, and Malcolm Gillis (1984), "The Indonesian Tax Reform of 1983," Cambridge, Mass.: Harvard Institute for International Development (HIID) Development Discussion Paper No. 162.

Due, John (1957), *Sales Taxation* (Urbana, Ill.: University of Illinois Press).

Gillis, Malcolm (1980), "Energy Demand in Indonesia," Cambridge, Mass., Harvard Institute for International Development (HIID) Development Discussion Paper No. 101.

——— (1984), "Episodes in Indonesian Economic Growth," in Arnold C. Harberger, editor, *World Economic Growth* (San Francisco: Institute for Contemporary Studies).

——— (1985), "Micro and Macroeconomics of Tax Reform," *Journal of Development Economics*, vol. 19, pp. 221–24.

——— (1987), "Lessons from Postwar Experience with Tax Reform in Developing Countries." Paper prepared for the 1988 World Development Report, World Bank (unpublished).

——— (1989), "Tax Reform and the Value-Added Tax: Indonesia," forthcoming in *World Tax Reform*, ed. Michael Boskin, International Center for Economic Growth.

Gillis, Malcolm, and David Dapice (1986), "External Adjustments and Growth: Indonesia since 1965," in Rudiger Dornbusch, ed., *A Policy Manual for an Open Economy* (forthcoming).

Gillis, Malcolm, Dwight Perkins, Michael Roemer, and Donald Snodgrass (1987), *Economics of Development*, 2d ed. (New York: Norton).

Kelley, Roy (1987), "Financing Urban Development: The Indonesian Experience." Paper presented at the ABD/UNCRD Regional Seminar on Major National Urban Policy Issues, February, Manila, The Philippines.

Shoup, Carl (1969), *Public Finance* (New York: Aldine).

Tait, Alan, Wilfred Gratz, and Barry Eichengreen (1979), "International Comparisons of Taxation for Selected Developing Countries," *International Monetary Fund Staff Papers* vol. 26, no. 1, March.

Tait, Alan (1986), "The Value-Added Tax: Revenue, Inflation and the Foreign Trade Balance," in Malcolm Gillis, Gerry Sicat, and Carl Shoup, eds., *The Value-Added Tax in Developing Countries* (forthcoming).

World Bank (1981), "Indonesia: Development Prospects and Policy Options," Report No. 3307-IND, April.

World Bank (1986), *World Development Report 1986* (New York: Oxford University Press).

5

·······

The Political Economy of the
Jamaican Tax Reform

·······

Roy Bahl

The policy analysis and implementation that led to the 1986 and 1987 Jamaican tax reform may be an important addition to the growing knowledge about taxation in developing countries.[1] The reform program was comprehensive: it covered the entire tax system, encompassing both the tax structure and tax administration (see chapter 1). And, like the Indonesian reform discussed in chapters 2 and 4 of this volume, it involved the development of a training program. Most important, however, the underlying research considered not only the reform of each tax in the system, but how the pieces of the new system would fit together. Among other things, this meant trying to find the right set of connections among tax policy, trade policy, and industrial policy. If the Jamaican tax reform study is to lay any claim to fame in this literature, it is due to this comprehensive approach.

This study might add to the literature in three other ways. First, Jamaica was reorienting its entire system in the 1980s and tax reform was to be a part of these broader changes. Edward Seaga was elected prime minister in 1980 with a mandate to replace the direct controls that had long governed the economy with an export-driven, private-sector-led economic growth strategy. The challenge to the project was to find a tax package that would fit this mandate and be politically acceptable. Second, the Jamaica reform was comprehensive enough to give an opportunity to observe the possibilities of "shocking" the tax system and still having a viable reform—something history tells us is not likely to be successful. Third, the experience in Jamaica can add something to what is known about the politics and the process of tax reform, i.e., how to go about involving interest groups and the general public in the design and "selling" of a comprehensive tax reform without compromising the integrity of the reforms. Fourth, this study gives some insights into how to get over the initial hurdles of implementation — "the science of implementation," if there is such a thing. In fact, just as in the Indonesian effort (chapter 4), the project stayed with the work through the public debate and to implementation, and was involved in the early stages of monitoring the performance of the new system.

This paper summarizes the results of this four-year effort. The goal is to fit the pieces together and to tell the story in a context of the politics and the economics of the Jamaican tax reform. The concluding section of this chapter lists the lessons learned from this work and draws some parallels with the conventional wisdom.

The Jamaican Economy

If the reform of a tax system is not in step with the goals of a government's economic and political program, it can have little chance for success. The best of tax reforms will not have the desired effects on the economy, and quite possibly will make matters worse, unless it is designed to reinforce the macroeconomic plan which the government intends to follow. The Jamaican tax reform was a continuing process of trying to stay up with the changes in the Jamaican economy and in the government of Jamaica's economic policies. To understand the work of the tax project and the factors that shaped the design of the reform program, it is necessary to understand the economic and political context.

Macroeconomic Performance

The Jamaican economy suffered a severe and sustained contraction from 1973 through 1980.[2] Estimates published in the International Monetary Fund's (IMF) *International Financial Statistics* show the following:

GDP (1980 prices) declined 18 percent
GDP per capita (1980 prices) declined 26 percent
the Consumer Price Index rose 304 percent
government expenditure rose 419 percent
government revenue rose 274 percent
net foreign assets dropped U.S. $582 million
estimated unemployment rose from 22 percent to 27 percent

There was no economic miracle in the first half of the 1980s. The Seaga administration lived up to its promises by turning government policy toward deregulating the economy and changing its orientation from import substitution to export-driven. However, there was a long way to go, foreign exchange reserves were short, the government treasury was all but bare, and the government had to ride out the collapse of the bauxite industry. Moreover, there was considerable pressure from foreign creditors to adopt more austere economic policies and there would be an election in 1984. Still, many felt that economic policy did not go far enough or fast enough.

The Jamaican economy grew slowly in the first half of the 1980s. Real GNP increased by only 2.6 percent between 1980 and 1986 (table 5.1). Though even this modest increase represented a turnaround from the real 18 percent decline between 1973 and 1980, Jamaica's growth has remained well below that of other developing countries and below that of most Caribbean countries. The 1980–86 period was also one of economic instability. There were real GNP declines in 1984 and 1985, the Jamaican dollar was devalued in 1983 and 1984, and the rate of inflation varied erratically between 5 percent in 1981 and 31 percent in 1984.

The foreign exchange shortage has remained acute in the 1980s, in spite of very sizable devaluations. Imports, particularly of consumer goods, fell significantly in response to the devaluation, but the current account balance of payments deficit was about 14 percent of GDP in 1984. Despite rescheduling, foreign debts outstanding grew relative to export earnings and external debt increased from the equivalent of 90 percent of GDP in 1983 to 145 percent in 1986.

Inflation increased by more than 30 percent in 1984. This was due to a 77 percent increase in the exchange rate, the removal of subsidies on certain foods and public utility rates, and the rapid monetary growth of past years. The U.S. dollar moved from an average J$2.76 in 1983 to an average J$4.00 in 1984. This devaluation was largely the initial response of market forces to the liberalization of a previously pegged undervalued exchange rate. The new system was a managed float operated through a biweekly auction system. The money supply (M1) grew by about 21 percent in 1983 and 14 percent in 1984.

The government deficit had reached more than 17 percent of GDP in 1983, by World Bank accounting, but had fallen to below 6 percent by 1986. The reduction was accomplished by a substitution of external for domestic borrowing, tax rate increases (especially the stamp duty on imports), and an expenditure reduction program. About 4,000 positions (4 percent of the civil service positions) were cut in 1984.

Table 5.1   Selected Indicators of the Performance of the Jamaican Economy

	1975	1980	1981
Per capita GDP (J$)			
Real	1,069.5	856.8	867.9
Nominal	1,292.0	2,226.9	2,439.2
GDP growth rate (percentages)			
Real	−0.5	−5.8	2.7
Nominal	20.5	11.1	11.0
Rate of inflation (percentages)			
CPI average annual (point to point)	15.7	28.7	4.8
GDP deflator	20.8	17.9	8.1
Fiscal deficit (in J$ millions)			
Real	211.3	319.5	313.8
Nominal	255.3	830.4	881.8
Percentage of GDP	9.8	17.5	16.7
Foreign debt outstanding			
Nominal (in US$ millions)	388.3	2,055.4	1,311.1
Percentage of export earnings	49.5	214.2	134.0
Percentage of government expenditure	37.6	164.5	172.7
Balance of payments (in US$ millions)			
Current account deficit	282.8	166.0	336.8
Percentage of GDP	9.9	6.2	11.4
Exports (in US$ millions)	784.0	959.2	978.1
Percentage of GDP	27.4	36.2	33.1
Imports (in US$ millions)	1,123.5	1,172.6	1,481.1
Percentage of GDP	39.3	44.2	50.1
Exchange rate (percentage average)	0.9091	1.7814	1.7814

Source: GDP—Statistical Institute of Jamaica, *National Income and Product 1986*; CPI —Bank of Jamaica, *Statistical Digest*, various years; fiscal deficit—World Bank, *Jamaica: Economic Situation and Public Investment*, vol. 1, p. 48, and Bank of Jamaica, *Statistical Digest*, various years; foreign debt—Bank of Jamaica, *Statistical Digest*, December 1981 and July 1987; exports—Planning Institute of Jamaica, *Economic and Social Survey*,

Social Conditions

The 1980–85 period was a hard one for most Jamaicans. Though the average per capita GNP was U.S. $940 in 1985, much of the population lives near a subsistence level of income. It is estimated that 40 percent

1982	1983	1984	1985	1986	Percentage change 1980–86
862.6	866.0	844.0	794.9	803.3	−6.2
2,658.8	3,114.4	4,089.5	4,852.4	5,706.0	156.2
1.1	2.3	−1.4	−4.5	2.2	n.a.
10.9	19.3	33.6	20.3	18.8	n.a.
7.0	16.7	31.3	23.3	10.4	n.a.
9.7	16.6	34.8	26.0	16.3	n.a.
313.2	335.6	144.1	106.1	84.7	−73.5
965.4	1,206.4	698.0	647.6	601.6	−27.6
16.5	17.3	7.5	5.8	4.5	n.a.
2,739.9	3,266.9	3,261.6	3,499.0	3,520.0	71.3
356.5	476.4	464.4	615.5	581.7	n.a.
188.1	213.4	350.9	429.5	344.4	n.a.
408.6	358.7	335.3	304.4	105.6	−36.4
12.4	9.9	14.2	15.1	4.3	n.a.
768.5	685.7	702.4	568.5	605.1	36.9
23.4	19.8	29.3	27.9	25.0	n.a.
1,375.9	1,281.0	1,183.3	1,143.7	976.4	16.7
42.1	40.7	48.4	54.8	40.3	n.a.
1.7814	1.9322	3.9428	5.5586	5.4778	502.6

1975, 1982, 1984, and 1986; government expenditures—World Bank, *Jamaica: Economic Situation and Public Institute*, vol. 1, and Bank of Jamaica, *Statistical Digest*, various years; balance of payments—International Monetary Fund, *International Finance Statistics*, and Planning Institute of Jamaica, *Economic and Social Survey*, 1986.

of the national income is earned by the top 10 percent of the population, and that this inequality has not been significantly reduced in the past two decades.[3] The distribution of land wealth, as might be expected, is even more skewed.[4] When it is reported, then, that *average* real per capita income decreased by J$62 between 1980 and 1985, one can imagine that there was some considerable worsening of living standards for the poor.

The inflation of over 30 percent brought on by the devaluation was led by an increase in food prices, and deregulation and removal of subsidies led to some increases in public utility charges, petroleum prices, and housing rents during this period. A food stamp program was put in place in 1984 to provide some relief to lower-income Jamaicans. The unemployment rate, though difficult to measure, appeared to be 15 percent or higher. Jamaican authorities report the percent of labor force employed to have risen from 72 percent in 1980 to 77 percent in 1984.

Jamaica's "brain drain" of the 1970s—educated Jamaicans migrating abroad in search of better economic opportunity—imposed a heavy cost on the economy. There was a net outmigration of 129,000, or 6 percent of the (average) population between 1974 and 1980. The outmigration has continued into the 1980s, although at a lower rate. Between 1981 and 1984, 1.4 percent of the (average) population (30,500 persons) migrated from Jamaica.

Economic Policy

The Seaga administration's economic program was outlined in the Ministry of Finance and Planning *Ministry Paper 9*, "Taxation Measures 1982–83." This program counted on controlled expansion of aggregate demand to bring order and real economic meaning to relative price movements in commodity, labor, money, bond, and foreign exchange markets, and to the distribution of income and wealth. Implicit in the program was the proposition that economic growth and efficiency would be improved if private markets and private decisions were permitted a larger role. Accordingly, *Ministry Paper 9* proposed to reduce public ownership of commercial enterprises, public sector control of prices (except the prices of foreign exchange), and regulation of imports, exports, and domestic investment.

The economic program which the government has actually followed since the issuance of *Ministry Paper 9* has been consistent with the strategy outlined, with a notable and important exception. Import licenses and price controls were for the most part phased out as promised. The government deficit has been reduced dramatically and the first phase of a comprehensive income tax reform has been undertaken. Most of these initiatives have not gone so far as some had hoped, but the program has generally been in the direction promised.

The notable exception is the foreign trade regime. The price of foreign exchange has not been decontrolled—except for a period during 1983–84 when there was a "controlled float" of the Jamaican dollar—and the foreign exchange shortages in the economy persist. As discussed below, the taxation of international trade has probably exacerbated the problem. The formulation of a consistent trade policy still remains at the top of the government's list of unfinished economic reforms.

Foreign Pressure

Jamaican economic policy since 1980 has been shaped, partly if not largely, to satisfy the conditions imposed by creditors. In some cases these actions compromised the design and implementation of the comprehensive tax reform.

The government negotiated separate loan agreements with the World Bank, the IMF, and the U.S. government in 1981–82. The agreement with the Fund provided for a target deficit level of 10 percent of GDP by fiscal year 1983–84. When the government did not meet this target, the IMF began to push for a deficit reduction program. With the unemployment rate in the 20 percent range and the bauxite sector declining, substantial public employment reductions seemed out of the question. The government turned first to tax rate increases on the perennial excise products—cigarettes and spirits—and in the following year to the major rate increases under the import stamp duty mentioned above.

These discretionary actions affected the planning for the tax reform in several ways. First, it seemed (at the time) to make it all the more clear that major tax reductions of any kind would be out of the question, and raised the possibility that the structural reforms would have to be introduced simultaneously with a tax increase. Second, the import duty rate increases effectively introduced a major new indirect tax and further distorted the pattern of relative prices. As a result, the simplified general sales tax (the general consumption tax, or "GCT") that would be proposed as a substitute for the existing system of several indirect taxes would be harder to sell because it would now be even more of a "shock" to the system.

An agreement with the World Bank led to a trade liberalization program beginning in 1987. This, in effect, recalled the stamp duty rate increases enacted in 1985 and 1986. The program called for a "flattening" of the duty rate structure and the elimination of most import exemptions, hence it moved the import stamp tax structure back in the direction of the proposed GCT. This would have made implementation easier except that the Bank and the government agreed to postpone implementation of the GCT and to consider a program of export rebates.

Another major influence was U.S. government policy. Though neither its balance of payments loans nor its project assistance carried conditions in the same way as did the Fund and Bank loans, U.S. foreign policy did play a role in shaping tax, trade, and industrial policy in Jamaica. First, it was the U.S. government that provided the funding for the comprehensive tax reform project. Second, there was always the implied threat that Jamaican economic policy, should it take a wrong turn, could dampen U.S. enthusiasm for supporting the programs of the Seaga administration. Third, and perhaps most important, was the U.S. tax reform of 1986. By lowering the corporate rate to 34 percent, it compromised the foreign tax credit position of U.S. firms investing in Jamaica and gave the tax reform program one more argument for lowering the corporate rate.

The Setting for Tax Reform

In some ways, Jamaica in the early 1980s was not the ideal setting for tax reform. Successful tax reform in almost everyone's eyes meant tax reduction, an understandable reaction to the slow growth in the economy, inflation, and the resulting income tax bracket creep. But given the size of the government deficit, tax reduction seemed a farfetched possibility. There was considerable pressure to hold the line on expenditure retrenchment. Such cuts would almost certainly mean reductions in government employment, and would have to take place at a time when unemployment was very high and when the private sector economy was performing too poorly to absorb the surplus labor. Major budget cuts in other programs seemed out of the question because of the potential disruption to the economy and because of the obvious political drawbacks.

This meant that if tax reduction was to be accomplished, it would have to come at the expense of an increase in the government's budget deficit or a reduction in some other cost of government. The former would not be a possibility for two reasons. First, increased domestic borrowing would put more pressure on domestic prices. Second, the IMF loan agreement required a reduction in the government deficit and a ceiling on domestic credit. The cost reduction route was only a little more promising. One possibility centered on the state enterprises, which were a known drain on the central government budget. There was a call for divestment in some cases and for increased user charges to cover operating costs in others. But divestment takes time, and increased user charges on some items (e.g., electricity) would have been even more unpopular than increased taxes. Another deficit reduction strategy would center on removing some costly government subsidies, for example, raising the price of petroleum products or eliminating import duty exemptions on a wide variety of producer goods. Though some of these measures were eventually taken, they proved to be as politically difficult as had been expected.

There were some favorable aspects of the setting for a comprehensive tax reform. First, and most important, the tax system was believed to be, and was in fact, unfair. This widely held public view turned out to mean that the horizontal inequities inherent in the present tax structure and accentuated by the way the system was administered had gone beyond tolerable limits. Piecemeal reform to fill this year's revenue gap, long the approach taken to the annual budget crisis in Jamaica, would no longer be acceptable. The public—business, labor, the press, and foreign investors—seemed to have given the Seaga administration a clear mandate to put forward a plan for a complete overhaul of the tax system. This dissatisfaction and the willingness of the government to think carefully through the problems with the present system were keys to the eventual implementation of the reform.

A second stimulus was the foreign donors. The IMF was pressing the government to reduce the fiscal deficit and limit domestic borrowing. The Fund took its usual position of being agnostic about whether a balanced budget balance should be achieved by tax increases or expenditure reductions, but it gave annual advice on which tax rates to increase in order to fill the fiscal gap. The World Bank was more aggressively pressing for tax structure change in the areas of tariff reform and indirect taxation. The U.S. government did not condition its aid package on tax reform, but it did urge changes in the tax system and financed the tax project that was eventually to lead to the reform. These external pressures made it urgent and politically beneficial for the government to embrace "its own" tax reform project.

Third, the Seaga administration's political hand was strengthened in the 1984 elections when its party (the Jamaica Labour Party) won parliament in an uncontested election. The issues that led to this political victory did not have to do with the economic reforms, but the control of parliament did mean that the reform program would eventually be reviewed and decided by a more friendly and unified parliament than otherwise would have been the case.

Table 5.2   The Changing Structure of Taxes in Jamaica, 1980–88
(as percentage of total taxes)[a]

	80–81	81–82	82–83	83–84	84–85	85–86	86–87	Budget 87–88
Taxes on foreign trade	44.7	45.5	38.5	34.0	40.5	44.2	42.2	44.8
On imports[b]	(17.2)	(20.0)	(22.5)	(23.6)	(21.2)	(32.1)	(30.0)	(35.8)
On exports[c]	(27.5)	(25.5)	(16.0)	(10.4)	(19.3)	(12.1)	(12.2)	(8.9)
Taxes on consumption	22.0	19.8	20.7	23.7	20.2	19.3	18.5	14.5
Sumptuary[d]	(12.4)	(10.3)	(10.5)	(12.2)	(10.5)	(10.1)	(8.6)	(n.a.)
Other[e]	(9.6)	(9.5)	(10.2)	(11.5)	(9.7)	(9.2)	(9.9)	(n.a.)
Taxes on income and wealth	33.3	34.6	40.6	42.3	39.3	37.8	39.2	40.8
On companies[f]	(11.8)	(12.6)	(17.2)	(13.4)	(13.8)	(14.1)	(17.6)	(16.9)
On individuals[g]	(19.4)	(20.1)	(21.3)	(27.2)	(24.5)	(22.8)	(20.9)	(22.3)
On property[h]	(2.1)	(1.9)	(2.1)	(1.7)	(1.0)	(0.9)	(0.8)	(1.6)
Total as percentage of GDP	23.4	26.9	26.1	23.3	25.4	26.2	30.6	30.6[a]
Memorandum items (as percentage of total taxes) Taxes collected at import[i]	9.0	13.9	16.1	16.1	15.5	26.3	19.6	n.a.
Bauxite taxes[j]	26.6	24.5	15.0	9.0	16.8	9.3	9.9	6.6
Total consumption taxes[k]	39.2	39.8	43.2	47.3	41.4	51.4	48.6	50.3

[a]Total taxes include the bauxite levy.

[b]Taxes on imports include customs duty, tonnage and warehouse fees, consumption duty on imports, stamp duty and additional stamp duty on customs inward warrants, and retail sales taxes collected on imports plus consumption duties on motor fuels and the balance of retail sales taxes.

[c]Taxes on exports include bauxite taxes (defined in note j) plus the following taxes on tourism: travel tax, tax de sejour, additional hotel tax, and hotel license duty.

[d]Sumptuary taxes are consumption and excise duties on alcoholic beverages and tobacco products.

[e]Other consumption taxes include other excise duties; other consumption duties; other stamp duties; entertainment duty; taxes on betting, gambling, and lotteries; and miscellaneous taxes and licenses such as motor vehicle licenses, telephone tax, and retail sales

tax on used vehicles.

[f]Taxes on companies exclude taxes on bauxite companies but include betterment taxes and bank and trust company surcharges.

[g]Taxes on individuals include individual income tax, PAYE, and the education tax. (Note that both this item and total tax revenues are understated because information on other payroll taxes—NIS, NHT, and HEART in particular—was not available for all years.)

[h]Taxes on property consist solely of the property tax.

[i]Taxes collected at import include customs duty, tonnage and warehouse fees, consumption duty on imports, stamp duty and additional stamp duty on customs inward warrants, and retail sales taxes collected on imports.

[j]Bauxite taxes include the bauxite levy and company taxes on bauxite companies.

[k]Total consumption taxes are the sum of taxes on consumption and taxes on imports.

Source: The basic source for most of the tax data is the monthly statement of revenues from the Collector-General. A few numbers for 1982–83 were estimated on the basis of preliminary data because the available final data did not contain as detailed a breakdown as desired. The figures for 1985–86 were for the most part estimated by the Board of Revenue. Collections for 1985–86 from the bauxite levy were assumed to decrease by the same proportion as projected output over the previous year (Planning Institute of Jamaica, *Quarterly Economic Report*, October–December 1984–85, p. 25). Other information on the bauxite levy came from the same source (p. 60), except that the out-turn for fiscal 1984–85 was estimated to be the same proportion of target as the results for the first three quarters of the year. GDP data on a fiscal-year basis came from the same source (pp. 24–25) for 1983–84 to 1985–86. The middle estimate is used for the latter year. Fiscal-year GDP for earlier years was estimated from calendar-year data in Statistical Institute of Jamaica, *National Income and Product 1983*, on the assumption that growth was even throughout each year.

Finally, it should be noted that at the time the first of the new reforms was to be put in place (1986), the Jamaican economic situation improved. The decline in oil prices, a lower rate of inflation, and a good tourist season all set the stage for the individual and, later, the company income tax reform to produce far more revenue than had been expected. The extent to which the tax program itself was responsible for this favorable economic performance is an issue that we take up below.

Fiscal Structure

At the time of the initiation of preparations for tax reform, Jamaica was taxing at a level equivalent to about 23 percent of GNP. Since 1983, this share has grown to 30 percent, primarily because of the increasing use of import taxes. We will see that by world standards this is a very high level of taxation.

The structure of Jamaican taxes is described in table 5.2. By 1983, the tax structure was relatively balanced in the sense that taxes on income, domestic production, and foreign trade were all important components. Between 1983 and 1986, however, the taxation of domestic production had declined in favor of increased taxes on imported goods. The current situation—with nearly half of all taxes derived from foreign trade—is that Jamaica's fiscal position is very sensitive to its foreign-exchange position. Individual income taxes have not increased as a share of total financing since 1983.

Problems with the Pre-Reform Tax System

Analysis of the Jamaican tax system indicated that there were three fundamental problems to be resolved. The first is that taxes were too high and, as a consequence, the investment of financial and human capital in the economy was being discouraged. Second, the tax system had badly distorted the structure of relative prices and therefore economic decisions. As a result, the economy was not performing as efficiently as would be the case under a system that was more neutral in its effect on relative prices. Third, a poor administration taxed only that income and consumption that could be easily reached, thereby narrowing the effective tax base and making the system unfair.

Were Taxes Too High?

It is the rare country where the public does not feel that it is overtaxed. At the beginning of the tax project in 1983, the tax ratio[5] was 23.3 percent and was thought to be "too high." But the complaint that taxes are too high can mean many things. It can signal a dissatisfaction with the quality and type of public services being provided, as was case of the U.S. tax revolt of the late 1970s. Another possibility is to argue that taxes are too high by international standards and this somehow makes Jamaica less competitive in attracting investment. Finally, and perhaps a more appropriate argument in the case of Jamaica, is that high taxes discourage work effort and savings and bias investment decisions in such a way that economic growth is slowed.

International Comparisons. To answer the question whether Jamaica taxes more heavily than do other countries, we make use of what has become known as "tax effort" analysis, where "tax effort" is defined as the extent to which a country utilizes its taxable capacity. This tech-

Table 5.3   Taxation Norms in Developing Countries

Measure	Jamaica Actual value	Jamaica Estimated value	Sample average	Sample size	Jamaica ranking	Source equations
Tax/GNP ratio						
1983	23.3	21.1	16.6	52	11	(1)
1972–76	19.0	17.9	16.1	47	13	(2)
1969–71	19.4	19.5	15.1	47	10	(3)
1966–68	16.9	16.9	13.6	49	12	(4)
Tax Effort Index						
1983	1.1037	—	—	52	19	(1)
1972–76	1.0640	—	—	47	18	(2)
1969–71	0.9930	—	—	47	23	(3)
1966–68	0.9986	—	—	49	25	(4)

Estimating Equations

1. $Ty = 0.1148 - 0.0215Ypa + .2116Ny + .096MXy - .004D + .0256D^*Ypa$
   $(7.435) (-4.198) \quad (1.813) \quad (4.91) \quad (-0.107) (2.28)$
   Adj $R^2 = 0.4681$

2. $Ty = 9.9949 - 0.0008(Yp-Xp) + 0.4068Ny + 0.1938Xy$
   $(6.15) \quad (-0.34) \quad (5.41) \quad (3.12)$
   Adj $R^2 = 0.413$

3. $Ty = 11.47 + 0.001(Yp-Xp) + 0.44Ny + 0.05Xy$
   $(7.84) \quad (0.38) \quad (5.45) \quad (1.17)$
   Adj $R^2 = 0.376$

4. $Ty = 14.95 - 0.0742Ay + 0.2951Ny$
   $(9.682) (2.074) \quad (3.678)$

where
  Ty = ratio of taxes to GNP
  Ypa = per capita income in thousands of U.S. dollars
  Yp = per capita income in U.S. dollars
  Xp = per capita export income
  Xy = share of nonmineral exports in GNP
  Ny = share of mining in GDP
  Ay = share of agriculture in GDP
  MXy = sum of imports and exports as a share of GDP
  D is the dummy variable = 1, if Caribbean; otherwise, $D = 0$

Source: Equation 1—see text; Equation 2—Alan Tait, Wilfrid Gratz, and Barry Eichengreen, "International Comparisons of Taxation for Selected Developing Countries, 1972–76," *IMF Staff Working Papers* 26 (March 1979):123–56; Equation 3—Raja Chelliah, Hessel Baas, and Margaret Kelly, "Tax Ratios and Tax Effort in Developing Countries, 1969–71," *IMF Staff Working Papers* 22 (March 1975):187–205; Equation 4—Roy Bahl, "A Regression Approach to Tax Effort and Tax Ratio Analysis," *IMF Staff Working Papers* 18 (March 1971):570–613.

nique of international tax comparisons was originally developed by Lotz and Morss[6] and extended by Bahl[7] as an ongoing project of the Fiscal Affairs Department of the International Monetary Fund. Since the early work, the Fund has continued on a periodic basis to make intercountry comparisons using basically this approach.[8]

The earlier Fund studies showed Jamaica's estimated taxable capacity, or taxable potential, to increase from 16.9 to 19.5 percent of GDP and then to fall off to 17.8 percent during the 1972–76 period (table 5.3). For other developing countries in these samples, however, estimated taxable capacity continued to increase. Jamaica was an "outlier" in the 1970s in the sense that its capacity to raise revenue was actually declining. However, the public sector did not retrench; in fact, the government expenditure-GDP elasticity averaged about 2.0 over the 1974–80 period. Jamaica's actual level of taxation and its tax effort (the actual ratio of taxes to GNP divided by estimated taxable capacity) increased through the 1970s with the result that tax effort was 6.4 percent above the international norm by 1972–76.

We have updated this analysis to 1983. In the regression model specified here, four determinants of taxable capacity are included. The tax ratio is hypothesized to vary directly with the level of per capita income and with two measures of the availability of "tax handles," the openness ratio (MX_y) and the share of mining and other extractive activities in GNP (N_y). The former, measured as the ratio of imports plus exports to GNP, enhances taxable capacity because of the relative ease of taxing the foreign trade sector; and the latter is meant to reflect the greater taxable surplus associated with mineral exports. A dummy variable is included for Caribbean location ($D = 1$ is Caribbean location) to account for the greater taxable capacity that comes with close proximity to the U.S. market.

This equation is estimated on 1983 data for fifty-two developing nations, with results shown in equation (1) of table 5.3. Nearly half of the variations in the tax ratio are explained. The openness ratio and the mining share are significant (at the 0.1 level) and have the expected positive signs (t-statistics are shown in parentheses). The negative coefficient on the per capita income variable suggests that after one accounts for the foreign trade and mining "tax handles," higher income LDCS appear to tax away a smaller share of GNP. This would be consistent with the hypothesis that a given share of GNP is needed to cover the "fixed cost" of government, no matter how small the country. Above this basic share, the effective tax rate may fall as income increases. A

Caribbean location does not significantly affect the tax ratio per se.

This equation has been used to estimate taxable capacity in 1983 for each of the fifty-two countries in the sample. By this measure Jamaica has a predicted taxable capacity of 21.1 percent of GNP. Its even higher actual level of taxation (23.3 percent), then, gives it a tax effort which is 10.4 percent above normal and ranks Jamaica nineteenth among these countries (table 5.3). Of the ten member nations of the Caribbean Common Market (CARICOM) included in this sample, only Dominica, Guyana, Trinidad, and Tobago show a higher tax effort. The regression approach tells us that by international standards Jamaica is a high-taxing country, and that its relative level of tax effort has been increasing during the last decade.

Narrow Bases. Another explanation for the dissatisfaction with the level of taxation in Jamaica is that nominal tax rates are too high. As shown above, Jamaica's 23.3 percent tax share of GNP in 1983 is high by world standards. This is a more onerous burden if GNP is not fully included in the tax base. A recurring theme in the Jamaica tax story is that the base of virtually every tax has been significantly narrowed by exemptions, preferential rate treatment, and administrative constraints. The result has been that nominal (marginal) rates had to be set very high to satisfy revenue requirements.

Before reform in 1986, the individual income tax base was narrowed by the exclusion of perquisites of "allowances" from tax, by sixteen personal tax credits, and by the preferential treatment of wages earned from overtime work. More importantly, poor administration meant that only the sector of the economy subject to witholding—the Pay-As-You-Earn (PAYE) sector—was effectively taxed. Dividend income was not fully reached because of poor administration, and interest income earned from bank deposits and capital gains was not taxable. The result was that only about 40 percent of the true taxable base was actually taxed. In order to raise the necessary amount of revenues the lowest marginal tax rate was set at 30 percent with no standard deduction and it reached 57.5 percent at the relatively low income level of J$14,000. The frequently heard complaint that the income tax system discouraged work effort and investment really meant that those who were included in the income tax net were forced to pay very high marginal rates.

A similar story may be told for five payroll taxes, none of which have yet been restructured. The education tax and the Human Employment and Resource Training (HEART) trust are not contribution programs, and

like the individual income tax, their base does not include allowances
for the self-employed sector. The base of the three payroll tax contribution programs—each of which contains a significant tax element—is
also narrowed by statutory exemptions (there is a ceiling on wages taxed
under the National Insurance Scheme) and allowances are not taxed.
Removal of the NIS ceiling and the taxation of allowances alone would
have permitted an equal yield reduction in the average rate on the three
contribution programs by over 1 percent of wages.

The base of indirect taxes was also limited by exemptions. In 1985,
only about 20 percent of the value of all imported goods was subject to
import taxes. As a result, the import stamp rate was over 200 percent
on some items, and was 30 and 16 percent on capital goods and raw
materials, respectively. The base for domestic indirect taxes was also
limited. Only about 16 percent of final consumption of services and
one third of domestic manufacturing output was in the tax base. If the
present indirect tax system, with the present base, were to be replaced
by a value-added tax of the manufacturer-importer type, comparable to
that of Indonesia (chapter 4), the rate would have to be in the range of 20
to 25 percent in order to maintain revenue yield. This rate would be
high by world standards.

The property tax base also falls well short of its legal goal of taxing
the full market value of land. The 1974 valuation roll is still in use,
hence less than half of the true land value base is under tax.[9] The tax
base is further narrowed by preferential assessment of agricultural and
hotel properties. As a result, the top statutory property tax rate is 4.5
percent, extremely high by international standards.

Allocative Effects

Neutrality is a basic maxim in taxation (see chapter 1). The tax system
should raise the desired amount of revenue in such a way as to leave
unaffected relative prices of commodities and services and factors of
production. The modern and more practical restatement of the neutrality goal is to minimize the excess burdens associated with raising a
given amount of revenue. Not every analyst or every economic planner
agrees that neutrality is a desirable goal. The polar view is that taxes
can and should be used as levers to stimulate economic activity in
desired directions. This interventionist approach underlaid the Jamaican philosophy of taxation in the 1970s.

The tax policy design proposed here departs from neutrality in recommending the retention of some differential tax treatments and the

adoption of others—for example, continuing some investment tax incentives to remain competitive, and exempting certain consumption items from sales tax on administrative grounds or to protect the real income position of low-income residents. The question is how far to go in using the tax system as a lever to guide economic choices, correct undesirable distributional impacts of the tax system, or simplify administration. In the case of Jamaica, the relative price distortions introduced by the old tax system went beyond the justifiable exceptions and likely weakened the efficiency with which the economy operates.

It is no simple matter to prove the case that tax-induced distortions in relative prices have resulted in a significant welfare loss. Roughly, the welfare loss is proportional to the product of the size of the distortion in relative prices and the compensated price elasticity of demand (or substitution) for the good (or factor) in question. It turns out that the magnitude of neither term is easily estimated. The net change in relative prices that is *caused* by the tax code is difficult to estimate because several different provisions in the tax structure may be involved and because all may not affect relative prices in the same direction. As for the second term, there is very little evidence on the compensated price elasticities of substitution in developing countries, but what there is suggests an inelastic response to relative price changes. One could have a nonneutral tax structure, then, and not suffer substantial welfare losses if only the relative price distortions are not very large.[10]

Implications for Equity. Relative price distortions not only impose an efficiency cost on the economy, they introduce an unfairness in the system that most taxpayers find even more objectionable. This clearly was the case with the previous income tax system in Jamaica. The self-employed were given favored treatment by the income tax administration and paid little or no individual income tax, while those enrolled in the PAYE system were forced to cope with what appeared to be onerous burdens. Even within the PAYE sector, private-sector workers had a better opportunity to avoid tax through the receipt of allowances and overtime earnings and paid a lower effective rate.

The price distortions in the system also compromise vertical equity. Those who gain the most from evasion tend to be in the upper-income classes. Allowances are concentrated in the higher-income brackets, and even overtime income was claimed heavily by those who one would expect to be salaried rather than hourly wage earners. Jamaicans with unearned income—interest and dividend income—paid a lower effective tax rate and, since they tended to be concentrated in the higher brackets, this tax preference tended to reduce the overall progressivity of the system.

Administrative Problems

The Jamaican tax system has long been plagued by administrative problems. The previous tax system was very complex and therefore difficult to administer, particularly given a shortage of skilled staff as well as inadequate assessment, collection, and recordkeeping procedures.

Complexity. The complexity of the system made the assessment and audit function of tax officials difficult, a problem compounded by the shortage of skilled staff in virtually all of the tax departments. Complexity also raised compliance costs for taxpayers and in so doing either wasted important private-sector manpower or provided an additional incentive for tax evasion and avoidance.

The individual income tax included two separate rate structures, and a preferential rate for income earned by working overtime hours. There were sixteen allowable income tax credits and an even greater number of nontaxable perquisites or "allowances." The forms that are used to establish an employee's credit entitlements were rarely if ever updated and almost never monitored by either the employee or the income tax department.

For those who file year-end tax returns, the forms and instructions are long and detailed, even by comparison with other developing countries. An analysis of the content revealed numerous errors in the instructions and that the income tax forms did not even reflect the present law. Moreover, it was difficult to obtain a copy of the current income-tax law.

Complexity extended far beyond the income tax. Five different payroll taxes levied on four different bases and administered by three different government agencies involve a substantial burden on employers who collect and remit such taxes. There are also five different indirect taxes: the external (CARICOM) tariff, the import stamp duty, an excise tax, consumption duty, and a retail sales tax. Within this family of sales, excise, and import levies, there are over 100 rates, some providing needlessly small gradations.

Staffing Problems and Outmoded Procedures. A shortage of skilled staff is a major bottleneck to improved tax administration. DeGraw reports that in 1983, a time when increased revenue mobilization was at a premium, there were 150 vacancies among the 449 positions authorized for the income tax department.[11] A disproportionately large number of these were technical positions. The reasons for the staffing problems were about the same in Jamaica as in other developing countries. Salaries were too low, even given the job security and prestige that a government post may offer. In 1983, a trained accountant making J$9,000 in the income tax department would make J$14,000 with a private-sector accounting firm. Moreover, there was no formal career development program, little opportunity for promotion, and the training program in place in 1983 was inadequate.

The methods used to assess and collect taxes in Jamaica were inadequate at the time the tax reform project began in 1983. There was no unique numbering system for either businesses or individuals, hence there was no up-to-date master file of taxpayers. The system was completely manual, i.e., there was little if any use of the computer other than to print bills. This effectively ruled out the use of third-party information, the cross-checking of sales and income tax returns, etc.

The income tax was essentially a PAYE levy and there was little if any use of presumptive assessments on the hard-to-tax sectors, such as self-employed professionals. The major problem was, and remains, record-keeping. The income tax file room is inadequate in size and all records are manually kept. Files are regularly misplaced or lost, and records are frequently out of date or incomplete.

Objectives of the Reform

One is tempted to claim all good things for the objectives of a comprehensive tax reform, i.e., to argue that the reformed system should be designed to meet all the maxims for a good tax system better than the old system did. Too many tax reform studies are unable to resist this temptation and end up falling into the trap of designing a system with multiple and often even conflicting objectives. In fact, there are important decisions to be made about exactly which objectives of tax reform are the most important and about what the government is both willing and politically able to give up.

The Jamaican tax reform took simplification and neutrality as its primary objectives. The goal was to put in place a system that the government will have some chance of administering efficiently and to "get the prices right." To be sure, there were important constraints that limit how much can be done: political resistance to taking back too much of the progressivity in the system, raising an adequate amount of revenue, and reckoning with the goals of trade and industrial policy. Still, the primary thrust was in the direction of restructuring the tax system so that it would have a less distortive effect on relative prices and therefore on economic decisions.

Both of these objectives point in the direction of proposing broader-based, flatter-rate taxes. The fewer the exemptions and "special features," the more easily are taxes assessed and collected. This will minimize the amount of time required to police those already in the system and give tax officials more time to expand the base by bringing the hard-to-tax into the net. Simplification also makes the tax system more understandable and therefore reduces compliance costs. It is also true that broader-based taxes can generate the same amount of revenues at lower marginal rates, which can reduce some of the harmful efficiency effects of the current tax system.

What about the place of equity in this comprehensive tax reform? Infusing the Jamaican project was the view that equity should not be a primary objective in the design of Jamaica's comprehensive tax reform. The steep progressivity of the individual income tax rate structure had the objective of increasing the vertical equity of the tax system, but it also increased the incentives for evasion and avoidance. Because the income tax administration was too weak to properly enforce the system, the loopholes and noncompliance grew, with the eventual result that individual income tax burdens came to be distributed quite regressively.

Another problem with taking vertical equity as a primary reform objective is that unacceptable efficiency costs may result. One example is the tradeoff between what are usually viewed as special "equity" features of a tax—high marginal income tax rates on the rich and higher taxation of more luxury type goods—and the disincentives to savings and investment that such measures might bring. Finally, there is the tradeoff between introducing selective tax treatments to enhance vertical equity and defining a tax base that is broad enough to provide adequate revenues.

None of this is to say that equity is not an important consideration in the design of the Jamaican tax reform. The following were taken as constraints in developing the reform program and form an important part of the research program. First, the overall system should not be made more regressive than it formerly was. Since analysis showed the system to be proportional over the first eight deciles and regressive at the top end, a program of broad-based, flatter-rate taxes would not seem to compromise this objective.[12] Second, there should be no increase in the tax burden on very low income households. Our low-income household survey identified the consumption baskets of the low-income and therefore the "necessities" that would have to be excluded from the base of the proposed new general sales tax.[13]

Horizontal equity is an equally important objective of the reform. The objectives of "getting the prices right" and equal treatment of equally situated individuals and businesses are very closely linked. Horizontal inequities not only may induce uneconomic behavior by firms and workers, they contribute to a general undermining of confidence in the tax system and encourage noncompliance (see chapter 1). There is probably no better rationalization for shirking one's taxpaying duty than to point at the unfairness in the tax system.

It is important to distinguish structural reform of the tax system from a revenue-raising program. The objective was a "revenue-neutral" system (see chapter 1). In truth, "one-period" revenue neutrality is about the best that can be promised. One might design a system that will yield the same revenue as the present system in the first year of reform, but it is quite unlikely that the revenue income elasticity of the restructured system will be the same. In the present case, the shift to flatter-rate, broader-based taxes is expected to lower the built-in income elasticity of the income tax system by eliminating the bracket creep induced by inflation. On the one hand, this will hold down the growth in the government share in GNP, but on the other it will not give the government the automatic increases in revenue that it so often wants in order to expand social programs. This is another of those important tradeoffs among policy objectives where a tax reform may force the issue.

Taxes, the Foreign-Trade Regime, and Industrial Policy

The foreign-trade regime and industrial policy have led to significant distortions in resource allocation in Jamaica, not all of which are unwanted. Some result from policies designed expressly to favor one industry or sector over another, others from the goal of discouraging the consumption of imported goods, and still others have been justified on grounds of protecting certain domestic production activities from foreign competition. In other words, taxation may not be the most important policy instrument in the hands of government. Clearly, the design of a comprehensive tax reform—especially one that sets out to correct distortions in relative prices—must take the goals and impacts of trade and industrial policy into account.

The problem is how this should be done. Should the basic taxation maxims of horizontal equity and neutrality be stressed, even though these might run counter to the objectives of the foreign-trade regime and the existing program of tax incentives to industry? Alternatively, should tax policy play a more supporting role and focus on reinforcing the allocative impacts of other government policies? Or, is it possible to design a tax reform that can be relatively neutral in its effect on the allocation of resources and at the same time keep in step with the government's goals of conserving foreign exchange, encouraging export development, and stimulating investment?[14]

Policies and Problems

Trade and industrial policies in Jamaica have the objectives of stimulating domestic and foreign investment and stabilizing the nation's external balance so as to ensure competitive international markets for exported goods, and allocating enough foreign exchange to support the demands for local industrial growth and "necessary" consumption of imported goods. Many different instruments have been used to support these policies since 1983: multiple exchange rates, devaluation, import licensing, tax incentives, protective tariffs, import duty exemptions, preferential tax rates for certain commodities, and special capital depreciation allowances. Sometimes the effects of these policies have been reinforcing, but other times they have been offsetting, and the net impacts have not always been in step with the stated strategy of the Seaga administration to support a private-sector-led, export-driven growth. To complicate matters, the government's approach to trade and industrial policy has been changing continuously over the past five years—in no small part due to the pressures brought by external creditors.

Probably a fair characterization of these policies as followed in Jamaica is that they have been targeted on favored activities and sectors and that they have been interventionist in spirit. The policy mix is designed precisely to affect economic choices and therefore to stimulate certain production and consumption activities and to discourage others. Horizontal inequities and relative price effects are at the very heart of this strategy. This leaves the tax policy strategist to face the possibility that a more "neutral" tax program would push the government to an even greater use of targeted, direct controls to reestablish any desired preferences that the tax reform may have taken away.

Trade and Tax Policy

By 1984, the Jamaican dollar was considerably overvalued,[15] thereby effectively taxing exporters by forcing them to sell foreign-exchange earnings at a low price and to buy imported inputs at world market prices or higher. Not surprisingly, the results were a shortage of foreign exchange and an active illegal currency market. The collapse of the Jamaican bauxite industry (a major earner of foreign exchange) in 1983 and the heavy drain on foreign exchange reserves caused by debt repayment and oil purchases combined to yield a precarious situation. The government responded to the foreign-exchange shortage first by establishing a parallel market for foreign exchange, then with an extensive system of import licenses, and finally with a devaluation. The Jamaican dollar has not been devalued further, and the system of import licenses has been gradually phased out.

Since 1985, the policy instrument most used to shape trade policy in Jamaica has been the stamp duty on inward customs warrants, essentially a surtax on the value of imported goods which is levied independently from the common external tariff. Beginning in 1984–85, the import stamp tax rates were increased dramatically as an emergency revenue measure. By 1985–86, the duty accounted for over 13 percent of total taxes, and collections had nearly tripled in one year. Revenues were derived principally from a 16 percent tax rate on raw materials, a 30 percent rate on capital goods and a 40 percent rate on consumer goods. While the 1984–86 surge in the importance of stamp duties was successful as a revenue measure, it may have harmed the Jamaican economy in other ways: it was protectionist, and because it was so complicated it was probably arbitrary in its application.

This led to a call for a trade liberalization program and a rationalization of the stamp duty rates. As a condition of a World Bank loan, it was agreed that beginning in 1987, a four-year reform would be aimed at broadening the base of the import duty and rationalizing the rate structure. In particular, the program called for the 1985 tax rate increases to be rolled back to 10 percent for raw materials, 20 percent for capital goods, and 30 percent for consumer goods. By 1991, 30 percent was to be the maximum duty rate.

Industrial Policy

Like many countries, Jamaica has sought higher national-income growth by increasing investment in the island's businesses. But there are many different ways to structure economic policy to encourage development and expansion of the private sector. At one extreme is a strategy that attempts only to improve the general climate for investment and employment generation, and leaves it to the market to determine the amount and mix of new economic activity. This approach attempts to avoid policy measures that will distort economic choices, and to restrict government interventions to those cases where inefficiencies arise from market failure. The policy tools consistent with this approach are the development of public infrastructure such as roads, ports, and public utilities, and possibly an increased investment in human capital. On the revenue side, this approach is most consistent with a set of broad-based, low-rate taxes—the tax policy strategy argued here for Jamaica.

Jamaica presently follows an industrial policy closer to the other extreme—a highly targeted policy where the government intervenes to encourage development in certain sectors of the economy. The program includes incentives to "approved" firms, under separate programs for firms producing for domestic and for export markets. The incentive package can include exemption from import duty, tax holidays, and special capital allowances. Prior to 1980, when the emphasis was on import substitution, these programs did not work well, i.e., they imposed a revenue cost and led to inefficient uses of resources that outweighed the gains from net new investment generated. Thirsk calculates welfare losses of between 3 and 38 cents per dollar of investment under the import substitution regime. The Seaga years have seen a shift in emphasis toward subsidizing labor-intensive exports and agriculture, with the result, Thirsk estimates, that this program, potentially, could generate net social benefits from anywhere between 1 and 29 cents per dollar of investment.[16] Such estimates are very difficult to make, but the Thirsk analysis is probably as close as one can get to quantifying these impacts. One might draw the conclusion that the evidence is not clear that the government gets a very large return even from its present tax incentive legislation.

There are, however, more implicit elements to Jamaica's industrial policy. Perhaps the most important is the way in which it alters the relative price of labor and capital and therefore the incentive to substitute capital for labor-intensive technologies. An unfortunate and unintended side effect of the present system of incentives is that they have encouraged the growth of capital-intensive enterprises. Here it might be argued that the government's intentions are unclear, that some of its policies have potentially offsetting effects on one another. For examples:

Tax holidays from the company tax have increased the after-tax rate of return to investors and stimulated aggregate investment. The provision for large writeoffs of capital expenditures gives an incentive to shift this investment toward shorter-lived capital investments.

Payroll tax contributions (employer and employee) have been substantial and probably introduce a bias against labor, as does the provision for a substantial severance allowance for employees who are laid off. The tax credit to firms for employing (newly trained) workers under the HEART program works in the opposite direction, but the amounts involved are very small. The substantial increase in stamp duty rates on capital equipment in 1985 gave an incentive to substitute labor for capital. This effect was somewhat offset by the reduction beginning in 1987, but the tax rate on capital goods remained at 20 percent of c.i.f. value.

The effects of lax income tax administration on capital-labor substitution are not easily seen. On the other hand, wages are taxed at a higher rate in the formal sector than in the self-employed sector; therefore, an incentive exists to substitute capital for labor in the PAYE sector. It is this sector where most industrial activity resides. On the other hand, interest income was not taxed at all before the 1986 reform, dividend income appeared to be substantially underreported, and there were income tax credits for investment in life insurance, a home mortgage, and a unit trust.

Compatible Tax Policies?

The problem became how to design a new tax structure that would not be out of sync with the government's other economic policies, but would stay with the principal tax reform objectives of neutrality and simplification. The above discussion of trade and industrial policy makes it painfully clear that a move to neutrality in the tax system has made the overall allocation of resources even worse—both because of the preexisting distortions and because the tax reform might be seen by the government as a call for even more targeting of trade and tax incentive policies in an attempt to restore the position of favored sectors. Far from getting the prices right, there was the real danger that tax reform could make matters worse.

On the other hand, it is possible to stay with the objectives of creating a "good" tax structure and not compromise the overall efficiency with which an economy operates. In fact, some parts of the proposed tax reform program could be seen as reinforcing the objectives of the government's trade and industrial policies. In some cases this is not true because the government's policies are unclear and in some instances are even contradictory. The proper strategy here is to urge changes in the economic policies, or at least a clarification of objectives. In other cases, there is simply an incompatibility between the proposed tax policy and the existing trade-industrial policy. This requires the government to face up to some important tradeoffs. There is also the possibility that defects in trade and industrial policies will prove transitory, and the tax reform ought to be pointed more toward the longer term where all of the government's economic policies are more in step with overall development strategy.

Three components of the tax reform package were at issue here: the introduction of a value-added type consumption tax, a reduced rate of company tax, and the disposition of the tax incentive programs in place prior to reform.

First, the project proposed replacement of the existing domestic indirect taxes with a general consumption tax (GCT) to be levied at a single rate on importers, manufacturers, and large distributors. Bird has suggested the possibility that the import stamp duty could also be brought under the GCT, but a temporary additional rate of 15 percent on imports would be necessary to protect revenues.[17] Some features of this proposal would fit the government's economic program as well as the wish list of the donors. Introduction of the GCT with its value-added feature will provide exporters (who would be zero-rated) with an automatic rebate for taxes paid on imported inputs. The proposed basic rate structure of the GCT—a single basic rate and a luxury rate—is consistent with the goals of an equal tax treatment of imported and domestically produced goods, and discouraging nonproductive uses of foreign exchange. However, the 15 percent tax on imports, even if temporary, reintroduces a significant element of protection.

The most important way in which the GCT does not fit government industrial policy is that it is not targeted to provide relief to particular activities (the single important exception being the zero-rate for exporters). All firms would face the same rate and all imports would be taxed according to the same rate schedule if the import stamp duty were subsumed with the GCT. The present practice of exempting certain imported goods and taxing others at preferential rates, or the proposals to give rebates to exporters on a partly judgmental basis, gives the government a latitude for stimulating activities in "favored" sectors that the GCT would not accommodate.

The conflicting objectives of trade-industrial policy and tax policy led to a significant problem in the design of the GCT. If the government was unwilling to simplify the rate structure applicable to imports, then incorporating the import stamp duty into the GCT would lead to a more complicated rate structure than before. The costs of such complication would be high; indeed one of the main justifications for amalgamating indirect taxes into a GCT was simplification. Bird goes so far as to argue that "if there is a prospect that one of the prices that may have to be paid for getting rid of the import stamp duty would be to incorporate similar rate differentials in the GCT, then the idea of including the stamp duty should be put aside."[18]

The centerpiece of the corporate income tax reform, as proposed and enacted in 1987, was a reduction in the tax rate from 45 percent (including the additional company profits tax, ACPT) to 33⅓ percent. This increases the after-tax return to companies, and thus meets one of the principal objectives of national industrial policy. Moreover, it reduces the rate to match the top rate in the reformed U.S. system, thus protecting the foreign tax credit position of U.S. investors in Jamaica.

The reform, however, is not totally compatible with industrial and trade policies. The principal reason is that a general rate reduction is not targeted, i.e., the lower rate is available to all firms and not just to those who are "approved" under the incentive legislation. Another way to look at the implications of the 1987 tax reform is that the lower tax rate effectively reduces the comparative advantage given to existing incentive firms, e.g., a tax holiday is now worth less.

Finally, there was the question of what to do about the tax incentive legislation. Various proposals to scrap the incentive programs were probably ill-advised. Most competitor countries give comparable subsidy packages and withdrawal by Jamaica might have been read as a sign of a less hospitable business climate. Jamaica's political climate is still considered risky by some investors, and its economy has only recently shown signs of reversing a long-term decline. The mid-1980s was not a good time to take any major actions that might shake investor confidence.

The Individual Income Tax

Prior to the 1986 reform, the individual income tax base, in theory, included all sources of income except bank deposit interest. In prac-

Table 5.4   Rate Structure of the Individual Income Tax Prior to Reform

Statutory income[a]	Marginal tax rate
If income is less than J$7,000	
J$ 0− 4,000	0
4,001− 7,000	.70
If income is more than J$7,000	
J$ 0− 7,000	.30
7,001−10,000	.40
10,001−12,000	.45
12,001−14,000	.50
14,001 and over	.575

[a]Statutory income is the tax base for the personal income tax. It is the amount that is entered on the personal income tax return and equals the sum of income from employments and offices; pensions; rent of land, houses, or other property; dividends, interest, annuities, discounts, estates, trusts, alimony, or other annual payments arising within Jamaica; sources outside Jamaica; sources not stated elsewhere; and trade, business, profession, or cultivation of land or farming; less capital allowances.
Source: Income Tax Department.

tice, there was no tax on capital gains and most self-employed income was outside the tax net. There were two rate structures—depending on whether income was above or below J$7,000. The top marginal rate was 57.5 percent (table 5.4). There was no standard deduction but taxpayers could qualify for sixteen separate tax credits. These credits had been added to the tax system over a period of years, for purposes that ranged from personal allowances to stimulation of savings to even employment of helpers in the home. Because the credits were not indexed to inflation, their value had been substantially eroded during the early 1980s. The income tax administration did relatively little monitoring of the credit system.

The base of the tax was further narrowed by the practice of permitting employers to grant nontaxable perquisites ("allowances") to employees. These perquisites were a matter of negotiation between employee and employer (including government ministries) and it was not required that they be reported to the income tax commissioner. The project's sample survey results showed that allowances averaged about 15 percent of taxable income, but were over 30 percent for those with incomes above J$18,000. Perhaps as important, there was a general perception that allowances were even greater—some prominent Jamaican analysts argued from anecdotal evidence that the ratio of allowances to taxable income averaged 40 percent.

Problems with the Preexisting System

The results of an exhaustive empirical analysis of the individual income tax system can be summarized in five general conclusions.[19] The first is that the income tax base was narrowed dramatically by the provision of tax credits, the exclusion of allowances, and various forms of evasion. More than half of potential individual income tax liability was not in the tax net in 1983. By our rough (and, we think, conservative) estimates, the full taxation of allowances and unreported income would have doubled individual income tax revenues. To give some idea of the opportunity cost of the administrative practice, this amount would have fully covered the government of Jamaica's deficit in 1983.

The second conclusion is that the income tax system was not as progressive as its statutory rate structure would seem to suggest. When measured against statutory income, the effective tax rates showed a pattern of graduation, but when tax liability is measured against a more comprehensive definition of income—including allowances and unreported income—the progressivity disappeared.

Third, we discovered substantial horizontal inequities in the system: a differential tax treatment of individuals in the same income bracket. This differential is somewhat arbitrary in that it depends on an individual's ability to hide income and to receive a larger share of income in allowances. For example, the average tax rate for individuals in the high income classes ranges from 50 percent for PAYE employees who comply with the tax law to zero for nonfilers, with an estimated average of less than 10 percent.

The fourth conclusion is that inflation raised effective tax rates via "bracket creep." Simultaneously, inflation had a (partially) offsetting effect on the vertical equity of the tax because the value of credits declined in real terms and because the effects of inflation in pushing taxpayers into higher tax brackets stimulated evasion and avoidance. We found that the three main avenues for escaping the high rates of individual income tax—evasion, allowances, and overtime—are all concentrated in the upper income brackets.

A fifth conclusion, more speculative than substantive, is that the marginal income tax rates were high enough to affect work effort, investment, savings, and compliance choices.

Evasion and the Hard-to-Tax Sector

Every income taxpayer faces the choices among tax evasion, tax avoidance, and fully reported income. The potential rewards for successful evasion or avoidance under the pre-reform system were considerable —the 57.5 percent marginal tax rate and the tax component of the various payroll levies. Although the opportunities for avoidance were certainly present—allowances and "overtime" income—self-employed Jamaicans more often captured these benefits by outright evasion.

As a first step in estimating the revenue loss to avoidance and evasion, we identified the population of Jamaicans working in six professions: accountants, architects, attorneys, physicians, optometrists, and veterinarians. From a random sample of this group, we determined that only about one in five paid income taxes in some year between 1981 and 1983, 60 percent did not even have an income tax reference number, and the revenue loss was equivalent to about half of total income tax collections in 1983. This analysis was extended to nine other self-employed occupations, with similar results. We concluded that fewer than one in five of the self-employed filed a return. A summary of the filing rates in these nine occupation classes is reported in table 5.5. Based on this sample of lower-income self-employed persons, the revenue costs from evasion were estimated to be on the order of 50 percent of income tax collections.

The Reform Program

The general direction for reform was to broaden the tax base by legal and administrative means, to lower top end marginal rates, and to protect the real income position of those at the bottom end of the income taxpaying population. All of this had to be done within a constraint of revenue neutrality and had to be mindful of the almost certain opposition of interest groups who had long since come to expect (and rely on) some of these tax preferences.

The key elements of the 1986 reform program were:

1. The credit system was replaced by a standard deduction of $J8,580.
2. A flat rate tax of 33⅓ percent replaced the progressive rate structure.
3. Fringe-benefit type allowances were made taxable as ordinary income, with some exceptions.
4. The preferential treatment of overtime income was eliminated.
5. Interest income, above a threshold level, was made taxable.

Table 5.5   Income Tax Filing Rates for Self-Employed Individuals: By Occupation

Occupation category	Percentage of self-employed who filed a return for 1982	Percentage of self-employed who filed a return for any year between 1982 and 1984
Service station	11.9	5.6
Customs broker	8.2	2.7
Auto repair	15.1	9.7
Auto parts	11.4	8.2
Hair care	11.1	5.8
Real estate	22.8	10.1
Contractor	11.4	5.3
Transport	21.5	13.3
Beverage and spirits	14.2	9.6
Total	17.3	10.9

Source: Roy Bahl and Matthew Murray, "Income Tax Evasion in Jamaica," Jamaica Tax Structure Examination Project Staff Paper No. 31, Metropolitan Studies Program, The Maxwell School (Syracuse, N.Y.: Syracuse University, November 1986).

Revenue and Tax Burden Impacts

One approach to estimating the structural impacts of the reform is to make use of historical data. At the time this proposal was being evaluated, the hypothetical question we asked was: what would have happened had these reforms been put in place in 1983?[20] The results show that the proposed system would have led to a reduction in the average rate of taxation from 14.5 percent to 9.8 percent of taxable income for those who actually paid income taxes in 1983. Enactment of the full program would have led to a revenue loss equivalent to about 26 percent of revenues. The distribution of tax burdens would have become more progressive because the impact of the interest tax, the taxation of allowances, and the relatively high standard deduction of J$8,580 would have offset the effects of the lower nominal rates.

Surprisingly, the revenue-income elasticity of the reformed system is not significantly less than that of the pre-reform system. This is because the standard deduction of J$8,580 is not indexed; hence average tax rates for all taxpayers rise with increases in income, and income growth also "bumps" previously exempt taxpayers into the taxpaying range. As a result of inflation, the distribution of burdens under the new tax system will become less progressive over time owing to the fact that neither credits nor the standard deduction are indexed and both weigh heavier in the tax calculus for lower-income taxpayers.

We also made out-year projections of the impact of the proposed reform, and compared these with projections of the pre-reform system. The results suggested that in 1987 the flat-rate tax would yield about 7 percent less than the pre-reform system, again with more progressivity in effective rates. For example, it was estimated that those in the over J$50,000 income class would face an effective rate of 32.5 percent under the new system in 1987—about twice the effective rate they would have paid under the pre-reform system. This increased progressivity was an unexpected bonus from the flat tax. Does this imply some sacrifice of the objective of reducing the marginal tax rate on productive activities? In fact, the increased marginal rates on higher income taxpayers is primarily due to the tax on interest. The effective tax rate on earnings actually drops in the top income brackets. Those who would emphasize the potential economic impacts of lower marginal rates on higher income taxpayers will applaud this change in the taxation of unearned income. Those who look to the tax system to reduce disparities in the distribution of income might be equally happy with the increase in the average rate of taxation in the top brackets.

Allocative Effects

Prior to enactment of reform, a major concern was whether income tax rate reductions would yield significant investment, saving, and work effort responses. Even if the short-run price elasticities of work effort, saving, and income tax compliance are very small (as the evidence suggests), the impact could be substantial because the marginal tax rates were reduced so dramatically. Though no solid evidence is available, it would not seem farfetched to argue that the after-tax return to investors and to increased work effort has been significantly increased. Under the proposed new 33⅓ percent flat rate schedule, the *incremental* tax cost of increased investment, etc., is much less than before. The benefits of outright evasion have also been lessened. Moreover, well-structured enforcement programs have a better chance for success than would be the case under the higher marginal rates.

Gauging the impact on saving is more complicated. One possible effect might be that since interest is brought into the tax base and one third of the gross return on savings accounts is taxed away, funds previously devoted to commercial bank savings deposits might be shifted to equities. Moreover, other preferential tax treatments of favored investments are removed with elimination of the income tax credit for the purchase of life insurance premiums and unit trust shares. These changes should have the effect of putting all types of investment on a more equal footing and *cet. par.* improving the relative attractiveness of purchasing stocks. Perhaps more important, the top marginal tax rate on income from all investments other than savings accounts will fall from 57.5 percent to 33⅓ percent. On the debit side, inclusion of interest in the tax base may encourage avoidance via capital flight, a shift to consumption, or a shift in investment to the more lightly taxed real estate sector.

First-Year Results

The first component of tax reform was enacted in January 1986. By May it was believed that most firms had switched their employee withholding to comply with the new system. Available data suggest a successful first year revenue performance of the new system—a 20 percent increase between 1986 and 1987. Despite this revenue productivity, the tax reform is not a tax increase in disguise. Barring offsetting discretionary reductions the old system would have yielded more. Revenues from the flat tax were more than we originally projected, but this is mostly due to the unexpected strong performance of the Jamaican economy. In fact, when we "backcast" using the true economic assumptions, the actual revenue performance of the new system falls short of expectations.

The Unfinished Reform Agenda

The Jamaican income tax reform, though it went much further than most tax structure revisions, has left some needed structural changes undone. Unless these issues are addressed, some of the important gains from the reform may be eroded. Moreover, there are the inevitable problems that creep into any reformed system in the first years of operation: administrative difficulties, ambiguities in the legislation, and loopholes that taxpayers are far more adept at identifying than were the tax reform designers.

The major structural problem with the Jamaican reform is that it leaves open some perquisite loopholes. The tax treatment of allowances for automobiles, housing, and especially uniforms and laundry gives away too much in some cases and is unclear in others. There is already evidence of abuse. A lesson that should have been taken from the experience in the late 1970s and early 1980s is that income taxpayers will take advantage of this type of loophole and there will be a migration of "legal allowances" to these categories. Predictably, our sample survey taken in the first year of the reform showed a movement in compensation toward the "nontaxable" allowances.

A second problem is that the reformed individual income tax is too income elastic, i.e., its revenues automatically increase at about twice the rate at which income increases. This will inevitably bring pressure on the government to enact discretionary changes to bring about tax relief. These discretionary changes, year to year and ad hoc, could eventually compromise the achievements of the reform program. The government should follow one of two courses of action in dealing with this problem. First, and probably best, the standard deduction could be indexed to the rate of inflation. This would get around the problem of having to make periodic discretionary adjustments in the standard deduction, it would hold down the increase in tax burden to match the growth in GNP, and it would hold harmless from tax increases those lower-income Jamaicans who have experienced no increase in their real income position. The second alternative is to make annual discretionary adjustments in the standard deduction *and* to lower the greater stimulative effect on the economy because of the lowering of the marginal tax rate, but it also has disadvantages. For example, it would politicize revisions in the tax structure to a much greater extent than is desirable, and it would raise pressures to make comparable reductions in the rate of corporation taxation.

Payroll Taxes

Five payroll tax programs use wages as the base for the tax contribution. These include the Education Tax, the Human Employment and Resource Training (HEART) Trust Fund, the National Housing Trust (NHT), the National Insurance Scheme (NIS), and the Civil Service Family Benefits Scheme (CSFBS).[21] The latter three are more properly viewed as contributions because individuals are entitled to benefits in proportion to their contribution.[22] The Education Tax and HEART are simply surcharges on the individual income tax. In total, these payroll taxes generate sizable revenues, equivalent to roughly half of individual income tax collections.

The Programs

The Education Tax was established to advance educational goals, but the collections from the tax go into the general fund and are not earmarked for education programs. The base of the tax is all earnings. The employee and his employer are each taxed at the rate of 1 percent on wages. Self-employed persons are taxed at the rate of 1 percent. Education Tax revenues were equal to about 7 percent of individual income tax revenue in fiscal year 1984–85.

The HEART fund was established in 1982 by the Human Employment and Resource Training Act to develop employee training schemes. Private-sector employees whose monthly payroll exceeds J$7,222 are required to pay a 3 percent tax on total gross emoluments of employees. By law, compensation in the form of allowances should be included in the tax base; we have seen, however, that in practice allowances are not taxed. Unlike the Education Tax, HEART payments are deposited in an account earmarked for use by the Trust, and do not go into the consolidated fund. In 1984–85, revenues from the 3 percent HEART tax were equivalent to about 4 percent of individual income tax revenues.

The National Housing Trust (NHT) was established to improve the existing stock of housing. The Trust imposes a contributory rate on the wages of workers, and then uses these contributions to finance a variety of housing benefit programs. For an employed individual the tax base is gross emoluments; the employee pays 2 percent and the employer 3 percent. The self-employed pay 3 percent of gross earnings, and domestic workers pay 2 percent of gross earnings. Allowances are in principle subject to the contribution, but in practice are excluded. An individual is exempt if annual wages are less than the minimum annual wage of J$3,120. An employee's contributions entitle the employee to a variety of benefits, all of which are related to the amount of the contributions. Employee—but not employer—contributions are vested with the employee. In 1977–78, NHT revenues were well over one third of income tax revenues.

The National Insurance Scheme (NIS) is a funded security system. Contributors are entitled to a variety of benefits which are based on past contributions. In 1986–87, total contributions were just over J$82 million, and the NIS Trust Fund of J$912 million generated J$124 million in income. The contribution rate for PAYE and self-employed workers is 5 percent of weekly gross earnings between J$12 and J$150 (split equally between the employee and the employer in the case of PAYE workers).

The Civil Service Family Benefits Scheme (CSFBS) is a forced insurance scheme for some Jamaican government employees. All persons in "pensionable offices" must contribute to the scheme. Coverage is in

fact very limited—less than 25 percent of government workers participated in 1985. A contributor must pay 4 percent of total salary to the
scheme. Revenues have grown erratically, but were only J$2.2 million in
1982–83.

Problems with the Present System[23]

Payroll taxes are closely linked to the individual income tax in terms of
economic effects and in the minds of the Jamaican worker who reads
the amount of deductions on his pay slip every week. But while the
income tax reform has gone forward with a program to broaden the tax
base and lower the marginal rates, the payroll taxes have not been
restructured. At the time of the income tax reform in 1986, the rate of
payroll tax contribution was frozen, and at the time of this writing no
permanent improvements have been made.

Structural reform of payroll taxes involves two major problems. The
first is the narrow base on which the payroll taxes are levied and consequently the high nominal rate of tax. The second problem is that administration is fragmented and there is little communication among the
five programs. There are five separate recordkeeping systems, each has
its own audit program, and (except for the Education Tax) each is responsible for its own audit program and for monitoring collection efficiency.
Compliance with the Education Tax is monitored by the revenue board,
but only two people are assigned exclusively to this task. NHT and NIS
officials have authority to audit company records and to obtain income
tax information, but their compliance staffs focus primarily upon the
internal consistency of the records. The monitoring division of the
HEART Trust Fund looks mainly at the training capacity of participants.
And for all of these programs, almost no attention is being paid to the
issues of bringing the self-employed into the payroll tax net.

Proposed Reforms

Payroll tax reform should concentrate on simplification of the system, a
broadening of the tax base and a lowering of rates, and a general overhaul of the administration of these five taxes. As a first step, the Education Tax should be abolished as a separate payroll levy and merged into
the general tax system. To protect revenues, if necessary, this would
require an increase in the individual income tax rate from 33⅓ percent to 35 percent. HEART is a more difficult case, because one might
argue the benefits principle as a justification for financing worker training with an employer tax on private-sector payrolls. Alternatively, it

might be argued that the benefits of such a program are economy-wide. That being the case, it is a good candidate for general fund financing. In general, the inclusion of these levies in the general income tax would improve the horizontal equity of the system because the income tax base is more comprehensive than the payroll tax base, and it would improve vertical equity because interest would be taxed and the standard deduction amount would not.

The government should consider a consolidation of the administration of the two largest contribution programs, NIS and NHT. Centralized assessment, audit collection, and recordkeeping can lead to substantial reductions in administrative costs and in compliance costs. This consolidation, and a simplification of the rate and base structure of the two taxes, would make the enforcement task easier and give officials more time to concentrate on bringing the self-employed within the payroll tax net.

If the base of the payroll tax could be broadened, the rates could be lowered. Even if base broadening were confined to taxing allowance income and eliminating the ceiling on NIS contributions, the combined tax rate on payrolls for the four remaining programs could be reduced from 11.4 percent of wages to 10.4 percent of compensation. Elimination of the Education Tax would further reduce this average rate to 8.8 percent. With a stronger enforcement program that concentrated on increasing the contributions from the self-employed, the rates could be dropped even further.

Company Income Taxation

The corporate income tax has been a reliable, growth-responsive source of revenue for the government of Jamaica. In recent years, however, the structure of this tax has come under scrutiny because of the preferential treatment given to certain types of income and to income earned by certain types of companies, the absence of any mechanism to adjust taxable profits for inflation, and the separate treatment of companies and their shareholders under the income tax.

Rate and Base Structure

Before the 1987 reform, the company income tax was levied at a basic rate of 35 percent. In addition, there was an "additional corporate profits tax" (ACPT) of 10 percent levied on the same base. Companies were required to withhold tax of 37.5 percent of the value of dividends paid, but could credit these withholdings against ACPT liability. Companies that had distributed 40 percent of their pretax profits would recover all of the ACPT they had paid on these profits.[24] ACPT credits could be carried forward indefinitely.

The tax base was defined in much the same way as that in other developing countries, with at least the same degree of complexity. Jamaican law permits deductions for capital allowances, rather than book depreciation. Enterprises could claim a prescribed initial allowance[25] and an annual deduction computed on a declining basis against historical cost. Inventories were valued using the first-in-first-out (FIFO) method. Losses could be carried forward five years but there was no provision for loss carrybacks. Capital gains on the sale of shares listed on the Jamaican stock exchange were not taxed.

There were many exceptions to this basic treatment of companies resident in Jamaica. Financial institutions were taxed under a separate and very complicated regime, as is the case in most countries.[26] Separate incentive legislation provided for a different rate and base of tax for incentive companies, and preferential treatment was given in the taxation of public enterprises.[27] With respect to the taxation of dividends, some resident shareholders received special relief, and dividends paid to nonresidents were generally subject to a special withholding tax rate, determined by treaties.

The company tax has actually accounted for about 15 percent of total tax revenues. This proportion has held approximately constant during the 1980–86 period, even with the substantial reduction in the payment from bauxite companies. Tanzi's comparative analysis for the 1980s shows that Jamaica has relied much less on the company income tax than other countries at a similar income level.[28]

Problems and Reform Needs

At the outset of the tax reform program in 1983, restructuring of the company tax was seen as essential. There were some areas where the tax was flawed, its structure was not totally compatible with the economic policies of the new administration, and revisions of other taxes almost certainly would change the way the company tax "fits" into the total system. The pre-reform company tax structure could also be criticized for its complexity, its bias toward certain types of investment decisions, and for the way it responds to inflation.

Complexity and Administration. Because of the many special features in its rate and base structure, the pre-reform company tax was not easily administered. The problems were magnified by a shortage of skilled staff and outmoded—in some cases flawed—operating procedures. Such difficulties of administration not only imposed administrative costs but led to more than a little arbitrariness in assessing the tax base and inevitably to some unfairness in the way different firms were treated.

Two good examples of how a complicated structure compromised administration relate to depreciation allowances and inventory valuation. The previous (and current) system of capital allowances is quite complex, involving numerous schedules for asset types, special types of allowances for different industries, and incentive laws providing special treatment to both favored industries and favored types of assets. As a consequence, income tax officers have spent too much time on classification issues at the costs of spending too little time with the important business of book audit, thus inviting abuse and leading to tax monitoring. Under such a complicated system, compliance costs are high. Large enterprises make use of accounting firms to assist them in compliance, but smaller enterprises almost certainly have had trouble understanding the available options. This introduces an unintended but potentially important non-neutrality into the system.

The law on inventory valuation requires that it be valued at the lower cost or market value, and most firms have used the FIFO method for determining the cost of their sales. However, some large firms have utilized the last-in-first-out (LIFO) method, which has neither been sanctioned in the courts nor approved by the Commissioner. Others have availed themselves of even more advantageous approaches, such as writing off stocks that are over a certain age and excluding the proceeds of their sales from chargeable income. They were successful because the income tax department lacked an effective audit branch.

Inflation. Brisk inflation during the 1980s, in concert with the present tax structure, has driven up real company tax rates, influenced investment choices, and provided additional incentives for tax avoidance and evasion. The law contained no provisions for inflation adjustments even though it was generally recognized that the base of the tax diverged substantially from real corporate income during periods of high inflation.

Under inflationary conditions the Jamaican approach to defining capital allowances understated capital consumption and LIFO accounting understated the cost of goods sold. Both of these factors caused profits to be overstated and, *cet. par.*, dampened the rate of investment. Wozny demonstrated that under the old tax structure the effective tax rate on an equity-financed capital investment in a basic industry increased from 42 percent to 60 percent when the inflation rate increased by 10 percent.[29]

The effects of inflation may also work in the direction of overstating profits and may cause firms to adjust their financing structures. Inflation causes a decline in the real value of corporate debt which results in untaxed gains that vary among companies according to the degree to which they are in debt. Moreover, the tax exempt status of interest income under the previous system allowed a firm to compensate for the fact that capital allowances were not indexed, by substituting debt for equity financing of its capital assets. In the example of the capital investment presented above, the effective tax rate would actually have been lower with a 10 percent higher inflation rate, if 80 percent of the investment had been debt financed.

Finally, the availability of three important avenues of tax avoidance —the preferential tax treatment of incentive activities, interest income, and capital gains—encouraged enterprises to undertake tax arbitrage: to engage in transactions whose sole purpose is reduction in tax liability. Among the many avoidance techniques observed in Jamaica are revaluation and sale of assets with leaseback arrangements: revaluation and sale of assets with a distribution of the (nontaxable) proceeds to shareholders and the leasing of capital equipment by incentive firms to affiliated nonincentive firms.

Debt-Equity Choice. In principle, full integration of personal and company income taxes would require that distributed and retained company profits be taxed at the same rate as other sources of income. Jamaica, as most countries in the world, taxes distributed and undistributed corporate profits under the company tax, and dividend income under the individual income tax.

This tax structure was widely criticized on grounds that it biased investment decisions in favor of debt and against equity investments. Before the 1986 individual income tax reform, the problem was further complicated by the exemption of interest income. The bias in favor of debt, it is argued, led to thin capitalization of Jamaican corporations, inhibited the development of the domestic capital market, and created horizontal inequities, i.e., investors pay different amounts of tax depending on the composition of the portfolio which they hold.

Empirical analysis on a representative sample of Jamaican companies supports some of these claims, but not others.[30] The 1984–85 tax system in fact did favor debt-financed investment, but this had nothing to do with a lack of dividend relief. Rather, it was due to the fact that borrowers were able to deduct nominal interest payments from their gross book income in computing taxable income, while true economic income would have been computed by deducting only payments of real interest. The tax penalty on dividends that existed under the 1984–85 tax system was due to the overly favorable treatment of retained earnings, not to an overtaxation of distributed earnings.

While it seems clear that integration and a lower tax rate would be a step in the direction of "getting the prices right," it is by no means clear how much economic loss has resulted from the distortions introduced by the present system. One could take the position that these price effects either are not significant or they are offset by some other distortion in the system. With respect to the latter, consider that the bias in favor of debt was to some extent offset by the absence of capital gains tax on securities. Moreover, all dividend recipients were not being subjected to double taxation in any case. Less than 10 percent of the self-employed—a large proportion of those whom we would expect to face marginal tax rates in excess of the withholding rate of 37.5 percent —even filed a return.

The Reform Program

There were important constraints to reforming the company tax. An initial charge was to assure revenue neutrality. Although this requirement was later relaxed, it was clear that any proposal that carried too great a revenue loss would have no chance. There were three other important constraints. First, the new system would have to be within the present administrative capabilities of the income tax department. Administrative improvements would come with a simpler, more rational system and with a better training program for the tax administration service, but these improvements could not be counted on immediately. Second, the reformed system of taxing companies and dividends would have to "fit" the new individual income tax structure. Third, it would have to be sensitive to the politics involved in tax relief for the business sector.

Proposed and Adopted Changes. The most important component of the proposed reform was to reduce the tax rate from 45 percent (including ACPT) to 33⅓ percent. The project and the tax reform committee further recommended that dividend distributions to residents be exempt from individual income tax. Among the strong arguments in favor of this proposal are that the system would be greatly simplified and thus more easily assessed and monitored.

This reform program would reduce the tax incentive to employ debt and all but eliminate the tax disincentive to distribute earnings. These improvements would not result from the elimination of double taxation, but rather from the lowering of the corporate tax rate to equal the new rate of the personal income tax. This rate equalization, combined with the recommendation to eliminate the transfer tax on capital gains arising from the transfer of corporate shares, meant that both distributed and retained corporate income attributable to resident Jamaican individuals would be taxed at the same rate as any other income earned by those individuals. In other words, full tax integration would effectively be achieved for this class of shareholders. The simplicity of the new personal-income tax would permit this without a complicated imputation and credit mechanism.

It was proposed that the withholding tax on profits remitted abroad be retained. The magnitude of the basic rate reduction meant that the overall tax borne by foreign investors would be lower than it had been under the existing system and lower than the taxes levied by Jamaica's closest competitors in the region. Most foreign investors would have received a real tax benefit from the elimination of the withholding tax (it would not simply have resulted in an offsetting increase in their home-country tax liabilities), but the line between investment attraction and revenue sacrifice had to be drawn somewhere.[31] It was decided that the greatest efficiency gains would be achieved by lowering the basic corporate rate as far as possible.

The government adopted the recommendation that the company tax rate be reduced to 33⅓ percent and that the ACPT be abolished, and that the withholding tax on dividend payments to nonresidents be retained. The proposal to exempt dividend payments from personal tax liability, however, was rejected. The government instead decided on a separate entity approach whereby company profits and dividends would be taxed at 33⅓ percent, the latter under a withholding system. The government thus "passed" on the opportunity to fully (and simply) integrate the income tax.

One reason given for rejection of the proposal to exempt dividends received by individuals was that the government was in a crucial stage of its negotiations with the IMF and was under pressure to minimize the revenue cost of the revenue package. A more likely explanation is political, i.e., the Jamaica Labour Party's sensitivity to the growing public perception that it had become the party of the "big Man." The government was still feeling the criticism over the taxation of interest income that had been introduced the year before. The prime minister and members of the cabinet fully understood that the exemption of dividend income and the taxation of interest income represented equivalent treatment, but did not believe this could be explained to the public.

Impacts. Wozny has modeled the impact of the system actually introduced by the government for 1987.[32] Corporate income will bear a lower overall tax burden than it had under the pre-reform system but, because the tax burdens on other forms of income have been reduced by a greater degree, corporate-source income will be relatively disadvantaged, especially when distributed. The end result of this discrimination will be a lower supply of funds for equity investments, compared to what would have existed if the full integration proposal had been adopted. The 1987 tax system will also discourage the distribution of earnings to resident shareholders to a greater degree than the pre-reform system. Wozny's estimates are that this reform will lead to a reduction in the payout rates of widely held companies from about 0.32 to between 0.23 and 0.26.

The lowering of the corporate tax rate from 45 percent to 33 ⅓ percent in 1987 will increase the post-tax return on corporate investment and stimulate growth in the sector and in the demand for corporate equities. The imposition of a higher tax penalty on dividends than existed before the reform will, however, impede the flow of investible funds out of established widely held companies and into the hands of investors who will find the highest returns available for these funds. The introduction of full double taxation of corporate income in Jamaica, even though both the corporate and personal tax rates are lower than they were before 1986, is antithetical to the government's long-range economic strategy of structural adjustment, which calls for a reallocation of resources out of the low-return import-substitution sector into the export-promotion sector.

It is clear that much remains undone and there are still important distortions to investment choices that are attributable to the tax system. In particular, the change in the relative tax treatment of debt versus equity investments is not in the direction of getting the prices right, because full double taxation of dividends has been adopted. Another problem is that the system has not been restructured to deal with the problem of inflation: depreciation allowances remain unindexed and FIFO valuation of inventories remains the practice. The move to either LIFO or to indexing asset values to price level changes are beyond the administrative capabilities of the Income Tax Department at the present time.[33]

Indirect Taxes

The history of changes in the structure of Jamaican indirect taxes has been one of piecemeal adjustment to cover annual revenue shortfalls. As a result, the underlying problems with the system have persisted and perhaps even worsened. The conclusion reached by virtually all who have studied the system is that it should be replaced with a general sales tax. Our conclusion was the same.

The indirect tax system had not been restructured through June, 1988. It remains a complex system of five separate taxes.[34] From the revenue standpoint, the most important component of the system is the consumption duty, which is levied on the value of imported and domestically produced goods and is collected at the import and the manufacturing stage. The other two domestic indirect taxes, retail sales tax and excise duties, are insignificant in terms of revenues raised. Two taxes are levied on the import base: customs duty and stamp duty on inward customs warrants. The customs duty proper is a relatively small revenue source by international standards (less than 10 percent of Jamaican revenues), primarily because of Jamaica's membership in CARICOM. However, with significant rate increases beginning in 1984, the stamp duty has become a major fiscal instrument.

Problems

The Jamaican economy has simply outgrown its indirect tax system. Basically, the same laws, regulations, and forms designed forty years ago for the duty on rum and a few other items are still being used even though the present system covers nearly all manufacturing activities. Cnossen describes the situation well:

As Jamaica's economy has grown more complex, the administration of its indirect tax system, which is largely based on production checks, has become more cumbersome, impeding the free functioning of business and trade. The inherently fragmented nature of the present indirect system's coverage, its multi-rate structure, and its complexity may have undesirable economic effects. Its distributional effects are largely undeterminable.[35]

Complexity

The administrative problems with the indirect tax system are in part due to its complexity. The five taxes are levied under separate acts, are administered by different divisions within the Customs and Excise Department, have different licensing and return requirements, and even require separate recordkeeping systems. The bases which are taxed are not the same, nor are the rate schedules which are a mixture of ad valorem and specific ones. Even the customs and excise officials have some problems fully understanding the system. The rate schedules are very detailed with many fine gradations, and tax officials spend far too much time classifying commodities for purposes of selecting the proper rate. Moreover, the base is not clearly defined in either the law or the regulations, and often the official must make a notional assessment of the taxable value of an object. The result is that the tax administration service, already understaffed, has much less time available to spend on the more important business of assuring a proper rate of compliance.

Efficiency

Jamaica's system of indirect taxation does not fit the neutrality goal. It distorts the relative prices of consumer goods from what would be the case in the absence of taxation, it gives enterprises an incentive to alter their methods of doing business, and it offers some degree of inefficient protection to domestic producers. As noted above, all of these concerns about the economic effects of the present system can be traced to a single underlying problem: the tax base is very narrow and revenue needs force a high effective tax rate and a concentration on those commodities where assessment and collection are relatively easy. Less than 20 percent of final consumption of services and less than one third of gross manufacturing sales are taxed.[36] The coverage of domestic value-added is thin because the consumption duty is essentially a manufacturers' sales tax and does not reach the distributive sector, small firms, or most of the services sector. Excluding the traditional excises, the average effective rate of indirect taxation on those commodities actually in the base is 36 percent (in 1983).

Much of the revenue from the domestic base comes from cigarettes, gasoline, and alcoholic beverages. About 40 percent of all indirect tax revenues, 20 percent of all tax revenue, and 5 percent of GDP in 1983 came from taxes on drinking, smoking, and driving. Relatively high tax rates on these items probably do not impose welfare losses in Jamaica because of the price-inelastic demand for these goods and the external costs associated with consumption of these goods. These taxes are easily assessed and collected, and consumption will not be enough to measurably affect revenues.

The problem with all of this is that the system becomes very dependent on this narrow base, perhaps to the neglect of fully developing the taxation of domestic produce and consumption. Reliance on the "perennials" for 85 percent of consumption duty has understandably dampened enthusiasm for developing a major training program in tax accounting and auditing. In Jamaica, the traditional excises have always been assessed on a specific basis, requiring the physical control expertise which is associated with an "excise man." But the ad valorem basis necessary to assess the broader domestic consumption and production sectors requires an ability to inspect the books of account of enterprises in the system. The consequence of not having a more solid tradition in ad valorem taxation is not only the shortage of skilled tax accountants but also the fact that domestic firms are not likely to have developed their accounts as properly as otherwise would have been the case. Both of these problems will haunt the implementation of the proposed general consumption tax.

Of perhaps more concern are the distortions potentially introduced by the consumption duty. Because the taxes are levied at the manufacturers and import stage, differential wholesale and retail margins are not recognized. As a consequence, the final tax burden on consumers varies by commodity in unintended (and probably unknown) ways. Using the Jamaica input-output table Bird estimates that the average (pyramided) effective tax rate on inputs was equivalent to 2.4 percent of the gross value of manufacturing output in 1983, compared to an average tax rate of 7.8 percent on total manufacturing output.[37] Since the rate of import taxation on raw materials and capital goods has been raised substantially since 1983, it is reasonable to expect that the proportion of tax that is hidden in the cascading has increased.

One would expect manufacturers—especially those who face a high rate of duty—to react to this by shifting functions such as blending, packaging, and warehousing to subsidiary distributors, thereby lowering their tax liability. We can only speculate about the importance of this problem, and draw upon anecdotal evidence of significant vertical integration in sectors where the indirect tax rates are high.

The Jamaican indirect tax system also protects domestic producers from foreign competition. Though a large proportion of imported goods enters the country tax-free, the stamp duty on imported goods is levied at a high rate. Bird estimates that in 1983–84, imports were taxed at a 19 percent higher rate than was domestic production. Moreover, consumer durables and capital goods were taxed at significantly higher rates than were other imports. With the shift in revenue reliance from consumption duty (which does tax imported and domestically produced goods at the same rate) to the import stamp duty, the rate of protection has increased. The tax incentive program, to the extent it favors domestic producers with lower rates for raw materials or outright exemption for intermediate goods, has accentuated this protection.

Inelasticity

The revenue-income elasticity of indirect taxes is low by comparison to that for public expenditures, for at least two reasons. First, the tax base excludes much of the rapidly growing service sector and about 80 percent of imports. Second, the tax rate structure has not fully shifted from a specific ad valorem basis, and so is not as "automatically" responsive to income and price level growth as otherwise would be the case. Bird estimates that over the 1978–84 period, the buoyancy of all indirect taxes was about unity and for the consumption duty it was 0.78. Were it not for discretionary rate and base increases for import stamp duties and traditional excises, indirect revenues would not have grown to keep pace with GNP.

There are some bothersome implications of an income-inelastic structure. If indirect taxes are not doing their part in financing public expenditures, there will be pressure to make up for the shortfall by making discretionary adjustments. This has been exactly the case in Jamaica where the income elasticity of public expenditures was on the order of 1.2 over the 1980–86 period. The discretionary changes to correct this imbalance have almost always been made under time pressure and in the context of an immediate problem with the budget deficit or the foreign trade regime. Almost inevitably, the "reform" amounted to little more than an upward revision in rates. The allocative, distributive, and administrative effects of these changes, if carefully evaluated at all, have taken a back seat to the revenue goals and the political constraints. The resulting reforms make the system increasingly complicated and introduce some new directions to the system of relative prices.

Administration

The indirect tax system is beset by serious administration problems. As noted above, some of these are traceable to the complexity of the system and can be addressed by nothing short of a restructuring of the tax. Beyond this, however, there are important shortcomings in the areas of personnel, record-keeping, and procedures that would compromise the effective operation of even the best-designed general sales tax.

Perhaps the major problem is the shortage of qualified staff. Under the present system, most of the inspectors lack the type of training necessary for effective auditing. The inspection program is also weak and burdened by operating procedures that are antiquated in some cases and weak in others. The ratio of the number of inspectors to the number of accounts is in an acceptable range, but the frequent visits to enterprises are not true audits. Due reports that "there is no system of priorities for inspection nor guidelines for the inspectors, no system for them to report their findings, and little supervision."[38] Even in the case of the traditional excises, where administration is relatively more manageable and physical methods of control are used, there is evidence that procedures are inadequate and that qualified staff are in short supply.[39]

Proposed Reform[40]

The goals of the reform program are to make the indirect tax system more neutral with respect to economic choices, less arbitrary in the way it treats similarly situated individuals and firms, to tie its revenue performance more closely to the performance of the economy and less to annual discretionary actions, and to improve its administration. To accomplish these objectives, the project proposed adoption of a general sales tax of the value-added type. The major constraints in designing such a reform program are revenue neutrality and protection of low-income Jamaicans from any substantial increase in burdens.

Value-added Tax

The general consumption tax (GCT), was proposed to replace the present system of consumption duties, excise duties, and retail sales tax. The base of the tax would include importers, manufacturers, and large distributors, with the value-added feature of allowing a credit for taxes paid on inputs. Exporters would be zero-rated[41] and the major consumption items for low-income families would be excluded from tax, but otherwise there will be few exemptions. This should lower the costs of administration and compliance, make the system less horizontally inequitable, and eliminate some unintended effects on methods of doing business.

For reasons of administration, much of the service sector will be outside the base, as will small, handicraft-type manufacturers, smaller distributors, and all but the largest retailers. Bird's estimate is that to retain a constant amount of revenue, the GCT rate will have to be on the order of 20 to 25 percent. This translates into a retail-equivalent rate of 10 to 20 percent.

It is proposed that the present system of taxing cigarettes, petroleum products, and spirits will remain unchanged for the time being in order to protect revenue and minimize the amount of disruption associated with the reform. Accordingly, only about 30 percent of what is presently collected from the present consumption duty, retail sales tax, and excise duty will initially come under the GCT. Eventually, these taxes should be included for the difficulties associated with the administrative transition and the potential short-run revenue losses would be too great to bring them in at the present time.

Imports

If the reform merged consumption duty, excise duty, and the retail sales tax into the GCT, imports would be taxed at the same rate as domestically produced goods. The common external tariff would, of course, remain unchanged. A special problem arises, however, in the case of the import stamp duty. Should it be subsumed with the GCT?

There are good arguments for keeping it separate. It is a proven revenue producer, it enables the government to keep rates relatively high on certain imports to encourage foreign exchange savings, and it enables a targeting of import tax relief on certain sectors of activity. Perhaps the most persuasive argument is that integration of the stamp duty on imports and the GCT would almost certainly lead to a more complicated GCT and could thus defeat one of the main purposes of the reform.

But there are advantages to bringing the stamp duty into the GCT, especially in light of the government's program to broaden the import tax base and lower and simplify the rate. It could provide for a similar tax treatment for imported and domestically produced goods and would thus improve economic efficiency. Unwanted consumption would still be discouraged by the luxury rate under the GCT and the common external tariff. Most important, however, it would be a better approach (than the proposed system of export rebates) to compensate exporters for the tax on imported inputs.

As a practical matter, it would be impossible at this time to fully merge the import stamp duty into a flat-rate GCT. The revenue loss could not be made up without a substantial increase in the rates of other taxes or a cut in expenditures. The protective element in the stamp duty, however undesirable it may be from a point of view of economic efficiency, is not likely to be abolished overnight and cannot be shifted to the common external tariff. The remaining alternative to discouraging imports and correcting external imbalance—devaluation —will have few strong supporters. One possibility is to merge the GCT and the import stamp duty with a flat 20 percent temporary stamp duty on basically the same range of imports as covered by the present stamp duty.

Lessons For Tax Reform

The Jamaican tax reform provides a real-world setting in which to rethink some of the principles of tax policy analysis in developing countries. In some cases, old lessons were relearned. But the Jamaican experience also suggested some areas where the conventional wisdom ought to be challenged. Perhaps as important as the substantive issues are the lessons learned here about how to do a tax reform in a developing country, i.e., about how to maximize the chances that the work will lead to an improvement in the tax system.

Tax Reform and the Economic Setting

The best time to do a comprehensive reform of the tax structure is when the economy is performing poorly. There is a sense that something must be done and tax policy is one area where the government can take aggressive action. In such times, it is easier to focus the attention of policymakers on the structural problems with the entire tax system and to think through the ways in which the tax system may be retarding economic growth. The same inefficiencies that are so visible when the economy is not going well tend to become invisible in periods of economic growth. Consequently, when the economy is growing, the attention of tax reformers shifts to piecemeal adjustments that are "popular" or that appear to improve vertical equity, and to administrative improvements. The attention of politicians shifts to the expenditure side of the budget during periods of economic growth, and this shift accelerates as elections approach.

Jamaica's tax reform began when the economy was in dire straits: real GNP was declining, a devaluation was quite clearly in the immediate offing, the external debt burden was heavy and the country was under pressure from the IMF and the World Bank to reduce its budget deficit and limit domestic borrowing, and the unemployment and inflation rates were at unacceptably high levels. Things were bad enough that the Seaga administration and the general public were in agreement that nothing short of a complete overhaul of the tax system would do. The stated focus of the tax reform was on a "revenue neutral" restructuring of the system and the government was willing to take its time in thinking through the issues. Had the economy been growing, the government may have been less enthusiastic about the comprehensive restructuring objectives. Indeed, when the Jamaican economy did improve in 1986 and 1987, the government began to slow the pace at which it pushed for further tax reform in introducing the remaining parts of the comprehensive reform.

The potential pitfall to doing tax reform in a context of economic decline is that the government's interest and the energies of the project will be siphoned away to deal with the exigencies of each year's fiscal crisis. In Jamaica, this problem was dealt with by keeping the work of the comprehensive tax reform quite separate from the annual revenue-raising exercise. This turned out to be crucial. Had it been otherwise, the work of the project would almost certainly have been diverted to "quick fixes" to generate enough revenue to meet annual budget needs and tax reform would have remained a piecemeal exercise.

How Much Can a Tax System Be Shocked?

The conventional wisdom suggests an incremental approach to tax reform, i.e., it argues that if the existing system is shocked too much, it will compromise the success of the proposed reform. Individuals and businesses have become accustomed to the system and even to its shortcomings, they understand how it works and how they may comply with its provisions, and they have long since capitalized on many of its features. To shock the economy with anything more than an incremental reform will impose significant transition costs as firms and individuals try to adjust to major administrative burdens (especially if the reform calls for a new approach to taxation), and will necessarily rearrange the distribution of tax burdens among sectors and individuals in the economy.

The Jamaica experience suggests not only that the tax system can be shocked under the right circumstances, but that comprehensive reform can only take place if the system is shocked. What are the "right" circumstances? First, the government and the public must have lost confidence in the present system. Certainly, Jamaica had reached the point where patchwork reform was no longer good enough. The tax structure and the tax administration had drifted so far out of line with the nation's goal for economic development, and with its notions of fairness, that only a complete overhaul of the system would work. Second, the government and the public need time to absorb the shock. There was a full six-month debate of the proposals in the Jamaican press and by the time of enactment the shock effect had pretty much dissipated. Third, there is the possibility of revenue shock—large first-year losses that might result from transition problems or from the appearance of unexpected loopholes. Some steps were taken to guard against this in the Jamaica reform. It was recommended that the traditional excises—alcohol, petroleum, and cigarettes—which bring in about two thirds of indirect taxes, not be initially brought into the GCT.

Fourth, the administrative system must be able to absorb the change. In the case of the income tax reform, the new simpler system did not require new skills in the income tax department, and if anything, it made taxpayer compliance easier. There were some problems because the revisions to the act were confusing in some cases, but in general the transition was relatively smooth. Finally, if a big change is to be enacted, the taxpayer must see a package that brings him or her gains and losses. For example, the adoption of a flat-rate individual income tax was favored by higher-income Jamaicans but could never have been accepted unless nontaxable perquisites (which benefited those with higher income) were abolished and a high standard deduction (which benefited lower-income workers) was imposed at the same time. There was little pleasure and a little pain in the new tax package for nearly everyone. If the Jamaican reform had been constrained to incremental improvements, this income tax reform could never have happened.

The Role of Equity Considerations

Vertical equity cannot be the driving force behind a comprehensive tax reform program in a developing country. In part this is because developing countries cannot implement progressive tax systems and in part it is because the costs of vertical equity are very high. It is one thing to recite the rhetoric linking progressivity in nominal rates of income tax to vertical equity, but quite another to show that such a linkage actually exists. The problem is with administration. The Jamaican individual income tax had the look of a progressive tax with a steeply graduated nominal rate structure, but in fact the tax was regressive because of the extent of evasion and avoidance at the top end. Giving up the progressivity in Jamaica's nominal rate structure had little if any effect on the distribution of income.

Indeed, the creation of a progressive distribution of tax burdens may not even be a primary consideration in formulating a tax structure revision because of the inherent tradeoff between vertical equity on the one hand and the goals of efficiency and simplification on the other. There are several dimensions to this tradeoff. First, the unbeatable combination of weak administration and the political power of higher-income residents will probably defeat the effort to restructure the income tax to make it more progressive. The corollary to this is that the addition of tax features to improve vertical equity often makes the system more complicated and difficult to administer, and imposes new costs on society. The addition of a family of special rates on luxury commodities, or the provision of tax credits for activities in which lower-income workers are thought to engage are cases in point.

Second, attempts to build vertical equity into the system may impose an efficiency cost on the economy. For example, the higher the standard deduction on income tax, the higher must be the tax rate, with whatever implications that may have for investment, productivity, evasion, and employment generation. The same is true for the exemption of commodities from sales taxation and the general sales tax rate. Third, tax preferences to achieve vertical equity have a revenue cost, either directly in terms of the tax relief, or indirectly in terms of the revenue sacrifice due to the greater complexity of the tax system.

What is the place of equity in comprehensive tax reform? The first goal ought to be to protect the lowest-income families in the society. This means that the issue is much less income taxation than interest taxes. The Jamaica project carried out a family budget survey to identify the market basket of low income families, and used these results to propose a short list of exemptions under the GCT.[42] This done, the goal in the Jamaica study was to work toward a system that was roughly proportional in its distribution of effective rates. Fine-tuning the distribution of tax burdens to achieve some particular pattern of progression was not considered.

Probably more important is the issue of horizontal equity, which the Jamaicans seem to have equated with fairness in taxation. The system was riddled with inequities: private sector workers received more income in nontaxable perquisites than public sector workers, self-employed workers paid lower taxes than those in the PAYE sector, those in certain industries had access to the preferential "overtime" tax rate while others did not, only some types of businesses could engage in arbitrage to avoid income taxes, etc. Such unequal treatment had undermined confidence in the tax system. The primary goal of the Jamaican study was to find a way to eliminate these horizontal inequities and the distortions in economic choices which they promoted.

The Power of Data

Empirical estimates of the impacts of proposed tax structure changes on revenue yield and on the tax burdens of variously situated individuals and businesses were key in selling the reform package in Jamaica. The quality of the underlying data was not without problems, but the data gave a basis for removing some of the guesswork in evaluating the options. Most important, the presence of the data lifted the debate to a much higher level than otherwise would have been the case. There was a reasonable basis to guess as the differential impacts of alternative relief programs and both the government and the tax reform committee focused on simulating the impacts of alternative specifications of the rate and base.

The individual income tax reform was particularly influenced by the data analysis. In fact, it is very doubtful that so sweeping a reform as this could have occurred in the absence of a rigorous statistical study. The proposed flat tax would change the entire system and it was not intuitively obvious how various taxpayers or even the government treasury would fare. Moreover, the revenue and burden impacts would depend on the exact rate and standard deduction chosen. About two hundred combinations of rate and base were eventually run through the simulation model before a final structure was chosen. Even then, the government specified particulars for over one hundred "hypothetical" taxpayers and the tax impact of the proposed reform was calculated for each. It was a textbook example of looking for the "right" effect on the median voter.

A similar experience can be recounted in the design of the GCT. The issue was the choice of a simple revenue structure, or even a single rate, that would give the same revenue as the previous consumption duty, retail sales tax, excise duty, and stamp duty on imports. The second question was: how would various commodities be affected? As in the case of income taxation, this analysis required gathering data that the government had never before assembled. The result was a reasonably clean estimate of the base of Jamaica's indirect taxes, an estimate of the options open in structuring the rates for the GCT, and some idea about how various commodities might be affected by the new tax. Finally, the survey of low-income families provided some hard evidence on the expenditure patterns of the poor and headed off proposals for long lists of exemptions in the name of equity.

First Policy, Then Administration

A first principle for successful tax reform is to get the policy right and *then* deal with the administrative problems. The consumers and sponsors of a reform often cannot see beneath a plethora of administrative problems to the real issue, which may well be a badly structured tax. Too often the call for technical assistance in tax administration from the IRS or from one of the international agencies is premature.

There are three good reasons for giving policy reform priority over administrative reform. First, administrative improvements can often generate a quick revenue impact. Because this may satisfy some of the urgency about "reforming" the tax system, the government may lose its enthusiasm about rethinking its tax policy. Second, the true, underlying "administrative" problem may be with the tax structure. It may be so complicated as to be beyond the capacity of the government to properly administer, or it may so unfair that payment of taxes will be resisted no matter how much the administration improves. Third, if the reform goes no further than administration, the government will not go through the invaluable exercise of questioning whether the tax system is affecting the economy in ways that reinforce government objectives.

The Jamaica case offers some good illustrations of why tax policy considerations should lead such work. The individual income tax was hopelessly complicated, with three rate schedules, sixteen tax credits, and a system under which employees could choose to grant nontaxable perquisites to their employees. It would have been virtually impossible to improve the administration of such a tax and resources spent in that direction would likely have been wasted. More to the point, why would anyone consider improving the administration of such an outrageously bad tax? Yet, the initial proposal for the Jamaica tax project was for IRS technical assistance in the area of income tax administration.

A second illustration relates to the introduction of the GCT. The present system is assessed primarily by physical methods and assumed notional prices. The skills required of an excise person have to do with physical control of inventory, so that measurement and training to improve administration would center on improving these skills. The proposed change to the GCT would require a different kind of expertise —primarily book-audit. An earlier program of technical assistance in the area of administration would almost certainly have strengthened the existing system, with all of its weaknesses, and the opportunity to switch to a more modern sales tax system might have been missed.

Monitoring

The results of a tax reform should be monitored in the first years after implementation. While it is essential that the reform study generate the possible forecasts of revenue yield, tax burden impacts, and economic effect, it is also essential that the tax planner know the actual outcome and be ready to adjust the new system as necessary. It is especially important that the monitoring begin immediately after the reform is implemented and before new avenues of avoidance become entrenched. Taxpayers (and tax evaders) are far more adept at finding loopholes in the new legislation than tax reformers are at closing off all the avenues for tax avoidance. The more dramatic the structural reform and administrative "shock," the more likely are such loopholes to appear and to be undetected.

This is an important problem with the Jamaica reform. The income tax reform should have resulted in a significant adjustment in the compensation package for PAYE employees—away from allowances and toward wages and salaries. However, some loopholes were left open with respect to uniform, housing, and automobile allowances and these apparently dampened the propensity to convert allowances to wages. To study the initial compensation adjustments, we randomly sampled firms and carried out an inspection of payroll books before and after firms had converted to the new system. The results suggest that the tax reform led to a base expansion of only about 8 percent because some allowances remain untaxed. Apparently, the initial adjustment to the reform was for allowances to migrate to those categories which remain untaxed. One might discount these results on grounds that May 1986 was too soon to measure the impact of the reform, i.e., that neither firms nor the income tax administration had adjusted. The other possibility is that these data do tell the true story—that allowances will not be brought fully into the base until the loopholes are closed off. Either way, it is clear that there have been some abuses, and consequently there is some need to tighten legislation, provide tougher enforcement regulations, and do further monitoring.

Another reason for monitoring is to determine whether the reforms have met revenue targets and consequently whether some base or rate structure revision is necessary. It is not enough simply to rely on the *ex ante* projections of the revenue impact of the reform. Forecasts, by their very nature, are conjectural and inaccurate. The underlying data used to make the projections are sometimes flawed and always dated, the behavioral model may not accurately predict the response of individuals and businesses to the tax changes, and the underlying economic assumptions used to drive the model may turn out to be far off the mark. The latter in particular was a problem with the projections of the revenue impact of the Jamaica reform. The revenue yield turned out to be much greater than had been expected because the economy grew much faster than had been assumed in the forecast. This resulted in revenues well above the first-year targets, and an increase in the average income tax burden. One possibility is that the individual income tax may be too income-elastic, and the government should reconsider indexing the standard deduction to head off the public discontent which will surely come with continued real growth and/or the resumption of a higher rate of inflation.

Tax Reform or Fiscal Reform?

It is better to do a comprehensive fiscal reform—which also includes consideration of the expenditure side of the budget—than a comprehensive tax reform. It is a more difficult job, requires more resources and time, and probably raises many more controversial issues, but it allows the government to get a better picture of the overall implications of the tax reform under consideration.

The Jamaica tax reform mandate was revenue neutrality. What does this mean? It implies that the first-year revenue target for the reformed system is fixed by the intended amount of government expenditures, but it does not provide guidance on the desired income elasticity of the new tax system. The latter, of course, depends on the desired income elasticity of public expenditures. The result in the Jamaica case was the design of a new tax system whose revenue yield may or may not grow at the desired rate. To the extent that there is a divergence, discretionary changes will be necessary and a return to piecemeal tax policymaking will be invited.

Fiscal reform is also more desirable because it allows a more comprehensive study of the options for getting the prices "right," balancing the budget, affecting the distribution of income through the budget process, evaluating least-cost methods of achieving certain objectives, etc. The Jamaica reform was more far-reaching than most tax studies in that it considered the financing of public enterprises, the benefits of tax incentive legislation, and the effectiveness of the government's food stamp program. Still, the work came up far short of considering even some of the most relevant expenditure-side issues, for example, the actuarial position of the payroll tax contribution programs, and the possibilities for user charge financing. The project did a reasonable job of estimating who pays for the Jamaican public sector, but it did not go very far in considering who benefits.

How to Get Successful Implementation

The Jamaica reform suggests five rules about how to get to successful implementation of a tax reform. First, the government must see the project as its own and not that of a donor or even that of a technical assistance research team. The personal and close involvement of the prime minister set the tone for the Jamaica work, and the chairman of the revenue board was an active participant in the research. A very important and beneficial development in the Jamaica work was the prime minister's appointment of an independent tax reform committee. The committee was comprised of twelve leading citizens and included representatives of most of the major public interest groups. The project staff worked directly with the committee in their review of the tax reform proposals and in the formulation of the alternatives which they put forth to the government.

Second, the technical-assistance team should have the right mix of skills and experience and, above all, should have expert credentials. Nothing short of well-known tax policy experts with extensive policy experience would have satisfied the Jamaicans. The government was understandably uneasy about the risks and uncertainties associated with the reform; moreover, some aspects of the reform were very complicated and others raised important issues of administration that appeared to be stumbling blocks. It was essential to have senior staff who could draw easily and confidently on knowledge of tax systems and of successes and failures elsewhere.

Third, tax reform should not be hurried. It takes time to get the technical proposals properly in place, and the public debate needs time. The Jamaican press and public-interest groups were all involved in the debate, at a surprisingly technical level, for a full six months before the income tax reforms were implemented. By the time the law was enacted, a very major change in the system was not seen by the public as a tax "shock."

Fourth, there is the important issue of timing. The income tax reforms have been enacted, but the government has not yet moved to introduce the GCT or restructure the sales tax. The lesson here is that a government is not willing to be associated indefinitely with tax reform, even good tax reform. Comprehensive reform tends to be associated with a particular administration and there is need to get on with it while the power is in place and while there is still enthusiasm for the reform program. Even the best of tax reform programs carries unfavorable connotations for most citizens and politicians, and the zeal for even so noble a goal as "getting the prices right" wanes as time goes by and election years draw close.

Fifth, implementation requires a great deal of attention—probably more attention than it received in the course of the Jamaica work. The project did have two income tax administration experts reside in the country to work out administration procedures and to assist in training, and a sales tax administration expert to do the same for the GCT. On the other hand, too little attention was paid to the need for carefully drafting the new legislation and implementing regulations.

Notes

1 The Jamaica Tax Structure Examination Project was sponsored by the government of Jamaica from 1983 to 1987. The project was carried out by the Metropolitan Studies Program of Syracuse University's Maxwell School under the direction of the Board of Revenue of the government of Jamaica. The author organized and directed the project from start to finish. Funding for the project was provided by the government of Jamaica and the U.S. Agency for International Development Mission to Jamaica (under contract 532-0095-C-00-3020-00). This paper is an abbreviated version of various chapters in Roy Bahl, ed., *The Jamaican Tax Reform* (Cambridge: Oegleschlager, Gunn and Hain, forthcoming).

2 See also Dawes (1982); Chernik (1978).

3 This is discussed in Michael Wasylenko, "Tax Burden Before and After Reform," in *The Jamaican Tax Reform*, ed. Roy Bahl (Cambridge: Oegleschlager, Gunn and Hain, forthcoming), chapter 28.

4 James Follain and Daniel Holland, chapter 23 in Bahl, ed., *The Jamaican Tax Reform*.

5 The ratio of taxes to GNP.

6 Lotz and Morss (1967).

7 Bahl (1971); Bahl (1972).

8 Tait, Gratz, and Eichengreen (1979); Chelliah, Baas, and Kelly (1975); Chelliah (1971).

9 Follain and Holland in Bahl, ed., *The Jamaican Tax Reform*, chapter 23.

10 An extensive discussion of the effects of the Jamaican tax structure on work effort, saving investment, and compliance is in Roy Bahl et al., "A Program for Reform," in Bahl, ed., *The Jamaican Tax Reform*, chapter 1.

11 See DeGraw (1984).

12 See Wasylenko in Bahl, ed., *The Jamaican Tax Reform*, chapter 28.

13 See Richard M. Bird and Barbara Miller, "The Incidence of Indirect Taxes in Low Income Households in Jamaica," in Bahl, ed., *The Jamaican Tax Reform*, chapter 29.

14 These questions are addressed in Carl S. Shoup, "Integrating Tax Policy, Industrial Policy and Trade Policy in Jamaica," in Bahl, ed., *The Jamaican Tax Reform*, chapter 25.

15 A discussion of the foreign trade regime before 1983 is in Whalley (1984).

16 Wayne Thirsk, "Jamaican Tax Incentives," in Bahl, ed., *The Jamaican Tax Reform*, chapter 26.

17 Richard M. Bird, "Taxation of Services," in Bahl, ed., *The Jamaican Tax Reform*, chapter 22.

18 Ibid.

19 The underlying data and empirical analysis are described in detail by Bahl et al., "An Evaluation of the Structure of the Jamaican Individual Income Tax" and "A Program for Reform," in Bahl, ed., *The Jamaican Tax Reform*, chapters 3 and 4.

20 At the time this work was done, the most recent available data were for 1983.

21 See Alm and Wasylenko, "Payroll Taxes in Jamaica," in Bahl, ed., *The Jamaican Tax Reform*.

22 Each of the three, however, has a tax element.

23 The allocative effects of this system of payroll are not discussed here. Alm and Wasylenko provide a careful discussion of the economic effects under alternative assumptions about the incidence of the employer share. Alm and Wasylenko, "Payroll Taxes in Jamaica."

24 James Wozny, "The Taxation of Corporate Source Income in Jamaica," in Bahl, ed., *The Jamaican Tax Reform*, chapter 8.

25 For industrial buildings and machinery are given an initial allowance of 20 percent, but other asset investments receive a lower percentage according to a complicated schedule.

26 This is described in Martinez, "The Taxation of Financial Institutions in Jamaica," and Brannon, "Tax Policies for Life Insurance Companies in Jamaica," in Bahl, ed., *The Jamaican Tax Reform*, chapters 10 and 11.

27 David Davies and Lauria Grant, "The Taxation of Jamaican Public Enterprises," in Bahl, ed., *The Jamaican Tax Reform*, chapter 13.

28 Tanzi (1987).

29 He defines the effective tax rate as the ratio of the present value of the tax payments (individual and corporate income) to the present value of the economic income arising from the investment. Economic income is measured as the difference between

revenues and economic depreciation. Wozny, chapter 8 in Bahl, ed., *The Jamaican Tax Reform*.

30 Ibid.

31 The international implications of the company tax reform are described in Oliver Oldman, David Rosenbloom, and Joan Youngman, "International Aspects of Revisions to the Jamaican Company Tax," in Bahl, ed., *The Jamaican Tax Reform*.

32 Wozny, chapter 8 in Bahl, ed., *The Jamaican Tax Reform*.

33 These issues are discussed in Break, Holland, and McLure (1986).

34 The system is described in John Due, "Jamaica's Indirect Tax Structure," in Bahl, ed., *The Jamaican Tax Reform*, chapter 15.

35 Sijbren Cnossen, "Future Development of the Sales Tax in Jamaica," in Bahl, ed., *The Jamaican Tax Reform*, chapter 20.

36 The latter excludes food, petroleum products, cigarettes, and alcoholic beverages.

37 Bird, chapter 16 in Bahl, ed., *The Jamaican Tax Reform*.

38 Due, chapter 15 in Bahl, ed., *The Jamaican Tax Reform*.

39 Cnossen, chapter 20 in Bahl, ed., *The Jamaican Tax Reform*.

40 The work on indirect taxation was coordinated by Richard Bird. The design of the proposed reform is found in his "Choosing a Tax Rate" (chapter 18), and "Taxation of Services" (chapter 22) in Bahl, ed., *The Jamaican Tax Reform*.

41 No tax would be due on value-added *and* all taxes paid on inputs would be refunded.

42 See Bird and Miller, chapter 29 in Bahl, ed., *The Jamaican Tax Reform*; and Miller and Stone (1985).

References

Alm, James, and Michael Wasylenko. "Payroll Taxes in Jamaica." Chapter 6 in *The Jamaican Tax Reform*. Edited by Roy W. Bahl. Cambridge: Oegleschlager, Gunn and Hain, forthcoming.

Bahl, Roy W. (1971). "A Regression Approach to Tax Effort and Tax Ratio Analysis." *IMF Staff Papers* 18, 3 (November): pp. 570–612.

——— (1972). "A Representative Tax System Approach to Measuring Tax Effort in Developing Countries." *IMF Staff Papers* 19, 1 (March): 87–124.

Bahl, Roy W., ed. (forthcoming), *The Jamaican Tax Reform*. Cambridge: Oegleschlager, Gunn and Hain.

Bahl, Roy W. et al. "An Evaluation of the Structure of the Jamaican Individual Income Tax." Ibid., chapter 3.

———. "A Program for Reform." Ibid., chapter 4.

Bird, Richard M. "Choosing a Tax Rate." Ibid., chapter 18.

———. "Sources of Indirect Tax Revenue." Ibid., chapter 16.

———. "Taxation of Services." Ibid., chapter 22.

Bird, Richard M., and Barbara Miller. "The Incidence of Indirect Taxes in Low Income Households in Jamaica." Ibid., chapter 29.

Brannon, Gerard. "Tax Policies for Life Insurance Companies in Jamaica." Ibid., chapter 11.

Break, George, Daniel Holland, and Charles E. McLure, Jr. (1986). "Private Sector Capital Investment and the Company Tax." Jamaica Tax Structure Examination Project Staff Paper No. 28. Metropolitan Studies Program, The Maxwell School. Syracuse, N.Y.:

Syracuse University, March.

Chelliah, Rajah J. (1971). "Trends in Taxation in Developing Countries." *IMF Staff Papers* 18 (July), pp. 254–331.

Chelliah, Rajah J., Hessel Baas, and Margaret Kelly (1975). "Tax Ratios and Tax Effort in Developing Countries, 1969–1971." *IMF Staff Papers* 22, 1 (March), pp. 187–205.

Chernick, Sidney (1978), ed. *The Commonwealth Caribbean: The Integration Experience.* Baltimore: Johns Hopkins University Press for the World Bank.

Cnossen, Sijbren. "Future Development of the Sales Tax in Jamaica." In Bahl, ed., *The Jamaican Tax Reform*, chapter 20.

Davies, David, and Lauria Grant. "The Taxation of Jamaican Public Enterprises." Ibid., chapter 13.

Dawes, Hugh N. (1982), *Public Finance and Economic Development: Spotlight on Jamaica.* Lanham, Md.: University Press of America.

DeGraw, Sandra (1984). "Current Administrative Procedure of the Income Tax Department of Jamaica and Some Recommended Changes." Jamaica Tax Structure Examination Project Staff Paper No. 4. Metropolitan Studies Program, The Maxwell School. Syracuse, N.Y.: Syracuse University, February.

Due, John. "Jamaica's Indirect Tax Structure." In Bahl, ed., *The Jamaican Tax Reform*, chapter 15.

Follain, James, and Daniel Holland. "The Property Tax in Jamaica." In Bahl, ed., *The Jamaican Tax Reform*, chapter 23.

Lotz, Joergen, and Elliott Morss (1967). "Measuring Tax Effort in Developing Countries." *IMF Staff Papers* 14, 3 (November), pp. 478–99.

Martinez, Jorge. "The Taxation of Financial Institutions in Jamaica." In Bahl, ed., *The Jamaican Tax Reform*, chapter 10.

Miller, Barbara, and Carl Stone (1985). "The Low-Income Household Expenditure Survey: Description and Analysis." Jamaica Tax Examination Project Staff Paper No. 25. Metropolitan Studies Program, The Maxwell School. Syracuse. N.Y.: Syracuse University, November.

Oldman, Oliver, David Rosenbloom, and Joan Youngman. "International Aspects of Revisions to the Jamaican Company Tax." In Bahl, ed., *The Jamaican Tax Reform*, chapter 12.

Shoup, Carl S. "Integrating Tax Policy, Industrial Policy and Trade Policy in Jamaica." Ibid., chapter 25.

Tait, Alan, Wilfred Gratz, and Barry Eichengreen (1979). "International Comparisons of Taxation for Selected Developing Countries, 1972–1976." *IMF Staff Papers* 26, 1 (March), pp. 123–56.

Tanzi, Vito (1987). "Quantitative Characteristics of the Tax Systems of Developing Countries." In David Newberry and Nicholas Stern, *The Theory of Taxation for Developing Countries.* New York: Oxford University Press for the World Bank, chapter 4.

Thirsk, Wayne. "Jamaican Tax Incentives." In Bahl, ed., *The Jamaican Tax Reform*, chapter 26.

Wasylenko, Michael. "Tax Burden Before and After Reform." Ibid., chapter 28.

Whalley, John (1984). "Tax Reform and Foreign Trade Regime in Jamaica." Jamaica Tax Structure Examination Project Staff Paper No. 7. Metropolitan Studies Program, The Maxwell School. Syracuse, N.Y.: Syracuse University, April.

Wozny, James. "The Taxation of Corporate Source Income in Jamaica." In Bahl, ed., *The Jamaican Tax Reform*, chapter 8.

6

....

The Tax Mission to Japan, 1949–50

....

Carl S. Shoup

I. Genesis of the Tax Reform

In mid-1947 General Douglas MacArthur and Harold Moss were discussing taxation in the general's Tokyo office. MacArthur was Supreme
Commander of the Allied Powers (SCAP), in charge of the occupation
forces in Japan. Moss, an official in the Internal Revenue Service of the
United States, was en route to Korea to serve as budget and tax adviser
to the Korean interim government. The two had known each other for
some ten years, since the days when they were in the Philippines
together.

MacArthur was clearly worried about the condition of the tax system
in Japan. The occupation had now been in force for nearly two years, yet
imposition and collection of taxes was still on a largely arbitrary basis.
The occupation military were still assuming responsibility for getting
tax revenue to the treasury. A U.S. officer would tell a Japanese district
collector of taxes how much he was expected to bring in, no matter
what methods he found it necessary to use.

MacArthur told Moss that his reading of history showed that the
collapse of nations was due often, if not always, to the mounting inef-
fectiveness of their tax systems. Japan, although then in a state of near
ruin, could in a few decades become one of the world's great democratic
powers if the necessary steps were taken, including the creation and
operation of a sound tax system. Moreover, if Japan were to become
democratic—one of the general's most intensely held aims—local government would have to be strengthened. To this end, prefectures and
cities would have to be granted more financial independence, which
implied stronger taxing powers than their own.

Moss went on to Korea, but three months later word came from Mac-Arthur calling him to Tokyo. The general had clearly decided to proceed with fundamental tax reform in Japan. Moss was given charge of the Internal Revenue Branch of the Finance Division of General Headquarters of SCAP. A few weeks later the Branch was made a Division, placing it on the same level as the Finance Division, in the Economic and Scientific Section of GHQ.

In the ensuing months, well into 1948, Moss succeeded in getting tax collection methods on a sounder basis, but the structure of the tax system badly needed repair, indeed, an overhauling. Moss suggested that someone versed in tax policy, as distinct from tax administration, be brought from the United States, preferably with a group of colleagues who would form a tax mission. MacArthur agreed, and in the fall of 1948 Moss went to the United States to find a director for such a mission.

II. Initiation of the Project

In October 1948, Moss called at my office at Columbia University in New York City to explore the possibility of my forming and directing a tax reform mission to Japan. The following terms were quickly agreed on, and I accepted the invitation. The mission would come to Japan in the summer of 1949, and complete its work by the fall. An earlier date, though preferred by General MacArthur, would be impracticable, since the potential members of the mission that I had in mind were committed to their academic assignments for the next six months. The members would be chosen by me, subject to the usual clearance requirements (no difficulty at all developed on that score). The report would be published by SCAP in both English and Japanese. There would of course be no censorship or other dictation of the contents of the report from anyone. Moss agreed to devote virtually full time on the logistics of the enterprise, on the entrees to SCAP and Japanese officials and others, and to similar matters. There was no need for me to draw up a budget and estimate a total cost of the project, since we would be assimilated into the military, with similar pay, and transportation and hotel accommodations would be provided, as well as secretarial assistance and the like. The mission would consist of seven persons including myself. Fortunately, I obtained an affirmative answer from each of the six individuals whom I approached as first choices. They were:

Howard R. Bowen, dean of the College of Commerce and Business Administration, University of Illinois

Jerome B. Cohen, professor of economics, College of the City of New York

Rolland F. Hatfield, director of tax research, Department of Taxation, State of Minnesota

Stanley S. Surrey, professor, School of Jurisprudence, University of California at Berkeley

William S. Vickrey, professor of economics, Columbia University

William C. Warren, professor of law, School of Law, Columbia University

The members of the tax mission were together, in the old Imperial Hotel, for the greater part of the summer of 1949. In August, after two months of intensive work, we repaired to a mountain resort hotel away from the heat of Tokyo to draft the report, which was finished by the end of August and appeared a few weeks later in four volumes with facing pages in English and Japanese (Shoup, 1949).

In August and September 1950, four members of the tax mission (Shoup, Surrey, Vickrey, and Warren) made a second trip to Japan, described below (Shoup, 1950).

General MacArthur discussed with me, shortly after my arrival in Tokyo, the program of the mission, but made no concrete suggestions except to request that the report not make a "guinea pig" of Japan by recommending many hitherto untried taxation measures. He received the mission members at luncheon, and again, in July, in his office, and had another discussion with me just before my departure at the end of the study. The impression he gave was that he wanted to facilitate the mission's work in every way feasible, but would not discuss specific recommendations and the like before the report was written —the report would be entirely our responsibility. In the event, General MacArthur accepted the report in toto and recommended to the prime minister that it be accepted and implemented without change, as a package.

The resources made available to the mission were of very high quality. Several of the younger Japanese officials in the finance ministry were assigned as interpreters, and their high level of general capability, including an excellent command of English, and knowledge of the Japanese fiscal system, made them invaluable colleagues. In later years these men went on to high positions: for example, one became finance minister and another, president of one of the large banks. Whatever success the mission had was due in considerable part to the contributions of these talented colleagues.[1]

The tax mission was the last of the several groups or individuals that had been called to Japan by SCAP to suggest or formulate reforms in the Japanese government and even social structure (for brief descriptions of these reforms, see Perry [1980], passim). The Dodge mission, in 1948–49, was instrumental in checking the postwar inflation: wholesale prices, which had risen from an index of 100 in 1934–36 to 350 in 1945, had leaped to 20,876 in 1949 (Perry [1980], 111).[2] But they had stabilized by the time the tax mission had arrived, and showed promise of remaining so. Thus another diversion of the mission's energies was prevented: its recommendations did not have to include elaborate measures to adapt the tax system to an inflationary environment.

Before considering the mission's report, let us look briefly at the tax system then in force in Japan. It was essentially a modern one, in structure. The following extract from Aoki (1985, p. 435) sketches the development of the Japanese tax system up to 1949:

> When Japan emerged as a modern state after the Meiji Restoration of 1868, the land tax accounted for more than 80 percent of the total tax revenue of the national government. With the advent of the capitalist economy, in 1887 Japan became one of the first states to initiate a national income tax. Under the schedular income taxation in 1899, the income tax was extended to corporations. Around the turn of the century, the liquor tax and other indirect taxes were established. In 1904, the production and sales of cigarettes and tobacco products were brought under the monopoly of the government, which lasted until March 1985.
>
> After World War I, the income tax was completely revised. By that time the revenue from income tax, including both corporate and personal taxation, as a percentage of the total tax revenue exceeded 20% while those from the land tax fell below 10%. Later in 1938, the predecessor of the commodity tax was introduced. On the eve of the Pacific War, a far-reaching reform of the tax system was put into effect. The former income tax was divided into the income tax (on natural persons) and corporation tax. Since then, in Japan, the term "income tax" means only the tax imposed on individuals under the Income Tax Law and the term "corporation tax" means the one on income of corporations under the Corporation Tax Law. The new income tax was featured by the bipolar system,

which employed schedular taxes and graduated global tax. Withholding tax at source which had been hitherto applied to interest and dividends was expanded to wages and salaries. The corporation tax was imposed on corporate profits at a flat rate. The share of the direct tax revenue in the total national tax revenues rose from 34.8% in 1934 to 36 average to 65.1% in 1941 . . . .

Immediately after World War II, various taxation measures were taken to curb inflation and to reorient the economy. The property tax with highly progressive rates was introduced. In 1947, the bipolar system of income taxation was replaced by the purely global tax with progressive rates and the American "self-assessment" system superseded the traditional method of government assessment and collection. Some national taxes such as land and business taxes were transferred to local governments. For a brief period from 1948 to 1949, the turnover tax was put in force.

III. The Tax Mission Report

A. Publication

Publication of the tax mission's report of 1949 was a remarkable achievement. The report appeared in October of 1949, in the form of photocopy of typescript. The first two volumes contained the report proper; the second two, appendices. Volumes I and II took up 227 pages of double space text. There were in fact twice that many pages, since the Japanese translation appeared on the (right) facing page.

The mission thought of its work as largely an educational task, as well as a direct guide to policy; care was taken to explain the reasons for every recommendation, and the report was widely distributed over the country. (Memory does not serve too well here, but I seem to recall being told that some 20,000 sets of the four volumes were sent out.) The definite intent was to bring the tax system out into the open, to give the public a chance to understand the system and its problems.

The second report of the mission was printed in 1950, again with facing pages in Japanese. It contained only 92 pages (184, counting the Japanese pages) and covered only certain selected topics, as described below.

Three and a half decades later, these two reports were retranslated[3] and published, in 1985, by the Kasumi Publishing Company, Tokyo, in a single volume, with a two-page preface written on request by Shoup.

Aside from this preface, there is no English text, naturally enough. The new translation is the work of "a group of some former and present officers of the Ministry of Finance . . . . For one thing, the importance of the Recommendations has recently been anew widely recognized and strongly emphasized in discussions for tax reform to be made. For another thing, Japanese language, both its terminology and expressions, has considerably changed for the past thirty-five years, and the original translation has become a little old-fashioned" (H. Kaneko to Shoup, July 15, 1985).

The authorities publicized the report in 1949 and 1950 and sought to educate the taxpayers in many ways.[4] For example, a wall calendar, 16 by 10 inches, showed a smiling young Japanese woman holding a copy of the report, while the leaves of the calendar beneath, upon being turned up, revealed exhortations alongside the month's calendar, from January to December, as follows (in translation):

> January: The final return of income tax shall be filed in January. Don't forget your filing and tax payment . . . . February: Finish your tax payment as soon as possible . . . . March: To prepare for tax payment, deposit money for that purpose . . . . April: Let us file returns for Commodity Tax by 10th of next month . . . . May: Correct bookkeeping for correct tax payment . . . . June: Let everyone file his provisional return of income tax . . . . July: Never let tax become delinquent, in order to establish a bright and cultural Japan . . . August: Let us subscribe "Zeino Shirabe (The Way to Tax)", top level tax. September: Let us exterminate illicit sake and illicit tobacco . . . . October: Don't forget the second term payment of income tax . . . . November: To prepare for tax payment, let us deposit money obtained through rice quota delivery . . . December: Finish your tax payment this year, and welcome a bright new year.

B. Contents, in General

The 1949 report proper (volumes 1 and 2) considered the revenue system on a tax-by-tax basis, except for three opening chapters dealing with the tax system as a whole, intergovernmental fiscal relations, and prospects for government expenditures with the corresponding changes in tax revenue to come from the report's recommendations for the tax system.

Of the several taxes, the income tax, individual and corporate, received by far the most attention. This reflected the mission's view that the income tax should be the largest single source of revenue and that it needed a great deal of reconstruction if it were to play this role.[5]

Separate chapters were devoted to the taxation of gifts and bequests, the local-inhabitants tax (counted in the income tax total above), the real estate tax, and to other local taxes. The indirect tax system, aside from a few local taxes, was covered in just two chapters, one on the tobacco monopoly and the liquor taxes, the other on the turnover tax, various excises, customs duties, social security taxes, and revenue from government monopolies other than tobacco. This brevity of treatment reflected the mission's view that the turnover tax should be repealed and should not be replaced, on the national level, by any other broad-based sales tax (the value-added tax suggested for the prefectures will be noted below), and that the excise taxes, in concept or in administration, did not call for much change, at least relatively to the income tax.

The four appendices in the last two volumes of the report dealt with: (A) Finance of Local Governments, (B) Treatment of Irregular Incomes under the Personal Income Tax, (C) Revaluation of Assets (for purposes of income taxation), and (D) Administration of the Individual and Corporate Income Taxes. Item (C) reflected the need for revaluation following the period of drastic inflation.

The 1950 report consisted of a press statement of the tax mission released September 21, 1950, and three supplementary memoranda: *The Equalization Grant, Administration of the National Income Taxes*, and *Local Tax Administration Problems*. The emphasis placed on tax administration is evidenced by these memoranda titles and by the devotion of a considerable part of the press release to administrative problems. Conceptual and tax-theory issues were restricted almost entirely to the paragraphs devoted to the proposed value-added tax (prefectural) and to the grants made by the national government to the local units.

Taking the 1949 and 1950 reports together, we find that, of a total of 492 pages, 121 pages, or 25 percent, were devoted to tax administrative and tax compliance problems, all but thirteen pages of the 121 being devoted to the income tax. Of course, the remaining 371 pages, on conceptual and substantive policy issues, contained some discussion of administration and compliance. Perhaps about one third of the two reports together are of special interest to the tax administrator, with respect to the activities of the administrator, and those of the taxpayer as he seeks to comply with (or evade or avoid) the tax laws.

C. Recommendations in the 1949 Report: Conceptual and Substantive Issues

The tax mission's recommendations were summarized in a press release distributed at a press conference on August 26, 1949.[6] They are given in detail in the four-volume report. We consider first the major recommendations on conceptual and substantive issues. They were as follows:

1. Total tax revenue to be decreased by 2.5 percent in the 1950–51 fiscal year from the 1949–50 fiscal year. Thus, the overall reform was intended to be virtually revenue-neutral, as that term is used in this volume (Gillis, chapter 1).

2. National government tax revenue would decrease by 9 percent, this being largely offset by a 27 percent increase in the much smaller total of local (prefectural plus municipal) tax revenue.

3. The personal income tax to continue to be the major source of revenue for the national government, slightly decreased by the net result of the following proposed changes:

   a. The bracket rates to be reduced somewhat, with the top rate to be only 55 percent compared with the existing 85 percent rate. This top-rate reduction to be partly offset by the introduction of a personal net worth tax on individuals with more than 5 million yen, at rates ranging from 0.5 percent to 3 percent on that part of the net worth over 50 million yen. This combination, it was argued, would reduce the disincentive to investment and entrepreneurial labor.[7] The starting rate would be 20 percent on the first 50,000 yen. The 55 percent rate would apply to that part of one's income over 300,000 yen.

   b. The personal exemption to be increased from 15,000 yen to 24,000 yen, part of this increase being to absorb a recommended reduction in the earned-income credit, which was deemed to give too great a tax advantage to the wage or salary earner over the farmer or small businessman.

   c. The allowance for a dependent to be increased somewhat, and its form changed from a credit against tax to a deduction from income, on the grounds that the tax differential due to a dependent should increase with income (degree of progressivity desired is obtained by the rate schedule).

   d. Deduction to be allowed for medical expenses and loss of property due to accident or theft, to the extent that the total of such expenses and losses exceeds 10 percent of net income.

e. Capital gains to be included in full, instead of only 50 percent, under existing law, and capital losses to be allowed in full. The net gain or loss would be averaged forward over five years. Gains or losses resulting from a change in the price level of more than 15 percent would not be taken into account.

f. Other types of fluctuating income, e.g., royalties, also to be averaged forward. The income would be divided into, say, five equal parts, one part to be included in each of the next five years' incomes.

g. An extra 12,000 yen of personal exemption to be allowed to the blind and, possibly, to those with similarly severe physical disabilities.

h. An individual stockholder to be given a tax credit equal to 25 percent of dividends included in his return, to compensate, more or less, for the 35 percent corporation tax (see below).

i. Contrary to a proposal being urged in Japan at that time, no favorable tax treatment should be given to interest paid on bank deposits or other savings accounts.

j. Again contrary to proposals strongly urged, no special income tax treatment should be accorded foreign nationals working in Japan.[8]

Certain recommendations affecting both the personal income tax and the corporation income tax are noted under number 5 below.

4. The role of the corporate income tax to be decreased somewhat.

a. The excess profits tax, introduced in 1947, to be repealed, as impairing incentives unduly and being difficult to administer.

b. The corporation income tax rate to remain at 35 percent.

c. Withholding tax of 20 percent on dividends paid to be repealed.

d. A new tax to be levied annually on total retained earnings of a corporation, at 1 percent. This would represent roughly an interest charge on personal income tax deferred by retention of earnings in place of paying taxable dividends. The tax would apply only to earnings accumulated after July 1, 1949. A higher rate, perhaps 9 percent, would apply to family corporations.

e. Repeal the tax on corporations levied when they liquidate, and tax the accumulated surplus and the portion of capital representing capital gain by the shareholder at the shareholder level.

5. The taxation of business profits, whether arising in a corporation or an unincorporated enterprise, to be modified as follows:

a. All depreciable business assets, and land, to be revalued to current prices to allow adequate depreciation, or basis, for computing taxable income. A 6 percent tax to be imposed on this recorded increase in asset values, as a matter of equity vis à vis firms that had been taxed in the past on realized paper gains and holders of fixed money claims who could not deduct their real losses, due to inflation, for income tax purposes. (The price level had increased since 1940 by something between 100 and 200 times.)

b. Repeal the 66⅔ percent tax levied on inventory profits whenever official prices are increased under the Price Control Law, except as as the increase can be traced to removal of a price subsidy (see pp. 131–33 of 1949 report).

c. Allow a two-year carry-back of business loss and an unlimited carry-forward.

d. Allow certain other methods of inventory valuation in addition to the sole method then allowed, the weighted average method (average cost method).

e. Allow certain other depreciation methods in addition to the sole method then allowed, the declining balance method.

6. The existing estate and gift taxes to be replaced by a cumulative accessions tax on the recipient of gifts inter vivos and property passing at death, with a top rate of 90 percent applicable to amounts in excess of 50 million yen. An exclusion of 30,000 yen would be granted each year with respect to property passing from any one donor (this, for administrative reasons), and, in addition, each recipient (each taxpayer) would be given a 150,000-yen lifetime exemption. The tax mission report explained that this move would avoid many of the problems that were undermining the estate-gift tax in the United States, and would promote a wider distribution of gifts and bequests.

7. The government tobacco monopoly to be continued, not to be replaced by putting that industry in private hands and then taxing it. The mission did not have the time or resources to compare these alternatives carefully. As soon as further national tax reduction was possible, it should include some slight decrease in prices of tobacco products. The monopoly was obtaining a profit on low-price cigarettes equal to a tax of 200 percent on a retail price net of tax or

profit, and 600 percent on high-priced cigarettes. Such high implicit taxation was aimed partly at reducing tobacco production severely, not for health reasons (scarcely an issue in those days), but to increase land available for producing food. The resulting monopoly profit was very large: in the national budget for 1949–50 it was estimated at 120 billion yen, which was 15 percent of total national and local tax revenue ("tax revenue" includes these monopoly profits, unless otherwise noted).

8. The tax rates on liquor (i.e., alcoholic beverages) to be increased substantially. They had been reduced in May 1949 on the assumption that revenue would be increased but with better administration. But the report conjectured that the maximum revenue rates had not yet been reached. Existing rates were the equivalent of about 300 percent of the retail price ex-tax, more or less; there were nine rates, all specific, varying with the type of liquor. The report based its maximum-revenue rates proposal on the luxury nature of liquor consumption generally, apart from the rationed supply that was allowed, at the lower end of prices, to farmers and certain workers. A further rise in the national tax rates on liquor was recommended to take effect if, as the report urged, the 5 percent tax on liquor sales levied by municipalities were repealed. Finally, the national government should resume control of the wholesale distribution of liquor. The revenue from the national tax on liquor for 1949–50 was estimated at 65 billion yen, about half the yield from the tobacco monopoly.

9. The general sales tax, a turnover tax on all sales (cascade tax), to be repealed if the national government's expenditures were reduced as recommended, or contemplated, in the report's chapter 3. This 1 percent tax, introduced September 1, 1948, was opposed by the tax mission partly because it burdened the poor to some extent (although staple food and dwelling accommodation were exempt), but also because the rate could not be raised without causing serious economic disadvantages. Further, at the 1 percent rate it was not being taken seriously enough by either administrators or taxpayers. The estimated yield of this "transactions" tax for 1949–50 was only 45 billion yen. No other type of general sales tax was recommended for the national government. In particular, a retail sales tax was deemed infeasible, in view of the fragmentation of retail trade among small firms. The value-added tax recommended for prefectures is discussed below.

10. A set of manufacturer's excises, levied on a large number of specified

goods, to be retained, but the tax rates in the two highest-taxed groups (100 percent and 80 percent of the manufacturer's price) to be reduced to 70 percent and 60 percent. The 50, 30, and 20 percent rates were to be retained. The specific tax rates on five other commodities were to be retained, also. Goods used wholly or chiefly by business firms should be exempt. The yield of all these taxes was estimated for 1949–50 at only 27 billion yen. They were acceptable because virtually all of them fell upon luxury or semiluxury expenditures.

11. The textiles tax to be repealed, as an undue burden on clothing, one of the necessities of life. The tax, levied on producers of silk, rayon, woolen, cotton, and staple fiber goods, was 40 percent on silk, rayon, and woolen goods, and 10 percent on the other two. The luxury element in silk was offset by the special difficulty the silk producers were experiencing in their export markets.

12. As to other indirect taxes, the tax on sugar was to be repealed, the new gasoline tax to be retained. Customs duties to be reconsidered later (largely because at that time practically all imports were either from the United States as aid, or for occupation personnel, or by the Japanese government's Foreign Trade Fund). For lack of time to study them no recommendations on a firm basis were made regarding several other taxes, including the tax on soft drinks, the tax on transfer of securities, the tax on mah-jongg and other playing sets, and the stamp taxes on legal documents and the like. The inclination of the tax mission was, however, clearly to repeal these taxes, save the one on playing sets.

13. Several taxes were being imposed on payrolls, to help finance various parts of the social security program. The report made no fundamental recommendations on these taxes, partly because of a thorough report on the social security system had already been made by a mission that visited Japan in 1947. The report did recommend consolidation of the various payroll taxes in the hands of the ministry of finance, to be integrated with the withholding of income tax from wages. The report gave no data on tax yields or tax rates in this area.

14. The report had little to say about the revenue aspects of government monopolies on salt, camphor, and betting on horse races, all of which involved insignificant tax collections.

15. One of the main local taxes, the inhabitant's tax, shared by the prefectures and municipalities (cities, towns, and villages), to be based

more on income and less on other factors, including per capita and ranking (for description, see chapter 11 of the report), and to be reserved entirely for the municipalities. Corporations should be excluded from this tax. The municipalities would get about 60 billion yen a year from it, under the mission's recommendations, a substantial increase from the existing yield of some 25 billion yen, shared about equally between the two levels of government.

16. Expansion of the tax base was recommended for the real estate tax, which, despite its label ("land and house tax"), applied also to business real estate. The revenue from the tax was negligible because the annual rental values on which the tax rate was imposed were those of the prewar period, before the 100- to 200-fold inflation. To be sure, rentals were under severe rent control, but half or more of the real estate was used by its owners, domestic or business. The report recommended that this tax (a) be reserved for the municipalities and administered entirely by them, (b) be based on capital value, and (c) be expanded to include all assets of a business firm subject to a depreciation allowance under the national income tax. The tax rate for 1950–51 should be 1.75 percent of the newly appraised capital values. The yield of the tax was expected to be, under these reforms, about 50 billion yen, all to go to the municipalities, representing a gain of some 40 billion yen for them.

17. The local-enterprise tax to be replaced by a tax on value added of business firms, the tax revenue to go entirely to the prefectures instead of being split 50-50 between the prefectures and the municipalities. This tax was levied on business profits as reported for the national income tax, although in practice some sort of standard rate of profit was often assumed. The standard rate of tax varied from 15 percent to 22.5 percent, among the prefectures. Agriculture, livestock breeding, forestry, and fishing were taxed, generally, at two thirds the standard rate, and income from staple foods was exempt. The cumulative tax rates on business profits of an unincorporated enterprise could, considering the national income tax and the inhabitant's tax, rise to a total of 70 percent. The tax mission deemed this too high, and sought a lower rate for the enterprise tax, something between 4 and 8 percent, which would be possible under the broader base of value added. This, the only major recommendation of the report that was never put in force, is discussed in more detail in section IV (A, 1) below. The revenue from this new tax would be about the same as that from the existing tax.

18. The admissions tax rate to be reduced from 150 percent to 100 percent, and to a still lower level in some later year. The entire yield of about 14 billion yen should go to the prefectures instead of one third to prefectures and two thirds to municipalities, since such a tax is a very uneven source of revenue as among different types of municipality. The 150 percent rate was an unfair discrimination against this economic sector, and induced much evasion.

19. The real estate acquisition tax to be repealed, as hindering unduly the transfer of such properties to their most economically efficient uses, especially at the standard rate of 20 percent (10 percent on small houses). This tax, yielding about 12 billion yen, was shared equally between municipality and prefecture.

20. The tax on amusement, eating, and drinking establishments (20 percent up to 150 percent) to be retained, but the 12 billion yen of revenue to go all to the prefectures in place of being split equally with the municipalities.

21. The 5 percent local tax on retail sale of liquor (half to prefectures, half to municipalities) to be repealed, taxation of liquor to be concentrated at the national level. Another group of 14 minor local taxes to be retained (report, p. 209), and another group of 7 to be repealed (pp. 209–10).

22. Some 40 billion yen, apparently, was being raised by municipalities through so-called voluntary contributions, chiefly for building schoolhouses, police stations, and the like. These contributions were a source of difficulty and unfairness, and the tax mission indicated a hope that they would decline, perhaps vanish, as the system of regular municipal taxes was strengthened.

23. In general, as to local taxation, the following changes (implemented by the recommendations above) to be made: (a) total tax revenue raised by local taxes to increase from 150 billion yen to 190 billion yen, all this increase to go to municipalities; (b) the device of municipal surtaxes on prefectural taxes to be abandoned, each of the two local levels to have its own kinds of tax; (c) the taxes to be fewer, at higher rates, in place of the existing medley of taxes; and (d) the three major local taxes to be extensively revised, the yield of the inhabitant's tax to be more than doubled, and that of the real estate tax more than tripled (the enterprise tax yield would remain about as before).

24. The system of grants-in-aid by the national government to the local governments to be revised as follows:

(a) The total of 143 billion yen to be increased to 165 billion yen.

(b) Almost all of the 100 percent grants (total, 10 billion yen) to be abolished since the citizen is confused as to which level of government is responsible for the activity in question, there is undue control from the national level, and friction is created between national and local officials.

(c) The more than two hundred less-than-100-percent grants (e.g., the national government pays 50 percent of the salaries of teachers in local elementary schools) to be replaced by a general-purpose equalization grant. Those partial grants designed to induce localities to pioneer in new services or better methods would be retained.

(d) Grants for local public works to be retained (30 billion yen).

(e) The percentage share of the localities in the national personal and corporate income taxes' revenue (33 percent in 1948–49, and 17 percent in 1949–59) to be replaced by the general purpose equalization grant, to avoid undue annual fluctuations in the amount of the grant. In 1948–49 the amount was 58 billion yen.

(f) The equalization grant to be computed for each locality separately, to equal the difference between (i) what would be yielded by local taxes at certain standard rates and (ii) the minimum cost of providing necessary local services in the locality. This grant would be about 120 billion yen.

25. A Local Finance Commission to be established, to gather information and to decide certain matters that cannot be regulated closely by law. The existing Local Tax Deliberation Committee and Local Autonomy Agency were not representing local interests adequately. A temporary Commission on Local Government Organization should be formed to allocate particular governmental functions among the national, prefectural, and municipal governments.

D. Recommendations in the 1950 Report:
Conceptual and Substantive Issues

In this 1950 report, submitted almost exactly a year after the first report, attention was centered on the question of what kinds of tax reduction should be voted, in view of the prospective national budget surplus for 1951–52. These recommendations, although important for short-term policy at that time, are of limited interest for the present study and are not reproduced here.

The only important conceptual or substantive issues discussed in the 1950 report concerned the as yet unimplemented uniform rate value-added tax to replace the income-based enterprise tax for the prefectures levied at multiple rates depending on the type of business. The report concluded that firms should be allowed to deduct, in computing value added, depreciation on property owned by them when the tax took effect, as well as deducting the amounts spent subsequently, immediately upon expenditure, on capital equipment. Complaints had been heard that firms, including government-owned railroad firms that would be subject to the tax, that had undertaken capital expansion programs just before the tax was introduced would otherwise be at a disadvantage competitively. (This argument now seems to me not as justified as it appeared then, unless the firm in question had paid the now-to-be-repealed turnover tax on purchase of that plant and equipment.)

In addition, any firm that preferred to go to a depreciation basis permanently, instead of deducting the cost of capital equipment in the year of purchase, should be allowed to do so. It might prove difficult to get a prompt payment from the government on negative value-added, as would occur if such outlay were large enough. (At this time the distinction between the income type of value-added tax and the consumption type had not yet been formulated. [Shoup, 1969, p. 251–57])

The proposed tax rate schedule of 3, 4, 6, and 8 percent for various types of business should be replaced by a single tax rate. Government railroads should pay this tax.

The new equalization grant was also given a thorough study in the second report, and several recommendations were made for further improvement; these are not summarized here (see pp. 19–20 and 27–46 of this second report).

E. Recommendations on Tax Administration:
1949 and 1950 Reports

"We get the impression," said the 1949 report (p. 15), "that total tax revenue might increase anywhere from 25 percent to 100 percent, if all taxes were fully enforced according to the law as it now stands." Therefore, although "The details of administrative reform are . . . outside the scope of this report," (p. 16), issues of "Compliance, Enforcement, and Appeal under the Income Tax" (the title of the sixteen-page chapter 14) were addressed, and, indeed, the 1950 report went into some detail in discussing these problems under the local property and inhabitants tax and again, the income tax. Moreover, the description and analysis of each of the other taxes usually contained discussion and some recommendations on these administrative issues.

The major recommendations were:

1. An income taxpayer agreeing to keep books and records as specified by the tax administration would be distinguished by filing his return on a form of a distinct color (blue) and would thereupon not be subject to reassessment until after an actual field investigation; if a reassessment were made, the specific reasons for it would be given. Other inducements might be offered: depreciation deductions and loss carry-overs might be denied to those who failed to keep books (pp. D58–D59). The 1950 report (pp. 53–55) returned to this proposal briefly, urging that administrators not put obstacles in the way of using the "blue return" form. At that time, this form had been chosen by 47.2 percent of the taxpaying corporations, but only by 4.4 percent of individual taxpayers.

2. The general aim for income tax administration should be to eliminate, or reduce to a minimum, "the use of goals and quotas, the collective allocation of tax amounts among associations . . . the allocation by an association of a group amount among its members [and] any extreme reliance upon standards to measure income. . ." (p. D4). Under the goal system, in widespread use in Japan at that time, a tax collection goal was assigned to, or computed by, each tax office (a given tax office covered a specified geographical area). The total of the goals was the budget figure of expected income tax collections.

3. Estimated income tax payable under the current-payment system should be based on the previous year's tax as a minimum.

4. An income tax return should be held confidential, not open to inspection, as it was then, by anyone willing to pay a nominal fee.

5. The income tax on farm income should be based less on standards and more on the particular farmer's actual income, and payment should be adjusted to seasonal farm income patterns.[9]

6. Anonymous bank accounts presented a major problem in enforcement of tax administration. The mission urged that all bank deposits should be in the real name of the depositor, and all securities should be registered (e.g., no bearer bonds).

7. Litigation by the taxpayer, scarcely in use at that time, should be provided for, and the system of penalties for income tax violations should be recast and the large amount of income tax delinquency

should be reviewed. Moreover, the procedure for taxpayer protest of assessment should be reformed and the procedure for tax refunds should be reexamined.

8. The internal administration of the income tax should be further improved, with regard to basic structure, caliber of tax officials, operating instructions, administrative interpretation of tax laws, and office procedures.

9. "The participation of the trade association in tax activities must be ended . . ." (p. D60). At that time, "trade associations often enter into a system of 'collective bargaining' with the Tax Offices by which an overall tax figure is arrived at for the business activity represented by the association . . . . The association then allocates such tax figures among its members" (p. D60).

10. The "Tax Practitioner," the taxpayer's representative, should be required to know more tax law and accounting, not be merely a skilled negotiator, and tax materials (laws, etc.) should be more readily available to the public.

The second report (1950) returned to several of these issues, but without strikingly new recommendations.

F. Recommendations on "Tax Atmosphere":
1949 and 1950 Reports

The tax mission recommended that an informative tax atmosphere (that term was not used by the mission) be developed in Japan. This would include: encouragement of professional and technical journals containing qualified articles on technical tax matters; textbooks on substantive provisions of the tax laws; and promotion of forums on taxation, by bar associations, accounting organizations, university organizations, and the like, to promote informed discussions in the tax field (pp. D66–D67).

In addition, the mission emphasized the importance of courses in tax law as a distinct subject in law departments of universities; access to foreign literature on both substantive and administrative aspects of taxation; and the introduction of accounting in Japan as an independent profession (there were virtually no independent certified public accountants in Japan) (see pp. D50–D56 for detailed recommendations in the 1949 report, and pp. 78–80 in the 1950 report).

Implied in these recommendations was one "of an informal nature, not spelled out in the report but which is well on the way to fruition.

This is the formation of a national body, meeting at least once a year, publishing a journal and a volume of proceedings, composed of professors and other instructors in public finance in the colleges and universities, tax administrators of the central and local governments, tax officials of corporations, tax lawyers and accountants engaged in tax work . . . . A preliminary meeting of some thirty prominent Japanese interested in taxation was held in the middle of August [1949], and the idea seems to have been taken up with genuine enthusiasm . . . . In the long-run, I should not be surprised if this, the formation of a Japanese National Tax Association . . . should prove the most fruitful of all the suggestions made by our tax mission" (Shoup, "Tax Reform in Japan," 1950, p. 16).

IV. Degree of Implementation of the Tax Mission's Recommendations

A. Conceptual and Substantive Issues

Almost all of the more important conceptual and substantive recommendations in the report were implemented over the short run, in the year or two following publication. Over the longer run, however, to 1987, some of these measures were repealed or substantially altered. Moreover, some of the less important recommendations remained unimplemented both in the short and long run.

As to the interim period from 1949 or 1950 to 1987, a year-by-year tracing of the fate of the report's recommendations would be lengthy and somewhat tedious, and, for most years, difficult to compile. There are two interim years, however, for which a comparison with 1949 has been made. One, by Bronfenbrenner and Kogiku,[10] refers to 1956, and the other, by the Tax Bureau of the Japanese Ministry of Finance, to 1981 (see references).

1. *Short-Run Results.* In a letter dated September 15, 1949, General Douglas MacArthur told Japanese premier Shigeru Yoshida that he "hoped the Japanese government will be able to 'formulate an appropriate program for effectuating the broad principles and objectives set forth in Dr. Shoup's recommendations.'" *The Mainichi* reported that this letter "virtually assured quick passage by the Japanese Diet of the Shoup recommendations" (*The Mainichi*, September 18, 1949; see appendix A below for the full text of the MacArthur letter and of Yoshida's reply).

The report was presented, in summary form, at a press conference on August 26, 1949. Even before then there had been indications that the Japanese government was in a receptive mood, prepared to enact most if not all of the as yet undisclosed recommendations. This receptivity may have been due in part to the apparent approval by the government and the Japanese public of the research techniques used by the mission, especially the wide-ranging interviewing of taxpayers. Some second thoughts a little later were less favorable.[11]

The Japanese Diet did in fact quickly enact the report's recommendations. The only major exception was the value-added tax (VAT) proposed for the prefectures to replace the use of income as a tax base for the enterprise tax. This tax was enacted later, but its application was suspended, and it was never put in force. Rejection of the VAT was due to several factors. First, the basic concept of value-added tax was unfamiliar then, not only in Japan. In addition, there was perhaps fear of inter-prefectural disputes over transactions crossing boundary lines. Finally, Japanese officials and the public were less concerned about the cumulated burden of the three levels of income taxation.

2. *Long-Run Results.* The long-run results of the mission's work are cast in terms of a comparison of the tax law as it stands in 1987 with that in effect in 1949. Admittedly, the term "results" may be too strong in some instances; a conformity of a certain part of the present-day law with a recommendation of the report may be no more than a coincidence.

A tax-by-tax comparison is followed by an overview comparison of the tax system as a whole, 1987 versus 1949, with respect to total tax revenue and the division of that revenue between national and local taxes. For a detailed description and analysis of the present Japanese tax system, the reader is referred to Aoki (1985), Homma, Maeda, and Hashimoto (1986), and Ishi (forthcoming).

(a) Particular Tax Provisions. The income tax base and rate structure have, after nearly four decades, departed substantially from the report's recommendations. There are a number of exemptions, deductions, and tax credits for this or that type of income or use of income presumed to be socially important, in the individual income tax. The top rate is 60 percent (national tax). Homma, Maeda, and Hashimoto (1986, p.1), who give details of these measures, remark that "Japanese income taxes are riddled with special provisions, which produce major inequities and distort economic activity."

Moreover, individual income is now classified into ten categories. The treatment of deductions differs somewhat among these categories. Special tax rates apply to capital gains (there is no tax on gains from the sale of securities except for "continuous traders"). Only half of retirement income is taxable income. Until April 1988, up to 3 million yen of principal amount per taxpayer, interest was in general exempt; however, interest and distributions accruing in an anonymous bank account were taxed at a flat rate of 35 percent.[12] And there are still more complexities in the individual income tax. Perhaps all these special rules and preferences help explain why the bulk of the Japanese individual income tax revenue comes from tax withheld at source.

Contrary to the mission's proposals, the present corporation income tax, too, now provides a number of tax preferences, including accelerated depreciation and tax-free reserves.

With respect to integration of the corporation income tax and the individual income tax, the present system appears to adopt the philosophy, if not the exact technique, of the report. Homma et al. (1986, p. 16) report that "In Japanese tax law, the corporation income tax is regarded as an advance payment of the individual income tax. A dividends-received credit is provided at the individual level and a dividends-paid deduction is provided at the corporate level, the former eliminating three quarters and the latter one quarter of the double taxation of distributed profits."

The wave of income tax reform proposals in Japan in 1987 and 1988 seems to be based largely on a desire to eliminate many of the tax preferences and to reduce the tax rates. The immediate stimulus for this kind of reform may have been the example set by the United States in 1986. The reform proposals also accord with the views set forth in the tax mission report, and in this sense we may say that Japan is perhaps on the road back to the type of income tax envisaged by the report. On the other hand, the government's proposal to introduce a value-added tax for the national government, a proposal rejected by popular protest, did not accord with the report, which advocated only a low-rate VAT for prefectural use in place of the prefectural income tax. Further discussion and appraisal of current tax reform proposals in Japan may be found in Aoki (1987) and Homma et al. (1986), and, from an American point of view, Teuber (1986).

The tax on retained profits of corporations, recommended at 1 percent by the tax mission report, but enacted at 2 percent, was repealed in 1952 except for family corporations. This was done "in view of the important role of profit retention in business financing."[13]

Capital gains and losses from the sale of securities were removed from the income tax base in 1953, because "the taxation of capital gains allegedly hampered the development of the securities market" and "technically the tax on such gains was found difficult to properly assess and collect."[14]

The net-worth tax was abolished in 1953 because it "proved inequitable because real property owners whose net worth is easily identified bore the full brunt while others escaped to some extent."[15]

The accessions tax (termed "inheritance tax" in the *Outline*) was revised in 1958. The tax had proved "unsatisfactory because the tax amount due varied depending on the method of dividing estates and taxpayers often made false reports as to shares received by heirs. In 1958, a revision was made so as to calculate the tax on the basis of the statutory shares of estates provided under the Civil Code."[16] The total tax to be paid by heirs and legatees is now computed by assuming the statutory heirs inherit property in accordance with the Code provisions, and this total tax is then allocated to each heir in proportion to his actual share. The rate schedule runs from 10 percent on the first 2 million yen (after deductions and credit) to 75 percent on the excess over 500 million yen. A separate gift tax, on properties acquired by gift over a lifetime, is levied by a rate schedule ranging from 10 percent on the first 500,000 yen to 75 percent on the amount in excess of 70 million yen.

Before moving on to the indirect taxes, we may ask, did the income tax in fact become the mainstay of the entire tax system, as the report hoped it would? Comparing 1949 revenue data with those for 1986,[17] we find that, somewhat surprisingly, the share of the individual income tax of the national government in total national and local tax revenue declined sharply, from 36 percent to 26 percent. That of the corporation income tax, however, rose from 8 percent to 19 percent. Finally, the share of the inhabitants tax, which is based largely on income, rose from 3 percent to 15 percent. All three income taxes together, therefore, raised 47 percent of total tax revenue in 1948 and 60 percent in 1986. But the rise of the corporation tax share and decline of the individual income tax share were directly contrary to what the report evidently favored; it seemed to regard the corporation income tax as a sort of necessary evil.

The decrease in the share of the individual income tax was caused chiefly by yearly increases in the personal exemptions and by new tax preferences rather than by reduction in the general rate schedule. Most

of the decline occurred in the period 1961–75 (Ishi, 1983). It was motivated largely by a desire to compensate for "bracket creep" under
inflation, but in fact did more than that (Ishi 1983, p. 27) and was made
possible by budgetary surpluses, which, however, turned into deficits in
the years following the "oil shock." The tax preferences, on the other
hand, were designed chiefly to increase personal saving. Ishi concludes
that they had a minor, if any, effect in increasing saving, compared with
other forces (Ishi 1983, p. 36). For the opposite conclusion, see Nakatani
(1986, p. 126). In 1984 the individual income tax was reduced for the
first time since 1977, chiefly by an increase in personal exemptions,
and the corporation income tax was increased, along with the liquor
tax. Certain other taxes were also increased (Miura 1984).

These data do not include contributions paid to the social security
funds, which are generally not counted as taxes in Japanese tabulations.
They are much more important now than they were in 1949–50. If they
are included in income taxes, the increase in income tax share since
1949 becomes considerably larger. Aoki (1987, p. 437) shows the following shares in total national and local tax revenue in Japan in 1982:
income and profits taxes, 45.0 percent (individual, 25.3 percent; corporation, 19.7 percent); social security taxes, 30.4 percent; property taxes,
8.9 percent; taxes on goods and services, 15.4 percent; other taxes, 0.3
percent. For a description and analysis of old-age social security in
Japan, see Murayama (1978).

We turn now to particular indirect taxes.

In April 1985 the government tobacco monopoly was replaced by ordinary companies and an excise tax was imposed on their output. The tax
rates were set so that the burden on each kind of tobacco product
remains basically the same as was previously reflected in the former
charge on the monopoly.

As to the taxes on alcoholic beverages, it is not clear from the data at
hand whether the tax rates have been changed substantially in real
terms from 1949 levels, since the changes in the specific rates must be
compared with changes in the selling prices, and the ad valorem rates
are imposed only on certain high-priced alcohols.[18]

The commodities tax now includes, besides the excises on certain
manufactured products, a 15 percent tax on the retail sales of certain
jewelry and furs, and a 10 percent tax on carpets. The maximum tax
rate under the excises is only 30 percent; the reduction of high rates has
thus gone even beyond the report's recommendations.[19]

Among the other taxes concerning particular products, that on textiles has apparently been repealed, as recommended.[20] The sugar excise tax, however, has not been repealed.[21] The gasoline tax has been retained.[22] The rest of these taxes, which the report was inclined to oppose, are still being levied except, it appears, the tax on soft drinks.[23]

As to the local taxes, the inhabitants tax has apparently not been wholly reformed as suggested in the report. It still contains a per capita element, though a small one for individuals, and is still imposed by both prefectures and municipalities. Corporations are still included.[24]

The real estate tax, in contrast, remains today the same as it was following the changes made shortly after the report was issued, to conform with the changes there suggested. The tax base has been broadened, it is levied on capital values, and is reserved to the municipalities.[25]

The enterprise tax—the local income tax on profits—is now reserved to the prefectures, as the report recommended, but its base has not been changed to value added.[26] The admissions tax rate has been reduced to a level even lower than the report implied, to 10 percent.[27]

The real estate acquisition tax has been retained, contrary to the report's recommendations. The other minor local taxes are not covered here. Apparently the custom of "voluntary" contributions has been discontinued.[28]

The rule of distributing a portion of grants money to localities according to need has been accepted to a degree, but the total amount of such grants is still linked to the yields of certain national taxes.[29]

In general, the report's recommendations as to local finance have been followed in some important instances, especially as to the real property tax and the use of a need index for distributing some grants-in-aid, but not, in others, notably for the enterprise tax.

(b) Size of tax system. In the almost four decades that have elapsed since 1949, total tax revenue in Japan, excluding social security premiums, has increased only moderately as a percentage of national income. But at the same time, national defense expenditures have, at only 1.3 percent of national income in 1986, remained low relative to the United States (6.1 percent of GNP). In 1949 national, prefectural, and municipal tax revenues came to about 20 percent of national income. At that time, national income data were fragmentary, and the total was but an educated guess. Using that guess, one obtained a percentage of 26, but since the national income seemed almost surely higher than that estimate (report, pp. 4–8), a figure of 20 percent was probably nearer the truth. A recent estimate for 1950 is 22 percent.

Although the estimated figure for 1986 is 25 percent,[30] the highest in the 37-year period, this level was reached by a series of yearly increases that began in 1978; in 1977 only 18.9 percent of the national income was taken in taxes. If, however, social security premiums are included in the tax total, that total, as a percentage of national income, rises from 25 percent to about 36 percent.

(c) National versus local tax totals. The share of local taxes (prefectural plus municipal taxes) in total tax revenue has doubled. It was 19 percent in 1949 and is now (1986) 37 percent. In general, this accords with the recommendation of the report (p. 35).

Of the three important local taxes, the inhabitants tax, based on individual incomes, accounted for two thirds of this increase in the local share. In 1949 it accounted for only 3 percent of total tax revenue; by 1986 this had risen to 15 percent. Hence this one tax contributed twelve percentage points to the eighteen-point total increase in local share. The tax on real property, greatly strengthened, contributing only 2 percent in 1949, accounted for 8 percent in 1986. The enterprise tax, wholly prefectural, and based on business profits, did not increase in share at all; in 1986, as in 1949, it accounted for 6 percent of total tax revenue.

Despite these substantial changes in the roles of two of the three chief local taxes, and despite the great increase in share of local tax revenue to total tax revenue, the relative importance of the prefectures and the municipalities with respect to each other was almost unchanged. In the earlier period the prefectures collected 47 percent of total local tax revenue; in 1986, 43 percent. Thus the report's recommendation that the municipalities notably increase their share in total local taxes (p. 23) has not been adopted. However, the large increase in the local tax share has been achieved by substantial increases in the two major local taxes that the report was inclined to favor: the inhabitants tax and the real property tax. But, the recommendation that the municipalities be given sole use of the inhabitants tax has not been adopted; they now get only 69 percent of the total revenue from that tax. On the other hand, the recommendation that only the municipalities should use the real property tax and that only the prefectures should use the enterprise tax is reflected in the present system (see *Outline*, pp. 306–7).

In terms of direct expenditures, local government in Japan is almost twice as large as the national government. This is because the latter transfers important amounts to the local units in the form of various grants, to be spent by the prefectures and municipalities: "the huge size of local public finance has a strong influence on national economy" (Japan, Ministry of Home Affairs, p. 110).

To be sure, there is still "strong administrative and financial control [over local governments] by the national government" (Shindo, 1982, p. 132), so that, in a sense, the almost two-to-one ratio just noted exaggerates actual local influence. The duties of the governor of the Tokyo Metropolitan Government, for example, despite the fact that he is elected by the residents, includes acting "as an agency of the central government." His execution of certain functions is "under the instruction and supervision of the competent [national] minister and is outside of the scope of the vote of the Metropolitan Assembly" (Nomura, vice governor of the Tokyo Metropolitan Government, 1982, pp. 141–42).

B. Tax Administration

1. All the report's recommendations as to the special blue return system advocated by the mission were adopted in 1950, except that which called for denial of deduction for depreciation if the blue return was not used.[31] In general, the blue return has flourished. By 1970, 48 percent of individuals whose main income consisted of business income and real estate income, excluding agricultural and forestry income, were filing such returns, and by 1979, 53 percent (Fukuda, 1981–82). In 1984, for a somewhat narrower group of individuals (excluding not only farming and forestry but also professions) the percentage was 51. Of all 7.1 million individual taxable returns (including those ineligible to file blue returns), 2.1 million (30 percent) used the blue return. As to corporations, the 47 percent of 1950 rose to more than 90 percent by 1979, and in 1984 was just 90. Sometime after 1949, Blue Return Taxpayers' Association was formed. By 1981, about 40 percent of blue-return filers were members of this association.

Evidently, the blue return, instead of being an intermediate kind of return, between the simplest form and the standard form for large enterprises with sophisticated accounting methods, has become a standard form, the only other type of form being the "white return," which is used only by the smallest taxpayers, including, supposedly, some small corporations. In a sense, then, the blue return may have outlived its usefulness, and, indeed, in 1981 the tax administration was considering asking for repeal of the blue-return system, perhaps on an assumption that it had accomplished its main task, i.e., bringing most taxpayers up to a reasonably sophisticated regime of bookkeeping.[32]

In 1984, the keeping of books became a requirement rather than a reward, for all corporations and for those individual business firms with income of more than 3 million yen, but the level of bookkeeping required is much simpler than that demanded of the blue-return taxpayer.

2. The goal system for tax collectors was abolished in 1950, except that, for some years, it was retained in allocating among district tax offices the amount of reduction of delinquent taxes.

3. A requirement that estimated income tax be based on the previous year's tax as a minimum was adopted in 1950; the district tax office could grant permission to pay less, upon a proper showing. Subsequently this estimated tax requirement was modified somewhat. It now applies to any taxpayer with estimated tax of 150,000 yen or more on permanent, ordinary income.

4. Income tax returns were made confidential except that each district tax office posts the names of individuals whose tax (until a few years ago, whose income) exceeds a certain amount: currently, 10 million yen of tax. Similarly posted are the names of corporations with more than 40 million yen of net income.[33]

5. A quote from Professor Kaneko (1985) illustrates continuing difficulty in taxation of farmers' incomes:

> Before the recommendation [of the tax mission report], a farmer's income was assessed by an estimate using the area of farmland as the standard. After the recommendation, the practice was changed to use gross sales as the standard, a method closer to the actual income. (Since farmers were required to sell all the rice and wheat products to their cooperatives, semi-official bodies, it was possible to check how much their gross sales were. Imputed sales—their own consumption—could be estimated by the number in each family.) However, it is extremely difficult to assess their actual income (nowadays they produce various things other than rice and wheat), and the blue return farmers are not many. Therefore, taxation by standard is still the ordinary and usual pattern. Nowadays, the standard of compliance of farmers is severely criticized by many people, and the tax authorities have been trying to improve the situation.[34]

6. The recommendation that all bank deposits should be in the real names of the depositors (rather than held anonymously, as was common) was not adopted, owing to strong objection from the business community, especially banks and other financial institutions, as well as the business section of SCAP (the occupation forces). In 1986 a small step was taken: the real name was required of any holder of a savings account entitled to tax-exempt interest.[35] The recommendation that all securities be registered, i.e., no bearer securities, was never accepted, also owing to opposition from financial institutions.

7. The procedure whereby the taxpayer can protest an assessment has been changed somewhat, as recommended in the report. Appeals from the district director now go to a national tax tribunal, established in 1970 as a quasi-independent organ of the National Tax Administration Agency. After appeal to the tribunal, the taxpayer can go to the ordinary courts. Professor Kaneko remarks, however, that, "Compared to American taxpayers, Japanese taxpayers are timid in suing tax authorities. Nevertheless, about 300 new suits are brought to courts by taxpayers each year. Among all suits against Government agencies, the number of tax suits exceeds the number of suits in any other field."[36]

8. Criminal penalties for tax evasion were strengthened somewhat. "However, sentence of imprisonment in tax cases is rare in Japan. Though in exceptional cases sentence of imprisonment is given,[37] it is usually suspended" (Kaneko, p. 4). The report's recommendations regarding penalties for failure to file on time or filing a deficient return or late payment of withheld tax were, on the whole, adopted, as were those concerning fraud. The excessive rates imposed for tax delinquency were reduced. Still, several years were required to reduce the large amount of income tax delinquency to a normal level.

9. No change was made in the procedures for tax refunds, although refunds presumably increased under adoption of a carry-back of business losses.

10. Substantial progress was made in improving the internal administration of the income tax. Professor Kaneko reports that:[38]

> (a) To improve tax administration according to the recommendation, funds have been generously allocated to the National Tax Administration Agency in the National Budget since 1950, and its administration was improved in every respect, although the basic structure of the National Tax Administration Agency was unchanged, except that the Collection Department was newly

established, replacing the former collection division in the General Department in order to strengthen the collection of delinquent taxes.

(b) To improve the calibre of tax officials, education at the Tax College was very much improved.

(c) Concerning operating instructions, various manuals were made to harmonize the tax administration of all the regions.

(d) Concerning administrative interpretation of the tax law, many detailed regulations and rulings were issued for each statute of tax law.

(e) Concerning office procedures, it became the policy of the National Tax Administration Agency after the recommendation to improve and strengthen the self-assessment system by encouraging the tax officers to avoid arbitrary assessment, to contact and assist taxpayers before the filing of a return, to encourage them to make an accurate return, and to encourage them to make an amended return when a deficiency was found (instead of making a deficiency assessment).

11. Participation of trade associations in tax matters was completely abolished. Also, important progress has been made regarding taxpayer representatives. The system was changed to one of "tax accountants" by the Tax Accountants Act of 1951. Professor Kaneko[39] reports that "To be a tax accountant, one should pass the national examination, which is rather difficult. Applicants should take exams in three fields of tax law (as, individual income tax law, corporate income tax law, and inheritance tax law) from the seven enumerated fields of tax law, and exams of bookkeeping and financial statements from the field of accounting. To practice, they should register with the Federation of Tax Accountants Associations. Discipline is maintained by the National Tax Administration Agency. There are now about 50,000 tax accountants. The scope of their activities is (1) representation for tax matters, (2) making tax forms and documents, and (3) consulting on tax matters. Only qualified tax accountants can practice these activities."

12. Finally, "Tax materials—law, administrative regulations and rulings, etc.—are all readily available to the public. These materials are published by many publishers (law, cabinet orders and ministerial orders are also published in the Official Gazette)." (Kaneko, letter to Shoup).

On the whole, the report's administrative recommendations were adopted, with the important exceptions of provisions on proper identification of all bank accounts and bearer securities. Some observers, e.g., Jason James (1987), consider the failure to require all bank accounts to be in the real names of depositors and the failure to abolish bearer shares as critical. In his view, this constituted a fundamental rejection of the report's administrative recommendations.

Despite improvements in tax administration, the individual income tax remains plagued, it would appear, by great differences in compliance among three groups of taxpayers: employees, non-farm self-employed, and farmers. A popularly received opinion is embodied in the phrase "ku-ro-yon," or "nine-six-four," which implies that while 90 percent of income that should be taxed is in fact taxed, as to employees (chiefly through withholding), that percent is only 60 as to the non-farm self-employed, and only 40 as to farmers. Ishi, testing this popular hypothesis, has concluded that "the 'ku-ro-yon' ratio does indeed seem to be approximated by these statistical procedures, although the results are far from satisfactory." He attributes these gaps both to outright evasion and to avoidance (1984, p. 22). Unless these gaps can be closed, it may prove quite difficult politically to call on the individual income tax to help reduce Japan's budget deficit appreciably.[40]

C. Tax Atmosphere

Some of the suggestions made in the 1949 and 1950 reports for improving the tax "atmosphere" in Japan have been accepted and vigorously developed.

The Japan Tax Association (Nippon Sozei Kenkyu Kyokai, or literally, the Japan Tax Research Association), was founded as a direct result of the tax mission's informal suggestion on this score in 1949. With the aid of some of the mission members, the association has developed into a substantial research and discussion organization. In an English-language brochure published in August 1982[41] the association notes that it "was established in 1949 by leading business men, scholars and government officials," to "research Public Finance Policy, Tax Policy and Tax Administration" and "make proposals and recommendations," as well as to "exchange information among the members and publish some results of its research works .... Since establishment, we have published a great number of reports ... of our research works."

The membership of the association appears to be somewhat more heavily weighted by representatives of the business world and the legal and accounting professions, and less by government tax officials and academics than its counterpart in the United States, the National Tax

Association.[42] The association is said to keep some distance between itself and the government by refusing to receive government subsidies and by never electing a current or former government employee to its presidency. The association meets annually, and publishes a volume of proceedings of each meeting, and also a monthly journal, *Tax Studies — Research on Fiscal Policies and Tax Problems* (*Sozei Kenkyu—Zaisei Sozei Mondai no Kenkyu Chosa*). It also publishes various ad hoc reports concerning, mainly, current and proposed tax legislation.

The nationwide trade association of tax consultants ("tax accountants" noted above) contains a section, the Japan Tax Matters Research Center (*Nippon Zeimu Kenkyu Center*) that publishes a journal, *T. R.* (*Zei Ken*), the initials for "Tax Research." A separate group, The Japan Tax Law Association (*Nippon Zeiho Gakkai*), has a membership consisting mainly of registered tax consultants. It publishes a journal, *Tax Law*.

The Tax Law Association (*Sozeiho Gakkai*), to be distinguished from the Japan Tax Law Association, is composed of mainly academic lawyers. It publishes an academic journal, "Tax Law Studies" (*Sozeiho Kenkyu*). Tax law professorships, recommended by the tax mission report, were instituted initially in Tokyo and Kyoto Universities. They were gradually increased until today they are found in five major national universities, out of a total of nine such universities (the successors of the former imperial universities), and in some thirty private universities. Certain of the junior colleges have professorships in tax accounting.

In general, then, it appears that the tax atmosphere in Japan has changed, since 1949, along lines suggested by the report, and is very different from that of the years before 1949, when tax policy and tax technique were hardly matters for public debate at all.

V. Some General Appraisals of the Tax Mission's Report

We turn now to some general appraisals of the tax mission's report, and to opinions as to whether the existing Japanese tax system is truly based, still, on that report, or at least coincides, except in some details, with the system recommended.[43]

The selection to follow is biased in that it includes only comments written in English or translated from the Japanese by English-writing commentators. It therefore provides a list of certain points to be considered rather than a balanced view of the report as seen by Japanese commentators.

1. Bronfenbrenner and Kogiku. In 1956 Martin Bronfenbrenner and his research assistant, Kiichiro Kogiku,[44] in two articles in the *National Tax Journal* appraised the tax mission's program as "only a limited and partial success" (p. 237), in terms of enactment, partly because it "included several novel fiscal experiments, which the Mission suggested for Japan without benefit of large-scale experience in other countries . . . [especially] the net worth tax; the accessions tax, and the value-added tax" (p. 240). (Here, they are partly incorrect: the net worth tax had a long and successful experience in several European countries.) Bronfenbrenner and Kogiku (hereafter, B-K) concluded that "through 1956 the Japanese national tax system retained the essential features of what one newspaper called the 'patched and tattered' Shoup plan, while the local tax system had departed further from the Shoup framework." B-K cite "Influential Leftist attacks on the Shoup Mission" (p. 241).

Of particular importance, in the present writer's view, is the comment by B-K that "The downward trend in self-assessed income tax receipts" gives "grounds to fear that it reflects . . . some deterioration of enforcement, so that the Japanese [personal] income tax may become in time little more than a disguised payroll tax . . . in the sense of hitting primarily wage and salary earners, while leaving the rest of the population relatively untouched" (p. 243).

B-K state that the 6 percent tax on book gains from revaluation of assets was repealed, but do not give the date (p. 244). They also state that "The Equalization Grant is gone; national grants to local units are largely ad hoc and have the traditional strings attached" (p. 245).

In the second article, Bronfenbrenner and Kogiku examine what in their view were the causal factors—political, economic, and social —that explain "the Japanese modifications of the Shoup tax system."

The report's "details never achieved the full support of the Japanese Government, the Japanese Opposition parties, or the Japanese administrative bureaucracy. Even the report's 'honeymoon period' (Autumn 1949) combined acclamation in the large with obstruction in the small" (p. 345).

"Keiichiro Hirata, who worked closely with the Mission . . . expressed what probably was the bureaucracy position in two separate volumes [cited]. He described the Shoup tax system as theoretically ideal, and possibly applicable to some future Japan with more highly developed capitalism, higher national income, and greater tax-consciousness, but poorly adapted to the Japan of 1949–50" (pp. 345–46).

"Perhaps because of the lukewarm enthusiasm for the *Shoup Report* shared by the Japanese Government and its higher bureaucracy, the Japanese tax administration never developed enough technicians adequately trained to administer the more novel and complex features of the system" (p. 346).

"Bills were drawn up, introduced, and in some cases passed on an overly aggressive basis, i.e., without sufficient attention to the special problems of the special interest groups affected most drastically by the Shoup program" (p. 347).

"On the economic side, the Shoup Mission's greatest handicap was in having been oversold. The Japanese expected a miracle man who could cut their taxes and prices simultaneously, and Shoup disappointed them" (p. 349).

The report challenged "the Japanese view that they were overtaxed," since tax-to-national-income ratios were not large compared with the United States and Great Britain. "This was anathema to the Japanese," who insisted that the comparison take into account official exchange rates, point to personal exemption levels, specify some prewar standard period, and be based on "supernumerary" income (p. 350).

Bronfenbrenner and Kogiku also ask "What might SCAP and the Shoup group have done or avoided doing to increase the long-term fruitfulness of the Shoup Mission? Four main groups of possibilities suggest themselves to the authors:

> 1. The Mission should have been summoned earlier, before deterioration of relations between SCAP and the Japanese had set in . . . .
>
> 2. Seven Supermen could not draw up in five months a document of the length and scope of the *Shoup Report* without some technical defects . . . .
>
> 3. . . . had time permitted, the *Shoup Report* might have been more palatable if presented in the form of *alternatives* among which the Japanese themselves might choose (perhaps within limits).
>
> 4. . . . the jurisdiction of the Mission should have included some over-all aggregative recommendations on the expenditure side. . . . The Mission might also have been permitted representation in policy decisions on money, credit and debt matters . . ." (pp. 359–60).

Bronfenbrenner and Kogiku offered a number of other judgments pertaining to the mission report. These are as follows:

1. Low marks must be assigned the Shoup Mission's efforts at inculcating tax-consciousness among the Japanese prefectures and municipalities. Herein lies an important economic reason for the submersion of the Shoup system of local finance in a sea of red ink (pp. 351–52).

2. . . . certain technical shortcomings of the Shoup system may explain why the increase in local tax-consciousness was somewhat disappointing (p. 353).

3. Passing on to fiscal sociology, the Shoup system's limited ability to improve taxpayer morale in connection with self-assessment might well have been forecast (p. 355). "The Mission may have yielded too much to rationalist predilections in overestimating the strength of logical argument in tax matters as against certain ingrown Japanese popular attitudes . . . . We may cite three folk prejudices with which the *Shoup Report* collided . . . . Both Japanese and Chinese have tended traditionally to prefer indirect over direct taxation because they associate direct taxation with inquisitorial methods of enforcement and with tyrannical government generally . . . . In Japanese history, periods of local independence have seen periods of lawlessness and civil war . . . the undivided family is felt by many Japanese to exercise a real function in reducing fragmentation of landholdings and . . . in assuring support for family members . . . . The accession principle in succession taxation flies in the face of this feeling . . . (pp. 356–57).

4. The ultimately damning ideological handicaps which the Shoup tax system never overcame were its American origin and the lateness of its imposition in Japan . . . . Had the Shoup Mission been summoned and submitted essentially its same plan in 1946 or even as late as 1948, a greater proportion of that plan would almost certainly have endured as well [as did earlier reform programs in the occupation] (pp. 357–58).

5. Three things had happened by 1949 to end the era of good feeling. The Occupation had overstayed its welcome . . . . It had also changed its primary function (without consulting the Japanese) from mopping up Fascism to holding back Communism . . . . Finally, the Japanese themselves had turned a corner economically . . ." (p. 358).

2. *The James Critique.* In a master's dissertation at King's College, Cambridge University, completed in 1987 and entitled *Japanese Tax Policy in the Wake of the Shoup Mission*, Jason C. James examines the changes in the Japanese tax system during the seven years following publication of the 1949 report. Only the mission's recommendations for the tax law are covered; James excludes from his study the recommendations on tax administration and tax education (tax atmosphere), though noting that in the latter two fields "The achievements of the Reports [1949 and 1950] . . . should not be underestimated" (p. 1).

Although James limits the time frame of his study to the period 1949–56, some of his conclusions seem to refer to 1987:

> . . . the reforms enacted following the . . . 1949 . . . Report are often held to constitute the basis of the present [*sic*] Japanese tax system. The present study aims to show that this is so only in a very limited sense . . . . I aim to show that . . . hardly any of what one may call the Report's 'strategic objectives' in the field of law were fulfilled in the longer term [1956? 1987?] . . . . By showing that almost all the major objectives of the Shoup Missions were dropped during this period, and that the structure envisaged by the Missions for most of the major taxes was lost, I intend to demonstrate that the effect of the Shoup Missions on the Japanese tax system in the long run was not great (pp. 1–2).

In his concluding section, James observes:

> The discussion above of the main aims of the Shoup Report and of how its recommendations fared in the next five years reached the following conclusions:
>
> The two criteria on which the recommendations were based, namely equity and simplicity, were both subordinated to another criterion which the Report did not recognize, namely, the achievement of a higher than market rate of economic growth.
>
> Turning to what I have defined as the broad objectives of the Mission, namely (i) the creation of a permanent tax system for Japan, (ii) increased local fiscal autonomy, and (iii) an increase in the proportion of direct relative to indirect taxation, the results were mostly negative. Looking at (i), it is of course easy to demonstrate that the Shoup system was altered afterwards, but not so simple to answer the question whether these alterations were significant in terms of the system itself, or just adjustments which

left the fundamental system unaltered. In view of the effect which the alterations had on the objectives of the Mission, I conclude that the Mission did not create a permanent tax system. I have described above how the Mission failed in its quest for greater local fiscal autonomy (ii). Objective (iii) was achieved in the long-term (although the results were not particularly visible in the time-period I have been discussing), but not in the way that the Mission had in mind. The subsidiary objective of making the income tax "the mainstay of the fiscal system" was not achieved.

The recommendations for the structure of the main taxes met with mixed results. Among the national direct taxes, which the Mission wanted to see raising the bulk of national tax revenue, the Individual Income Tax soon lost the structure envisaged by the Mission, returning to higher top rates and no Net Worth Tax, and moving back towards a schedular rather than a unified treatment. The Corporate Income Tax did not move so far away from the Mission's recommendation but the fundamental principle that corporations should be taxed according to the 'legal fiction' view was dropped, and many special provisions of which the report would not have approved were added to the corporate tax law. The procedure for asset revaluation, however, which affected several other areas of the tax law apart from this one, can be said to have been the greatest success among the Mission's recommendations. It was only an on-off operation rather than a part of the tax system, but it achieved its aims and was carried out more or less according to plan. The Estate and Gift Taxes survived in roughly the form envisaged by the Mission during the time period under consideration (although they reverted to the old format in 1958).

Among the National Indirect Taxes, the proposed increase in the proportion of revenue raised from the liquor tax and reduction of the proportion raised by the tobacco monopoly were never carried out. The Transactions Tax was, however, repealed as recommended.

The Shoup system of local finance never really got started. The biggest blow to it was the abolition of the Equalization Grant in 1954, but the system was already severely endangered by the fact that the Enterprise Tax was never imposed on a value-added basis as recommended, thus depriving local governments of 18 billion yen in the very first year after the Report was published. The recommended, relatively minor, alterations to the Inhabitant's Tax and Real Estate Tax were, however, carried out.

I conclude therefore that while a great number of the detailed suggestions contained in the Report were implemented, it did not have a great impact on the Japanese tax system in the longer term. It is going too far, though, to conclude that consequently the Report was a failure. It was asked to provide detailed recommendations for the Japanese tax system and this it did. The blame, if any, for failure to incorporate the recommendations into Japan's tax system lies not with the Mission but with the Japanese political process.

James's evaluations are to be taken seriously, especially his analysis of why the outcome was as it was; his facility in the Japanese language has enabled him to tap sources not accessible to the present writer.

James's general conclusions rest, however, on a scale of implicit weights that he gives to the several recommendations that differs from my own. I attach great importance, for example, to repeal of the turnover tax without replacement by any general sales tax at the national level, to repeal of the excess profits tax, to strengthening of the local real estate tax, and to the provisions for revaluation of assets. James seems to view the first two rather casually, and, while agreeing that the last two were important, weighs them lightly compared with certain income tax provisions adopted, or not repealed, in 1950–56 that went counter to the report's recommendations or philosophy.

James also identifies two other recommendations which seem to him to have been discarded out of hand. They were the abolition of anonymous accounts and the recordkeeping requirement for wealthy individuals.[45]

The former was passed as a Ministry of Finance Ordinance in 1950, but was repealed in 1951 without ever being enforced. The latter was never included in the Tax Bill as passed by the Diet. These omissions were particularly unfortunate since they made effective enforcement of the Net Worth Tax, Individual Income Tax and taxes on capital gains (treated on the same footing as ordinary income under the recommendations) impossible and thus undermined the whole logic of the Shoup system of individual and corporate income taxation. Shoup was well aware of the implications of anonymous accounts in particular and denounced them in no uncertain terms.[46] The explanation for this serious omission from the reform programme as passed into law can be found in Bronfenbrenner & Kogiku.[47] In the deflationary environment of 1949–50, there was thought to be the possibility of a banking and securities crash if enforcement of rules on anonymous accounts caused large withdrawals. SCAP was too easily convinced of this danger by the fact that it was in any case trying to encourage expansion (and thus democratization) of the securities markets. If there had really been a will to enact these record-keeping requirements into law, then the boom from the latter part of 1950 caused by the outbreak of the Korean War, when there was no likelihood of a stock market or banking crash, would have been the perfect opportunity. That resistance to such a law is well entrenched in Japan, however, is demonstrated by the fact that nearly forty years later this nettle has still to be grasped (pp. 12–13).

Other measures that ran counter to the report's recommendations or philosophy had to do with equity, simplicity, and the corporation income tax (James, pp. 14–15):

[*Equity*] The principle of equity, which the Report insisted on as being of paramount importance, was gradually subordinated to other concerns by Japanese policy-makers. Once equity in enforcement had been dealt a serious blow by the discarding of the Mission's recommendation on anonymous bank accounts, etc., the case for equity in the law itself was severely weakened. The law began to discriminate between different forms of income for a mixture of two reasons: (i) that taxation of certain types of income was particularly difficult to administer, so in these cases, taxation should be at lower rates to encourage compliance, and (ii) that certain activities (e.g. saving, investing in certain types of equipment, exporting) should be encouraged by favorable tax treatment.

[*Simplicity*] "The simplicity of the tax system was somewhat impaired by alterations between 1950 and 1956. Income tax, for instance, began to move back towards a schedular form, with bank interest, dividends, retirement income, and forestry income all receiving special treatments. An additional top rate of 65% was added to the income tax rate scale in 1953. Capital gains were given special treatment, also in 1953. Corporate income tax was being levied on ordinary corporations at two rates instead of the recommended single rate by 1956. A lower rate for special corporations was introduced in 1952. The only corresponding moves *toward* simplicity were the abolition of some recommended taxes.

Unhappily for local autonomy the Equalization Grant system was abolished in 1954 precisely because of budgetary problems at the national level. The recession caused by the cease-fire in the

Korean War from July 1953 necessitated a reining back of budget-ary expenditures, and the Equalization Grant was the preferred target.[48] The Mission's formula plan for distribution of the Grant was still used by the Local Autonomy agency in the distribution of shared taxes,[49] but the amount distributed to local authorities became once more dependent on the national government's deci-sion as to how much was available, rather than on an independent assessment of how much was necessary. "The Equalization Grant should have been a system for fiscal support of local autonomy 'from below,' but on the pretext that it was 'not suited to condi-tions in Japan' it disappeared completely in just four years."[50]

The Municipalities were never given control of the rate of the Real Estate Tax, and by 1957 the Inhabitant's Tax rates were also nationally controlled. Given the fiscal pinch felt by the local authorities all through the intervening period, they never had any option but to set their tax rates at the nationally fixed ceilings in any case.

More importantly, the income tax structure as envisaged by the Mission simply unravelled between 1949 and 1953. The Net Worth Tax could not be effectively enforced without the banning of anon-ymous accounts and the record-keeping requirement on wealthy individuals. It was thus repealed in 1953. It, therefore, followed that to maintain the progressiveness of the income tax, the top bracket rates had to be raised (to 65%, also in 1953). The Mission itself had stated: "We should certainly not recommend lowering the top income tax rate to 50 or 55 percent (national tax) if a net worth tax were not available."[51] The lack of effective administra-tion procedures also made it impossible to tax capital gains effec-tively, so, again in 1953, the law was changed such that capital gains of less than 150,000 yen became tax-free, and only half of capital gains above that figure were taxable. Inconsistently capital losses continued to be fully deductible. Capital gains and losses on securities transactions were to be ignored altogether for tax pur-poses because of the particularly great administrative difficulties involved, and because of pressure from banking and securities inter-ests. Even the official Ministry of Finance account sounds less than wholly convinced of the case for making capital gains from securi-ties transactions completely tax-exempt: "[T]he taxation of capi-tal gains *allegedly* hampered the development of the securities market."[52]

[*Corporate Income Tax*] The Mission's procedures for revaluation of assets were carried out, although they took rather longer than the Report anticipated. They were carried out in three stages and were not completed until 1954.

Corporation tax rates have remained relatively low in Japan in accordance with the Mission's recommendation. But withholding tax on dividend payments had to be restored in 1952 as a result of the lack of effective records of securities holdings, meaning that the "legal fiction" approach which the Shoup Missions took towards corporations had effectively had to be abandoned. More importantly, between 1951 and 1956 the Corporation Tax became riddled with special measures intended to promote economic growth. There were over 50 of these on the statute books by 1956.[53] Nakamura Takafusa argues that already by 1951 tax exemptions had replaced direct subsidies as the government's preferred method of implementing industrial policy.[54]

The history of the "income surcharge" is interesting. The Mission recommended its imposition at 1% p/a for ordinary corporations, but it was in fact imposed at a 2% rate and then repealed altogether in 1951 "in view of the important role of the profit retention in business financing."[55] One may suppose that pressure from bureaucratic policy-makers (e.g. MITI) and from business interests led to the repeal of this tax, but why was it introduced at a double rate in the first place? The double rate meant an effective interest charge on deferred taxes of 6.6% p/a on a 55% rate (national and local combined) taxpayer and as much as 13.2% on someone paying at 40%.[56] Moreover, doubling the rate exacerbated the regressiveness of this tax as noted by Hayashi.[57] One is almost tempted to conclude that the tax was deliberately made harsh in order to make it easier to repeal later.

C. Pechman and Kaizuka

Another, somewhat negative appraisal of the report's influence was that written in 1976 by Pechman and Kaizuka (1976). Their assessment was embedded, in bits and pieces, in their detailed description and analysis of the Japanese tax system. "Japan began its postwar recovery with a blueprint by the Shoup Mission that would have made its tax system a model for the rest of the world. But the Shoup blueprint was quickly discarded, and a Japanese brand of taxation was substituted" (p. 371). As to local finance, "The Shoup Mission recommended a greater local autonomy than was traditional in Japan, but this advice was virtually disregarded" (p. 336). On the positive side, "The major legacies of the Shoup proposals have been to make income taxation acceptable as the basic source of revenue in Japan, to raise the level of tax sophistication, and to improve tax administration" (p. 321).

D. Tax Bureau, Japanese Ministry of Finance

In its annual *Outline of Japanese Taxes*, the Tax Bureau of the Japanese Ministry of Finance, in reviewing the history of Japan's tax system, has commented on the influence of the report. In the 1986 edition, it says that "the intentions [of the tax mission] seemed somewhat too idealistic to fit in with the reality of the Japanese economy and standard of living of the Japanese people. The tax reforms made year to year since 1951 have represented the efforts to readjust the taxation system to actual conditions prevailing in the country" (pp. 7–8). It continues: "The Shoup recommendations were founded on the general principle of equitable share of the burden to meet government expenditures . . . . Many concerned persons in the Government, however, felt that, in view of the conditions of the Japanese economy then prevailing, vital economic policies might override certain general principles of taxation" (p. 8).

E. Other Appraisals

Other appraisals of the tax mission's report tend to view the present-day tax system of Japan as being, in some sense, based on that report.
   Hiromitsu Ishi (1987, p. 246) concludes that

> In retrospect the reforms were only a partial success, largely because subsequent modifications [after 1950] gradually made the tax system more inequitable and complicated. In spite of these drawbacks, the mission's contributions to reconstructing the postwar tax system in Japan are considerable. Throughout the postwar period, the Japanese tax system has retained major features of the Shoup framework. In this sense many would support the view that the Shoup reform should be considered one of the most successful in the world.

Yukio Noguchi (1986) puts it this way:

> It is not easy to evaluate whether the Shoup reform has, in fact, formed the basic structure of the postwar Japanese tax system.

Some recommendations, such as the wealth tax and the capital gain tax (on profits from sales of securities), were abolished a few years after they were implemented. Proposals such as the introduction of the value-added tax were not adopted at all. Also, some reforms were modified significantly by subsequent amendments which aimed at promoting capital accumulation. This is especially true for the corporate income tax. However, the implications of the Shoup reform were quite profound, especially in that the income tax did become the most important tax. In this sense, the reform established the basis of the Japanese tax system in the postwar period. (p. 38)

John Curtis Perry (1980), in his description and appraisal of the Occupation, devotes a few pages to describing the tax mission and the conditions under which it worked, and, without going into technicalities, concludes that "The tax system in any nation is likely to change in thirty years, and Japan is no exception. Yet 'the spirit or essence' of the Shoup recommendations remains . . ." (p. 155).

News dispatches in United States journals, dealing with current tax reform efforts in Japan, have on occasion described the existing system as being based on the report's recommendations: "Advocates of tax revision point out that Japan's tax system has changed little from the one established by the Shoup Commission in 1950 . . ." (Chira, 1986); "Japanese know their current tax code as the Shoup system . . ." (Burgess, 1986). In fact, the truth may be closer to the reverse of such statements. The current tax reform movement in Japan seems in large part an effort to remove most of the tax preferences that have been introduced into the income tax in the period since 1950.

VI. Some Retrospective Observations

A tax mission is a technical assistance group. Its chief task is to lay before the relevant government officials and the public the tax problems that they face and the solutions to those problems that the mission favors, with a full explanation of why these particular measures are recommended. In addition, the mission should stimulate interest in improving what has been called here the tax "atmosphere" so that tax policy becomes a widely discussed and well understood part of the political and social arena of debate.

Of course, education is not enough. No matter how lucid and widely read the report turns out to be, it is a failure if its authors so misunderstand the environment they are dealing with that virtually none of the recommendations are ever accepted. At the other extreme, however, can one say that success is marked by almost complete and immediate acceptance of the report's recommendations? Perhaps not; after all, no foreign-staffed mission, however capable its members, is likely to learn enough about the country in question to be right, in one sense or another, on all issues. Complete and immediate acceptance would seem to imply that the mission has failed in its educational aim. It has not taught the country to think for itself, and think clearly, on tax matters. (I was not only surprised, but somewhat uneasy, when, shortly after returning to the United States in 1949, I learned that almost all the mission's recommendations had, it was said, been put into law. As it turned out, I need not have been quite so uneasy.)

Another test for success or failure of the mission might be the degree to which the mission's recommendations, if adopted, did achieve the goals the mission had said they were aimed at. Here, answers are hard to get. Japan's economic recovery after the war is a matter of record. But would it have been much the same, if the tax mission's recommendations had been ignored? Perhaps the only assertion we should make is the very modest one that at least those of the mission's measures that were adopted did not block a strong and rapid recovery.

Economic consequences, however, are not the only measure of success or failure. If gross inequities, as perceived by taxpayers, are greatly reduced by the tax reform, there is a corresponding increase in well being, or decrease in dissatisfaction, that is as important, in its own way, as a measurable increase in economic well being. Whether a tax restructuring accomplished this aim is something that has to be inferred; the data are not usually among those collected and publicized. A fair inference here would seem to be that, yes, Japanese taxpayers as a whole felt better about their tax system, or less hostile toward it, as a result of the reform.

This feeling, however, has probably weakened over the nearly four decades since 1950. The income tax, as noted above, has been studded with a number of exemptions and low rates, to stimulate certain types of economic activity. Apparently, also, application of the tax law has been much less effective with regard to the self-employed (professions, small business, farming in general) than with respect to the wage and salary earners, whose tax is collected largely by withholding. One gets the impression that the tax reform movement sweeping Japan in 1987 and early 1988 reflects a desire to end tax inequities rather than to tailor the income tax still further to stimulate economic growth.

In any event, an appraisal of the tax mission's report must take account of the emphasis placed on fairness. In my brief preface to the 1985 retranslation of the report, I expressed the opinion that "Important though economic goals are, fairness (equity) in the tax system is even more important. 'A tax system can be successful only if it is equitable, and the taxpayer must realize that it is equitable' (p. 16, vol. I, 1949 report). Without perceived equity, a tax system becomes prey to elaborate avoidance devices developed chiefly by disgruntled taxpayers, and to outright evasion. Then, no matter how efficient economically the tax system was initially, it soon loses this attribute, too, as evasion and avoidance alter the very structure of the system. Without a high degree of perceived equity, a tax system will ultimately fail to reach any of its goals" (pp. 5–6).

To say that a tax mission is a technical assistance group is not to imply that it shall concern itself only with the technical aspects of tax administration and compliance, offering no advice on the structure of the tax system or tax policy generally. Yet it now appears that just that point of view was held by some high-ranking Japanese officials in 1949. The minister of finance at that time, Ikeda, in a book called *Kinko Zaisei* ("Balanced Budget"), wrote in 1949:

> I had no particular intention that Shoup should give me theoretical recommendations for the Japanese tax system. The tax *system* as such was based on a fairly careful study of various European systems, and its theoretical underpinnings were well developed, so there was no particular need to seek the guidance of foreigners on the system itself. But there was at that time quite a lot of confusion in the operation of the tax laws, that is, in tax administration. But this was the result not so much of defects in the tax system as of other factors, such as the general social disorder of the time, the fact that increases in the basic exemptions had lagged behind the severe inflation, thus greatly increasing the number of taxpayers, and the consequent fact that large numbers of new and inexperienced tax officials had to be employed. (Translated by Jason C. James, letter to Shoup, Jan. 20, 1987.)

This was certainly not the assignment outlined for the tax mission by Moss on behalf of MacArthur, in October 1948, at Columbia University, and nothing that I learned from conversations with Ikeda and other Japanese officials in 1949 (conversations carried on through inter-preters) suggested that they thought the mission's task should be so restricted in scope.

Looking back from the vantage point of nearly four decades later, what do we see that appears dubious or erroneous in the mission's activ-ities and recommendations?

Among the recommendations, that of a value-added tax for the pre-fectures now seems at least dubious.[58] First, the mission's fears that the cumulated income tax charge of three levels of government would dampen enterprise unduly have been proved unwarranted. Second, to the tax administrator and taxpayer, the value-added tax was the great unknown, however clear in concept and neutral in its economic pres-sures the tax may have appeared to mission members. This prospective newcomer evoked uneasiness if not fear. Third, even the pure theory of the value-added tax had not yet been worked out completely; it was not until 1955 that the basic distinction between a consumption-type VAT and an income-type VAT was made evident (Shoup, 1969, pp. 252–54). Finally, the question of just how to allocate a given firm's value-added between two or more prefectures in which the firm was active was not seriously addressed. On these and other points, the reader is referred to Bronfenbrenner's analysis of 1950, "The Japanese Value-Added Sales Tax."

Second, although the mission went into considerable detail on how the personal income tax might best be administered, the existing pat-tern today is certainly not what had been hoped for. It was not intended that the bulk of personal income tax revenue should come from simple withholding without any filing of a personal return by wage earners and salaried persons. On the contrary, the mission's aim was to get the aver-age Japanese family closely engaged in the process of tax determina-tion. Allied to this issue is that of unfairness as between these taxpay-ers and the self-assessed professionals, small businessmen, and farmers who are said to be evading or avoiding personal income tax to a consid-erable degree. What else might have been recommended, however, to assure the goals the mission sought, is by no means evident.

Third, the minor innovations of the net wealth tax, the low-rate "interest charge" tax on undistributed profits, and the substitution of inheritance for estate in the death tax (and the cumulation with gift tax) might have been recommended only for some future year when these novelties could have been accommodated more readily than in the chaotic days of 1949–50. These innovations were minor, not in the sense of principles at stake, but in the revenue implications, and so might have been postponed. Postponement, however, would probably have meant negation, in fact.

What of the four suggestions by Bronfenbrenner and Kogiku as to how the tax mission might have been more effective (1957, pp. 359–60)? "1. The Mission should have been summoned earlier, before deterioration of relations between SCAP and the Japanese had set in." B-K recognize the difficulties such an earlier mission would have encountered (e.g., inflation had not begun to subside), and in my opinion those disadvantages would have far outweighed the "sociological" advantages they claim for an earlier mission. "2. The Mission should have remained in Japan long enough to make the most pressing corrections" of "some technical defects" in the report. Such defects, however, do not seem to have been numerous or important enough that correcting them before the report was published would have made much difference in the outcome. Moreover, early publication of the report, before public interest in the tax mission had subsided, was important. B-K recognize that it would have been impracticable for the entire mission to have stayed in Japan longer, in view of their commitments elsewhere, but the alternatives they suggest seem to me also largely impracticable. "3. Had time permitted, the *Shoup Report* might have been more palatable if presented in the form of *alternatives* among which the Japanese might choose (perhaps within limits)." But we might have ended up with a textbook on taxation, which was not our assignment. Each recommendation was accompanied by arguments pro and con, and the tone was that of giving our own best judgment, not laying down a law that had to be accepted. "4. After SCAP had the Shoup Mission advertised to the Japanese as purveyors of tax reduction, the jurisdiction of the Mission should have included some over-all aggregative recommendations on the expenditure side . . . [and] on money, credit, and debt matters . . . ." If indeed SCAP so advertised the mission, it erred, but we were not aware of such advertising. Adding the other items to the mission's task would have swamped it.

This rather unsympathetic appraisal of the B-K suggestions does not imply that they were completely off target, but rather that the explanation of why the mission was not (even?) more successful than it was must be sought elsewhere. But is that "elsewhere" clear?

Appendix A

1. MacArthur and Yoshida on the Tax Mission Report
The Mainichi, Sunday, September 18, 1949
SCAP Hopes Japanese Government Would Form Appropriate Program to Effectuate Shoup
Recommendations

Letter to Premier Virtually Assures Quick Diet Approval

TOKYO, Sept. 17—General Douglas MacArthur has told Japanese Premier Shigeru
Yoshida in a letter dated September 15 that he hoped the Japanese Government will be
able to "formulate an appropriate program for effectuating the broad principles and objectives set forth in Dr. Shoup's recommendations."

This virtually assured quick passage by the Japanese Diet of the Shoup recommendations.

The text of General MacArthur's letter follows:

> Dear Mr. Prime Minister:
> I transmit herewith the report on Japanese taxation prepared by Dr. Carl Shoup and
> the members of his Mission, who were invited by me to come to Japan to conduct a
> comprehensive survey of the existing Japanese tax structure with the view of submitting recommendations which would assist in the establishment of a more equitable tax system.
>
> This Special Mission, after four months of intensive study which included interviews with taxpayers in all walks of life and investigations of many different types of
> business or agricultural activities, has evolved a body of recommendations which,
> taken together, should provide a vehicle for placing the finances of the national and
> local governments of Japan on a sound foundation.
>
> I trust that the Japanese Government will be able to formulate an appropriate program for effectuating the broad principles and objectives set forth in Dr. Shoup's
> recommendations in sufficient time to permit the Japanese Diet to consider that
> program simultaneously with the related budgetary and stabilization programs in
> order that the Japanese people may at the earliest possible time have the benefits of a
> sound fiscal system.
> Sincerely yours,
> DOUGLAS MACARTHUR

2. Yoshida Replies to SCAP
TOKYO, Sept. 17—Upon receiving General MacArthur's letter on the Shoup recommendations, Prime Minister Shigeru Yoshida sent a reply to SCAP today at noon.

Given below is the text of the prime minister's reply, which was later announced by the
cabinet:

> My Dear General:
> I desire to acknowledge the receipt of your letter of yesterday's date and the Report on
> Japanese Taxation by Dr. Carl Shoup and the members of his Mission.
>
> The report is literally a monumental work, which is bound to mark a new era in
> Japan's fiscal policy. I fully realize the fact that the recommendations are not to be
> accepted selectively, but they should be taken as a whole if they are to serve as the

basis for a rational and equitable tax system such as is envisaged by Dr. Shoup.

It is with this fact in mind that my Government will study the Report and formulate a taxation program to be submitted to the coming Diet.

On behalf of my Government I avail myself of this opportunity to express our profound appreciation of the arduous labors of the Shoup Mission as well as your unfailing solicitude toward the welfare of our nation.

Yours very sincerely, SHIGERU YOSHIDA

Appendix B

Extracts from letters by Shoup from Japan, May and August, 1949
The following extracts are from letters by Shoup to his family, from Japan, in the summer of 1949:

[May 12, 1949] At Guam at 10 A.M., then on another cargo plane [MATS] at noon, reaching Tokyo 8 P.M. Lots of newspaper men and flash bulbs, and the Finance Minister . . . and Moss and others. To the Imperial Hotel, where I have a 2-room suite, very comfortable. Wednesday morning I visited Moss' offices; at 12:30 I went alone to see MacArthur, and talked with him in his office for about an hour. He was very pleasant, informal, and promised full support of our mission. In the afternoon we had a courtesy-call meeting with Ikeda (Fin. Min.) and 3 other high Japanese officials in Moss' office—rather awkward at first, as it all had to be done through an interpreter, but we all relaxed a little after a few minutes. Polite expressions of appreciation, etc.

[May 14, 1949] . . . we are learning of the enormous gap between the tax laws on paper and how taxes are actually assessed and collected. It's more striking even than in France. Doctors in an area (say a city, or a part of Tokyo) belong to a "union," whose "boss" negotiates with the tax collector how much the doctors should pay as a group; then the members of the group divide up the tax bill among themselves somehow. Japanese firms either keep no books at all, or several sets of books (one for creditors, one for the tax collector, one for management purposes, etc.) . . . . At noon today the four of us [Cohen, Hatfield, Shoup, Vickrey] and Moss and Gen. Marquat, have lunch with Gen. and Mrs. MacArthur.

[May 15, 1949] Saturday's lunch at the former American Embassy, now the MacArthurs' home, was easy and informal, mostly small talk, except they told us of the details of their escape from the Philippines and the General gave us his analysis of why Japan went to war and why she lost. . . .

[May 25, 1949] We've just returned from a trip to Osaka, Kyoto, and Nagoya . . . . A Japanese official from the Finance Ministry who speaks English, a Mr. Hara, and an assistant of his came along on the Japanese section of the same train. Segregation is strictly enforced in all travel; ordinary trains, street cars and buses are marked "Off Limits to Occupation Personnel," some of the trains carry an "Allied Coach" . . . . At the Osaka station there were the Governor of the Prefecture, the Mayor, and other assorted officials; about a dozen news photographers and another dozen news correspondents. (This scene was substantially duplicated two days later at Nagoya). Also the U. S. Internal Revenue man in charge, and one or two other Military Government officials. At the hotel, deluxe as usual, breakfast was followed by a news conference I almost got out of, but the Military Gov't man said the papers had helped them in their drive for taxes and they wanted to keep on the good side of the press; also, he said this was the first thing he'd ever seen bring the Governor out to the station as early as 7 A.M. . . . after this we got to work, talking with the Japanese tax officials in their tax offices most of the day. We dug into tax files, examining actual returns.

That evening we all went to the Governor's house for dinner. It was an odd mixture of East and West. We sipped whiskey or sake in the living room and ate an American-style dinner in the dining room, sitting in chairs, but wearing slippers . . . . while four geisha entertainers hovered around, pouring sake and later on doing tricks with matches . . . .

We engaged chiefly in light conversation with our Japanese hosts through an interpreter, which is not quite, but almost, as hard as it sounds. We also got in some tax discussion . . . . That evening the Governor, the Vice-Mayor (the Mayor was ill) and various other officials gave a real Japanese dinner in a real Japanese restaurant. In a room about three times the size of our living room the Japanese hosts squat along one side of the room, their American guests along the other side. This effactually bars all conversation between hosts and guests . . . . The next day, more courtesy calls; discussions with military Gov't men; a session with heads of large Japanese manufacturing concerns and department stores; and a meeting with a (Japanese) Kyoto Area Economic Development Committee, or something like that: 30 or so around a large table, reporters and news photographers in the back of the room. Too formal to be very informative. In the afternoon we wandered through the alley-ways of a district of small shops, picked one out at random (a retail tea store) and asked the owner what his chief tax problems were. We were surprised at the results. For nearly an hour he discussed the issues lucidly . . . . Just as we started talking with him I noticed a young man grab the phone and talk earnestly for some minutes. Sure enough, the Kyoto paper next day carried a report on the interview. The reporter had been trailing us all afternoon . . . . Next morning we went by train (coach) to Nagoya . . . . At the Nagoya station we were met by the Governor, the Mayor, and other assorted officials; about a dozen news photographers and (see previous description). I got by with a 5-minute press conference this time. The Governor invited us to his house for dinner.

[June 11, 1949] We attended a special showing of a new Japanese film last night and were startled by its excellence . . . . This was a pre-preview, given for our benefit, in the private projection room of the film company . . . . Why the intense interest in our mission? There is a 150% (not 15%) tax on all movie admissions . . . . Yesterday I was offered drinks at the formal opening of the new Japanese Internal Revenue Bureau (sake, beer, 3 P.M.), at the cocktail party for a visiting group of U. S. tax agents (cocktails, 5 P.M.), at a dinner given for us at a nearby club (7 P.M.), and in between the first and second parts of the movie (10 P.M.). Can't say that I'm not keeping in practice. Next week we have only 3 dinner engagements.

[June 30, 1949] The trip has been successful in gathering information, and our group has gotten along without friction, altho packed pretty close in the private car for 10 days. I've been quite well all the trip, although pretty tired after some days of interviewing, especially when they were topped off by an official Japanese dinner . . . . This morning Surrey, Takahashi, and I descended unannounced on the Communist headquarters at Nagano, this region being noted for Communist activity, and got their views on the tax problem. We came on them so suddenly they didn't even stick close to a party line—they weren't prepared . . . . Next week we have a series of discussions with the Finance Ministry experts at Tokyo.

[July 9, 1949] Last night we had dinner at the Prince & Princess Takamatsu's. He is the second younger brother of the emperor . . . . Mrs. Harada [wife of a family friend] was there, and since Mr. H. was out of town I was asked to drive her home in my car. It was only a few minutes from the Prince's. But she got completely lost, and the driver couldn't figure it out either. We drove around an hour before she found Avenue K. It's a good demonstration of what every one says of Tokyo—the most confusing city to find anything in.

[July 12, 1949] In a few days I've learned what I could about the Okinawan tax system, and made some recommendations for change. This afternoon I presented them to a dozen or so army and civilian MG men. If I stayed here a day longer I'd learn too much to permit myself these snap judgments . . . . I talked with the Okinawan Minister of Finance a couple of afternoons . . . .

[July 24, 1949] Bowen, Surrey, and Warren and I went to MacArthur's office today, to give them a chance to see him, especially Bowen and Surrey, who leave the 27th. The General seemed quite interested in our work, and intelligently so . . . . He ended up by asking, then insisting, that our whole mission come back in a year for a short stay to check up on the results of our reform . . . . It is getting really hot and humid now, like Washington at its worst. Luckily, all the big conference work is over by now. The Minister of Education today, the "Economic Stabilization Board" Monday.

[July 25, 1949] We are meeting just with ourselves every day now, reaching conclusions. Today it was the transactions tax (sales tax), tomorrow the income tax . . . . All Saturday morning we spent "talking" with Dodge and others in Washington over the "telecon" system, which uses typewriters and a screen something like a stock ticker screen . . . . We discussed (and argued) about the current financial situation in Japan—is it too deflationary or is inflation still the danger? . . . This week in Tokyo, then a week up at a hotel near Nikko.

[July 27, 1949] We discussed the tax program among ourselves until 1 A.M. this morning, to cover all we could with the 3 departing members [Bowen, Cohen, Surrey] before they left . . . . Present idea is that Hatfield leaves Aug. 15, Warren and I on Aug. 27 . . . . We leave Monday for a week at the hotel above Nikko, to write up the report, at least first draft.

[August 2, 1949] We leave for Nikko in a few minutes. We are a little uneasy as the deadline for completion of the report nears, and it's not done, to say the least. But somehow we'll get it finished. We've shown parts of our conclusions already to MacArthur & Marquat & Whitney, and have had a good reaction so far.

[August 3, 1949] This is a very pleasant place—4000 ft. high, cool, quite away from the sweaty weather of Tokyo. The four of us are using this chance, where it's cool and quiet, to work morning noon and night getting the report written. It is still going to be a tight squeeze but we'll make it all right.

[August 7, 1949] We are still at the Nikko Kanko, working on the tax report all day and every evening. Representatives of a coal miner's union showed up at the hotel the other day to present their views on the tax system, but we just accepted their written memorandum and wouldn't even go into the lobby to say hello. We plan now to stay here until Wednesday. Today we sent by messenger to Tokyo the first part of Ch. 1, ready for translation into Japanese.

Appendix C

Comparison of Present-Day Income Tax Law in Japan with Recommendations in the Report: Certain Specific Issues

Present-day income tax law in Japan coincides, at least fairly closely (Y) or does not so coincide (N) with the following recommendations in the Report (for details, see *Outline*, and Price Waterhouse): (1) dependent allowance to be a deduction instead of a tax credit (Y); (2) deduction, at least partial, to be given for medical expenses (Y) and property loss through accident or theft (Y); (3) irregular incomes to be averaged over the years (N); (4) extra allowance to be given to the blind (N) and (5) disabled (N); (6) foreign nationals to be given no strongly favored treatment (Y); (7) corporation tax rate to stay at 35 percent (N); (8) withholding rate of 20 percent on dividends to be repealed (Y); (9) tax on liquidating corporations to be repealed (N); (10) tax of 66⅔ percent on inventory profits to be repealed (Y); (11) losses to be carried back two years and then carried forward indefinitely (Y); (12) for inventory accounting, allow more methods than just average cost (Y); (13) for depreciation, allow more methods than just declining balance (Y).

The individual income tax law now allows several deductions or exemptions, completely or partially, that the report opposed, explicitly or implicitly: social insurance premiums; premiums for small-scale enterprise mutual aid; premiums for life insurance and fire or other casualty insurance; extra personal exemption for the aged.

Notes

For information, comments, and suggestions in connection with this project I am indebted to many persons, but especially to Martin Bronfenbrenner, Lorraine Eden, Hidaki Fujimura, Jason C. James, Hiroshi Kaneko, Harold Moss, and Hirofumi Shibata. I thank them for their help, so generously given.

1 In other respects, too, the mission was well served. Adequate secretarial assistance was provided. Automobiles, chauffeured by skilled drivers, were available, and were used for several trips through the countryside and to other cities. A private railway car, to be attached to scheduled trains, and on one occasion, indeed, with its own locomotive, facilitated travel. All of these arrangements were made by or through the good offices of Harold Moss; this left the mission members free to concentrate on their task. Without this excellent logistical aid much of the mission's time and energy would have been diverted from its main purpose.

2 For a summary of the postwar inflation in Japan, see Shoup, "Tax Reform in Japan," 1950, pp. 4–5.

3 The research group for the new translation numbered fourteen. The work was started in 1983. The volume contains a few pages of material supplied by this group to supplement the Report, including a schematic map of the travel within Japan by the mission (dates and places, p. 454). Letters from H. Date, October 1985, and I. Inouye, January 1986.

4 A news dispatch from Tokyo in the September 12, 1949, edition of *The Mainichi*, an English-language daily in Tokyo, read in part as follows: "Seventy percent of the nation has read the Shoup recommendations on the tax system, according to a Kyodo News Service public opinion survey. A majority regarded the recommendation as 'satisfactory,' while 40 percent considered the present tax as 'too heavy.' The survey

was conducted immediately after the Shoup recommendations were made public. Two thousand five hundred and sixty-eight persons in every regional, vocational, and sex division were interviewed directly. Replies obtained numbered 2,528."

5   The income tax took up 120 pages of the total in the first two volumes, the Report proper, which ran to 226 pages. The two appendix volumes were almost entirely devoted to income taxation: 142 pages out of 173.

6   See, e.g., *Nippon Times*, August 24, 1949.

7   For the reasoning leading to this conclusion, see *Report*, pp. 81–84, and Shoup, "Tax Reform in Japan," 1950, pp. 8–9.

8   For a discussion of this and alternatives, see Shoup, "Tax Reform in Japan," 1950, pp. 10–11.

9   "Collections [of the income tax] from the farmers was . . . fairly good considering that farmers in Japan seldom till more than an acre or two and keep almost no records. They have been supposed to make out their own income tax returns, but in practice they simply enter what the local tax office broadcasts as being an estimate of average net income per acre for that area." Shoup, "Tax Reform in Japan," 1950, p. 6.

10 See Bronfenbrenner and Kogiku (1957). Professor Martin Bronfenbrenner, then of the University of Wisconsin, was requested by SCAP, upon my recommendation, to assist the Japanese government in implementing such of the report's recommendations as they adopted. Bronfenbrenner was engaged in this task for several months, from September 1949 well into 1950.

11 These statements are based on news dispatches, chiefly in Tokyo English-language newspapers.

12 As from April 1, 1988, all interest is taxed at a uniform rate of 20 percent, except that exemption continues for persons over 65, surviving spouses, and disabled persons.

13 From Japan, Government of, Ministry of Finance, *An Outline of Japanese Taxes, 1986*, pp. 8–9.

14 For further details on present-day income tax law compared with the Report's recommendations, see appendix C.

15 *Outline*, pp. 8–9.

16 Ibid., p. 272.

17 Percentages for 1949 are from Kaneko (note to Shoup, April 29, 1988) and are actual 1949–50 fiscal year collections, instead of budget estimates used in the mission Report. For 1986 tax revenues, see Ibid., pp. 304–7.

18 Ibid., pp. 128–35.

19 Ibid., pp. 138–42.

20 Ibid., passim.

21 Ibid., pp. 150–51.

22 Ibid., pp. 143–44.

23 Ibid., passim.

24 Ibid., pp. 189–91, 199–204.

25 Ibid., pp. 204–6.

26 Ibid., pp. 191–93.

27 Ibid., pp. 157–58.

28 Ibid., passim.

29 Ibid., pp. 187–89. The general-purpose equalization grant, distributed largely by formula, is termed the "local allocation tax" and consists of 32 percent of the yield of

the individual income tax, the corporation income tax, and the liquor tax. In 1954, the initial year of this grant, the percentage was only 20. It reached 32 in 1966. The national government also distributes substantial amounts for specific purposes, allocated by discretion rather than by formula. There are also certain other distributions. For details, see Yonehara (1986), 160–68, Yonehara (1981), and Ishihara (1986).

30 Japan, Ministry of Finance, *Financial Statistics*, p. 37.

31 For this information, for the 1984 data on blue returns, and for all the information given in nos. 2 to 14 below, I am indebted to Professor H. Kaneko.

32 The discussion of the blue return's effect on encouraging a sophisticated bookkeeping system needs to be qualified as follows. A taxpayer who uses a "simplified accounting system," i.e., one that does not employ double entry, need not include with his blue return a balance sheet. About 50 percent of blue return taxpayers fell in this class as of 1981.

33 On this practice, see Pechman and Kaizuka, pp. 333–34.

34 Correspondence from Professor H. Kaneko (1985).

35 However, with adoption of the uniform separate tax on interest in 1988, the real name is no longer required.

36 Kaneko (1985), Correspondence.

37 "'Violence,' says a Japanese gangster '. . . is obsolete. Today we go to prison for tax evasion.' The fine art of underreporting income, and the equally fine art of nabbing those who do, is the all-embracing subject of 'A Taxing Woman,' the solemnly funny new satire by Juzo Itami." Vincent Canby, *New York Times*, September 26, 1987.

38 Kaneko (1985), Correspondence.

39 Kaneko (1985), Correspondence.

40 "The New Salaried Men's Party, created on the single issue of income tax fairness (or current unfairness) for salaried workers, won two seats in a Japanese parliamentary election last year [1984]" (Ryan, p. 10).

41 Japan Tax Association (1982), p. 1.

42 As of mid-1986 the membership classification was: nonindividual, 613 (business, 493; nonprofit, 80; university research groups, 10; law offices, 17; local governments, 11; a Diet committee, and a Korean government representative) and private (individual), 89 (professors, 50; tax consultants, 17; certified public accountants, 17; tax lawyers, 5), for a total of 702. I am indebted to Professor Hirofumi Shibata for obtaining this information.

43 For still other appraisals of the report, see the References in Ishi (1983); Yamamura (1967).

44 Bronfenbrenner, Martin, and Kiichiro Kogiku, "The Aftermath of the Shoup Tax Reform," *National Tax Journal*, vol. X, no. 3, September 1957, pp. 236–58 and no. 4, December 1957, pp. 345–60.

45 E.g., Carl S. Shoup et al., *First Report*, p. 99.

46 James, *Japanese Tax Policy in the Wake of the Shoup Mission*, p. 85.

47 Bronfenbrenner and Kogiku, p. 348.

48 Nishi, p. 140.

49 Bronfenbrenner and Kogiku, p. 252.

50 Nishi, p. 139.

51 Shoup et al., *First Report*, p. 84.

52 *Outline of Japanese Taxes*, 1986. Tax Bureau, Ministry of Finance, Tokyo.

53   Pechman and Kaizuka, "Taxation," in Patrick, H., and H. Rosovsky, *Asia's New Giant: How the Japanese Economy Works*. Washington, D.C.: Brookings Institution, 1976.
54   Nakamura Takafusa. "Sengo no Sangyo Seisaku" ("Postwar Industrial Policy"). In Niida Kenji and Ono Akeda, eds., *Nihon no Sangyo Soshiki (Japan's Industrial Organisation)*. Tokyo: Iwanami Shoten, 1969.
55   *Outline*, p. 8.
56   These calculations use the method described in *First Report*, pp. 109–10.
57   *Outline*, p. 229.
58   The value-added tax proposed by Prime Minister Nakasone in 1986 was far more complicated that the one recommended by the Report, for the prefectures: for example, fifty-one categories of goods and services excluded (Darlin).

References

Andic, Suphan, and Alan Peacock. "Fiscal Surveys and Economic Development," pp. 89-104. In *Readings on Taxation in Developing Countries*, 3rd edition. Edited by Richard M. Bird and Oliver Oldman. Baltimore: Johns Hopkins University Press, 1975.

Aoki, Torao. "Ongoing Tax Reform [in Japan]." *Bulletin for International Fiscal Documentation*. Part I: March, 1987, vol. 41, pp. 111–16. Part II: May, 1987, vol. 41, pp. 224–31.

———. "The National Taxation System [of Japan]." In *Public Finance in Japan*, chapter 7, pp. 103-22. Edited by Tokue Shibata. Tokyo: University of Tokyo Press, 1986.

———. "A Survey of the Japanese Tax System." *Bulletin for International Fiscal Documentation* 39 (October 1985), pp. 435–45.

Bronfenbrenner, M. "The Japanese Value-Added Sales Tax." *National Tax Journal* 3, no. 4 (December 1950), pp. 298–313.

Bronfenbrenner, M., and Kiichiro Kogiku. "The Aftermath of the Shoup Tax Reforms. Part I." *National Tax Journal* 10, no. 3 (September 1957), pp. 236–54.

———. "The Aftermath of the Shoup Tax Reforms. Part II." *National Tax Journal* 10, no. 4 (December, 1957), pp. 345–60.

Burgess, John. "Japan Moves Toward Tax Revision," *Washington Post*, December 14, 1986.

Canby, Vincent. "Film Festival: 'Taxing Woman,' From Japan." *New York Times*, September 26, 1987.

Chira, Susan, "Japanese Leaders Propose Overhaul of the Tax System," *New York Times*, December 4, 1986.

Darlin, Damon. "Tax Uproar Threatens Japanese Premier." *Wall Street Journal*, March 19, 1987.

Fukuda, Yukihiro. Director-General, Tax Bureau, Ministry of Finance, Tokyo. Correspondence with the author, 1981–82. (On June 1, 1982, Mr. Fukuda was appointed commissioner of the National Tax Administration.) He is now (1988) a member of the Diet, House of Councillors.

Homma, M., T. Maeda, and K. Hashimoto. *The Japanese Tax System*. Washington, D.C.: Brookings Institution, June, 1986. Brookings Discussion Papers in Economics.

Ikeda, Hayoto. *Kinko Zaisei*. Tokyo, 1949. (Section translated by Jason J. James for Carl Shoup.)

Ishi, Hiromitsu. "An Overview of Postwar Tax Policies in Japan." *Hitotsubashi Journal of Economics* 23, no. 2 (February 1983), pp. 21–39.

———. "The Impact of the Shoup Mission." In *Proceedings of the 41st Congress of the International Institute of Public Finance, 1985*, pp. 237–49. Edited by Hans W. van de Kar and Barbara Wolf. Detroit: Wayne State University Press, 1987.

———. "International Tax Evasion and Avoidance in Japan." *Hitotsubashi Journal of Economics* 25, no. 1 (June 1984), pp. 21–29.

———. *The Japanese Tax System*. London: Oxford University Press, forthcoming.

Ishihara, Nobuo. "The Local Public Finance System [of Japan]." In *Public Finance in Japan*, chapter 9, pp. 132–55. Edited by Tokue Shibata. Tokyo: University of Tokyo Press, 1986.

James, Jason C. *Japanese Tax Policy in the Wake of the Shoup Mission*. Dissertation for part two of the Tripos in Oriental Studies: Japanese Studies at Cambridge University, King's College. Cambridge, U.K.: Cambridge University, 1987.

Japan, Government of. Ministry of Finance. Institute of Fiscal and Monetary Policy. *Financial Statistics of Japan: Fiscal Year 1986*, October 1986, and *Monthly Finance Review*, December 1986, No. 162.

———. Ministry of Finance. Tax Bureau. *An Outline of Japanese Taxes, 1986*.

———. Ministry of Finance. Tax Bureau. "Shoup Mission Recommendation and Its Implementation (Comparison between The Recommendation and the Present Tax System)." September 9, 1981. Photocopy of typescript, 13 pages.

———. Ministry of Home Affairs. "Local Administration and Finance." In *Public Administration in Japan*, pp. 99–120. Edited by IIAS Tokyo Round Table Organizing Committee. Tokyo, 1982.

Japan Tax Association. *An Outline of Japan Tax Association*. Tokyo, August 1982.

Kaneko, Professor H., personal correspondence (1985).

Kato, Mutsuki. Member, Japan House of Representatives and chairman, Tax Council of Liberal Democratic Party. Interview, October 26, 1985.

Kubo, Shintaro. Staff correspondent, Yomiuri Shimbun, Tokyo. Interview, March 6, 1985.

Miura, Makoto. "The 1984 Tax Amendments [in Japan]." *Bulletin for International Fiscal Documentation* 38, no. 6 (June 1984), pp. 251–54.

Moss, Harold. Interview, September 18, 1986.

Murayama, Saeko. "Retirement and Post-Retirement Work of the Japanese Elderly," *Journal of the Institute for Socioeconomic Studies* 3, no. 4 (Winter 1978), pp. 28–37.

Nakatani, Iwao. "Towards the New International Order—The Role of Japan in the World Economy." Sec. III, "Proposal for a Tax Summit." *Hitotsubashi Journal of Economics* 27 (October 1986, Special Issue), pp. 124–32.

Nishi, Kazuo. *Showa no Zaiseishi (A History of Public Finance in the Showa Era)*. Tokyo: Kyoikusha, 1985.

Nomura, Shinici. "Problems of Local Administration: The Case of Tokyo Metropolitan Government." In *Public Administration in Japan*. Edited by IIAS Tokyo Round Table Organizing Committee. Tokyo: Institute for International Administrative Studies, 1982, pp. 120–32.

Oldman, Oliver, and Stanley S. Surrey. "Technical Assistance in Taxation in Developing Countries." In *Modern Fiscal Issues: Essays in Honor of Carl S. Shoup*, pp. 278–91. Edited by Richard M. Bird and John G. Head. Toronto: University of Toronto Press, 1972.

Pechman, Joseph A., and Keimei Kaizuka, "Taxation." In *Asia's New Giant: How the Japanese Economy Works*, pp. 317–82. Edited by Hugh Patrick and Henry Rosovsky.

Washington: Brookings Institution, 1976.

Perry, John Curtis. *Beneath the Eagle's Wings: Americans in Occupied Japan*. New York: Dodd, Mead & Co., 1980, pp. 152–55.

Price Waterhouse. *Information Guide: Doing Business in Japan*. New York: Price Waterhouse, 1983.

———. *Supplement to the 1983 Edition of the Information Guide*, 1986.

Ryan, Ray. "Personal income tax . . ." *Frankly Speaking* (Japan Air Lines), April 1985, pp. 10–15.

Shibata, Hirofumi. Professor of Economics, Osaka University. Interview, October 1, 1986.

Shindo, Muneyuki. "Relations Between National Government and Local Government [in Japan]." In *Public Administration in Japan*, pp. 121–34. Edited by IIAS Tokyo Round Table Organizing Committee. Tokyo, 1982.

Shoup, Carl S. *Public Finance*. Chicago: Aldine Publishing, 1969.

Shoup, Carl S. "Tax Reform in Japan." *Proceedings, Forty-Second National Tax Conference*, September 19–22, 1949. Sacramento, California: National Tax Association, 1950.

Shoup, Carl S., Howard R. Bowen, Jerome B. Cohen, Rolland F. Hatfield, Stanley S. Surrey, William Vickrey, and William C. Warren. *Report of Japanese Taxation by the Shoup Mission*. Tokyo: General Headquarters, Supreme Commander for the Allied Forces, September 1949. Four volumes. In English and Japanese. Retranslated into Japanese and published in 1985 by Kasumi Publishing Co., Tokyo.

Shoup, Carl S., Stanley S. Surrey, William Vickrey, and William C. Warren. *Second Report on Japanese Taxation by the Shoup Mission*. Tokyo: Japan Tax Association, 1950. In English and Japanese.

Surrey, Stanley S. "When American Tax Reformers Devised Japan's Tax System." *People and Taxes* II, no. 11 (November 1963), pp. 4–5.

Teuber, Jack. "Japanese Tax Reform Effort Underway," *Tax Notes* 31, December 22, 1986, pp. 1094–96.

Togashi, Tom. Japan Broadcasting Co. Interview, September 29, 1986.

Ueda, Yoshihisa. First Secretary, Embassy of Japan, Washington, D.C. Interview, October 26, 1985.

Yamamura, K. *Economic Policy in Postwar Japan*. Berkeley and Los Angeles: University of California Press, 1969.

Yasuda, M. Correspondent, *Tokyo Post*. Interview, September 15, 1986.

Yonehara, Junshichiro. *Local Public Finance in Japan*. Research Monograph No. 36, Centre for Research on Federal Financial Relations, The Australian National University. Canberra, London, and Miami: ANU Press, 1981.

———. "Financial Relations between National and Local Governments [in Japan]." In *Public Finance in Japan*, chapter 10, pp. 156–68. Edited by Tokue Shibata. Tokyo: University of Tokyo Press, 1986.

Yoshida, Satoshi. Staff writer, Kyodo News Service. Interview, October 3, 1986.

For ten references in the Japanese language bearing directly on the topic of this paper, see the bibliography in Jason C. James, which also contains other general references in English not cited here.

7
·······

Tax Changes Before Tax Policies:
Sri Lanka, 1977–88
·······

Glenn P. Jenkins

Abstract

This study examines a series of changes in tax policies that occurred in Sri Lanka after the change in government in 1977. These policies are evaluated in the context of the major reforms that were carried out on most aspects of the economy. These successive, partial reforms (see chapter 1) have experienced significant success in terms of economic growth and employment. The numerous tax incentives and tax holidays initially weakened the income tax system, but significant progress was made with regard to indirect taxation for both domestic and traded goods. After a number of years of consistent economic management, steps have been taken to apply more economically oriented policies to strengthen and rationalize the tax system. One result of these changes is that the administration cost of the tax system in terms of revenue collected has been reduced by about 50 percent.

I. Introduction

The year 1977 was a major turning point in the modern economic history of Sri Lanka. In that year a new government assumed office and challenged the basic assumption on which economic policy had been made over the previous two decades. The result was a series of major policy changes in ten areas of the economy:

a. The adoption of a realistic exchange rate.
b. The liberalization of foreign exchange markets.
c. A shift from quantitative restrictions on imports to tariffs as a means

of protecting domestic industry.

d. The lifting of price controls.

e. Relaxation of interest rate controls to encourage greater savings.

f. Shift from consumer subsidies to producer incentives.

g. Creation of favorable business climate for foreign investment.

h. Removal of excessive administrative controls over investment.

i. Creation of tax incentives for investments in real assets and for export sectors.

j. Special tax incentives and technical assistance for small business.[1]

The objectives of these economic policy changes were to promote rapid economic growth, create employment, and stabilize and rationalize the economy. A clear shift was made in economic management from the highly interventionist policies of governments of the previous decade to a much greater reliance on the private sector and the use of market forces to guide the allocation of resources.[2]

These policy changes were badly needed at the time. With a few exceptions, they have generally been effective. The tax system in 1977 was a prime example of where two decades of misguided tax policies fueled by interventionist tendencies can lead a country. While the economic philosophy of the government changed dramatically and many tax changes have been made, the basic approach to tax policy remained largely unchanged until just recently. Under this approach the income tax system was used more as a political tool than a fiscal tool, with an incentive for almost every interest group. At the same time, the government relied on a poorly designed indirect tax system to raise revenues for the public sector. Evidence is beginning to emerge, however, that this approach has been supplanted by more soundly based tax policy.

II. The Tax System in 1977

The Sri Lankan tax system in 1977 contained seven categories of taxes: an income tax system that contained both a corporate and a personal income tax, a wealth tax, a business turnover tax, a set of excise taxes, a set of import duties, a set of export taxes, and sales of Foreign Exchange Entitlement Certificates (FEEC).

This tax system was typical of that found in a highly regulated economy. It was very interventionist with high and differential tax rates, while being largely ineffective as a system for raising revenue.

From table 7.1 we find that from 1971 to 1977 the combined personal

Table 7.1   Tax Revenue, 1971–77 (percentage composition)

	1971	1972	1973	1974	1975	1976	1977
1. Taxes on income and profit	19.9	17.7	21.7	15.3	18.6	20.4	17.3
Corporate	—	—	14.1	10.4	12.4	14.9	12.0
Personal	—	—	7.6	4.9	6.2	5.5	5.3
2. Taxes on property and property transfer	2.2	2.3	2.4	1.8	2.3	1.9	2.0
3. Taxes on goods and services	37.6	42.5	38.9	36.9	38.1	37.7	40.0
Business turnover tax	14.6	15.4	16.6	15.4	15.6	15.5	12.2
Liquor	7.4	10.4	7.7	5.5	5.0	4.1	4.4
Tobacco	11.1	12.2	10.6	9.5	11.1	9.8	10.9
Tea	1.7	1.7	1.2	4.1	4.0	6.0	10.6
Other	2.7	2.7	2.7	2.3	2.4	2.2	1.9
4. Taxes on imports	12.6	10.1	6.9	7.1	8.1	10.4	9.6
5. Taxes on exports	11.9	9.1	12.1	16.9	10.4	9.2	11.4
Tea	7.3	6.4	5.3	4.0	4.3	3.6	4.9
Rubber	0.6	0.4	4.5	7.3	3.4	4.4	4.9
Coconut	2.5	1.1	1.0	4.1	1.6	0.1	0.5
Other	1.6	1.2	1.2	1.4	1.1	1.1	1.2
6. FEEC	15.7	18.3	18.2	22.1	22.5	20.4	19.7
7. Total tax revenue	100.0	100.0	100.0	100.0	100.0	100.0	100.0
8. Tax revenue as a percentage of total current revenue	86.0	87.2	89.2	91.6	91.1	89.6	88.9

Note: Totals may not add up because of rounding.
Source: Central Bank of Sri Lanka.

and corporate income taxes were in the order of 20 percent of total tax revenue, with wealth taxes amounting to about another 2 percent of tax revenues. The business turnover tax and excise taxes generated about 15 and 24 percent of total tax revenues, respectively.

Because of the heavy reliance on quantitative import controls to ration the use of foreign exchange, the average revenue yield from import duties was relatively small. They amounted to about 9 percent of total revenues, while export duties averaged about 1 percent. These taxes greatly underestimate the total taxes on the export sector because of the highly overvalued exchange rate. From the sale of the rights to use foreign exchange (FEECs) the government obtained additional funds equal to about 19 percent of total revenue.

Income Taxes

The basic structure of the corporate income tax system in 1977 was a 69 percent rate of tax on taxable income of resident and non-resident companies. In addition, resident companies were required to pay a dividends distribution tax of 33⅓ percent. Nonresident companies were required to pay an additional 6 percent of taxable income in lieu of estate duty and also a tax of 33⅓ percent on dividends remitted abroad.[3]

Offsetting this seemingly harsh corporate tax system was a set of tax incentives that allowed for immediate expensing of a major portion of new investments. The proportion that could be deducted immediately from taxable income ranged from 50 percent for assets with long lives to 80 percent for assets with short lives. In addition, five-year tax holidays were given for a wide range of activities including industrial undertakings employing more than twenty-five people, activities engaged in the export of goods and services, deep sea fishing enterprises, tourist hotels, and paddy milling. Given the difficulty of defining what was a "new" activity, and the difficulty of administration of conditions laid down by law, there was plenty of room for creative tax avoidance activities.

The personal income tax had characteristics similar to that of the company income tax. Until 1979 the taxable unit was the family. The income of children under the age of 21 and that of the spouse were aggregated with that of the head of the family. In the early 1970s there were twelve tax brackets, with the top income bracket facing a marginal tax rate of 65 percent,[4] and in 1975 there were thirteen tax brackets with a top tax rate of 75 percent. The size of tax brackets and rates were changed almost annually, dropping to eleven tax brackets with a top tax rate of 50 percent in 1975.[5] Then they were increased to fifteen brackets with a top tax rate of 70 percent in 1978.[6]

There were a number of tax incentives, including the exemption of dividends arising from companies enjoying tax holidays, and for interest (subject to limits) received from the National Savings Bank. In brief, declared taxable income was taxed at very high rates, but the opportunities for tax avoidance were abundant.

The Wealth Tax

The wealth tax was introduced in 1959 with the objective of increasing the degree of progressivity of the tax system. Like other wealth taxes in developing countries, it has not been effective either as a revenue producer or as an instrument to bring about a better distribution of income. But unlike many such wealth taxes in developed and developing countries, it has not been abolished.

It is applicable to both the movable and immovable property of resident and nonresident individuals, but only immovable property of nonresident companies in Sri Lanka. In addition to a basic deduction, there are further deductions for a house, furniture, jewelry (subject to a limit), and an automobile. The asset values that make up the base of the tax have been frozen at their 1977 levels. This provision, along with generous opportunities for tax avoidance and evasion, has resulted in a steady decline in the importance of this tax.

The Business Turnover Tax

The business turnover tax (BTT) was originally introduced in 1964. It is a multistage sales tax that is applied to gross quarterly receipts from sales at all stages of production and distribution. When it was initially implemented it was highly cascading, but measures to permit tax credits on purchases of current inputs have reduced this characteristic of the tax. It has always had several rates of tax depending on the commodity and stage of distribution. In 1977 there were six rates of tax ranging from 1 to 35 percent.

Selected Sales and Excise Taxes

These taxes have been traditionally on alcoholic beverages, tobacco, tea, and coconut oil. Except when the price of tea has been extraordinarily high, the bulk of the revenues have been obtained from tobacco and alcoholic beverages. The application of these taxes and their role in the fiscal system have been fairly consistent for the entire period of the 1970s and 1980s.

Import Duties and FEECs

Until 1977 foreign exchange controls were pervasive. Although tariff rates were high, the principal device for rationing the available foreign were quantitative controls and the sale of Foreign Exchange Entitlement Certificates (FEECs). The FEECs raised quite a large amount of revenue, but a large proportion of this amount had to be turned over to producers in order for them to be willing to produce for the export market. Due to the stagnation of the economy, and in particular the exporting sectors, there was not much foreign exchange available. As a result, the growth in imports and tariff revenues was small.

Export Taxes

Export taxes on tea, rubber, and coconut have been traditional features of the Sri Lankan system. Furthermore, the government's nationalization policies during the early 1970s ensured that these once dynamic sectors would stagnate and experience disinvestment. The combination of an overvalued exchange rate, export taxation, and incompetent economic policies during this period have inflicted damage on these agriculture export crops that has not been rectified to date.

III. Tax Changes 1978–88

Taxes on Trade

In the years immediately following the change in government in 1977 there have been dozens of tax changes that have shifted the fiscal system further from direct taxes toward indirect taxation. The first step was taken following the devaluation in 1978, when large export taxes were imposed on tea and rubber to capture most of the short-run gains that would have accrued to these sectors from the devaluation. Between 1977 and 1978 the proportion of total tax revenues raised by export taxes (table 7.2) rose from 11.4 to 40.8 percent. Since that time the reliance on export taxes has gradually decreased to the point where they are now less important than they were in 1977.

Since the removal of exchange controls and the reduction in the use of quantitative controls to restrain imports, the tariff system has become a much more important source of tax revenue. From table 7.2 we find that since 1979 tariffs have consistently provided more than 20 percent of total tax revenues to the government.

The Presidential Tariff Commission (PTC), set up in 1977, has played a very positive role in rationalizing the tariff system over time. In particular, the recommendations that were implemented in 1985 went a long way toward reducing the level and degree of dispersion of the effective rates of protection given to domestic producers of import substitutes.

Although the overall levels of effective protection are quite high, their trends (and recommendations of the PTC) have been fairly consistent at

Table 7.2   Tax Revenue, 1978–85 (percentage composition)

	1978	1979	1980	1981	1982	1983	1984	1985	1986
1. Taxes on income and profit	10.6	12.2	16.7	14.4	19.0	16.3	18.4	19.4	15.3
Corporate	6.9	8.7	13.7	10.3	13.8	12.0	12.5	15.2	10.5
Personal	3.7	3.5	3.0	4.0	5.2	4.3	5.9	4.2	4.8
2. Taxes on property and property transfer	1.4	1.3	2.1	2.0	2.1	1.9	1.5	1.3	2.0
3. Taxes on goods and services	29.9	28.8	28.8	34.9	42.0	46.7	42.9	48.4	47.2
Business turnover tax	10.4	10.7	13.1	19.9	26.3	30.1	27.3	33.6	32.2
Liquor	5.3	4.5	5.5	5.6	5.2	4.2	3.4	3.9	
Tobacco	7.3	7.2	8.0	7.9	8.5	6.9	10.8	6.9	– 14.1
Tea	4.9	2.0	0.8	0.6	1.0	4.5	0.7	3.3	
Other	2.0	4.4	1.4	1.2	1.0	1.0	0.7	0.6	0.9
4. Taxes on imports	14.1	20.4	23.4	22.7	21.0	23.4	22.1	24.4	30.1
5. Taxes on exports	40.8	37.4	29.1	26.0	16.1	11.9	10.6	6.6	5.2
Tea	26.8	22.4	15.4	13.2	9.4	6.2	5.9	4.1	3.4
Rubber	9.6	11.1	11.1	10.1	4.9	4.1	3.4	1.2	1.0
Coconut	3.3	3.0	1.7	1.7	1.2	1.2	1.0	1.0	0.8
Other	1.0	0.9	1.0	1.0	0.6	0.4	0.3	0.3	0.0
6. FEEC	3.2								
7. Total tax revenue	100.0	100.0	100.0	100.0	100.0	100.0	100.0	100.0	100.0
8. Tax revenue as a percentage of total current revenue	93.3	92.7	94.3	93.0	92.8	90.5	87.8	87.3	83.2

Note: Totals may not add up because of rounding.
Source: Central Bank of Sri Lanka.

moving the tariff system toward a more rational allocation of resources between the production of import substitutes and the other sectors of the economy. The proposals made in the 1988 budget are consistent with this trend. In it the minister proposed to reduce all import duties that were above 60 percent to 60 percent.

Income and Wealth Taxation

Accompanying the very positive set of economic reforms in 1978 that removed many of the controls on international trade and other areas of the market economy, the government started a process whereby almost every conceivable form of tax incentive has been introduced into the company and personal income tax systems. In the case of company taxation, a 100 percent investment deduction was given for expenditures on assets in housing and hotel development and for various capital expenditures on new plant machinery, equipment, and furnishings. These 100 percent deductions were withdrawn in 1983, but very generous accelerated depreciation allowances are still given for selected capital expenditures.

Tax holidays have been the preferred brand of tax incentive. If approval was granted before March 31, 1983, a five-year tax holiday is granted for the development of hotels. If granted to a quoted public company, the tax holiday can be extended to ten years. A ten-year tax holiday is also given to any new company engaged in property development so long as it becomes a quoted public company within two years after starting business. Tax holidays are also available for new industrial activities including agribusiness, animal husbandry, and offshore or deep-sea fishing. Companies producing exports are completely tax exempt for the first five years. Even with substantial tariff protection, new enterprises engaged in import substitution activities are given a five-year tax holiday.

As many of these tax holidays are given for approved rather than actual operating businesses, there are many authorized, but not yet built, projects that will be eligible for tax holidays in the future. The impact on the corporate income tax revenues has been quite substantial. Although the amount of activity undertaken by the private sector has increased dramatically since 1977, the share of tax revenues from the company income tax has by the mid-1980s only reached what it was during the mid-1970s.

Another innovation of the new government was the development of a large free trade zone. When Greater Colombo Economic Commission (GCEC) was set up in 1978 to administer Export Promotion Zones, authority was given to it so that it could disregard the Inland Revenue Act, the Customs Ordinance, and other regulatory procedures. Hence, tax administration was determined by negotiation between GCEC and the investing companies. A 100 percent tax holiday for up to ten years was available at the commencement of the project, and later a further concessionary tax period up to fifteen years was available. During this period an income tax at the rate of 2 percent to 5 percent based on the turnover was to be imposed. During this period, wages of foreign personnel, dividends, and royalties were exempt from tax. There were, however, only thirty-nine projects (including seven projects in trial production) which were in commercial production with an estimated investment value of Rs. 840 million. The gross number of jobs created in the zone was around 14,740, but no estimate has been made of the number of jobs that have been simply shifted into the zone.

Since the early 1970s the company income tax law has also given preferential treatment to small business. In this case the tax rates start at 20 percent on the first Rs. 50,000 of taxable income, and increasing 10 percentage points on each additional Rs. 100,000 of taxable income until it reaches 50 percent.[7] The same rate of advanced company tax applies to the dividends of small business companies as large business.

In 1979 the government took a positive tax policy step by reducing the rate of company tax from 60 to 50 percent. At the time, this rate reduction brought the Sri Lankan company tax system in line with the tax rates of many other developing and developed countries. Since then, it has not attempted to follow the tax policies of a great many countries engaged in tax reform by reducing its company tax rates further while simultaneously eliminating tax incentives.

In the 1988 budget it is proposed to increase the degree of integration of the corporate and personal income tax systems. This is to be done by allowing the advance company tax on dividends to be available to offset company income tax due, and to give a tax credit to individual taxpayers who receive dividends equal to 50 percent of the value of the dividends.

The personal income tax system has never been a very effective fiscal tool in Sri Lanka. At the present time less than 4 percent of total tax revenues are raised from this tax. As it is unlikely that the personal income tax can ever be an effective fiscal instrument in a country with a per capita income as low as that of Sri Lanka, a number of the measures taken since 1977 can be viewed positively. First, adjustments were made in the structure of the basic personal deduction to eliminate low-income taxpayers from the tax net. Second, since 1980 steps have been taken to lower the top marginal tax rates, first to 55 percent, and in 1986 and 1988 to 50 and 40 percent, respectively. The basic exemption has also been increased to about 2.5 times the per capita income. The net result is that only about 200,000 people either file tax returns or come under the PAYE (pay-as-you-earn) system.

Although the basic rate structure and personal deductions are realistic, the personal income tax still suffers from the same kind of wide array of deductions and exemptions that is characteristic of Sri Lanka's company tax. For example, the wages of all public servants are exempt from taxation. Although many of the public servants earn income of less than the basic deduction, it also means that those with substantial income from other outside sources also enjoy lower tax rates on that income. In a move that facilitated income splitting among members of a family, the law was changed in 1979 to tax personal income on an individual rather than on a family basis.

The ability of a taxpayer to avoid paying significant personal income taxes is enhanced by a wide range of possible deductions. For example, the first Rs. 12,000 of dividends are exempt from personal taxation, as is the first Rs. 2,000 or ⅓ (whichever is larger) of interest income from National Savings Certificates. For administrative reasons, most other interest income avoids taxation. However, since 1986 this is controlled by requiring the depositors to furnish the national identification numbers and also imposing a withholding tax of 20 percent on interest income of taxable persons.[8] Rental income from houses is largely exempt. Capital gains realized on the sale of shares in quoted public companies is exempt from tax, as is the capital gains from immovable properties. However, exemption for houses is restricted to first sale of the house, and to the first sale by an individual, after 1978. One is also able to deduct a wide range of expenditures from taxable income including the purchase of selected ordinary shares, expenditure for the construction and lease of houses, insurance premiums, mortgage interest for houses, pension fund contributions, and the expenditure on the overseas eduction of a child.[9]

Positive steps have been taken over the past ten years to introduce a more realistic rate structure in the company and personal income tax systems. In tax policy terms, however, these tax systems are still extremely weak. Unless steps are taken to reduce the rates of company tax further and to systematically broaden the tax bases of these taxes by the elimination of tax holidays, exemptions, and excessive deductions, they will primarily serve to misallocate resources rather than to obtain financial revenues for the public sector.

Although the wealth tax, with a tax yield of about 1 percent of tax revenues, could be classified as a "nuisance tax," it has been retained to the present. By fixing asset values at their 1977 levels, this tax will continue to decline in significance and should become a candidate for elimination in the not-too-distant future.

Business Turnover Tax

In the evolutionary process of tax policy formation in Sri Lanka over the last ten years, it is the indirect tax system that has experienced the greatest advances. Not only have steps been taken to rationalize the indirect taxes on exports and imports, but the business turnover tax (BTT) has been developed as a central fiscal instrument. In 1978 it generated only about 10 percent of total tax revenues, but at present, more than 30 percent of total revenues are raised by this tax. Over time, the range of goods and services subject to the BTT has been greatly broadened and the rates of tax increased.

The administrative costs of the tax are quite low, at less than 0.4 percent of total revenues. It is far, however, from being a neutral tax. Prior to 1988, there were ten different rates ranging from 3 to 20 percent on manufacturing enterprises and importers. A tax rate of 1 percent is applied to wholesalers and retailers, and many services are taxed at rates of 1, 3, and 5 percent, depending on the item. In the most recent budget, there has been a partial rationalization of the turnover tax by reducing the number of rates to four categories for commodities and to three rate bands for services.

Although the BTT is a tax on the gross quarterly receipts from sales, it has some features of a value-added tax. There is a credit mechanism that allows manufacturers to deduct the tax they have paid on inputs from the taxes that are payable on their sales. At all other stages the tax is cascading, and in addition, capital assets are subject to tax. As a result, the effective rates of tax on value-added across industries vary greatly. It has been estimated (prior to the 1988 budget proposals) that the effective rates of taxation on the value added of an industry range all the way from the 20 to 50 percent range on metal products, chemicals, and paper products to the 1 to 2 percent range on such items as textiles, construction, and transport.[10]

In the context of indirect taxation in developing countries, the BTT has the important feature of being broad-based. It is almost unheard of even in developed countries to have a sales tax that covers the basic food necessities such as fish, rice, flour, and salt at a 5 percent rate.

With this basic policy feature in place it should be a relatively easy task to bring about a greater uniformity in the rate structure and the extension of the credit for taxes paid on capital inputs. If it was thought to be important to have higher tax rates on some items, then a uniform set of excise of luxury taxes could be fairly easily imposed on these objects in addition to the basic rate of BTT.

IV. Process and Results of Economic Reforms

The series of economic reforms undertaken by the Sri Lankan government from 1977 has made a major change in the direction of economic activity in the economy. Over a period of about three years not only were the foreign exchange markets and prices largely decontrolled, but the widespread consumption subsidies were eliminated.

At the same time, gross capital formation increased dramatically as a percentage of gross domestic product. In 1976 and 1977 this gross capital formation averaged 14.5 percent of GDP, while for the period from 1978 to 1982 it averaged 28.9 percent. Even in the next two years at the beginning of the period of serious communal conflict, this ratio still averaged 27.5 percent.[11]

Role of Foreign Assistance

Throughout this period Sri Lanka has received a tremendous amount of support from both the bilateral and multilateral aid agencies. From table 7.3 we see that government capital expenditure amounted to 14.7 percent of GDP over the period from 1978 to 1984. Over this period about 38 percent of these investment expenditures were financed by foreign grants and foreign project loans. In total, foreign assistance and loans financed about 56 percent of all government capital formation, or an amount equal to 8.2 percent of GDP.

With this degree of foreign financing (with very favorable terms) the government was not required to use the tax system to mobilize resources for the public sector to the same degree as it would have had to if it were not the recipient of this massive amount of foreign assistance. This situation cannot be expected to last for an extended period of time. Greater reliance will eventually have to be placed in the future on the mobilization of domestic resources to finance development expenditures; recent steps to rationalize the tax system were essential for this purpose.

Technical assistance via the international aid agencies has played an

Table 7.3   Financing of Government Capital Expenditure from 1978–84
(percentage of GDP at current market price)

	1978	1979	1980	1981	1982	1983	1984	1978–84
Capital expenditure	12.8	14.8	18.6	13.8	16.2	13.6	12.8	14.7
Among which financed by:								
Government savings	−1.3	0.4	−3.6	−1.8	−1.4	0.1	3.9	−0.5
Foreign grants	1.5	2.6	4.0	3.2	3.4	2.8	2.2	2.8
Foreign project loans	3.5	1.3	1.5	2.3	3.0	4.0	4.2	2.8
Foreign commodity loans	2.4	2.1	1.6	1.6	1.0	0.8	0.4	1.4
Foreign other loans	1.8	1.1	2.1	1.9	0.8	0.4	0.4	1.2
Domestic non-market borrowing	1.8	1.1	2.1	1.9	0.8	0.4	−0.4	1.1
Domestic market borrowing	0.7	1.7	−0.7	0.4	1.7	1.8	0.5	0.9
Monetary expansion	3.8	4.4	3.1	1.7	4.0	3.3	3.4	3.4

Note: Repayment of public debt is excluded.
Source: Central Bank of Sri Lanka.

important role in assisting the analysis of policy options in the fiscal area. In the case of taxes and regulations affecting international trade a number of major studies have been sponsored by the World Bank and other agencies. On domestic tax policy, a series of mission reports made by the IMF and the World Bank have addressed the tax structure and administration issues on a regular basis. Unlike most tax reform programs discussed elsewhere in this volume, at no time has a formal tax reform study been undertaken. Perhaps the economic policymakers in Sri Lanka learned an important lesson from their previous high-profile tax reform effort in the 1950s. That partial reform was famous both because it was done by Nicholas Kaldor and because most of the implemented tax policies were abolished within five years.[12]

Over the past decade the business community, both small and large businesses alike, has had a very large influence in the formulation of company and personal income tax policies. After being the focus of government regulation and nationalization for the previous decade, the private sector needed maximum encouragement from the tax system in order to build business confidence and the desire to make long-term investments. This was reflected in the outpouring of tax incentives and tax holidays. On the other hand, the international assistance agencies have been consistently encouraging the development of a strong domestic tax system that would be capable of mobilizing domestic resources. Recent budgets seem to indicate that the government is adjusting its position with respect to direct taxation to recognize that many of the tax incentives were counterproductive and that a system with fewer distortions might be better for both the business community and the treasury.

Impact on Revenues and Administration

From 1971 to 1977 government tax revenues as a percentage of GNP averaged 16.2 percent, with a slight downward trend to 15.0 percent in 1977. Since 1978 this variable has averaged 19.2 percent. If the values for 1978 and 1979 are removed because of the high values for export taxes during those years, the ratio becomes 18.0 percent.[13] From these aggregate statistics it would appear that the changes in the structure of taxation increased the performance of the system by about 20 percent or 3 percentage points of GNP. With the changes that have recently been introduced to simplify the structure of the BTT and remove some of the tax preferences from the income tax, the performance of the tax system may be further enhanced.

By international standards, Sri Lanka has a fairly efficient tax administration, although at the present time it has fallen behind in its development of computerized information systems. In this context it is surprising to see the significant drop in the administration costs of the tax system that followed the deregulation of the economy in 1978 and the shift of the tax system away from income tax and toward the business turnover tax.

In table 7.4 we examine the administrative costs of the Inland Revenue Department from 1973 to 1985. This department administers the income tax, the business turnover tax, the wealth tax, and other ad hoc tax levies. In this table the administrative costs are expressed as a percentage of tax revenue collected. From 1973 to 1976 the administrative costs averaged about 1.0 percent of tax revenues, but from 1978 to 1985 they averaged only 0.52 percent of tax collection. Furthermore, the trend has been clearly downward with the costs of administration for these taxes from 1982 to 1985 only amounting to 0.37 of tax collections.

This is a clear indication of the relative administrative efficiency of the use of a BTT as compared to an income tax in the context of a

Table 7.4   Comparison of Administration Costs to Tax Collections
(Income Tax, Business Turnover Tax, Wealth Tax)

Financial year	Percentage
1973	0.90
1974	1.05
1975	1.06
1976	1.02
Average 1973–76	1.00
1977	n.a.
1978	0.82
1979	0.82
1980	n.a.
1981	0.50
1982	0.47
1983	0.40
1984	0.28
1985	0.33
Average 1978–85	0.52

Source: *Administration Reports of the Commissioner General of Inland Revenue* (Colombo, Sri Lanka, 1973 to 1985).

developing country. In these calculations of administrative cost, we have not been able to estimate the relative costs of tax compliance. Yet the compliance costs of income taxes are generally much higher than indirect taxes where the determination of the tax base is relatively easy. If this holds for Sri Lanka, administrative and compliance costs probably have fallen by an even greater amount since 1978 than is indicated by the estimates in table 7.4.

Impact on Economic Growth

Another important objective of the economic reforms was to facilitate economic growth. Although the various tax incentives introduced from 1978 to 1985 were motivated by considerations of accelerating economic growth, it is difficult to assess the incremental contribution they made as compared to the other fundamental reforms. The tax policies probably had their most important impact on business confidence through the strong message they carried to the business community of the government's support and belief in the private sector. The tax incentives for many activities do little to alter the relative rate of return of investments. The tax holidays are particularly ineffective for undertakings

Table 7.5   Annual Real Growth Rates of GDP and Selected Sector from 1978–85 (at constant 1970 factor prices)

	1978	1979	1980	1981	1982	1983	1984	1985	1978 –85
Agriculture	5.4	2.0	3.1	6.9	2.6	5.0	−0.4	8.7	3.8
Paddy	12.7	1.4	11.9	3.6	−3.4	15.2	−3.5	9.9	5.1
Tea	−4.3	3.5	−7.5	10.0	−10.7	−4.5	16.2	2.9	−0.2
Rubber	5.6	−0.9	−13.0	−6.7	0.6	12.3	3.7	0.7	−1.2
Coconut	15.4	6.4	−11.0	11.5	11.3	−8.3	−7.0	46.4	2.9
Other agri- culture	0.7	0.2	4.7	8.0	6.7	6.2	7.2	n.a.	5.9
Mining	20.2	5.3	4.9	4.2	4.1	7.8	1.5	1.5	6.2
Manufacturing	7.8	4.6	0.8	5.2	4.8	0.8	12.3	5.2	4.6
Export processing	2.1	4.4	−9.8	7.6	−5.3	−4.6	9.0	8.0	0.3
Factory industry	11.0	4.0	5.0	4.0	8.9	2.0	14.0	5.0	6.2
Small industry	13.2	9.8	0.0	5.1	10.1	4.0	4.2	3.0	5.6
Construction	28.3	20.9	11.0	−3.0	−2.0	1.0	−0.1	0.5	5.8
Services	7.6	7.8	8.0	6.4	7.0	6.7	7.0	3.9	6.7
GDP	8.2	6.3	5.8	5.8	5.1	5.0	5.0	5.0	5.5

Source: Central Bank of Sri Lanka.

such as hotels where the profits are usually low or negative during the first few years of operation.

As shown in table 7.5, during 1978 to 1985 the growth in real GDP averaged 5.5 percent. This is a substantial improvement over the performance of the economy from 1971 to 1977 when the real growth in GDP averaged only 2.8 percent. From 1978 to 1985 the average growth rates of manufacturing, mining, construction, and services were all between 4.6 and 6.7 percent. In contrast, agriculture grew by only 3.8 percent even though massive investments were being made in irrigation and infrastructure.

While rice production grew quite well at 5.1 percent, the performance of the tree crop sector including tea, rubber, and coconut was very poor. The combination of higher export taxes, a softening of international prices, and the continuation of a high degree of public-enterprise activity in these crops was sufficient to cause tea and rubber to have negative average growth rates during this period.

Impact on the Distribution of Income

In the 1950s the tax reform efforts in Sri Lanka were characterized by an emphasis on income redistribution. The Kaldor proposal for expenditure taxes and wealth taxes in Sri Lanka was a typical example. Sri Lanka tried an expenditure tax but discontinued it because the administration proved to be excessively difficult. A second trial was attempted in 1976, but was repealed in 1977, characterized as "unworkable and impractical in an economy like that of Sri Lanka."[14] Clearly, the redistribution of income was not a stated objective of tax reforms in 1978, except for the overall objective of creating economic activity and employment. On this criterion the government was highly successful in that the rate of unemployment was reduced from rates of about 20 percent to less than 10 percent between 1977 and 1982.[15]

From an examination of the legal structure of the tax system after 1978, it would appear that the tax changes gave more relief, through both lower tax rates and tax incentives, to the high-income individuals. This need not be the case. The administration of the tax system also plays a central role in determining who actually pays more or less tax. In addition, the shifting of the tax system toward the BTT might add to the progressivity. Much higher tax rates and broader coverage have tended to be placed on the goods that are consumed more intensely by the higher-income groups. Furthermore, the administration of the business turnover tax is much more effective at collection of the tax from the legal tax base than is the personal income tax.

V. Lessons from the Sri Lankan Experience

The process that Sri Lanka used in the late 1950s and the one policy-makers took from 1978 to 1988 to bring about tax policy changes are stark contrasts. In the 1950s a bold attempt was made to bring about a new tax structure of experimental design. This followed a high-profile, academically driven tax reform study. The result was a total failure of the tax reform.

The recent experience was quite different. Following a change in government many tax measures were taken that, in the first instance, were not clearly positive tax policies. This was followed by a relatively long period of sound economic leadership during which time the tax system evolved slowly in a positive manner. Tax changes such as the lowering of marginal income tax rates for individuals, and the development of a broad-based BTT might not have been politically possible if the tax changes that took place over the decade were all put into one contemporaneous "tax reform" package. Thus Sri Lanka in recent years provides one example of moderate success in implementing "successive" tax reform (see chapter 1).

Although the BTT is far from being an ideal value-added tax, it again supports the view that broad-based indirect taxes are preferred to income taxes or taxes on trade as fiscal instruments to raise revenues in developing countries. Economic policymakers in Sri Lanka now should assess how their BTT system can be improved. Emphasis should be placed on not trading off too much of the broad nature of the tax in order to ease the administration of a more neutral value added tax.

Finally, the tax changes made during the 1980s in Sri Lanka are an example of the benefits of continuous tax policy analysis by both local officials and international agencies over an extended period of time. Through this process the government was able to take the very poor tax system of the 1970s and to gradually transform it into a workable fiscal instrument.

Notes

The assistance of Mr. U. Dharmawasa, Mr. Jehan Perera, and Mr. Xeronog Fang in the completion of this study is greatly appreciated.

1 Ministry of Finance and Planning, *Public Investment 1980–1984* (National Planning Division, Colombo, Sri Lanka), p. 3.
2 Minister of Finance and Planning, *Budget Speeches, Republic of Sri Lanka,* 1978 and 1979, and Central Bank of Sri Lanka, *Annual Reports and Reviews of the Economy,* 1977 and 1978.
3 Inland Revenue Act (I.R.A.) #4, 1963, Secs. 25(1)(a) and (b) and Sec. 26(1) as amended by Sec. 8 of I.R.A. #17 of 1972.
4 I.R.A. #4, 1963. Secs. 18, 19, 20, 20A, 21, 22, 23, 23A, and 24 of Chapter V and Secs. 44, 45, and 46 of Chapter XI as amended from time to time and also Sec. 129 (definitions) as amended by Sec. 28 of I.R.A. #16 of 1976.
5 I.R.A. #4 of 1963, 2nd schedule, parts v, vi, and vii, as inserted by Secs. 30 (1) and (2) of the I.R.A. #16 of 1976.
6 I.R.A. #4, 1963, 2nd schedule, part viii, as inserted by Sec. 44 of I.R.A. #30 of 1978.
7 I.R.A. #28 of 1979; Sec. 33, parts II–IV, 2nd Schedule as amended by I.R.A. #27, 1982; Sec. 35, parts II–IV, 2nd Schedule.
8 I.R.A. #28 of 1979, Sec. 113A–J as inserted by Sec. 15 of I.R. (amend) Act #56 of 1985.
9 Until 1984 the amount of deductions of this type, except few specified items which enjoyed full benefits, was restricted to one third of accessible income. In 1985 an annual limit of Rs. 500,000 was imposed which was further reduced to Rs. 150,000

in 1986, and it included those items specifically excluded. In the 1988 budget it is proposed to lower the annual limit to Rs. 50,000. I.R.A. #28 of 1979; Secs. 31(5), 31(5A), and 31(5B) as amended by Sec. 12 of I.R.A. #16 of 1985 and Sec. 6 of I.R.A. #56 of 1985.

10 Shah, Anwar, *A Review of Selected Taxation Issues in Sri Lanka* (Mimeograph, February 1988), p. 27, table 7.

11 Central Bank of Sri Lanka, *Annual Reports*, 1971–86.

12 *Report of the Taxation Inquiry Commission*, Colombo (1968).

13 Source: Central Bank of Sri Lanka, *Annual Reports*, 1971–86.

14 Minister of Finance and Planning, *Budget Speech*, Republic of Sri Lanka, 1978.

15 Central Bank of Sri Lanka, *Annual Reports*, 1977–85.

References

Aquirre, C. A., L. H. De Wulf, A. Feltenstein, and G. Cox. *Selected Taxation Issues in Sri Lanka*. Washington, D.C.: International Monetary Fund (IMF), 1985.

Central Bank of Sri Lanka. *Annual Reports*. 1971–87.

——. *Review of the Economy*, Colombo, 1975–87.

Commissioner General of Inland Review. *Administration Reports*, Colombo, 1970–85.

Inland Revenue Act #4 of 1963, #28 of 1979, and Amendments.

Kappagoda, Nihal, and Suzanne Pains. *The Balance of Payments Adjustment Process — The Experience of Sri Lanka*. Marga Institute, Sri Lanka, 1981.

Gillis, Malcolm. *Tax Reform in Developing Countries*. Mimeograph, 1988.

Kaldor, Nicholas. *Suggestions for a Comprehensive Reform of Direct Taxation*. Sessional Paper IV—1960 Government of Sri Lanka.

Ministry of Finance. *Public Investment 1980-1984*. Colombo, Sri Lanka: National Planning Division, 1986, p. 3.

Minister of Finance and Planning. *Budget Speeches*, Republic of Sri Lanka, 1971–88.

Report of the Taxation Inquiry Commission. Colombo, 1968.

Shah, Anwar. *A Review of Selected Taxation Issues in Sri Lanka*. Mimeograph, February 1988.

8

Retrospectives on Tax Missions to Venezuela (1959), Brazil (1964), and Liberia (1970)

·······

Carl S. Shoup   Introduction by Malcolm Gillis

I. Introduction

This chapter consists of a retrospective look at two ambitious tax reform missions (Venezuela and Liberia) and one tax reform study (Brazil) organized and undertaken by Carl Shoup in the two decades following his tax mission to Japan (chapter 6). The background, genesis, contents, and degree of implementation of each set of reform measures are discussed, and in each case hindsights are offered that might be helpful in the design and execution of future tax reform initiatives.

In all three cases factors other than fiscal crisis prompted requests for expatriate assistance in tax reform. The Venezuelan government, for instance, acted out of concern for four revenue related issues: In pre-OPEC 1958, when oil prices were moving toward $1.00/bbl, and when reserves of Venezuelan heavy crude were uncertain, it seemed important to have in place a tax system that could be called upon to supply large increases in non-oil taxes when petroleum reserves dwindled. (The old Venezuelan non-oil tax system consisted primarily of indirect taxes, particularly tariffs and sumptuary excises, and could *not* be counted upon to replace oil revenues, should they eventually decline.) The government was also interested in collecting enough taxes to greatly expand public expenditures for human capital, in education primarily (only 50 percent of the school age population was in school), but also in public health. While officials expected no *immediate* fiscal crisis, they anticipated a sizable deficit in 1958–59, so they needed to address medium-term revenue needs. Ultimately, they were interested in increasing progressivity, at least to a limited degree.

Nineteen sixty-four may have been the only year in recent Brazilian history in which the government budget deficit was not viewed as a high-priority problem. Because Brazil's government was not clearly committed to tax reform at this time, the Shoup tax mission report did not explicitly report on the goals sought by the government where it did enact tax reform. Instead, the report identified problems in taxation and resource allocation, taxation and income distribution, multilevel government finance, and tax *structure* issues in general.

Liberia also faced no immediate threat of fiscal crisis in 1969—and, for reasons discussed in section IV, could not increase tax rates for most existing taxes anyway. In this case the tax mission focused on restructuring the tax system to achieve equity, to reallocate resources, and to promote economic growth.

In none of the three cases did the work of the mission have much significant immediate impact on tax policy: in Venezuela, it was only in the tax reform of 1966 that the recommendations of the tax mission were clearly apparent. Since 1966, a number of the mission's proposals (including those on capital gains taxes, on the taxation of foreign source income, and a few administrative reforms including self-assessment of income taxes) have been enacted, but only on a piecemeal basis.

Although Brazil did act on the report's recommendation of a state-level VAT, it has adopted only small bits and pieces of the rest of the Shoup program in the last twenty-three years. However, Brazil was influenced by the Shoup reports more than any other assessment of its tax system, in that the only major taxes it has repealed are those that Shoup recommended be abolished.

One final similarity between the three programs was that in each case the author agreed to undertake the projects only after receiving assurance that all tax reform studies would be published, so that the reports would facilitate open and wide-ranging discussion of tax reform issues in each of the countries.

Naturally, there were also significant differences between the tax reform undertakings. For example, the Shoup report on Brazil was a one-man show, while both the Venezuelan and Liberian reform proposals were the product of a team of well-known economists and legal specialists in taxation and government spending. The reform proposals also varied because each committee was provided with different sorts of resources.

II. The Tax Mission to Venezuela 1958–59

A. Genesis of the Project

By 1957 Venezuela had experienced more than one hundred years of dictatorships. It had become an independent state in 1830, and was then mainly controlled by *caudillos* from the landowning class. From 1908 till his death in 1935, Juan Vicente Gomez ruled with "total and absolute tyranny" (*Columbia University Encyclopedia*, p. 2875). In 1948 a repressive military dictatorship seized power; by 1952 Colonel Perez Jiménez had become dictator. After ten years of Jiménez's police state techniques, revolutionaries supported by liberal units of the armed forces caused Jiménez to flee, and formed a presidential junta.

In late 1957 and early 1958, Thomas Enrique Carillo-Batalla, first imprisoned and then exiled by Jiménez, was living in New York City, taking graduate work in economics at Colombia University. In January 1958 Carillo asked me if I would consider forming a tax mission to Venezuela. By this time his Venezuelan friends were in control of their government, and Carillo-Batalla informed me that they were interested in reforming the tax system.

B. Initiation of the Project

Early in May 1958 Professor Stanley Surrey and I accepted the invitation of the Venezuelan minister of finance, Dr. Arturo Sosa, to travel to Venezuela to ascertain whether the prospects for a useful study were sufficiently bright. Dr. Surrey and I concluded that they were, and planned to arrive in Venezuela early in the summer and submit the report before the end of August. The Venezuelan government was to pay for the mission, while the director would choose the mission members. Venezuelan tax and finance experts (with Dr. Carillo as chair) would form a Fiscal Reform Commission, and would both help the mission and comment on its preliminary proposals. The report itself would be made available in book form in both English and Spanish.

Dr. Carillo urged that the members of the mission not be solely from the United States; and that the report present some background material on the Venezuelan economy, notably distribution of income, rate of investment, sources of its finance, and optimum uses of capital. Later we decided to add sections in which we estimated the cost of certain goals of education and public health, and analyzed the government's accounting system with a view to changes that would facilitate gathering data for the national income accounts and integrating the two sets of accounts. In these respects the mission's work extended well beyond the tax field proper.

The members of the mission,[1] aside from the director, were:

John F. Due, professor of economics, University of Illinois
Lyle C. Fitch, first deputy administrator, City of New York
Sir Donald MacDougall, Official Fellow, Nuffield College, Oxford University
Oliver S. Oldman, assistant professor of law, Harvard Law School
Stanley S. Surrey, professor of law, Harvard Law School

The mission's report was submitted August 22, 1958, then mimeographed, translated into Spanish, and circulated within the government. With the feedback we obtained we revised and expanded the report in June 1959.

C. The Tax Mission Report

1. Publication. The revised report was published later in 1959 by Johns Hopkins Press, and complimentary copies were distributed among public finance scholars and libraries. The government of Venezuela printed a Spanish-language edition.[2] Although the government did not widely distribute the Spanish-language edition, professor Oliver Oldman concluded (1968) that publication of the report in Spanish "was crucial to the Report's having substantial impact. The Report has been and is probably still being used in Venezuelan universities . . . . The role of the Report in stimulating interest in tax structure reform and in identifying problem areas ought not to be underestimated. Moreover, the impact of the Report in other countries ought not to go unnoticed. The Report received wide distribution in Latin America and no doubt had a bearing on the Conferences on Tax Administration (Buenos Aires 1961) and Tax Policy (Santiago 1962), as well as on the formulation of the tax planks of the Alliance for Progress. Reforms which have already taken place in such countries as Mexico and El Salvador and are in progress in such countries as Brazil and Chile parallel many of the Report's suggestions with respect to income taxation. Finally, the Report continues to serve as a model in the preparation of fiscal surveys for other countries."[3]

2. Contents, in General. For the most part the tax mission report was a straightforward description and analysis of the tax system, tax by tax. However, because the mission felt that Venezuela's previous government had failed to consider all relevant factors in devising its tax system, it devoted one quarter of its report to nontax background material. This material included sections on capital requirements, the actual rate of investment in Venezuela, sources of finance for investment, the importance of the oil industry and of other foreign capital and know-how, and tariff protection. The dictatorship had also neglected to formulate goals in the areas of education and public health, so the report considered the costs and benefits of such concerns.

The first two chapters consisted of an estimate of the distribution of income by income class in Venezuela (MacDougall) and a discussion of the problem of capital accumulation, and economic development in general (also MacDougall). Sections of the second chapter covered taxation of the higher-income groups, budget surpluses and deficits, and considerations affecting the future level of taxation as they related to general issues of development.

Much of the chapter on Venezuelan national government accounts and accounting reports also encompassed more than a traditional tax study would include, since it presented detailed descriptions of the accounting and reporting systems in offices dealing with expenditures. It dealt with the practice of completely separating the functions of tax administration and tax collection, and the usefulness of the accounting reports in the task of compiling national income accounts and formulating fiscal policy.

The concept of "tax" was extended to cover the government's profits from a certain kind of exchange control: the petroleum companies operating in Venezuela were required to satisfy their needs for bolivars by purchasing them from the central bank at a rate slightly above three to the dollar, and the central bank then resold those dollars to the commercial banks and the public at a substantially higher rate.

Although the mission report described the special tax measures that aimed at a 50-50 sharing of oil profits between the companies and the government, no recommendation was made on whether to change that ratio, since it was felt that "this matter of national policy involves so many important issues other than taxation that it lies outside the scope of the commission's technical recommendations" (p. 2).

A chapter was devoted to a question of aggregate fiscal policy: use of the tax system in stabilizing the economy in booms and depressions through appropriate changes in tax rates.

A detailed examination of the income tax, personal and corporate, occupied about one third of the report. Of this segment, about 20 percent was given over to administration of the tax, testifying to the importance the mission attached to this aspect of tax policy and practice. Indirect taxation, although of far greater current revenue importance, was allotted only about one eighth of the total pages; the technical issues were less complex, and the mission's aim was to show how the direct-tax part of the system might carry a larger share of the total load.

3. *Recommendations: Substantive and Structural.* The chief structural and substantive changes in the Venezuelan tax system recommended by the commission's report (administrative changes are covered in section 4 below) concerned the income tax, the customs duties, the 0.5 percent turnover tax (to be repealed), the gasoline tax (to be increased), and a strengthening of the municipal real estate tax in urban areas. Suggestions were also offered for revision of the grants-in-aid system. Costs were computed for a program of enhanced education and the increases in income tax rates that would cover this cost were specified.

a. The nine schedular income taxes and the overall complementary income tax levied at progressive rates were to be replaced with a single, unified tax. Under the existing law, income was classified into nine schedules (rents from real property, interest and royalties, business profits, etc.) and each schedule had its own rules for deductions and its own flat rate. The complementary tax was applied at a progressive rate scale to the sum of the amounts entered under the schedular computations. The schedular rates, in percentages, were: 1 (salaries and wages), 2 (agricultural profits and profits from noncommercial professions), 2.5 (oil and mining profits, business profits, rents from real property), 3 (interest and royalties and gains from sales of real property), and 10 (lottery prizes). An inordinate amount of time and effort was taken up in deciding under which schedule a given item of income and, especially, expense, should be placed. The basis of the mild progression, type of income, was deemed inferior to size of total income. Personal exemptions under the unified tax would take account of family status, which they did not under the schedular taxes.

b. The corporation income tax was to be henceforth a distinct, separate tax, not a virtual duplication of the personal income tax. At that time, corporations were subject to the same set of schedular taxes and the complementary tax, at the same rates, as individuals. Dividends were not included in the taxable income of the shareholder. "The present system would be understandable perhaps in an economic society in which corporations were family-owned and family-managed" (p. 112). But when individuals started to receive income from various sources, the progressive feature was weakened by the flat schedular rates; moreover, the progressive rate of the complementary tax led to the splitting of a family corporation into two or more corporations. The advent of the modern widely held corporation also negated the rationale of the identical-rates treatment of the corporation and the individual. Moreover, if tax policy required an increase in the rates applicable to individuals, that same rate change would probably not be deemed appropriate for corporations. Accordingly, a separate rate scale was recommended for the corporate tax: 10 percent of the first 50,000 bolivars (Bs.) of profits, or perhaps the first 100,000 Bs.; 20 percent on the next block of profits up to, say, Bs. 10,000,000; and a top rate (not specified) on profits above that. The existing reductions in tax rates for the top three brackets (complementary tax) for reinvested earnings were to be repealed.

c. Double taxation of dividends, or something close to it, would occur under the new regime, unless measures were spelled out to prevent it, and the commission report went into great detail in proposing the best method for averting or mitigating such extra taxation (pp. 114–25). The technique of allowing corporations to deduct dividends and that of allowing shareholders to credit company-level taxes against those due at the personal level were closely compared, and seen to be virtually the same in the more important results; administratively, the credit method was thought to be somewhat simpler. In either case the aim, for reasons given, was to reduce double taxation, but not to eliminate fully the effect of the corporate tax.

d. At some later date, a worldwide principle of taxing income was to be adopted, to replace the existing territorial (or "source") principle of taxing only income arising in Venezuela. Credit would be given for foreign income taxes paid. This issue was not urgent, because in 1958 Venezuelan individuals and corporations were apparently receiving little income from abroad. A change to the worldwide principle would discourage the use of Venezuela by "base companies" established there to control foreign operating subsidiaries or branches and to receive income from such foreign sources. Also, continuation of the territorial principle might give an undesirable incentive to Venezuelans to invest abroad. Meanwhile, the actual application of that principle in Venezuela was too strict, in disallowing some expenses that were properly allocable to income earned in Venezuela simply because they were incurred abroad. Nonresidents, of course, would in any case be taxed only on their income arising within the country. The report goes into some detail regarding certain troublesome conceptual and accounting problems on this score.

e. Exclusion of certain types of interest from taxable income, and certain rents, should be "re-examined," and, the report implied, probably repealed.

f. Capital gains should continue to be taxed, but with the benefit of an averaging formula. Gains accrued at death should be reached, perhaps indirectly through a special regime under the death or gift tax.

g. Certain recommendations were made concerning the existing limit on deduction of corporate salaries, loss carryovers, worthless-stock losses, and deductions for certain personal expenses (pp. 169–71). Some liberalization of the accounting rules permitted taxpayers was suggested, and certain changes in the statute of limitations (pp. 172–74).

h. Regarding property passing at death or by lifetime gift, the report made no firm recommendation for change from the existing succession tax, levied on the donee, to an estate tax, levied on the donor. The pros and cons were spelled out, and at least some doubt was expressed on the advisability of making the amount of tax depend on the relationship of the recipient to the donor.

i. Venezuela, the report recommended, should move away from the existing pattern of raising some 70 percent of non-oil national tax revenues from indirect taxes. Instead, efforts should be focused on strengthening the income tax, repealing the general sales tax, and reducing many of the customs duties. Also, the admittedly moderate taxes on liquor, tobacco, and motor fuel were to be increased only because additional revenue might well be needed to finance education and health and balance the budget. The case for decreasing the overall share of indirect taxation was particularly strong for Venezuela, given that it had an important source of tax revenue in its natural resources, and that the income tax, apart from the oil sector, was "little more than a token levy" (p. 5).

j. As for the particular excises, there were "no obvious features of liquor taxation which appear to warrant drastic revision" (p. 257). The cigarette tax, instead of being at a uniform specific rate, might well be graduated in two to four brackets according to the retail selling price. The tax on gasoline, collected at the refineries, was also to be raised.

k. The customs duties not levied for protection, i.e., imposed on articles not produced in Venezuela, should be removed, except for luxuries (see next paragraph). Many of these items were producer goods and the tariff burden on the consumer goods was haphazard. Especially appropriate for such exemption were various food items, paper, industrial machinery, and chemicals.

l. On a specified list of articles regarded as luxuries, the import duties should be kept, but transferred from a specific basis (so much per pound, usually) to a percentage-of-value (ad valorem) basis. If the article were also produced in Venezuela, a similar rate would be imposed: the same, if no protection was sought. The rates suggested by the report, as examples, were low (10 to 30 percent) compared with usual luxury-tax rates.

m. The so-called consular fees, levied on imports at ad valorem rates progressive with the size (value) of a shipment, should be imposed at a single rate, with exemptions, possibly, of a few basic goods consumed in large amounts by lower-income groups.

n. The general sales tax, a turnover tax of one half of one percent on all sales, with no allowance for tax paid at earlier stages of production or distribution ("cascade tax"), was to be repealed. The many well-known faults of this type of tax were cited, including its burden on the poor, its artificial inducement to vertical integration of business firms, and the difficult administrative tasks it posed. The revenue loss would therefore be on the order of only 3 percent of total tax revenues, owing to the very low rate of the tax. If Venezuela desired to retain some form of general sales tax (an action not recommended by the commission), it was advised to consider a wholesalers' sales tax, since a retail sales tax would be hard to administer in this country of small shops and stands. (The report spelled out in some detail how such a wholesalers' tax should be constructed and administered.)

o. On the question of whether the Venezuelan states and municipalities should be given substantially more taxing power, or exercise more of the power they already had, the commission did not take a stand one way or the other (p. 350). The states had virtually no taxing power of consequence, and the municipalities controlled only the business license tax (*patente*), the urban real estate tax, and the automobile license tax. For the fiscal year ending June 30, 1959, the national government was estimated to collect Bs. 3.809 billion in what the commission considered tax revenues; the state governments, only a few million; the federal district (this includes Caracas), between Bs. 50 and 100 million; and the rest of the municipalities (strictly, *distritos*), less than Bs. 100 million (p. 3).

p. While at the time the only taxes imposed by the states were very minor ones (on raffles and sales of lottery tickets of other states, and the anomalous unconstitutional tax on imports imposed by the state of Zulia) (p. 317), the commission concluded that there were few feasible tax sources which the states could effectively administer. The commission did suggest a new state tax that would be a supplemental income tax assessed on residents of the state, or a percentage of taxable income as defined for national income tax purposes, reported by residents of the state. This tax, imposed by the states, would be collected by the national government and turned over to them. This is to be distinguished from a state-collected tax based on what the taxpayer shows on his national income tax return, or expressed as a percentage of the national tax. Another potential state tax was a tax on agricultural land holdings, which paid no tax at all.

q. As to municipal taxes, the commission was not happy with the *patentes* on industry and commerce, which took two main forms: a per millage of gross sales or gross revenues, the rate depending on the type of business, and a system of flat-sum taxes, the amount depending on the "class" of the particular firm. But if the tax were retained, it should be removed from manufacturing and wholesaling firms, eliminating the flat-sum feature and restricting the rate structure to two basic rates. The tax law should be revised and codified, through a national "model" tax law.

r. The urban real estate tax, in contrast, was regarded favorably: it was "the only state or municipal tax source capable of yielding substantial increased revenues" (p. 336). It was recommended that the tax continue to be based on rents rather than on capital values (the federal-district tax rate on rents was 6.5 percent), including imputed rent. It was, however, recommended that taxes on agricultural land should be reserved to the states, or possibly to the national government, in connection with a general land reform program" (p. 340).

s. It was argued that the rates of the municipal tax on automobiles, which varied among municipalities and induced many car owners to register falsely in low-rate municipalities, should be made uniform throughout the country and collected by the national government.

t. The national government should make general-purpose grants directly to the municipalities, according to need and financial capacity. Specific-program grants might also be instituted. The report offered some suggestions as to the particular structures of possible grants.

u. In any case, the report advised that "the national government must continue to raise the bulk of the nation's public revenues" (p. 348). The pressing needs of the federal district could readily be met by increasing the rate and enforcement of its real estate tax. The potential increases in local tax revenues would be chiefly from better administration and expanded use of the real estate tax, partly offset by repeal or improvement of the *patentes*. The report presented a number of reasons for granting more spending powers to the local units, along with several reasons to the contrary, but did not make a firm recommendation on this point. More cooperation among the three levels of government was badly needed, in view of overlapping responsibilities for supplying education, water supply, sanitation, health and medical facilities, rural roads, and measures to increase farm productivity; the report offered some concrete suggestions to this end.

v. Only about one half of the children aged 6–12 years were attending elementary school and kindergarten in Venezuela in 1957–58. The dropout rate was high: the number of those completing sixth grade in the 1956–57 school year was only 18 percent of the number who had entered first grade in 1950–51. Many schools were offering no more than two or three grades. Data gathered and analyzed by Lyle C. Fitch on comparative earning power by level of education, and on the cost of supplying education (including earnings foregone) indicated that in Venezuela at that time the incremental rate of return on an additional dollar spent on education in the primary schools would be between 82 percent and 130 percent per annum—far higher than could be obtained by almost any business investment. For additional secondary school education the annual rate of return was estimated at only 17 percent, rising somewhat to 23 percent for university education. The difference was due in large part to the earnings-foregone cost for the older students. The cost of the expanded education program proposed could be met, in the first year, by a moderate increase in the corporation income tax rate, along with an increase in the unified personal income tax rates that resulted in bracket rates ranging from 6 percent to somewhat above 14 percent for total revenue from this tax. For the longer term, increases in the liquor and tobacco taxes could be called on (letter j above).

w. Public health expenditures were seen to be another sector where additional expenditure could be easily justified, but the data did not permit the kind of cost-benefit computations made for education.

x. Each of the tax measures recommended by the commission was examined, in chapter XIII ("The Tax System and Economic Stability"), to ascertain whether it increased (+) or decreased (−) the sensitivity of the national tax system to fluctuations in business. Such sensitivity was deemed desirable, if the fluctuation occurred in the non-oil sector, since an increase in tax revenue would automatically tend to check a boom and a decrease in tax revenue, and would dampen a business depression (changes in oil-sector tax revenue would have modest or no

Table 8.1   Recommended Tax Measures Classed by Their Effect on the
Sensitivity of the Non-Oil Segment of the Venezuelan Tax System

Income tax	Increases in sensitivity	Decreases in sensitivity
1. A more progressive rate	+(?)	
2. Lower personal exemptions	+(?)	
3. Carrybacks of business loss	+	
4. Taxation of dividends		−
5. Higher rates but less progression in corporate income tax		−
6. Current payment of tax on estimated income of current year; and extension of withholding	+	
7. Averaging of capital gains over several years and carryforward of unabsorbed capital losses		−
Customs duties		
1. Higher tax rates on certain luxuries	+	
2. Lower tax rates on certain necessaries	+	
3. Extension of ad valorem basis in place of per kilo basis	+	
Gasoline tax		
1. Higher rates	+	
Real estate tax		
1. Improved administration and increased rates		−(?)

(Question mark indicates considerable doubt as to which category the item belongs to.)
Source: Commission Report, table 13-1, p. 362.

effects, given the degree of foreign ownership of the oil companies).
Non-oil tax revenue was so small, however, relative to national income,
that the automatic effect would be slight. The plus or minus ranking of
the proposed tax changes is reproduced here from table XIII-1, p. 362.
All of these changes were recommended for reasons other than
sensitivity.

4. Recommendations on Tax Administration

(a) Income taxation. The report's recommendations on tax administration were especially lengthy and detailed with respect to the income
tax. Only the major recommendations are listed here.

i. The declaration form was to be redesigned, to encourage and in
some cases require that the taxpayer himself compute his net taxable

income and the tax due (both of these tasks were being performed by the tax administration, on the basis of declarations of income submitted by the taxpayer, and information at source).

ii. Major taxpayers were to pay the tax at the time of submitting the forms, instead of awaiting a bill computed and sent by the tax office.

iii. A list of potential taxpayers was to be drawn up, and kept current.

iv. Collection of delinquent accounts was to be improved by (a) visits by a specially trained group of tax officials to delinquent taxpayers to determine capacity to pay and use of installment payments; (b) garnisheeing wage or other payments made to delinquent taxpayers and attaching liens against their properties; (c) gradually ending the existing system of turning over large overdue accounts to private lawyers on a commission basis.

v. A system was to be built up for gathering information from payers of various types (other than those withholding tax) regarding payments made to individuals and business firms.

vi. The field audit function was to be expanded and systematized, a function "now largely performed in an inadequate, haphazard fashion" (p. 212), and the office auditing was to be improved also. Some tax agents would be especially trained to handle cases involving fraudulent reporting.

vii. The system of certificates of solvency was to be streamlined. The certificates, attesting that the individual was not delinquent on income tax, were then being required of anyone entering into a contract with a governmental agency, obtaining a license to operate a business, getting permission to go abroad, and the like. "It seems that this type of sanction is quite acceptable to Venezuelan social political philosophy, while direct sanctions, such as jail sentences for tax violations, are not acceptable" (p. 217). The solvency system "should as nearly as possible require certificates of only those persons who are obligated to declare their income and to pay tax" (p. 217). Therefore the requirement should be cast in terms of various groups of persons that are likely to consist largely of taxpayers. "Businessmen of almost all kinds constitute a likely group. So too do purchasers of homes above a certain price. Buyers of expensive cars . . . . Members of the legal, medical, engineering, and accounting professions . . . ."

viii. The withholding of income tax on wages and salaries was to "be made into a more effective collection device" than the existing 1 percent withheld under one of the schedules (p. 220). This could be readily done under a unified income tax. Tax refunds would occasionally be necessary, and the report suggested details for such a procedure.

ix. To put other taxpayers on a par with those withheld from, a pay-as-you-go system should be introduced: payment, in quarterly installments, of the estimated tax on the current year's income.

x. The taxpayer was to be allowed to appeal within the tax administration against any claim for additional tax asserted against him, instead of having to go directly to court. The tax court was working well, but it should have all of its decisions published regularly.

xi. "The present system of penalties, based on a range of 10 percent to 100 percent and 200 percent of the amount of tax involved, . . . involves too much administrative discretion" (p. 228). The report therefore suggested a series of penalties largely automatic in their gradation, for failure to file a declaration on time, late payment of tax amounts admitted to be due, and increase in tax owing to failure to report items of income or to disallowed deductions.

xii. The work of the Technical Division, a section of the Income Tax Administration, was to be recast. "This division should essentially be a group of skilled technical experts, legal and accounting, charged with the tasks of interpreting the statute and regulations and dealing with the complex technical problems arising at the administrative level," and with supplying information to the public (pp. 230–31).

xiii. A reorganization of the tax work within the Ministry of Finance was to be carried out as suggested in a chart on p. 234 of the report.

xiv. More specialized training was to be given to the tax personnel, including some training in courses abroad.

xv. Much more statistical information, obtained from the income tax returns, needed to be assembled and published.

xvi. The practice of disbursing to tax personnel funds collected from delinquent taxes was to be discontinued, and a direct increase of salaries substituted.

xvii. More information was to be made available to the public on the structure of the tax system, methods of administration, and the public's tax responsibilities. Special tax courses would to be made available in law schools and business schools. ". . . [I]t would be helpful to form an organization interested in the subject of taxation, such as a Venezuelan Tax Association," to "hold meetings devoted to discussions of tax subjects and publish a periodical containing articles on tax policy and technical tax issues" (p. 241).

(b) Other taxes. Administrative and compliance problems of taxes other than the income tax took up relatively little of the report, only

some seventeen pages scattered throughout several chapters, and reform proposals are not detailed here. The commission's emphasis on the income tax reflected our view of this tax as the chief source of additional revenue for future years if the budget deficit were to be eliminated and if large additional funds were to be made available for education and public health. It also reflected, to a moderate degree, the weighting of expertise among the commission's members toward the income tax, in terms of the professional backgrounds of those members. This weighting was deliberate, however, in the choice of the commission membership.

D. Degree of Implementation of Tax Commission's Recommendations

1. The Pace of Tax Reform, 1958–87. As background for assessing the extent to which the commission's recommendations were adopted, we first take a general view of tax reform in Venezuela in the nearly thirty years that have elapsed since the report was written.

The year 1958 saw adoption of one of the most important recommendations, that is, repeal of the general sales tax (*cinco por mil*). Thereafter, tax reform languished, except for a 1961 law that adopted a separate income tax rate schedule for corporations. In late 1966, however, the core of the commission's reform for the income tax was adopted, when schedular taxes and the complementary tax were replaced by a unified income tax. Oil and mining companies continued to be taxed under a special regime. In 1973 customs duties were changed to accord with the Andean Pact. In 1983 the Commission on Fiscal Study and Reform, chaired by Dr. Carrillo, submitted its report, which was debated in Congress but has not yet led to extensive change in the tax system (this report covered a wide range of government fiscal activities besides taxation: government expenditure, public debt, budget and administration, accounting, and control, areas that are not covered in the present research project). In 1986 a fairly comprehensive stamp tax was enacted, which some have seen as a type of general sales tax. A few other changes were made in the 1958–87 period that will be noted in the appropriate sections below.

This summary does not include reforms in tax administration, to be treated separately below.

2. Extent of Adoption of Report's Tax Recommendations: Substantive and Structural Matters. The following paragraphs consider substantive and structural tax recommendations listed earlier, to ascertain the extent to which they became incorporated into Venezuelan tax law.[4]

Schedular taxes. The schedular income taxes and the complementary tax were replaced by a unified income tax on individuals and a separate income tax on corporations. This reform has been maintained to the present. Individuals, including partners and sole proprietors, pay a progressive-rate tax on total income, including their shares of partnership profits, computed under "Tariff 1." General partnerships are not taxed, being treated as conduits (Price Waterhouse, p. 70). Corporations and similar entities pay tax under a separate progressive-rate "Tariff 2." Iron mining and petroleum companies were nationalized in 1975 and 1976 respectively; when in private hands they had been subject to a third type of income tax regime.[5] This transformation of the income tax structure was the single most important income tax recommendation in the commission's report.

Family status, not taken into account in the schedular taxes, is allowed for by personal tax credits: a basic credit, plus a smaller credit for a dependent wife not filing separately and for each other dependent that is an ascendant or descendant.

Corporation tax. The graduated rate schedule applicable to most corporations (s.a.s) and limited liability companies (s.r.l.s) ranged, in 1984, from 18 percent on the first Bs. 300,000 to 50 percent on taxable income over Bs. 20 million. In 1986 it was simplified to 15 percent (first Bs. 500,000), 35 percent (next Bs. 4,500,000), and 50 percent (all above). This schedule did not apply to foreign corporations engaged in exploitation of hydrocarbons or minerals.

The rules for determining taxable income for a corporation are the same for all types of business income, and of course no distinction is made in the tax rate schedule. (This practice is in contrast to the practice in force in 1958, when different types of corporate income were taxed at different rates under the schedular taxes.)

A problem not foreseen in the 1958 report emerged when the progressive rate schedule induced the split-up of many substantial corporations into a number of smaller corporations so as to take advantage of the lower tax rates of this graduated scale. This avoidance technique was countered in 1986 by legislation requiring that "companies having the same shareholders and similar or supplemental objectives must declare one single income." But this system of compulsory consolidated returns "has serious technico-legislative defects" and high administrative costs, and the Fiscal Study and Reform Commission in

1983 recommended a single flat rate of 30 percent for the corporation tax (Carrillo, 1987, pp. 2–3). This recommendation has not yet been adopted.

Dividends. Double taxation of dividends, under the new regime of a corporate tax and an individual tax, was mitigated in the 1966 law by allowing a tax credit of 40 percent of the dividend, in the individual's return, but without a "gross-up" (Gittes, p. 150). At present, however, no such credit is allowed, hence dividends are currently taxed twice: once by the corporate tax and again by the individual tax. For a two-year period starting December 29, 1982, an individual shareholder could deduct 50 percent of dividends received from corporations registered on the stock exchange (Price Waterhouse, pp. 88, 104). Dividends received by a corporation are not subject to the corporate tax. The commission's recommendation on dividends has therefore in general not been adopted.

Worldwide and territorial principles, income tax. Nearly thirty years later, Venezuela has accepted, in part, the report's recommendation that the income tax be extended to income derived from abroad by Venezuelan residents, with some allowance for foreign taxes on such income. The 1986 tax law provides for taxation of interest, dividends, royalties, and lease income arising abroad, but at a reduced flat rate: 40 percent on 35 percent of such income (i.e., a rate of 14 percent on full income). Moreover, a regulation of November 26, 1986 (Reglamentary Decree No. 1369) limits this tax to income arising from capital obtained in the foreign country, or earnings obtained there and reinvested (Carrillo, 1987, p. 3).

Partial exclusion of interest and rents. The report's implied suggestion that the partial exclusion from taxable income of certain amounts and/or types of interest and rents should be ended has on the whole not been accepted. Individuals are exempt from paying tax on time deposits made for periods of at least ninety days in national finance or banking institutions and, within established limits, on savings accounts (Price Waterhouse, p. 105). Moving from the recipient to the payor, we find that deduction is allowed to the individual taxpayer for "Interest on loans to purchase or enlarge the principal residence . . . or for rental of the principal residence" (ibid.), with a ceiling (for this and three other types of deduction, apparently, together) of 30 percent of total income if not over Bs. 200,000, plus 1.5 percent on the portion of income from Bs. 200,000 to Bs. 500,000.

Capital gains and losses. Capital gains are included as ordinary income to both corporations and individuals, and capital losses are deductible under specified circumstances (Price Waterhouse, pp. 75, 104). Thus the commission's recommendation has been accepted, aside from the absence of an averaging provision and, apparently, taxation of gains accrued at death.

Limits on corporate salaries. The report, while agreeing that some limits had to be put on deduction of corporate salaries, at least those salaries that went to officers who were also stockholders, pointed out several unsatisfactory features of the existing limitations (pp. 169–70). These features have been, on the whole, removed in the present law (Price Waterhouse, pp. 78–79).

Loss carry-overs. The report proposed that business losses should be carried forward two to three years and that loss carry-back be allowed. The recommendation on carry-forward was accepted, but no loss-carry-back is allowed (Price Waterhouse, p. 82). Carrillo (1987, p. 3) observes that the refusal to allow a carry-back is perhaps due to "administrative complications" in reimbursement of tax, which a carry-back sometimes requires.

Deduction of personal expenses. More, not less (as recommended in the report), deduction is allowed for personal expenses than in 1958 (Price Waterhouse, p. 105; report, 170–1).

Accounting rules. Installment-method accounting and deferred-payment accounting were not allowed in 1958; both were recommended by the report. The former method is now allowed and, apparently, the latter also under the completed-contract and percentage-of-completion methods (Price Waterhouse, p. 74).

Statute of limitations. The point in time at which the obligation for payment of tax and the right of the government to impose fines lapse has been shifted somewhat from that in 1958, but apparently not closely in line with the report's suggestions on this score (Price Waterhouse, pp. 115–16).

Death and gift taxes. The succession type of tax has been retained for transfers at death and by living gifts, and, with it, the variation in tax rates according to the relationship of the donee to the donor (the report doubted the usefulness of this relationship variation). The report's recommendation for cumulation of transfers from any one donor to any one donee, over time, has been partly accepted. Such cumulation, used to determine the tax applicable under the progressive rate scale, now is required for a five-year period (Price Waterhouse, p. 107). The report was favorably disposed toward higher rates, at least at the upper part of the rate scale, for this tax, and, over the years, the rates have indeed been raised, so that they are about double what they were in 1958, in the upper ranges at least (Price Waterhouse, p. 129; report, p. 244).

Pattern of taxation in non-oil sector. The structure of that part of the national tax system applied to the non-oil sector has developed in line with the report's recommendation in 1958. The non-oil income tax, instead of being "little more than a token levy," (see above) is now "the linchpin of the non-oil tax and fiscal system" (Carrillo, p. 61), though, indeed, "its proceeds come largely from the tax on business income and the tax on income from games and betting" (Carrillo, p. 63)—the individual income tax is still modest, by international standards. No general sales tax has been levied to replace the turnover tax repealed in 1958, though the stamp tax passed in 1986 may prove an important revenue source. Customs revenues have declined from their 1958 degree of importance, though apparently more from restriction of trade due to protectionism rather than, as the report recommended, through lowering of duties. The excise taxes have not increased, relatively, enough to alter the general picture that shows a shift of the structure to direct taxation.

Social security and other payroll taxes were unimportant in 1958, and were not studied in detail in the report (p. 10). However, by the 1980s they had developed to the point where the two major payroll taxes (one contributing to the Venezuelan Social Security Institution (IVSS), the other, to the National Institute of Educational Cooperation (INCE) supplied more than twice the revenue produced by the personal income tax. The rate of the former was 11 to 13 percent on the employer, and 4 percent on the employee, a total of 15 to 17 percent, while the education institute tax was only 1 and 0.5 percent on employer and employee, respectively (Carrillo, pp. 89–90). The proceeds are paid, not into the national treasury, but directly into the respective agencies.

Excise taxes. As this is written, information is not at hand on the two of the recommended changes noted above: graduation of the cigarette tax according to retail price, and increase in the gasoline tax. Since nationalization of the hydrocarbons industry in the 1970s, the latter tax, as such, no longer exists.

Customs duties. The recommendation that customs duties not levied for protection be removed, except for luxuries, has been followed to some extent (López, p. 37), but its relative importance has been overshadowed by the growth in protectionist duties. (The commission report did not take a stand for or against protection.)

Duties on luxuries. Information is not at hand on the degree, if any, to which specific duties have been restated as ad valorem duties, on luxury imports. The chief influence on these and other duties has been the Cartagena agreement adapting the duty structure to the Andean Pact, under a decree effective from January 1, 1973 (López, p. 37).

General sales tax. The commission's recommendation to repeal the low-rate general sales tax was adopted immediately, in late 1958. The 1986 stamp tax, on the other hand, seems like a step back toward that tax.

Degree of taxing power for states and municipalities. Evidently the states and municipalities have not been granted significant increases in their taxing powers. The commission made no firm recommendation on this issue, aside from concluding that the states' powers would have to remain minor aside from, possibly, a supplemental income tax; this latter has not been adopted.

Restructuring and restricting of municipal patentes. The industrial and commercial license tax levied by municipalities has not been reformed along the lines recommended by the commission, although its collection has been improved (Carrillo, 1987, p. 6).

Real estate tax. The only major change recommended for the urban real estate tax was differential taxation of two kinds of real estate, land and structures. Carrillo reports that "lots with no construction or (lots) insufficiently constructed are more highly taxed, in order to avoid idle tenancy of urban property, and thus increase the offer of constructible land and produce a decrease in its price" (Carrillo, 1987, p. 6). The tax rate on land is approximately 10 percent of the market value. A series of tax rates has been adopted for improvements on such land (buildings, etc.), depending on location, market value, and other variables (ibid.).

E. Extent of Adoption of Report's Tax Recommendations: Administrative Matters

(1) The Record. As with section 2 above, the present section attempts to ascertain the extent to which administrative changes now in force coincide with the major recommendations of the report. The information in the present section has been obtained chiefly from the *Final Report of the Commission on Fiscal Study and Reform: Reform of the Venezuelan Fiscal System* (English edition), 1983. This English-language version is now (May 1988) about to be published by the Iowa State University Press. This report devotes 49 single-spaced typed pages to "Administrative Features" of the Venezuelan tax system. In the following paragraphs of this section 4, numbers in parentheses, unless other-

wise noted, refer to page numbers of this 1983 report. The number at the beginning of each paragraph corresponds to the similar number in section III, 4 above.

(a) Income taxation

i. *Self-assessment*. The recommendation that the income tax payer himself compute his net taxable income and the tax due was adopted, apparently nearly twenty years after the 1958 report, and implemented in 1980 (112). "The introduction of self-assessment has caused severe administrative problems, mainly as a result of the shortcomings that were already present in the tax administration but also because of tactical errors in implementation" (114). Part of the trouble no doubt stems from ignoring the 1958 recommendation that the declaration form be redesigned to facilitate self-assessment. "The layout of the forms gives the taxpayer little help in avoiding mistakes, the accompanying instructions are rudimentary, inadequate for advising taxpayers even to a minimum extent . . ." (114).

ii. *List of potential taxpayers*. The listing of potential taxpayers is still somewhat of a problem. On the other hand, "the use of identity card numbers as the basis for the Fiscal Information Register" has not caused major problems (113).

iii. *Collection of delinquent accounts*. Delinquent accounts seem still to pose a problem. The 1983 report says that the problem is "critical" because "the collection system, which is undergoing a comprehensive reorganization up to the stage of standard collection, has proven to be wholly inadequate for bringing delinquent debtors to heel," and because "mismanagement of accounts, coupled with an inefficient legal mechanism, has led to a chaotic situation regarding the State's claims. If a taxpayer intends not to pay his taxes, there is a strong likelihood that he will succeed" (115). While private lawyers are sometimes assigned to collect delinquent taxes, nothing is said about garnisheeing wage or other payments made to delinquent taxpayers.

iv. *Field audits*. The appraisal of the audit procedure given in the 1983 report seems no more optimistic than that found in the 1958 report. In the six pages devoted to this subject, the following passages are typical: "There is no coherent selection system that is able to embrace general criteria and specific tactics with the aim of maximizing auditing coverage. The surveys that have been carried out suggest that the greater the degree of evasion, the lesser the likelihood of being audited. . . . Standards or instructions concerning the way to make the selection [of taxpayers to be audited] are not known" (119). There exists "an unsatisfactory policy regarding the use of [auditing] personnel." The "reduced complement of specialized trained personnel" is due partly to the fact that "earnings are frozen at low levels," with a consequent "constant drain of personnel" (118).

v. *Certificate of solvency.* The certificate of solvency, to which the 1958 report attributed much importance, is still in use. The income tax law as of October 1986, Article 102, requires that it be shown (a) by "Venezuelans to obtain approval for leaving the country when they are not residents of Venezuela and by foreigners whether or not residents of this country," (b) by those incorporating, dissolving, etc., companies, (c) for real estate transfers, (d) upon contracting with the government, (e) when obtaining patents, trademarks and the like, and (f) to take up public office.

vi. *Withholding of tax from wages and salaries.* The withholding of income tax from wages and salaries is more significant now than it was under the old low flat rate of the schedular tax. The 1958 recommendation that withholding be adjusted to a degree of accuracy that would require occasional refunds seems not to have been heeded; the 1983 report nowhere mentions a refund procedure or refund problem.

vii. *Pay-as-you-go (estimated tax) system.* Payment of estimated income tax on current year's income by installments during the current year has been adopted in Venezuela. Aside from income on which tax is withheld, the current year's estimate may not be less than 80 percent of the preceding year's income. "This system entails the declaration of taxable gains at the lower levels of the progressive scale," and "The tax paid in advance will always tend to be lower than the tax for the previous year" (p. 115).

viii. *Taxpayer appeal within the tax administration.* The taxpayer may now, evidently (in contrast to 1958), appeal within the tax administration instead of having to go directly to court, since the 1983 report recommends that he also be given the option of doing just what he had to do formerly: obtain "direct access to appeals litigation without passing through administrative appeal" (p. 143).

ix. *Compensating tax officials from delinquent tax payments.* Information is not at hand as to whether there still exists the practice of pooling 10 percent of collections of delinquent taxes, additional taxes, and fines for distribution to field agents, lawyers, other technical personnel and all chiefs of sections (p. 239, 1958 report).

x. *Information available to the public.* Despite the recommendations of the 1958 report that the public be informed as to the structure of the tax system, methods of administration and compliance, and the public's tax responsibilities, there has been little progress here; the 1983 report contains some uncomplimentary comments on this area. Strangely, even the private sector makes little or no effort here. ". . . [T]here is no sustained work by professional associations, major consultants, and private publishing houses in the area of taxation" (p. 123; see also p. 143). There is no "Venezuelan Tax Association" (p. 241, 1958 report).

(b) Other Tax Issues

Customs administration. The 1983 report devotes fourteen pages to customs administration: ten pages of description and four of recommendations. It would require a more intensive study of this sector than is feasible for the present report, to ascertain the degree to which the particular recommendations in the 1958 report have been adopted. In general, the 1983 report seems not to concentrate on the particular reforms that the 1958 report advocated (1983 report, pp. 127–39, 145–48).

Administration of municipal taxes. We may infer that little or no progress has been made in improving the administration of municipal taxes along the lines recommended by the 1958 report, from the general tone of the 1983 report on this sector (148–51): Many of the tax regulations "are antiquated, use obsolete systems." "Few municipalities use computers." "Municipal land Registers, if they exist at all, are out of date, and there are no vehicle registers." "Auditing is non-existent for some taxes . . . . [E]vasion is widespread even for taxes . . . with a high yield." As to collection, "primitive procedures survive."

(2) Appraisal. No "score sheet" of the kind given for substantive and structural recommendations will be attempted here for the administrative sector, but a general appraisal may be as follows:

Under the income tax, the adoption of self-assessment and of pay-as-you-go (estimated tax) can be regarded as major achievements that coincide with the 1958 report's recommendations. These are features of what may be termed external administration, or even compliance, as distinct from internal administration. On other external-administrative matters the record of achievement is not encouraging: audit procedures (perhaps), statistical information for external use, provision of information to the public.

The following observations by Carrillo in 1987 indicate that there is much yet to be done, administratively: "The administrative inability in the collection of taxes not subject to withholding permits one to affirm that Venezuelan income tax is only imposed on those earning a salary and is collected by withholding." The withholding system has recently been extended to some other types of income, and indeed "currently includes almost any payment, reaching limits of doubtful legality, since a legislative authorization is required" for such extension of withholding.

F. An Overall Appraisal of the Report

There was an eight-year gap between the report and any implementation of most of its suggestions, with the result that it may be argued that any causal connection between the report and later changes may be implausible. A more subtle interpretation, made by Gittes, writing in 1968, is that some sort of tax reform would have occurred in 1966 whether or not the 1958 report had been written, but that the decisions as to what the reform should consist of were influenced by the report (pp. 171–72). On the other hand, the 1983 report of the Commission on Fiscal Study and Reform (Carrillo Commission) suggested that "The history of Venezuela's tax system, written by a group of experts for the Commission on Fiscal Study and Reform, shows that the guidelines and point of reference for reforms implemented in the 1960s and early 1970s were based on the recommendations contained in the work of the 1958-60 [Fiscal Reform] Commission and those made by Professor Shoup and his colleagues" (p. 4).

Professor Carrillo, in a commentary on the first draft of the present paper, remarks that:

> There is no doubt whatsoever that the "report on the Venezuelan 1958 fiscal system" constitutes the most valuable technical analysis ever made of the Venezuelan tax system. The recommendations contained in the same have shown the way to the national fiscal reforms since 1958 up to 1986 . . . the principal merit of the Shoup Report has been its permanent applicability in the last thirty years as fundamental technical orientor of the Venezuelan fiscal system. (Carrillo, 1987, pp. 1, 2)

One of the commentators (López) on the 1958 report correctly points out that any such document starts with two handicaps. First, the very fact that the recommendations are made by outsiders, foreign experts, tells against them in any socially sensitive field (López, p. 23), because "potential domestic contributions, typically characterized by a deeper analysis of national realities, are ignored and at the same time local egos are bruised. Examination by insiders, whether tinted by partisan or ideological considerations or not, means a better grounded interpretation of existing internal tendencies" (p. 25).

On the other hand, there were some advantages to be gained by getting assistance from outsiders. "A new and up-dated view of its topics changed the predominantly institutional approach so far used to deal with them. A joint economic, administrative and legal approach that appears from its text pioneered new studies. Founded on the Venezuelan reality, the 'case study' nature of the Report pointed out problems detected in the course of the research at different levels of the public powers, making fiscal matters less theoretical and more solidly grounded" (López, p. 26).

The economic and political climate of a given time, of course, affects the degree to which any tax reform will be undertaken. In Venezuela in 1958–59 there was no urgency for improving the tax system—the oil revenues formed a comfortable fiscal cushion, the deficit seemed to have no immediately alarming consequences, and the need for more education and public health measures was not immediately apparent to everyone. At the other extreme, where fiscal crisis is present the pressures are not uniformly in favor of tax reform. For example, in May 1987 the minister of finance was preoccupied with discussions on how to restructure a large external debt. But since any workable solution to the debt service problem will likely require strengthening of the revenue system, recent factors exerting pressures for tax reform seem stronger than was the case in 1958, when longer-term aims dominated discussion of tax reform. Accordingly, some of the proposals of the 1983 report will be adopted with less delay than was the case for all but two chief recommendations in the 1958 report.

G. Hindsights

The major suggestion as to how the work of the Commission to Study the Fiscal Commission of Venezuela might have been differently structured to advantage is probably that of Gittes, who implies that a continuing effort was needed after release of the report. Specially needed was "a continuing process of analysis and development of alternatives to the end of creating a new law." Indeed, Gittes implies that the report itself was of secondary importance compared with the continuing technical help that he thought essential: "More often than not, it is in the working out of technical details that expert help is needed; today foreign technicians will not be the first persons in the host countries to suggest broad policy changes such as the elimination of schedular taxes or the taxation of dividends" (p. 172).

The "continuing process" that Gittes envisaged implies that one or more mission members should stay in the host country for some time after the report proper had been submitted, to be available for technical questions. This suggestion was in fact followed in the recent Indonesian and Jamaican reforms (see chapters 4 and 5). The procedure adopted in the Venezuelan study was, however, thought to be one that largely eliminated this need. Administrative problems were discussed at length by professors Oldman and Surrey with a group of tax officials on many days and for rather long periods. None of the members of this mission could have stayed into the autumn and winter months owing to other engagements, chiefly academic posts. Another alternative seems to be to have a somewhat larger mission, not all the members being together in the host country at all times. This technique has been used successfully in recent years (cf. *also* the Indonesian experiences, chapters 4 and 5).

III. The 1964 Brazil Study

A. Introduction

This is a retrospective look at a brief one-man survey of the tax system of Brazil, in 1964. The following extracts from the foreword to the published report, by Luiz Simoes Lópes, president of both the Vargas Foundation and the Reform Commission of the Ministry of Finance, give some of the background of this project:[6]

> *The Tax System of Brazil*, now presented to the public in the form of a book, is another contribution of the Reform Commission of the Ministry of Finance to the Brazilian literature on the modern aspects of taxation . . . . It contains a study conducted by Professor Carl Shoup . . . for the benefit of the Commission.
>
> . . . At the invitation of the Getulio Vargas Foundation and under the auspices of usaid, he came to Brazil in August 1964 in the . . . capacity of tax expert.
>
> . . . the Reform Commission . . . held two round tables . . . . The first round table dealt with the Brazilian tax system as a whole, its origin, its evolution, and its present structure. The second dealt with the income tax . . . . [S]everal experts on tax policy and tax administration attended these round tables [names follow] . . . .

Even though it was prepared in a very short time (Professor Shoup had only four weeks to examine the basic legislation, interview authorities and experts in the Finance Ministry and write the text) the present report presents a fairly comprehensive picture of the shortcomings, inconsistencies and anachronisms of the Brazilian tax system. It points out as well, under the form of specific recommendations, the institutional measures that Professor Shoup prescribes to remedy the problems. As he himself confesses, some of his recommendations are in conflict with certain constitutional provisions, being consequently infeasible unless the Brazilian Constitution is amended. (XIII–XIV)

The report was published in Portuguese and English editions, in 1965 (see References), by the Vargas Foundation and the Reform Commission of the Ministry of Finance.

Perhaps the main occasion for the study of the Brazilian tax system was a supposition (which I conjecture but cannot document) that at last there would be a period of economic and financial stability in Brazil that would allow rational tax reform. The grounds for this belief, insofar as it existed, were perhaps based on the military insurrection in April 1964 that ousted President Goulart, who had succeeded, as vice-president, an elected president (Quadros, 1960), who had resigned within seven months of taking office. When Goulart took office, the military and conservatives had forced constitutional changes that created a parliamentary form of government and weakened the president's powers. Nonetheless, full powers were restored to him by a plebiscite in 1963. Goulart's insistence on further radical constitutional changes was apparently one factor that promoted the military takeover. Meanwhile, a high rate of inflation (rise in prices) had been a characteristic of much of the two preceding decades, stimulated in part by President Kubitschev's massive spending on the creation of the new capital, Brasília (1955–60). (See *Columbia Encyclopedia*, "Brazil.")

There was no immediate fiscal crisis that required heavy new tax measures to raise large sums of revenue; estimated tax revenue for the federal government in 1965, at Cr$3.2 billion, compared with estimated expenditures of Cr$3.8 billion (pp. 10–11).[7] Inflation had subsided (but not disappeared). No quantitative goals were set for the tax reform study, and technical problems of tax administration were not to be covered. The aim seemed to be, rather, a qualitative appraisal of the tax structure, to identify shortcomings, inconsistencies, and anachronisms.

Against this background, it is perhaps understandable why this report, far more so than those on the other three countries, contained little more than "soft" recommendations: of frequent occurrence are the terms "might," "sooner or later," "ideally," "seems to be," and the like. But softness does not imply vagueness; the recommendations were specific enough so that one can check on whether subsequent changes in the tax system accorded with them.

One reason for having an outsider appraise the Brazilian tax system in 1964 may be found in the fact that a draft of a new income tax law had just been presented by Dr. José Luiz Bulhoes Pedreira, as a member of the study committee on tax reform of the Getulio Vargas Foundation, to this committee, at its request. The draft was designed to replace in its entirety the present series of laws, amendments to laws, and amendments to amendments, which in the view of some Brazilian tax lawyers was no longer possible to work with adequately; besides being a complete recodification, the project introduces several new conceptual and administrative ideas of importance, which will be noted in the appropriate sections below (p. 28). On balance, the report favored repeal of the old income tax law and introduction of a new code based on the Bulhoes Pedreira draft.

B. Composition of the Report

The report was divided into four sections: a Background and Summary (18 pages); Part I, The Income Tax (36 pages); Part II, The Federal Government's Consumption Taxes, Stamp Taxes, and Taxes on Motor Fuels, etc. (7 pages); and Part III, The National (i.e., Overall) Tax System of Brazil (6 pages).

The relative amount of space devoted to the income tax in the report did not reflect its proportionate share in total revenue. It accounted for only about 28 percent of federal tax revenue, against 50 percent from the consumption taxes (exclusive of revenues from the gasoline tax). The space—and effort—allocation partly reflected my own greater familiarity with the income tax, but was chiefly the result of the fact that there are so many structural decisions to be made in building an income tax; they are often problems that are exacerbated by inflation (a long-standing problem in Brazil).

The Background and Summary section concluded with recommendations made in the report in a two-way classification. The first classification, reflecting a time dimension, divided the recommendations into three groups: those that could be enacted within the coming few months, those that had to await amendments to the constitution, and those that could be introduced only gradually over a period of years as tax administration improved (p. 16). The second classification divided each of these three first classifications into two subgroups: those measures that were designed primarily to check inflation, and those designed for other purposes. It happened, perhaps not unexpectedly, that all the primarily anti-inflation measures fell in the first time group: measures that could be enacted during the remaining months of 1964.

A considerable part of the report was devoted to tax structure and tax policy problems caused by inflation. Also noted and commented upon was the way in which the personal exemption under the income tax had been fixed, since 1961, not in cruzeiros, but in units of the "fiscal minimum wage." The six pages devoted to inflation and the taxation of business income (pp. 52–58) discussed the conflict between equity and the financial needs of business firms, concluding that "the economic consequences probably have to be given some priority" (p. 54). The result would be an income tax system that would avoid taxing paper gains, but would not allow deduction of real losses (e.g., depreciation in real value of debt holdings). As to intergovernmental fiscal relations, "the theory of public finance contains no formulae for a stable system of federal-state-local fiscal relations in a world of unstable prices" (p. 79).

The report did not cover Brazil's social security system, which included a 3 percent tax on payrolls introduced in July 1964, and certain other taxes. Nor did it describe the revenue gained by the government from differential exchange rates. It did, however, include discussion of Brazil's system of compulsory loans.

C. Recommendations: Overview

A summary of the report's recommendations and suggestions is reproduced at the end of this section. The proposals called for repeal of four important levies: excess profits tax, compulsory loans, schedular income taxes, and the legal-entity tax on sole proprietorships and partnerships. The revenue loss would be recouped by raising rates of the basic income tax.

The only new tax suggested was a value-added tax for the states, to replace the cascade turnover tax they were collecting.

Certain changes in state and local taxing powers were proposed, along with introduction of a formula type of grants-in-aid, to replace the sharing of income and consumption taxes.

A number of changes in the income tax base, exemptions, and rate scale were suggested.

The excess profits tax had become, under the rise in nominal profits due to inflation, largely a tax on ordinary profits, until assets were allowed to be written up in 1964, and, with inflation continuing, further write-ups would be needed. In any case, the definition of "excess" was deemed so difficult that "[t]he administrative effort that would be needed to develop a true excess profits tax could better be devoted to improving the regular corporation income tax" (p. 59).

The compulsory loan was condemned as carrying a hidden tax element, even when indexed to the price level (as it had not been, until shortly before 1964). This tax element was to be measured, conceptually, as the amount the taxpayer would be willing to pay outright in tax to be free of the loan requirement. This hidden tax was almost surely regressive with respect to income.

The schedular rates called for segregating the individual's income into eight categories, with six different rates, including a zero rate. The chief distinction desired could be better obtained by an earned income credit, and much administrative effort would be released to more important tasks if the schedule system was repealed (p. 31).

The value-added tax for the states was recommended with some diffidence, but at least as being better than the cascade tax:

> If the states are to retain the sales tax, consideration could be given to transforming the turnover, cascade-type taxes into the value-added type employed by the federal consumption taxes, or possibly into a single-stage tax. The single-stage tax, however, might favor the producing states over the consuming states. But so too would a value-added tax, unless it could be extended to the retail level, which seems administratively impracticable, at present. A higher tax rate would be required but if evasion were reduced it might not need to be much higher. (p. 79)

The federal value-added tax should in any case give credit for tax paid on purchase of machinery and other items not tax-creditable under current law (pp. 21, 65).

For reasons underlying the other changes recommended, the reader is referred to the report itself, to avoid unduly lengthening the present chapter.

D. Summary of Recommendations and Suggestions

1. Recommendations capable of enactment within six months
   a. Measures designed primarily to check inflation
      i. Income Tax:
         1. Lower the basic (single-person) exemption to Cr$756,000, starting with 1965 incomes, adjust withholding scale accordingly.
         2. Raise the 3 percent, 5 percent, and 8 percent bracket rates to 10 percent, starting with 1965 income.
         3. Put the progressive-rate scale for 1965 incomes into terms of cruzeiros at the same scale as for 1964 incomes.
         4. Replace the compulsory indexed loan of 15 percent to 25 percent by a supplementary tax designed to yield about half the revenue of the loan, and expressed as a percentage of the entire regular tax due (not of that part paid directly) and with bracket rates (not effective rates).
         5. Replace compulsory loan of corporations by an increase in corporation income tax of somewhat smaller amount.
         6. Raise the regular rate on corporations, for 1965 incomes only, by say, 5 percentage points.
      ii. Consumption Tax:
         1. Increase tax rates on cigarettes, distilled spirits, effective as soon as possible.
         2. Extend the rate increases of the Law of August 28, 1964, indefinitely (Part II-A).
         3. If rate of inflation has not greatly decreased by November 1964, increase rates of consumption tax by average of 100 percent, as temporary measure for 1965.
   b. Measures designed for purposes other than checking inflation
      i. Income Tax
         1. Increase allowance for each dependent from three eighths of the basic exemption to half that exemption, starting with 1965 incomes.
         2. Do not extend the 1963–64 compulsory indexed loan.
         3. Allow revaluation of inventories to 1964 price levels free of tax, but retain traditional valuation method from this level.
         4. Replace excess profits tax by equivalent revenue increase in regular corporation tax.
         5. Put corporate income tax on a current-payment (pay-as-you-go) basis, over a three-year period.

2. Recommendations that cannot readily be enacted until 1965 or later, often because amendment of the Constitution is required.

   a. Measures designed primarily for purposes other than checking inflation.

      i. Income Tax

         1. Repeal present income tax code and substitute code based on draft code of July 30, 1964, after discussion and amendment.

         2. Repeal the normal (schedular taxes) and increase progressive-rate scale to recoup revenue loss.

         3. Call in all bearer shares and replace them with nominative shares; forbid issuance of bearer shares henceforth.

         4. Adopt modified split for family income.

         5. Repeal legal-entity tax as to sole proprietorships and partnerships.

         6. Do not require or permit revaluation of fixed assets after 1965.

         7. Include capital gains and losses from shares, real estate, and other assets in individual income; adopt an averaging device; and possibly allow a slight reduction of tax (gains) and tax relief (losses).

      ii. Consumption Taxes

         1. Give credit for tax paid on purchase of machinery and other items not now creditable.

         2. Extend the consumption tax to certain services, after amending the Constitution.

      iii. Taxes on Motor Fuels, etc.

         1. Increase rates if more revenue is needed for highway expenditures.

      iv. State and Municipal Taxes

         1. Transfer export-tax power from states to federal government, transfer rural-land-tax power from municipalities to state governments, transfer death-duties power from states to federal government.

         2. Introduce formulae type grants-in-aid: repeal present sharing of income and consumption taxes and the 30 percent rule for state sharing with municipalities.

         3. Reduce tax on transfer of real estate to almost 1 percent.

3. Recommendations that cannot be made fully effective until administration is greatly improved.

   a. All measures were designed primarily for purposes other than checking inflation.

    i. Income Tax
       1. Refine withholding on wages and salaries, using either U.S. or U.K. methods, or a compromise.
       2. Give prompt refund on overpaid tax.
       3. Amplify regulations on capital gains and losses.
       4. Improve assessment of agricultural incomes (Part I-O).
    ii. State and Municipal Taxes
       1. Replace state turnover (cascade) sales taxes with single-stage or value added taxes.
       2. Reform assessment of municipal real estate tax.

E. Twenty-Two Years Later

There was no follow-up visit to Brazil, as occurred in Japan and Venezuela (one year later) or Liberia (five years later). Nor have I kept in touch with my colleagues in Brazil in subsequent years to the degree I have done in the cases of Japan and Venezuela. Accordingly, the task of ascertaining the extent to which the report's recommendations were adopted, or followed, purposely or coincidentally, year by year since 1964 posed a substantial research problem, one beyond the resources available for this part of the tax missions study.

What we can do, however, is look at the Brazilian tax system as it exists today and note the changes from the 1964 system that coincide with the changes recommended in the report, and the corresponding lack of change. The present section makes precisely these types of observation, with the aid of the Price Waterhouse booklet on Brazil in its *Information Guide* series, containing material assembled at May 31, 1986, and material supplied on request by the International Bureau of Fiscal Documentation.

No claim of cause-and-effect linkages is made here. Possibly, all of the "agreeing" changes have been coincidental; almost surely, some of them have been. Lack of an agreeing change, on the other hand, does always imply a rejection of that part of the report (even not reading the report is a form of rejection).

The recommendations for repeal of certain taxes and for introduction of a value-added tax at the state level have all taken effect, except that the legal-entities tax still applies to partnerships. In addition, partnerships pay a withholding tax of 25 percent (23 percent for liberal professions) when distributing profits. The partners thereupon include these distributed profits in their personal income tax returns, taking credit for the withholding tax. They may elect to exclude these profits and forgo the credit (Price Waterhouse, p. 102). The same procedure applies to dividends received by shareholders of companies.

There is no longer an excess-profits tax or a compulsory loan based on income. An individual's gross income is distributed among eight schedules, but only to classify for related deductions (ibid., p. 98) and to avoid a general definition of income, since whether an item is taxable or not depends on whether it is to be found among the enumerated items in the eight schedules. The same tax rate schedule embraces all these incomes.

The states' turnover tax has been transformed into a value-added tax (ibid., p. 109). With one exception, no new taxes other than the one recommended in the report are in force today, and all of the 1964 taxes not recommended for repeal are still in force. The one exception is a tax on the ownership of a motor vehicle. It is a state tax, but 50 percent of the revenue is transferred to municipalities.

Passing now to substantive changes in particular taxes, we find that two of the three chief recommendations for the corporate income tax are in force today. The statutory rate of the tax on legal entities (corporations, chiefly) has been raised from the 28 percent of 1964 to 35 percent, but there has been added another 10 percent applicable to that part of profits over a certain figure (about $300,000 U.S. dollars). This additional 10 percent seems to have been viewed by some as a sort of substitute for the old excess profits tax.[8]

An accelerated payment requirement was adopted for large-profit entities, which had to file semiannually, instead of annually, and had to pay the tax on the half-year's income within three months (Price Waterhouse, p. 104, and Tax News Service [TNS], Jan. 31, 1986, p. 8). But a 1987 decree-law requires that taxpayers must now file on a more complex schedule: (1) some prepayments in September to December of the income year, (2) "twelfths" from January to March of the filing year, and (3) remaining installments, April to August. Other legal entities pay in monthly installments from April to December of the filing year. The 1985 law required current payment even by individuals, but this has not been substantially implemented.

In contrast, the chief recommendations with respect to the individual income tax have not been adopted, with a minor exception: the initial bracket rates of 3, 5, 8, and 10 percent have been consolidated, not into a 10 percent rate, but into two rates: 5 and 10 percent (Price Waterhouse, p. 116). The rate schedule continues upward with 5 percent intervals. The allowance for dependents has been made smaller, not larger, relative to the primary allowance, than it was in 1964 (ibid., pp. 116, 119). Bearer shares are still allowed (ibid., p. 32).

Capital gains and losses are still not taken into account in computing an individual's taxable income when they are from shares in "quoted companies" ("public corporations"), or, if the asset has been held five years or more, from other shares (ibid., p. 99). Capital gains from other share-holdings or from real estate are taxable, with an optional 25 percent rate. Withholding of income tax from individuals' incomes has apparently not been refined as suggested (3[a] in the summary table).

There are only two structural recommendations under "consumption taxes" in the summary table (group 2, items [h] and [i]). Neither of them has been adopted. The federal value-added or "excise" tax gives credit for tax paid on raw materials and component parts (Price Waterhouse, p. 110), but apparently not on machinery and plant, etc. As to services, a tax reform that was said to be "under way" in 1985 (TNS, July 31, 1985, p. 101) included "extension of VAT to services: services, currently subject to the municipal tax on services (ISS) at rates between 2 percent and 5 percent, will be subject to VAT (ICM) [the state tax] at the rates applicable to the suppliers of goods," but Price Waterhouse describes that tax as still applying only to "physical movement of merchandise" (p. 109).

As to stamp taxes and "taxes on motor fuels, etc.," no structural recommendations were made by the report.

The record on the tax measures listed under "State and Municipal Taxes" in the summary table is mixed. The tax on transfer of real estate has been reduced from its highest rate of 12 percent (p. 80), not to about 1 percent (p. 22), but at least to 2 percent, and, for transfers at death or by gift, to 4 percent (Price Waterhouse, p. 112). (This tax is now a state tax; in 1964 it was reserved for municipalities.)

Taxation of rural land has been transferred from the municipalities to the federal government (p. 22; Price Waterhouse, p. 112). As to death duties proper, "There are no (comprehensive) wealth, gift or inheritance taxes" in Brazil (ibid., p. 101). The report remarked that "The state tax on transfers at death will be kept at low levels because of interstate competition for wealthy decedents as long as it remains reserved to the states" (ibid., p. 76). Did competition in fact reduce the rates to zero? Transfer of real estate, however, is still taxed, on death or gift.

Although the compulsory loans based on income are no longer levied, there is now in effect a compulsory loan that uses a purchase figure, rather than net income, to determine the amount of the loan. A decree-law of July 23, 1986, imposes a compulsory loan on buyers of alcohol and gasoline for motor vehicles, and buyers of private passenger cars. The loan is repayable, to these buyers, together with accumulated interest, in three years, but it is repaid, not in currency, but in shares of the Fund for National Development, which can be sold in the market. This measure is therefore more of a compulsory loan. The amount to be paid upon purchase is: 28 percent on the cost of alcohol or gasoline, and 30 percent, 20 percent, or 10 percent of the cost of cars that are, respectively, not older than 1, 2, or 4 years (TNS, Aug. 31, 1986, p. 114). The seller adds the loan amount to the price of the fuel or the car and remits that amount to the treasury. This is apparently the first time in any country that a compulsory loan has been based on a purchase figure.

F. Hindsight

Had the forthcoming periods of renewed severe inflation in Brazil been foreseen, perhaps most of the report would have been devoted to methods of maintaining real revenue from a tax system in such periods without gross inequities. The ensuing inflations might not then have been as severe. This was not the task set for the report, however. Today (mid-1987) that problem could scarcely fail to dominate a similar study. Inflation at an annualized rate of more than 400 percent in early 1986 was followed by the "Cruzado Plan" (the cruzado was the name given to the new currency) involving wage and price freezes. Inflation was greatly reduced. But the fiscal measures needed to make such freezes last were not adopted, and by early 1987 inflation was again running at about 400 percent a year (Cohen, p. 1).

In fact, this experience with high-rate inflation in Brazil has led to construction of an indexing regime for income tax that is said to be, if far from perfect, less imperfect than any similar regime elsewhere. It goes under the name of "monetary restatement." It was repealed when the Cruzado Plan was adopted but has recently been reinstituted. Bracket boundaries for the personal income tax are updated annually, along with all figures in the income tax law expressed in cruzados. Similarly, the historical basis for reckoning capital gain or loss is increased by the price index.

Another direction the report might have taken would have been to set forth in more detail the problems and possibilities of new forms of tax that were suggested in the report. A special case is the value-added tax recommended for the states. To have made such a contribution, the report would have had to depend largely on introspection and speculation, since no country, in 1964, imposed a value-added tax that extended through the retail stage. Indeed, when the Brazilian states, three years later, introduced such a VAT, they were the first (Shoup, September, 1986, pp. 2–3). For a VAT restricted to stages prior to retail, experience could in 1964 be drawn from only one country, France, aside from Brazil itself (federal tax).

A more drastic judgment would be that no project at all should have been undertaken with such restricted resources and time period. But this seems unduly conservative a view, considering the several recommendations that were in fact adopted (or at least duplicated). The Brazilian tax system has improved.

To be sure, the very high rate of inflation might seem to imply that the Brazilian tax structure is still somehow deficient, that it is unable to produce the greatly increased tax revenue that would be needed to check inflation—the system would break down under a sharp increase in tax rates. However, this view seems unwarranted. The Brazilian tax structure appears sound enough to supply whatever revenue is needed, under higher tax rates, to stop inflation. If inflation continues, it is not because the Brazilian tax system is structurally deficient, but because of deep divisions within the society as to how the burden shall be distributed among the income classes, between urban and rural inhabitants, and the like.

> Even the uncertainty that characterizes inflationary finance speaks in favor of it to legislators in a country where social and economic conflicts are so great that consensus on how to distribute the burden, beyond a modest level of taxation, is virtually impossible to achieve . . . . The overriding distributive feature (of inflationary finance) is . . . the absence of any need ever to make an explicit decision on how the burden shall be distributed, even initially. It is this freedom from the need to make up one's mind in order to reach an explicit compromise that is so attractive in a turbulent political environment. (Shoup, 1969, p. 459)

The reader is warned that of the statements above concerning the Brazilian tax system "as it exists today," many may soon be obsolete, since "a new Constitution" is being drafted containing between four hundred and five hundred articles; "the chapter on taxation is going to change completely the present system" (letter from Xavier Ferreira to Shoup, Feb. 11, 1988).

IV. Liberia

A. Genesis of the Project[9]

The need for tax reform in Liberia in the late 1960s was apparently first advanced by the secretary of the treasury in his annual report for the year 1966–67. He was opposed to any "new taxes on nationals" for fear of "adverse effects on the level of spending power . . . in a low income economy such as ours." Instead, he saw a need for "rationalising" the tax system, after "determining the incidence of the existing tax structure on different levels of income earners." To this end, he proposed establishing a tax commission "to review and analyze our entire tax law," and to make the incidence study. In his next annual report the secretary published some incidence figures, "based upon a limited analysis." Taxpayers earning less than $300 a year or more than $6,000 per year were found to be paying more than 7 percent of their incomes in taxes, while those in the $300–$6,000 group were paying from 6 to 7 percent.

In 1968 the president of Liberia appointed a tax commission, under the chairmanship of the secretary of the treasury, using terms of reference suggested by the secretary in his 1966–67 report.

The chairman of the new tax commission consulted with Harold Moss as to methods of getting the tax reform study under way. In the 1960s Moss had developed and directed a system whereby the United States Internal Revenue Service assisted developing countries—and some others too—in creating efficient tax administrations by supplying IRS personnel on loan for extended periods to those countries. Moss suggested a technical tax reform mission similar to the one he had been so influential in originating and implementing in Japan. Since Liberia was about to be given assistance in this or a similar manner by Moss and his colleagues, this seemed an appropriate occasion for advancing the idea of a mission that would deal with problems of broad tax policy and substantive details with which the administrative teams could work.

In January 1969 Secretary Weeks asked me to come to Liberia as soon as possible to discuss arrangements for a study, on behalf of its tax commission, of the Liberian tax structure. I went to Liberia early in June to talk with Weeks and his officials, and then to meet President Tubman (who was in London at the time), to insure his personal commitment to the proposed tax mission.

In my files I find a brief note I made on the June 11 meeting with Weeks et al.:

Debt service is about $15 million or about one-quarter of total government expenditure. Education takes about 10 percent to 11 percent; farm improvement, only about 2 percent to 3 percent, much too low (Weeks) in a largely agricultural country. Debt service rises about 1972 . . . . The several types of poll tax should be replaced in part (Weeks), perhaps by increasing the income tax. Top rate of income tax is 35 percent, but that doesn't matter, since nobody pays the top rate (Kennan). Mining companies reduce their income tax by capitalizing largely with debt . . . . Customs revenue is about $20 million out of the $56 million total tax revenue . . . . The present revenue system's yield probably won't grow as much as 5 percent a year, and may even not grow at all (K). With a change in structure and better administration we would hope it might grow at 5 percent a year (W)—but the increase might be just once for all (K) . . . . Customs collections cost about 2 percent (Greaves) . . . Illegal *octrois* [it seems to me that is what they are] are collected on transit of goods by some tribal groups or chiefs, and are tolerated, some of them at least. There are nine counties, each with its superintendent, but no local financial autonomy, not even for Monrovia, the capital city. Police and fire protection are provided by the central government. Much remains to do, to improve tax administration (G) . . . . Liberia tried to harmonize its tax system (and also agricultural policy and other matters) with three or four of its neighboring states a few years ago, but political developments destroyed the technical agreements that had been reached . . . . There is no central bank in Liberia. The government borrows from commercial banks, at an interest charge one percentage point above the U.S. prime rate . . . .

The proposed tax mission was not to deal intensively with tax administration, but was deemed necessary chiefly, it appears, because the authorities feared that in the years ahead the existing tax system would, as in the past, fail to keep pace with the growth in the monetized sector of the Liberian economy. This growth was expected to demand increasing amounts of government services such as education of the work force, the building of highways and other transportation facilities, and assurance of fire and police protection. Moreover, even apart from growth, the existing tax system needed some strengthening if grants from abroad and borrowing from banks were not to be depended on continually. (In 1967 these two sources had accounted for 17 percent and 23 percent, respectively, of total sources of funds, the remainder coming from taxes and a small amount of nontax current revenue [report, p. 54].)

The immediate fiscal picture was not threatening enough to warrant a crash program of tax reform, but the report did find that the $55 million estimated yield of the tax system for the calendar year 1969 would need to increase so that for 1970 it would be some one or two million dollars more than it would be if the system were left unchanged (report, pp. 14, 55). The existing tax system was deficient with respect to the criteria that the mission proposed to use in formulating a restructuring, quite apart from total revenue: horizontal equity, efficient allocation of resources, reduction of involuntary unemployment, vertical equity, and economic growth (p. 10).

As the Progress Report of the Tax Commission put it: "in a growing and developing society the government needs tend to increase much faster than private needs . . . . Public support of governments . . . can be directly related to tax equity and the belief that the tax system is fair . . . . Where the . . . non-monetary segment of the economy is large, a tax program is needed which does not discourage entry into the urban-monetary labor force" (pp. 3–4).

Moreover, there were two other reasons for restructuring the tax system, rather than simply raising rates. First, much of the tax revenue came from large foreign companies operating concessions within Liberia. This revenue arose chiefly from the iron ore extractors, whose tax obligations, in terms of tax rates, were fixed in the concession agreements. Second, no matter how much administrative help and advice was received from the Internal Revenue Service and other foreign sources, increased rates under the existing tax structure and "tax atmosphere" would probably induce even greater tax evasion (pp. 4–8). Although the tax mission would not focus on techniques of administration as such, it was hoped that it might be able to suggest structural changes and improvements in the tax atmosphere that would reduce evasion somewhat.

B. Initiation of the Project

Initiation of the project proceeded rapidly after the June conference in Monrovia, referred to above. As I recall, there had been no difficulty in reaching agreement with secretary Weeks on terms of the contract. There were, to be sure, certain restrictive clauses: "at least three other public finance experts from the field of economics [sic] to be chosen by [Shoup] . . . with the approval of the Government," and the "understanding" that "the printed version of the report will not contain any material from the typewritten or duplicated report that, in the opinion of the Government, as expressed by the Secretary of the Treasury, should be treated as confidential." Given the reassuring atmosphere in which the June conference in Monrovia had been conducted, there seemed no reason to fear that these restrictions would undermine the mission's usefulness.

The typewritten or duplicated report was to be submitted by September 20, 1969; the printed copies were to be available by March 31, 1970 (this date was later extended by a few months).

Secretary Weeks thought it would be advisable to have at least one of the members of the mission from outside the United States, and I agreed. Otherwise I do not recall anyone offering any suggestions as to membership on the mission. There were four of us: Douglas Dosser, York University, England; Rudolph G. Penner, University of Rochester; William S. Vickrey, Columbia University; and myself. All were professors in the field of public finance.[10]

C. The Tax Mission Report

1. Publication. Arrangements for publication of any studies were my responsibility. I first sent the report to Johns Hopkins Press, which had published the Venezuela report, but they declined it on the grounds that it lacked enough comparative material (other countries) and supporting theory on economic development. I then approached the Columbia University Press, and on March 26, 1970, reached an agreement whereby the Press would, not "publish," but "manufacture and distribute the WORK exclusively throughout the world, and to advertise, catalog, and promote it to the same degree as a regular PRESS publication." The Press was paid $5,400 from the mission's budget. They agreed to provide me with 800 free copies (600 of which I sent to Liberia for distribution).

2. Contents, in General. A substantial part of the study was given over to nontax matters: a section of nearly forty pages on the economy of Liberia, with emphasis on the national income accounts, and one of twenty-four pages on nontax revenues. It was nevertheless possible to treat substantially structural and conceptual issues of various taxes in the remaining space, since the report did not need to analyze intergovernmental relations (there being none), or to describe in detail tax administration.

The report treated in detail the tax ratios derived from national income accounting, important because in Liberia there was a much greater difference in the totals of gross *domestic* product and gross *national* product than is usually found in larger or more developed economies. The domestic product was nearly half again as large as the national product, indicating that a substantial portion of the value produced in Liberia flowed out of the country to foreign investors and other outside factor owners. A comparison of a tax total with an economic flow total needed to distinguish taxes paid out of value flowing abroad, and of course the flows themselves. This was done in chapter II and in the appendix and tabular appendix to that chapter.

The problem of how to tax the large nonmonetized sector of the economy (the "subsistence sector") was also important to this particular report. The subsistence sector in Liberia was large compared with the monetized sector, at least in terms of population: an estimated 700,000 persons in the subsistence sector against only 400,000 in the monetized sector.

3. Recommendations

a. Revenue from concessionary enterprises. Liberia's income tax revenue was derived largely from a few foreign-owned corporations operating iron-ore concessions. The concession agreements stipulated the terms on which the taxable profit of these enterprises was computed. The mission report therefore developed a set of rules to be followed in such computations, if the concession agreements were to be reviewed so that existing practice could be changed. This was probably the first attempt in taxation literature to develop systematically the issues of taxation of profits that arise under a concessionary enterprise subject to the income tax (chapter IV).

The importance of this problem to Liberia can be seen in the fact that in 1968, out of a total income tax revenue of $19.1 million, $7.6 million, or 40 percent, took the form of government shares in the profits of four large iron ore concessions (p. 59). This was 15 percent of total revenue from all taxes. Another $4.8 million was corporate income tax paid by two large concessionaires outside the iron-ore extraction industry (pp. 58–59).

The report questioned the appropriateness or fairness of the following practices found in the terms of the concession agreements: (1) financing heavily by debentures owned by those with an equity interest with deduction of interest on these debentures in computing taxable income; (2) reducing selling price of the concession's product to those who had helped finance the enterprise; (3) deductions or allowances contrary to accepted principles of accounting, e.g., deduction for "depletion" when the concessionaire had paid nothing for possession of the natural resource and had been allowed deduction of exploration and other development expenses, deduction of two or more duplicating charges: depreciation, cost of replacement or renewal (or contributions to a reserve for that purpose), and debt amortization, and use of actual sales prices that were in fact below an arm's length transaction price because the buyer had an interest in the seller or in some way aided the seller; (4) deductions or exclusions not granted to the general taxpayer, e.g., carry-over of losses (eight other items were noted); (5) tax holidays so lengthy that the present value of the benefit to the enterprise was much less than that of the loss to the government, assuming a higher discount rate to be applied by the enterprise than by the government; (6) extension of tax privileges to suppliers to the concessionaire, e.g., financial institutions; (7) guarantee to the concessionaire of tax treatment as favorable as any given in a later year to another concessionaire in the same industry; (8) exemption from import duties of goods not used by the concessionaire in its business (in general, this was not the practice); (9) stipulation that the government must accept the findings of an audit of the company's books for tax purposes that is made by an auditor of the company's own choosing.

Although the tone of the report was restrained (pp. 67–69), the inference was clear: sophisticated foreign investors may well have taken advantage of the government's relative lack of expertise in the tax field in the drawing up of the concession agreements, and if the concessions could be reopened, these tax anomalies should be rectified.

The report also discussed the pros and cons of special tax treatment for concessionaires under other taxes, including widespread customs exemptions, exemption of dividend and interest payments by concessionaires to residents of Liberia, and exemption from user taxes on motor fuel and vehicles, without making specific recommendations for the Liberian tax system. Royalty payments to the government in lieu of income taxation were also analyzed (pp. 69–74).

(b) Personal and corporation income taxes. The report recommended that the "austerity tax" be allowed to expire as scheduled at the end of 1969. This was a tax of 4.2 percent of the total earned income for annual incomes of $600 or more, and 2.1 percent for lesser incomes, and, together with the per capita tax and the hut tax, injected a regressive element in the lower ranges of income. It also caused duplication of administrative effort and was difficult to enforce uniformly among small taxpayers. It also did not reach unearned income.

Partly to make up for this revenue loss, the report recommended that the flat $1,500 exemption under the personal income tax be reduced to $1,000 and the rate schedule that ran from 2 percent to 35 percent be compressed to one of 8 percent to 20 percent (on 1967 incomes, no one had paid personal income tax at a marginal rate of over 25 percent, and only two taxpayers at rates exceeding 20 percent). A lower exemption for a single person and allowances for dependents should not be introduced, owing to difficulties of administration and compliance. The low ceiling rate of 20 percent was recommended partly to aid in the country's announced policy of inducing a flow of persons and resources from the subsistence sector into the monetized sector, and partly to enhance compliance and taxpayer morale. If these and other tax lowerings depleted the revenue below the goals set, the initial rate could be set at 10 percent and the top rate at 25 percent (on that part of one's income over $10,000).

The report had little to suggest as to changes in the definition of taxable income: "The definition of income provided in the Liberian income tax law is admirably comprehensive. Especially important is the inclusion of capital gains" (p. 80). The existing deduction for personal taxes was deemed undesirable, and the deduction for losses from fire, theft, etc., should be allowed only for large losses. Refunds of overwithheld tax should be given promptly. A loss carry-over for businesses should be introduced, at least a loss carry-back, if not also a loss carry-forward.

Partnerships were taxed separately on their income at the same rates as individuals. Change to the more usual system of attributing to each partner his share of the partnership's income was not recommended for Liberia, for administrative and compliance reasons, except where an individual divided his income among a number of partnerships in order to put more income in the lower brackets.

Regarding the corporation income tax on concerns other than concessionaires, the report had little to add, except that the existing double taxation of dividends might be mitigated by allowing "individuals to include in their taxable income only . . . say, half of the dividends they receive from Liberian corporations . . . . Given the small amount of dividend income currently reported by individual taxpayers, not much revenue would be lost by such a provision . . . . A more thoroughgoing form of integration might be worked out at a later time when administrative problems are better in hand" (p. 86). At that time, corporations were taxed at graduated rates generally 5 percentage points higher than those on individuals, with a minimum rate of 10 percent, no exemption, and a maximum rate of 45 percent on that part of the income over $500,000.

(c) Per capita taxes, hut taxes. To get the full flavor of the analysis of these taxes, unfamiliar to developed country economists, we reproduce the mission's paragraphs on the main points (pp. 89–90):

> The "per capita" tax, at present $6, is levied throughout Liberia except in the tribal [subsistence, nonmonetized] areas. It is composed of a $2 tax per lot—hence not actually a tax per capita —and a consolidation of four formerly distinct taxes: the development tax ($1), the health tax ($1), the Coast Guard tax ($1), and the relief tax ($1). In addition, residents of Monrovia pay a $2 water tax. On top of these taxes there is a temporary tax of $10 per capita on all adults outside the tribal areas, to finance an emergency relief fund for education.
>
> In the tribal areas these same taxes apply (except the Monrovia water tax), but on a hut basis instead of on per lot or per capita basis. No matter how many adults are in a single hut, the total tax is still $16. Theory would suggest that huts would be larger and fewer under this kind of tax pressure, and, indeed, we have been informed that this tendency is observable in some areas, more persons per hut and larger huts than was the case before the $10 education tax was imposed.
>
> The combination of hut tax and "per capita" tax is a slightly, but erratically, progressive tax, since those who live in huts are on the average somewhat poorer than those who live in houses, and the hut tax comes to less per person (except for the single-occupant hut) than does the "per capita" tax . . . .
>
> About the only reasons for keeping the hut and per capita taxes are: (1) they are relatively easy to collect; (2) the hut tax maintains a link between the government and the local chieftains, who obtain a commission for collecting the hut tax. To repeal the hut tax now would be to force too abrupt a change in the relationship of the national government to the tribal areas. And if the hut tax is retained the "per capita" tax on the rest of the country can hardly be repealed.

As a step toward eventual repeal of these taxes, however, we recommend that the $10 education levy be discontinued, its revenue to be replaced from part of the changes recommended for the personal income tax.

(d) Real Estate Taxes. Only three pages were devoted to real estate taxation in the report, not because the subject lacked interest, but because "our recommendations concerning the taxes on real estate are made with somewhat more diffidence than others in this report. This form of taxation appears to be deeply involved with the social and political character of the country, and we have not been in Liberia long enough to explore the problem to the depth that it would require if definitive recommendations were to be made" (p. 95). Earlier in this chapter: "Moreover, in a context where any vigorous attempts to enforce the payment of the property taxes are inhibited by political considerations . . ." (p. 89).

The recommendations, or perhaps suggestions, were:

Move gradually toward more equal taxation of land with that of improvements, and eventually even toward heavier taxation of land, in place of the system that taxed town lots at $2 per quarter-acre lot while imposing taxes on the value of commercial improvements at 2 percent, of industrial improvements at 1 percent, and of residential, farm, and other improvements at 0.5 percent. Farmland was taxed at up to 6 cents per acre. No attempt had been made to assess the value of land, either urban or rural.

The tax on all rents, at 10 percent of the rent paid, should at least be mitigated by eliminating the double and triple taxation that occurred when both land and improvements were leased (the rent of the latter of course including the value of the use of the land) and when subleases existed. Eventually, the lease tax should be repealed; it had been enacted as a temporary tax to pay off the debt incurred in establishing the Coast Guard.

Impose a uniform rate on industrial and commercial improvements.

It will be recalled that these real estate taxes were national taxes, not revenues of a municipality.

(e) Taxes on imports. A relatively lengthy (twenty-six pages) and detailed description and analysis of import taxes was given in the report, partly because such taxes, the second most important source of revenue, provided about 35 percent of total current government revenues

during 1966–68, and partly because the nature of this field lent itself to a number of very specific recommendations.

The major recommendations on tariffs were: first, that rates on capital and intermediate goods should be reduced significantly or eliminated, but the revenue loss should be held to $2 million and should be partly recouped by tariff increases on consumer luxury items, and, second, that the Investment Incentive Code should be phased out. This code gave the government great power to discriminate on a firm-by-firm basis; that is, it allowed reduction of tariffs on goods used by particular firms, thus increasing "effective protection" for those firms. Several reasons were given for finding "the enormous powers of discrimination inherent in the present Investment Incentive Code disturbing . . ." (p. 106).

In addition we proposed that "a highly paid group of expert customs inspectors should be created in the customs administration, and they should be assigned to ports of entry . . ." (p. 122). The report's analysis of import taxes devoted nearly three pages to administrative problems.

Other recommendations were that the government should gradually eliminate its own duty-free privileges, more use should be made of the computations of duty-free imports by institutions, future concession agreements should not exempt companies from consular fees, and, if the Industrial Code were not phased out, future contracts should limit duty-free imports of each item and impose restraints on the prices charged by monopolists.

(f) Export taxes. Export taxes provided only a small amount of revenue for Liberia: in 1968, only $1.2 million out of a total of $50 million tax revenue. The report's recommendations were (pp. 126–27):

Suspend the rubber export tax, which burdened the Liberian producers, not the world consumers, until the price of rubber exceeds 25 cents a pound (in 1968 the average price was 19 cents). When the price equals or exceeds 25 cents a pound, the tax should be 10 percent of the amount by which the price exceeds 20 cents. The tax should be deductible from taxable profits and no longer a credit against income tax. In fact, "only the highest grades of rubber have seen prices above 20 cents over the last three years, and as a result, the rubber export tax has been largely irrelevant . . ." (p. 125). (By June, 1974, however, rubber had in fact reached 39 cents.)

Maintain the other export taxes at their existing levels. These consisted chiefly of export taxes on minerals, precious metals, and gems, at

10 or 15 percent, and on wood products at $3 or $5 per 1,000 board feet. "The bulk of the revenue comes from the export of diamonds and some comes from wood exports" (p. 125).

If existing coffee conditions continue, the government should negotiate with the Liberian Produce Marketing Association (LPMC) "to siphon off a higher share of coffee profits" (p. 127).

The existing stumpage tax should be integrated with the export tax on wood and wood products.

(g) Business and occupation licenses. A mercantile license "fee" of 1.5 percent of the maximum inventory held by any business that sold merchandise and a series of fixed license "fees" for occupations, both levied yearly, were supplying about 3 percent of total tax revenue. The report showed no enthusiasm for either but concluded that, lacking any better alternative, they had better be kept, with the tax rate and the fixed amount increased by 50 percent. The tax on inventory was judged to be "a desirable, if crude, substitute for a retail sales or value-added tax, because it is relatively easy to administer even where the establishment keeps no records or keeps multiple records for tax and other purposes" (p. 129). The license applicant, under either type of "fee," should be required to prove that income tax forms have been filed for the previous year, unless the applicant is exempt from filing. From a sample of the fixed license fees for occupations, we see that, for example, tailors and barbers paid $10, architects $15, accountants $25, drivers $50, and physicians $100. In Monrovia, 1967–68, the record of fees paid included 17 accountants, no architects, 48 lawyers, and one surveyor.

(h) Excise taxes. "Various laws impose excise taxes on a number of domestically produced goods and services in Liberia, but many are not collected" (p. 130). Those collected were taxes on beer (50 cents a gallon), carbonated beverages (30 cents a gallon), and cinema tickets (10 cents a balcony seat, 5 cents an orchestra seat). Those not being collected were on paint, certain footwear, liquor, cement, and jewelry. "The government expects soon to be collecting the taxes on cement and domestically produced liquor. Thus far collections have been retarded by a series of administrative lapses, the most recent being the failure to publish regulations to accompany the tax legislation. The tax on paint is irrelevant at the moment because the country's sole paint producer has a seven-year tax holiday, and the tax on shoes does not apply because the only shoe producer recently went bankrupt. The lack of jewelry tax collections is somewhat more mysterious. Many officials were not aware

that the jewelry tax was on the books, and one suggested that in any case it would be foolish to tax an industry which has recently been showing great promise as an exporter" (p. 131).

"The tax on beer was imposed on the country's only beer producer to recoup some of the customs revenue lost when domestic production began to replace imports. The excises on paint, gasoline, domestic liquor, and cement have a similar philosophy . . . . We believe that this strategy should be examined carefully" (p. 131).

The report came to the following conclusions: there should be a doubling of the excise tax on liquor, of license fees for sellers of alcoholic beverages and owners of stills, and of the cinema tax. The taxes on jewelry, shoes, and paint should be repealed; and, in the longer run, the cement tax, too. Bottle counters and/or meters should be installed at soft drink producers, distilleries, and bottling plants for distilled spirits.

(i) User taxes on automotive transport. The total tax on an ordinary car was $39.25 a year, and on a driver's license, $7.50. The first "is quite low compared with many other countries, especially developing countries" (p. 139). The report recommended an increase of 50 percent in the car tax. As to the gasoline tax, to be collected from the newly constructed sole domestic refinery (fully protected), "the proportion that the excise duty of 12 cents bears to the pump price of motor gasoline [about 40 cents per U.S. gallon] is quite low in Liberia . . . . We see no reason why the excise duty may not be progressively raised over the next few years . . . so that the tax rate would approximate 32 cents per U.S. gallon on a gallon sold for 60 cents tax-inclusive at the pump" (p. 143). The increased revenue should be dedicated to a highway development fund. The report went on to point out the important developmental results that could be obtained by increasing the road network. Eventually, tolls should be charged on long-distance paved roads and on entry to, and possibly movement within, Monrovia.

(j) Possible New Taxes

Death and gift taxes.

> . . . in a country that, like Liberia, has no net wealth tax and—so far—only a very light tax on real estate, a death tax seems especially appropriate, provided it can be administered without too much inequity within this group of taxpayers . . . . An estate tax levied on the decedent's aggregate transfer would be the preferable form, administratively. Property not passing at death would, of

course, pay no tax. An important example is land in the interior held under tribal rights. In the cities the ownership of many properties is unclear, but . . . tax reform, either in the real estate tax or if a death tax is adopted, cannot wait upon title reform. Tax reform must force title reform . . . . A gift tax should not be introduced until experience has been gained with the death tax." (pp. 150–51)

The report noted that apparently few, if any, of the countries of tropical Africa imposed a tax upon transfer of property at death or by gift, whereas such a tax, at death, was common in the countries of Southeast Asia.

General sales taxes, including value-added tax.

On the face of it, there is no case for a general sales tax in Liberia, where consumer commodities for the middle and upper income groups are almost entirely imported, and those for the low-income groups are domestically produced and in large part produced by the consumer himself . . . customs duties imposed for revenue . . . are, in principle, the preferred method for taxing consumer commodities. Consumer services remain untaxed, to be sure, but aside from domestic service they seem to be less important in the Liberian consumption pattern than in developed countries . . . . In practice, however, the administration of the ad valorem rates of the customs duties encounters difficulties of valuation so severe . . . . Should the existing $18 million of customs revenue be collected instead under two taxes, that is, part of it from customs and part of it from retailers? There would be less pressure for dishonesty at any one point in the [tax] system . . . . But the very number of retailers makes administration expensive per dollar of revenue . . . . Many retailers are said to keep no books . . . . Much consumption is never preceded by a retail sale, notably "subsistence" consumption . . . . The full tax would still have to be levied upon import when the goods were brought in directly by a consumer . . . . To concentrate all the pressure of the $18 million at the retail level would make the tax unworkable . . . . But if the customs duties were continued, although reduced by, say, one-half from their present level, and if the retailer were given a credit against his retail sales tax in an amount equal to the tax paid at customs on the goods he sells at retail, the retailer would have less chance of success in underreporting his sales . . . . Meanwhile, it would not matter much, if at all, how far evasion had proceeded at the import stage . . . . A system resembling the one just described has been tested and found successful, over the past two years, in several European countries, under the name of "value-added" tax . . . . A complete value-added tax system . . . imposes a tentative sales tax not only on retailers but also on wholesalers, manufacturers, farmers, and raw material producers . . . . But in the Liberian economy, where imports predominate, it might not be worth the extra administrative effort to extend the scope of the tax in this way . . . . [Moreover] this split tax system . . . has one grave limitation. It cannot work well unless it is kept simple . . . . [T]here must be just one tax rate at retail on all goods, whether luxuries or necessaries . . . [Hence] the progressive elements in other parts of the tax system would need to be strengthened.

The report thus ended on an uncertain note, with respect to the possible introduction of a general sales tax, specifically a value-added tax, and offered no firm recommendation.

(k) Nontax revenues. In a chapter on nontax revenues, the report went into some detail in analyzing gross and net revenues from the Port of Monrovia, the Vessel Registration Tax, Liberian Corporation Fees, Postal, Telephone, and Telecommunications, the Roberts International Airport, Domestic Airports, the Public Utilities Authority, and the Liberian Produce Marketing Corporation, to ascertain whether there was justification for raising prices or fees charged in these activities so that, through smaller losses or larger profits the government would need to raise correspondingly less in tax revenue for general purposes.

In general, it appeared that little help could be expected from these sources. We concluded that port charges would probably have to be increased merely to meet the payments due by the government to the United States in coming years on the purchase price of the Port, which had been constructed by the United States. Moreover, the structure of rates charged by the Port of Monrovia was "economically inefficient, horizontally inequitable, and self-serving from the point of view of some of the owners of the Monrovian Port Management Company . . . . [T]his aged, distorted [rate] structure appears about to be revised" (p. 160). The vessel registration and tonnage taxes, a major source of revenue (Liberia had one of the largest registered fleets in the world) could not well be increased because of potential competition from other countries, and, indeed, existing competition from Panama. Postal charges on foreign mail might be raised without too much loss of traffic, but this was not certain (domestic-mail revenue was relatively small). Rates could and should be raised for telephone and telecommunication service, but current revenues were only about half a million dollars. Landing, handling, and parking fees at Roberts International Airport would need to be increased anyway to meet costs of expansion in the near future, but there might be a half-million-dollar surplus available for the government. The Public Utilities Authority was profitable, but needed the money for expansion and possible reduction of the high rates. The Liberian Produce Marketing Corporation, half owned by the government, could not be counted on for an increase in profits in the years ahead.

D. Degree of Implementation of Tax Mission's Recommendations

1. Progress Report of Tax Commission, October 30, 1970. The Progress Report of the Tax Commission, submitted about a year after the Tax Mission had delivered its report, concluded that "Although the Commission recognized the merits and quality of the [tax mission] . . . recommendations it was generally believed that the Shoup Report best served as a long-run guide toward which the Liberian government could move after more careful and intensive study, but that it was not a tax package to be implemented in its entirety at this time" (p. 5). This first report of the commission would therefore be restricted to "high priority items," and the recommendations would in total be revenue-neutral. The commission recommended:

> In line with the Mission report, the austerity tax and the education tax should both be repealed, the revenue loss being made up from a lowering of the personal exemption under the income tax (to $600) and a redesign of the rate schedule for individuals so that the top rate would drop from 35 percent to 25 percent. The lower rates were to be more steeply graduated than before. A partnership, aside from zero exemption, would use the same rate scale. An individual who was a member of more than one partnership and had an income of more than, say, $20,000 would have to include his share of the profits in his return, taking credit for his share of the partnership tax. (p. 11)

As to the business and occupation license "fees," the commission agreed with the mission that the occupational license charges should be increased by 50 percent. For the mercantile licenses, the commission went well beyond the mission's view and recommended their replacement by a "business trade levy" based on gross income or gross sales and covering "a wider group of businesses" (p. 8). Rates within the mercantile and service categories "would be allowed to vary . . . in accordance with ability to pay" (p. 8). This tax would now include financial institutions, service industries in general, and liquor dealers, among others.

The commission accepted the mission's recommendation that motor vehicle licenses should be raised 50 percent (with a graduated fee for large vehicles) (p. 12).

On the other hand, the commission said nothing about reforming the tax rules for concessionary enterprises, repealing deduction of personal taxes under the income tax, providing loss carry-overs, reducing the double taxation of dividends, repealing the education flat tax, and, eventually, the hut tax, reforming the real estate tax, altering the pattern of taxes on imports, suspending the rubber export tax, increasing the tax on liquor, or raising the gasoline tax. Nor was introduction of a death-and-gift tax suggested. Nontax revenues were not covered.

At no point did the commission report flatly disagree with a recommendation of the mission, except, implicitly, in venturing into a general sales tax against the mission's warning.

2. *Revenue Symposium, August 1974.* In December 1973 Byron Tarr, assistant minister of finance of Liberia, invited me to give a paper at a Revenue Symposium to be held in Monrovia August 21–23, 1974. My assigned topic was "Liberia's Tax Structure: Are Material Changes Desirable? Its Role in Economic Development." Eight other speakers were to give papers on income tax, customs and excise duties, sales tax, real estate tax, and tax harmonization for Liberia and Sierra Leone. The following remarks are based on material received from the Ministry of Finance before the symposium, incorporated in my paper submitted June 30, 1974.

All in all, it appeared that

> Liberia's tax system is very much the same as it was in 1969. . . . A
> 1 cent per gallon motor fuel tax came into force August 25, 1971,
> the proceeds apparently to be dedicated for agricultural expansion.
> A $3 "airport/seaport service charge" became effective August 27,
> 1971, on every person's travel fare abroad from Liberia (except those

in transit within 48 hours). A law effective April 26, 1972, provided for "an excise tax on either the production, sale, or consumption of all products manufactured within the Republic of Liberia," as Chapter 47, "Excise Tax"; apparently further steps had to be taken before this tax would be implemented. In laws effective February 23 and March 20, 1973, an annual development tax of $5 per capita or $5 per hut in Tribal Jurisdictions was imposed. Finally, in a law effective March 20, 1973, a 5-year carry-forward of business losses was allowed under the income tax.

The information in this paragraph is from my paper.

The United Nations Development Programme started a project in Liberia in February 1973 "to uplift the real estate tax area," with the result, by July 1974, that

> a major part of the properties in Monrovia have been revalued on a current market value basis and these will have effect for tax purposes from January 1, 1974 . . . . [A] substantial number of properties not previously taxed have been brought to account. A systematic valuation field book system has been utilized in this work; . . . the rate of tax on let out apartment buildings and houses has been increased from the residential ½% rate to the 2% business rate; . . . quite a number of tax loopholes have been closed, e.g. several well improved "farm" properties have been valued (for the first time) and taxed . . . likewise by a systematic search at the Deeds Registry Office many undeclared leases have been discovered and tax bills prepared to recover the "Coast Guard" tax due on these. (An attempt was made to consider whether to drop this tax but met with no encouragement). (Letter of July 12, 1974, from H. J. Manning to Shoup.)

3. The Period 1975–87. Information on changes in the Liberian tax system since 1974 has proved difficult to obtain, but thanks to four sources,[11] enough has been learned to indicate that although a few of the 1969 report's recommendations have become law, in general they have not been accepted, and some tax measures quite contrary to those recommendations have been enacted.

Income tax and poll tax. In 1980, the individual income tax rates were increased and the personal exemption was lowered. The increase in rates was far greater than the mission report would have considered practicable: the schedule now went from 11 percent on the first $2,000 to 65 percent on the amount in excess of $99,000 (TNS, 1981, p. 33). The report had suggested a top rate of only 20 percent (p. 77). This 1980 rate schedule is evidently still in force.

The personal exemption was reduced from $1,500 to $1,000 (TNS, 1981, pp. 21, 33). This $1,000 was the level recommended in the mission report, but the rise in prices since 1969 makes this exemption much lower in real terms than the report called for. In line with the report, the practice of giving no other type of personal exemption, e.g., for dependents, has been continued. The $1,000 exemption is apparently still in force.

A poll tax of $10 a year, called a "development and progress tax," was introduced in 1977. It strikes all individuals over 18 (and under 61: *African Tax Systems*). The proceeds were to be used for development projects (TNS, 1977, Non-Europe, p. 57). Apparently the old "education tax" thus reappeared, with a differently stated objective.

A "national reconstruction tax" was imposed on all wages and salaries and on the income of the self-employed, effective August 1, 1981. The tax rates ranged from 2 to 10 percent, but were lowered, as of January 1, 1982, to 1 to 8 percent (TNC, 1982, p. 13). But the rates appear to be linked, not to annual earnings, but to monthly earnings, as follows: 1 percent on $1 to $200; 4.5 percent on $201 to $500; 7.5 percent on $501 to $1,000; and 8 percent over $1,000. Presumably these are bracket rates. Apparently the old austerity tax had been repealed, only to reappear in this form.

A "health tax" of $5 per month (not per year) was imposed in the fiscal year 1984–85 on all persons in employment and on all foreign residents.

As to the other personal tax in force in 1969, the $6 per capita tax ($6 per hut in the tribal areas), information is not at hand as to whether it is still in force, but since it is not mentioned in *African Tax Systems*, we may perhaps assume that it was repealed.

The personal-tax segment of the Liberian tax system, therefore, is a mixture of taxation of personal income in general, personal earned income, and of poll taxation on an age group and on employed persons.

When we move to taxation of business organizations we see, first, that partners are now required to include in their taxable incomes their shares in the profits of the partnerships, an advance from 1969 that the tax mission thought was not advisable at that time. The partnership itself is still taxable, but a tax credit is given each partner in respect of his or her share in the tax paid by the partnership (but is a tax refund given if that share exceeds the partner's tax attributable to the profits?).

The corporation income tax seems to be about the same now as it was in 1969. No change at all appears to have been made from 1980 to 1986. The graduated rate scale is somewhat stiffer now, in money terms, than it was in 1969: 20 percent on the first $10,000, rising to 50 percent on that part over $100,000. This change took effect July 1, 1977 (TNS, 1978, Non-Europe, p. 20).

The only corporation tax recommendation in the 1969 report was that double taxation of dividends be mitigated, and this has not been adopted.

In 1980 the TNS reported that the investment code was being revised with the hope that "investments can be better spread geographically and over the various sectors of the economy" (p. 91).

Real estate tax ("land tax"). The real estate tax is evidently much the same as in 1969, except that undeveloped town lots, instead of being taxed $2 per quarter acre, are now taxed at 5 percent of assessed value. The two recommendations of the report as to the lease tax and uniformity of tax rates have not been adopted.

Taxes on imports. A new customs tariff came into effect October 1, 1977; it "alters the rate of duty on almost all items" (TNS, 1977, Non-Europe, p. 57).

In the period 1980–81 to 1985–86, an increased dependence on import taxes can be noted, although some reductions were made. In 1980–81 two increases were enacted. A variable-rate surcharge of 25 percent was imposed on dutiable luxury items and one of 15 percent on all other dutiable nonessentials. An invoice entry fee was levied: 7.5 percent on duty-free and transshipment goods and 5 percent on dutiable goods (lowered to 2.5 percent on transshipment goods in 1981–82, but put back to 7.5 percent in 1983–84).

In 1982, "the duty-free exemptions on imported equipment and materials for foreign companies" were "suspended" (TNS, 1982, p. 93).

In 1982–83 the import surcharge of 1980–81 was eliminated for several nonluxury goods. The stamp tax on bills of entry for duty-free goods processed by concessions was increased, in 1983–84, from $0.25 to $0.75 for each $100 or a fraction thereof. All ad hoc duty-free privileges granted to corporations were suspended on July 6, 1984, but were reinstituted at 50 percent of the previous levels in November of that year. Finally, an across-the-board increase in all import duties by 10 percentage points was introduced May 1, 1985, but several exemptions to this were introduced in 1985–86.

It is not known to the writer whether any of the mission report recommendations on tariffs have been adopted, but the across-the-board increase may indicate that little attention has yet been paid to the need to reduce tariffs on business goods (producer goods) relative to consumer goods, especially consumer luxury items.

Taxes on exports. The export tax on rubber, applied to foreign concessions, was withdrawn, in 1983–84, but was reimposed in 1984–85 (15–25 cents per pound). The 1969 recommendation was scarcely applicable here in view of the great change in world prices subsequently.

Business license fees. The recommendation of the tax commission to convert part of the license fee area into one subject to a sales tax has evidently been accepted; thus the advice of the tax mission was not followed. As of 1984 there is a "business registration license" of $400 a year, and a series of "miscellaneous licenses" fixed fees on hotels, restaurants, diamond brokers, prospectors, etc., but there is also an annual trade levy varying from 0.5 percent to 1 percent on total sales in the preceding calendar year. "This levy also applies to banks, insurance companies, insurance brokers and similar financial institutions but slightly different rates and rules are applied" (IBFD, Liberia, p. 11). In 1985–86 the business registration fees for various categories were increased.

Excise taxes (ex gasoline tax). In 1980–81 excise taxes on several items, including beer, were increased, and the beer tax was raised again, on August 1, 1981, by 59 cents to $1.10 per liter, but was subsequently lowered to 90 cents per liter. In 1983–84 a special low rate (50 percent of the normal rate) was accorded to certain items sold by military PXs: beer, stout, soft drinks, domestic spirits, and tobacco; and customs duties were lowered to 25 percent of the normal rate for imported spirits and tobacco.

Information for comparison with the 1969 rates is not at hand, in general. The specific-rate tax on beer has been almost doubled, a step the mission recommended for liquor.

User taxes on automotive transport. The mission recommendation that the gasoline tax be raised, from 12 cents a gallon to 32 cents, has been more than followed. We recall again that the price level has risen greatly since 1969. The tax rate was raised to 32 cents in 1981 and in 1983–84 was increased to $1.25. This evidently proved too drastic, as the rate was subsequently lowered to 82 cents, but on May 1, 1985, this reduction was more than recouped by an increase to $1.50 a gallon.

A 10 percent tax on international air travel was introduced in 1980–81.

Tonnage tax. Probably in line more or less with the rising general price level, the annual tonnage tax on ships registered under the Liberian flag was raised from the 1969 level of 10 cents to 30 cents per ton in 1981–82, to 35 cents in 1982–83, and to 40 cents in 1984–85. Presumably Panama and other competitors have enacted somewhat similar increases.

E. A General Appraisal

In chapter 6 (tax mission to Japan), I remarked that a tax mission report "is a failure if its authors so misunderstand the environment they are dealing with that virtually none of the recommendations are ever accepted." By this test, the Liberian tax mission report must be considered a failure. The responsibility for this failure, or degree of failure, rests on the director of the mission, not on his colleagues, who pursued their research within the framework agreed on by the director with the Liberian officials.

In the income tax field, the failure of the tax mission to influence policy seems to have been almost total. For the real estate tax the record is somewhat better, but not by much. The mission's warning against attempting a general sales tax has apparently been ignored. Eventual repeal of the per capita and per hut taxes seems as far away as ever. Excise tax changes may have been more in line with the mission recommendations, but this is not certain. No tax on transfer at death has been imposed. Acceptance of the mission recommendations on import duties seems to have been at least partial, in the distinction drawn between luxury and nonluxury items, but that had been somewhat in force initially, and the recent across-the-board increases run counter to this recommendation. More importantly, there is no record available as to whether the import duty load has been lifted from, or at least reduced for, producers goods. As to highway user taxes, the gasoline tax has certainly been increased, but it is not known whether the mission's recommendation that the car tax also be increased has been implemented.

The violent overthrow in 1980 of the Tolbert government by Doe and his associates, and the decline in Liberia's economic fortunes, have probably made much of the description and analysis in the 1969 report inapplicable today. Acceptance now of any of these 1969 recommendations could scarcely be considered, automatically, a "success" for the tax mission. The financial extremity to which Liberia has come is indicated by its acceptance of a group of seventeen United States "operational experts" who have

> co-signing authority in several key ministries and state corporations: finance, commerce, planning, the central bank, the national oil company and the produce marketing company . . . . Liberia was cut off from assistance last year by the World Bank, the International Monetary Fund and the African Development Bank for nonpayment of its debts. Last fall, the United States Agency for International Development halted money for projects pending payment of overdue loans. (*New York Times*, April 26, 1987, dispatch by James Brooke from Monrovia)

F. Hindsights

The relative failure of the Liberian tax mission may have been due to one or more of the following circumstances.

First, tax reform may not have been a truly urgent matter in the minds of either the Liberian officials, the business community, or the populace in general. Most of the government's revenue was coming from taxes on concessionaires, operating under agreements that could not be unilaterally changed. Further aid from abroad always seemed to be a possible way of avoiding hard choices in taxation. There had been no revolution to induce a rethinking of, among so many other things, the tax structure. A major portion of the population, those in the nonmonetary sector, were little influenced, at least directly, by taxes other than the hut tax. There were no problems of intergovernmental tax relationships.

Second, the total of resources put into the tax mission's effort may have been too small: five persons, working in Liberia for only five weeks or so, and, except for the director, not more than another two weeks back home. In particular, if substantial resources had been employed in analyzing tax administration problems, a better understanding might have been obtained as to what substantive recommendations would be appropriate (where considerable effort was made to appraise administrative techniques, that is, in customs and excises, the record of acceptance of substantive recommendations seems to have been better).

Third, the obligational pattern of the Liberian culture may have been so different from that of the Anglo-Saxon culture reflected by the tax mission that certain suggestions from the latter could scarcely be taken seriously enough for thorough implementation. In American society, no widespread obligation is felt by the elite to select some one or more of the younger persons in a disadvantaged group, say in the inner city, and assure that individual a full education and cultural contacts and even family life that will open the door to a position in the upper class. In Liberia, such a quasi-adoption, or even legal adoption, was not uncommon. The more impersonal obligation to pay one's taxes promptly and in full, on the other hand, seems to have been taken more seriously in the Anglo-Saxon culture (to say nothing of the minds of five individuals trained in public finance) than in the Liberian. Our mission members were somewhat startled to learn, from the files freely made available to Vickrey along with a computer to analyze them, that on 1967 incomes no individual in Liberia reported a taxable income of over $76,500, and only two reported taxable incomes between $51,500 and $76,500 (pp. 75, 78). The government offered no objection to printing these findings (they might have objected under the "confidential" clause—see p. 3 above).

I quote from the opening chapter of the report:

> [T]he tax system [in Liberia] must compete with an informal system of more or less voluntary contributions to family, friends, political party, local political chiefs, charitable organizations, and the like. This informal, or "quasi-tax system," as it may be called, is not inherently an evil; it is to some degree a necessary social cement that binds the community together . . . . The extended family and, to some degree, various secret societies obligate those who gain to share with others. However necessary this attitude might be in a nonmonetary economy where the individual is dependent on community action, it dampens incentives to enter the monetary economy permanently . . . . Another example is the strong pressure on Government employees to make political contributions that have on occasion amounted to as much as one month's salary. Equally serious are the informal and arbitrary levies said to be made by country officials, chiefs, and others, without statutory authority, to finance amenities for traveling officials, to defray fines incurred by the country officials, chiefs, etc.—to name but two instances. Under these circumstances it is understandable that the formal sanction for not paying taxes may be often less severe than for not participating in the informal contributions . . . . [If] the load of informal contributions . . . continues in its present intensity

and extent, meaningful reform of the formal tax system will probably not be possible. (pp. 6–7)

Liberian officials did not object to this statement.

A somewhat different cultural pattern may have developed under the Doe regime. The *Tax News Service* stated in its 1984 edition (pp. 83–84): "It has been reported that a tax collection force has been set up in a new effort against tax evasion and bribery. This force will be backed up by soldiers and policemen. Anyone receiving or giving bribes to avoid paying tax could be summarily executed. Foreigners who do not comply may be deported and are liable to have their property confiscated."

TNS contains no information on Liberia in 1985, 1986, 1987, and through April 15, 1988, except (1) "abolition of the progress and development tax . . . as part of a package of tax concessions announced on July 6, 1987. The package also includes a proposal to abolish the health tax as from January, 1988" (1987, p. 160) and (2) a proposal by Sweden to terminate its tax treaty with that country, among others (1987, pp. 70, 81).

Notes

1   Contributions were made to various factual and analytical sections of the mission's report by Dr. Jean Due, research associate, Anthony H. Pascal, research assistant, and Consuelo Maldonado, director of the Office of Accounting Systems of the Treasury Department of Puerto Rico.

2   *Informe sobre el Sistema Fiscal de Venezuela: Mision Shoup*, 2 vols. (República de Venezuela, Ministerio de Hacienda, Comisión de Estudios Financieros y Administrativos, 1960).

3   Foreword to Enrique F. Gittes, "Income Tax Reform: The Venezuelan Experience," *Harvard Journal of Legislation* 125 (1968), pp. 125–27.

4   The sources used are chiefly those listed in the references below as follows: Carrillo, Gittes, International Bureau of Fiscal Documentation, López de la Roche, and three Price Waterhouse publications.

5   However, there continues to exist a separate income tax rate applicable to mining and hydrocarbon activities of 60 percent (PW, pp. 70, 124), and 67.7 percent (PW, p. 131), respectively.

6   For information, comments and suggestions in connection with this project, I am indebted especially to Prof. Alcides Jorge Costa, Dr. Arthur Soares Xavier Ferreira, Dr. Ives Gandra da Silva Martins, Prof. Ruy Barbosa Nogueira, Dr. Joseph A. Pechman, and Dr. Henry Tilbery.

7   In the present paper, numerals in parentheses refer to page numbers of the Shoup Report. Numerals in parentheses with "PW" refer to the Price Waterhouse *Information Guide* of 1986 on Brazil.

8   For example, this addition to the regular entities tax is termed a "permanent excess

profits tax" by TNS (Jan. 31, 1986, p. 8). But Dr. Henry Tilbery sees no element of excess profits taxation in this extra 10 percent, and Dr. Alcides Jorge Costa considers that only the extra 5 percent of a special extra rate of 15 percent, in 1983, on financial institutions should be viewed as a substitute for an excess profits tax.

9   The first three paragraphs of this section are based on conversations with Harold Moss, and on the *Progress Report of the Tax Commission to the President of Liberia*, October 30, 1970, p. 1.

10   Dr. Donald S. Shoup (my son), of the National Bureau of Economic Research in New York City, agreed to come with the mission as research consultant; he had obtained an extensive background in Liberia in economics by a study, at Monrovia, of the Liberian port system. "Although the report is a joint effort of our entire group, there was division of labor along the following lines: Douglas Dosser, Liberia's economy, and user taxes; Rudolph G. Penner, customs duties, excises, stamp taxes, and export taxes; Carl S. Shoup, tax reform in Liberia, Liberia's public finance system, concessions agreements, per capita and hut taxes; Donald S. Shoup, nontax revenues; William S. Vickrey, concessions agreements, income taxes, and real estate taxes. Mrs. Carolyn S. Scott, as Secretary to the mission, typed the report and assisted in the logistics of our task" (p. xii). Cooperation by Liberian tax and other officials was excellent, and our group had ready access to files, taxpayers records, and the like. We also had informative conversations with some of the larger taxpayers (corporations).

11   I am indebted to Michael Frankel of the International Monetary Fund for a list of new revenue measures enacted in Liberia in the fiscal years 1980–81 through 1985–86, and to the International Bureau of Fiscal Documentation (IBFD) for a copy of the chapter on Liberia in their publication, *African Tax Systems*, and a copy of the 1977 Revenue and Finance Law, with amendments and regulations currently in the IBFD file. As will be seen, substantial use has also been made of the IBFD's *Tax News Service* ("TNS"), a loose-leaf updated source on tax changes in countries around the world. A letter from me to the minister of finance in Liberia elicited no response. For the most recent compilation, see Price Waterhouse, *Worldwide Summaries of Individual Taxes and Corporate Taxes*.

References

Brooke, James. "U.S. Will Oversee Liberian Finances." Dispatch from Monrovia to *New York Times*, April 26, 1987.

Carrillo Batalla, Dr. Tomas Enrique (chairman of the Commission on Fiscal Study and Reform and of the Coordinating Committee) et al. *Reform of the Venezuelan Fiscal System: Final Report*. Caracas: Republic of Venezuela, 1983.

———. *Memorandum* (to Shoup) on *Retrospective Appraisal of the 1958 Venezuelan Tax Study*. August 14, 1987. Typescript, 7 pages.

Cohen, Roger. "Anatomy of Failure: The Collapse of Brazil's Cruzado Plan." *Wall Street Journal*, February 13, 1987.

Columbia Encyclopedia, 1975 ed. S.v. "Brazil."

Gittes, Enrique F. "Income Tax Reform: The Venezuelan Experience." *Harvard Journal of Legislation*, 1968, 125–73.

International Bureau of Fiscal Documentation. *African Tax Systems*. Chapter on Liberia,

1984. Supplement No. 57, Autumn 1985.

———. *Tax News Service*. Bimonthly reports (various issues). Amsterdam.

International Monetary Fund. "Liberia: New Revenue Measures, 1980–81—1985–86." Typescript, courtesy of Michael Frankel.

Liberia, government of. Tax Commission. *Progress Report*. 1970. Monrovia.

López de la Roche, Carmen A. *El Informe de la Misión Shoup:* 28 Años Después. Maracaibo, December 1986. (English version: *The Shoup Mission Report: 28 Years After*. Maracaibo, January 1987).

Oldman, Oliver. "Foreword," in Gittes, "Income Tax Reform: The Venezuelan Experience." *Harvard Journal of Legislation*, 1968, pp. 125–27.

Oldman, Oliver, and Stanley S. Surrey. "Technical Assistance in Taxation in Developing Countries." In *Modern Fiscal Issues: Essays in Honor of Carl S. Shoup*, pp. 278–91. Edited by Richard M. Bird and John G. Head. Toronto: University of Toronto Press, 1972.

Price Waterhouse. *Corporate Taxes: A Worldwide Summary*. 1987 Edition. New York.

———. *Doing Business in Brazil (Information Guide)*. New York City, May 1986.

———. *Individual Taxes: A Worldwide Summary*. 1987 Edition. New York.

Shoup, Carl S. *Criteria for Choice Among Types of Value-Added Tax*. World Bank Discussion Paper, Report No. DRD191. New York: World Bank, September, 1986.

———. "Liberia's Tax Structure: Are Material Changes Desirable? Its Role in Economic Development." Paper given at Revenue Symposium, Monrovia, 1974.

Shoup, Carl S., Douglas Dosser, Rudolph G. Penner, and William S. Vickrey. *The Tax System of Liberia*. New York: Columbia University Press, 1970.

Shoup, Carl S., John F. Due, Lyle C. Fitch, Donald MacDougall, Oliver S. Oldman, and Stanley S. Surrey. *The Fiscal System of Venezuela: A Report*. Baltimore: Johns Hopkins Press, 1959.

———. *Informe sobre el Sistema Fiscal de Venezuela: Misión Shoup*. 2 vols. Caracas: Ministerio de Hacienda, República de Venezuela, 1960.

The Tax System of Brazil. Rio de Janeiro: Getulio Vargas Foundation, 1965. (Portuguese translation also in 1965).

Venezuela, government of. *Venezuelan Income Tax Law*. In Spanish and English. Code 200. October 1986. Caracas: Traductores Téchnicos.

9

The Administrative Dimension of Tax Reform in Developing Countries

·······

Richard M. Bird

The importance of good administration has long been as obvious to those concerned with taxation in developing countries as has its absence. Over thirty years ago, Stanley Surrey (1958, pp. 158–59) noted that "the concentration on tax policy—on the choice of taxes—may lead to insufficient consideration of the aspect of tax administration. In short, there may well be too much preoccupation with 'what to do' and too little attention to 'how to do it.'"[1] Although Surrey's paper has been frequently cited, and presumably read, there is surprisingly little evidence in the hundreds of articles, books, and reports on tax reform written over the last few decades that this warning has been taken sufficiently seriously.[2] It thus seems time to sound the alarm again, before we launch into another thirty years of misguided attempts to reform tax structure while largely ignoring tax administration.[3]

The basic message of this paper is that the administrative dimension should be placed at the center rather than the periphery of tax reform efforts. The overwhelming importance of the administrative dimension in developing countries is first stressed: as Casanegra (1987, p. 25) put it, ". . . tax administration *is* tax policy." Some solutions that have been proposed to the pervasive malaise characterizing developing country tax administrations are next reviewed and, for the most part, found wanting.[4] It is argued that the most rewarding approach to tax reform in most countries is likely to be to design a tax system that can be acceptably implemented by the existing weak administration. Miracles being always in short supply, any other course of action is, in the end, unlikely to prove successful. Finally, the appendix contains a brief case study of Papua New Guinea: the argument is that the tax system with which

Papua New Guinea was launched into the world a decade ago is completely unsuited to both its economic structure and its administrative capabilities, and needs to be drastically reformed in recognition of the probable persistence of these constraints.

The Importance of Administration

Limited administrative capacity is a binding constraint on tax reform in many developing countries. A recent survey by Richupan (1984a), for example, cites studies of tax evasion in different developing countries indicating that it is not uncommon for half or more of potential income tax to be uncollected.[5] Matters are not much better with respect to indirect taxes (Rao and Pradhan, 1985; National Institute, 1986; Bird, 1985b) or property taxes (Bahl and Linn, 1985).

This scanty quantitative evidence accords with the common perception that there is widespread tax evasion in most developing countries. Moreover, even when there is not outright evasion, the tax structure in these countries is often designed, administered, and judicially interpreted in such a way as to ensure the emergence of a huge gap between the potential and the actual tax base. Sometimes this result is achieved crudely, as through the continued use in Guatemala after a major devaluation, of values converted at the old exchange rate for purposes of customs duties (Bird, 1985a). Sometimes it is achieved through more subtle (and usually peripherally legal) exploitation of the peculiarities of banking and tax laws, perhaps particularly with respect to the widespread availability of tax "incentives."[6] And sometimes it is achieved by the functioning—or nonfunctioning—of the appeals system.[7] However it is accomplished, whether at the legislative, administrative, or judicial levels, the result in most developing countries is that there is a great discrepancy between what the tax system appears to be on the surface and how it actually works in practice (Gray, 1987).

The effects of this discrepancy are more important and pervasive than seems generally to be recognized. Not only is revenue "lost" but the elasticity of the tax system is also reduced—particularly, of course, in inflation when administrative lags alone will usually suffice to yield this result (Tanzi, 1977). The result is that additional revenue must continually be secured through a series of discretionary ad hoc rate increases and new taxes. The "patchwork" character of the tax system of many developing countries arises in large part from their inability to administer the taxes they legislate, which leads to a continual need to legislate new tax changes.

The incidence and effects of the tax system are as sensitive to how it is administered as is its yield (Archaya, 1986). Tax evasion inevitably undermines the horizontal equity of the tax system.[8] Recipients of equal income, like consumers of similar products and owners of similar properties, are not in fact taxed alike, whatever the law may say.[9] The income tax in most developing countries is in practice a schedular tax, with the effective tax rate depending largely on the source of the income and almost always heavier on wage than on self-employment or capital income (Rezende, 1976; Oldman and Bird, 1977). Taxes on property are even more sensitive to administrative interpretation, with old buildings being favored over new, and so on (Bahl and Linn, 1985). Even in the case of sales and excise taxes (Cnossen, 1977), in practice the products of small firms are usually favored.[10]

Moreover, most divergences between law and reality also serve to undermine the vertical equity of the tax system. It is the well-to-do who can most readily arrange for the law to contain convenient loopholes in the first place, and to exploit such loopholes once they are there with the aid of the "rent-seeking" skills of tax accountants and lawyers (and the consequent waste of scarce resources). The same group receives much of its income in the forms that are hardest to track down; people in this group may also more readily hold their wealth, and even spend it, in ways hard to detect (e.g., offshore). Finally, they can not only most readily bribe and subvert administrators but they have the most to gain from doing so. Since the incidence of a tax is the result of the interaction of statute law, the opportunities different groups have to evade it, and the rigor with which it is enforced—and the rich come out ahead on all three counts—it seems clear that taxation in developing countries is, as a rule, unlikely to cause much disturbance to the inhabitants in the upper ranges of the income distribution.

For similar reasons, the real incentive effects of the tax system may be quite different from those that may be surmised from the statute. The global progressive personal income tax established by law is in practice likely to amount to little more than at most a mildly progressive tax on wage earners in the modern sector.[11] The equally formidable-looking modern corporate income tax may turn out to be a crude gross receipts tax in practice.[12] Even an apparently general ad valorem sales tax may in practice amount to little more than a collection of specific excises on a small fraction of consumption.[13] In these circumstances, comparisons of the merits of general income or consumption taxes, or lamentations about the heavy burden imposed on capital by nominally progressive income and corporate taxes, may sometimes represent more obeisance to current trends in the academic literature than serious analysis of tax reform.

The tax administration—and hence feasible tax policy—in any country inevitably reflects to a large extent the nature of the country itself.[14] If the country is a sea of corruption, as some are, the tax administration will not be an island of incorruptibles, and it is foolish to pretend it is. If most traders in the country are illiterate and keep no written records, no accounts-based tax (such an income or general sales tax) can effectively be levied on them, and it is futile to pretend to be doing so. Similarly, if land titles are in chaos or nonexistent in rural areas, no effective rural land tax can be levied. If officials are judged solely by the tax revenue they produce and little else—as was long the rule in the western world (Webber and Wildavsky, 1986) and is still true in some developing countries—they are likely to get that revenue from the politically weaker sectors of the population (such as ethnic minorities), regardless of what the law says. If the only way for an honest official to make a living wage is to claim travel allowances, then he or she is forced to travel even if it is a complete waste of time. If only the incompetent and the untrained are left to deal directly with taxpayers, as is the case in many administrative systems where advancement comes only in the form of being promoted to a desk job, then taxpayers will meet only the incompetent and the untrained.

This catalog of woes is not easily remediable even in principle, let alone in practice. In many developing countries, the honesty of both taxpayers and tax officials is suspect (Virmani, 1987). Governments have little control over officials, little information as to what is going on, and no easy way to get it (Gray, 1987). Even if the information were available, the problem is inherently complex: market structures (and hence adjustment costs) vary widely, as do risk and time preferences, so that the costs, probabilities, and benefits of detecting evasion and corruption vary widely (Virmani, 1987). Administrative cost functions are discontinuous and hard to interpret (Bird, 1982b). Tax schedules, the interpretation of the law, the penalty schedule, and the appeals process all vary over time, as do enforcement efforts—and the reaction of taxpayers to such efforts.[15]

In the circumstances, it is not surprising that many tax analysts ignore the problem of tax administration—a problem epitomized in many countries in the phrase of Gray (1987, p. 32), "All taxes are negotiable"—perhaps in the hope it will go away on its own. Even some of those most aware of these problems have in effect done this. Taylor (1967), for example, who wrote a perceptive piece on tax administration in Nigeria two decades ago, began his paper by saying these were only short-run problems which would undoubtedly be resolved in twenty or twenty-five years. An official report in Papua New Guinea (1971) similarly said of the income tax that doubtless, by the end of the decade, its reach will have extended throughout the population. Both these predictions, like similar ones made in other countries, have turned out to be wildly optimistic, proving once again that "the first law of finance is inertia" (Webber and Wildavsky, p. 214).

Many tax reform proposals in developing countries have not paid even this passing obeisance to the problem of tax administration. Indeed, some reform proposals would make the life of administrators even more difficult. As Surrey (1958, pp. 160–61) put it in his seminal paper:

> The tax administrator on the one hand sees new burdens falling on his shoulders—new taxes being imposed and existing levies becoming more severe. He must collect more taxes, at higher rates, and from an ever expanding body of taxpayers. On the other hand he finds himself saddled with a staff which is insufficient, inexperienced, and poorly paid. He faces a public in large part unfamiliar with the tax knowledge and record keeping requirements which a developing state must inevitably demand of its citizens. He cannot obtain the needed support from the legal and accounting professions . . . . Finally, he often must demand the taxes from businesses and individuals with a deep-rooted suspicion ranging to contempt of the tax collector, for a public whose antagonism to tax payment, arising from a basic lack of confidence in the government, is almost the very antithesis of the attitude which must be the cornerstone of every successful democratic tax system—that taxes are the price necessarily paid for civilized society.

It is no wonder that tax administrators often view would-be tax reformers to be little more than residents of an ivory tower, who descend after the battle is largely over to shoot the wounded.[16]

One reason for this apparent disinterest in administration may be, as McLure (1982, p. 54) suggests, that it seems hard to go beyond platitudes on this subject. A more basic reason, however, has less to do with platitudes than with attitudes. As has been noted with respect to budget reform: "It may finally dawn upon observers that the peoples involved must not want to succeed all that much if they keep failing."[17] To put the point another way, if after thirty years of persistent nagging there has been so little perceptible improvement in important aspects of tax administration in many developing countries, it may perhaps be safely assumed that the next thirty years are likely to mean more of the same.[18] Whether this administrative inertia shows that a society gets the tax administration it wants (or deserves)—perhaps because taxation reflects the reality of political power (Best, 1976)—or whether it simply shows that no administration can be much different from the society of which it is a part, is less important than the fact of its existence. Neither quick fixes nor head-on confrontations seem likely to change matters much in the foreseeable future in most countries. Tax administration will thus remain a binding constraint on tax reform. In these circumstances, what can be done?

Coping with Administrative Reality

Broadly speaking, the solutions to the administrative problems of tax reform found in the literature may be divided into three groups: those that would change the environment, those that would change the administration, and those that would change the law.

Changing the Environment

Academic economists discussing policy issues sometimes sound as though they are, in effect, advocating that the way the world works should be changed to fit the conditions assumed in their models. Tax reformers discussing the need to change the institutional context within which a tax system functions often sound equally futile.

It is a commonplace, for example, that modern direct taxes depend to some extent on what is usually called "voluntary compliance." Even if such compliance is perhaps often motivated less by civic conscience than by the fear of being caught, it would clearly be exceedingly difficult, perhaps impossible, to administer such a tax if every hand were always raised against it. One cannot put the entire population into jail. Equally, however, one cannot will into being a spirit of compliance that is not there. If, as has often been said, the willingness of taxpayers to comply with their obligations depends to a large extent upon their perception that the funds thus taken from them are put to some good use and that they are treated fairly when compared to other taxpayers, then the fiscs of most developing countries are in deep trouble indeed.[19] These conditions do not now prevail, and in many cases are not likely to prevail in the near future.

Several ways of attempting to remedy this serious "environmental" defect have been mooted. One is simply to undertake a campaign of "taxpayer education," to convince taxpayers that—in Justice Holmes's phrase (cited earlier in the quote from Surrey)—taxes are the price paid for a civilized society, that they live in such a society, and that the tax system is equitable. Such campaigns to encourage compliance are unlikely to do much good, however, if reality is too obviously different. As another famous American, Abraham Lincoln, once said: "you may fool all the people some of the time; you can even fool some of the people all the time; but you can't fool all of the people all the time."

Words alone are unlikely to change basic attitudes. Deeds may do so, however, so another approach is obviously to turn government into something which people see as adding to their lives rather than a burden.[20] Thoroughgoing expenditure reform, increased use of devices such as earmarking and benefit taxes that link taxes and expenditures in some believable way, the devolvement of functional and financial responsibilities on local communities—such fundamental changes in the way government is conducted may indeed lead to a change in the attitude to taxation over time, and hence make the work of the tax collector, if never pleasurable, at least acceptable.[21] The perceived fairness of the tax system may of course also be a factor in shaping attitudes.

Fundamental changes in such matters, however desirable, by definition cannot be made easily or quickly, so there is little immediate hope for relief from this source. On the other hand, one should not overdo the importance of securing any particular concept of equity in the context of the tax system. Most developing countries are at best limited democracies or constrained autocracies. Even in the most democratic such countries, as a rule only limited groups are both tax-sensitive and politically significant. Most governments seem more concerned with the tax concerns of the few who matter than with the burden on the many: the "horizontal equity" emphasized in tax reform discussions seems often to be viewed solely from the perspective of those sufficiently well-off to be subject to direct taxes.[22] The tax treatment of the population as a whole sometimes seems to be considered primarily in terms of how to secure the necessary revenues with the least fuss.[23] The "ability to pay" doctrine as it applies in some countries thus seems concerned more with the ability of the government to make people pay than with abstract notions of equity.

The appropriate role for tax policy advisers in such circumstances is probably to trace out as carefully and convincingly as possible the consequences of particular measures, leaving the decision about their acceptability up to the presumably responsible authorities.[24]

Changing the Administration

Another approach to relieving the constraints imposed on tax reform by administrative limitations is to tackle those limitations directly. Some proposals for administrative reform, however, seem to amount to little more than looking reality squarely in the eye and passing on. An example is the common suggestion that an elite corps of tax administrators should be created—an idea which dates back at least to Kaldor (1956) and perhaps in part has its roots in some fuzzy notion of the great days of the British Raj and the Indian Civil Service. This hoary chestnut deserves to be put aside for once and all.[25]

In the first place, any tax administration is part of the public service generally. Consequently, it is, as a rule, no more than a fantasy to think that it can for long be pulled out of the ruck of political favoritism, employment-generation, and the myriad other factors that account for the masses of low-paid, poorly trained, poorly motivated public servants found in most developing countries (Goode, 1981). Secondly, even if such an elite could be created, it cannot do the job properly without both good soldiers (the front-line clerks, tellers, and so on) and adequate tools (computers, communication systems, etc.), neither of which is likely to prove easy to procure in developing countries, particularly for usually low-status revenue agencies.[26] An even more popular way of ignoring the administrative problem is to pretend it can all be handled by a small staff equipped with appropriately up-to-date computers. There is no doubt that in certain areas of tax administration, good use can be made of computers and that, indeed, they may in some instances obviate the need to acquire the skills of many highly trained specialists (Lane and Hutabarat, 1986).

On the other hand, as experience has shown in all too many countries, the computerization of tax administration is a complex task that has as yet been successfully accomplished by few. Computers must be programmed and operated by people; they must rely on information obtained and inputted by other people; and their output must be acted upon by still other people. Since the motivations and incentives of all these people are unlikely to be altered by the introduction of new equipment alone, it is by no means obvious that the dawning of the computer age has significantly reduced the importance of the administrative constraint on tax reform in developing countries. Indeed, it is not hard to find instances in which the inappropriate introduction and use of computer systems has in some ways made matters worse. On the whole, computerization is clearly most useful where the tax administration is already well organized (Corfmat, 1985).

Too often, as was recently noted in India—sometimes thought to be among the best of all developing countries in this respect—the tax administration is "neglected" and "archaic," characterized by poor training, low status, poor salaries, and poor equipment (Archaya, 1986, p. 362). An obvious remedy is to tackle these and other organizational and procedural problems head on: to see that the law is properly drafted and codified; that the administration is properly organized, staffed, and trained; that taxpayers are located, placed on the rolls, and their returns adequately examined and audited; that relevant information is obtained from other government departments and elsewhere and properly utilized; that controversies between taxpayers and the administration are satisfactorily resolved; that taxes due are collected; and that penalties are properly applied. This is the approach taken by Surrey in the seminal paper cited earlier; it is also the approach suggested in an interesting recent paper by McLure (1982).

The discussion of why the high hopes held for the 1974 tax reform in Colombia (McLure and Gillis, 1974) were so quickly undermined —not least by the judicial overthrow of critical administrative parts of the reform package—led him to propose the establishment of a high-level commission focusing on the reform of tax administration rather than tax structure. What is interesting about this logical proposal is that it appears unique in the tax reform literature: no one, anywhere, has done much along these lines. Even if someone did, however, it is by no means clear that any useful action would result, as experience with attempts at administrative reform have shown in many countries.[27]

Interestingly, perhaps the oldest means of dealing with the administrative problem is to "privatize" tax collection. "Tax farming," as this practice is known, has a bad name in view of the gross injustices to which it led, but it also had real virtues in many countries during the centuries when it was the dominant form of tax collection. In particular, it ensured a reliable and steady stream of revenue into state coffers.

The practice went out of favor in Europe when modern public administrative structures began to emerge in the seventeenth and eighteenth
centuries.[28]

Of course, no one would recommend the revival of tax farming today.
Some important features of tax administration in many developing
countries, however, are not dissimilar to tax farming in both their good
and their bad aspects. Moreover, the recent spread of what is in effect
private administration of important customs functions in countries
such as Indonesia and Jamaica may signify a new legitimacy for this
practice.[29]

As yet, not many developing countries have opted to hire foreigners,
let alone local private firms, to collect their taxes on a commission
basis as opposed to the fixed fees characteristic of traditional tax
farming.[30] In practice, however, some aspects of how tax administration
works in many countries are not dissimilar. In some countries (e.g.,
Senegal), tax inspectors are rewarded in accordance with the amount of
additional tax and fines they collect. The earmarked taxes common in
Latin America are sometimes shared between the collecting agency and
the state (Musgrave, 1981; Bird, 1984b). The "third party" collection
systems that are the backbone of most effective taxes in all countries
also have a commission aspect, since the collecting agent (the withholding employer, the sales taxpayer) has the use of the funds for a
legally or customarily agreed period before remitting them to the
government.[31] Finally, in all too many countries tax collectors are more
or less expected to make up for their poor salaries by supplementary
collections from taxpayers—collections which are not accompanied by
a corresponding remittance to the government. In many such "corrupt"
situations, indeed, there is a conventionally accepted level of private
reward to the fortunate possessors of official positions which is regarded
as no more criminal than the equivalent rake-off by a cook from the
household budget.[32]

Yet another interesting variant of "official tax farming" which exists
in some countries is to establish revenue targets for each auditor, tax
official, or district tax office.[33] If such targets are used as the sole basis
of evaluating performance, and if compliance with such targets is considered essential to ensure an adequate flow of revenue to the central
authorities, clearly such a system has both the virtue (stable revenue)
and the vice (a license for extortion) of traditional tax farming. Moreover, unless the targeting system is altered, tax changes intended to
alter allocative or distributive outcomes will not have much effect in

reality, however refined their design, since the basic incentive of officials will still be to meet their targets by collecting the most they can from those least able to resist.

In other instances, of course, "targeting" may be simply a relatively innocuous device used as one part of an array of measures intended to keep administrators up to the mark. Indeed, one of the main purposes of such a system—and perhaps even its effect if there are adequate controls to restrain excessive zeal—may be to provide a higher degree of certainty to both the state and taxpayers. With respect to public as to private tax farming, full understanding of the possible merits and demerits of the practice requires a detailed examination of its context and effects.[34] Labels alone are not grounds for condemnation.

Although what we think we have learned from history tends to turn most of us against such practices, many countries for many centuries have found it useful, even necessary, to thus employ private cupidity to serve public needs. Rather than outright condemnation of the desire of tax officials to feather their private nests, and pleas for the invention of "new model" men to replace the present unworthy vessels, one important component of a realistic study of tax administration in developing countries should be to devise incentive systems, perhaps at times including financial rewards, that will lead to a better matching of public and private interests.[35]

Should this advice be acted upon, it would of course be important to have an effective system of controls to ensure that tax administrators do not steal the state (and the taxpayers) blind. As Webber and Wildavsky (1986, p. 39) say, ". . . a tax collector's very function tempts him to cheat." Indeed, much of their lengthy history of fiscal administration is devoted to detailing the many ways over the centuries that sovereigns have tried to restrain this natural impulse of their servants. Rewards for good performance and penalties for poor performance; overlapping, duplicative, and redundant administrative structures;[36] the division of functions among different officers, both to use each as a check on the other and to make it more difficult and costly to bribe them;[37] the use of internal and external "spies" to check on the honesty of tax officials —all these devices and others have long been employed for this purpose in different countries.

The most basic way to ensure that tax officials do what they are supposed to do, and no more, however, is simply to reduce to a minimum the amount of discretion they have in dealing with taxpayers. The more room there is for negotiation between official and potential taxpayer, the more scope there is for bribery by the one, arbitrary exaction by the other, and collusion by both. The more the tax to be paid is based on some readily measurable, observable, and verifiable base, the less scope there is for such maneuvers. If tax administration is to be effective and seen to be fair in the context of many developing countries it is thus necessary to apply clear, known, objective standards—however rough the ensuing justice—rather than leaving the application of a fine-sounding general statute to negotiations between taxpayers and officials.[38]

Changing the Law

The best way to cope with the administrative problem is to design tax reforms for developing countries in full recognition of the severe limitations imposed by administrative realities. The administrative dimension is central, not peripheral, to tax reform. Without significant administrative changes, the alleged benefits of many proposed tax reforms will simply not be achieved, and, as a rule, it is unrealistic to expect such changes. Too many tax reform efforts have regarded tax policy and tax administration as quite separate matters. The world is not like that. No policy exists until it is implemented, and it is the manner of its implementation which really determines its impact. Those who would alter the outcomes of a tax system must therefore understand in detail how it is administered, and adjust their recommendations accordingly if they want to do good rather than ill.

There are at least three ways to approach the question of modifying the legal structure to accord with the administrative realities of developing countries: the first, to develop some gadgetry to bypass the problem, is a false lead; the second, to provide an adequate legal structure for administration, is obviously important but in itself inadequate; while the third, to design the basic tax law properly in the first place is, in the end, the only sensible procedure.

Gadgets. At least three types of tax "gadgets" have been suggested to get around the administrative problem. The "lottery" approach in effect uses the cupidity (or gullibility) of taxpayers to make their interests congruent with those of the administration. Perhaps the best example of this approach is a scheme suggested by Hart (1967) to encourage customers to collect their sales receipts, so that they could enter them for lottery prizes.[39] The idea is to obtain more reliable information on both the gross receipts of business and the expenditures of taxpayers.

One problem with such schemes is that it is unlikely the probability of a prize would be great enough to make it worthwhile for most people to comply. Even if it was, the seller could easily offset this incentive by offering two prices, with and without receipt (Casanegra, 1987). Another, even more serious, problem is that there is no conceivable way most tax administrations in developing countries could use the information thus provided, since they are already swamped with usable but unused information. An example is the provision found in some countries permitting the deduction of (e.g.) professional fees only on the submission of appropriate receipts. The idea, of course, is to aggregate such receipts and match them with the declaration (or nondeclaration) of the professional in question. Unfortunately, this never seems to happen.[40]

For much the same reasons, the much-touted "self-checking" feature of the value-added tax has in fact amounted to little in most countries. This is one area, however, where computerization in principle could be the answer, although it does not as yet seem to have amounted to much in the case of other "information return" reporting systems (such as bank interest in Canada and the United States). Korea, for instance, at first matched all value-added returns on the computer (Han, 1987), although it seems unlikely that this elaborate exercise was more productive than a properly designed selective audit system would be.[41]

Another "gadget" is the proposal by Kaldor (1956), subsequently elaborated by Higgins (1959), for a "self-enforcing" tax system consisting of personal and corporate taxes on income and capital gains, combined in various ways with taxes on wealth, sales, gifts, excess inventories, and expenditures. Since this scheme has, quite properly in my view, been characterized by such authorities as Shoup (1969) and Goode (1981) as unworkable, and has in any case not been taken seriously anywhere, it will not be further discussed here. Much the same fate has been suffered by the proposal for a "self-assessed" property tax suggested by Harberger (1965) and elaborated by Strasma (1965), although in this case variants of such systems have in fact been employed in some countries, albeit without much success (Bird, 1984c). Once again, there seems to be no relief for the hard-pressed tax administrator in clever design. In the end, the only way to administer a tax is, alas, to do so.

A final tax "gadget" is the tax amnesty. Recently there has been a revival of interest in this shopworn device as a result of some apparent success in, of all places, the United States (Jackson, 1986; Lerman, 1986). On the whole, however, there seems no reason to change the traditional view that this approach too is a loser unless, of course, the new day really has dawned and henceforth the tax in question will be fiercely and strictly administered. Leonard and Zeckhauser (1987), for example, suggest that an amnesty may be needed to facilitate tougher enforcement. As Zweifel and Pommerehne (1985) have shown, however, many of those who support amnesties are willing to do so only if there is no subsequent tightening of administration. More importantly, history suggests that such tightening seldom follows in any case and that those who miss out on one amnesty can likely count on another one in the future.[42] For these reasons, tax amnesties will doubtless continue to be more popular with politicians than with tax analysts.

Legal framework. In contrast to the false hopes of gadgetry, there is clearly much to be gained by ensuring that the basic legal structure of tax administration (Yudkin, 1973) is set out properly. This path too will not lead to Nirvana. In particular, while it is obviously important to have a correct, and enforceable, set of sanctions (Oldman, 1965; Gordon, 1988), the notion that some seem to have derived from the theoretical tax evasion literature—that all that is needed to deter evasion is a correct penalty structure—is simple fantasy.[43] The one-off game between a rational tax evader and a two-instrument administration postulated in this literature is too far removed from the real world to provide much useful guidance to tax designers or officials. So long as the probability of being caught is close to zero, as is the probability of being subjected to a severe penalty if one is caught, then even within the framework of this model, there would seem to be little penalty design can do to alleviate real-world problems. Why would anyone who can costlessly evade a 50 percent tax rate hesitate to dodge one of 30 or even 10 percent?[44]

Adapting the tax structure. As with earmarking and tax farming, schedular taxation has long had a bad press, much of which has been well deserved. As in the other cases mentioned, however, wholesale condemnation of the schedular approach is by no means justified. The simple fact is that not only is the income tax in every developing country schedular in practice, but that the very nature of most such countries means that this outcome is inevitable, no matter what the law may say (Rezende, 1976; Oldman and Bird, 1977). It is not really possible to apply a "global" income (or consumption) tax in the circumstances of most developing countries. In reality, there are perhaps four income taxes in most countries: (1) a more or less progressive tax imposed through a withholding system on money wage income in the modern sector; (2) a set of more or less ineffective levies on the self-employed; (3) flat-rate withholding taxes on certain forms of capital income; and (4) a tax on the profits of large, and especially foreign, business.

The administrative case for a properly designed set of presumptive taxes is especially strong in most developing countries (Bird, 1983). Obviously, such crude methods should not be applied in the more organized sector, from which most taxes are likely to be collected in any event.[45] What can be done, however, is to concentrate the scarce administrative skills available in most tax administrations—the "detective" skills needed to uncover accounting fraud, for example—on those firms, seldom more than a few hundred in number, from which most taxes are collected, whether in the form of corporate income taxes, withheld personal income taxes, or sales, excise, and payroll taxes, rather than dissipating them uselessly across a vast sea of noncompliant small and medium traders (Muten, 1981). This may not be fair, but it is reality.[46]

For similar reasons, the concern often manifested with increasing the number of tax filers may well be misconceived. Experience in the Philippines with respect to both income and property taxes, for example, suggests that most nonfilers were too small to warrant the cost of tracking them down. In such cases, scarce administrative resources should be concentrated on ensuring that the larger taxpayers, who are generally already on the rolls, comply fully with their fiscal obligations.[47] In the case of the well-off and notoriously elusive "professional" class, whose noncompliance brings direct taxation into disrepute in so many countries (see, for example, Bahl and Murray, 1986, on Jamaica), the best approach, as with small traders and farmers, is to impose as stiff a presumptive system as can be implemented, with the better-trained officials being used to devise and adapt the standards rather than to deal directly with individual taxpayers.[48]

The moral of this story is of course not that there is no place for an income (or other general direct) tax in any developing country. Indeed, it may even prove useful to package the diverse set of levies described above in a single income tax law (Oldman and Bird, 1977). The moral is simply that those who would design a better direct tax system for such countries should realize that the economic and administrative realities are usually such that what is really being done is to design a schedular tax. The tax analyst who approaches his task in this way is unlikely to make the same reform proposals as one who does not so take into account the way the world works.

In the income tax field, for example, the key to success in any country is as comprehensive a withholding system as possible, in most cases supplemented by some sort of legally based presumptive assessment method on the "hard-to-tax" groups: both of these approaches will likely work best if rates are not too high or steeply progressive (Bird, 1983; DeGraw and Oldman, 1985). In the sales tax field, for many less developed countries the best that can be done may be a well-designed, physically controlled excise system (Cnossen, 1984), though in other cases a simple, uniform value-added tax may be both feasible and desirable to reduce cascading (Bird, 1985b). In the case of some small, open countries with little domestic production and relatively low tariffs on most items, much the same results may be achieved by simply levying a uniform tariff on imports (see appendix). As for wealth taxes, simple flat-rate taxes on urban and rural property are perhaps all that can be expected in all but the most advanced developing countries (Bird, 1974).

Conclusion

The basic conclusion to which the preceding discussion leads is thus simply that those proposing tax reforms in developing countries should both understand thoroughly the existing administration and assess realistically the possibility of rapid improvement. Since many tax reforms that have been proposed in developing countries would complicate rather than simplify the work of already overloaded administrations, the failure to adopt or implement them successfully is not surprising.

The only real solution to this problem is to design a tax reform that will "work," that is, produce better results than the existing system with an administration similar to that now in place. Complex schemes simply will not work in the conditions of most developing countries. Too often would-be tax reform-mongers have been led astray in the futile search for the perfect fiscal instrument in theoretical terms. The "perfect" in this sense, however, is too often the enemy of the "good" in the sense of a roughly acceptable tax system, that is, one which can be administered roughly and still produce acceptable results.

The "brave new world" of tax reform sketched in this paper may not sound either very brave or very new, but it is the world in which most developing countries are found. Moreover, since those who would change the world must first understand it, starting from such a basis appears to offer a better prospect of attaining an acceptably fair and generally efficient tax system than the adoption of the latest up-to-date model of fiscal perfection from the academic drawing board.

Appendix. Tax Reform in Papua New Guinea:
Backward to the Future

The range and variety of conditions found in developing countries are so great that lessons derived from the experience of any one country may be applied to others only with considerable care. In some ways, Papua New Guinea is so different from any other developing country that this warning seems particularly appropriate: what other country of less than 3 million people has over 700 languages, a population which ranges from Stone Age farmers to sophisticated Western businessmen, a functioning democracy, and twenty-two partly autonomous provincial governments? In other ways, however, Papua New Guinea's experience seems close to that of many African countries in the postcolonial era (Wedderspoon, 1969). In particular, Papua New Guinea illustrates the often unhappy consequences of implementing in one country the ideas currently fashionable in another, without paying adequate attention to the vast differences in the economic and administrative situations of the two.

Indeed, the misfit between the relatively "advanced" tax (and expenditure) structure Papua New Guinea inherited at the time of achieving its independence from Australia in 1975 and its economic and administrative realities is so great that the only sensible direction for future tax reform appears to be, so to speak, to go backward in time and to introduce some of the sorts of crude, but workable, devices that may function better in such an environment.[49] Experience elsewhere with respect to collecting taxes with very limited administrative resources in a highly fragmented, largely illiterate, poorly developed rural economy would seem to provide a more relevant basis for the development of a workable tax structure in Papua New Guinea than the latest fad in the developed world —whether it be the highly progressive income tax of the 1960s or the flat-rate tax of the current era.

Like all developing countries, Papua New Guinea faces increasing budgetary demands simply to provide services to its rapidly expanding population. In addition, the Australian government has recently announced that the level of its foreign aid, which currently finances one third or more of Papua New Guinea's total budgetary expenditures, may well be decreased in the next few years. There is thus no alternative to strengthening the national revenue system if the current level of government expenditures is to be maintained, let alone improved and extended.[50]

The Changing Structure of Taxation

Many of the reports written on how to deal with this problem have urged increased use of indirect taxes, especially those on imports (Lent, 1976; Mathews, 1980; Collins, 1985). An income tax cut and tariff reform introduced in 1987 (Chan, 1986) in fact went some distance in this direction. Under the colonial regime in 1952 most of Papua New Guinea's (much smaller) revenues did in fact come from taxes on foreign trade. At that time, the fiscal structure basically matched the very underdeveloped nature of the economy. By 1961, however, following the introduction of an income tax and the abolition of the export tax by the Australian administration, the relative importance of trade taxes declined. Nonetheless, as late as 1971 the revenue structure remained more or less as one might expect to find it in a largely underdeveloped, rural, fragmented, and dependent country: relatively high dependence on import duties, traditional excises, and stamp duties, with the balance coming from income taxes paid almost exclusively by a small enclave of expatriate companies and employees.

By the time of independence in 1975, however, there had been a startling change in this situation. Although almost half the company taxes collected in that year came from Bougainville Copper (BCL), the effects on revenues of very substantial increases in both company and personal income tax rates were clearly apparent. Although income taxes did not long retain this prominence in the total revenue picture, their decline over the subsequent decade is almost entirely attributable to the fall in revenues from BCL. Indeed, personal income taxes not only retained but increased their importance, as did both excises and customs duties, the latter largely as a result of the growth of imports relative to GDP. On the other hand, the growth of personal income taxes was entirely attributable to increased effective tax rates, owing to the highly visible interaction of increased nominal incomes and the progressive rate schedule (Thac and Lim, 1984; Lim, 1987).

The result has been considerable unrest in recent years in the ranks of the relatively small band of income taxpayers, especially the politically important, though numerically very small, group of national (in contrast to expatriate) taxpayers. Nevertheless, the extent to which there has already been a substantial shift toward increased reliance on indirect, and particularly import, taxes since independence is striking. Despite the narrowness of the indirect tax base in the largely rural economy of Papua New Guinea,[51] the desired move to greater reliance on indirect taxes is well on its way. Nonetheless, the prospects for direct taxation are so bleak that still further moves in this direction seem necessary.

Revising the Present System

Personal income tax. Personal income tax revenues are dominated by the proceeds of the fortnightly tax on wages and salaries. Introduced in 1980 largely to relieve the processing burden on a tax administration creaking under the strain of losing almost all its experienced (expatriate) officials, this tax accounted for almost 95 percent of all personal income taxes collected in 1985. Indeed, since 1981 the amount of income taxes collected from individuals other than by wage withholding has actually declined, even in nominal terms! The efficacy of the income tax in reaching such recipients of nonwage income as landlords, small businessmen, and self-employed farmers and professionals is low, and decreasing.

Similar administrative deterioration is apparent in increasing arrears figures with respect to both personal and company income taxes. These poor results, in the face of a substantial increase in the numbers of staff in the tax office (from 108 in 1980 to 213 in 1985), a sharp fall in the number of returns with which they have to deal,[52] and a consequent drastic reduction in the number of assessments issued per tax official (from over 900 in 1980 to less than 90 in 1985), do not appear to augur well for the future of the personal income tax in Papua New Guinea.[53]

Even more importantly from a revenue point of view, the base of the wage tax is shrinking. In 1986, some 55 percent of wage taxes were paid by expatriate employees, who constituted less than 9 percent of the taxpaying population.[54] At the time of independence in 1975–76, the corresponding proportions were 82 percent of taxes and 16 percent of taxpayers. When this decline is combined with the rapid increase in personal income tax revenues over the last decade, it appears that Papua New Guinea has managed to triple the amount of income tax collected from national taxpayers over the course of a decade of very slow real income growth (and almost no inflation). The political resistance to which this rate of expansion has given rise virtually ensures that it will not be.

Personal income tax revenues thus remain precariously dependent on the base provided by a small, and declining, expatriate population. In 1986, for instance, the average tax rate on expatriate taxpayers was 28 percent, compared to 9 percent on national taxpayers. Should localization proceed more rapidly at the higher levels—an important political objective—and the salaries at these levels become more realistic in local terms—an economic necessity—or should events induce an even faster outflow of expatriates than is already taking place, the income tax base will evaporate even more quickly. The prospects for expanded personal income tax revenues in the future in the face of a shrinking expatriate base, increasing taxpayer resistance by nationals, and apparently deteriorating administrative capacity are thus bleak.

In addition, the prevailing wage structure also has important implications for income tax reform, which do not seem to have always been appreciated. One recent report, for example, recommended the introduction of a flat-rate tax as a simpler, equally equitable, and more efficient means of raising around the same revenues from the personal income tax (Collins, 1985). Many good things can obviously be said in support of this proposal, not least on administrative grounds. If the same revenues are to be obtained from the income tax, however, moving to a flat rate in Papua New Guinea would imply a substantial increase in taxes on nationals and a reduction in taxes on expatriates—a combination with no apparent economic benefit and obvious political problems. No doubt the 1,200 expatriates and 200 nationals affected by the reduction of the top marginal rate in 1987 were duly grateful, but absolutely nothing seems likely to have been gained in terms of equity, efficiency, or even administrative simplicity as a result of giving up this revenue.

Import duties. In the end, if any new revenues are to be squeezed from the existing tax system, the only real possibility appears to be through increased taxes on imports. Increasing the basic tariff rate (which is applicable to all imports except for a very few "basic" consumption items) from the present 7.5 percent to 10 percent or more is probably the simplest and most acceptable way to increase revenues quickly. The tariff increase implemented in 1987 will thus in all likelihood be followed by others in the near future. One problem with this scenario, of course, is that Papua New Guinea may begin to tread the slippery path of import-substitution in a way it has so far largely managed to avoid.[55] On the whole, however, there is little alternative to higher import taxes if more revenue is to be obtained from the existing tax structure in the near future. The revenue structure by 1991 may thus look more like that in 1971 than that in 1981.

Matching Tax Structure to Economic Structure

Such increased reliance on import taxation clearly represents a step backward in the "normal" evolution of fiscal structures in developing countries. If Papua New Guinea is to levy any effective taxes on the growing "informal" sector of urban traders or rural smallholders, however, it will almost certainly have to go even further back in developmental time.

Taxing the "informal" sector. The only practical way to extract significant revenues—

or, indeed, in many instances any revenues at all—from the growing urban national small business sector of traders, microbus (PMV) owners, landlords, and the like is through the introduction of some form of "presumptive" taxation based on hard-to-conceal external indicators of activity (Nield, 1980; Chelliah, 1981; Bird, 1983). To date, there has been only one limited experiment along these lines in Papua New Guinea, with respect to PMV owners—and this effort was aborted in 1986 as soon as it showed any sign of being effective. Political support for still more efforts in this direction seems unlikely.

Moreover, although an ambitious program of assistance to the tax administration is currently under way with the aid of the Australian government, those involved do not seem particularly aware either of the problems of taxing the urban informal sector or of the sorts of approximate solutions developed in other countries. Further refinement and more assiduous application of techniques to track down revenues in the small, organized sector that keeps accounting records, as is mainly envisaged in the current plans, while obviously useful, will not help in the basic tasks of identifying, assessing, and enforcing taxes in the informal sector.[56]

Even if a major effort were launched to reach these hard-to-tax groups, little revenue can realistically be expected from this source. Nevertheless, unless the income tax is to be converted irredeemably into a discriminatory tax on wages, thus probably accentuating even more its already marked unpopularity with high-salaried employees in government and elsewhere, the development of crude presumptive methods of tapping other incomes in the urban sector must constitute an essential component of tax reform in Papua New Guinea.

Taxing the rural sector. Papua New Guinea is one of the most rural countries in the world, with perhaps 95 percent of its population still residing outside the few small urban centers. It is also a federal democracy, which means it has an elaborate political superstructure of provincial governments where other countries might have unorganized rural municipalities. Experience everywhere suggests that direct taxation in rural areas works in nonauthoritarian states only when those taxed perceive real benefits to themselves from the taxes. What this means in Papua New Guinea is that such taxes almost certainly have to be provincial in character, which in turn means that the likelihood of developing and implementing such taxes is inextricably entwined with the need for a general revision of provincial finance, especially given the practical impossibility of levying land taxes in any case (Bird, 1984a; Axline 1986). What this means is that there is simply no feasible way to tax the rural sector directly.

The only way to increase revenues from the rural sector, if desired, is through increased taxes on agricultural exports, notably the principal ones of coffee, cocoa, and coconut products. A low flat tax (now 5 percent) on these products was reintroduced in 1975, but a number of experts have subsequently recommended that this tax should be increased, altered to a sliding-scale basis, and treated as a prepayment of income taxes for those plantations that are subject to the income tax (Lam, 1984). Heavy export taxation may clearly have undesirable effects on both agricultural development and the level of well-being of many rural people (though mainly the better-off ones). Nevertheless, if necessary, the yield of the present export taxes could be increased, particularly in years of increasing commodity prices, without unduly severe consequences in either equity or development terms. In any event, the complete absence of any administrative capacity to collect taxes in the rural areas in any other way means that export taxes are the only means available if rural taxation is to be increased.

Conclusion

To sum up, if Papua New Guinea's fiscal prospects are as bleak as they seem to be in the absence of substantial new mineral revenues, then an essential ingredient of any solution must be to adjust its tax structure to match its economic structure. The principal tax "handle" in the economy is clearly trade. Both exports and especially imports could bear somewhat heavier taxes than at present without inducing severe distortions in development patterns and without putting too much strain on the country's exceedingly limited administrative capacity.[57] If even rough justice is to be achieved in direct taxation, increasing use will have to be made of technically crude but feasible presumptive methods that do not depend for their efficacy on either good record-keeping or the ready compliance of taxpayers. Only by thus turning back the fiscal clock does Papua New Guinea have much hope of developing a tax system that better matches its true economic and administrative conditions.

Notes

The first version of this paper was prepared while I was at the University of York, U.K., and the final version was prepared at Erasmus University, Rotterdam. I am grateful to both these institutions for their hospitality. I am also grateful to the following for comments that have led to substantial changes and, I hope, improvements, although of course none of those named are responsible for what I have done with their ideas: Milka Casanegra, Gordon Cox, Sijbren Cnossen, Dennis Frampton, Malcolm Gillis, Charles McLure, Oliver Oldman, Cedric Sandford, Carl Shoup, and Wayne Thirsk.

1 This paper was originally delivered in 1954 to the International Institute of Public Finance; it was subsequently reprinted in all three editions of Bird and Oldman (1964, 1967, 1975).

2 Naturally, there are exceptions to this assertion—as to most of the more sweeping generalizations made in this paper. The early report by Shoup (1959) on Venezuela, for example, paid considerable attention to administration (Surrey was a member of the research team). The later Musgrave reports on Colombia (1971) and Bolivia (1981) are more typical in confining their concern with administration mainly to the vexed issue of the "hard-to-tax" groups. Even more characteristic of much tax policy work is the view epitomized by Kaldor (1980) that administrative deficiencies can and must be rectified to permit desirable policy changes. In contrast, the present paper argues that as a rule such problems will persist for a long time to come in most countries and that successful policy reform must take this reality into account.

3 Surprisingly few studies have been made of the actual functioning of tax administrations in developing countries. Much of the best work by outside analysts is essentially nonquantitative (Joint Tax Program, 1965; Wilkenfeld, 1973; Radian, 1980); the same is true of most of the better published country studies (India, 1960, 1969; Joint Legislative-Executive Tax Commission, 1961), although there is at least one interesting exception (Colombia, 1985). Most of the available literature is essentially prescriptive (Public Administration Service, 1961; United Nations, 1967, 1968; Nowak, 1970; Kelley and Oldman, 1973). There appear to be almost no published empirical studies in developing countries of many of the key administrative issues touched on here: the costs and benefits of tax amnesties, the costs of rate differentia-

tion and exemptions under sales taxes, administrative and compliance costs, the incidence and allocative effects of appeal procedures, the effects of revenue quotas and incentive systems, the costs and benefits of refund systems, audit selection procedures, and so on. This research agenda obviously requires systematic exploration if the propositions asserted in this paper are to be tested properly. For a useful beginning, see Yitzhaki and Vaknin (1987).

4   Despite the extensive references in this paper, it will be obvious to the careful reader both that this survey of a vast subject is selective and, more controversially perhaps, to some extent more impressionistic than based on hard evidence. One reason for this state of affairs is mentioned in note 3 preceding. In addition, it may be worth mentioning that every statement made can be supported by reference to at least one and often several examples, although I do not think it appropriate to bring out for public display the numerous instances that I have encountered over the last twenty-five years in various parts of the world of corruption, of incompetence, of low morale, and—surprisingly common, and most tragic of all—of able and willing administrators starved of the tools and support they need to do their job properly. Indeed, I want to emphasize that nothing in this paper should be read as a criticism of tax administrators: their job is hard enough at the best of times and in the best of places. My point is rather that administrators in developing countries are never in these fortunate circumstances and that tax policy designers have not, as a rule, taken this reality adequately into account in recommending tax reforms in developing countries.

5   For additional evidence, see Richipuan, 1984b; Archaya, 1986; Bahl and Murray, 1986; Virmani, 1987. An earlier survey may be found in Herschel, 1978.

6   As McLure (1982, p. 57) says, a tax advisor needs "... an appreciation of how the finest tax structure can be subverted by tax avoidance made possible by carelessly drafted statutes and regulations and especially by tax evasion facilitated by poor tax administration." Almost every technical assistance report contains other instances of defective structural design and poor administrative implementation which result in substantial revenue losses.

7   The clearest instance of the judicial "perversion" of a tax system of which I am aware is actually in a developed country (Australia, under the "Barwick" court in the late 1970s: Lehman, 1983). Although it would be invidious to name less-publicized names, it is not difficult to find similar instances in developing countries of judges apparently bound and determined to find in favor of taxpayers, or at least those rich enough to wait out the appeal process.

8   Tax evasion also adds to the conventionally estimated excess burden of taxation, as Yitzhaki (1986) demonstrates—although the significance of this finding is not clear when the basic competitive conditions assumed in making these estimates are so obviously violated in most developing countries.

9   Skinner and Slemrod (1985), taking the view that old inequities are in fact capitalized, argue that heavy penalties on evaders will themselves violate horizontal equity. The conclusion that such penalties are inequitable seems unwarranted, however. At most, a case may be made for phasing in or signalling in advance the launching of an anti-evasion campaign to permit those in the wrong to regularize their affairs (for example, through an initial tax amnesty).

10   In some instances, as in India and (formerly) in Indonesia, such favoritism was delib-

erate. Whether deliberate or not, however, this outcome also reflects the inability of the administration to tax smaller firms effectively.

11 This is a good description, for example, of the situation in Bolivia a decade ago (Musgrave, 1981). In 1986, however, Bolivia followed a path quite different from that proposed by the Musgrave mission when it abolished the income tax and replaced it by a set of consumption and asset taxes, calling the latter "presumed income" taxes (American Chamber of Commerce, 1986). Some aspects of this reform seem close to the lines suggested in this paper for very underdeveloped countries, although I have no idea of how (or whether) it is actually functioning.

12 The best description of this process at its extreme remains Hinrichs (1962). To some extent, the alternative minimum taxes of some countries in francophone West Africa as well as Colombia also work in the same direction: in Colombia in 1984, for example, one third of all companies were taxed on a presumptive basis and about 13 percent of company taxes were assessed on this basis. For two thirds of those taxed on this basis, the presumption was based on net wealth and for the others on gross receipts. The new Bolivian tax mentioned in note 11 preceding goes further, taxing all companies at a rate of 2 percent on net assets at the end of the year.

13 This is the characterization of the Jamaican consumption tax that emerges from Cnossen (1984). Tanzi (1987, p. 227) has noted that most so-called "general" sales taxes in developing countries amount to little more than a levy on imports and a few "excisables" and seldom cover more than 20 percent of domestic value-added.

14 While it would be invidious to name names, it may be of interest to mention that each of the examples in this paragraph is drawn from personal experience in a wide variety of countries—including Colombia, Bolivia, Panama, Guatemala, Venezuela, Jamaica, Egypt, Senegal, Philippines, Indonesia, Papua New Guinea, and India.

15 A particularly interesting discussion of this interaction is Boyd (1986), who draws an analogy with the analysis of "predator-prey" relations. See also Mayshar (1986) who takes a longer time perspective, referring to "a slow Darwinian process of mutation and adaption."

16 This characterization is adapted from the reaction of the Australian commissioner of taxes to a critical report on his office by the auditor-general, as reported in Australia (1986a, p. 64). It may be worth noting parenthetically that Australia—like most developed countries—suffers from some of the administrative ills stressed here, e.g., inability to utilize existing information effectively (Australia, 1986b, 1986c) and the lack of a satisfactory taxpayer identification system. Of course, Australia also has a well-trained tax administration: nonetheless, its most significant difference from the typical developing country is that most taxes are collected through the agency of large, well-organized, and basically trustworthy companies. Obviously, there is a wide range of administrative experiences and competencies among developing countries. As a rule, however, they all face inherently more difficult problems with, by definition, fewer resources than more developed countries—and even the latter can by no means administer whatever policymakers may dream up (see, for example, the land development taxes in postwar Britain).

17 Webber and Wildavsky (1986), p. 609. Or, as Witt (1987, p. 140), puts it: "Efficient and inefficient tax systems are not the result of some kind of 'happy' coincidence but of social and political power constellations."

18 The slow course of administrative improvement may be illustrated by referring to

three studies of Colombia over the years (Caldwell, 1953; Bird, 1970; and McLure, 1982). There have clearly been substantial improvements in Colombian tax administration over these three decades, but progress has been slow and episodic and there is still a very long way to go. See also Colombia (1985).

19 As Adam Smith put it: "In those corrupted governments where there is at least a general suspicion of much unnecessary expense, and great misapplication of the public revenue, the laws which guard it are little respected" (quoted in Skinner and Slemrod, 1985, p. 353).

20 It is particularly clear that governments should not, as some now do, burden even willing taxpayers with such unnecessary discomforts as the need to stand in long queues to file returns or pay taxes, needless requirements to submit numerous copies of returns, and even charges for supplying returns in the first place.

21 Earmarking was traditionally employed more as a means of controlling the purposes to which tax collectors put the funds they extracted than as a means of encouraging taxpayers to tolerate their exactions (Webber and Wildavsky, 1986), but it has also been advocated at times in part for the latter reason. For further discussion of this and most of the other points mentioned in this paragraph, see Bird (1984b).

22 Tax advisers who have found themselves involved in interminable discussions on the fine points of income taxes which affect at most 1 percent of the population, while being unable to get anyone to listen to their concerns about the effects of some much more important tax on the other 99 percent, should understand this remark. On the other hand, even the most autocratic regimes are restrained in their exactions by the fear of revolt, either by the masses or their more powerful supporters.

23 Webber and Wildavsky (1986) provide various examples of the various sayings to this effect that have come down through the years, although they somehow manage to omit the famous remark, usually attributed to Colbert, about geese, feathers, and hissing.

24 Moreover, as Wedderspoon (1969, p. 55) put it: "It is a question whether truer equity could not be achieved (and the other consequences more realistically anticipated) by an instrument which was less zealously aimed at the abstract, which was more closely oriented to the immediate capacity of available administrative resources, and which paid greater attention to the prevention and detection of fraud—a factor which experience shows can have greater relevance to equity than tax policy itself."

25 A more promising approach is to establish what is in effect a new tax administration, for example, by contracting collection of export taxes to the central bank or some other "reliable" organization, or by creating a new quasi-independent revenue authority (such as the Revenue Board in Jamaica). Such measures may be effective for a period, but over time the bad old ways are likely to creep in again—except, of course, in the unlikely event that the underlying factors creating the problems in the first place have been corrected.

26 In a private communication, Sijbren Cnossen makes the interesting argument ". . . that tax administration should take a back seat in the modernization process. Modern taxes, like the income tax and a broad-based sales tax, are accounts-based taxes. To enforce these taxes properly, tax departments need auditors. But auditing skills are hard to acquire and auditors are a scarce commodity. Even if auditors can be found they should probably be employed in roughly the following order: private sector, public enterprises, government expenditure programs—before they are put to work in a tax department."

27 In Jamaica, for example, there have been at least seven attempts to reform important aspects of the public administration since independence: none has succeeded to any noticeable extent.

28 This brief history is based largely on Webber and Wildavsky (1986), who trace this practice back to Mesopotamia. One example is the English customs tax, which was farmed until 1671, and even later in Scotland (Carson, 1972): indeed, until well into the nineteenth century many officials were still paid on a fee basis.

29 In some ways, however, the use of a private Swiss customs service seems more equivalent to the famous Chinese Maritime Customs (largely established by expatriates)— an example Kaldor (1980, p. x) suggested should be emulated by India—than to the tax farming familiar from ancient and European history.

30 This change in the fee basis obviously obviates some of the worst problems with tax farming. The basic problem with privatizing monopolies like revenue collection, however, is to specify the terms of the contract, especially since the most economic methods (from the contractor's point of view) are unlikely to be acceptable to modern governments. Indeed, if the contract is adequately specified, and compliance with it sufficiently monitored, it would probably be as efficient for the government to do the job itself!

31 Sandford (1981) analyzes this aspect of VAT carefully. See also Due (1987) who notes that a number of European countries allow small-sales taxpayers to retain some of the tax for their trouble.

32 It should perhaps be emphasized that paying officials by a mixture of fees and bribes need not be inconsistent with those officials doing a good job. To take an historical example, Samuel Pepys has come down in history as one of Britain's greatest naval administrators; he was also, however, by modern standards an avid seeker and taker of bribes, gifts, fees, and commissions—as witnessed by countless references in his famous diary—and was, the same source makes plain, acting entirely as expected in so doing.

33 This description is in part based on Indonesian practice in the early 1980s. (Until 1971, an explicit bonus was paid to those exceeding collection targets.)

34 In the case of Indonesia, for example, targeting may be condemned as arbitrary, inequitable, and discouraging administrative effort. Alternatively, it may be accepted as conforming to local standards of fairness and administrative probity while providing a modicum of oversight and not affecting administrative effort adversely (since close examination suggested that the effort tended to establish the targets, rather than vice versa).

35 For example, a "performance bonus" system proposed in Ghana would have established a fund (based on 0.1 percent of revenue, 0.5 percent of additional revenue from audit, and higher shares of penalties imposed for various offenses) from which a (taxable) bonus was to be paid to established staff in proportion to their basic salary.

36 Such devices may in practice often hinder the honest more than they deter the unworthy. A classic example is the Contraloria system in some Latin American countries (Bird, 1982a).

37 A good example is the development in the British customs service (Carson, 1972) of the "triangular control" system—valuation, collection, and checking—which is still in use in much of the world. For similar reasons, the separation of assessment and collection functions is often recommended for other taxes.

38 Even in developed countries, "provisions which rely unduly on administrative discretion risk being applied arbitrarily, unfairly, and selectively" (Ireland, 1985, p. 55).

39 Such schemes are actually employed to various extents in some Latin American countries, Turkey, and Taiwan.

40 Similar problems are not unknown in developed countries: witness the recent condemnation in Australia (1986b) of the collection of useless (and unused) information in the "naive belief" that it will ensure compliance.

41 Interestingly, although it is clearly possible in principle to develop an "optimal" audit system (Balachandran and Schaefer, 1980), in practice it appears that the most rewarding way to proceed is still the old method of "leads and experience" (Due, 1985).

42 In fact, it might even be suggested that to the extent an amnesty successfully increases revenues, it often tends to reduce administrative efforts! As no comprehensive analysis of tax amnesties in developing countries appears to be available (but see Pepper, 1966), this conclusion is necessarily based on limited personal experience, particularly in the Philippines and Colombia. (See also note 9 preceding for reference to amnesties.)

43 The theoretical literature has now become so large that all that can be done here is to note that it started with a paper by Allingham and Sandmo (1972) and has since grown like wildfire. For three useful summaries by the IMF's Fiscal Affairs Department, see Sisson (1981), Richupan (1984c), and Mansfield (1987). As Mansfield (1987) notes, the basic problem with the theoretical literature is that for the most part it ignores the constraints that permit the system to function at all.

44 For a formal argument suggesting that evasion is basically independent of the tax rate, see Yitzhaki (1986).

45 But note the case of Bolivia (American Chamber of Commerce, 1986).

46 Casanegra (1987) seems to illustrate some of the confusion many feel on this issue: at one point, she says there should be no special enforcement focus on the larger taxpayers in order not to weaken compliance by others; but at other times she notes most of the revenue comes from these sources, and that a "special control" system of filing and collection is needed with respect to such taxpayers. The only way I can see to reconcile these positions is to assume that there is no enforcement problem at all with large taxpayers, since it would seem that even a small infraction by a large taxpayer might be more important in revenue terms than large infractions by many small taxpayers.

47 In Bolivia, for example, the main tax "gap" arose from the ineffective taxation of capital income rather than the failure to tap the self-employed (Musgrave, 1981, pp. 292–3).

48 That is, what is proposed is a presumptive rather than a *forfait* (negotiated) system: for further discussion, see Tanzi and Casanegra (1987); Morag (1957); Lapidoth (1977); Bird (1983).

49 In the long run, of course, as Webber and Wildavsky (1986) have recently shown in detail, in an important sense the tax system of every country reflects its own political culture (see also Hinrichs, 1966). Since in many ways Papua New Guinea's nascent political culture is unique, its tax system too, when fully developed, may be unique in some respects. At least for the next few decades, however, the argument in the text seems valid.

50 In addition, and probably more importantly, the present scale and structure of public

expenditure needs to be curtailed (unless perhaps the revenues from several new mineral projects come in much more quickly than seems likely). These and many other matters are discussed in more detail in Bird (1987), from which the present brief account is abstracted.

51 In particular, the consumption pattern of the (diminishing) expatriate population is much more import-intensive than that of nationals. In 1976–77, for example, 25 percent of all imported final goods were consumed by expatriates, who at that time constituted less than 2 percent of the population (Baxter, 1982).

52 The number of tax returns processed by the tax department fell from 115,818 in 1980 to 10,581 in 1981. These figures, like the others in this paragraph, are taken from Papua New Guinea (various).

53 Incidentally, both the equity and the efficiency of the fortnightly wage tax are suspect, as discussed in Bird (1987).

54 The 1986 figures are based on an unpublished survey kindly made available by the Chief Collector of Taxes; the earlier figures come from Papua New Guinea (1983).

55 Robson (1985), for example, expresses concern on this score. In principle, to avoid resource misallocation similar taxes should be levied on domestic equivalents. Given the severely limited administrative capacity, the absence of an industrial base, and the relatively low and uniform tariff structure, however, this danger is much less imminent than in many countries. This point—as well as why there is no revenue potential in company taxes, excise duties, or sales taxes—is discussed further in Bird (1987).

56 The assessment of the tax administration assistance program in the text is based on discussions in both Australia and Papua New Guinea (and reinforced by previous experience with similar projects in countries as different as Colombia and Egypt).

57 For an assessment of development policy in Papua New Guinea by a well-known economist which similarly pinpoints administrative capacity as the binding constraint, see Reddaway (1986).

References

Allingham, M. G., and A. Sandmo (1972). "Income Tax Evasion: A Theoretical Analysis." *Journal of Public Economics*, 1 (November), 323–38.

American Chamber of Commerce of Bolivia (1986). *Tax Reform Law: An Explanation of its Contents*. La Paz.

Archaya, S. N., et al. (1986). *Aspects of the Black Economy in India*. New Delhi: National Institute for Public Finance and Public Policy.

Australia (1986a). Auditor-General. *Efficiency Audit Report. Australian Taxation Office: Prescribed Payment System*. Canberra: Australian Government Publishing Service.

Australia (1986b). Parliament. *Report of the Auditor-General on an Efficiency Audit. Australian Taxation Office: Unpresented Group Certificates*. Parliamentary Paper No. 192/1986. Canberra: Australian Government Publishing Service.

Australia (1986c). Parliament. *A Taxing Problem*. Review of 5 Auditor-General's Audit Reports into the Australian Taxation Office. Report from the House of Representatives Standing Committee on Expenditure. Canberra: Australian Government Publishing Service.

Axline, A. (1986). *Financial Foundations of Provincial Policy Making in Papua New*

Guinea. Research Monograph No. 45. Canberra: Centre for Research on Federal Financial Relations, Australian National University.

Balachandran, K. R., and M. E. Schaefer (1980). "Optimal Diversification among Classes for Auditing Income Tax Returns." *Public Finance* 35 (no. 2), 250–58.

Bahl, R., and J. Linn (1985). "Urban Public Finance and Administration in Less Developed Countries." Unpublished; World Bank.

Bahl, R., and M. N. Murray (1986). "Income Tax Evasion in Jamaica." Jamaica Tax Structure Examination Program, Metropolitan Studies Program, Syracuse University, Staff Paper No. 31.

Baxter, P. T. (1982). *An Input-Output Matrix for Papua New Guinea 1976–77*. Waigani: National Planning Office and National Statistical Office.

Best, M. (1976). "Political Power and Tax Revenues in Central America." *Journal of Development Economics* 3, no. 1, 49–82.

Bird, R. M. (1970). *Taxation and Development: Lessons from Colombian Experience*. Cambridge, Mass.: Harvard University Press.

——— (1974). *Taxing Agricultural Land in Developing Countries*. Cambridge, Mass.: Harvard University Press.

——— (1982a). "Budgeting and Expenditure Control in Colombia." *Public Budgeting and Finance* 2 (Autumn), 87–99.

——— (1982b). "The Costs of Collecting Taxes: Preliminary Reflections of the Uses and Limits of Cost Studies." *Canadian Tax Journal* 30 (November–December), 860–65.

——— (1983). "Income Tax Reform in Developing Countries: The Administrative Dimension." *Bulletin for International Fiscal Documentation* 37 (January), 3–14.

——— (1984a). *The Allocation of Taxing Power in Papua New Guinea*. Discussion Paper No. 15. Port Moresby, Papua New Guinea: Institute of National Affairs.

——— (1984b). *Intergovernmental Finance in Colombia*. Cambridge, Mass.: Harvard Law School International Tax Program.

——— (1984c). "Put up or Shut up: Self Assessment and Asymmetric Information." *Journal of Policy Analysis and Management* 3 (Summer), 618–20.

——— (1985a). "A Preliminary Report on the Guatemalan Tax System." Local Revenue Administration Project, Metropolitan Studies Program, Syracuse University.

——— (1985b). "The Reform of Indirect Taxes in Jamaica." Jamaica Tax Structure Examination Project, Metropolitan Studies Program, Syracuse University, Staff Paper No. 24.

——— (1987). "Taxation in Papua New Guinea: Backward to the Future?" National Centre for Development Studies, Australian National University.

Bird, R. M., and O. Oldman (1964, 1967, 1975). *Readings on Taxation in Developing Countries*. Baltimore: Johns Hopkins University Press.

Boyd, C. (1986). "The Enforcement of Tax Compliance: Some Theoretical Issues." *Canadian Tax Journal* 34 (May–June), 588–99.

Caldwell, L. K. (1953). "Technical Assistance and Administrative Reform in Colombia." *American Political Science Review* 47 (June), 494–510.

Carson, E. (1972). *The Ancient and Rightful Customs: A History of the English Customs Service*. London: Faber and Faber.

Casanegra, M. (1987). "Problems in Administering a Value-Added Tax in Developing Countries: An Overview." Development Research Department, World Bank, Report No. DRD246.

Chan, J. F. (1986). *Budget Speech and Related Bills*. Port Moresby, Papua New Guinea: Government Printer.

Chelliah, R. J. (1981). *Public Finance and Tax Reform*. Discussion Paper No. 8. Port Moresby, Papua New Guinea: Institute of National Affairs.

Cnossen, S. (1977). *Excise Systems: A Global Study of Selective Taxation of Goods and Services*. Baltimore: Johns Hopkins University Press.

Cnossen, S. (1984). "Jamaica's Indirect Tax System: The Administration and Reform of Excise Taxes." Jamaica Tax Structure Examination Project, Metropolitan Studies Program, Syracuse University, Staff Paper No. 8.

Collins, D. (1985). *Designing a Tax System for Papua New Guinea*. Discussion Paper No. 18. Port Moresby, Papua New Guinea: Institute for National Affairs.

Colombia (1985). "Diagnóstico operaciónal de la administración tributaria." *Informe financiero*. Contraloria General, Bogotá, June, 31–50.

Corfmat, F. (1985). "Computerizing Revenue Administrations in LDCs." *Finance and Development* 22 (September), 45–47.

DeGraw, S., and O. Oldman (1985). "The Collection of the Individual Income Tax." *Tax Administration Review* (March), 35–48.

Due, J. F. (1985). "Trends in State Sales Tax Audit Selection since 1960." *National Tax Journal* 38 (June), 235–40.

——— (1987). "The Tax Treatment of Farmers and Small Firms under Value-Added Taxes." Development Research Department, World Bank, Report No. DRD223.

Goode, R. (1981). "Some Economic Aspects of Tax Administration." *International Monetary Fund Staff Papers* 28 (June), 249–74.

Gordon, R. (1988). "Income Tax Compliance and Sanctions in Developing Countries." *Bulletin for International Fiscal Documentation* 42 (January), 3–12.

Gray, C. W. (1987). "The Importance of Legal Process to Economic Development: The Case of Tax Reform in Indonesia." World Bank.

Han, S. S. (1987). "The Value Added Tax in Korea." Development Research Department, World Bank, Report No. DRD221.

Harberger, A. C. (1965). "Issues of Tax Reform for Latin America." In Joint Tax Program, *Fiscal Policy for Economic Growth in Latin America*. Baltimore: Johns Hopkins University Press.

Hart, A. G. (1967). *An Integrated System of Tax Information*. New York: Columbia University School of International Affairs.

Herschel, F. J. (1978). "Tax Evasion and its Measurement in Developing Countries." *Public Finance* 33, no. 3, 232–68.

Higgins, B. (1959). *Economic Development*. New York: W. W. Norton.

Hinrichs, H. H. (1962). "Certainty as Criterion: Taxation of Foreign Investment in Afghanistan." *National Tax Journal* 15 (June), 139–54.

Hinrichs, H. H. (1966). *A General Theory of Tax Structure Change during Economic Development*. Cambridge, Mass.: Harvard Law School International Tax Program.

India (1960). *Report of the Direct Taxes Administrative Enquiry Committee*. New Delhi.

India (1969). *Report of the Working Group on Central Direct Taxes Administration*. New Delhi.

Ireland (1985). *Fifth Report of the Commission on Taxation. Tax Administration*. Dublin: Stationery Office.

Jackson, I. A. (1986). "Amnesty and Creative Tax Administration." *National Tax Journal*

39 (September), 317–23.

Joint Legislative-Executive Tax Commission (1961). *A Study of Tax Administration in the Philippines*. Manila.

Joint Tax Program (1965). *Problems of Tax Administration in Latin America*. Baltimore: Johns Hopkins University Press.

Kaldor, N. (1956). *Indian Tax Reform: Report of a Survey*. New Delhi: Ministry of Finance, Department of Economic Affairs.

——— (1980). *Reports on Taxation II. Reports to Foreign Governments*. London: Duckworth.

Kelley, P. L., and O. Oldman, eds. (1973). *Readings on Income Tax Administration*. Mineola, N.Y.: Foundation Press.

Lam, N. V. (1984). *The Commodity Export Sector in Papua New Guinea*. Monograph No. 22. Boroko: Institute for Applied Social and Economic Research.

Lane, M. G., and H. Hutabarat (1986). "Computerization of VAT in Indonesia." Development Research Department, World Bank, Report No. DRD194.

Lapidoth, A. (1977). *The Use of Estimation for the Assessment of Taxable Business Income*. Amsterdam: International Bureau of Fiscal Documentation.

Lehman, G. (1983). "The Income Tax Judgements of Sir Garfield Barwick: A Study in the Failure of the New Legalism." *Monash University Law Review* 9 (September), 115–56.

Lent, G. E., A. Premchand, and R. J. Niebuhr (1976). "New Revenue and Economy Measures for Papua New Guinea." International Monetary Fund, Washington.

Leonard, H. B., and R. J. Zeckhauser (1987). "Amnesty, Enforcement, and Tax Policy." In *Tax Policy and the Economy*, vol. 1, 55–85. Edited by L. H. Summers. NBER and MIT Press Journals.

Lerman, A. H. (1986). "Tax Amnesty: The Federal Perspective." *National Tax Journal* 39 (September), 325–32.

Lim, D. (1987). *The Spending and Taxing Behaviour of Governments of Resource-Rich Countries: A Study of Papua New Guinea*. Discussion Paper No. 28. Port Moresby, Papua New Guinea: Institute of National Affairs.

Mansfield, C. Y. (1987). "Tax Administration in Developing Countries: An Economic Perspective." International Monetary Fund, Washington.

Mathews, R. (1980). *Problems of Tax Reform*. Discussion Paper No. 5. Port Moresby, Papua New Guinea: Institute of National Affairs.

Mayshar, J. (1986). "Taxation with Costly Administration." University of Wisconsin, Social Systems Research Institute 8616.

McLure, C. E. (1982). "Income and Complementary Taxes: Structure, Avoidance, and Evasion." World Bank.

McLure, C. E., and M. Gillis (1974). *La reforma tributaria en Colombia*. Bogotá.

Morag, A. (1957). "Some Economic Aspects of Two Administrative Methods of Estimating Taxable Income." *National Tax Journal* 10 (June), 176–85.

Musgrave, R. A. (1981). *Fiscal Reform in Bolivia*. Cambridge, Mass.: Harvard Law School International Tax Program.

Musgrave, R. A., and M. Gillis (1971). *Fiscal Reform for Colombia*. Cambridge, Mass.: Harvard Law School International Tax Program.

Muten, L. (1981). "Leading Issues of Tax Policy in Developing Countries: The Administrative Problems." In *The Political Economy of Taxation*. Edited by A. Peacock and

F. Forte. Oxford: Basil Blackwell.

National Institute of Public Finance and Policy (1986). *Evasion of Excise Duties in India.* New Delhi.

Nield, R. (1980). *Tax Policy in Papua New Guinea.* Discussion Paper No. 4. Port Moresby, Papua New Guinea: Institute of National Affairs.

Nowak, N. (1970). *Tax Administration in Theory and Practice.* New York: Praeger.

Oldman, O. (1965). "Controlling Income Tax Evasion." In Joint Tax Program, *Problems of Tax Administration in Latin America.* Baltimore: Johns Hopkins University Press.

Oldman, O., and R. Bird (1977). "The Transition to a Global Income Tax: A Comparative Analysis." *Bulletin for International Fiscal Documentation* 31, no. 10, 549–56.

Papua New Guinea (1971). *Committee of Inquiry on Taxation.* Port Moresby, Papua New Guinea: Government Printer.

Papua New Guinea (1983). Bureau of Statistics. *Taxation Statistics 1975/76.*

Papua New Guinea (various). Chief Collector of Taxes. *Annual Reports.*

Pepper, H. W. T. (1966). "Tax Amnesties." *British Tax Review*, pp. 284–96.

Public Administration Service (1961). *Modernizing Government Revenue Administration.* Washington: International Cooperation Administration.

Radian, A. (1980). *Resource Mobilization in Poor Countries.* New Brunswick, N.J.: Transaction Books.

Rao, M. G., and G. Pradhan (1985). "Excise Duty Evasion on Cotton Textile Fabrics." *Economic and Political Weekly* 20 (November 2), 1877–89.

Reddaway, B. (1986). *Some Key Issues for the Development of Papua New Guinea.* Discussion Paper No. 26. Port Moresby, Papua New Guinea: Institute of National Affairs.

Rezende, F. (1976). "Income Taxation and Fiscal Equity." *Brazilian Economic Studies* no. 2, 105–45.

Richupan, S. (1984a). "Measuring Tax Evasion." *Finance and Development* 21 (December), 38–40.

——— (1984b). "Income Tax Evasion: A Review of Measurement Techniques and some Estimates for the Developing Countries." International Monetary Fund, Washington.

——— (1984c). "A Survey of the Determinants of Income Tax Evasion: Role of Tax Rates, Shape of Tax Schedule and Other Factors." International Monetary Fund, Washington.

Robson, P. (1985). *Trade and Trade Policy Issues in Papua New Guinea.* Discussion Paper No. 21. Port Moresby, Papua New Guinea: Institute of National Affairs.

Sandford, C., et al. (1981). *Costs and Benefits of VAT.* London: Heinemann Educational Books.

Shoup, C. S. (1969). *Public Finance.* Chicago: Aldine.

Shoup, C. S., et al. (1959). *The Fiscal System of Venezuela.* Baltimore: Johns Hopkins University Press.

Sisson, C. A. (1981). "Tax Evasion: A Survey of Major Determinants and Policy Instruments of Control." International Monetary Fund, Washington.

Skinner, J., and J. Slemrod (1985). "An Economic Perspective on Tax Evasion." *National Tax Journal* 38 (September), 345–53.

Strasma, J. (1965). "Market-Enforced Self-Assessment for Real Estate Taxes." *Bulletin for International Fiscal Documentation* 19 (September), 353–65, and (October), 397–414.

Surrey, S. S. (1958). "Tax Administration in Underdeveloped Countries." *University of Miami Law Review* 12 (Winter), 158–88.

Tanzi, V. (1977). "Inflation, Lags in Collection, and the Real Value of Tax Revenue." *International Monetary Fund Staff Papers* 24 (March), 154–67.

——— (1987). "Quantitative Characteristics of the Tax Systems of Developing Countries." In *The Theory of Taxation for Developing Countries*. Edited by D. Newbery and N. Stern. New York: Oxford University Press.

Tanzi, V., and Casanegra, M. (1987). "Presumptive Income Taxation: Administrative, Efficiency, and Equity Aspects." International Monetary Fund, Washington.

Taylor, M. C. (1967). "The Relationship between Income Tax Administration and Income Tax Policy in Nigeria." *Nigerian Journal of Economic and Social Studies* 9 (July), 203–15.

Thac, C. D., and D. Lim (1984). "Papua New Guinea's Tax Performance, 1965–77." *World Development* 12, no.4, 451–49.

United Nations (1967). Department of Economic and Social Affairs. *Manual of Income Tax Administration*. New York.

United Nations (1968). Department of Economic and Social Affairs. *Manual of Land Tax Administration*. New York.

Virmani, A. (1987). "Tax Evasion, Corruption and Administration: Monitoring the People's Agents under Symmetric Dishonesty." Development Research Department, World Bank, Report No. DRD271.

Webber, C., and A. Wildavsky (1986). *A History of Taxation and Expenditure in the Western World*. New York: Simon and Schuster.

Wedderspoon, W. M. (1969). "Simplifying Taxes in East Africa." *Finance and Development* 6 (March), 51–56.

Wilkenfeld, H. C. (1973). *Taxes and People in Israel*. Cambridge, Mass.: Harvard University Press.

Witt, P.-C. (1987). *Wealth and Taxation in Central Europe*. Leamington Spa: Berg.

Yitzhaki, S. (1986). "On the Excess Burden of Tax Evasion." Development Research Department, World Bank, Report No. DRD211.

Yitzhaki, S., and Y. Vaknin (1987). "On the Shadow Price of a Tax Inspector." World Bank.

Yudkin, L. (1973). *A Legal Structure for an Effective Income Tax Administration*. Cambridge, Mass.: Harvard Law School International Tax Program.

Zweifel, P., and W. W. Pommerehne (1985). "On Preaching Water and Drinking Wine: An Analysis of Voting on Tax Amnesty and (Under) Reporting of Income." University of Zurich.

10

....

Lessons for LDCs of U.S.
Income Tax Reform

....

Charles E. McLure, Jr.

I. Introduction

It is commonly said that a wave of tax reform is sweeping the world, largely in response to the massive reform enacted in the United States in late 1986 (and in the United Kingdom, even earlier). Developing countries, always pressed for public revenues and plagued by tax systems that distort economic decisionmaking, contain substantial inequities, and strain scarce administrative capabilities, can be expected to look to the United States and other developed countries for suggestions on improving their tax systems. Moreover, it is only appropriate that bilateral donors of foreign aid and multinational organizations should urge LDCs to benefit from the tax reform experience of developed countries.

Translating tax reform from developed countries to LDCs involves substantial risk. Most obviously, economic conditions and administrative capabilities differ considerably between developed countries and nations of the Third World. In general, in LDCs there are many more impediments to the efficient operation of markets, the distribution of income is much less equal, and both taxpayers and tax administrators have substantially less capacity to deal with complex tax laws. At the same time, the need to mobilize resources, to encourage savings and investment, to stimulate development, and to earn foreign exchange may be more urgent than in the more developed nations. Even if one knew with certainty the appropriate tax policy for a highly advanced nation, it is by no means clear that the same policy would be appropriate for a country at a substantially lower level of development. In fact, considerable disagreement exists even regarding the appropriate tax policy for developed countries.

This paper is an attempt to indicate the relevance for LDCs of income tax reforms recently enacted or considered in the United States. It begins with a brief exposition of the reasonable objectives of tax reform and then proceeds to an examination of particular issues. While roughly the same objectives should motivate tax reform in both developed and developing countries, the weight attached to various objectives will differ, depending on economic and administrative realities; for example, in a country severely lacking in the human resources necessary to cope with complex tax provisions, the fine-tuning that might be justified on equity grounds in a developed country must often give way to the achievement of "rough justice."

Similarly, the discussion of particular tax issues will not be equally applicable in all LDCs. Issues of rate reduction and determination of the tax threshold (the level of income at which liability for income tax begins) will be generally relevant in all countries, regardless of their level of income. The discussion of excluded sources of income and preferred uses of income is also generally useful, though in some low-income countries even efforts to implement some of these reforms may be doomed. Much of the discussion of issues in the taxation of income from business and capital may be of little relevance to the poorest countries; even among those LDCs with relatively high levels of income, implementation of many of the reforms considered or enacted in developed countries may be infeasible for administrative reasons.

In most instances the judgments made here are probably generally accepted, at least by experts on tax reform in developing countries. But in other cases the conclusions are more controversial. These should provide an ample research agenda for those working on tax reform in developing countries.

The primary thrust of this paper is an examination of the feasibility of reforming a tax based on income in the light of experience in developed countries.[1] Among the most difficult problems revealed by this examination are those of inflation adjustment and the timing of recognition of income and allowance of deductions. These difficulties lead some observers to suggest that direct taxation should be based on consumption, rather than on income.

Space (and lack of expertise) also precludes discussion of the question of improved administration, including changes in withholding, advance payments, and the structure of penalties.[2] Silence on this issue should not be interpreted as implying that it is unimportant. Neither the need for improved tax administration nor the extreme importance of withholding needs emphasis in most developing countries.

The Tax Reform Act of 1986 enacted in the United States represents one of the most ambitious income tax reforms ever undertaken by a developed country. Even so, it falls far short of the potential for reform offered by the Treasury Department's November 1984 report to President Ronald Reagan entitled *Tax Reform for Fairness, Simplicity, and Economic Growth* (hereafter Treasury I), which was perhaps the most comprehensive set of proposals for fundamental tax reform since the Carter Commission issued its report in Canada in 1966.[3] It thus seems appropriate to include in the present discussion the reforms proposed in Treasury I, as well those enacted in the 1986 Act. Of course, the U.S. reforms share many common elements with those enacted earlier in the United Kingdom and those being discussed in other developed countries, including Australia, Canada, France, Japan, New Zealand, and West Germany.

II. Objectives of Tax Reform

A. Economic Neutrality

Many prominent advocates of tax reform in the United States and other developed countries believe strongly that free markets do relatively well —and certainly better than central planning or attempts by politicians and bureaucrats to guide economic decision making—in allocating the scarce resources of the nation. In particular, they believe that markets can generally be relied upon to indicate fairly accurately what consumers want, the least expensive means of satisfying consumer demands, and the best way to organize and finance production, if only there is little governmental intervention. As President Reagan stated the proposition in a 1981 address to the Congress, "the taxing power of government . . . must not be used to regulate the economy or bring about social change." In the realm of income tax policy nonintervention translates loosely to uniform and consistent taxation of all real economic income. For expositional convenience this absence of tax-induced distortions can be called "economic neutrality."

Even in developed countries legitimate concern can be expressed about whether a comprehensive income tax is truly optimal or even neutral. It can be argued, for example, that a tax that is neutral may not be optimal because it violates the conventional dictates of the theory of optimal taxation. A detailed discussion of this issue would take us far afield from the assigned topic of this paper.[4] Suffice it to say that both difficulties of implementation and perceptions of inequity cast considerable doubt on the practical utility of optimal taxation.[5]

A related line of reasoning having its foundation in the theory of the second best raises more troublesome issues, particularly in the context of a developing country. That theory indicates that it is generally difficult to know whether reducing some economic distortions will actually improve resource allocation, rather than worsening it, if not all distortions can be eliminated. Applied to questions of tax policy, this implies that reducing tax-induced distortions in the interest of greater neutrality may not actually improve resource allocation. Nonetheless, most economists probably would agree that tax reforms of the type introduced in the United States are generally likely to improve the allocation of resources, at least in a static sense. (Dynamic issues are discussed immediately below.) Because distortions are much more pervasive in developing countries, one must be somewhat more wary of naively assuming that a seemingly more neutral tax system would be better from a resource allocation point of view. Even so, there are some theoretical reasons to believe in the case for neutrality, even under the conditions prevailing in most LDCs.[6] Certainly there is little reason to believe that bureaucrats and politicians can do better than market forces in directing economic resources in LDCs.

Potentially the most telling argument against the neutrality of the income tax rests on the fact that such a tax is not neutral in its treatment of saving for future consumption.[7] Whereas a tax based on consumption does not alter the terms on which present consumption can be sacrificed in exchange for future consumption, an income tax does alter these terms, making saving for future consumption relatively less attractive. Offsetting considerations include the fact that a higher tax rate is required to yield a given revenue under a consumption-based tax than under an income-based tax; as a result, remaining distortions will be magnified, including notably those against work effort. Whether the efficiency gain from neutrality toward the saving/consumption choice outweighs the loss due to these distortions is problematical. (It is a classical application of the theory of second best.) U.S. advocates of consumption taxation have argued that the gains from static neutrality in the allocation of resources across sectors achieved by the 1986 Act (or by any comprehensive income tax) are outweighed by the efficiency losses resulting from more general application of the income tax to income from business and capital. However, it may be more difficult to achieve goals of vertical equity under a consumption-based tax than under a tax based on income. In addition, important noneconomic concerns may properly dominate the result of economic inquiry into this matter.

B. Tax Equity

A second major objective of tax reform is the achievement of equity or fairness. Equity has two important aspects: vertical and horizontal. Vertical equity involves the variation in average tax rates (tax as a percentage of income) across income brackets. Horizontal inequities occur whenever tax burdens at a given level of income differ significantly.

There is little scientific basis for judgments about what constitutes vertical equity in the tax system. Most observers agree that at least some progressivity (increase in average tax rates as income rises) is appropriate and that regressivity is to be avoided. But there is little agreement on the proper degree of progressivity, and significant support exists for a flat-rate (proportionate) tax, especially if taxation is limited to income in excess of some minimal level. Those who favor a low degree of progressivity may fear the adverse incentive effects caused by high marginal tax rates; by comparison, those who favor a high degree of progressivity may play down such disincentives.[8] It should be noted, however, that concern with incentive effects, at least in a static framework, are more appropriately characterized as being based on a desire for neutrality, than on concern for fairness.[9]

The income tax laws of many countries treat income quite differently, depending on how it is earned and how it is spent. For example, in the United States interest on general purpose obligations of state and local governments is tax-exempt, even though interest on similar corporate debt is taxable. Similarly, many fringe benefits provided by employers are tax exempt, although an employee wishing to provide similar benefits for himself of herself would generally be required to provide them from after-tax income, without the benefit of either an exclusion from taxable income or a deduction for the expenditure. Besides distorting choices between sources and uses of income, depending on their tax treatment, such differences create substantial variations in the amount of tax paid by families of equal income who are otherwise similarly situated. One of the important objectives of U.S. tax reform was to reduce these horizontal inequities.[10]

It should be noted that difference in taxation may not actually result in horizontal inequities. If, for example, incomes from two investments are treated differently, investors can be expected to reallocate savings among them until they earn the same after-tax rate of return in each. No horizontal inequity results, but resource allocation is distorted.[11] In many important cases differences in taxation do, however, cause horizontal inequities. In any event, considerations of both horizontal equity and neutrality point in the same direction, to comprehensive taxation of all income.

Inequities of the type described do not just reduce the actual fairness of the income tax. They also undermine the perception that the tax system is fair. A particularly important source of perceived inequities in the United States, as well as the cause of real unfairness, was the proliferation of tax shelters. Many affluent taxpayers were combining rapid deduction of expenses and/or postponement of the recognition of income, conversion of ordinary income to preferentially taxed capital gains, and deductions for interest payments to produce artificial accounting losses used to offset or shelter income from other sources, including employment and professional practice.

Deterioration of the perception of fairness must cause concern in a tax system based on "voluntary" compliance.[12] Taxpayers can reasonably be expected to be troubled by the awareness that high-income individuals and profitable corporations pay little or no tax, even if methods being used to avoid taxes are totally legal. The expert's distinction between legal tax avoidance and illegal tax evasion may have little meaning for a taxpayer being ridiculed by a friend or neighbor who is using tax shelters to avoid paying taxes. Unless the perception that the tax system is unfair can be reversed, taxpayer morale is undermined and evasion may become uncontrollable.

Tax reform in the United States has commonly been advocated by liberals interested in using tax reform to increase the overall progressivity of the income tax. As a result, battle lines have often been drawn along boundaries between income classes, and relatively little attention has been devoted to issues of economic neutrality and horizontal equity. By comparison, Treasury I adopted as a working hypothesis the view that tax reform should not change the distribution of tax liabilities across income brackets; that is, the tax reform proposed would be distributionally neutral.[13] Rather than pitting the wealthy against the middle class, for example, this approach was intended to draw attention to the waste of economic resources induced by the tax system and to rally those in all income classes who were paying their share of taxes against others with the same income who were using various tax preferences to pay less than their share. In other words, it focused on economic distortions and horizontal inequities rather than on issues of vertical income distribution.

This discussion of horizontal and vertical equity probably cannot be carried over directly to LDCs without substantial modification. First, the U.S. income tax is a "mass tax," in that it affects a majority of all households; by comparison, in most developing countries the income tax is paid only by an elite and relatively affluent group comprising only 10 to 20 percent of all households. Thus in LDCs much of the contribution the income tax makes to overall progressivity results from the mere existence of the tax, rather than from its graduated rate structure. (Of course, the existence of tax thresholds, as well as administrative realities, are important in reducing the coverage of the income tax and creating this phenomenon.)

Second, in many developed countries tax evasion is a relatively unimportant source of inequities; by comparison, in developing countries evasion may rival (or surpass) poor tax structure as a source of inequities.[14] In LDCs attention must be given to improving taxpayer compliance and administration, as well as to improving the underlying tax structure.

Third, the income tax, being paid by most families, has symbolic importance in developed countries that it lacks in LDCs. Moreover, the typical developing country relies less heavily on the income tax for revenues than does the typical developed country. For both of these reasons, loss of taxpayer morale that results from perceived inequities is probably less of a problem in LDCs; it pales by comparison with other perceptions of inequity found in LDCs.

Fourth, the taxpaying population at a given income level may be more homogeneous in LDCs than in developed countries; if so, there may be somewhat less horizontal inequity. Finally, there is almost certainly much less awareness of the nature of various abuses in LDCs than in developed countries. Thus perception problems may be less important than in developed countries.

C. Lower Rates

The single feature of the 1986 Act that has received the most attention is the reduction in marginal tax rates. Reducing marginal rates was an extremely important objective of tax reform in the United States, for both political and economic reasons. Whereas arguments about economic neutrality may not be persuasive to most taxpayers, the prospect of lower rates is quite appealing. Of course, average tax rates (including the effects of taxes on corporations) could not be reduced overall in a revenue-neutral tax reform. But expansion of the tax base would make it possible to apply lower marginal rates while leaving revenues unchanged. Lower marginal rates have the obvious advantage of reducing disincentives to a wide range of economic activities, including work effort, saving and investment, and efficient operation of enterprises. Moreover, any distortions that might survive tax reform would be less important if marginal tax rates could be reduced. Finally, the lower the tax rates, the less gain there is from tax evasion.[15]

D. Simplification

Because of the proliferation of tax preferences accorded various sources and uses of income through exemptions, exclusions, deductions, credits, and special rates, the tax system of the United States has become increasingly complex over the years. In addition, by distorting economic choices the system complicates economic decisionmaking. One of the important forces initially underlying U.S. tax reform was the desire to simplify the system.[16]

There are at least three elements to the simplification argument for tax reform. First, compliance with the law—understanding the provisions, keeping the records, and completing the forms—would be easier under a simpler system with fewer tax preferences. Second, economic decisionmaking would be simpler if choices were not so heavily influenced by tax considerations. Finally, it appears that many American taxpayers wanted simplification for others as much as for themselves; that is, many Americans apparently felt that under a simpler system the "other guy" would be less able to take advantage of tax breaks to pay less than his or her fair share of taxes. For convenience, these three arguments can be identified as simplification per se, simplification of decisionmaking, and the "other guy" case for simplification. The last two of these arguments for simplification can be seen to be closely akin to the neutrality and horizontal equity arguments described earlier.

To some extent these three arguments are also relevant in developing countries. But, as noted before, because the income tax is not a "mass tax" in most developing countries, the "other guy" argument for simplification probably has less force. And, as suggested above, there are enough nontax impediments to rational economic decisionmaking in developing countries that the complexity created by tax influences on decisionmaking may also be of relatively less concern than in developed countries. Moreover, since it is also easier to avoid taxes (or even to evade them) in LDCs, the tax system presumably interferes less with decisionmaking than in developed countries.

In LDCs simplification per se is important for reasons beyond those in the United States, where concern centers on the inability of a high percentage of the population to cope with the income tax law. In developing countries low levels of literacy and accounting skills and lack of economic and legal sophistication pose serious problems for taxpayer compliance. But even more serious is the inability of the tax administration of most LDCs to implement a complex law. Given severe limitations on administrative resources it makes sense for developing countries to utilize relatively simple income taxes to raise money in a way that achieves rough justice, rather than to enact complicated systems that cannot be administered effectively.[17]

E. Other Objectives

Tax policy is often advocated as a means of encouraging saving, investment, innovation, economic growth, and international competitiveness. Explicit incentives for saving and investment were accorded relatively low priorities in the formulation of Treasury I for several reasons. First, there was a strong feeling that economic growth and international competitiveness would take care of themselves if the tax system could be made more neutral. It is extremely difficult to provide investment incentives that do not discriminate across industries and types of assets, and therefore distort economic decisionmaking. Moreover, such incentives are an important building block of the tax shelters that undermine both actual and perceived equity.

Second, structural tax policy is a relatively blunt and ineffective instrument to use in attempting to increase aggregate saving. A far more direct and effective approach would be to reduce the federal budget deficit. In addition, using tax policy to increase investment may be a mixed blessing if saving cannot also be increased. Manipulation of national income accounting identities reveals that a nation's deficit on current account in its international payments is equal to its excess of aggregate investment over total saving, including that by governments. Investment incentives may therefore simply aggravate short-run problems of international competitiveness, rather than solving them, as is commonly thought.[18]

Finally, structural tax policy did not, in any event, appear to be the appropriate means of combating problems of international competitiveness at a time that the dollar was generally agreed to be substantially overvalued. Reducing the federal budget deficit, which should produce a lower value of the dollar, appeared to be a more appropriate response.

There is reason to believe that in LDCs, as in developed countries, reducing tax-induced distortions to economic decisionmaking would have a beneficial effect on the efficiency of resource allocation and economic growth—particularly if nontax distortions could be reduced at the same time. Even so, there is more reason to be concerned explicitly about economic growth as an objective in LDCs than in developed countries.

F. Revenue Neutrality

The recent debate on tax reform in the United States occurred within the context of revenue neutrality. This constraint—that tax reform could not result in markedly higher or lower revenues—had an important influence on the debate. It helped prevent irresponsible raids on the treasury by those who would retain or increase tax preferences; if the tax rates were to be reduced substantially, it would be necessary to eliminate many tax preferences including popular ones. That tax reform would not be used to raise taxes provided at least limited comfort to those who saw their tax preferences being taken away. Though they feared that higher rates might eventually be imposed on the new reformed base in order to reduce the federal budget deficit, they knew that revenue neutrality would place a cap on the damage they would experience, at least for the immediate future.

Whether revenue neutrality makes tax reform easier or more difficult to achieve has long been subject to debate. Arguments can be constructed for either view. Fundamental tax reform might appear to be more attractive in an environment in which total revenues are being reduced, because there will be relatively fewer losers than in a revenue-neutral context, the losses that do occur will be smaller, and tax reductions for those who gain from tax reform will be greater. On the other hand, it is sometimes easier to raise additional revenue by curtailing tax preferences than by raising rates, especially if only moderate amounts of revenue are needed and the loopholes involved are particularly egregious or if a sudden drop in revenues creates a fiscal crisis that forces unpopular action to be taken. One might conclude from this that revenue neutrality is the worst context in which to attempt tax reform. All in all, it appears that no general judgment can be made about the importance of revenue neutrality for tax reform in developing countries.

U.S. tax reform was intended to be revenue neutral in the aggregate, but not for individuals and for corporations, considered separately. All the tax reform proposals beginning with Treasury I, up to and including the 1986 Act, involved massive transfers of marginal tax rates for individuals to corporations.[19] Reductions of liabilities from individuals were thus substantially greater than would have been possible if the reform had been revenue neutral for individuals and corporations considered separately. This presumably increased the attraction of tax reform to individuals.[20]

Although the economic and political factors that produced the shift of liabilities from individuals to corporations in the U.S. tax reform are also operative in developing countries, there are important differences. The fact that the private sectors of most developing countries import foreign capital has important implications. First, to the extent that such capital comes from equity investment by corporations headquartered in countries allowing foreign tax credits such as the United States (or from countries that provide tax sparing), there is an important question of whether increased corporate taxes would be allowed as credits (or spared), rather than resulting in increased aggregate (LDC and home country) taxes on income from investment in LDCs. To the extent that increased corporate taxes really represent increased real burdens on the corporations in question, it might be unwise to raise corporate taxes in order to reduce individual taxes. The recent reduction of U.S. rates, together with changes in U.S. rules for determining the source of income from multinational operations and for calculating foreign tax credits, will put downward pressure on corporate rates around the world. On the other hand, economic rents may constitute a relatively more important component of the corporate tax base in developing countries than in developed ones. Where this is true it may be possible to derive greater revenues from the corporate sector without driving out capital and retarding development. But this is risky business, as going too far can destroy the investment climate of a country.[21]

G. Sacred Cows

During the 1984 presidential election campaign Ronald Reagan promised not to eliminate the deduction for home mortgage interest. Surprisingly enough, this was the only instance in which a "sacred cow" was publicly identified and placed off-limits prior to the release of Treasury I. As a result, the authors of Treasury I had a relatively free rein in formulating proposals for tax reform that approximated taxing real economic income.

The tax reform debate identified many more examples of preferential treatment that could not be touched for political reasons. Among provisions removed fairly quickly from the tax reform agenda were veterans' benefits, housing allowances of the military and the clergy, most employer-provided fringe benefits, and most ordinary itemized deductions for charitable contributions. While some of these exceptions to the tax reform process can be defended on policy grounds (deductions for charitable contributions being perhaps the best example), for the most part the result was less equity, higher rates, and unnecessary distortion of economic decisionmaking.

Some notable sacred cows were injured, if not slain, in 1986. The itemized deduction for sales taxes, one of three major broad-based sources of general revenue of state and local governments, was eliminated. Further inroads were made into the tax-exempt status of securities issued by state and local governments both for themselves and on behalf of nonprofit organizations. Unemployment compensation was made part of taxable income.

Certain types of organizations and particular types of income have long been given undeserved or questionable preferential treatment in many developing countries. These include certain fringe benefits, housing, income of the military, government enterprises, the income of nonprofit organizations, and various taxes paid by individuals. Eliminating these loopholes is crucial if tax reform is to be truly effective in many countries. Thus U.S. experience in this area is highly relevant for LDCs, for it shows that progress can be made in reducing the tax-preferred status accorded such organization and income. But there is a much more important lesson in the resistance of these and other loopholes to reform. It would be far better never to have enacted the preference in question.

III. The Taxation of Individuals

The discussion that follows covers the following types of reform of the taxation of individuals: rates, tax thresholds, excluded income, preferred uses of income, income shifting, and simplification. Within each of these topics the organization is roughly as follows: what was done in the United States, what was not done or was done wrong, and the relevance of the U.S. experience for developing countries.

A. Tax Rates of Individuals

Rate reduction is one of the most important benefits of the 1986 Tax Reform Act. Previously there were more than a dozen rates, from 11 percent to 50 percent; the new law has only four rates; 15, 28, 33, and 28 percent. (The 33 percent rate occurs because a 5 percent surcharge is applied to income of upper middle-income taxpayers—those with income between $71,900 and somewhat in excess of $170,000 for a married couple filing jointly—in order to take back the benefits of the 15 percent rate and the personal exemptions for those with incomes in excess of the lower figure.)

It is anomalous that the marginal rate should rise to 33 percent for the upper middle class before reverting to 28 percent.[22] A commonly heard political judgment is that it would have been difficult to adopt a more traditional three-rate system with a top rate of about 33 percent; without the promise of the eventual reversion to a 28 percent marginal rate, much support (or at least tolerance) of tax reform by high-income taxpayers would have evaporated, and preferential treatment of long-term capital gains would have been inevitable. An alternative would have been to adopt a pure two-rate system of perhaps 15 and 28 percent. This, however, would have substantially reduced revenues and the progressivity of the income tax; even further closing of politically sensitive loopholes, such as those for the oil and gas industry, probably would not have been enough to offset this.

Marginal tax rates now prevailing in many LDCs are high enough to cause serious disincentives and distortions, and incentives for brain drain and capital flight have been increased by rate reduction in the United States and other developed countries.[23] It thus seems appropriate that developing countries consider reducing their top marginal rates, perhaps to the range of 30 to 40 percent. Doing so need not reduce significantly either tax revenues or the progressivity of income taxation, since the effects of rate reduction can be offset by base broadening that maintains revenue and distributional neutrality. LDCs presumably should not follow the U.S. lead in applying higher marginal tax rates to the upper middle class than to the wealthy.[24]

B. Tax Thresholds

During the 1970s historically high rates of inflation eroded the real value of tax thresholds—the lowest level of income at which income tax is paid. This problem was not addressed in the 1981 tax reform.[25]

The 1986 Act eliminates the taxation of incomes below the poverty level by increasing deductions for personal exemptions and the standard deduction allowed those who do not itemize. In addition, the earned income tax credit—a refundable credit available only to low-income families with children that first increases with earned income and then declines as income exceeds a certain figure—was increased and indexed for inflation. As noted earlier, the benefits of the personal exemption are phased out at very high levels of income.

Increasing the tax threshold to eliminate tax on poverty-level incomes was one of the few tax reform proposals that encountered little serious opposition. There was, however, some debate on the best technique for achieving this objective. Tax credits are more efficient than deductions (in terms of revenue loss) in achieving a given tax threshold. But their effects are probably substantially less transparent to many taxpayers than those of a deduction.[26]

Issues of tax administration must figure more prominently in the LDC decision on tax thresholds than in developed countries. It would be hopeless to attempt to collect income tax from a percentage of the population approaching that in the United States. Tax thresholds limit the size of the tax-paying population, as well as saving an important equity goal. For administrative reasons LDCs might usefully consider curtailing somewhat the differentiation of tax thresholds based on numbers of dependents.[27] This troublesome and controversial suggestion flies in the face of commonly accepted principles of tax equity. It is made in recognition that tax administrators have little ability to verify the number of exemptions claimed; as a result, such differentiation creates a tax on honesty and rewards dishonesty.

Though the issue deserves further study, it does not appear appropriate in most LDCs to introduce a system such as the earned income tax credit (with or without limiting it to families with children). Besides involving potentially substantial revenue costs, such a proposal would add yet another layer of administrative complexity to systems that generally already suffer from excessive complexity that strains administrative capability. Moreover, such a scheme would benefit primarily those fortunate enough to find employment in the more advanced sectors that come in contact with the tax administration, and not the truly poor, who tend to be employed in other sectors.

C. Excluded Income

Despite the fanfare that accompanied passage of the 1986 Act, little progress was made in dealing with the most important exclusions from taxable income of individuals, aside from elimination of the partial exclusion of long term capital gains (to be discussed in section IV). For the first time unemployment compensation was made fully taxable, the tax treatment of social security was tightened somewhat, deductions for meals and entertainment were reduced, and the living allowance component of scholarships was made taxable. By comparison, veterans' benefits remain fully tax exempt.

Interest income on debt securities issued by state and local governments has historically been exempt from federal income tax. Though this exemption may have originally resulted from the view that it is constitutionally required, more recently it has been defended primarily as a form of federal support for the activities of state and local governments. Indeed, based on that reasoning, the exemption is also applied to interest on debt issued on behalf of certain nonprofit organizations. Though the 1986 Act continued the basic exemption for interest on general obligation bonds of state and local governments, it did restrict somewhat the availability of the exemption for interest on bonds used to finance private-purpose activities.

There are few areas in which disadvantages of tax exemption are more obvious than in the case of interest on government debt. Yet many developing countries provide such an exemption, even for interest on debt of the national government itself.[28] The presumed reason for such exemptions it to reduce the cost of borrowing. But at best it is likely that the reduction in interest rates resulting from the exemption no more than compensates for the lost tax revenues. More likely, the interest saving falls short of forgone tax revenues, with high-income bondholders pocketing the difference. This is the expected result if foreigners who receive no benefit from the exclusion are marginal purchasers of the bonds. In extreme cases, taxpayers may be able to borrow on a tax deductible basis in order to invest in tax-exempt securities, earning a substantial after-tax premium via tax arbitrage.

The 1986 Tax Act did little to correct one of the most important omissions from the income tax base of the United States, fringe benefits provided by employers. Such benefits include health insurance, a limited amount of group life insurance, and a variety of less important benefits. Moreover, employees can be allowed to choose between tax-preferred benefits via "cafeteria plans." Of particular interest to many developing countries is the fact that housing allowances of the military and the clergy benefit from tax preferences.[29]

Besides causing marginal rates to be higher than necessary, preferential treatment of fringe benefits creates inequities and distorts compensation packages and consumption choices in favor of goods and services that can be provided in tax-preferred forms. The availability of cafeteria plans makes quite explicit one major defect of the failure to tax fringe benefits: removing a portion of income from the tax net via fringe benefits and cafeteria plans necessitate higher rates on income that cannot escape tax.[30]

Developing countries should not follow the unfortunate pattern of the 1986 Act in perpetuating exclusions for fringe benefits. In some cases there are admittedly administrative and conceptual difficulties of valuing fringe benefits and allocating them to particular employees; in such instances it may be preferable to disallow business deductions for the cost of providing fringe benefits, rather than attempting to levy the tax on individual beneficiaries. Of course, in some cases such problems will not be important.

A related area of concern that falls between "excluded income" and "preferred uses of income" involves the tax treatment of such items as travel, meals, entertainment, and the provision of housing and automobiles for employees. These problems are often particularly troublesome in the case of the self-employed, who generally have relatively high incomes. There is no doubt that some business expenditures for meals and entertainment and those for most deductible travel constitute reasonable business expenses; but it is also clear that business deductions for meals, entertainment, and travel often provide substantial subsidies for private consumption. Similarly, tax-deductible provision of cars and housing reduces the tax base, distorts economic choices, and generates inequities. In most developing countries it would be advisable to limit severely the availability of such deductions or to include (at least part of) such expenditures in taxable income of the employee.

The 1986 Act tightens substantially the so-called nondiscrimination rules intended to prevent top executives from providing tax-advantaged fringe benefits for themselves without making them widely available to lower-level employees. Although this approach deals with cases of abuse, it does not address the underlying problem of overly generous tax treatment of fringe benefits. Moreover, the nondiscrimination rules are incredibly complex. It would be far better for LDCs to deal directly with the underlying problems than to attempt to prevent abuses via nondiscrimination rules.

Probably the most important item of tax-preferred income in most countries is the imputed income from owner-occupied housing. In the United States, the imputed income from such housing is not taxed; however, two of the important costs of generating that income, interest expense and property taxes, are allowed as deductions. In short, income from owner-occupied housing is effectively subject to a negative rate of income tax; that is, it is subsidized.[31] Besides reducing the tax base and leading to higher marginal tax rates, the preferential treatment of owner-occupied housing is unfair, and it results in too much capital being invested in such housing, at the expense of socially more productive investment in other sectors.

It may be unrealistic to attempt taxation of net income from owner-occupied housing, even though some countries have attempted to do so. Problems of valuation that plague implementation of property taxes would be encountered, but they would be accentuated because the stakes would be higher. At the very least the home mortgage deduction should be eliminated in order to reduce the tax advantage of owner-occupied housing.[32]

There may be a tendency to suggest the provision of tax subsidies to rental housing, in order to create a more equitable and neutral tax relationship between homeowners and renters. Although there is something to be said for this proposition, following this approach would create additional administrative problems and perhaps accentuate horizontal inequities. More important, especially in an LDC context, it would aggravate distortions of investment decisions in favor of housing and against other sectors. Tax benefits provided directly to taxpayers as renters would benefit only the minority of the population that is subject to income taxation. It would be difficult even to use tax subsidies flowing to providers of housing to benefit the poorest households most in need of assistance.

D. Preferred Uses of Income

Treasury I proposed elimination of itemized deductions for all state and local taxes, one of the largest "tax expenditures."[33] By comparison, the 1986 Act only eliminated itemized deductions for sales taxes, leaving intact those for state and local income and property taxes. The deduction for state and local taxes causes taxpayers to favor the activities of such governments, relative to those of the private sector.[34] Moreover, its effect on equity is highly regressive, since the benefits of the deduction depend on the marginal tax rate of the taxpayer. Whereas for someone in the 50 percent bracket the federal government effectively pays one half the cost of state and local government, someone who pays no federal income tax or who utilizes the standard deduction pays the full cost of such activities. Thus the deduction is neither fair nor neutral.

Although the 1986 Act opened the door for more rational treatment of state and local taxes, the solution it provides is by no means satisfactory. Eliminating the deduction only for sales taxes discriminates between residents of states that rely heavily on sales taxes and those that do not, and it encourages sales tax states to shift reliance to the income tax. A far more appropriate response would have been to allow a deduction or a credit for some uniform percentage of all state and local taxes, if the deduction could not be eliminated entirely. Such a recommendation is equally applicable in developing countries. Of course, it is most relevant to those countries with federal systems of government.

In the United States nonprofit organizations undertake many activities that are assigned to the public sector in other countries. At least part of the explanation for this can be traced to the deductions allowed both corporations and individuals for contributions made to such organizations. In recent years a deduction has been allowed even for individuals who do not otherwise itemize deductions, in order to encourage contributions. This provision has been an open opportunity for abuse since it is not economical to audit the small amounts claimed; much the same can be said for small amounts claimed by those who do itemize, but may lack adequate documentation. Another form of abuse can be traced to the tax treatment accorded the donation of appreciated property. Deduction has been allowed for the full value of such property, even though appreciation on the property is not reflected in taxable income. Though such treatment provides substantial incentive for contributions of appreciated property, it violates basic rules for income measurement. Moreover, it creates substantial opportunities for abuse through the use of inflated deductions based on overvaluations of donated assets.

Treasury I would have eliminated the deduction for nonitemizers and allowed the deduction for itemizers only for contributions in excess of two percent of adjusted gross income. While this provision might have reduced incentives for charitable giving somewhat, incentives for marginal giving by itemizers with gifts in excess of the floor would have remained intact, except to the extent reduced by rate reduction; it was believed that the gains in simplification and equity justified its proposal. The 1986 Act eliminated the deduction for nonitemizers, but did not impose a floor on contributions by itemizers. Treasury I also proposed taxation of the appreciation on assets donated to charity. Though the 1986 Act did not follow this proposal, it did subject such appreciation to the alternative minimum tax (described later in this essay).

Given the relative unimportance of the tax-exempt sector in most developing countries, it may not be necessary to devote considerable attention to tax reform issues affecting charitable contributions. A reasonable solution would be to follow the Treasury I approach. In addition, closely controlled nonprofit foundations that are used to avoid taxes or that provide unfair competition for taxable entities should be scrutinized carefully.

E. Income Shifting

In most countries the existence of graduated rates creates incentives to shift income between family members. (An exception would be the use of the family unit as the taxpaying unit, rather than either individuals or only the parents.) Where the taxpaying entity is the individual, the shifting of income is between spouses, often through transfers of the ownership of assets or the use of artificial transactions between husband and wife. The United States provides for joint returns, effectively treating the income of a married couple as if earned equally by the two spouses; the usual abuse in the U.S. therefore involves shifting of income to children. This problem is further accentuated by the use of trusts, which in the United States have traditionally been taxed under the graduated rate schedule applicable to individuals.

The 1986 Act reduces the possibility of shifting income to minor children and using trusts to minimize taxes. First, it applies the marginal tax rate of the parent to nonlabor income of children under the age of fourteen in excess of $1,000. Second, more income of trusts is construed to be that of the grantor of the trust, and the rate schedule applied to income of trusts is compressed, making use of that device to avoid taxes much less attractive.[35]

Attention to issues such as these would be appropriate for many developing countries, particularly those with well-developed commercial, financial, and legal systems. Fairly simple and obvious ways can be found to shift income between family members, in the absence of explicit prohibitions. Moreover, techniques can often be utilized to avoid limitations of the type recently enacted in the United States. In particular, a closely held business owned by the parents could pay a large deductible salary to a child. Such salary deductions might be disallowed as unreasonable if discovered, but the discovery of abuses may not be simple in a country in which administrative resources are scarce. This is especially true if there is no easy way to link the tax returns of children to those of their parents or to those of businesses controlled by their parents.

F. Simplification

There seems to be an irrepressible urge throughout the world to provide tax benefits to virtually every activity man can conceive as being "good." Besides interfering with equity and efficiency, yielding to this urge reduces the tax base, necessitates higher rates, and increases complexity. Whereas a developed country may be able to afford the luxury of a complex tax code, developing countries generally cannot. It is often best to forgo tax preferences, even for activities that are universally agreed to be worthwhile, in order to assure the administrative feasibility of taxation.

In the United States any individual with income in excess of $5,000 is required to file an income tax return.[36] A high percentage of all tax liabilities of individuals are discharged through withholding at source on wages and salaries. A claim for refund (in the case of overpayment) or a check for underpayment is filed with the return. Though a small fraction of returns are audited and the calculations of taxpayers are verified, returns are generally accepted as accurate.

In several other developed countries a substantially smaller fraction of taxpayers actually file tax returns, their liabilities having been discharged through withholding at source. Treasury I included a proposal for a "return-free system," under which the Internal Revenue Service would calculate income tax liability for many taxpayers, based on information on filing status supplied by the taxpayer and information returns supplied by employers, lenders, state and local governments, financial institutions, and others currently providing such information on income and potentially deductible expenses. This proposal was not accepted by the U.S. Congress.

A return-free system of the type proposed in Treasury I is not feasible in developing countries because of the lack of adequate reporting of taxpayer information. But many such countries should strive to reduce the number of taxpayers who must file returns. For those with only labor income subject to withholding who do not itemize deductions, it should be possible to rely almost entirely on withholding, eliminating any need for the processing of tax returns. (Whether by law or by practice necessitated by administrative realities, many developing countries already follow such an approach.) Implementing such an approach requires careful attention to the design of the withholding system. That, in turn, rests on careful consideration of system design and the benefits of fine-tuning; it is clearly easier in a system with such characteristics as individual taxpaying units, a single rate covering much of the taxpaying population, and few itemized deductions.

G. Other Provisions

The income tax of the United States is perhaps the most complicated of any in the world. It contains provisions with no counterparts in the income taxes of many developing countries. Some of these provisions make very little sense on policy grounds, regardless of a country's level of development. Although others are potentially appropriate for a highly developed country with the administrative skill required to deal with the implied complexities, most such provisions are probably best avoided by developing countries.[37]

IV. Taxation of Business and Capital

Assuring that the taxation of income from business and capital is at the same time fair, economically neutral, relatively simple, and conducive to economic growth is exceedingly difficult, especially in an environment of high and variable inflation—a situation commonly found in developing countries. Though the tax reform proposals submitted to President Reagan in November 1984 by the Treasury Department made a concentrated effort to achieve these objectives, the 1986 Act fell short of realizing them in several important respects.[38] This section deals with the following general topics: corporate rates, the relationship between taxes on individuals and those on corporations and other business entities, timing issues such as depreciation allowances, the need for inflation adjustment, and provisions intended to curtail the use of tax avoidance and tax shelters. There is no discussion of reforms affecting the taxation of foreign-source income of multinational American firms; though these changes have highly relevant "implications" for the design of tax systems in LDCs, they contain few "lessons" for such countries, which are almost universally importers of capital.

A. Corporate Tax Rates

U.S. tax law has long provided graduated corporate rates, presumably to encourage small businesses. The idea is that the owner of such a business can pay corporate tax rates below both that paid by large corporations and the rate that would be applicable if the income were to be taxed at the marginal rate of the owner(s). For reasons to be spelled out below, Treasury I proposed that a single rate be applied to all corporations, except those electing to be taxed as partnerships.[39] By comparison, the 1986 Act continues the practice of applying a graduated rate structure to corporations.

This approach to encouraging the development of small business has obvious flaws. First, activities that might otherwise be included under one corporate structure may be broken down into numerous separately chartered corporations in order to take multiple advantage of graduated rates. In principle it would be possible (as in the United States) to restrict substantially this type of manipulation by allowing corporations subject to common control to benefit only once from rate graduation. But this is likely to be a counsel of perfection in a developing country, where information on the ownership of closely held corporations is often fragmentary.

Second, there is no necessary relationship between the size of a business and the total income attributable to its owner(s). Large corporations may be owned by individuals with low incomes. This is especially true in developed countries, where pension funds hold substantial stakes in the equity of large corporations. Conversely, companies qualifying for the benefits of graduated rates may be owned by wealthy individuals with high incomes. Thus graduated rates for small corporations are likely to do little to improve the equity of an income tax system, and they may harm it. Moreover, because of the ease of manipulation of organizational structure, graduated rates may be an extremely inefficient way of encouraging small business; that is, wealthy taxpayers may take advantage of such provisions to such a degree that the revenue cost of encouraging small businesses through this means may be unbearable.

Depending on the relationship between individual and corporate rates and the ease of using illegal means to evade taxes, professionals such as doctors and lawyers may use "professional corporations" to take advantage of the graduated corporate rate structure. In many countries evasion is so easy for these professionals that use of the corporate form is superfluous. It seems safe to say that in LDCs, tax benefits of this type are generally not necessary to elicit an adequate supply of professional services.

In short, developing countries generally should not employ graduated corporate tax rates. Certainly they should not do so unless they have the administrative capacity to prevent the types of abuses just described.

B. Integration of Corporate and Personal Taxes

The United States is one of relatively few developed countries that do not provide meaningful relief from the double taxation of income from corporate equity. Under the "classical system" found in the United States such income is taxed first when received by the corporation and again when distributed to shareholders. As a result, there are incentives for corporate managers to prefer debt over equity finance and to retain earnings rather than distributing them; in addition, this system generally discriminates against investment in the corporate sector and against the use of the corporate form of business.[40]

Treasury I attempted to rectify this situation by allowing corporations a deduction for 50 percent of dividends paid to individual shareholders. In addition, it proposed that large limited partnerships be treated as corporations, in recognition that they have many of the economic attributes of corporations. (Some are even listed on the New York Stock Exchange.) The dividend-paid deduction approach was chosen over the much more common shareholder credit method (also called the imputation or withholding method) because of its greater simplicity.[41] An explicit decision was made in Treasury I to break with common practice and extend the benefits of dividend relief to tax-exempt shareholders and foreigners.[42] Taxation of dividends can be implemented effectively in developing countries only if there is a withholding tax. But if there is, there may be relatively little practical difference between the shareholder credit and the dividend-paid deduction.[43]

Dividend relief did not have strong support and is not provided in the 1986 Act. If anything, the defects of the classical U.S. system have been aggravated. For the first time in history the marginal rate paid by high-income individuals (28 percent) lies well below that paid by most major corporations (34 percent). This rate differential, which applies to retained earnings, as well as to income distributed as dividends, will accentuate the traditional advantage enjoyed by noncorporate investments. The rate differential will also accentuate the bias toward debt finance created by the classical system.[44] It would not be surprising to see corporations use the proceeds of large issues of debt to retire their shares or to buy the stock of other corporations.

A corporate deduction only for dividends paid on new issues has all the allocative advantages of a deduction for all dividends, without the loss of revenues and windfall gains to owners of existing shares.[45] It does, however, suffer some administrative difficulties. Whether developing countries could implement a deduction only for dividends paid on newly issued shares, without encountering severe administrative problems and abuse, deserves consideration.

Under a flat-rate income tax applied at the same rate to corporations and individuals, the equilibrium effects of allowing a deduction for dividends paid and taxing such dividends in the hands of shareholders can be duplicated by allowing no corporate deduction and excluding dividends from the taxable income of shareholders. Similarly, the standard practice of allowing corporations (and unincorporated businesses) a deduction for interest expense and taxing interest income is equivalent to exempting interest income and allowing no deduction for interest expense. There is, however, a crucial administrative difference in these two approaches. (Significant differences also exist in the tax treatment of interest and dividends paid to tax-exempt organizations and foreigners; these are not considered at this point.) It is far simpler and more certain to disallow corporate deductions for dividends and interest expense than to attempt to assure that dividends and interest are included in the taxable income of shareholders. Although this approach suffers from perception problems, some countries might wish to consider adopting it.[46]

Of course, matters are not so simple if, as is common, income tax is levied at graduated rates. Disallowing a business deduction for interest involves more taxation than subjecting interest income to the marginal rates of low-income recipients of interest. But in most developing countries the concentration of wealth is such that most dividends are probably paid to individuals who are (or who should be) subject to the top marginal rate. Interest income may be more widely distributed. But in many countries the taxation of such income via disallowance of deductions may be less important than the "tax" implicit in interest rates set at below market levels.

C. Timing Issues

If an income tax system is truly to be fair and neutral, income for tax purposes must resemble closely economic income. If the timing of the recognition of income and the deduction of expenses does not track economic reality fairly closely, there will be opportunities to reduce the present value of taxes by postponing recognition of income and accelerating deductions for expenses. The postponement of taxes can be a quite valuable benefit if interest rates are high, as they commonly are in developing countries.[47] The result is a tax system that is unfair and that distorts the allocation of resources toward activities offering the greatest opportunities for this type of mismatching of the timing of income and expense. In addition, the reputation of the tax system suffers as high income individuals and profitable corporations are seen to pay little or no taxes.[48]

In many cases current expenditures create assets of lasting but diminishing value. Proper income measurement requires that the costs of creating such assets be capitalized and deducted as the resulting assets decline in value, rather than being deducted in the year costs are incurred. For convenience we might call such activities "point input, phased output."

Probably the most familiar question of timing of this type involves depreciation allowances. If taxable income is to track economic reality, depreciation allowances must be based on economic depreciation, the time pattern of loss of value of a depreciable asset. Implementing this rule is difficult, at best, because accurate information on patterns of economic depreciation are not readily available.[49] Moreover, in many countries depreciation allowances are deliberately accelerated. First, it may be thought necessary to allow accelerated depreciation to compensate for inflation; otherwise, depreciation allowances for tax purposes will not allow tax-free recovery of capital. Second, many countries use such techniques as accelerated depreciation and investment tax credits to provide incentives for investment. This approach has been followed in the United States since 1962. From 1981 to 1986 the combination of highly accelerated depreciation allowances and the investment tax credit produced capital recovery allowances for many assets that at 1981 levels of inflation were roughly equivalent to expensing (first-year write-off) in real present value. Some contend that this is appropriate, noting that expensing is a standard component of proposals for basing taxation on consumption, rather than income, without noting that income tax treatment of debt and interest expense is inconsistent with consumption-based taxation.

This system came to be widely viewed as overly generous, in part because it resulted in the proliferation of tax shelters for individuals and elimination of income tax for many profitable corporations. This problem was aggravated when the drop in the inflation rate caused the real present value of capital cost recovery to exceed that of expensing. Moreover, the economic effects of these investment incentives differed widely across industries, with the degree of nonneutrality depending on the rate of inflation.[50] Treasury I proposed that the investment tax credit be repealed and that depreciation allowances for tax purposes be based on the best available evidence of economic depreciation. The depreciable basis of assets would be explicitly indexed for inflation. Although the 1986 Act repealed the investment tax credit, it did not reduce substantially the acceleration of depreciation allowances for equipment, perhaps in part because it provides no adjustment for inflation.

The principles underlying the Treasury I proposals for real economic depreciation are generally applicable to a much wider range of issues. The cost of discovering and developing natural resources should be capitalized and recovered through depletion allowances based on output.[51] Thus Treasury I proposed repeal of the existing provisions under which so-called "intangible drilling costs" (IDCs) in the oil and gas industry and analogous mine development costs are deductible in the year incurred. It proposed elimination of percentage depletion, an irrational system under which taxpayers in natural resource industries are allowed to deduct a given percentage of income, without regard to the relationship between the total amount of such deductions and the capital expenditures ostensibly being recovered. Reflecting political pressures, the 1986 Act retains expensing of IDCs for independent operators, though it does tighten somewhat the alternative maximum tax relating to IDCs and makes deductions for IDCs by major oil companies and analogous expenditures in hard mineral development less generous.

Successful research and development (R & D) creates assets having value extending beyond the current period. The same can be said for expenditures on advertising and public relations. For accurate income measurement such expenditures should, in theory, be capitalized and amortized. Reflecting both the difficulty of valuing such assets and the perceived social benefits of R & D, under U.S. law such expenditures may be deducted in the year incurred. Of course, current expensing of advertising and similar expenses creates a bias in favor of this type of investment, relative to investment in productive assets. The same argument may apply to expenditures on research and development, but with less force, depending on the validity of external economy arguments.

By comparison with the activities just discussed, there are activities in which costs are incurred over time to create assets of increasing value that are then harvested or sold intact. A clear example would be timber. For such assets characterized by "phased input, point output" the conceptually correct approach under an income tax would be to tax the increase in value on an accrual basis.[52] Under such an accrual approach all costs of creating increases in value would be deducted as incurred. Such an extreme approach is politically unlikely and perhaps administratively infeasible in most cases. Thus in the case of timber Treasury I adopted the alternative of requiring capitalization of the costs of phased inputs, allowing their deduction only at the time income is realized through the sale of the resulting assets. Because recognition of income is deferred until timber is cut, this approach would not fully eliminate the timing problem.

When applied in other areas the logic just described produces unacceptable tax postponement. For example, it has been applied in the construction industry as the "completed contract method" of accounting for multiyear projects. Under this method no income is recognized until a contract is completed, even though progress payments have been received. An alternative that reflects economic reality more closely would be to require that income be recognized for tax purposes on the basis of the estimated percentage of completion. The 1986 Act requires that this "percentage completion method" must be employed for at least 40 percent of the calculation of income from multiperiod contracts. In addition, the completed contract method is not available for the calculation of income under the alternative minimum tax.

Some assets are characterized by both phased inputs and phased outputs. For example, vineyards, rubber trees, coffee plants, and fruit trees are characterized by unproductive gestation periods extending over several years, followed by lengthy productive lives. In such cases it would be appropriate to combine the Treasury I treatment of timber and of depreciable assets, requiring capitalization of pre-production expenses and subsequent amortization of such expenses over the productive life of the asset. A similar situation exists in the case of construction activities extending over several years, including self-construction of assets by the taxpayer. Construction-period costs, including interest and taxes, should be capitalized and then recovered through depreciation allowances, whether by a taxpayer-constructor or by a third party. Inventory accumulation provides another example of phased input and phased output. The 1986 Act provides that many costs of inventory accumulation that were previously expensed must be capitalized.

Accurate income measurement requires the use of accrual accounting. It may be necessary and appropriate to allow small businesses to employ cash accounting, to ease compliance burdens. But allowing the use of cash accounting creates opportunities for abuse. For example, it has been common practice in the United States for cash-basis taxpayers to incur large expenses near the end of the fiscal year in order to generate tax deductions, even though the expenditures are for purchases related to the earning of income to be reported in the next year. Similarly, it is common for cash-basis taxpayers to postpone billing for sales and services rendered late in a year in order to postpone realization of income. In extreme cases an accrual-basis taxpayer takes a deduction in one year for obligations that will not be recognized until a year later by a cash-basis taxpayer. The same taxpayer may even be on both sides of such a transaction, for example, operating through one cash-basis partnership and another partnership reporting on an accrual basis.

Another abuse of cash-basis accounting has been particularly prevalent in the construction of housing. (The problem is, however, more widespread.) A housing contractor sells a home but accepts a note providing for deferred payment, which is then discounted to a financial intermediary. The contractor reports income only as the note is amortized, even though by discounting the note he has, in effect, realized cash from the sale of the home. The 1986 Act contains strong restrictions on the use of such "builders' bonds" and other instances of borrowing by those making installment sales.

If all forms of income are not taxed uniformly, substantial incentives exist for recharacterizing income and expense. If, for example, interest income is taxable but capital gains are taxed preferentially, there is an incentive to convert interest income to capital gains. One way this can be done in the absence of rules preventing it is by issuing debt for less than its value at redemption and paying little or no interest explicitly. Much of the return implicit in the bond would be realized as a "capital gain" upon redemption. (By comparison, an accrual-basis taxpayer may be deducting this implicit interest as it accrues.) Of course, the manipulation inherent in such "original issue discount" bonds is fairly transparent, and rules have existed in the United States since 1954 to deal with this problem. In order to measure taxable income and expense correctly, it is necessary that lenders report the implicit interest on transactions of this type as it accrues. Use of a straight-line amortization schedule for tax purposes is too generous to the borrower, since it fails to take account of the effects of compound interest.

The rules dealing with timing issues are among the most complex features of the 1986 Act. One would advocate their adoption in toto by a developing country only with trepidation. Full consideration of the possibility of transplanting these rules to LDCs requires further study, but is beyond the scope of the present paper.[53]

D. Inflation Adjustment

A well-designed income tax must make allowance for inflation in the measurement of income from business and capital. Otherwise, high and variable rates of inflation can produce grossly inaccurate measurement of taxable income. These inaccuracies can cause considerable inequity and distort the allocation of resources. In addition, they may generate disincentives for saving and investment and stifle capital formation and growth.[54]

Some countries use ad hoc substitutes for inflation adjustment; these include acceleration of depreciation allowances, LIFO (last in, first out) accounting for inventories, and preferential treatment for long term capital gains. Such ad hoc approaches are defective in several respects. Most obviously, they are appropriate, at best, for only one rate of inflation. At any other rate they may be either too generous or not generous enough. Ad hoc provisions enacted when inflation is high can result in enormous tax loopholes and opportunities for tax shelters when inflation declines; this has been the experience in the United States since enactment of overly generous accelerated depreciation allowances in 1981.

Second, while it is common to introduce ad hoc responses to inflation in the case of depreciable assets, capital gains, and goods sold from inventory, it is much less common to make similar adjustments for the erosion of the real value of debt resulting from inflation. If interest income and expense (or the principal of debt obligations) are not indexed, inflation may undermine incentives to save, increase incentives to borrow, and aggravate opportunities for tax shelters. To be satisfactory a system of inflation adjustment must reflect fairly accurately actual experience with inflation and must be applied to interest income and expense (or to the principal amount of debt), as well as to depreciable assets, capital gains, and inventories.

Treasury I included a comprehensive system of inflation adjustment. The basis of depreciable assets would have been adjusted to reflect inflation, the basis of capital assets would also have been adjusted, so that only real capital gains would be taxed (and real losses would be deductible, up to a limit), taxpayers would have been given a choice between using indexed FIFO (first in, first out) or LIFO accounting for inventories, and an inflation adjustment would have been applied to interest income and expense.[55]

The primary defect in this system was the method proposed for dealing with interest income and expense. The conceptually correct approach would be to allow taxpayers to exclude from income (and disallow interest deductions for) an amount equal to the product of the inflation rate and the principle amount of debt. Because it was feared that compliance with this approach would be too difficult, the Treasury Department proposed an alternative ad hoc substitute. The exclusion (and disallowance) would be the product of nominal interest income (and expense) and the percentage that the inflation rate represents of the sum of 6 percent plus the inflation rate.

This approach suffers from several shortcomings.[56] First, the indexing formula proposed would be accurate, strictly speaking, only for new debt yielding a real rate of return of 6 percent. In general the inflation adjustment would be much too small, because the 6 percent real rate of return implicit in the formula substantially overstates real rates of return historically experienced. Moreover, the accuracy of the inflation adjustment would vary considerably, depending on the nominal interest rates on various debts.[57] It can be argued, however, that even with this design flaw the interest indexing in Treasury I would be a significant improvement over current law, which makes no allowance for inflation.

Second, the Treasury I proposal would exclude from tax a percentage of the spread of financial institutions (and others with positions on both sides of debt transactions).[58] It would have been appropriate, but more complicated, to limit interest indexing to income from loans financed from equity.

None of these proposals for inflation adjustment were included in the 1986 Act. Capital gains are now taxed as ordinary income, despite the lack of inflation adjustment. LIFO continues to be available; indexed FIFO is not allowed. Inflation adjustment is not allowed for depreciation; although the investment tax credit was repealed, depreciation allowances remain somewhat accelerated, perhaps because of the lack of inflation adjustment. Nominal interest expense remains fully taxable and fully deductible, subject to a variety of limitations intended to prevent tax avoidance.

Unless they can realistically expect very low and constant rates of inflation, developing countries that continue to levy traditional income taxes should seriously consider providing inflation adjustment. The need for inflation adjustment is probably greater than in the United States, since inflation is generally more rapid in such countries than in the United States. Unfortunately the ability to deal with the complexity of inflation adjustment is also generally much more limited. Further attention should be devoted to alternative techniques of inflation adjustment and to experience in other countries. The most difficult problems occur in attempting to adjust interest or debt for inflation. To avoid the difficulties with the Treasury I approach described above, the conceptually correct approach requires knowledge of the average principal amount of debt during the year. A third alternative would be that used in Chile, proposed by Harberger for Indonesia and proposed more recently by the current author in Colombia.[59] It involves inflation adjustment of both the value of "real" assets and net wealth.[60] Experience in Chile suggests that such an approach has been workable.

E. Tax Avoidance Measures

Because of inaccuracies in income measurement resulting from timing issues, the preferential treatment of capital gains, and the full deduction of nominal interest expense, many high-income taxpayers in the U.S. have been able to avoid substantial amounts of taxes.[61] A common approach is to invest in a limited partnership established for this purpose. Because deductions are accelerated and recognition of income is deferred, current income for tax purposes is understated. Further understatement occurs because deductions are allowed for the full nominal amount of interest, rather than only the real component. When income is finally realized, it is often characterized as preferentially taxed capital gains. The partnerships' artificial accounting losses are passed through to the partners, who use them to offset (or shelter) income from other sources.[62] A less elaborate means of sheltering income involves borrowing to make long-term investments. Nominal interest on the debt is fully deductible, while long-term capital gains benefit from preferential treatment.

Treasury I would have eliminated most of the opportunities for tax shelters by attacking the provisions that make them possible. It would have made the timing of the recognition of income and the allowance of deductions match much more closely the underlying economic reality. Deductions for interest expense would have been adjusted to take account of inflation, albeit in a very rough manner. Finally, real capital gains would have been taxed in the same way as other income. In short, the only generally available preference remaining would have been the

advantages of deferral and step-up of basis at death for purposes of calculating capital gains.[63] While important in their own right, these probably would not have been enough to perpetuate seriously abusive tax
shelters.

The 1986 Act followed a circuitous route in curtailing tax shelters,
rather than the direct approach of Treasury I. While dealing with many
timing issues and providing for the taxation of nominal long-term capital gains as ordinary income, it left in place several building blocks of
tax shelters, including accelerated depreciation, expensing of intangible drilling costs for independents, deferral and step-up of basis at death
for capital gains, and full deduction of nominal interest expense. Being
worried about the inequities, distortions, and perception of unfairness
created by tax shelters, the Congress introduced several new anti-shelter
provisions.

First, it essentially divided income and expense into three separate
"baskets." In one basket is income from employment and the active
pursuit of a trade or business. The second contains investment income
such as interest, dividends, royalties, and capital gains on investment
assets and interest expense incurred to finance such investments. The
third basket contains passive income and losses. In general this basket
includes income and expenses from business activities in which the
taxpayer is not an active participant, except for those from working
interests in oil and gas properties (an exception explained by powerful
political forces). Income and losses from limited partnerships (except
for those of the general partners) and rental income and losses, including those from real estate, are presumed to be passive, but income from
portfolio investments is presumed to be investment income.

Passive losses can only be deducted to the extent of passive income;
they cannot be used to offset investment income or income from
employment or the active pursuit of a trade or business. Similarly,
investment interest can only be deducted to the extent of investment
income; it, too, cannot be deducted against income from employment
or a trade or business. These rules effectively prevent the use of passive
losses from tax shelter investments and excess interest expense from
offsetting employment income and income from the active pursuit of a
trade or business. These benefits have been purchased, however, at a
high cost in terms of complexity. It is necessary to draw many arbitrary lines between similar transactions in order to distinguish between
various types of income and various types of interest.[64] It would have
been far simpler to adopt the straightforward scheme proposed in Trea-

sury I, which would have substantially eliminated the building blocks of shelters.

Seen from the perspective of traditional public finance theory, the "three-basket" approach recently adopted by the United States seems highly anomalous. It converts a tax on global income into a schedular income tax. Schedular taxes have traditionally been opposed on the grounds that income from all sources should be taxed equivalently. Of course, that view rests on the (usually implicit) presumption that taxable income from various sources is measured accurately, that is, that it reflects economic income. At the heart of the U.S. retreat to a schedular system is the reluctance (or political inability) to eliminate tax preferences, as proposed in Treasury I. Given this fact of life an attempt to implement a global system would leave the door open for tax shelters and other avenues of tax avoidance. The schedular approach adopted in the 1986 Act is perhaps a reasonable response to this state of affairs, although a second-best one.

Since 1969 the United States has imposed an alternative minimum tax (AMT) on individuals. The AMT has a base that is much broader than that for the regular income tax. Because certain itemized deductions and excluded sources of income are included in the base of the AMT, the effect of the AMT is potentially somewhat more far-reaching than those of the anti-shelter devices described above. As a result, the AMT helps to prevent high-income individuals from paying no tax. The 1986 Act extends the AMT concept to corporations. In a sense, the alternative minimum tax is evidence of congressional schizophrenia: preferences that allow taxpayers to avoid tax are enacted, but the alternative minimum tax is imposed to prevent taxpayers from making excessive use of those preferences. Because of its proposals to eliminate virtually all opportunities for tax shelters and to severely restrict the availability of itemized deductions, Treasury I proposed repeal of the alternative minimum tax.

Because many itemized deductions and opportunities to avoid taxes were continued, the 1986 Act makes the AMT much more stringent. More items of tax preference are included in the base of the AMT, and the 21 percent AMT rate for individuals is 75 percent of the 28 percent rate applicable to high-income taxpayers under the regular tax. (By comparison, the previous AMT of 20 percent was only 40 percent of the top marginal rate of 50 percent.)

Many high-income individuals will be forced to calculate liability under both the AMT and the regular tax. Since many items of income and expense are treated differently under the two taxes, this reform increases substantially the complexity facing those potentially liable for AMT. The corporate AMT in the 1986 Act contains a particularly peculiar feature: liability is based in part on the "book" income used for financial accounting purposes.[65]

It is difficult to know how to appraise the relevance of U.S. experience in this area. The best approach for LDCs, as in developed countries, is to adopt an economically sensible and comprehensible definition of income. While administrative constraints may preclude a totally correct definition of income, it should at least be possible to avoid the most glaring deficiencies and thus the need for either a schedular approach or an alternative minimum tax. Failing that, the proper solution is not obvious. As in the United States, a schedular approach would prevent the most egregious abuses. But it would do so at substantial costs in terms of added complexity.

Introduction of an alternative minimum tax appears to be even less attractive for an LDC. The already thin administrative capabilities of the fiscal authorities would be stretched even further. Moreover, as a practical political matter it seems fairly unlikely that much progress could be made in reaching through the AMT income that cannot be reached through the regular tax.

V. Concluding Remarks

Limitations of space preclude an extensive summary appraisal of the lessons for LDCs of U.S. tax reform. Suffice it to say that in many cases reforms enacted in the United States would be equally appropriate for LDCs; especially important is the fundamental approach of broadening the tax base in order to reduce marginal tax rates. In many developing countries it would be appropriate to adopt reforms proposed in the United States, but not enacted; these include more comprehensive taxation of fringe benefits, elimination of exemptions for interest on governmental securities, and reduction of the tax benefits of owner-occupied housing.[66] In the area of taxation of income from business and capital, problems that deserve attention by any LDC expecting to rely on a traditional tax based on income include relief from double taxation of dividends, inflation adjustment, and timing issues.

The complexities of inflation adjustment and timing issues, as well as concern about saving, investment, and economic growth, lead one to ask whether continued reliance on income taxation is preferable to personal taxation based on consumption. Consumption-based taxation has the substantial administrative advantages for LDCs that inflation adjustment is not necessary and that most timing issues disappear. Moreover, by eliminating the tax on the marginal return to investment, a consumption-based tax would reduce the relative attraction of tax-preferred investment, in the United States and elsewhere.[67] Further attention should be devoted to the relative merits of personal taxation based on income and on consumption.[68]

Notes

1 For thorough analysis of the use of value added taxes in developing countries, including discussions of the European experience and the VAT recently enacted in New Zealand (called a "general sales tax" for cosmetic reasons), see Gillis, Shoup, and Sicat (forthcoming).

2 See, however, Bird (1983). Space also precludes examination of a long list of other features of the U.S. income tax, including special exemptions for the blind and elderly, the child care credit, the second earner deduction, deductions for moving expenses, energy credits, allowances for political contributions, the presidential check-off, income averaging, and a variety of tax incentives for activities such as investments in pollution control equipment and rehabilitation of historical buildings. Most of these would strain the administrative capacity of LDCs, and many would be bad tax policy. Finally, I do not discuss the tax treatment of nonprofit organizations. While the nonprofit sector is substantially smaller in most developing countries than in the more-developed ones, there is reason to believe that nonprofit organizations related to and controlled by firms in the regular private sector may play a role in avoidance (or even evasion) of income taxation in some developing countries. It is interesting to note that in Colombia the activities of nonprofit organizations have come under increased scrutiny in recent years.

3 Other comprehensive studies of tax reform options for the United States include U.S. Department of Treasury (1977) and the analysis underlying the 1969 tax reform.

4 See, however, Atkinson and Stiglitz (1980) and Newberry and Stern (1987).

5 Difficulties of implementation include lack of knowledge about the relevant parameters, including elasticities of factor supply and product demand. Attempting to base taxation on such parameters, even if they were known, would probably not seem fair to most taxpayers. For efforts to implement the theory of optimal taxation in India, see Newberry and Stern (1988).

6 For an argument to this effect, based on Harberger (1964), see Thirsk (1987).

7 See Feldstein (1978), Bradford (1980), or King (1980). McLure (1980) provides a simplified discussion of this issue.

8 Application of one rate to all taxpayers has the further advantage that there is no advantage in shifting income and deductions between taxpayers to take advantage of differences in rates.

9 In a dynamic context, responses to incentives created by the tax system can affect both the rate of economic growth and the distribution of economic output, and

therefore have implications for equity.

10   It might be noted, however, that the two sources of inequities mentioned in the text, tax-exempt securities and fringe-benefits, were largely unaffected by the 1986 Act.

11   See Bailey (1974) and Feldstein (1976).

12   Some might argue that compliance with the U.S. income tax is voluntary in the same sense that the failure to rob banks is voluntary. But there is a substantial difference. Each year some 100 million U.S. taxpayers calculate income tax liabilities and file returns, claiming refunds for overpayment or remitting residual liabilities, despite the well-known fact that only a minute percentage of tax returns are audited. Of course, the majority of revenue comes from withholding on wages and salaries.

13   See U.S. Department of Treasury (1984), vol. 1, page 15. This is only one of several alternative definitions of distributional neutrality; see also McLure and Zodrow (1987), p. 44.

14   This may surprise American readers accustomed to hearing estimates of the "tax gap," the amount of revenue that should be collected that is not. Much of this gap can be traced to illegal activities; in such instances it seems inappropriate to characterize the inability to collect taxes as primarily a problem of tax evasion.

15   There is little reason to believe that tax evasion would drop dramatically if tax rates were reduced. Yet there must be some truth to the notion that tax evasion and higher rates follow each other in a vicious circle, with evasion necessitating higher rates and higher rates stimulating more evasion.

16   It may be worth noting at the outset that the simplification objective was sacrificed early in the tax reform process in order to salvage tax preferences of particular benefit to politically important groups. There is, of course, little reason to expect experience to be different elsewhere.

17   For an eloquent description of this thesis, see Bird (1987).

18   For further description of the mechanism by which incentives that stimulate increases in investment not matched by increases in saving can cause worsening of the competitive position of a nation, see McLure (1986b) or Summers (1987).

19   In judging such matters it is important where one starts. For example, in appraising the shift of liabilities from individuals to corporations in the 1986 Act it is important to recall that corporate income taxes were reduced substantially in 1981. To some extent it may be more sensible to look at the combined effect of the reforms that occurred over the entire period beginning in 1981 than to focus only on the 1986 Act. But that is true only if the pre-1981 pattern of taxation was acceptable—a view that does not attract universal agreement. See also McLure (1986c).

Most estimates of the revenue effects of tax reform concentrate on the five-year budget period following enactment. This tends to overstate the long-run increase in corporate tax liabilities, since many of the reforms involved one-time acceleration of liabilities through the correction of timing problems (discussed in section IV). For the same reason, revenue neutrality during the budget period may not imply long-run revenue neutrality.

20   Individuals may not have fully appreciated that the higher taxes collected from corporations would ultimately be paid by individuals in their capacities as shareholders, workers, consumers, or owners of capital in general; they may have simply seen the corporate tax as being borne by "someone else," including wealthy shareholders and foreigners. This appreciation was not facilitated by the failure of the estimates of

distributional effects reported in Treasury I to take account of the increase in corporation income taxes. See U.S. Department of the Treasury (1984), vol. 1, pages 46–61.

21 This appears, for example, to have happened in the case of Jamaica's extraordinarily high tax on bauxite. See also Gillis and McLure (1975).

22 This "humpbacked" rate structure is, however, consistent with the dictates of optimal taxation theory that low marginal tax rates should be applied to the income of those with relatively elastic labor supply. Even though equity is ordinarily thought to be primarily a matter of variations in average tax rates (which increase monotonically with income under the 1986 Act), many taxpayers subject to the 33 percent rate probably wonder about the fairness of their paying a higher marginal rate than those with incomes substantially above their own. Moreover, this pattern of rates creates unusual pressures on the timing of discretionary receipts and deductions. Where possible, taxpayers will push income from 33 percent years into 28 percent years and move deductions into 33 percent years.

23 The reduction in individual tax liabilities can be expected to accentuate brain drain. Even if liabilities were not reduced there might be an inducement to brain drain if lower marginal rates held out the promise of lower taxes on incremental effort.

24 Again on the basis of the theory of optimal taxation it might seem appropriate to follow this course, considering especially that high-income individuals are presumably the ones most likely to be attracted to the United States by the prospects of lower marginal rates.

25 It is ironic that the across-the-board rate reduction of the 1981 Act was sold, in part, as a means of offsetting increases in marginal tax rates resulting from inflation-induced "bracket creep." Rate reduction does little to reduce the inequitable effects of the worst form of bracket creep, the movement of poverty-level families onto the tax rolls.

26 Moreover, if the intent of personal exemptions is to remove from the tax base some minimal amount of income, the deduction is preferable to a credit on conceptual grounds.

27 In the U.S., some thought was given to a system of personal exemptions other than an equal per capita exemption and to basing the standard deduction on family size. Whether rightly or wrongly, these were rejected because of concern over their complexity. Of course, the standard deduction does depend on the filing status of the taxpayer (joint return, single return, or head of household).

28 Though the United States does not exempt interest on the federal debt, it does defer tax on interest on savings bonds until such bonds are redeemed.

29 Housing and housing allowances provided by employers in the U.S. are generally subject to tax, except for relatively unimportant cases in which housing is provided in remote places or on the business premises for the convenience of the employer.

30 Thus, for example, it is better to levy a tax rate of 30 percent on all income than to be forced to impose a rate of 40 percent because 25 percent of economic income takes the form of tax-exempt fringe benefits. Some may argue that this difference is more apparent than real, since in both cases tax revenues are 30 percent of income. But it seems likely that in most cases fringe benefits do not increase proportionally with fully taxable income. For example, the benefits of employer-provided health insurance do not increase because an employee has a higher salary or works overtime. To

the extent that fringe benefits and other tax-preferred sources and uses of income are inframarginal, the hypothetical example above is relevant.

31   In order to calculate the net imputed income from owner-occupied housing, it is necessary to deduct mortgage interest, property taxes, and other expenses from the gross rental value of such housing. Since gross rental income is not subject to tax, but mortgage interest and property taxes are deductible, the net contribution of owner-occupied housing to the calculation of taxable income is negative.

32   Basing taxation on the taxpayer's net equity would not be much better because it would also require valuation of houses. As the preceding footnote makes clear, the basic problem is the inability to subject gross rental income to tax; the deduction for mortgage interest would be quite appropriate, if only gross rental income could be taxed. David Bradford (1986) has suggested that it might not be inappropriate to continue the mortgage deduction, since it makes the benefits of the exclusion of imputed income more widely available and thereby improves the equity of the tax system. The logical conclusion of this line of reasoning would seem to be that tax benefits should be extended to rental housing. The wisdom of this advice for a developed country is debatable. Primarily the well-to-do would benefit significantly from the mortgage deduction, and even those who would benefit from a deduction for rent would be among the relatively few who file tax returns. Given this and the need for nonhousing investment in LDCs, the case for allowing mortgage interest deductions is even more limited than in developed countries.

33   For a thorough discussion of the concept of tax expenditures and further references to the literature, see Surrey and McDaniel (1985).

34   There are, of course, reasons that services of state and local governments may be underprovided (or overprovided) in the absence of such tax subsidies. This may justify some federal subsidy for state and local expenditures. Neither it nor the fear of tax competition between the states justifies use of the tax deduction vehicle; see McLure (1986b).

35   As before, there is no personal exemption for trusts. Only the first $5,000 of taxable income benefits from the 15 percent rate; the remainder is taxed at rate of 28 percent. Even the benefit of the 15 percent rate is phased out between $13,000 and $26,000 of taxable income.

36   This is the figure for 1988, when increases in the personal exemption and standard deduction are fully phased in; it is based on the $3,000 standard deduction for single persons and the $2,000 personal exemption.

37   See note 2 for a partial list of such provisions.

38   It bears repeating that the single most important shortcoming of the Treasury I attempt to achieve fair and neutral taxation of all income from capital resulted from the retention of preferential treatment of housing; see McLure (1986a).

39   Under U.S. law, there is no separate tax on partnerships; their income is attributed to the partners and taxed as part of the income of the partners.

40   See McLure (1979). Strictly speaking these propositions do not necessarily hold because of the preferential treatment accorded long-term capital gains; see Slemrod (1983) and literature cited there. Nonetheless, they accurately describe general tendencies. See also the discussion at note 45.

41   The dividend paid deduction has the obvious benefit on simplicity grounds that only the corporation paying dividends needs to contend with the mechanics of divi-

dend relief. By comparison, under a shareholder credit each recipient of dividends must include in taxable income the grossed-up amount of dividends and then take credit for the imputed withholding tax implicit in the corporation tax. In principle this is no more difficult than implementation of withholding on wages and salaries, once taxpayers have gone through the learning process. It would, however, necessitate the filing of tax returns by low-income taxpayers who might not otherwise file, in order to claim refunds. Moreover, the widespread existence of Individual Retirement Accounts and pension plans for the self-employed would further complicate matters. If the benefits of dividend relief were to be extended to owners of such plans it would be necessary for each plan to file a tax return for the sole purpose of claiming the shareholder credit. The implied avalanche of paperwork could be avoided by denying the shareholder credit to such plans. But substantial confusion might still result; since corporations would presumably report dividends and imputed taxes to all shareholders, individuals would need to distinguish between reports pertaining to shares held on personal account (for which inclusion of dividends and claiming a credit would be appropriate) and those pertaining to IRAS and pension plans for the self-employed. To some extent a similar distinction must be made now. But the United States does not currently apply withholding to most dividends and interest received by individuals, as it should, due in large part to a successful public relations campaign by financial institutions in the early 1980s that resulted in a repeal of a law requiring withholding. This could constitute a major problem under the dividend-received deduction.

42   Under common (but not necessarily sensible) international practice, as embodied in current interpretations of foreign tax treaties, these benefits can be denied by allowing shareholder credits only for domestic shareholders; the equivalent effect cannot be achieved by providing a dividend-paid deduction and a correspondingly higher withholding tax only on dividends paid to foreign shareholders without provoking claims that treaties have been abrogated. See also Sato and Bird (1975) and McLure (1979). It was expected that other countries providing dividend relief would extend their benefits to U.S. shareholders; there was a thinly veiled threat that if such reciprocal treatment was not forthcoming the benefits of dividend relief would be denied residents of offending countries. Of course, achieving this result would likely involve abrogation of some U.S. tax treaties. Most developing countries would probably feel somewhat less constrained than most developed countries in dealing with the problem posed by foreign shareholders. Since there are relatively few double taxation treaties between developed and developing countries, LDCs adopting a deduction for dividends paid could compensate in the case of dividends paid to foreign shareholders by raising withholding taxes on such dividends. In most developing countries the tax treatment of dividends paid to tax-exempt organizations would probably be a relatively unimportant issue.

43   Colombia has recently followed an approach to the integration problem that is probably quite appropriate, although it violates the dictates of standard policy advice. It has excluded dividends from the individual income tax base, while continuing full taxation of corporate profits. To the extent that shareholders are in the top (30 percent) bracket, profits are taxed in the same way as under a standard approach to dividend relief (the dividend-paid deduction or imputation systems).

44   Each dollar of interest paid to taxpayers in the 28 percent bracket by a corporation

subject to a 34 percent marginal rate results in a tax saving of 6 cents. By comparison, under pre-1987 law such a payment to a shareholder in the 50 percent bracket by a corporation subject to a 46 percent rate would cost an additional 4 cents.

45   For a general explanation of this proposal and its benefits and for further references, see Andrews (1984). It would be necessary to impose a tax on nondividend distributions, as well as on dividends on new shares, in order to prevent existing shares from being converted to "new" ones eligible for the dividend deduction.

46   This is the approach advocated in Hall and Rabushka (1983) and (1985). For further discussion of this type of tax, see McLure, Mutti, Thuronyi, and Zodrow (1988), chapter 9 or Zodrow and McLure (1988). An alternative would be to continue the usual approach (deduction of expense, taxation of income), but collect a nonrefundable withholding tax on the payment of dividends and interest. This is economically equivalent to allowing no deduction and not taxing income. In either event it is difficult to deal with the possibility of structuring loans as rental agreements in order to gain deductions; this is especially important with graduated rates.

47   Interest rates are often high because of the expectation of rapid inflation. The need to combat the effects of inflation in causing income to be measured inaccurately is discussed in the next subsection. The remainder of this subsection discusses problems of timing that would exist even in the absence of inflation.

48   In a steady-state situation without inflation or real growth merely postponing taxes probably would not cause perception problems, even though it would be distortionary. Taxes not paid yesterday would simply be paid today and today's taxes would be paid tomorrow. But in an economy in which nominal income is growing, whether because of real growth or inflation, taxes postponed today will exceed taxes postponed from yesterday (which would perhaps be offset by deductions accelerated from tomorrow), creating perception problems.

49   Treasury I proposed depreciation schedules based on the estimates contained in Hulten and Wykoff (1981). Although these estimates are the best available and are widely accepted by economists, taxpayers complained vigorously about their deficiencies.

50   For estimates of the dispersion of marginal effective tax rates across industries, see U.S. Department of the Treasury (1984) vol. 2, p. 165.

51   The proper treatment of "dry holes" and other costs of unsuccessful exploration raises interesting and important conceptual issues. From an economic point of view costs resulting in abandonment of exploration in a particular area should reasonably be expensed. By comparison, those that help to determine the boundaries of existing known resources or that provide valuable information leading to nearby discoveries should be capitalized.

52   Tax experts will recognize this proposition—like most of the present discussion—as an implication of the so-called Haig-Simon definition of income based on consumption plus increase in net wealth.

53   See, however, McLure, Mutti, Thuronyi, and Zodrow (1988).

54   See Steuerle (1985) and McLure, Mutti, Thuronyi, and Zodrow (1988), chapter 7.

55   It is generally necessary to limit the amount of capital losses that can be deducted. Otherwise taxpayers can pursue a strategy of realizing losses but letting gains "run" to take advantage of deferral. If both gains and losses could be constructively realized on an accrual basis, all losses should be deductible.

56 For a discussion of ways to overcome these problems, see Halperin and Steuerle (1988).

57 If, for example, the inflation rate was 4 percent, interest income and expense would be reduced by 40 percent under the Treasury I proposal. For a bond yielding 10 percent, the adjustment would be appropriate. But for one with a nominal yield of 5 percent the inflation adjustment should be 80 percent, rather than 40 percent. For any bond with a nominal yield in excess of 10 percent the inflation adjustment would be too great.

58 Suppose, for example, that a bank borrows at 8 percent and lends at 10 percent, realizing a spread of 2 percentage points. Presumably this spread is more or less independent of the rate of inflation, and it would be preserved by the conceptually correct approach to interest indexing. The Treasury Department approach would have eliminated a portion of the spread (40 percent in the case of a 4 percent inflation rate) from the tax base.

59 See Harberger (1982) and McLure, Mutti, Thuronyi, and Zodrow (1988).

60 For a more complete discussion, see McLure, Mutti, Thuronyi, and Zodrow (1987), chapter 7.

61 See U.S. Department of the Treasury (1985).

62 For a useful discussion of the mechanics of tax shelters, see U.S. Congress (1984).

63 In addition to the deferral advantages inherent in cash-basis taxation of long-term capital gains, the U.S. income tax provides a further benefit, step-up of basis at death. That is, when an appreciated asset is transferred at death, no income tax is paid on gains accruing before that time, and the recipient of the transfer takes the value at the time of death as the basis for calculating future capital gains. It is sometimes proposed that these benefits be reduced or eliminated through the use of constructive realization, either periodically or at the time of death. Besides being politically controversial, such an approach would raise severe administrative problems of valuing property.

64 It might be noted that seven types of interest expense can easily be identified; it has been said that there are as many as ten.

65 For a more complete discussion of the AMT and other anti-shelter provisions contained in the 1986 Act, see McLure (1987).

66 It is an indictment of the 1986 Act that the list of potentially important reforms not adopted is far longer than the list of important reforms that were adopted.

67 See McLure (forthcoming) for a description of U.S. tax laws that induce capital flight from developing countries.

68 This is the topic of McLure, Mutti, Thuronyi, and Zodrow (1988). Zodrow and McLure (1988) report a similar analysis of the consumption-based tax. The tax treatment accorded income from foreign sources by developed countries must be considered carefully in any such examination. The United States, for example, allows foreign tax credits only for taxes based on net income. It is not unlikely that the United States government would not classify as a tax on net income a tax that allowed no deduction for interest expense, even if immediate expensing were allowed for depreciable assets. Developing countries that rely heavily on American investment might be unwilling to change to a tax system based on consumption in the absence of assurance that the U.S. Treasury Department would allow a foreign tax credit for such taxes paid by American multinational firms.

References

Aaron, Henry J., and Harvey Galper. *Assessing Tax Reform*. Washington, D.C.: The Brookings Institution, 1985.

Andrews, William D. "Tax Neutrality Between Equity Capital and Debt." *Wayne Law Review*, vol. 30, no. 3 (1984), pp. 1057–71.

Atkinson, Anthony B., and Joseph E. Stiglitz. *Lectures on Public Economics*. McGraw-Hill, 1980.

Bailey, Martin J. "Progressivity and Investment Yields Under U.S. Income Taxation." *Journal of Political Economy*, vol. 82, no. 6 (November/December 1974), pp. 1157–75.

Bird, Richard M. "Income Tax Reform in Developing Countries: The Administrative Dimension." *Bulletin of the International Bureau of Fiscal Documentation*, vol. 37, no. 1 (January 1983), pp. 3–14.

———. "The Administrative Dimension of Tax Reform in Developing Countries." 1987 (photocopied).

Bradford, David F. "The Case for a Personal Consumption Tax." In *What Should Be Taxed: Income or Expenditures?* pp. 75–113. Edited by Joseph A. Pechman. Washington, D.C.: The Brookings Institution, 1980.

———. "The Economics of Tax Policy Toward Saving." In *The Government and Capital Formation*, pp. 11–71. Edited by George M. von Furstenberg. Cambridge, Mass.: Ballinger, 1980.

———. *Untangling the Income Tax*. Cambridge, Mass.: Harvard University Press, 1986.

Feldstein, Martin. "On the Theory of Tax Reform." *Journal of Public Economics*, vol. 6, nos. 1, 2 (July/August 1976), pp. 77–104.

———. "The Welfare Cost of Capital Income Taxation." *Journal of Political Economy*, vol. 86, no. 2 (April 1978, Part 2), pp. S29–S51.

Fullerton, Don. "The Indexation of Interest, Depreciation and Capital Gains and Tax Reform in the United States." *Journal of Public Economics*, vol. 32, no. 1 (February 1987), pp. 25–51.

Gillis, Malcolm, and Charles E. McLure, Jr. "The Incidence of the World's Taxes on Natural Resources with Special Reference to Bauxite." *American Economic Review*, vol. 65, no. 2 (May 1975), pp. 389–96.

Gillis, Malcolm, Carl S. Shoup, and Gerardo Sicat. *VAT in Developing Countries*. Forthcoming.

Hall, Robert E., and Alvin Rabushka. *The Flat Tax*. Stanford, Calif.: Hoover Institution Press, 1985.

Hall, Robert E., and Alvin Rabushka. *Low Tax, Simple Tax, Flat Tax*. New York: McGraw-Hill, 1983.

Halperin, Daniel, and Eugene Steuerle. "Indexing the Tax System for Inflation." in *Uneasy Compromise: Problems of a Hybrid Income-Consumption Tax*, pp. 347–72. Edited by Henry J. Aaron, Harvey Galper, and Joseph A. Pechman. Washington, D.C.: The Brookings Institution, 1988.

Harberger, Arnold C. "Taxation, Resource Allocation and Welfare." In *The Role of Direct and Indirect Taxes in the Federal Revenue System*, pp. 65–70. Edited by John F. Due. Princeton, N.J.: Princeton University Press, 1964.

———. "Notes on the Indexation of Income Taxes." Prepared for the Ministry of Finance of Indonesia, under the auspices of The Harvard Institute of Economic Development,

August 1982. Summarized in Uneasy Compromise, pp. 380–83.

Hulten, Charles R., and Frank C. Wykoff. "The Measurement of Depreciation." In *Depreciation, Inflation, and the Taxation of Income from Capital*, pp. 81–125. Edited by Charles R. Hulten. Washington, D.C.: Urban Institute, 1981.

King, M. A. "Savings and Taxation." In *Public Policy and the Tax System*. Edited by G. A. Hughes and G. M. Heal. London: George Allen and Unwin, Ltd., 1980, pp. 1–35.

McLure, Charles E., Jr. *Must Corporate Income Be Taxed Twice?* Washington, D.C.: The Brookings Institution, 1979.

———. "Taxes, Saving, and Welfare: Theory and Evidence." *National Tax Journal*, vol. 33, no. 3 (September 1980), pp. 311–20.

———. "The Tax Treatment of Owner-occupied Housing: The Achilles' Heel of Tax Reform?" In *Tax Reform and Real Estate*, pp. 219–32. Edited by James R. Follain. Washington, D.C.: Urban Institute Press, 1986. (a)

———. "Tax Competition: Is What's Good for the Private Goose Also Good for the Public Gander?" *National Tax Journal*, vol. 38, no. 3 (September, 1986), pp. 341–48. (b)

———. "Where Tax Reform Went Astray." *Villanova Law Review*, vol. 31, no. 6 (1986), pp. 1619–63. (c)

———. "U.S. Tax Reform." In *Australian Tax Reform*, the proceedings of a conference at Monash University, Melbourne, December 8–10, 1986. Edited by John Head.

———. "The 1986 Act: Tax Reform's Finest Hour or the Death Throes of the Income Tax." *National Tax Journal*, vol. 42, no. 3 (September 1988), pp. 303–15.

———. "U.S. Tax Laws and Capital Flight from Latin America." Forthcoming in *InterAmerican Law Review*, 1989.

McLure, Charles E., Jr., John Mutti, Victor Thuronyi, and George R. Zodrow, *The Taxation of Income from Business and Capital in Colombia*. A Report to the Finance Minister of Colombia, 1988, Durham, N.C.: Duke University Press, forthcoming.

McLure, Charles E., Jr., and George Zodrow. "Treasury I and the Tax Reform Act of 1986: The Economics and Politics of Tax Reform." *Economic Perspectives*, vol. 1, no. 1 (Summer 1987), pp. 37–58.

Newberry, David, and Nicholas Stern, *The Theory of Taxation for Developing Countries*. Oxford: Oxford University Press for the World Bank, 1987.

Sato, Mitsuo, and Richard M. Bird. "International Aspects of the Taxation of Corporations and Shareholders." International Monetary Fund *Staff Papers*, vol. 22 (July 1975), pp. 384–455.

Slemrod, Joel. "A General Equilibrium Model of Taxation with Endogenous Financial Behavior." In *Behavioral Simulation Methods in Tax Policy Analysis*, pp. 427–58. Edited by Martin Feldstein. Chicago: University of Chicago Press, 1983.

Steuerle, C. Eugene. *Taxes, Loans, and Inflation: How the Nation's Wealth Becomes Misallocated*. Washington, D.C.: The Brookings Institution, 1985.

Summers, Lawrence H. "Tax Policy and International Competitiveness." National Bureau of Economic Research Working Paper 2007 (August 1986).

Surrey, Stanley S., and Paul R. McDaniel. *Tax Expenditures*. Cambridge, Mass.: Harvard University Press, 1985.

Thirsk, Wayne R. "Taxes, Welfare, and Effective Tax Rates." DRD Discussion Paper no. 237, World Bank, Washington, D.C., 1987.

The President's Tax Proposals to the Congress for Fairness, Growth, and Simplicity. Washington, D.C.: U.S. Government Printing Office, May 1985.

U.S. Congress, House Committee on Ways and Means. "Proposals Relating to Tax Shelters and Other Tax-Motivated Transactions." Washington, D.C.: U.S. Government Printing Office, 1984.

U.S. Department of Treasury. *Blueprints for Basic Tax Reform.* Washington, D.C.: U.S. Government Printing Office, 1977.

U.S. Department of Treasury. *Tax Reform for Fairness, Simplicity, and Economic Growth.* Washington, D.C.: U.S. Government Printing Office, 1984.

U.S. Department of the Treasury. "Taxes Paid by High-Income Taxpayers and the Growth of Partnerships." Reprinted in *Tax Notes,* vol. 28 (August 12, 1985), pp. 717–20.

Warren, Alvin C., Jr. "The Timing of Taxes." *National Tax Journal,* vol. 39, no. 4 (December 1086), pp. 499–505.

Zodrow, George R., and Charles E. McLure, Jr. "Alternative Methods of Implementing Direct Consumption Taxes in Developing Countries." 1988 (photocopied).

11

On Using Computable General Equilibrium Models to Facilitate Tax, Tariff, and Other Policy Reforms in Less Developed Countries

·······

Edward Tower and Thomas Loo

1. Introduction

This paper is a guide for policy advisers on how to use computable general equilibrium models (CGEs) in the policy process. It draws heavily on Tower's work for the World Bank and USAID and on joint work of Loo and Tower. Discussion of this work is used to illustrate important elements of strategy in the use of computable general equilibrium models and the productive and efficient use of modelers. We argue that very useful linearized CGEs can be built and used effectively in very short periods of time. To be useful, they need only capture the most important interactions in an economy, because that is enough to illustrate economic principles that policymakers may be unaware of, and to give us better ideas of the costs and benefits of both good and bad policy initiatives. We also argue that the modeler should be closely linked to the policy advising process, because the links between model building, economic theory, and politics are critical. We note that distortion indicators like the effective rate of protection (ERP) and its variants have an important role to play, and we discuss the link between the newer CGEs and these older tools. We also discuss how one ought to formulate, build, debug, calibrate, and present a CGE, and the insights that emerge from the process.

Specifically, we draw on two World Bank Working Papers which deal with effective rates of protection (ERPs), domestic resource cost coefficients (DRCs) and shadow pricing. These papers develop refinements of the ERP concept and new ways to use them in the policy process, discuss pitfalls in the standard use of the domestic resource cost concept, and argue that shadow prices should always be presented next to a discussion of the CGE model which generated them.

We also draw on applied work with USAID in Sudan and Malawi, with the Harvard Institute for International Development in Indonesia, and joint work with a Malaysian national on tariff reform and shadow pricing in Malaysia. All of the work on particular countries has consisted of suggesting to policymakers what models, i.e., sets of assumptions, would be appropriate for solving pressing problems, and what kind of trade-offs they would imply. The work in Indonesia consisted of using ERPs in lieu of a full-fledged CGE to get at some of the same results that a CGE would have provided, but with an economy of effort. The work on Malaysia consisted of taking a sophisticated model of the Malaysian economy and paring it down and rearranging it to generate interesting cost/benefit ratios for hypothetical policy reform and project selection. The Sudanese work is similar, consisting of a CGE built by Kiyoun Han to analyze policy reform, with particular attention paid to alternative tax policies. The Malawian work assesses the subsidy on smallholder fertilizer. It features a CGE built to calculate the taxes which would be needed to finance the subsidy, and the effects of this package on efficiency and income distribution. The most recent work is an analysis of the effects of agricultural liberalization by the developed world on prototype less-developed countries. All of this work has generated some interesting cost/benefit ratios and provides approaches which we feel would be useful to others analyzing problems in particular LDCs.

This paper distills lessons for policy advisers who want to know what this modeling can be used for and how to direct it to get useful results quickly. It is also an attempt to pass on to other model builders some of the truths that we and our colleagues found as we worked to discover interesting questions and appropriate techniques for answering them.

2. A Short History of Modeling and Guide to the Current Literature

Much of the progress in the science of economics since the Mercantilists has consisted of replacing demand and supply curves with tools designed to capture the effects of economic policy on the entire economy. Early on, the analysis consisted of the discovery of truths like the fact that the Hume specie-flow mechanism will automatically generate balance of payments equilibrium and the Lerner symmetry theorem which notes that a tax on imports has the same effect on all real variables as a tax on exports. As a consequence of these theorems, an import tariff causes any import decline to be matched by an identical shrink-age in exports. Then, to capture the effects of perturbations in one market on economic welfare and its distribution, simple general equilibrium models like those by Stolper and Samuelson (1941), Solow (1956), and Jones (1965) were developed. Also, elements of interrelations between markets were introduced into structures that retained much of the simplicity of partial equilibrium modeling in Johnson (1960), Corden (1966), Tower and Pursell (1987), and others. Thus, until the advent of widespread low-cost computing capacity, especially PCs, the skill of model-building consisted of couching the problem at hand in a tractable way which permitted solution.

In the 1970s computer modeling techniques were developed which generated two important books on the subject: Dervis, deMelo, and Robinson (1982), henceforth DMR, who focus on modeling LDCs, and Dixon, Parmenter, Sutton, and Vincent (1982), henceforth DPSV, who present the ORANI model of the Australian economy. DMR present the approach which they developed and was used at the World Bank at the time. It consists of laying out all of the equations describing an economy and using numerical methods to simultaneously solve them. DPSV start out with a similar equation system, but to make solution easier, they differentiate it about its initial equilibrium in order to reduce their model to a set of simultaneous linear equations in the policy changes (e.g., taxes, tariffs, subsidies, exchange-rate changes, and government procurement policies) and the variables they influence (e.g., wages, outputs, and employments). The DPSV computational technique is easier, for one can build and solve a linearized model of this sort on a personal computer using common spreadsheet software with matrix capacities (such as Lotus 1-2-3, Excel or Quattro), and if one is satisfied with analyzing the effects of small changes, i.e., calculating multipliers, then it is perfectly adequate. Software has now become available which makes work with finite changes in models of the DMR type easier. Moreover, as DPSV note, it is possible to solve linearized models for large changes by thinking of them as a succession of small changes and updating the parameters of the model after each small change.

Both books are well worth skimming in order to develop a sense of the power and usefulness of these modeling techniques. Shoven and Whalley (1984) survey applications in general and Newberry and Stern (1987) contain a set of applications to tax policy in LDCs. For other recent contributions see Piggott and Whalley (1985), Stoeckel (1988), and Whalley (1985). Probably the most effective introduction is Robinson (1986) which discusses the logic of CGE modeling and the choices facing modelers. Then for examples of particularly sensible applications of these tools to important issues, presented in easily readable format, the reader should see Browning and Johnson (1984), Imam (1985), Judd (1987), de Melo (1978), Stuart (1984), Stoeckel (1985), and Taylor and Black (1974).

Interestingly, there have been relatively few applications of computable general equilibrium modeling to problems of LDCs at USAID. This is presumably because it is perceived as not being cost-effective. Since the simplest calculations are likely to be the most cost-effective in that they focus the policy debate on the important issues and produce immediate results, we will focus in this paper on the potential usefulness of relatively small linearized models.

3. Using CGEs to Illustrate Opportunity Costs of Projects and Policy Reforms

a. The Issues

In this section we discuss several policy experiments which we have undertaken using simple linearized models. In each case, we kept the model simple in order to keep down the costs of building the model, working with it, and understanding the results. Our goal was to teach an understanding of the economy, to develop a recognition that indirect effects of policy are important, to foster a sense of how important these effects are, and to encourage policymakers to contemplate better ways of achieving their targets. In each of the cases below we shall see how the exercise facilitated achievement of these targets.

b. Tariff Reform in Malaysia

Malaysia is a relatively free trader by the standards of low-income and lower-middle-income LDCs, although its protection is slightly higher than normal by the standards of upper-middle-income LDCs, which is the group in which it lies.[1] In 1971 its average import tariff on manufactured items was a mere 14.7 percent, although its export tariff on agricultural goods was a substantial 22.0 percent. Thus Malaysia would appear to be a fairly poor platform on which to demonstrate the benefits of tariff reform. Yet Malaysian data were in good shape as they had been assembled for a model developed for the Economic Planning Unit of Malaysia by Frank Lysy et al. While the Lysy model was quite disaggregated both by sector and types of consumer, it had never been used to simulate the effects on economic welfare of alternative policy initiatives—an example of wasteful misuse of model-building resources. Consequently, Gan and Tower (1987) (henceforth GT) used these data to build a simple 5-sector model of Malaysia with a representative consumer and intermediate inputs used in fixed proportions in combination with a value-added composite comprised of labor, land, and capital to assess the consequences of changed tariffs. Two models were simulated. In the short-run model, capital was assumed to be sector-specific, and in the long-run model, it was variable with investment proceedings until the after-tax rate on investment in Malaysia was driven to equality with that in the rest of the world. Labor was assumed to be homogeneous when measured in efficiency units and domestic wages and prices were perfectly flexible, so that resources were fully employed. Also, Malaysia was assumed to trade internationally at fixed world prices.

In order to get results that would mean something to policymakers GT couched all of their results in terms of interesting cost/benefit ratios rather than absolute magnitudes of effects measured in currency units, a strategy that we believe is effective if one is to have a policy impact. GT's criterion for the impact of policy was the change in Malaysian real income or welfare, measured as the change in consumption valued at the prices paid by consumers, which is the extra amount of money which would need to be given to Malaysian households at constant prices in order to result in the same utility change for them as the policy change does.

GT found that the welfare cost of using tariff protection to maintain employment in import-competing was 91 percent of the value of employment created at the margin in the short run and 113 percent in the long run. The welfare gain from creating agricultural employment by cutting the agricultural export tax was 76 percent of the value of employment created in the short run and 73 percent in the long run. GT found it surprising that the welfare costs of using import tariffs to create import-competing employment would be as high as they were, and that the welfare gains from export tariff reductions would be so great. However, these results are not so surprising in light of the fact that these tariff rates created ERPs of 55 percent and −26 percent for import-competing manufacturing and agriculture respectively in the short run with corresponding figures of 2.7 percent and −48 percent in the long run. Also, the import and export tariffs combine to yield a domestic relative price of import-competing manufactured items relative to agricultural goods of 147 percent of the world relative price. This is to say that the import and export taxes on international trade combine to yield an implicit tax on international trade of 47 percent, which is quite substantial.

Several lessons emerge here:

The cost/benefit ratios turned out to be quite similar under very different specifications of the model, so that uncertainty as to how a model should be specified is not enough to disregard the use of such calculations.

It is important to perform both short- and long-run calculations. Recall Keynes' remark, "In the long run we are all dead," and as others have observed, the long run is just a succession of short runs. Thus it is misleading to present the results for just one adjustment mechanism, just as it is important for policy advisers to think seriously about both long- and short-run consequences. It is misleading to take ERP calculations at face value. In the long run the capital stock is an intermediate input, rather than a fixed factor, and should be treated as such in ERP calculations, and making the adjustment in this case had a profound impact on the numerical values for the ERPs.

Another reason to impose tariffs besides employment creation could be to collect tax revenue. Lowering the agricultural export tax was found to raise both revenue and real income in both the long run and short runs while raising the tariff on import-competing manufacturing raises revenue in the short run, but shrinks revenue in the long run. But even in the short run the marginal welfare cost of using a hike in the tariff on import competing manufacturing to raise revenue is 224 percent, which makes it a very costly revenue-raising instrument. This is clear evidence of the Laffer curve, which GT had not anticipated. Thus GT found that their intuition had not been a particularly good guide to general equilibrium orders of magnitude. Having a sense of proportion is important to successful policymaking, and these sorts of calculations are necessary to achieve such a sense.

There is a serious danger that once a model is built, it will be used to answer the question at hand, but will have no usefulness subsequently. For this reason, GT argue strongly that policy advisers should present in matrix form the entire set of their multipliers for the effect of each policy they consider on each variable which policymakers might be concerned about. In this way others can use the simulations to explore the implications of other closure rules. For example, with such a set of multipliers from the GT paper, they could calculate the effect on economic welfare and its distribution of increasing the excise tax on consumption of manufactured items, while adjusting the import tariff by just enough to leave revenue unchanged, even though this precise calculation was not performed in the paper itself. Alternatively, they could calculate how much increased unemployment (modeled as withdrawal of labor from private sector economic activity) could accompany a reduction in the import tariff and still leave economic welfare no lower that it was initially.

Another use to which GT put the model was to calculate shadow prices of goods, labor, and, in the short run, the capital stocks in various sectors. The shadow price of an item is the impact of economic welfare of a unit increase in the quantity of that item provided by the government to the private sector, assuming that the economy adjusts fully to the change in the quantity, using a postulated adjustment mechanism. These calculations are useful for assessing the welfare implications of hypothetical government projects. For example, the welfare impact of a government project which absorbs two worker-years of time to produce a manufactured item would be the shadow price of the manufactured item minus the shadow price of two worker-years of labor time.

To the extent that distorting taxes are used to raise revenue to finance government projects, shadow prices will depend on the revenue sources used to finance government projects, and the GT paper shows how the shadow-price calculations of a linearized model under one revenue assumption can be modified by the user to calculate shadow prices under other revenue assumptions without performing new matrix inversions. While it might seem that such shadow-price calculations would have policy implications which are relevant only for specific hypothetical projects, they are also important tools for assessing the role of import substituting versus export promoting strategies.

For example, GT calculated a short-run shadow price for investment in import-competing manufacturing of $.13, which is to say that an investment in import-competing manufacturing which earns $1 annually will make an annual contribution to Malaysian welfare of only 13 cents.[2] This reflects the fact that increased import competing manufacturing investment will draw labor out of exportable agriculture where it is earning less than its marginal product at world prices and move it into import-competing manufacturing where it is earning more than its marginal product at world prices. This results in substantial loss of export revenues and a small savings of foreign exchange spent on manufacturing imports, for a small net gain in economic welfare. By contrast, the shadow price of the fixed factor in the agricultural export sector was $1.82, which is to say that an investment in agriculture which earns $1.00 annually will make an annual contribution to Malaysian welfare of $1.82. These calculations stress the importance of investing in export promotion as opposed to import-competing activity in the event that incentives cannot be adjusted to make this occur naturally.

c. Trade, Tax, and Agricultural Policy Reform in Sudan

Sudan is an example of a highly distorted economy. In fact, the economy is so distorted that clear thinking about it is difficult without explicit modeling of the sort that Kiyoun Han (1988) has done. Because of the very substantial tax and subsidy distortions, the desirability of any policy initiative depends critically on the manner in which taxes are handled in the simulations. The wheat market is highly distorted. Some wheat is imported and other wheat is grown domestically. Farmers are permitted to sell some proportion of their crop at market prices but are required to sell the rest to the government at below market prices, which the government then sells, again at subsidized rates. Agricultural nonwheat exports plus foreign aid pay for the import of intermediate inputs and final consumption goods. The multiple exchange rate, the wheat procurement policy, the import tariff on final goods which averages 76.4 percent, and the export tax on agricultural goods which averages 4.4 percent, together imply very different effective rates of protection in Sudan: 422 percent for industry, 22.6 percent for wheat, and −4.7 percent for other agriculture.

For years, USAID has been trying to convince the Sudanese to devalue the official exchange rate at which agricultural exports and certain intermediate imports are valued in order to bring it into line with the free market exchange rate which applies to final goods. The effect of the exchange-rate policy has been to disadvantage agriculture relative to industry. Recently, USAID has also been trying to convince the Sudanese to privatize the wheat sector.

Using a model containing only the three tradeable sectors mentioned above and nontradable services, where agricultural labor moves freely between the two agricultural sectors, urban labor moves freely between industry and services, labor is always fully employed, and lump-sum taxes are used to hold the exchange rates constant, Han has derived some striking results. Some of the most interesting are the following.

Industry is so highly protected that the import tariff on final industrial goods exceeds its maximum revenue level. Thus lowering it raises both revenue and welfare.

The multiple exchange rate regime serves as a tax. The government in effect taxes agricultural exports by giving farmers few Sudanese pounds for each dollar's worth of exports. It then uses the foreign exchange obtained for its own purposes and for specially selected imports. The foreign exchange which is not used up is then in effect auctioned off to the private sector at the free rate. Thus the only way to appreciate the free pound is to draw resources out of the economy by raising tax revenues, so that the number of pounds which will be bid for foreign exchange shrinks. He finds that the marginal welfare costs of raising revenue via a less favorable exchange rate for industrial imports or agricultural exports are 3,500 percent and 2,200 percent respectively! Thus they are both close to their maximum revenue levels.

The marginal welfare cost of using higher agricultural export taxes to raise revenue is 538 percent. This reflects the already high taxes on imports and exports, and dramatizes the need to improve the exchange rate for agricultural exports or else cut the explicit agricultural export tax.

Raising the official wheat procurement price or lowering the required proportion sold in the official market will encourage wheat cultivation. Whether this is a good idea is uncertain, since the ERP for wheat lies between that of industry and other agriculture. Thus, his calculation that the welfare cost of using either of these policies to attract labor to the wheat sector is 197 percent of the labor attracted is an important one. Privatization of the Sudanese wheat market is in effect a reduction of the official procurement percentage. Thus USAID should be wary of this policy without accompanying it with its sister policy of a better exchange rate for agriculture.

Moreover, the desirability of depreciating the official exchange rate at which agricultural exports are valued is reflected in Han's calculation that for each additional Sudanese pound's worth of increased agricultural exports made possible by the exchange-rate change, Sudanese real income rises by 2.07 Sudanese pounds. Han finds that the gain in real income from driving the free market rate closer to the official rate is 346 percent of the reduction of Sudanese industrial output which it makes possible. This illustrates the importance of unifying the two exchange rates in order to drive resources from industry back into agriculture, which is also consistent with reform efforts of the IMF.

Han finds that cutting import tariff protection raises real income by 3.7 times the value of industrial employment thereby destroyed, which illustrates the importance of freer trade.

In each of these simulations the free market exchange rate was assumed to be maintained by varying nondistorting taxes, and not surprisingly the figures varied when the adjustment was assumed to be accomplished with taxes with very large positive or negative marginal welfare costs. This in itself is an important lesson to be stressed about the functioning of the Sudanese economy. Appreciating the free market exchange rate to be closer to the official one will be undesirable if the necessary withdrawal of purchasing power from the economy is effected by increasing highly distorting taxes. Finally, assuming that the government budget is financed at the margin by adjustment of the free exchange rate, the shadow price of dollars in the hands of the government is an exchange rate of 158 Sudanese pounds/$ compared with an agricultural rate of 2.5 Sudanese pounds/$. Moreover, the shadow prices of urban and rural labor are market values multiplied by 34 and 66 respectively! This means that in the absence of fiscal reform or adjustments in existing taxes, the government should scrutinize very carefully the projects that use up these resources. Similarly high shadow prices emerge for other resources. Thus some shrinkage of existing government activities would be good.

d. Tax Finance of a Fertilizer Subsidy in Malawi

In 1987 USAID sponsored a study of the desirability of proceeding to remove the subsidy to fertilizer purchased by Malawian smallholders. Tower's contribution was a series of short (three- to five-page) essays on various aspects of the issue, which were discussed with policymakers as soon as they were written. Tower became convinced that the focus of the policymakers was partial equilibrium in the sense that the costs of raising the revenue and increasing exports by enough to finance the importation of subsidized fertilizer was not being adequately reckoned with in the policy debate, and that the most important role of the team was to enable the policymakers to understand the issues involved. Consequently, Tower and Christiansen (1987) built a model to illustrate the tradeoffs.

Distortions in the Malawian economy included an inefficient agricultural marketing board, restrictions on private agricultural trading, import restrictions, and foreign exchange licensing. To build a model which reckons with all of these distortions was daunting, and it seemed to us to be perverse policymaking strategy to use a fertilizer subsidy to correct distortions elsewhere in the economy. Therefore, we chose to model the Malawian economy as if (1) the tax reform, which is designed to replace variable excise taxes and import tariffs with a value-added tax (VAT) on industrial output, had already been enacted, (2) foreign exchange licensing, which the Reserve Bank of Malawi intends to eliminate, had already been eliminated, and (3) the government of Malawi had already acted on its officially stated plan to open up agricultural trading to the private sector. This left the value-added tax on the industrial sector as the only distortion in the economy, and we modeled the increase in the fertilizer subsidy as being financed by an increase in this tax. From start to finish we had only a week to work on the model (including learning how to use the Lotus 1-2-3 software necessary to invert our matrix), so we kept it very simple, assuming a representative consumer, a single industrial sector, two industrial sectors whose exports paid for imported fertilized and industrial inputs, and fully employed labor which migrated between the industrial and agricultural sectors in response to wage differentials.

Out of this simple 33-equation model we still generated some sensible results which served to focus the debate. For example, we found that

the marginal efficiency cost of using a higher fertilizer subsidy financed by an increase in the VAT to create increased employment in agriculture was 57 percent of the wages paid out to new hires
the marginal efficiency cost of using a higher VAT-financed fertilizer subsidy to create increased agricultural consumption was 43 percent of the increased agricultural consumption created
the marginal efficiency cost of using a higher VAT-financed fertilizer subsidy to create increased real income for those initially in the smallholder sector was 34 percent of the increased real income created.

Finally, our intention initially had been just to focus on efficiency cost of the fertilizer subsidy. But the income distributional effects also turned out to be instructive. We found that a 10 percent reduction in the smallholder fertilizer price would raise the real rental rate on smallholder land by 1.4 percent while decreasing the real industrial wage by 0.22 percent, decreasing the real agricultural wage by 0.04 percent, decreasing the real after tax rent on industrial capital by 0.6 percent, and decreasing the real rental rate on estate sector agricultural land (which was not eligible for the fertilizer subsidy and suffers a drain of labor to the smallholder section) by 2.0 percent. Since real wages fell, it was hard to argue that the fertilizer subsidy had desirable income distribution effects. We were delighted when in response to our paper one member of the Malawian Ministry of Agriculture mentioned that he had never thought before about the fact that the fertilizer subsidy would impose costs elsewhere in the economy, as driving that one message home was our primary goal.

In thinking about the fertilizer subsidy we were faced with a number of imponderables:

How big are the distortions in agriculture due to lack of knowledge by smallholders?

How big is the implicit tax levied on agricultural output by fixing output prices at parity prices denominated in local currency prior to planting, in the face of anticipated inflation and currency depreciation?

How will the fertilizer subsidy be financed?

Will the additional fertilizer imports be financed by currency depreciation or more stringent import licencing of industrial intermediate inputs or additional foreign aid?

To model every contingency would require excessive resources. Thus, we adopted what seems to us to be a reasonable strategy for all model builders. We simulated one model as a bench mark, and discussed how deviations from that set of assumptions would be likely to affect the results.

e. The Effects on LDCs of Agricultural Policy in Developed Countries

The useful applications of simple linearized CGEs specifically tailored to address particular issues in economic development are not confined to tax and tariff questions in LDCs themselves. General equilibrium modeling can also be used to clarify the impact of policymaking with regard to tax, trade, and industrial policy in developed countries on LDCs, so that the tradeoffs between various policy options can be quantified. Recently Loo and Tower (1988) examined the effects of developed countries' agricultural policies on LDCs in the context of a general equilibrium model designed to apply to all LDCs, and there is no reason why developed country tax reforms of various forms could not be examined as well. Our model was a simple one which recognized four sectors: agriculture, industry, services, and mining and petroleum. All sectors use a sector specific factor in combination with labor and an imported intermediate input to produce output. Exports of all three traded items plus net transfers to the country in the form of aid minus debt service paid for imports of intermediate and final goods. Labor was always fully employed and partially mobile between sectors, production functions and consumption functions used inputs in variable proportions, and the ratio in which goods were consumed depended solely on relative prices.

Before we started to model, we knew the story we wished to tell. Agricultural protectionism is an issue of critical importance to LDCs, since most of them are net exporters of agricultural commodities and have the potential to export considerably more should developed countries liberalize their agricultural policies. But the importance to them of liberalized agricultural markets extends beyond a casual glance at the numbers describing their trade and production. Anne Krueger (1983) and the 1986 *World Development Report* (among others) both document that less-developed countries typically tax their agriculture through export taxes and the activities of agricultural marketing boards and subsidize their industry through trade, tax, and credit market policies which bestow high effective rates of protection on them. Krueger argues that in addition to imposing an efficiency cost, such policies also serve to worsen the income distribution, because the poorest members of LDCs are typically those employed in agriculture.

All of these factors mean that gaining extra earnings of foreign exchange via increased agricultural production is a particularly effective way of generating resources for LDCs. The reasoning is the following: the taxation of the agricultural export sector in LDCs means that in agriculture considerably less than a dollar's worth of resources at domestic prices is required to earn a dollar's worth of foreign currency at the margin, whereas the subsidization of industry means that in industry, considerably more than a dollar's worth of resources at domestic prices is required to save a dollar's worth of foreign exchange. Thus, if resources are drawn from industry into agriculture to meet increased external demand, for each extra dollar earned considerably less than a dollar's worth of resources needs to be transferred into agriculture, and the transfer of these resources costs the industrial sector considerably less than a dollar of increased industrial imports in order to make up for the lost domestic production. The result is a considerable increase in foreign exchange earnings at given world prices.[3]

Moreover, the rise in both imports of industrial goods and exports of agricultural goods means that government tariff and export tax revenues rise. To the extent that this enhanced revenue enables LDC governments to reduce the level of distorting taxes, and/or tariffs, there will be a further gain in economic efficiency, which raises the standard of living.

We modeled agricultural liberalization in the developed world as 10 percent across the board in all world agricultural prices, including the prices of LDC agricultural imports. The poorest LDCs are those which discriminate most markedly against agriculture. Thus we will focus on our results for them. Our most striking results for them were:

Each dollar transferred from developed countries to the LDCs via higher agricultural prices raised LDC real income by $7.87, where the transfer is defined as the initial level of LDC net exports multiplied by the price change, which is simply the first-order term of a consumers' surplus expression, and the change in real income is defined as the change in consumption at initial prices. This indicates the importance to LDCs of keeping world agricultural markets open.

For each dollar transferred to the LDC via better agricultural prices, LDCs could increase their payment of interest or principal on their debt by $6.38 and still leave their real incomes unchanged. Thus, trade is 6.38 times as effective as debt forgiveness. If all of these repayments went to failing banks, then the need for developed countries to collect tax revenues to bail out their banking systems would be reduced, which would result in a further increase in their real income. Assuming (somewhat arbitrarily) a marginal welfare cost of tax collection in developed countries of 40 percent which would be needed to finance foreign aid, transferring a dollar through better agricultural prices means that this reduction in foreign aid would result net in an increase in $7.93 in developed country real income.

Assuming that debt repayment is held constant, so that the LDCs spend their increased real income on increased imports, every extra dollar's worth of net agricultural imports (at initial prices) accepted from LDCs by developed countries enables developed countries to export an additional $1.08 worth of industrial goods. This illustrates the importance of recognizing that agricultural protectionism in developed countries in effect taxes their exports.

A transfer through higher agricultural prices also has a more salutary impact on increasing the real income of the poorest workers in the economy, who are those in agriculture, than does the same size of debt forgiveness. We found that its impact on the agricultural real wage is 5.9 times that of the same debt forgiveness and its impact on the real incomes of all factors initially employed in agriculture is 10 times that of the same debt forgiveness.

A 10 percent increase in world agricultural prices should increase real incomes of all less-developed countries by $25.9 billion if there were no change in aid or debt repayment.

A 10 percent increase in world agricultural prices should increase the real income in the developed world by $12.38 billion if debt repayment is increased by enough to leave LDC real income unchanged. This is $69.36 per citizen of the United States or 0.416 percent of U.S. GNP.

f. Conclusions

The major points that we have tried to illustrate above are that with tax reform as in trade policy reform it is possible to build highly aggregated models in order to illustrate economic trade-offs and to develop plausible estimates of how important they are. A well-constructed study can develop the simulation results in such a way that policymakers are forced to see how policy reforms can facilitate achievement of the ends they seek. Unfortunately, many modeling efforts are undertaken without a clear goal in mind. Consequently they generate little political action. In *The Game Plan* the Centre for International Economics (1987, p. 71) reminds us, "If research is not worth doing, it is not worth doing well." This message's lessons for model builders is that any expenditure of resources on modeling should be directed at an important policy initiative. Our experience is that it makes sense to build the model solely for the purpose at hand in order to keep costs low. Then when other answers are needed the model can be modified accordingly. For example if one wishes to calculate the impact on exports of import tariff and quota restrictions, in the first instance it makes no sense to disaggregate either the import bill beyond those items feeding into a highly aggregated model.[4]

4. On Modeling

Now let us turn to some aspects of how to select and implement a model to deal with a policy problem. We view modeling as a dialogue in which policymakers express their goals and concerns, and the model builder places them all into a framework that incorporates economic truths in order to generate a set of policy recommendations.

a. Model Formulation

There are three stages in the process of model formulation. First, the modeler must learn the conventional wisdom or rationale for the existing policy. This involves talking with policymakers about how they view the economy and what they perceive the consequences of policy changes would be. Second, the modeler must pick a story that describes how the economy works, so that he can model how it will respond to the policy initiative that he wishes to examine. This may involve focusing on elements that policymakers have ignored like the effects of a particular aspect of tax policy on income distribution or of import barriers on export levels. Third, the minimal model that will tell the story must be selected. The minimal model is selected because simpler models are easier to construct and explain, and the more quickly the model can be constructed, the more time will be left to explore variations of it, either formally or in informal discussion about how the real world differs from the bench mark model. It is important that the model address the specific concerns of the policymaker in the country. Therefore, it is important for the modeler to start with a simple model and show what can be done in a reasonable period of time coupled with an offer to explore other questions. Discussions of the mechanisms that would be germane to model construction is a good way to get policymakers and others who are concerned about the efficient functioning of the economy thinking about the mechanisms that drive it and for the model builder to learn about how it works.[5]

b. Model Building

The purpose of model building is to stretch the intuition and to calculate tradeoffs. A model that cannot be understood is of little use, because no one will believe the results. Economists and policymakers are accustomed to thinking in terms of a demand-and-supply framework, and it is desirable to start with a model that the client can easily understand. The general equilibrium model that fits this intuition most closely is a specific factors model of the kind developed by GT, discussed above, in which the capital stock is fixed in each sector while labor is allowed to move relatively freely between sectors. Such a model also describes the kind of short-run equilibrium that is relevant to the three- to five-year time horizon that is likely to be important to policymakers. The results of this sort of model tend to fit quite closely with intuition and to develop the client's trust.

However, the modeler should not stop here, because elasticities of demand and supply will be lower in the short run than they would be over a longer time horizon, so that simulations may be qualitatively quite different over the two horizons. Thus, for example, a short-run focus will lead policymakers to conclude that they have more capacity to levy taxes in order to raise revenues and affect the income distribution without markedly influencing efficiency than is in fact the case. Thus policy based on short-run modeling is likely to trap the economy in an inefficient trajectory. Consequently, we advocate following up the specific factors modeling exercise with one in which savings depends on the after-tax rate of return and capital and labor are perfectly or highly mobile between sectors. Such a strategy will generate the conclusions that taxation imposes a high welfare cost and that broad-based taxation is best, but these conclusions are the appropriate ones over a long time horizon.

c. Debugging

The modeling experience that we have had is building linearized models from scratch, using Lotus 1-2-3 without the use of a canned program. Thus, our advice should be interpreted accordingly. We have found that new modelers should start with simulating a model that is so simple that they can intuit it completely or solve it analytically, so that they can master the problems associated with the computer software in a context where error search consumes little time. In simulating both this simple version and the final model it is important to isolate the parameter specification from the equation system. An important role of modeling is to find how policy multipliers depend on parameters and initial conditions. Therefore, we construct the coefficient matrices in the Lotus spreadsheet to consist of parameters and initial levels whose particular values are specified elsewhere in the program. Our strategy is to construct the algorithm so that the modeler can specify the requisite parameters and initial levels with the program calculating the remaining parameters and initial levels so as to generate an internally consistent equilibrium. This facilitates learning about how policy multipliers depend on the structure of the model. It makes modification of the model easy. It makes it easy to use numerical integration of the type discussed by DPSV (1982) to assess the impact of finite tax policy changes, which, of course, characterize changes in policy regimes. Finally, it facilitates debugging of the model.

We have found that in guiding others in the building of models it is too time-consuming and boring to check on every equation in their model. Rather, we discuss the structure of the model and the closure rules used. We then ask the modeler to simulate the distortionless case, where there are no tax or trade distortions in the model whatsoever and world prices are fixed. In this case, the marginal welfare cost of any incremental change in taxes will be zero, and all shadow prices will equal market prices. Any deviation from these results indicates a bug in the model, and the pattern of deviations provides useful clues in figuring out where the bugs are. We refer to this process as global error-checking.

The next step is to develop an intuitive mastery of the distortions involved. Thus, we ask the modeler to present a table of the distortions involved along with a table of effective rates of protection (calculated according to the technique of GT [1987] when there are nontraded goods). We then perturb the model in various ways, using lump-sum taxation to balance the government budget, and checking to be sure that the results correspond with intuition. When the effects on economic efficiency are inconsistent with intuition, we decompose the change in real income as the sum of the incremental flows of goods and factor services across distortions, with each change multiplied by the size of the distortion à la Tower (1984a) and Loo and Tower (1988). This enables us to break down the real income change into a series of production, trade, and consumption effects, which is a useful way of describing the intuition of the calculation and facilitates further intuitive description. As part of this stage of the investigation we calculate the marginal welfare cost of raising revenue via various taxes, where this ratio is defined as the incremental change in real income per incremental change in total real revenues collected and rebated via a lump sum tax as a result of an incremental increase in the tax rate in question. The final stage is to simulate the model using feasible tax closures.

The lesson of this section is that the debugging process is carried on in concert with development of the intuition. As Deardoff and Stern (1986, pp. 221–22) put it ". . . the modeling effort is not complete until it yields only *expected* results—in general terms, of course, since we do not require that specific numerical answers be altogether predictable . . . . [But] the feedback phase of modeling is as often as much a process of revising expectations as it is of revising the model itself."

d. Calibration

One of our colleagues is fond of saying, "One should be familiar with computable general equilibrium models, but shouldn't believe in any numbers they generate." This is because such models are sensitive to parameter values, specification, and closures used. In fact, one could make the same remark about economic analysis generally. How do we make our results believable and useful? We need to assure the client that the model has "reasonable" properties. What properties are reasonable depend on the time horizon considered. Factor mobility and savings supply elasticities are likely to be larger in the long run than the short run. Thus, we have found it useful to perform a variety of simulations designed to approximate short and long runs, although we have been content to work with our best point estimate of parameter values, whose values we believed would be relatively constant through time. It may well be that the policymaker has a near-term budgetary problem, so he is interested in near-term benefits and that his proposed solution will achieve these at a cost of long-term prosperity. In such a case two models or two sets of parameter values would be needed to evaluate the trade-off.

Also, results should be consistent with results from other state-of-the-art studies. In some cases, the modeler is able to draw on econometric work or the judgment of experts to develop a good sense of plausible values for general equilibrium elasticities of demand or supply, and it is desirable to experiment with underlying elasticities of substitution so that simulations of the model are consistent with this extraneous evidence. For example, Loo and Tower (1988) asked various experts what they believed the marginal welfare cost of tax collection to be and adjusted the micro parameters of the tax collection process to be consistent with these estimates.

e. Presentation

Typically, a modeler has many relatively uninteresting decisions to make about the exact specification of the model, and the number of parameters, variables, and equations tends to be large, and tedious to explain. Therefore, in common with other model builders, we prefer to lay out the precise mathematical specification in appendices. Then the body of the paper consists of (1) a description of the basic idea of the model, (2) a description of the broad outline of the model, accompanied by a schematic diagram which describes goods and factor service flows, (3) discussion of how the economy responds to various shocks to facilitate intuition about how the economy works, and (4) tables which present the important cost/benefit calculations which emerge accompanied by descriptions of the mechanisms which explain their signs and sizes.

In Loo and Tower (1988), we found it desirable to present the change in real income from selected perturbations of the model as the sum of the incremental flows of goods and factors across distortions multiplied by respective distortions. This demonstrates the extent to which the results are driven by the various distortions. It also facilitates making reasonable estimates about how the results would have been affected had different distortion levels been selected. We also presented a simple geometric analysis of a simplified version of the model in order to characterize the forces which lead to our major results. In fact, when the paper is presented in person, this simple geometric version serves as the focal point of the seminar, and once the participants have mastered the basic issues involved, they readily understand the calculations emerging from the detailed model. Finally, we like to close the paper with a discussion of which assumptions are driving the results and how the conclusions would differ under other circumstances. This presentational strategy differs considerably from that used by many authors, but we believe that it is a useful one to follow generally.

5. What Can Distortion Indicators Tell Us?
In Defense of ERP-Type Concepts

A consensus seems to have developed that the ERP is a partial equilibrium concept, and that CGEs have made use of the concept archaic. There is one mathematical formula for the Corden ERP, which involves integrating tradable goods sectors with the nontradables sectors which feed into them, and which we believe is the most generally useful definition of the ERP.[6] Although there are four different ways to interpret the concept as GT note, there is one particularly useful one: The incremental cost-benefit ratio approach thinks of the Corden ERP coefficient as the ratio of the value of primary factors at domestic market prices attracted into a sector at the margin divided by the change in foreign exchange earned or saved, assuming that inputs and outputs in all other tradeable goods sectors, the consumption bundle, and world prices are frozen. (For references to the literature see Tower 1984b, p. 128.) Thus it can be calculated as the product of a simulation which assumes that the government releases one unit of a primary factor of production from a project into the economy, where the output of each tradeable goods sector but the ith is held constant by (say) an immobile labor force or direct controls, and consumption is frozen by excise tax adjustments or the combination of a fixed-proportions consumption function and lump-sum tax variation which leaves real expenditure unchanged.

The ERP coefficient for the ith sector is then given by the ratio of the primary factor absorbed by the ith sector and the nontradeables that feed into it to the change in the economy's balance of trade (net earnings of foreign currency) evaluated at the market exchange rate. Moreover, while we have some difficulty figuring out how the Corden ERP should be modified when distortions and the tax system are complete, this approach leads us to a useful and easy-to-remember way to calculate the ERP, and is the technique that GT (1987) used to calculate their ERPs.

This interpretation of the ERP is a measure of the efficiency of the sector in converting primary factor services into factor exchange. Moreover, it is the product of a well-defined simulation, so it is a general equilibrium calculation in the sense that we know conceptually how policy instruments are being manipulated in our thought experiment, and we have left nothing out. Thus, we feel that it is best to describe the ERP as a simple general equilibrium concept, reserving the term partial equilibrium for those analyses where the analyst has not figured out what things he is holding constant, or where he has recognized that he is only approximating the truth.

The implication of this incremental cost/benefit approach is that shifting a dollar's worth of primary factors from sector m to sector X will result in increased net foreign exchange earnings equal to:

$$1/[1 + \mathrm{ERP_X}] - 1/[1 + \mathrm{ERP_m}]$$
$$= [\mathrm{ERP_m} - \mathrm{ERP_X}]/\{[1 + \mathrm{ERP_X}][1 + \mathrm{ERP_m}]\}$$

Thus, any policies which drive primary factors from sector m into sector X will be beneficial. For example, if sector m is an importable with an ERP of 422 percent and X is an exportable with an ERP of -5 percent (to use Han's figures for industry and agricultural exports in Sudan), cutting protection to m while devaluing the currency to maintain aggregate competitiveness would be desirable, in that for every 100 Sudanese pounds worth of labor and capital shifted net foreign exchange earnings would rise by 86 Sudanese pounds, which could then be allocated to expenditure on other needed goods. To conclude, the ERP can be useful in discussions of the potential benefits from policy reform, and it is a perfectly respectable rigorous concept.

Finally, no one is impressed by results from CGES which cannot be explained, because such exercises do not tickle the intuition, and in explaining the results of a CGE simulation it is often helpful to draw on sector by sector estimates of ERPs in combination with the factor flows that result from perturbations of the model.

Although we find the ERP to be a useful tool for policy analysis in the senses mentioned above, we are much more wary about using the DRC. Tower (1984b, 1987, and 1988b) argues that the DRC has been used to mean very different things by different investigators, who have not always realized that they are using different concepts from one another. Consequently, a DRC per se has no meaning unless the user describes exactly what he means by the concept. Moreover, to calculate a DRC requires estimates of shadow prices of primary factors, which can only be obtained from a general equilibrium model, so it is hard to see how DRCs can do anything that cannot be more easily done with appropriate use of multipliers from a general equilibrium model as described in GT (1987).[7]

6. Conclusion: On the Definition of an Economist

This paper has covered a number of disparate points about the use of CGEs in the tax and policy reform process. We have used a large number of subheadings for easy access. Thus, we will dispense with a detailed summary. Instead, let us finish with two truths which provide a useful focus for thinking about CGE modeling.

It is sometimes said that all one must do to train a parrot to be an economist is to teach him to say "supply and demand." Not so, we argue. What he needs to say is "opportunity cost." The critical role of an economist is to point out the hidden costs or benefits of policy initiatives, and the appropriate use of CGEs is to formulate policy issues in terms of opportunity costs that matter and to measure them.[8]

We tend to view our role as economists as providing answers as to how the economy works, and to judge our worth in terms of how good an answer we provide. Taken to its extreme, this could turn economics into a very dismal science indeed as we attempt to disaggregate our CGEs until every sector of conceivable importance is covered. But what economists are remembered for is not the answers they provide but the questions they ask. For example, once a policymaker is convinced to think about the effects of import restrictions on exports, much of the battle against protectionism is won, and while different ways of closing the CGE, selecting data for it and picking parameter values will generate different answers as to exactly how import barriers will affect exports, once the policymaker is trained to ask this particular question, he is much less likely to advocate protectionism as a way to serve the social good. Remembering that "it is the question you ask rather than the answer you provide" allows the modeler to use his questions to focus on the important mechanisms in the development process, and to set the policy debate on a firm intellectual foundation. Building CGES to calculate opportunity costs using intellectually respectable causal mechanisms raises the level of policy debate to consider the right issues. Once that is done, and policymakers have been convinced that basic truths have been captured, then perhaps larger, more disaggregated models which trace out multisectoral development paths will have a role to play; but it is more fun and profitable to ask the right questions and expose the wrong myths using manageable and easy-to-construct-CGES before disaggregating them to obtain micro-level predictions.[9]

Notes

Thanks go to Malcolm Gillis, Arnold Harberger, and Glenn Jenkins for comments.

1   See Loo and Tower (1988) for the definitions of LDC groups, which are drawn from the *World Development Report*, and for informed guesses about protection levels in each country group.
2   Strictly speaking, the figures reported here are conversion factors rather than shadow prices, conversion factor being the ratio of the social value to the market value of an item.
3   The argument is more fully developed in Tower (1984b).
4   As Harberger (1988, p. 3) puts it, "Another bit of wisdom on which most of the giants in our heritage would probably agree is the absolute necessity of oversimplifying. The world is far too complicated to understand in its full detail. We *cannot* win by trying to replicate its full complexity. As we deal with different problems we use simple models specifically designed or adapted to meet these problems. . . . It is the insights that tens or hundreds of examples with these simple models give to economists [read policymakers for our purposes] that help make them perceptive observers of events in the world, sharp diagnosticians, and even good inventors of new, simple theories to deal with new problems as they arise."
    He continues (p. 5): "Big-model estimation was another fad. People had huge expectations from models like the Brookings, the Wharton-EFU, etc. They seemed to really think such models could replicate the economy. It turned out that hardly a single issue of policy design (on things like taxes, tariffs, financial regulation, welfare, defense, social security—you name it) could be enlightened by reference to such models. In every case one had to turn to smaller models suited to the specific task at hand."
5   Harberger (1988, pp. 14–16) writes: "I think a graduate program [for our purposes read modeling exercise] should emphasize the need for economists to communicate what they are doing to noneconomists. I feel this deeply because I work so much with ministries, central banks, and other government and international agencies. The key

people there are rarely economists by training, let alone high quality economists of the type that one would like to produce or to hire. Mostly they are from other professions; very often they are extremely able and perceptive people. In my experience, such people will never 'buy' any result that comes out of a 'black box.' They want to know exactly what it is they are buying, what it will do for them, and why they should expect it to work. Economists who also know how to package and 'sell' good economic ideas to such people have a far higher marginal social product than those who are somehow restricted to the jargon of our trade.

"Related to the above is the idea of recognizing the virtues of what I call 'minimalism' in economics. By this I mean always using the simplest and most elementary way of making a point, or of extracting a result from the data. A more high-powered technique, according to this way of thinking, should be used only when it is required. It should never be used to simply show off what one can do.

"To me 'minimalism' has aesthetic values as well as operational ones. But I would emphasize its virtue as a device for helping those in the profession communicate with those outside of it. By aiming at stating our case in the simplest possible terms, we have our best shot at maximizing the usefulness of economics in the real world."

6   See Tower (1984b) for a discussion of the various ways of treating nontraded goods in ERP calculations.

7   An analogy to indicate the relationship of the ERP to a full-fledged complex general equilibrium simulation is appropriate. Suppose that a new drug is discovered which will cure the common cold. But the euphoria and hallucinations induced by this drug cause some patients to do crazy things, so that accidental death is likely. A full-fledged general equilibrium type analysis of the efficacy of the drug would have to take into account the probability of dying from these side effects. But in assessing the efficacy of the drug it is also interesting to report the probability of recovery with no side effects of those who are tied to their beds, where the side effects do no harm, even though in the real world there is no plan to tie the patients down. This latter measure of the drug's efficacy is like the ERP in that both measures assume a closure rule that simplifies the mechanisms under consideration, and help the intuition.

8   As Harberger (1988, p. 4) writes: "The big insight of general-equilibrium models is, of course, 'sources-and-uses' . . . . That is, whatever we get has to come from somewhere (even if it is from the leisure time of men and machines) and has to go somewhere (even if it is to the idle inventory shelf or to the automobile graveyard)."

9   Credit for these two truths belongs to Andy Stoeckel, director of the Centre for International Economics, Canberra.

References

Browning, E. K., and W. R. Johnson (1984). "The Trade-Off Between Equality and Efficiency." *Journal of Political Economy* 92 (April), 175–203.

Corden, W. M. (1966). "The Structure of a Tariff System and the Effective Protective Rate." *Journal of Political Economy* 74 (June), 221–37.

Corden, W. M. (1974). *Trade Policy and Economic Welfare*. Oxford: Oxford University Press.

Deardorff, A. V., and R. M. Stern (1986). *The Michigan Model of World Production and Trade: Theory and Applications*. Cambridge, Mass.: MIT Press.

Dervis, K., J. A. P. de Melo, and S. Robinson (1982). *General Equilibrium Models for Development Policy*. Cambridge: Cambridge University Press.

Dixon, P. B., B. R. Parmenter, J. Sutton, and D. P. Vincent (1982). *Orani: A Multisectoral Model of the Australian Economy*. Amsterdam, The Netherlands: North-Holland Publishing Co.

Dreze, J., and N. Stern (1986). "The Theory of Cost-Benefit Analysis." In *Handbook of Public Economics*, volume 2. Edited by A. Auerback and M. Feldstein. Amsterdam, The Netherlands: North-Holland Publishing Co.

Gan, K. P., and E. Tower (1987). "A General Equilibrium Cost-Benefit Approach to Policy Reform and Project Evaluation in Malaysia." *Singapore Economic Review* 32 (April), 46–61.

Han, Kiyoun (1988). "Trade, Tax, and Agricultural Policy in A Highly Distorted Economy: The Case of Sudan." Ph.D. dissertation, Duke University, in progress.

Harberger, A. C. (1988). "Notes of the Economics Program at Duke University." Typescript.

Imam, H. (1985). "The Welfare Cost of Interest Rate Ceilings in Developing Countries: A General Equilibrium Approach." In *New Developments in Applied General Equilibrium Analysis*. Edited by J. Piggott and J. Whalley. Cambridge: Cambridge University Press.

Jenkins, G. P., and C. Y. Kuo (1985). "On Measuring the Social Opportunity Cost of Foreign Exchange." *Canadian Journal of Economics* 18 (May), 400–15.

Johnson, H. G. (1960). "The Cost of Protection and the Scientific Tariff." *Journal of Political Economy* 73, 557–72.

Jones, R. W. (1965). "The Structure of Simple General Equilibrium Models." *Journal of Political Economy* 95 (August), 675–709.

Judd, K. L. (1987). "The Welfare Cost of Factor Taxation in a Perfect-Foresight Model." *Journal of Political Economy* 95 (August), 675–709.

King, M. A., and D. Fullerton, eds. (1984). *The Taxation of Income from Capital: A Comparative Study of the United States, The United Kingdom, Sweden, and West Germany*. Chicago: University of Chicago Press for the National Bureau of Economic Research.

Krueger, Anne O. (1983). *Trade and Employment in Developing Countries: Synthesis and Conclusions*. Volume 3. Chicago and London: University of Chicago Press for the National Bureau of Economic Research.

Loo, Thomas, and Tower, E. (1988). "Agricultural Protectionism and the Less Developed Countries: The Relationship Between Agricultural Prices, Debt Servicing Capacities and the Need for Development Aid," in Stoeckel (1988).

de Melo, J. A. P. (1978). "Estimating the Costs of Protection: A General Equilibrium Approach." *Quarterly Journal of Economics* 92 (May), 209–26.

Newberry, D., and N. Stern (1987). *The Theory of Taxation for Developing Countries*. Oxford: Oxford University Press.

Piggott, J., and J. Whalley, eds. (1985) *New Developments in Applied General Equilibrium Analysis*, Cambridge: Cambridge University Press.

Robinson, Sherman (1986). "Multisectoral Models of Developing Countries: A Survey." Draft of a chapter to appear in H. B. Chenery and T. N. Srinivasan, eds., *Handbook of Development Economics*. Amsterdam, The Netherlands: North-Holland Publishing Co.

Shoven, J. B., and J. Whalley (1984). "Applied General-Equilibrium Models of Taxation and International Trade." *Journal of Economic Literature* (September), 1007–51.

Solow, R. M. (1956). "A Contribution to the Theory of Economic Growth." *Quarterly Journal of Economics* 70 (February), 65–94.

Stoeckel, A. (1985). "Intersectoral Effects of the CAP: Growth, Trade and Unemployment." Australian Bureau of Agricultural Economics (BAE) Occasional Paper No. 95. Canberra: Australian Government Printing Service.

Stoeckel, A., ed. (1989—forthcoming). *Macroeconomic Consequences of Farm Support Policies.* Durham, N.C.: Duke University Press.

Stoeckel, A., and A. Cuthbertson (1987). *The Game Plan: Successful Strategies for Australian Agriculture.* Canberra, Australia: Centre for International Economics.

Stolper, W. F., and P. A. Samuelson (1941). "Protection and Real Wages." *Review of Economic Studies* 9 (November).

Stuart, C. (1984). "Welfare Costs Per Dollar of Additional Tax Revenue in the United States." *American Economic Review* 74 (June), 352–62.

Taylor, L., and S. L. Black (1974). "Practical General Equilibrium Estimation of Resource Pulls Under Trade Liberalization." *Journal of International Economics* 4 (February), 37–58.

Tower, E. (1984a). "On A Quick and Dirty Approach To Estimating Second Best Optimum Tariffs." *Revista Internazionale de Science Economiche E Commerciale* 31 (March), 212–19.

Tower, E. (1984b). *Effective Protection, Domestic Resource Cost and Shadow Prices: A General Equilibrium Perspective*, World Bank Staff Working Paper, No. 664, September 1984.

——— (1987). "On Domestic Resource Cost." Typescript.

——— (1988a). "On the Symmetry Between Effective Tariffs and Value Added Subsidies." In *Industrial Policy and International Trade*, Volume 62 in Contemporary Studies in Economic and Financial Analysis. Edited by V. Canto and J. Kimball. Greenwich, Conn.: Dietrich JAI Press, 1989.

——— (1988b). "Review of Newberry and Stern (1987)." *Southern Economic Journal* 55 (July): 249–50.

Tower, E., and R. E. Christiansen (1987). "A Model of the Effect of a Fertilizer Subsidy on Income Distribution and Efficiency in Malawi." Working Paper Number 27, Duke University Program in International Political Economy, October.

Tower, E., and G. G. Pursell (1986). *On Shadow Pricing.* World Bank Staff Working Paper, No. 792. January.

——— (1987). "On Shadow Pricing Labor and Foreign Exchange." *Oxford Economic Papers* 39 (June).

Whalley, J. (1985). *Trade Liberalization Among Major World Trading Areas.* Cambridge, Mass.: MIT Press.

World Bank (1986). *World Development Report 1986.*

12

Risk, Politics, and Tax Reform: Lessons from Some Latin American Experiences

....

William Ascher

A. Uncertainty and the Nature of Tax Reform

One powerful organizing principle emerges from examining the politics of tax reform efforts in Latin America. *The effective political[1] management of tax reform rests on the limitation of risk so that affected groups will be willing to bear some additional—but predictably contained —costs.* This principle seems to go far in accounting for the tax reform experiences of Chile, Colombia, and Peru, and seems to be consistent with other, more casually perused Latin American cases. In addressing the question of what it takes to accommodate the potential victims of a tax reform, we assume that accommodation that goes so far as to completely eliminate costs and risks is useless; someone must pay more or receive less benefits. Some accommodation comes from reducing the immediate costs that potential opposition has to bear. However, the most compelling imperative is to maintain a tolerable level of risk for the potential opposition. The successes in Chile and Colombia, and the frustration in Peru, bring out this principle quite clearly.[2]

This principle is clearly relevant only when the protestations and reactions of potential victims cannot simply be ignored. Occasionally the political calculations of a government intent on economic policy reform may be simplified by the powerlessness of the opposition, even if the latter stand to lose significantly. Following a revolution, an overwhelming electoral victory, or a system-transforming coup d'état, a government may be able to dispense with accommodation. Yet, while such cases are conceivable for tax reform initiatives, and held to a certain extent for the 1974 Chilean tax reform, the ability to dispense with accommodation is unlikely in most circumstances. The multiphase nature of changes in tax structure and tax implementation afford numerous opportunities to minimize or undermine the implementation and impact of tax changes. And these opportunities provide for the effective use of different sources of power: electoral support; legislative strength; social prestige convertible into policy influence; money to buy votes, bureaucratic dispensations, or to mount campaigns in opposition to policy proposals; and the potential to disrupt in reaction to unwanted policy changes. Given this diversity of resources to influence policy formulation and implementation, it is very unusual for the advocates of a particular reform to monopolize all of the abovementioned sources of power relevant to a process as complicated as tax reform. Therefore, without precluding the possibility of tax reform via *force majeure*, the tactician typically must face the need for some accommodation.

A1. Characteristics of Tax Reform and Its Risks

Several characteristics of tax reform, explained below, yield the peculiar political importance of maintaining a tolerable level of risk. Typically, tax reforms will be viewed as both redistributive and open-ended in terms of policy innovations; they present both indeterminate levels of risk as to how tax policies will be formulated (complicated by the frequent presence of foreign missions and sometimes foreign pressures) and administrative uncertainty in their implementation—and the operative penalties for evasion are also indeterminate. Some of these qualities are intrinsic to taxation and tax reform in general; others are more applicable in the Latin American context.

The Redistributive Connotation. Tax reform is typically perceived as redistributive. After all, taxation is the direct extraction of wealth from particular individuals and firms. Prudent interest group representatives could hardly operate on any other working assumption than that tax reform could redistribute wealth *from* them. Although all economic policy instruments have the potential to change the levels of income and wealth accruing to different individuals and firms, taxation is among the most blatant of such instruments. Tax *reform*, with its connotation of major shifts in the structure of taxation, is thus particularly likely to be seen as entailing major shifts in the burden of taxation. Thus, several tax reform initiatives have been undertaken with the explicit renunciation of intent to change the burden of taxation,[3] so as to neutralize the perception that vertical redistribution was at stake. However, even these efforts are at best only partially successful. Typically, suspicions of a redistributive motive on the part of the reform's initiators are widespread and often justified.

There are peculiar asymmetries in the attitudes toward the redistributive potential of tax changes. For one thing, it is nearly impossible to find interest group representatives who leap enthusiastically into the tax debate with the expectation that they are likely to gain through redistribution. This is due, structurally, to the fact that there are so many steps between revenue collection and expenditures that no group can count on a sure and significant increase in benefits. It is very difficult to establish who benefits from governmental expenditures, let alone to anticipate who would benefit under uncertain future changes in expenditure policies. Moreover, the groups organized well enough to be involved in the tax debate (with the possible exception of labor unions) consist of upper-income businesses or individuals who are obvious targets for greater extraction. Where tax avoidance and evasion are common, the possibility of improved tax administration is also a threat —though it may be offset by the opportunity for reducing both red tape and the need to pursue suboptimal tax-avoidance investments. Thus, even if tax reform may hold benefits for particular private-interest groups, such groups typically operate in a basically defensive mode of damage control on the tax reform issue.

An offsetting factor, however, is that the redistribution perceived in tax reform can often be confined to the upper-income groups. Unless the government goes out of its way to arouse the organized labor sector, unions tend to be relatively inactive on tax reform issues.[4] Union leaders and rank-and-file union members act as if they assume that both their risk and their potential advantage in the typical tax reform are low. Whether this assumption is correct is debatable, since tax reforms frequently end up with heavier reliance on easily collected payroll taxes. Nonetheless, tax reformers often have the luxury of proceeding without the full range of economic interest groups mobilized to exert pressure.

Finally, tax reform is distinctive as a redistributive issue in that both horizontal and vertical equity are involved and are highly interrelated. "Horizontal equity" is fairness in the burdens of taxpayers at the same income or wealth levels; "vertical equity" is fairness in the tax burdens across income or wealth classes. The relationship between the two is very important in that greater horizontal equity, a virtually consensual objective, can serve as the explicit objective of tax reforms that also have a vertically redistributive impact. Or, greater horizontal equity can be the "reward" for income classes that may lose through moderate vertical redistribution from the same tax reform. Moreover, existing horizontal inequality poses a risk of future reprisal for the individuals, firms, or activities currently subject to accusations that they are not paying their fair share.

Tax Reform as Innovation. A distinctive quality of tax reform is the potential for the introduction of *new types* of taxes. The potential for innovation is very high, and, while not unique to tax reform (new forms of government-guaranteed savings arise with great frequency), it differentiates tax reform from other potentially redistributive instruments. Instruments such as land reform, price controls, credit regulation, and spending policy generally follow standard formulae, but it is the magnitude that varies.

A large part of the desire for innovation of tax laws stems from the prevalence of poor tax administration. Poor administration leaves a huge gap between the theoretical yield of a tax and its actual yield. This means that a large part of the challenge of tax reform, and one of the major foci of the creativity mentioned above, is to devise taxes that will extract the desired amount of revenue through taxes that are easier to administer and are harder to evade.

Other implications flow from the distinctive "creativity" of many tax reforms. There is a strong appeal for the technical teams to exercise their ingenuity and sophistication. They are often engaged in professionally interesting experimentation, even if this experimentation is intrinsically risky for others. Tax specialists are often the champions of tax reform even when no private-sector group is willing to push for the reform.

Creativity also opens up a cat-and-mouse game between tax reformers and taxpayers. New taxes hold the promise of closing off prior avenues of avoidance and evasion, if only the tax formulators are more clever than the targeted firms and individuals. This is a game in which the taxpayers' economic standing is vulnerable to machinations by sometimes very clever *técnicos.*

As a result of both of the above qualities, innovation creates uncertainty: a new tax has uncertain impact even without avoidance and evasion; and whether the tax reformers succeed in closing the loopholes creates further uncertainty.

Indeterminacy of Tax Reform Risk. Tax reform does *not* represent a predetermined degree of threat to any particular group; indeed, the essence of the politics of tax reform is the indeterminacy of the impact the reform will have upon particular classes and types of taxpayers.

This indeterminacy is present until the final details of formulation and implementation are worked out and the economic actors have had time to react. Taxation has the theoretical capacity to destroy a given taxpayer economically, yet tax reform may produce mild or moderate changes in tax burdens. Thus tax reform is not typically the ultimate threat as is the classic land reform. Tax reform may be less risky to a high-income individual or firm than other policy changes.

However, tax reform initiatives may have the effect of opening up other issues, such as the nature of property, that hold their own risk for various economic groups. Therefore *some* tax reform initiatives bear risk beyond the planned or predicted tax policy changes per se.

Involvement of Foreign Missions. The technicalities of tax reform lend themselves to the participation of foreign missions. These missions may be perceived as reducing the possibility that the government will enact a damaging tax reform. Sometimes the foreign tax mission will be seen as guaranteeing the fairness of tax reform changes. However, the members of the mission may also be seen as an affront to economic nationalism, or as hired apologists for the government's preferences. Thus the contribution and image of the foreign technical mission add to the political complexity of the tax reform.

Poor Tax Administration, Uncertainty, and "Bureaucratic Politics." This uncertainty is, in a sense, increased by the common condition in Latin America of inefficient tax administration. Not only does poor administration provoke innovation of uncertain outcome, but also the question of whether administrative reform will increase tax burdens introduces an additional source of uncertainty.

Bureaucratic politics, pitting the tax administration bureaucracy against the technical team and the top-level economic policymakers initiating tax reform efforts, also puts the state bureaucracy at risk. Tax reform in developing countries is typically (but not always, given the current Chilean situation) an implicit affront to the competence of tax administrators. Their job tenure, let alone prestige, is at risk. Given the poor tax administration of most developing countries, the very initiative of tax reform typically puts the tax administrators on the defensive. Moreover, the reformers are often bent on making tax changes that require more difficult administration. Except for strengthening tax administration and moving to more easily administered taxes, tax changes represent additional burdens to tax administrators. When significant tax changes occur frequently, tax administrators find it difficult to consolidate and streamline their procedures; action to improve the administration of existing tax mechanisms can be crowded out by the scramble to meet new administrative demands.

However, poor tax administration does not necessarily increase risk to taxpayers. Inefficient (or corrupt) tax administration reduces the risk that a given initiative will require the payment of a surprisingly large increment in tax liability. With the latitude effectively permitted by poor administration, the taxpayer can, to a certain extent, adjust accordingly. By the same token, improvements in tax administration, as laudable as they might be in the long run, typically reduce the tolerance toward new taxes that imply possibly dangerously high burdens under improved administration.

Taxation, Fairness, and Illegality. The tax issue makes many individuals and firms peculiarly vulnerable with respect to the legality and fairness of their current tax payments. A seriously distorted tax system virtually forces many taxpayers into formal illegality in their tax declarations. They are thus subject to the risk of prosecution, even if evasion is widespread. These taxpayers, and those who represent them in the policy debate, are also naturally constrained from direct references to these transgressions. They typically cannot invoke counterarguments to tax reform initiatives if their responses amount to admissions of evasion. For example, on one occasion (elaborated below) Chilean tax reformers enacted a huge increase in the value-added tax by arguing that an "honest" taxpayer would already have been paying that amount in transactions taxes. To cite the fact that hardly anyone had been paying that full burden would have been extremely awkward.

A2. The Broad Political Context

The uncertainty of the entire political economy is one component of the risk facing groups when a tax reform initiative is undertaken. Tax reform risk is a function of both the specific formulation of the reform in a particular arena *and* the overall political climate that might override the limits that pertain to that specific initiative. The relevance of this distinction is that perceived risk may or may not be influenced by the tactics or design of the specific reform. For any case of success or failure, then, the reform design can be credited or blamed only to the degree that the macroclimate does not make the microanalysis irrelevant. For example, if a key group believes that the government is out to destroy it, or that the government's own survival is in doubt, or that the government lacks the basic competence to carry out the reform in its anticipated form, then the details of the reform will make little difference to that group's behavior. Therefore, in assessing the tax reform initiatives in the three countries under examination, it is necessary to gauge the extent of perceived overall uncertainty in each case over time.

Colombia. The basic political situation in Colombia since the mid-1960s has reduced policy risk by dictating a preoccupation with avoidance of political polarization. The preference for radical policy departures existed in some quarters, but the likelihood that any administration would act on this preference was assumed to be very low.

Although the two major political parties have shown little overall difference in policy preferences, there was (and still is) a wide divergence in the policy preferences among factions within each party. Thus a new administration, or at least some of the activists within it, might very well *hold* policy preferences that could present a threat to various economic-interest groups. However, the imperative of avoiding destabilizing conflict was accepted by the top leadership of all major factions within the two parties.

This was because the specter of "La Violencia," the extreme instability and violence of the 1940s and 1950s, was still very much alive in the minds of the Colombian elite, even if the political system had been stabilized by the time the reform took place. "La Violencia," like the Mexican revolution, was the kind of nightmare of uncontrolled mass mobilization that drives political leaders into an overwhelming preoccupation with maintaining elite cohesion. The "National Front" arrangement of alternating administrations between the two parties had temporarily neutralized some of the interparty political conflict, but the arrangement had come to an end with the 1974 campaign.

Under the National Front, severe policy swings were discouraged by the consideration that the other party would soon get its chance to retaliate. After the National Front, the need for cohesion remained, as the two traditional parties faced not only the possibilities that their own conflict would reescalate, but also both electoral challenges from populist movements and the continuation of guerrilla activity.

The net result of this need to avoid open conflict with major factions in both parties was a built-in limitation on the extremeness of policy outcomes. Thus, with respect to the major 1974 reform discussed below, interest groups still had to worry that new policies might have extreme unanticipated consequences, but they also knew that López Michelsen and other top Liberal administration officials would moderate the intended impacts of policy. Thus the decision to use economic emergency powers to formulate the tax reform may have reflected López

Michelsen's desire to end up with a tax reform (and a recognition that his rather left-leaning tax specialists ought to be allowed to have a tax reform), but the moderation of the reform through the Council of Ministers compromise process was a predictable political imperative.

Chile. Chile has shown the greatest variation in perceived uncertainty of the three countries examined here. For the period from the mid-1960s, the Frei administration (1964–70) was faced with a challenge from the communist-socialist Left that pulled Frei's own rhetoric, and many of his concrete initiatives, in that direction. In retrospect—and in obvious contrast with the Allende administration—Frei's policies were moderate, limited as they were by the middle-class basis of support for his Christian Democratic Party. Yet, when Frei sought to win over the labor movement, and when he unveiled his land reforms, spending program, tax reforms, constitutional amendment to redefine property, etc.—all in the context of the seemingly open-ended reformism of the Alliance for Progress, it was very difficult for anyone to predict the limits of the changes under Frei, let alone the direction after Frei.

Moreover, the ability of the Frei administration to fine-tune its policy impacts was very much in doubt. Major policy departures were being won or lost, often by close votes, on the floor of Congress, rather than being hammered out—and moderated—in closed-door negotiations. So many changes were being implemented by a bureaucracy being pushed into an activist role that the usual assumption of bureaucratic resistance to rapid change could not be held with confidence.

Under Salvador Allende, whose presidency and life were ended in September 1973, the only certainty was that drastic changes were afoot. Although Allende promised at the outset that the only targets of expropriation would be the "foreign exploiters and the monopolists," there were many other takeovers, often triggered by work stoppages designed to invoke a law allowing the state to intervene in firms with reduced production, and peasant land takeovers that were also validated by the state. Although the government's planners announced that 9.7 percent of national income was targeted to shift to wage and salary earners over the six full years of the Allende administration, nearly that much had been redistributed by 1972 (Ascher 1984:236; Stallings 1978:56).

All of this came to an abrupt end with the Pinochet coup of 1973. The Pinochet government was certainly expected to redress the perceived economic injuries imposed on former property owners by the Allende administration. Chile entered into the period of greatest systemic certainty.

Yet even this clear reversal in the treatment of these groups did not spell out a definitive balance among economic groups. Many military governments in Latin America had populist leanings, and Pinochet, treading in unknown territory with a working class known to be highly mobilized and thought to be capable of open revolt, had to be mindful of both the risks of further antagonizing the low-income classes and the possible gains of a conciliatory stance. To be sure, Pinochet promised to "eradicate Marxism," but whether this meant crushing or wooing the working class was not totally clear at the time. Indeed, when Pinochet consolidated his personal power in 1981 by taking the position of president, the regressivity of previous economic policies was somewhat reversed.

And it should be kept in mind that the longevity of the Pinochet administration, now known in retrospect, was by no means certain at the beginning. It is easy to exaggerate the confidence that the Right had won for an indefinite period. It was not known whether the blue-collar and peasant groups that had backed the Allende administration would or could undermine any government economic initiative seen as highly retaliatory. It was not known when the transition to civilian government would occur, nor what the nature of that government would be.

Peru. Since the 1960s Peru has been an almost archetypical case of political *and* economic insecurity for nearly all actors. The Alianza Popular Revolucionaria Americana (APRA), of unpredictably populist orientation, won the 1962 election but was promptly ousted by the military. The Belaúnde administration (1963–68) was widely viewed as more predictably progressive-reformist in its preferences, but Belaúnde himself was regarded by many as a dangerously romantic naif when it came to economics. While few believed Belaúnde to be a radical, there was great wariness about the possible misfirings of his economic policies, and doubt about who would end up bearing the burden of greater state expansion into economic activity and social services. This first Belaúnde administration was punctuated by a misguided education expansion that practically bankrupted the treasury and a series of fiscal crises, exacerbated by congressional obstruction, that ultimately led to another military intervention in 1968. From this turmoil, General Juan Velasco Alvarado emerged as an enigmatic and seemingly contradictory leader.

This military government confounded the early predictions and launched the "Peruvian Revolution," a hastily constructed program of state-promoted mobilization of peasants and urban workers, expropriation of foreign property, and partial collectivization. If the Peruvian revolution did not go as far as its opponents feared, it was not for lack of extraordinarily threatening rhetoric and seemingly irreversible challenges to the old economic structure. How far this revolution could have gone in the context of economic decline and the military's ambivalence about allowing truly independent mobilization of peasants and urban workers is much debated, but it is clear that the business sector, labor leaders of the nongovernment unions, and landowners had no choice but to presume that they were facing a total threat to their entitlements.

When a more moderate military regime under General Morales Bermúdez took over in 1975 after the economic debacle of the Velasco period, there was probably much more confidence that the government was motivated to restore continuity and security. Nonetheless, the Morales Bermúdez government was a transitional regime, and had little interest in raising the potentially threatening issue of tax reform. Hence, in order to maintain the feeling of security that Morales Bermúdez would not further threaten beleaguered groups, the government was loathe to initiate any serious tax reform at all.

With the restoration of civilian government, Belaúnde was again victorious, but economic chaos, a split government economic policy team, and the uncertain longevity of the Belaúnde administration left economic groups as uncertain about the magnitude of threat they faced as during the Morales Bermúdez years. Finally, the APRA victory in 1986 put a practically unknown young populist, Alan García, into the presidency. It is widely believed that careful economic calculus plays a small part in President García's thinking in comparison with political considerations, and that these political considerations conceivably could take a radical turn.

B. The Sequences in Colombia, Chile, and Peru

By the mid-1960s, technical knowledge about Latin American public finance made it clear that radical improvements in tax systems were both important and technically feasible. Tax reform had been a priority of the Alliance for Progress planning, and many technical studies were undertaken by the Organization of American States and other standing and ad hoc technical bodies.

In the three countries central to this paper, the tax systems had some strikingly similar problems:

Inflation was seen as an extremely pressing problem, and, although there was dissent both then and later, it was widely believed that the budget deficit was a major causal factor.

Existing tax systems were universally condemned for their bewildering arrays of different rates, exemptions, and special categories, violating norms of efficiency, horizontal equity, and vertical equity. Taxes were earmarked for specific purposes and private investment was distorted. Marginal direct tax rates were high, having been elevated in the previous struggles to increase revenues, but (because of exemptions and evasion) tax revenues remained inadequate.

Yet there were important differences:

Although all three countries faced inflation, Chile's hyperinflation was a major problem per se for tax collection.

The Chilean tax administration was already superior to the Colombian and Peruvian, and capable of rapid improvement.

The size and depth of the technical expert pools were greater in Chile and Colombia than in Peru.

B1. Colombia

The most ambitious tax reform carried out in the three countries was the Colombian reform of 1974. It was ambitious not only in its drastic simplification of the tax structure, entailing unification of tax categories and elimination of myriad exemptions and special treatments—the Chilean reform of the same year had the same objective—but also in its explicitly redistributive thrust. Considering that Colombia was (and still is) a highly competitive political system with strong representation of high-income groups, the progressivity of the tax reform presents a fascinating political riddle.

Antecedents to the 1974 Reform. During the 1960s, fundamental tax reform in Colombia was far more an idea than a reality. However, when Carlos Lleras Restrepo of the Liberal Party assumed the presidency in 1966, he initiated a major study of the tax system, with the expectation that a coherent set of recommendations would emerge. This culminated in the "Musgrave Report" (Musgrave and Gillis 1971), the results of two years of Colombian government-financed work by a mixed team of Colombian and foreign experts headed by Harvard economist Richard Musgrave. Apparently Lleras had no particular priority for a tax reform during his own administration. There had been a tax reform in 1966[5] that did little to streamline the tax system but did manage to increase revenues moderately, and taxation of increasing exports and imports also raised revenues. Yet high government spending led to an increasingly serious budget deficit. Lleras believed that a thorough and systematic study of the fiscal policy was overdue. The 1967–68 Musgrave Report was to be a blueprint for reform in the mid-1970s.

The Musgrave Report called for more streamlined, efficient tax collection in order to increase revenues and to do so more progressively. The tax reform was not conceived as subservient to other policy objectives such as control of inflation or the stimulation of investment. Naturally, it was asserted that a sound tax system was important for sound monetary policy and efficient investment, but the Musgrave Report did not advocate making any sacrifices in the integrity of the tax structure in order to pursue these other goals.

Whether the objective of greater progressivity was Musgrave's idea or that of the young, relatively left-wing Colombians on the study team is a matter of dispute. Indeed, the direct impact of the Musgrave Report is difficult to assess. The study was completed, the book was written, and the documents then sat on the shelf during the next administration of President Misael Pastrana Borrero (1970–74). However, two things are clear. First, the study was "on record" as evidence that a thorough technical analysis of the Colombian tax structure had been accomplished. Second, the study established the young Colombian participants as tax experts with standing, important for their subsequent reputations as much as for the experience they gained.

Yet, during the second half of the Lleras administration and the Pastrana administration, no fundamental tax reform efforts were undertaken. In the case of Lleras, it may seem surprising that there was no concerted effort to enact the reforms recommended by his own study mission. But, by the time the Musgrave Report was completed and digested, the Lleras administration was facing the decline in political power characteristic of single-term presidencies in their last years. Furthermore, Lleras' emphasis on the battle for classical land reform created so much hostility from the agricultural sector that this sector's acquiescence to tax reform (which was perceived as a stalking horse for further inroads against large-scale farmers and cattle raisers) seemed quite remote. Finally, it is possible (particularly given Lleras' later opposition to the 1974 reform based on his own mission's recommendations) that Lleras did not concur with the generality of impact on the higher-income groups that the Musgrave Report called for. Although Lleras' support for land reform and the taxation of wealthy landowners could certainly be construed as progressive in terms of income distribution, his support for and by the industrial sector was not consistent with greater taxation of industrial entrepreneurs engaged in import-substitution industrialization.

In the case of the Pastrana administration, the terms of trade for Colombia's exports improved markedly during the 1970–74 period (Perry and Cárdenas 1986:61); the economy was expanding and so were tax revenues—although increases in public spending led to a fiscal deficit. The tax side of fiscal policy may simply not have been the focus of concern for the Pastrana team. Politically, the Pastrana administration was in the awkward position of relying (in part) on the support of large-scale agriculture during a period of continued pressure for land reform. To relieve this pressure, a 1973 tax law (Ley 3) imposed a presumptive income tax on agricultural land.[6] However, the Ministry of Agriculture was given the authority to suspend the application of this tax for given regions and for a host of reasons. Given that in Colombia (as in many other countries) the minister of agriculture is traditionally drawn from the agricultural sector itself, it should not be surprising that the presumptive income tax on agriculture was suspended totally from that time until it was superseded by the tax reforms of the López Michelsen administration. Moreover, in compensation for this effectively fictitious presumptive income tax on agriculture, accompanying tax laws (Ley 5 and 6) expanded the exemptions and deductions for the agricultural sector more than for other sectors, even while tax retention on salaries and dividends was strengthened (Urrutia 1986:35; Perry and Cárdenas 1986:18).

Even so, enacting any sort of presumptive income tax for the agricultural sector was far from a trivial event, especially by an elected government. Several attempts during the 1950s and 1960s, urged on by World Bank missions of 1950 and 1956, were aimed at both increasing the agricultural sector's tax burden and forcing *hacienda* owners to increase production. To counter the owners' evasive tactic of undervaluing their land, some of these proposals called for giving the government the option of purchasing the land at the declared value or at some multiple (e.g., 140 percent) of the declared value. These initiatives were resisted strongly by the agricultural sector, and none succeeded (Hirschman 1963:116–33; Herschel 1971:411). This is not surprising, given the apparent open-ended risk. Yet the path of the related land reform issue improved the prospects for a presumptive tax. Whereas a presumptive agricultural tax that in effect threatens expropriation for undervaluation links the risk of new tax structures to greater risk of expropriation, bowing to new tax structures could also reduce the risk of expropriation. President Alberto Lleras Camargo put it bluntly in 1959: "Either the forcible distribution of landed wealth with the natural violence that this method brings with it, or the patient, continuous, and inflexible action of the state through taxation which converts the land into a means of production, whose ownership is justified by the income it produces. Faced with this alternative I am sure that Colombians shall not hesitate."[7]

The greatest threat to the large-scale agricultural sector had clearly been land reform. Various governments, including the Carlos Lleras Restrepo administration, had made land reform a high rhetorical priority, even if the actual redistribution of land was minimal. Before this administration, the land reform strategy had been to balance modest land expropriation (and the fears of greater expropriation) by granting tax exemptions and other incentives to large landowners, justified in the name of productivity stimulation. This may have been a good deal for the large-scale agriculturalists, as long as the land reform did not go too far, but the risk represented by the apparently growing momentum of land redistribution was perceived to be great. If the government found land reform to be politically popular, there were enough other cases, ranging from Cárdenas in Mexico to Allende in Chile, for landowners to worry about peasants and government encouraging one another to carry land expropriation further. Land takeovers by squatters, with what was seen as the implicit support of certain government agencies, were already not uncommon in Colombia. If the government shied away from significant land reform—as seemed to be the case to that point—then the danger of peasant disruption and land seizures in frustration with government policy was the other possibility.

Therefore, when an agrarian reform bill was blocked in Congress in 1972, a compromise more to the liking of the large-scale agricultural sector was reached through negotiations with representatives of *both* parties. The "Chicoral Accord" basically renounced land redistribution in exchange for the presumptive tax (Bagley and Edel 1980: 277, 283; Urrutia 1986:38). Through this accord, the government reversed its stated agrarian policy. Rather than encouraging greater productivity through tax exemptions, the government decided to emphasize fiscal extraction—again in the name of promoting productivity, since the presumptive income tax was thought to encourage fuller land utilization. The new burden for the wealthy landowners was to be higher taxes, but their risk of land expropriation would be reduced. The presumptive tax was the lesser of the two threats. Moreover, large landowners knew that their representation in congress was, and in all probability would remain, very strong. As long as the application of the presumptive tax remained partly under the control of congress, the risk would also be limited.

The 1974 Liberal Party candidate Alfonso López Michelsen made tax reform a prominent campaign issue. For López Michelsen, the appeal of tax reform was that it could be cast as an explicitly redistributive issue, thus enhancing his populist reputation, *and* it provided the means to highlight the rising inflation that tarnished the preceding Conservative administration. López Michelsen's lopsided electoral victory not only gave him enormous power, it also gave the issues of fiscal redistribution and inflation the prominence of electoral endorsement—a vote for López Michelsen could be read as a vote in favor of his campaign pledges.

The landslide also made it a foregone conclusion to the bulk of Colombian politicians of both parties that the López administration could have its way on tax issues. Even if the usual legislative process afforded opportunities for opponents to snag the procedures, there was a legitimate[8] procedure of invoking economic emergency powers that could secure some degree of tax reform for the new administration. The questions were: how strong a tax reform; who would bear the burden; and at what political costs to the López administration?

Immediately following the election, López Michelsen established a technical team to develop tax reform proposals.[9] Many of the key participants had been members of the Musgrave team, and the Musgrave studies clearly shaped their approach to tax reform.

The experts' recommendations included:

increasing revenues principally by raising overall sales tax rates—but with five different tax rates distinguishing among goods according to whether they are consumed by the rich or the poor

elimination of almost all income tax exemptions and special treatments for the oil depletion allowance, inheritance tax, capital gains, and previously tax-exempt government bonds and private financial instruments—income from these sources was to be taxed at the marginal income tax rate

substitution of tax credits for personal tax deductions, in order to eliminate the regressivity of tax deductions, which have a greater value for high-income taxpayers

higher top marginal rates for both income and net wealth
automatic adjustments for inflation—but not full adjustments, as the
tax policy was intended to help control inflation[10]
a *general* presumptive income tax
consolidation of treatment of different types of corporations
assorted measures to improve tax administration.

According to the constitutional provisions regarding the economic
emergency powers, all cabinet ministers had to agree to each decree.
Understandings between the Liberal and Conservative parties on the
transition from the National Front arrangement to strictly competitive
elections still called for the president to include opposition party members in his cabinet.[11] Overall, the cabinet represented urban and rural
interests, liberal and conservative outlooks (albeit not a major distinction in terms of policy in Colombia), and economic views ranging from
center-left to center-right. Yet even the Conservative ministers in López
Michelsen's cabinet owed some personal loyalty to the president. And
the deliberations within the closed-doors Council of Ministers kept out
both formal party representatives and the interest groups. Therefore the
process of policymaking under the emergency economic powers may
have resulted in a compromise position, but it also greatly reduced the
chances of stalemate that would have blocked any tax reform.

It was widely believed within the cabinet, even by the Conservative
Party ministers, that López' popularity and electoral margin made it
inevitable that the tax reform, to which the president gave so much
personal emphasis, would succeed. This, of course, became a self-
fulfilling prophecy (in addition to being a correct political assessment),
inasmuch as the ministers, even if they were philosophically opposed
to the direction of the reform, believed that they had to come to terms
with the president. Since the president was strongly committed to the
direction of the technical group's proposals, the Council of Ministers'
negotiations ended with all of the elements of the technical groups'
recommendations, although many of them were moderated.

Following the technical work and the government's initial tax decrees
under emergency powers (but still subject to modification and still vulnerable to congressional rejection), top government authorities met with
representatives of agricultural interests to mitigate the impact of tax
changes on the large-scale agricultural sector.

The background to these meetings was that the technical team was
known to be rather unsympathetic to the large-scale agrarian interests,

in part out of prior commitment to land reform that pitted the large-scale landowners against the smallholders and the landless. For some members of the technical team, change within the agrarian sector, whether land reform or governmental benefits to the rural poor, could best be financed by taxing the wealthy within that sector. The organized agricultural sector responded, however, by asserting that this approach was a disguised form of continued industrial and urban bias, and that Colombian agriculture, of whatever ownership, would decline under significantly greater taxation. In addition, although the major executive policymaking authorities were widely believed to be antagonistic toward large-scale agrarian interests, congress was seen to be just the opposite. Therefore the administration's leaders saw a need to soften both the intersectoral transfer and the political impact of the tax reform.

These consultations with agrarian interests did not yield very much significant change in the tax laws themselves. However, the *practical* impact on the agricultural sector was considerably softened by changing the rules of implementation. Most importantly, the planned revaluation of agricultural property was dropped (though added again in 1983). Since the agricultural interests feared most the implications of the presumptive income tax, the cancellation of property reassessment represented a major reduction in risk. The reduction in the presumed profit rate also lessened the possibility that an agricultural producer would have to pay taxes based on the presumptive income calculation beyond what would have been declared as earned income. The industrialists had even less to fear from the broadening of the presumptive tax to cover their earnings, since their ratio of earnings to property was typically well over 8 percent, and the possibility of plausibly reporting lower earnings was minimized by the better monitoring of industrial activity as compared to agricultural activity.[12] In short, what seemed to be a very frightening tax rehauling had some implicit but widely recognized constraints. The 1974 reform had enough of the Llerista attack on the landed property owners to assure the urban sectors that they were not the big losers. Yet it steered far enough away from land reform to placate the agricultural interests that things could have been much worse.

The net result was that the 1974 tax reform succeeded in introducing novel forms of taxation, simplifying the tax system, eliminating some loopholes, and increasing revenue. Its limitations included the relatively small contribution to overall revenues that the new forms of taxation made at that time, the perhaps inevitable failure to foreclose the long-term capability of the wealthy to learn ways to reduce their direct-tax liabilities, the administrative court's nullification of parts of the reform as impermissible under emergency powers, and the opening for later counterreforms brought on by the tax system's remaining weaknesses in inflation adjustment.

The technical group planned to use the sales tax (applied progressively) to provide the bulk of increased revenues. This reliance on an existing tax was in keeping with the concern for reducing uncertainty and risk. While the future potential for using innovative taxes such as the presumptive income tax was established, the potential cost facing interest groups for the moment was concentrated in the much better understood behavior of the sales tax. At the same time, this also served to ensure the government of greater confidence that the changes would not erode revenues.

This increase in indirect taxation did not arouse much opposition from organized groups, despite the fact that it was to be both progressive *and* the major source of new revenues. Manufacturers could pass the costs through to the consumer, as indeed happened (Urrutia 1986:46). However, some decline in the demand for more heavily taxed luxury goods could be expected, adversely affecting some manufacturers, and a decline in the purchasing power of high-income consumers was also implicit in higher taxes on their purchases.

The lack of opposition can be attributed to three factors. First, fighting the sales tax was not a good "consumer" issue.[13] The only potential defenders of the "general consumer interest" were the unions and the political parties. Neither had a strong motive to object to a sales tax weighted heavily against luxury goods. The opposition party also had minimal power following its electoral defeat. Thus, the ensuing rapid (though short-term) inflation was criticized, but there was no concerted attack against the sales tax per se by the unions or the political opposition. Second, high-income consumers were simply not organized along the lines appropriate either to identify a progressive sales tax as a serious threat or to fight such a tax. Third, although the economic emergency powers still required ultimate congressional approval, they did reduce the intermediate steps of committee hearings in which interest groups could have had more input. As long as López Michelsen could sell the package to the cabinet, and gain final congressional approval — a task aided greatly by his electoral popularity — he could bypass much of the public protests by interest groups.

The overall absence of effective opposition (other than loud complaining by most business and agricultural groups) was, however, matched by a striking lack of enthusiastic support from any nongovernmental quarter. Although Colombian labor unions are not controlled by the major political parties, and typically have ideologically radical-leftist leadership, their participation in the debate over tax reform has been minimal, except when the reform seems to pose a clear threat to their economic standing (Urrutia 1986:60). In 1965 there had been a general strike to protest tax changes that were seen as strongly regressive. Yet since that time, the apparently progressive tax reform initiatives have elicited little support from the labor sector.

Even without labor support, though, the government did not bow to the protestations of business, commercial, and agricultural associations (gremios). President López simply announced that the emergency did not permit policy changes to respond to their complaints, and rejected appeals to hand the tax reform over to a tripartite commission that would have given the business sector a direct corporatist role in formulating the reform package (Urrutia 1986:65). Thus, although the tax reform was redistributive along class lines, it was not won through anything resembling a struggle among classes. Rather, it was the state versus the business sector, and the former used the president's power and the mechanism of the emergency decree to carry the day.

Results and Denouement of the 1974 Reform. As planned by the technical group, the sales tax, rather than the presumptive income tax on agriculture, yielded the greatest revenue increases. Since this sales tax was made progressive through the different rates applied to different goods categories, it was an example of a progressive indirect tax.

The streamlining of the income tax also yielded significantly higher revenues for the first few years. The general presumptive income tax, which clearly went beyond the Musgrave Commission's recommendation of an agricultural presumptive income tax, was not only very popular politically but also produced very large yields in the first two years (Perry and Junguito 1978). Yet the increases were not permanent. For one thing, the failure to revalue agricultural land reduced the bite of the presumptive tax. For another, high-income taxpayers managed to reduce their tax burdens by avoidance or evasion (Urrutia 1986: 45; Perry and Junguito 1978). This was a good example of the limited half-life of reforms on direct taxation.

With respect to the failure to adjust fully for inflation, the Colombian reform represents an example of trying to do too much with a single policy instrument. Several members of the technical group had argued strenuously in favor of full inflation adjustments, and retrospective analyses of the 1974 reform point to this as its biggest mistake;[14] the subsequent distortions due to "bracket creep" were so great that tax relief measures in 1976, 1977, and 1979 received intense support, thus providing the opening wedge for other measures that watered down the force of the 1974 reform. Each of the tax relief measures prior to 1979 provided for only partial adjustment for inflation—only the 1979 changes enacted 100 percent adjustment. Thus, from 1974 up to the 1979 change, tax policy was partially directed to combat inflation, at the cost of jeopardizing the effectiveness of the tax system itself.

But this was more than a simple technical blunder or a case of trying to do too much with a single element of economic policy. Since the 1974 election campaign had focused on the problem of inflation, and the tax reform itself was rationalized as an anti-inflation measure (on the argument that inflation was due to the budget deficit), there was strong pressure on and by the minister of finance to try to use tax policy as another weapon against inflation. The rhetorical linkage of the two issues ultimately had some undermining effect on the coherence and persistence of the 1974 reform.

In accordance with the Colombian constitution, the emergency-power decrees were also subject to scrutiny by the Supreme Court to assess their constitutionality. Interestingly, the provisions struck down by the Supreme Court featured changes in procedures of tax administration, on the questionable (Urrutia 1986:53) grounds that the economic emergency had nothing to do with tax administration but rather with overall revenue levels. In this case, and later with the 1982–83 reforms, there seemed to be an unstated understanding that a serious tightening up of tax administration would have been a more drastic step—and much more threatening—than a change in the tax rates and even in the types of taxes!

With respect to tax administration, the curious denouement of the 1974 reform was the uproar when Guillermo Perry, a leading expert in the technical group and newly appointed director of the National Tax Administration, tried to gain greater administrative compliance by placing his own team into this bureaucratic structure. The old guard within the administration and several opposition politicians protested that Perry was trying to "infiltrate" the tax administration with leftists. After a "strike" by some tax administrators, Perry was reassigned. The idea that tax administrators could constitute a leftist threat may seem curious, but in fact lax tax administration was a feature that, along with the elimination of many exemptions, kept the high marginal income tax rates (raised to 56 percent for the top group by the 1974 reform) from being confiscatory.

The Colombian reforms of 1982–86. The 1974 tax reform was so strong that it triggered several counterreforms through 1980. The need for revenues kept the changes to a rather modest level in terms of overall tax incidence, but the changes, justified largely on the need to relieve the distortions due to the inadequate treatment of inflation adjustments, did dilute the coherence of the 1974 reform (Urrutia 1986:69). Thus the reform launched in 1982 was initially designed to restore coherence, not to increase revenues or change the vertical distribution of tax burden. Ironically, the 1982–83 reform was successful in terms of increasing revenues, but made less progress than anticipated in restoring the coherence of the 1974 reform. The reform went through despite the fact that the Supreme Court ruled that tax reform was too important and potentially too long-lasting to be subject to executive authority under emergency powers. Although the administration of newly elected President Belisario Betancur initially feared that tax reform pursued through the legislative route would be sabotaged, it was indeed enacted through the standard congressional procedures.

Two factors helped the enactment of the tax reform. First, considerable effort was needed to reshape the tax structure to improve its technical performance. Second, an unexpected fiscal crisis brought on by the unprecedented rise in real interest rates for foreign borrowing posed the danger of both severe recession and a frightening fiscal deficit that, without increased revenues, would require highly inflationary financing. Betancur was hampered by the narrowness of his electoral victory, and the fact that he had not campaigned as an advocate of a stronger tax effort. Indeed, Betancur had promised the industrialists relief from double taxation and promised lower tax rates to the public (Perry and Cárdenas 1986:277–78), yet the immediate crisis required both action to reduce inflation and stimulation of economic recovery.

The administration established an advisory commission attached to the Ministry of Finance, charged with the task of suggesting how tax revenues could be increased rapidly *and* economic recovery could be stimulated. Because a team had been working on a tax-reform analysis, the work of this commission did not have to proceed in a vacuum. Much of the analysis reflected in the Betancur commission's recommendations had been done by a technical team operating under the previous administration, aided by external technical advisers (in this case a team of the Inter-American Development Bank) (Urrutia 1986:54). The internal Colombian tax commission established under the previous administration was initiated by the director of National Planning, Eduardo Wiesner, who had been a member of the Musgrave Commission.

However, the principal objective of the tax changes had shifted from streamlining to increased revenue collection. When Wiesner had been finance minister under President Julio César Turbay, he followed the stance taken by Turbay's earlier finance minister, Jaime García Parra, that taxes ought not be raised further, but rather the system of intergovernmental transfers should be rationalized. Foreign loans had been available at very attractive real interest rates, which led both finance ministers to resist absorbing more private income when foreign capital seemed so cheap. Therefore the economic situations confronting tax reformers before and during the 1982 crisis were quite different. It is quite significant that the analytic preparation could be accomplished even though the short-term objectives of the reform had changed.

Initially, the Betancur administration planned to proceed, as with the 1974 reform, through economic-emergency decrees. In fact, the economic emergency was more acute in 1982–83 than it had been in 1974. Over the strenuous objections of some of his own cabinet ministers, Betancur approved a series of emergency decrees. Although many of the recommendations of the advisory commission were accepted, there were also significant modifications. These included providing exceptions to specific industries (e.g., housing construction) and to agriculture (the 1983 measures actually reduced the burden of the presumptive tax on agriculture [Urrutia 1986:69]) that were opposed by the commission on the grounds that they detracted from the coherence of the tax system (Perry and Cárdenas 1986: 278).

The economic-emergency decrees were annulled by the Supreme Court. The 1974 episode had shown that tax reform could have very long-lasting impacts, and hence was much more than an emergency response to the crisis of the moment. Therefore, the Supreme Court ruled that the economic emergency decrees were not appropriate for tax reform. Then, too, there was much less conviction that the Betancur administration could get its way on tax reform, whereas the overwhelming electoral victory of López Michelsen had made it clear that, one way or another, López's tax reform would go through. Thus in the Betancur case, the resort to emergency powers seemed to be a tactic that could change the basic outcome, and therefore was of more questionable legitimacy, whereas in the López case the only difference in outcome was that the result was likely to be somewhat more coherent.

President Betancur responded to the Supreme Court ruling by reverting to the normal channel of congressional approval and opening up a public debate on the tax reform. The result was that the gremios made greater inroads in getting modifications in the reform package, and therefore did not press congress to the same degree as they would have if given the opportunity in 1974. Even so, congress was surprisingly accommodating to the Betancur reform, especially in light of the fact that it was dominated by the opposition Liberal Party.

This time the manufacturing and commercial gremios felt the threat. The 1974 reform had been seen as directed against the agricultural sector, and the adjustments of the mini-reforms of 1977 and 1979 had favored the industrial sector by alleviating "double taxation." But the 1982–83 changes were clearly not going against the agricultural sector, and by 1983 it was clear that the reform would have to increase revenues from some source.

The business sector's response was extremely negative and combative. As in 1974, the associations of all sectors opposed the changes in the procedural tax laws that would make evasion more difficult. The industrial sector's explicit attack on the tax reform was that it reduced horizontal equity through inconsistent treatment of profits and financial loans (Perry and Cárdenas 1986:279), and its macroeconomic effect of worsening the recession.

Many Colombian observers explain the business sector opposition by pointing out that the "carrot was smaller than the stick": the promised relief for "double taxation" did not make up for the elimination of existing exemptions and higher tax rates. However, there is a different explanation that seems to capture the mood more accurately. Once it was clear that the fiscal emergency would negate the government's campaign commitments, and that the tacit commitment to revenue neutrality was abrogated, the business sector faced a risk of unpredictably higher tax burdens, and thus the gremios attacked the reform with full force. What had started out in 1982 as an initiative for horizontal equity became, in the eyes of the business sector, a hurried and open-ended reaction that entailed considerable risk to the profitability of industry and commerce.

The reason why the reforms went through congress despite business sector opposition illuminates not only why it is essential to distinguish between political and economic-sectoral groups, but also how important the timing of reform is to gaining the support of the political opposition. The Liberal Party, lacking executive control but with bright hopes for 1986, became interested in changing the regime that gave rise to expectations that a budget deficit could be financed through monetary emissions—and in getting the change enacted under a Conservative regime so that the austerity effects could be laid to the Conservatives. A newly established Interparliamentary Fiscal Commission of the Liberal Party announced its commitment to the principle of forbidding inflationary deficit financing in 1983. If the government succeeded in its reforms, future fiscal management would be easier for any government; if the government did not succeed, then the standing of the Liberal Party would be all the more strengthened in the contrast.

Congress actually eliminated some of the exemptions that the president had allowed for particular bank deposits, some of the relief for double taxation, and hastened the application of the value-added tax. Yet it also allowed for exemptions that the administration opposed for agriculture (reflecting the well-known pro-agricultural tendencies of the Colombian congress), automobile purchasers, and oil and mining companies (Perry and Cárdenas 1986: 281). Thus, from the congressional perspective, especially that of the Liberal Party congressmen, the tax reform resolved the short-term revenue crisis, made progress on long-term safeguards against inflation, acceded to some of the most effective business-sector pressures, and left most of the business-sector antagonism targeted against the Betancur administration. The costs to Betancur of introducing the tax reform as an open-ended threat were, first, the incoherence of the reform that resulted from having to accommodate the high level of mobilization of opposition by industrial and commercial groups; and, second, the erosion of political support that Betancur otherwise might have expected from the business sector with respect to all of his other policy initiatives.

The tax laws passed by congress also introduced greater flexibility to the administration than had been requested to revamp the sales tax in order to bring the system closer to a coherent value-added tax. With the technical support of both the Inter-American Development Bank and the Organization of American States, the administration extended the VAT to the retail level (Perry and Cárdenas 1986: 282). The immediate response was a threat of non-compliance by the large-scale retailers' association Federación Nacional de Commerciantes (FENALCO), which claimed that the measure would violate horizontal equity by placing a lesser burden on smaller retail establishments that could get away with evading the tax, and that it would be inflationary. Betancur's response was to force the retailers to choose between the lesser and greater threats: he offered to introduce the retail-level VAT gradually, but promised to punish severely any defiance of the new tax regime. The gremios moderated their opposition.

The Post-1974 Colombian Reforms. Two more "tax reforms" in Colombia are worth touching on briefly. In 1984 Minister of Finance Roberto Junguito went to Congress with a series of ad hoc proposals to increase tax rates in order to meet World Bank and International Monetary Fund conditions. By invoking the need for an austerity program, Junguito was able to effect an increase in real revenues of over twenty per cent by 1985. In a sense, the administration appealed to the nationalistic sentiment to avoid being placed in a vulnerable position vis-à-vis these international agencies. In another sense, the Bank and the Fund played the role of prodding the Colombian politicians to carry out the major increase in revenues (and marked improvement in the fiscal balance) that otherwise might have provoked another bitter fight.

Finally, the 1986 tax reform initiative of the new administration of Liberal President Barco represents another illuminating demonstration of the management of risk and uncertainty. The government had swept the presidential election with a majority of 2 million votes, giving it a far greater mandate than the preceding Betancur regime. This left President Barco in a position similar to that of López Michelsen, in that a sweeping reform, if so desired by the president, could rely on the political strength that follows a landslide victory.

Yet this time the president began with an open process, rather than having to open up the debate on a controversial reform that had already raised hackles because it had been developed strictly from within the administration and pursued initially through decrees. Instead of trying the economic emergency route—which would have had no plausibility in 1986, in any event—Barco initiated the deliberations over the reform through an Advisory Commission of the Liberal Party, which involved party members who informally represented practically every organized sector. Moreover, Barco had a better balance of carrot and stick than Betancur even though Barco had more power; the pursuit of greater efficiency of the tax system through further elimination of exemptions and special treatment was balanced by lowering of the top marginal tax rates to thirty percent. Thus the Barco reform was both the least costly in terms of the erosion of the president's power and goodwill, and, according to many observers, more successful than Betancur's in terms of surviving intact through the congressional process. Of course, one could argue that the Barco agenda itself is less ambitious and therefore less threatening to the interests mobilized on the tax reform issue.

The 1986 initiative also raised the issue of balancing the capability of the tax administration with the "theoretic" advisability of (and, in the Colombian case, political mileage accruing to) further tax reform. After substantial reforms in 1974 and 1982, as well as many more modest changes in other years, the question of whether improvements in the tax laws were causing administrative confusion in tax implementation became part of the debate. The controller general published several articles calling for a moratorium on new tax reform. He argued that the success of tax changes in Colombia over the previous twelve years had resulted in satisfactory legal provisions that now required consolidation and improved administration. Here we see a signal from the state that the pursuit of further tax reform was yielding diminishing returns.

Lessons of the Colombian Reforms. The Colombian successes at tax reform show that although the government may be the initiator of tax reform, the reduction of risk to nongovernmental groups calls for finding a way for these groups to express their concerns within governmental policymaking. As noted in the introductory section, in Colombia there is a striking certainty (relatively speaking) that an administration must balance its policies to avoid antagonizing its multiclass, multisectoral constituency. Through the Council of Ministers negotiations of the 1974 reform, various interests were inserted through the views of the ministers identified with them (e.g., agriculture and big industry). Through these discussions some of the measures were moderated, especially with respect to the agricultural sector, but certainly not eliminated. This was, in a sense, a two-way street: the presence of sectoral spokesmen in the cabinet, such as the former president of the Cotton Growers Federation and a former senior administrator of the Coffee Growers Federation, also made it more difficult for the agricultural associations to oppose the measures. The 1986 Liberal Party deliberations accomplished the same function.

The Colombian case also tells us that even bombshells have to be carefully manufactured before they are dropped. Although President López Michelsen implemented the tax reform under "economic emergency powers" and as part of a "Stabilization Plan," the groundwork had been laid by years of work by Colombian economists and a major foreign tax mission (the 1967–68 Musgrave Commission). The relevant governmental policymakers were engaged in working out the details of the executive's reform proposal well before López's inauguration and the selection of his cabinet (Urrutia 1986:34). Similarly, the 1982–83 reforms benefited from considerable prior analysis even though the purpose of the reform changed from the time of Betancur's inauguration to the specific formulation of the tax reform package.

Although poor tax administration is generally taken as a given, in fact it has a politics of its own, both as "bureaucratic politics" and in terms of the broader political economy. It is important—though perhaps ironic—that the weak tax administration can strengthen the political prospects of tax reform by reducing the short-term risk. In Colombia, for example, it is commonplace to shrug off the possibility of being unexpectedly burdened with a much greater tax burden by saying that one decides beforehand on one's "fair contribution" and adjusts one's tax return accordingly. Naturally, such adjustment or evasion has its limits. In the future, the tax administration could prosecute some flagrant evasions. For large firms, even a weak tax administration can afford rather careful monitoring. This is not to say that weak tax administration is desirable, but rather that the unfortunate situation of a weak tax administration may offer a political opportunity for improving tax legislation.

Even though the Colombian tax reforms have been accompanied by their share of confrontation and combative rhetoric, it is important to note how regularized tax reform has become in Colombia. By 1986, periodic tax reforms in Colombia seemed to be a political staple—a politically rewarding way for the government to project itself as active and responsible in economic policymaking. This represents an interesting counter-example to Urrutia's (1983:45) complaint that there is no political mileage in tax reform.

The passage of tax reforms under powerful presidents raises a very interesting and important issue of policy appraisal. If the tax reform was an "easy thing" given the political climate and distribution of power, the sense of economic emergency due to the rise of inflation, and the traditional power of a Colombian president elected by an impressive majority, then it does not make sense to call the tax reform a political success simply on the basis of its enactment. While we may still usefully ask what it is about Colombia or about that particular era that made tax reform politically viable, those questions do not address the issue of whether the government's strategies can be considered effective and efficient. For that sort of question, we must use the more demanding criterion of whether the political, policy, and economic costs to the government and the country were minimized in bringing about a reform of given benefits, or the even more demanding criterion of finding the best cost-benefit result.[15]

For example, the 1974 Colombian tax reform, though justified as a means of reducing the fiscal deficit, was accompanied by an expansion of social expenditures and marked increases in the wages of state employees. Whatever one thinks of the advisability of these changes, they certainly diminished the achievement of the stated priority of controlling the fiscal deficit. If deficit reduction was a serious objective of the Colombian government, *and* the increased expenditure was part of the price that the government paid for the political support for the tax reform, then the reform must be seen as a somewhat less impressive political accomplishment. Similarly, many Colombians believe that the combativeness of the government's approach to forcing through the tax reforms of 1974 and 1982–83 shut off opportunities to pursue reforms in other areas, because economic policymakers felt that they could not afford to antagonize the agricultural and business sectors any more than they did with these tax reforms.

Finally, the Colombian case tells us that there may be tradeoffs between the reliance on open, normal policymaking channels and the technical coherence of the resulting tax structure. There seems to be a consensus in Colombia that the 1974 tax reform, whether or not judged to have the correct objectives, was more coherent for its circumvention of the normal congressional modifications than subsequent reforms that went through the full congressional process.

B2. Chile

The tax reform experiences in Chile span the political conditions of competitive democracy and military dictatorship: both relatively low and high levels of contextual certainty. In the Chilean case, the level of certainty, imparted either by the broad political context or by the specifics of the tax reform initiative, seems more important in accounting for the degree of success than does the nature of the political regime.

In Chile, unlike Colombia, all three major tax reform efforts that achieved a modicum of success (under Alessandri in 1964 and in 1974 and 1984 under the Pinochet administration) were conceived by their initiators as neutral with respect to both income distribution and the volume of government revenues at the time (Arellano and Marfan 1987:20). That is, although it was surely known that improvements in the tax system would ultimately have impacts on the capacity of the government to alter the distribution and overall level of taxation, such changes were not explicit objectives of the tax reforms. It was left to the annual changes in the tax law to shift the total volume of tax revenues or the distribution of the burden. In contrast, the two major "open-ended" efforts at tax reform under Eduardo Frei (1964–70) and Salvador Allende (1970–73), while having very significant impacts on tax burdens, were not successful in bringing either greater consistency or efficiency to the tax system.[16]

Jorge Alessandri, a center-right president, approached tax reform near the end of his administration with the objectives of establishing a better basis for tax *administration*. This may seem like a very modest goal, but in retrospect it permitted much more ambitious reforms later on. And unlike most "streamlining" efforts at tax reform, the Alessandri reform created further distinctions in tax-treatment categories of incorporated and unincorporated firms. Preferential treatment was given to income earned by incorporated firms, in order to reduce the number of the less easily monitored, presumably more evasion-prone unincorporated firms. Many incorporations resulted from the tax law change (which was a governmental objective for other reasons as well), but there was no discernible immediate decline in tax evasion (Arellano and Marfan 1987:21). While the new distinction between incorporated and unincorporated profits implied greater complexity, the reform also reduced the number of separate treatments for different sources of income from six to two: profits and labor. Other simplifications in the reform included the elimination of tax exemptions that were viewed as having outlived their usefulness as investment incentives, yet the reform was not conceived as a total overhaul as were the later efforts under the Pinochet government.

Two notable features relevant to risk-reduction can be detected in the 1964 reform. First, after the reform initiative had been examined and debated in the Chilean congress for two years, the time was drawing near for a new administration. By 1964 it had become obvious that the Christian Democratic Party and its leader Eduardo Frei would assume power in the following year. The congressional followers of Frei could therefore see the tax reform as cleaning up problems that otherwise would have to be handled, at some political loss, by the incoming administration.

Second, the reform initiative was presented and pursued as a project that would not change the vertical progressivity of tax incidence. The Alessandri tax reform was presented as improving efficiency without depriving anyone. To the considerable degree that Alessandri could convince private-sector groups that the tax reform was sufficiently justified as an effort to bring more coherence to Chile's confused tax structure —and hence not a pretext for redistribution—*and* that the administration could formulate a tax reform without major surprises in terms of effective incidence, the distributionally neutral initiative presented little risk.

Frei himself had more ambitious goals for tax reform. He oversaw a major expansion of governmental spending to respond to the challenge of the Marxist Left. To finance this spending without disastrous inflation clearly required a dramatic increase in government revenues. By the same token, Frei made it clear that the changes in taxation were intended to increase the relative burden of the "upper classes" (Sigmund 1977: 50; Ffrench-Davis 1973: 252, 329). Frei's first tax reform initiative in 1964 was presented to a legislature still dominated by the opposition of Alessandri's followers and the Left. Invoking the anti-inflationary objective, the tax package included across-the-board increases in tax rates. Frei also emphasized reducing the budget deficit by introducing new spending programs only with adequate provisions for their funding (Arbildua and Luders 1968:37). Since this meant violating the stricture against "earmarking" taxes—a widely criticized practice—it is worthwhile to explore the political rationale for this action.

Earmarking taxes for specific funding obligations affected the policy-making structure by intensifying the interests of the beneficiaries of any given measure and limiting its burden for the general taxpaying public. Of course, the whole set of earmarked taxes could entail a much greater tax burden, but on any given measure the support from potential beneficiaries was intense and the opposition diffuse. The cost of this tactic is that by making explicit connections between specific taxes and specific expenditures, the directly redistributive nature of taxation becomes all the more obvious.

Linking specific taxes to social-service expenditures would seem a risky approach, considering the ability of the rich to obstruct legislation. Yet for Frei (unlike Belaúnde in Peru, who faced a similar challenge), two factors tipped the balance in favor of seeking separate financing for programs in education, health, and housing. First, the budget process allowed for considerable political credit to redound to the Chilean congress only when new funds were created. Second, the middle-class groups that would administer or supply the goods and services for extending social services to the poor could be expected to support not only the expenditures but also the taxes clearly linked to them.

The result was not a confrontation between rich and poor, but rather between a *coalition* of social service recipients and middle-class service providers, and the particular interests threatened by the specific tax obligations involved in greater expenditures.

The Frei administration also introduced a far more controversial Chilean version of the wealth tax (*impuesto patrimonial*) on the presumed income of capital assets including real estate, vehicles, and company shares. The wealth tax revenues were earmarked for a broad "program of transformation" for health, education, housing, and agrarian reform. The tax was to apply to individuals with incomes at least nine times greater than the minimum wage, at rates from 1.5 to 3.0 percent of the assets.

The right wing in congress objected to the entire tax package, but especially to the wealth tax. A campaign was launched to convince the public that the wealth tax would apply to peasants and small proprietors, when in fact its incidence would have extended to only 3 percent of the population. The campaign did indeed create considerable furor, and contributed to the defeat of the tax package in 1964. On the other hand, the defeat of the tax legislation in 1964 contributed to the strength of Frei's appeal for a legislative majority in the upcoming elections.

The wealth tax proposal opened up the highly contentious issue of the legal and even constitutional status of private property. The tax reform initiative was accompanied by both a government-sponsored land reform initiative and the openly discussed plan of the socialist and communist left to transfer industrial property to the state. Thus the risk of permitting a change in the status of property, even if ostensibly only for the purpose of a mild tax, was seen as very great in broader perspective. Not even the likelihood that such a property tax could easily be avoided or evaded was enough to soften the opposition.

Moreover, the broad Frei project of increasing the state's role in both social spending and direct economic activity had no discernible ceiling when viewed by the private business sector. Frei seemed to be intent on preempting the appeal of the left by expanding the state to an unpredictable magnitude. The tax reform was overtly geared to increase the burden on higher-income groups, and whatever technical corrections were entailed were viewed as serving that end rather than the more politically neutral end of the Alessandri reform.

When Frei resubmitted the tax package in 1965, it still could not gain passage intact, despite a Christian Democratic majority in the Chamber of Deputies. At this point (in contrast with López Michelsen in Colombia), Frei decided that a confrontation over tax reform would jeopardize the success of the other contentious objectives of economic redistribution, namely land reform and nationalization of copper. Frei's finance minister Sergio Molina (1972:127) later wrote: "The governmental measures were consciously designed *not* to open many simultaneous fronts in the struggle [for income redistribution], because it was known that the affected sectors would become tenacious enemies out to frustrate them."

Therefore the Frei administration accepted several dilutions to the wealth tax: it was restricted to the year of 1965; the rates were cut back to 1.2 percent–2.1 percent; and other tax liabilities were deducted from the wealth-tax base. Yet later that year an earthquake and flooding occasioned a reconstruction program that secured funding through an extension of the wealth tax at rates of 1.6 percent–2.8 percent. In 1968, when that tax expired, the wealth tax was again legislated, albeit at a lower rate of one percent.

Amid the furor over the wealth tax, many of the earmarked taxes were passed, and the overall rates of sales taxes and income taxes increased. The controversy over the wealth tax distracted attention and resistance away from these more mundane—but no less important —developments. From a level of less than 13 percent of gross national product in 1964, tax revenues rose to 18 percent by 1967 and over 21 percent by 1970 (Ffrench-Davis 1973: 252, 329). New taxes, increased tax rates, and stricter enforcement of existing penalties for evasion (e.g., the first prosecutions for tax fraud in Chilean history!) more than doubled tax revenues under the Frei administration.

These changes came at some substantial cost to the coherence of the Chilean tax system. The short-lived Allende administration (1970–1973) proposed to streamline the tax system in order to eliminate loopholes that provided the opportunity for high-income taxpayers to avoid taxes. The budget and the tax package were submitted together in an effort to force the legislature to meet the financing needs of the expanded spending program. It was presumed that the onus for inadequate taxes would be laid to congress, thus strengthening the administration's position should it call for a plebiscite. Allende's approach to tax reform was openly confrontational, a choice of little cost given the polarization that already prevailed.

The congressional opposition reacted in the same manner as did the opposition to Belaúnde in Peru during the 1964–68 period (see the discussion of Peru below). Instead of refusing to allow for higher taxes and cutting government spending accordingly, or acceding to tax increases, the legislative opposition exaggerated the spending burden without allowing for higher tax rates. The discrepancy between revenues and spending increased. By 1972, the last full year of the Allende administration, the fiscal deficit reached over 40 percent of central government expenditure, compared to less than ten percent during the 1967–69 period. The deficit was financed largely through internal borrowing, which contributed greatly to domestic inflation (Cauas 1974:133).

In 1973, with hyperinflation already underway, the congress passed higher state-sector wage increases than the Allende administration had requested; when Allende vetoed that bill, congress rejected his tax-increase proposals. Congress flaunted its control over taxation by passing a simplified tax structure, as the administration had proposed, but with *lower* burdens for high-income taxpayers. Less than half of the increased spending was covered by revenues (de Vylder 1976: 92–93, 223). By that time, the plebiscite threat was irrelevant, because the Allende administration had lost the support of middle-class voters necessary for a decisive victory. By September the Allende regime was toppled by the military.

In retrospect, it seems obvious that any sort of coherent tax reform under Allende was illusory. The Allende economic team took over without a carefully crafted economic plan, much less a well-prepared tax reform. The drastic economic fluctuations that ensued, and the uncertainty of the risk associated with going along with a tax reform, would have undermined the technical feasibility of true reform as well as compliance to such a reform.

The 1974 Pinochet Reform. The context facing the incoming military government was, of course, drastically different. The Left was definitively crushed for the time being—or so it appears after the fact. There was certainly a widespread belief among the victors that the Chilean entrepreneurial class had to be restored, rather than burdened further. Therefore the tax reforms under the Pinochet administration might be thought to be politically uninformative because the power of the regime was so great as to guarantee their successful implementation. Yet the 1974 reform and subsequent modifications are enlightening for what the management of risk implies about limits to reform even under those politically extreme circumstances.

In 1974, under the leadership of the newly appointed minister of finance, Jorge Cauas, a fundamental tax reform was enacted that has remained basically in effect ever since. Although there have been adjustments, a few "dilutions" of the principle of neutrality, and much improvement in tax administration, the 1974 reform still constitutes the basic tax system in Chile.

From late 1973 through mid-1974, a technical team from the Planning Office and the Ministry of Finance addressed what they saw as the three major problems of the existing tax structure. First, Chile's chronically high inflation created many serious problems. On the one hand, tax brackets for income tax rates were rendered almost immediately obsolete by high inflation. On the other hand, delayed tax payments obviously yielded much smaller real revenues. This lack of proper means to adjust for inflation was diagnosed as a major factor in propagating inflation, as declining real revenues required the financing of the public debt through money creation (Cauas 1974:131).

Second, there was the problem of "double taxation" of business, which in the Chilean context meant the taxation of nominal increases in capital in addition to their real profits. The multiplicity of direct taxes on income had reached a point where obvious problems with horizontal equity were encountered. It was felt that some individuals were subject to double or treble taxation. Moreover, "bracket creep" had elevated the tax burden of manual laborers excessively, according to the judgment of the Finance Ministry. Since there was a basic income tax rate, a "global complementary" add-on, *and* an "additional tax," all figured on different bases, individuals with the same income level could be subject to widely differing overall income taxes. The 1974 reform made the bases of these taxes coincide, in order to enhance horizontal equity, and lowered the maximum wage tax rates so that the maximum marginal tax rate would not exceed 60 percent (Cauas 1974:145). Direct taxation of corporations was also seen as grossly distorted. To avoid corporate profits taxes, companies were reinvesting profits in ways the government judged to be suboptimal, companies were maintaining large raw material inventories in order to avoid holding taxable liquid assets, and many forms of business assets were vulnerable to reduction through taxation of their inflationary increase in nominal terms.

Third, the technical team addressed the problem of a multiplicity of indirect taxes that added one tax on top of another to the same item without regard for the value added in each step or transaction. The technical team wanted to apply the value added tax globally.

More generally, the Chilean tax code was encumbered by countless exemptions and exceptional categories that had no clear justification in terms of desirable investment incentives. In 1974 Finance Minister Cauas judged this complexity as tantamount to "complete anarchy in matters of taxation." But beyond the difficulties of tax administration per se, these exemptions created distortions in investment incentives that "seriously limited the possibility of using the tax policy as one of the most important tools in the economic and social development of the country." (Cauas 1974:122). While recognizing that a tax incentive could theoretically be desirable, the diagnosis was that the bulk of existing exemptions were counterproductive.

The Junta's Adoption of Technical Team Recommendations. Whereas one might think that the Chilean situation as of 1974 was a perfect instance of the bureaucratic authoritarian fusion of the military and the technocrat, there were still considerable differences between what the tax-reform team recommended and what the Pinochet-led junta believed to be politically advisable. To be sure, the greatest accomplishment of the 1974 reform was to offset the distortions resulting from inflation, by adopting the technical team's ingenious approach to inflation adjustment. Yet the uniformity desired by the technical team and the Finance Ministry was only partially achieved. Some special treatments remained, although they were somewhat simplified and unified. For example, regional development laws were to be applied without discrimination in terms of the type of activity, and sectoral exemptions were to be granted without discrimination in terms of the region. All "discretionary" application of tax laws was formally eliminated. No new exemptions to the global complementary single wage or additional taxes were permitted, and all existing exemptions eliminated.

The sales tax was replaced in 1974 by the value-added tax (VAT or IVA). Whereas the technical team had recommended a global VAT, certain exceptions were made. Except for processed foods, sales of articles in the agricultural sector were exempted, and an excise tax remained on some luxury items including nonalcoholic beverages and (with a different rate) alcoholic beverages. On the other hand, with few exceptions, services were included at the same rate as products.

A 20 percent value added tax is high by international standards. But it was justified on the grounds that this had already been the level of transactions taxes that the nonevading (and apparently largely hypothetical) "honest" taxpayer would have been paying. Of course, actual evasion of the prior transaction taxes had been substantial enough to make the less avoidable value-added tax a much greater effective tax burden. On the rhetorical level, the comparison with the prior "honest" level had the advantage of neutralizing the issue of whether greater actual reliance on a flat-rate direct tax would have redistributive implications.

While the value-added tax was chosen in part because it makes evasion difficult (for example, value added was calculated as the difference between sales and purchases, thus providing incentive for intermediate purchasers to report fully on the sales of their suppliers), there was far less effort to ensure full compliance and even horizontal equity with respect to the income tax. Marginal rates remained very high for high brackets (50 percent even after the 1984 reduction), making it practically mandatory for the rich to resort to tax shelters or evasion. Income earned from different sources (a common occurrence for professionals) was taxed at the marginal rate for each source of income rather than at the marginal rate for the combined income; income earned on interest, typically evaded in an open way, remained untouched despite proposals to withhold tax on it. There were some modest improvements in direct taxation (e.g., corporations were made to collect a dividend withholding tax), but the generally greater weakness of direct tax collection reduced the weight of direct taxation and, according to many critics, undermined the vertical equity of the tax structure. Income taxes soon accounted for only 4 percent of government revenues (Arellano and Marfan 1987:28–30).

Many of the 1974 Chilean reforms entailed the elimination of special treatment for groups that had received politically motivated concessions under previous administrations. For example, individuals involved in passenger transportation and trucking, who could easily engage in economically disruptive strikes or slowdowns, had been placed in particularly favorable tax status. That was no longer politically necessary under the Pinochet government.

It is a very interesting twist that the 1974 Chilean tax reform made very little provision for the adequate taxation of high-income landowners. The sweeping land reform of the Allende era had left the countryside nearly empty of large landowners in current possession of their former property, and the idea of trying to impose complicated tax-filing procedures upon the new small-plot owners or agricultural collective members seemed counterproductive. However, the restoration of the property rights of the former large landowners was already under way. Yet they were both allies of the new government, and still appeared to that government to be the dispossessed rather than a target of extraction. Over the years, the tax system's lack of mechanisms to tax agricultural income effectively has emerged as a major problem.

Considering the political strength of the Pinochet government and the commitment to fundamental tax reform of the Pinochet economic team, one may ask why the 1974 reform did not accomplish even more; why did it not approach the issues addressed by the 1984 reform? If in 1974 the military had enormous political dominance, and yet many thought that the opportunity for drastic reform may soon pass, why did the reform go no further?

One of the constraints faced by the 1974 Chilean economic team, given its desire to make a sweeping change in the direction identified with the "Chicago boys," was the skepticism toward such radical changes within both the government and the military. The tax specialists, even if they were convinced of the reasonableness and predictability of going all the way with such reforms as the complete elimination of the personal income tax, could not fully relieve the anxieties of the "non-Chicago boys" and the nonexperts that such changes might be quite risky.

The Chilean tax experts were the first to admit that the vertical incidence of the tax system prior to the 1974 reform was very difficult to estimate, owing to the fact that two thirds of the tax revenues were from indirect taxes on products whose consumption patterns had not been examined in terms of the income levels of consumers (Aninat 1975:167). The lack of either fact or myth on the vertical incidence of the existing tax system made it more compelling to leave the issue of vertical distribution aside.

There were parallel political concerns. The military itself was not monolithic in terms of its views on income distribution and the general direction of economic strategy. For example, some high-level officers were attracted to the reform not because it ultimately had the effect of reducing the weight of direct taxation, but on the contrary because they believed that it would have the effect of clamping down on high-income earners' evasion of corporate and personal income taxes. As one observer put it, "The military, after all, were salaried, and had everybody else's resentment against the flaunting of the tax system by profit-earners."[17]

In addition, the military was not oblivious to the need to cultivate some popular support. Since large segments of the population had become thoroughly disillusioned with (and antagonistic toward) the Allende administration, it was not out of the question that the military might be able to win over hearts and minds by rationalizing the revenue system so as to be able to provide a solid basis for social service expenditures.

The 1984 Reform. Whereas the Chilean tax reform of 1974 was impelled by the disastrous state of Chilean public finance, and the need to cover public expenditures that could not be avoided in the short run, the reform of 1984 was formulated in a context of continuing efforts to diminish the role of the state in the Chilean economy. It was believed that reducing the still high marginal tax rates and corporate taxation would encourage private savings (Cheyre 1986a). The objective to stimulate savings was also presented as noncontroversially technical. Yet critics, principally those identified with the Christian Democrats and the prominent research center CIEPLAN, disputed the assertion that transferring more savings potential from the public sector to the private sector would enhance overall investment. The critics were quick to point out that there was no evidence, nor much theoretical rationale, to expect this to occur (Marfan 1987).

The 1984 reform deliberately eschewed technically complex ways of taxing spending (e.g., basing a spending tax on declared income less declared savings, or on directly declared spending) as impracticable (Cheyre 1986b:14), although it had been part of the original proposal. Therefore the emphasis remained on making the VAT a more significant source of revenues. Yet here, too, the critics attacked the global VAT as regressive, on the grounds that lower-income individuals consume a larger proportion of their incomes. Tax specialists within the government and at the economics department of the University of Chile call the same phenomenon "neutral," on the grounds that eventually all income ends up in consumption. The striking aspect of this dispute is that a basically ideological difference can create disagreement on such an important, seemingly technical issue of what constitutes neutrality.

Yet the critics making a fundamental theoretical attack of the approach had only one channel for circulating this rather complex argument—their own technical publications. In Chile, where the depth of technical capacity is quite impressive and "technopolitics" is as important as "bureaucratic politics," "opposition" experts have very little access to the policymakers. Of course, the opposition's appraisal of Pinochet's policies, whether economic policies or otherwise, has been so consistently negative that the government interprets any criticism as part of the political campaign against it.

Thus the constraints on going further with the VAT—or even to the point of moving totally to indirect taxes (a "theoretical" preference of a considerable number of Chilean tax specialists) was a form of self restraint rather than manifest political opposition. In the discussions over the 1984 Chilean tax reform, the concern of the private business sector to manage its risk took on an even more exotic form. Some businessmen objected to the elimination of the corporate tax because its disappearance would leave open the *future* danger that a new government might turn on the corporate sector with higher, even punitive taxes rationalized on the grounds that the business sector had been unfairly favored by having to pay nothing before that.[18] It was felt that a safer course was to live with a moderate corporate tax, moderated even more by legal exemptions (which could in part or in whole be passed on to the consumer in any event), than to risk the possibility of future reprisals.

The same attitude held in many quarters among high-income individuals with respect to the possibility of eliminating the personal income tax. Although some tax theorists believe that the system would have much more coherence if the value-added tax were virtually the sole source of internal taxation, there is the counterargument, based on political judgment, that this would make high-income earners more vulnerable to future attack—even assuming that the total elimination of the personal income tax were politically possible.

It might seem that these fears do not coincide with the observed indifference to tax issues of the pressure groups representing lower-income individuals. Yet it is widely believed that basing a tax system predominantly on indirect taxation, without high apparent marginal income tax rates to impart the impression of progressivity, would trigger strong opposition.

Lessons of the Chilean Reforms. The key lesson in Chile's experiences with tax reform has been the avoidance of direct confrontation over redistribution by the successful tax reform initiators even when they seemed to hold dominant political power. As in the Colombian case, low-income taxpayer groups do not become mobilized unless tax changes are blatantly regressive. Yet the anticipation that this mobilization could occur was an inhibiting factor even for the Pinochet government. The tempting simplification of assuming that a rightist government would willingly adopt the most pro-business tax structure that its political power would permit is simply not borne out by the Chilean case.

Another lesson of the Chilean reforms is that improved tax administration changes the politics of tax reform dramatically by limiting the capacity of evasion to limit the impact of changes in tax burden. According to one Chilean economist, "The incredible strength now of the tax administration is a political danger for the government, because what the tax law says is what will happen. So the government has to build in explicitly the loopholes that are politically required. Otherwise their allies in the business sector could be seriously hurt."[19]

Finally, the debate over the Chilean tax system reveals that there is no "technical consensus" even on the fundamental definition of vertical neutrality. The separation between the overtly value-laden formulation of tax reform by political leaders, and the "technical" work that also drives the explorations of tax reform options, is blurry indeed.

B3. Peru

It is safe to say that there has been no fundamental tax reform in Peru in the last three decades. This is certainly not because of a lack of need for tax reform, and economic policy reform in general. The paradox is that tax change is often fundamentally important for the long-term health of the economy and yet a secondary issue in circumstances of instability and generally bad economic policy. When government spending is out of control, foreign reserves are dwindling, and other economic catastrophes threaten, tax reform typically gets little attention, even if inadequate tax policies are partly to blame for the negative state of affairs.

The inadequacy of the Peruvian tax system is manifested in several ways. There is unanimity of opinion that the base for direct taxes is too narrow: less than half a million Peruvians, in a country of nearly 20 million, pay personal income taxes. This is not a case of the failure (or the unwillingness) to extract direct taxes from individuals lower down in the income distribution, but rather a failure to collect taxes from many middle- and high-income earners.

Second, the complexity of the tax system, with modifications piled upon previous modifications, is extreme. Tax lawyers who in other circumstances would be expected to brag about their mastery of the tax system openly admit that they cannot fully understand the Peruvian tax laws.

Third, the tax system is simply incapable of generating the level of revenues that Peruvian governments have wished to extract. The results of the narrowness of the tax base, the problems of collection, and other weaknesses are reflected in revenue shortfalls. While export booms now and then reduced the gaps between revenues and government spending, budget deficits have been a chronic source of economic instability, leading governments to face politically costly or economically counterproductive options. This is clear from the García government's recent need to resort to forcing private corporations to purchase government bonds, coming at a time when the government is supposedly firmly committed to stimulating investment to match the demand stimulated by monetary expansion. More generally, the inability to fine-tune the revenue level is continually apparent in the frequent reports that the government's tax changes have resulted in unanticipated revenue declines.

If we begin our analysis with the Belaúnde administration of 1963– 68, we see a recurrent pattern of initial preoccupation with economic stimulation, with low priority given to the overall coherence of the tax structure, followed by a fiscal crisis (often tied to exogenous shocks) culminating in ad hoc adjustments even if it could have been mitigated by a prior fundamental reform. Between the revenue-increasing options of expanding the tax base through aggregate growth or increasing the tax rates on the existing base, Belaúnde's initial policies strongly favored the former. The industrial promotion policies of previous governments were expanded. Tax changes to encourage industrial investment, rather than to raise revenues, became the focus of fiscal legislation. Without definitive economic criteria for deciding which industries really warranted preferential treatment, and motivated to avoid antagonizing any business groups, the Belaúnde government granted exemptions on virtually an ad hoc basis (Kuczynski 1977:80–85). To reduce the declines in revenues, the government raised import tariffs (sold politically as part of the campaign to promote domestic industry) and sales taxes (Webb 1977:51–52), but without placing these measures within a broad reform. The sales tax increases were very costly politically, because of the prevailing belief in Peru (in contrast to Colombia) that indirect taxation is inherently regressive. Webb (1977:50–53) argues convincingly that this belief is false for Peru as well.

As the need to raise revenues mounted, the Belaúnde administration pressed congress for increases in direct taxes but in fact settled for further increases in import duties. Since the rules allowed for "administrative updating" of import categories, changes in import duty rates were barely visible and did not require congressional approval.

The epitome of government futility came in 1966, when the Belaúnde administration's finance minister Sandro Mariategui finally submitted a significant tax reform embedded in the 1967 budget, calling for higher income taxes and new taxes on real estate and enterprise capital shares. APRA leader Haya de la Torre mobilized his supporters with the slogan, "No more taxes!" Congress rejected the taxes but approved the spending package. Instead of withdrawing the bill, forcing an acute crisis, and exposing the APRA to political risk of being party to an economic paralysis, the administration accepted an outcome that made the fiscal problem even worse.

The congressional opposition to increased direct taxation was both ironic and puzzling because the major thrusts of the tax reform were increases in income and profits taxes applicable to fewer than 40,000 individuals and firms. The personal income tax was applicable only to the top 1 percent of income earners because of the high exemption levels (Kuczynski 1977:87). This was hardly the mass public that the APRA intended to mobilize. The public's opposition to higher taxes was due in part to its identification of further tax increases with the highly visible previous increases in the sales tax. There was little recognition that further changes would place the burden on different groups.

In 1968 the APRA opposition finally relented to tax reform. Two important aspects of the political context must be emphasized. First, if democratic government could have been preserved through the upcoming elections and transition to the next democratically elected regime, the APRA stood a very good chance of winning. Thus the resolution of chronic fiscal problems, with the Belaúnde administration taking the heat, was very attractive to the APRA leadership. The tax changes would not have enough time to endear the voters to the Belaúnde administration; if anything, the short-term costs could have cost the Belaúnde administration some support during the election campaign. Second, the fiscal situation had become so bad that the military's confidence in the Belaúnde government was fast declining. APRA realized—too late —that Belaúnde's fiscal crisis could lead to military intervention. Until military intervention became a clear threat to the upcoming election, the opposition found greater risks either in the tax change, or in the political costs of a tax reform going through, than in the economic chaos of the fiscal crisis.

The way the opposition allowed the Belaúnde administration to carry out the reform is also illuminating. Rather than reversing their opposition publicly, the APRA and Unión Nacional Odriísta (UNO) granted authority to the executive in June 1968 to "take the emergency measures needed to solve the structural imbalance in public finances, to strengthen the balance of payments, and to encourage the integrated development of our economy . . . . The measures taken under the authority of this law will be in the form of Supreme Decrees approved by the Council of Ministers, with the obligation of advising the Congress of each measure so taken" (text of Peruvian Law 17044, 1978, cited in Kucinski, 1977, p. 266). Thus the opposition agreed to move tax policy out of the open arena of congress, so that responsibility for the sacrifices necessitated by the reforms would not be laid to the opposition.

During the two-month period of emergency power authorization, the Ministry of Finance and Commerce under Manuel Ulloa enacted many tax reforms that would have been important if they had endured. In the much more closed arena of the ministry, in an atmosphere of crisis, Ulloa decreed higher or altogether new taxes on profits, interest income, real estate, corporate net worth, gasoline (with much steeper taxes on the higher octanes used by automobiles rather than buses), and various other items. The net effect was strongly progressive (Kuczynski 1977:230–33; Webb 1977:53), although it was hardly a coherent streamlining of the Peruvian tax system. The imperative of coming up with revenues to reduce the deficit, exacerbated by the short time period, squeezed out efforts to rehaul the entire system for the sake of coherence.

The left-leaning Velasco military government that ousted Belaúnde in 1968, and the more centrist Morales Bermúdez military government that ruled from 1975 to 1980, could have pursued tax reform without any of the legislative obstructionism that seemed to doom Belaúnde's efforts. Yet there is broad consensus that the Peruvian military governments of the 1970s did not succeed at tax reform (Webb 1977: chapter 4; Thorp and Bertram 1978; Ugarteche 1980); indeed, it is widely accepted that the Velasco and Morales Bermúdez administrations did not push for fundamental tax reform despite the relatively easy political path for enacting one (Thorp 1983:49; FitzGerald 1983:77–79).

The Velasco administration announced a basic tax reform in its 1971–75 National Development Plan, that would have entailed a very significant increase in the direct tax burden from 19 percent to 22 percent of GDP by 1975, but never carried out the reform (FitzGerald 1983:78). The Morales Bermúdez administration did not even get that far; the 1975–80 period was marked by myriad piecemeal tax adjustments that did not amount to more than trying to maintain the level of revenues in the face of fluctuating export prices. Thus in 1977 the Morales Bermúdez government accepted the International Monetary Fund's insistence on reducing the budget deficit by cutting public spending, especially in cutting back on the operations of the state oil enterprise Petroperu. Whether or not the IMF's focus on budget cutbacks rather than revenue expansion was simply a case of bowing to the real-counterreforms.

ity that tax reform was not in the offing, the result was that compliance was pursued through expenditure contraction rather than by confronting the tax issue.

The failure of these military governments to enact tax reform allows us to look beyond the legislative obstruction to explain why, if tax reform is so essential for Peru, so few efforts at fundamental reform have been launched, let alone accomplished. The neglect of tax reform by Peruvian regimes unencumbered by legislative opposition implies a second answer: the severe imbalances of the Peruvian economy heightened the government's risks in undertaking a tax reform, while these same imbalances (as well as other conditions) diminished the apparent immediacy of the need for reform as well.

On the risk side, both Velasco and Morales Bermúdez viewed the support and compliance of middle-sized industrialists ("independent industry") as pivotal for maintaining economic normalcy. For Velasco, the populist rhetoric and some expropriation had supplanted or at least antagonized the large-scale industrialists ("oligarchic industry"), leaving any remaining dynamism to the up-and-coming entrepreneurs. Since the latter were moving into areas made attractive by government subsidies via tax exemptions and cheap credit, the announcement of a fundamental tax reform initiative could have jeopardized this dynamism. For Morales Bermúdez, the challenge was to restore investor confidence in general, and to convince the business sector that the Velasco days were behind them. Since Velasco's style had been characterized by sweeping gestures, Morales Bermúdez opted for a thoroughly incrementalist approach to economic policy in order to distance his own administration from Velasco's.

What minimized the perceived need to proceed with tax reform despite these risks was the combination of hopes for state-promoted industrial expansion, export growth, improved state-sector performance, and cheap foreign capital. There was an expectation in the early 1970s that both industrial production and export earnings would rise enough to meet revenue-need projections (FitzGerald 1983:78). Under Velasco, companies taken into the "social property" sector were expected to add to savings rather than constitute a drain on savings. Under Morales Bermúdez, there was optimism that the drain that did occur under Velasco could be reversed through greater discipline. To fill any investment gaps, foreign capital was available at very low real interest rates.

Nor was tax reform seen by the military governments as a necessary condition for effecting the improvements in income distribution that both Velasco and (though to a lesser extent) Morales Bermúdez prom-ised. During the military governments lasting from 1968 to 1980, the principal means of redistribution in Peru was the direct subsidy. Once the land reform had been largely completed, the governments of Velasco and Morales Bermúdez relied heavily on low gasoline prices, low health-care prices, and so on, to bolster the purchasing power of the poor—at least the urban poor. Thus there seemed to be little concern over tax reform, despite the fact that the tax system was increasingly riddled with inconsistencies. Thus in January 1980 the National Congress of Manufacturing Industries was still calling for "the integral revision of the tax system" (Centro de Estudios y Promoción del Desarrollo 1982: 3781).

Thus when Belaúnde took over again in the 1980 restoration of civil-ian government, his highly trained, antistatist economic team took sev-eral steps to liberalize the economy. State investment in productive sec-tors was redirected from competition with the private sector to infra-structure in support of private-sector initiatives. To launch these huge infrastructure projects, Belaúnde's economic team still looked to foreign borrowing rather than fundamental improvements in revenue collection —a choice made possible by the fact that the Morales Bermúdez auster-ity program had reduced inflation, improved the external trade balance, and balanced the budget. The creditworthiness accorded to Peru at the beginning of the Belaúnde term, and momentarily high export prices, once again seemed to vitiate the need for tax reform. By the time the explosion in real interest rates reduced the viability of additional for-eign borrowing in the early 1980s, the Belaúnde administration was battling the recessionary effects of another downturn in export prices, while trying to hang onto the large public works projects that Belaúnde claimed as his hallmark. Thus, while a tax overhaul in the name of supporting these large projects may have gained some political support, the need to counteract the recession put tax reform off the agenda.

What was done with respect to tax changes was characteristically hemmed in by other considerations far removed from rationalizing the tax structure. For example, the Belaúnde team saw the elimination of market-distorting subsidies as an important aspect of economic reform. This was thought to hold a political risk, inasmuch as urban disruption in reaction against the withdrawal of such subsidies might be expected. The Belaúnde government hit upon a way of softening the blow of elim-inating the subsidy on gasoline, by tying it into changes in the tax structure. With much fanfare, the increases in gasoline prices were announced as part of the effort to increase the profits of Petroperu, which then would be more heavily taxed to underwrite general government expenditures.

The very heavy reliance on the taxation of Petroperu that emerged was the politically easy way out for the Belaúnde government. It was certainly a narrower political battle to fight than taking on a private-sector group, or trying to make painful (and uncertain) changes in tax administration. The "bureaucratic politics" confrontation between Petroperu and the central administration was the only hurdle, and Belaúnde could choose the Petroperu head. Petroperu had never made the fortunes that could make it a power unto itself like Mexico's PEMEX. The very fact that "taxing" Petroperu was discussed in the same vein as taxing the private sector was a bit disingenuous, since Petroperu's profits were the state's.[20]

The Aprista administration of President Alan García was elected in 1985, following a horrendous economic contraction; austerity measures and drops in copper and oil prices left industry running at 40 percent of installed capacity. Whereas several aspects of economic imbalance were sure to continue (such as inflation exceeding 200 percent in 1985), the opportunity to revive the economy was far more attractive—politically as well as economically—than confronting a tax reform that would create uncertainty for all concerned in direct proportion to its depth. Here again, the initial conditions of economic contraction could be traced back to poor revenue collection and the budget deficits that brought about an austerity program as the policy response, but the immediate reaction was to restimulate the economy—hardly what a thorough and deliberate tax reform would encourage—in order to take advantage of the untapped potential for economic expansion.

The García administration, as part of its anti-inflation program, has artificially kept down the price of gasoline, among other basic consumption goods, thus eliminating the possibility of relying so heavily on the taxation of Petroperu. Yet coming to grips with the inadequacy of the tax structure seems to remain a low priority for the Peruvian administration.

Carol Wise (1986:5) points out that "the last three austerity programs (in 1967–68, 1977–78 and 1983–84) signified a final deathblow for the government that implemented each. Usually, it has been the succeeding government that has enjoyed the economic benefits, in terms of a greater financial flexibility; nevertheless, the final results of this additional 'margin of maneuver' have not been particularly favorable." It seems that one very unfortunate result of the sacrifices made by Peruvian administration in the last gasps of their tenure is that their successors see little immediate need for fundamental tax reform and considerable costs to undertaking such a reform. In these acute stop-go cycles, fundamental tax reform seems to be the last thing on the minds of top policymakers trying to cope with deterioration or taking advantage of expansionary opportunities. Moreover, as long as government economic policymakers believe that the rather heavy-handed policy tools of direct subsidies to consumers and manufacturers, augmented by price controls, will solve the distributional issue and increase the revenue base, the logic of fundamental tax reform will hardly seem compelling.

The Peruvian case also shows quite clearly that formal authority to make tax changes, which appears so important in Colombia because of the complicated circumventions that tax reforms had to employ in order to overcome congressional opposition, is not only insufficient to ensure constructive reform, it can even be counterproductive. Peruvian law permits the president to adjust even tax rates *during* the fiscal year, without legislative approval. This obviously creates considerable uncertainty for business planning and investment, inasmuch as the after-tax rate of return of a given investment remains uncertain even if the business side of the investment is well understood.

C. Some General Lessons

The experiences of the three countries examined above, and the importance of risk and its management, yield several lessons for each phase of tax-reform policymaking.

With regard to *initiation*, uncertainty of success is often a serious inhibition against the investment of significant effort by private groups, even if certain private groups may ultimately benefit greatly from tax reform. For reasons of complexity and the apparent indirectness of impact, organized labor exerts little effort over tax issues unless there is a clear danger (as opposed to opportunity).

One implication of the typically defensive stance of interest groups vis-à-vis tax reform is that tax reform, whether to increase revenues or to improve distribution, tends to be an initiative of the state. There are instances of private groups petitioning for more favorable tax treatment and for a rollback in what they argue are excessive rates, and there are cases of private sector initiatives to reduce the red tape and distortions of particular tax regulations. Yet these are relatively rare and modest efforts, because they too have the potential to open up an unpredictable chain of events. In short, without the government as the prime mover behind fundamental tax reform, it would be a very quiet field.[21]

Another implication is that the potentially redistributive nature of tax changes, combined with the uncertainty inherent in any new taxation, makes *risk avoidance* a very high priority for the typical interest group. Of course, change and innovation necessary to improve tax systems necessarily entail some uncertainty and risk for all taxpayers. The key to understanding the politics of tax reform is to appreciate the uncertainty of the impact of even moderate tax changes that persists during and even after the formulation and implementation of the reform. The frequently negative "reflex" reaction to a new tax reform initiative on the part of many groups is typically due not just to expected losses but also to the risk of incurring costs that cannot be anticipated.

Hence, much of the "artistry" of designing and negotiating tax reforms is in introducing innovations that nonetheless involve a tolerable degree of risk for politically and economically powerful interests.

State initiatives may be motivated by the obvious consideration that more efficient tax collection increases the power of the state. In some cases, tax reform can even become an issue of positive political payoff for the administration. This temptation can go too far, as too many tax changes to cash in on the political appeal of tax reform activism can be inefficient if tax administration cannot settle down to administering the same set of tax regulations.

In other cases, a seemingly ripe moment for tax reform can be squandered because more serious economic policy problems distract from concern over tax reform. Even if the government favors tax reform "in theory," serious economic disequilibria drive out initiatives for fundamental tax reform.

In electorally competitive systems, "ripe" moments for introducing tax reform are:

a. the beginning of an administration, if the electoral margin was large, and the solid prior studies exist
b. a financial crisis prevails, *if* the government maintains both credibility and good macropolicy
c. the political opposition, if not in principle opposed, foresees winning the next election and hence prefers the current administration to bear the costs of imposing a painful reform.

The promotional appeal of some tax reforms rests heavily on the attractiveness of horizontal equity. Striving for horizontal equity (except between sectors) is the consensus point for tax reform because it seems ethically compelling, technically straightforward, and does not raise the issue of class conflict. Vertical redistribution can sometimes be achieved as a consequence of measures explicitly designed to promote horizontal equity.

However, the issue of horizontal equity is often a sectoral issue, especially on the dimension of industry vs. agriculture. The politics of "sectoral clashes" is quite distinctive from class politics. By bringing in the debate over development strategies, sectoral champions can argue in favor of (cross-sectoral) horizontal inequality (e.g., by arguing that overall growth would be enhanced by providing more investment and income in one sector rather than another).

Although tax changes may be understood in terms of their impacts on income classes, interest group structures simply are not organized in terms of income classes. Typically they are organized "functionally" within industries and, as they aggregate through umbrella organization, within functional sectors such as manufacturing, agriculture, banking, mining, etc. Thus much of the politics over economic policy is structured around "sectoral conflicts."

Sectoral politics may be accentuated by social and political cleavages among the sectors (e.g., the "landed oligarchy" vs. the "nouveau riche" industrialists), but it is also fundamentally embedded in interest group organization. Even if individuals and families mix their investments among different sectors, their organizational spokesmen are still expected to lobby only for the interests of the particular sector or industry formally represented by that organization. Thus, no matter whether the Peruvian fishmeal processing is capitalized by landowners or industrialists, the fishmeal processors' association by and large pursues policies perceived as beneficial to the fishmeal industry and its profitability.

A final point on the definition of the tax reform issue is its linkage with other potentially redistributive initiatives. Economic groups react to the risks of a given prospect of policy change in the context of other risks. Thus a key factor in securing the acquiescence of economic groups facing risks from tax reform, beyond clarifying the limits of tax reform per se, is to tie the tax reform to guarantees that other risk-laden policy changes will be held in abeyance.

It may seem that fundamental tax reform—even if it is defined modestly as reform that has long-lasting impact—requires careful cultivation and therefore is incompatible with such short-term reactions to emergency situations as stabilization programs. Yet the prod of emergency is a resource of great potential importance for overcoming or discrediting opposition. Furthermore, it is often of great advantage to implement economic reforms at the very outset of a new administration's term, not only to take advantage of the political clout of a president with a full term left to punish recalcitrant opposition, but also to catch the opposition unprepared. It is therefore significant that several tax reforms were successfully imposed as part of emergency stabilization programs or as "lightning bolts" of a new government. How can this be done effectively?

It should be obvious that if the key to effective reform through immediate or emergency action is careful prior contingency planning, then either the existence of an established cohesive technical team is essential, or the government must accept a blueprint of a preceding regime or earlier external mission. The Colombian reform benefited from the former, while the Peruvian military regime that came to power in 1968 essentially capitalized on initiatives of the preceding civilian regime of Fernando Belaúnde. If the current government does not share the objectives of previous administrations, and lacks the resource of a previously established technical team, then its chances of being ready with a viable tax reform are much reduced.

Yet in the *estimation* (or technical design) phase of tax reform policymaking, it is unlikely that there will be consensus among experts. Not even the concept of "vertical neutrality" is consensually accepted by technical specialists. The chronic problems of tax evasion and avoidance (see implementation below) encourage innovativeness of tax design. Yet some evasion-minimizing forms of taxation add to complexity; and complexity adds to uncertainty. Complexity facilitates evasion and avoidance. Those tax changes that are designed to effect greater redistribution by cutting off all avenues of escape for the high-income taxpayer tend to increase complexity, with the obvious but ironic effect of creating new opportunities for evasion and avoidance, as well as jeopardizing political consensus.

The tax specialist may be asked to "design in" several objectives for the tax reform. However, too many objectives can undermine basic purposes, inasmuch as complexity, whether for the sake of accomplishing multiple goals or not, increases uncertainty and hence risk. Experienced policymakers and technical specialists recognize this fact, and often design the bulk of the real tax change to be borne by existing taxes.

The involvement of foreign tax missions in the technical work of a tax reform can have positive or negative effects on its feasibility. A strong technical reputation must be clear to the actors most concerned about the tax reform, lest the foreign mission be seen as yea-sayers for the government. Foreign tax missions have contributed most by preparing domestic experts, and background analyses, to be available when the domestic political and economic conditions are ripe for the reform.

With respect to *selection* (i.e., the authoritative choice of tax policy), no government can afford to be oblivious to opposition. Such groups' *perception* of specific burden incidence depends on many factors beyond the actual incidence. These factors include the perception of overall "environmental" threat; thus narrower policy differences among economic groups and political movements can be an important advantage insofar as a narrower range of possible outcomes increases certainty. While a government may not be able to do anything about that range, its breadth or narrowness may help to account for the success or failure of tax reform. But the perception of future burden is also influenced by factors over which the government does have some control, such as the perception of governmental competence to design and carry out a reform as specified in the formulation stage, and the perception of evasion by various groups.

The actual burden depends to a large degree on final details. This is a major reason why support for tax reform during the formulation phase is so thin. The reduction of risk to potential opposition—a crucial requirement for successful selection—can be accomplished either by constraining the risk of the tax reform itself or linking it with constraints on "greater evils" (e.g., land reform from the perspective of large-scale land owners).

Even the seemingly most technical tax reforms will have political and ideological overtones. This is a direct result of both the indeterminacy of what "equity" means and the fact that any significant reform will have distributional implications.

With respect to *implementation* (i.e., tax administration), success and failure both have rather counterintuitive implications. Although weak tax administration propels the search for innovative taxes, weak administration limits the innovations that are truly feasible. Although much of the attention and furor over major tax overhauls focuses on novel taxes, the changes in tax incidence typically come from existing taxes applied at different rates.

From a static perspective, the distributive liability of weak tax administration is that it generates pressure to tax the most easily taxed. However, from a dynamic perspective, weak tax administration, in reducing short-term risk, may allow for tax changes where political opposition could otherwise be fatal.

Efforts to strengthen a weak tax administration pose political issues, because: (a) stiffer anti-corruption rules may be interpreted as an attack on the bureaucrats as a group, and (b) the insertion of new personnel may be interpreted as "infiltration" by whatever ideological line is attributed to the initiators. However, it is difficult to oppose a strengthening of tax administration if it is carried out in the name of horizontal equity.

With respect to *appraisal* (i.e., evaluating the quality and success of the tax reform and the tactics used to pursue it), the first lesson is that success must be gauged relative to the political resources of the initiators. Thus the Colombian reform of 1974, while certainly impressive, must be evaluated in light of the tremendous clout of the López Michelsen administration.

A similar lesson of comprehensiveness of evaluation is that equity is most usefully considered in terms of overall fiscal policy. For example, a tax change that reduces progressivity may nonetheless increase revenues to such a degree that the lower-income groups are better off in net terms.

In terms of how the actors themselves appraise tax reform initiatives, it is clear that no tax reform will get universally high marks. There is always a different sort of sweeping reform that could be proposed as an alternative — to distribute differently, to promote investment rather than just savings, etc. Since the appraisal will necessarily depend at least partially on formal incidence rates rather than actual incidence, and on impressionistic evidence, there will always be disagreement.

With respect to *termination* (i.e., ending or changing a tax reform), we find that: (a) because incidence is a matter of late-settled details, the technical estimation at the outset is invariably somewhat in error, or at best somewhat irrelevant; (b) reform of a very messy tax system inevitably fails to address some problems; and (c) even well-designed reforms deteriorate in effectiveness as target groups learn how to avoid or evade their burdens. Therefore, tax reform is never a once-and-for-all phenomenon. Weaknesses in tax policy leave open the opportunity for counterreforms.

Notes

1   A political analysis is also distinctive in its focus on the question of why policy initiatives succeed or fail, without necessarily making a judgment on the economic advisability of the reform. Lacking any reason to believe that "intrinsically good" policies face a different politics than other policy initiatives, the examination of all initiatives adds to our understanding of how politics affects the fate of reforms. And clearly, we do not want to eliminate from consideration those many cases for which expert opinion is mixed about their technical quality. Thus, initiatives of various objectives and approaches are considered, without prejudging their advisability. And, for this analysis, a "successful tax reform initiative" means that a large part of the initiator's objectives were achieved, at rather low costs, rather than a demonstrable improvement in the tax system.

   This focus requires us to concentrate predominantly on "serious" efforts at major tax changes. Knowing when a tax reform effort is truly serious—i.e., when the initiators have great enough commitment to be willing to expose themselves to costs and risks—is not always straightforward. After all, in the rhetoric of policy, leaders rarely say that any initiative is less than serious. Yet the effort to identify serious efforts is important, because the inquiry into the requirements of successful tax reform can be seriously misled by mixing serious initiatives with efforts understood by the actors involved to be windowdressing.

2   The success of tax reform depends, of course, on its objectives. These can be classified as universal, typical, and particular.

   On the level of *universal* objectives, a tax reform initiative succeeds to the degree that the tax structure:

   comes closer to imposing the distribution of tax incidence on activities, individuals, and firms desired by the initiators;
   more easily permits adjustments in the volume of revenues and the distribution of incidence desired by top-level economic policymakers to adapt to changing macroeconomic conditions;
   minimizes the costs (foregone revenue or suboptimal distribution of incidence) required to achieve non-revenue ends.

   Typically, tax reformers, especially in developing countries, also want: enhancement of horizontal equity; i.e., to treat all activities and individuals of a given income or wealth equally, unless there is a particular reason to deviate from horizontal equity; simplification of tax administration, so as to reduce administrative costs, taxpayer resentment, evasion, and unwanted avoidance.

   Particular objectives of some tax reform initiatives include: greater progressivity (or regressivity) in tax incidence; greater (or lesser) stimulus of economic activity (e.g., savings, investment, consumption, importation, exportation); increased (or decreased) tax revenues.

3   Particularly in Chile. See the account of tax reform sequences below.

4   With the exception of one episode in the mid-1960s, the Colombian labor movement is virtually absent from the accounts on debates over tax reform. Miguel Urrutia goes so far as to bemoan the fact that such groups cannot be mobilized on the tax reform issue (see the section on Colombia). In Peru and Chile, the independent involve-

ment of the labor movement, apart from its participation in partisan movements, has also been very low as judged by the absence of prominent actions or pronouncements.

5 This reform and others in Colombia are described in Perry and Cárdenas 1986.

6 A presumptive income tax requires a property holder to pay a minimum income tax based on calculations of how much income would be generated by a property of given value. Obviously, the yield ratio and the property valuation are critical to whether such a tax is high or low.

7 Cited in Hirschman 1963:133.

8 "Legitimate" here is used to mean "accepted as normatively appropriate." Invoking emergency powers was regarded as a constitutional step, even though it was still up to the Supreme Court to decide whether the justification was adequate and the measures in keeping with the constitutional limitations of its use.

9 The events are covered extensively in both Urrutia 1983 and Perry and Cárdenas 1986. Both Urrutia and Perry were key members of the technical group.

10 Inflationary increases in asset values were thus taxable. The advocates of this policy believed that it would create pressure against inflation, while its opponents protested that it was confiscatory of accumulated wealth. (Urrutia 1986:36). The latter may also have been an intention of the more radical members of the technical group.

11 At the time, the president was expected to choose opposition cabinet members in rough proportion to the electoral split. See Dix 1987 for a description of these arrangements.

12 Interviews, Bogotá, May 12, 1987: nos. 3, 4, 5, 6.

13 Compare this with the lower middle class APRA objections to tax increases in Peru in the mid-1960s.

14 Urrutia 1986:34; interview with Ivan Obregon, May 14, 1987.

15 There are three kinds of costs. First, the government may sacrifice other policy gains in order to gain sufficient support for the tax reform. Second, the government may use up some of its "political capital" in accomplishing the tax reform, thereby leaving it with less power to accomplish other objectives. Third, the tax reform may lead to adverse economic reactions by nongovernmental actors.

16 Detailed descriptions of these episodes can be found in Molina 1972; Ffrench-Davis 1973; Sigmund 1977; Ascher 1984.

17 Interview Chile-11, Santiago, Chile, April 26, 1987.

18 Interview Chile-8, Santiago, Chile, April 26, 1987.

19 Interview Chile-10, Santiago, Chile, April 27, 1987.

20 The taxation of Petroperu was not entirely "show," though, because it was tied to the elevation of gasoline prices.

21 One could argue that all groups calling for greater governmental spending are essentially pressing for tax changes insofar as expenditures create pressure for greater revenues. Yet pressure for greater spending does not address several central tax reform issues: the form of taxation, its efficiency, or its equity. Moreover, the lobbying for greater spending typically does not engage the negotiations over tax policy. For better or for worse, they are largely separate interchanges.

References

Aninat, Eduardo. 1975. "Aspectos distributivos de la reforma tributaria." In Universidad de Chile, Departamento de Economía, *La reforma tributaria: Sus efectos económicos.* Santiago.

Arellano, José, and Manuel Marfan. 1987. "25 Years of Fiscal Policy in Chile." Santiago: CIEPLAN.

Arbildua, Beatriz, and Rolf Luders. 1968. "Una evaluación comparada de tres programas anti-inflacionarias en Chile: una década de historia monetaria." *Cuadernos de Economía* 5(14): 25–105.

Ascher, William. 1984. *Scheming for the Poor: The Politics of Redistribution in Latin America.* Cambridge, Mass.: Harvard University Press.

Bagley, Bruce, and Matthew Edel. 1980. "Popular Mobilization Programs of the National Front: Co-optation and Radicalization." In R. Albert Berry, Ronald G. Hellman, and Mauricio Solaun, eds., *Politics of Compromise.* New Brunswick, N.J.: Transaction Books.

Cauas, Jorge. 1974. "The Role of Tax Policy in National Economic Development." Santiago: Ministerio de Hacienda.

Centro de Estudios y Promoción del Desarrollo. 1982. *Peru 1980: Cronológia Política.* Lima.

Cheyre, Hernan. 1986a. "Análisis de las reformas tributarias en la década 1974–1983." *Estudios Públicos* (Chile) no. 21 (Summer): 141–83.

Cheyre, Hernan. 1986b. "Editorial", *Revista de Economía y Administración* (Chile) (April), no. 44.

de Vylder, Stefan. 1976. *Allende's Chile: The Political Economy of the Rise and Fall of the Unidad Popular.* London: Cambridge University Press.

Dix, Robert H. 1987. *The Politics of Colombia.* New York: Praeger.

Ffrench-Davis, Ricardo. 1973. *Políticas económicas de Chile 1951–1970.* Santiago: Ediciónes Nueva Universidad.

Fitzgerald, E. V. K. 1976. *The State and Economic Development: Peru since 1968.* Cambridge: Cambridge University Press.

———. 1983. "State Capitalism in Peru: A Model of Economic Development and Its Limitations." In Cynthia McKlintock and Abraham Lowenthal, eds., *The Peruvian Experiment Reconsidered.* Princeton, N.J.: Princeton University Press.

Herschel, Federico. 1971. "Taxation of Agriculture and Hard-To-Tax Groups." In Musgrave and Gillis: 387–415.

Hirschman, Albert O. 1963. *Journeys toward Progress: Studies of Economic Policy-Making in Latin America.* New York: Twentieth Century Fund.

IDE-ESAN. 1983. *El sistema tributario del Peru.* Lima: Mosca Azul Editores.

Kuczynski, Pedro-Pablo. 1977. *Peruvian Democracy under Economic Stress.* Princeton, N.J.: Princeton University Press.

Marfan, Manuel. 1984. "Una evaluación de la nueva reforma tributaria." *Colección Estudios Cieplan,* no. 13, Estudio no. 86 (June): 27–52.

———. 1987. "El conflicto entre la recaudación de impuestos y la inversión privada: Elementos teóricos para una reforma tributaria." *Collección Estudios Cieplan,* no. 18, Estudio no. 110 (December): 63–93.

Molina, Sergio. 1972. *El proceso de cambio en Chile: la experiencia 1965–1970.*

Santiago: Editorial Universitaria.

Musgrave, Richard, and Malcolm Gillis, eds. 1971. *Fiscal Reform for Colombia.* Cambridge: Harvard International Tax Program.

Perry, Guillermo, and Roberto Junguito. 1978. "Evaluación del régimen de la renta presuntiva mínima en Colombia." *Coyuntura Económica* (October).

Perry, Guillermo, and Mauricio Cárdenas. 1986. *Diez años de reformas tributarias en Colombia.* Bogotá: Centro de Investigaciónes para el Desarrollo/FEDESARROLLO.

Sigmund, Paul. 1977. *The Overthrow of Allende and the Politics of Chile, 1964–1976.* Pittsburgh: University of Pittsburgh Press.

Stallings, Barbara. 1978. *Class Conflict and Economic Development in Chile, 1958– 1973.* Stanford, Calif.: Stanford University Press.

Thorp, Rosemary 1983. "The Evolution of Peru's Economy." In Cynthia McKlintock and Abraham Lowenthal, eds., *The Peruvian Experiment Reconsidered.* Princeton, N.J.: Princeton University Press.

Urrutia, Miguel. 1983. *Gremios, política económica y democracia.* Bogotá: Fondo Económico Cafetero.

———. 1986. "The Politics of Fiscal Policy in Colombia." Tokyo: United Nations University.

Webb, Richard. 1977. *Government Policy and the Distribution of Income in Peru.* Cambridge, Mass.: Harvard University Press.

Wise, Carol. 1986. "Economía política del Peru: Rechazo a la receta ortodoxa." Instituto de Estudios Peruanos Working Paper, no. 15 (May) Lima, Peru.

13

A Political Scientist Looks at Tax Reform

·······

Robert H. Bates

Introduction

A major purpose of conferences such as this is to infer the lessons that
can be learned from past experience. For the subject at hand, some of
the key issues concern politics. Questions that naturally arise would
include: What are the political preconditions for successful tax reform?
On the basis of past expenses, what kinds of reforms are likely to succeed? What is the optimal timing, from a political point of view, for a
major tax reform? What is the best sequence? What advice would you
want to give to a reform minded politician, so as to enhance the likelihood of implementing successful fiscal policies?

I share with the other contributors to this conference a concern with
securing answers to such questions. But the basic issue I address is
more fundamental; it is the question of what we *can* know and therefore what we can advise.

When we address the question of methodology, we encounter powerful reasons for caution. By the standards normally adopted in the social
sciences, we find that there is little we can say with confidence. The
empirical foundations are lacking. And an exploration of the relevant
theory underscores the existence of problems that appear to confound
our ability to infer useful lessons or to formulate, even in principle,
valid prescriptions for reform minded practitioners.

By addressing methodological issues, however, we learn about the
political origin of tax reform. We learn why tax reform is demanded and
why it is needed. Perhaps even more important, we also learn what
constitutes useful knowledge to a tax reformer and the nature of such

knowledge. The lessons we learn do not take the form of universal pre-scriptions; but they should, nonetheless, prove useful.

Empirical Inference

Altogether the papers presented data from fifteen case studies. Given that Chile pre-1973 should in all likelihood not be treated as independent of Chile post-1973, and that Japan and the United States should not be regarded as developing countries, then the number of cases reduces to twelve.

The experience of the authors exceeds that of the case studies that they presented. Many have been involved in other instances of tax reform. All have studied the wider literature. Their insights therefore reflect as well their knowledge of other cases.

On the basis of these experiences, many of the participants confidently endorse formulas for success. Bird, for example, stresses that administrative reform lies at the root of successful tax reform. Jenkins calls for incrementalism; he suggests as well that reforms are best achieved when the economy is doing poorly. And Harberger calls for economic professionalism.

For the sample of cases in which Bird, Jenkins, and Harberger have been involved, these lessons may well stand uncontradicted by the facts. But what, then, are we to think of Bahl's equally confident assertion that policy reform is a necessary preliminary to good administration; of Gillis's stress on the importance of comprehensive reform; and of the apparent implication of the Indonesian case that tax reform can be successfully achieved when it is done prior to economic crisis? And for each professional economist who confidently takes a stand on one side of a knotty issue, we note, *pace* Harberger, the existence of another who asserts the opposite.

Throughout the papers there runs a highly prescriptive tone. The papers strive to develop useful insights for policy makers. But, in key instances, the lessons posited by one expert appear to be contradicted by the lessons prescribed by another.

One way of proceeding under these circumstances is to reinterpret the status of the formulas prescribed by the paper givers. They could be treated not as conclusions but rather as hypotheses. The degree of confidence with which they would be asserted would then be proportional to the level of confidence with which they could be accepted when subject to empirical confirmation.

Such a tactic has much to recommend it. But it clearly faces difficulties, for the case studies prepared for this conference do not furnish an adequate data base for implementing such a strategy. The number of cases is small. But the number of variables that affect the success of a policy reform is large. We therefore lack a sufficient number of cases to hold critical variables constant while altering single features of the policy package; as a consequence, we cannot investigate in a controlled fashion the impact of particular features of the tax reform package. Nor can we employ nonexperimental methods. The sample is too small to support with any confidence inferences drawn from correlations within it. In addition, the sample was drawn unsystematically, reflecting more the experience of well-known practitioners in the tax reform field than the experiences of the developing nations themselves.

The implication of these remarks is that while much wisdom is reflected in these papers, they do not yield propositions that can be empirically tested and confirmed on the basis of the data they offer.

What makes this particularly painful for a political scientist such as myself is that there was in fact one area of consensus among the conference participants, at least in the two (of six) sessions I attended. Many underscored their conviction that the basic variables affecting the success of tax reform lay outside their control. The impact of the studies they conducted, the training programs they put in place, or the advice they offered, they indicated, was largely determined by domestic politics. For Harberger, it was the wise leadership of a few distinguished politicians and civil servants that made all the difference; for Gillis, the core group of technocrats who maintained positions of leadership in the making of economic policy. For Jenkins, Shoup, and Bahl, the decisive force was the leadership brought to power by recent changes in government.

If there was any consensus in the fifth and sixth sessions of the conference, then, it was that domestic politics is decisive in affecting the success of tax reform. But the papers do not provide an empirical basis for distinguishing the specific political forces or conditions that make a difference in implementing tax reforms.

An Alternative Tactic

If empirical inference fails to enlighten then we must attempt an alternative tactic: taking recourse to theory. In the sections that follow, I introduce a "dialogue" between theory and data in an effort to elicit systematic lessons concerning the politics of tax reform.

I begin by making three assumptions. The first is that people are rational and that, in reacting to a change in taxes, they compare the costs and benefits. The second is that governments seek to maintain and to strengthen political support. The third is that when the benefits of a change in taxes exceed the costs, then people give greater support to the government; conversely, when the costs exceed the benefits for a given set of persons, then government support weakens among them.

In pursuing this line of analysis, I start with the least realistic framework and move in stages to greater realism. I begin by analyzing the behavior of rational actors. I then add the feature of public goods. Lastly, I move to a multiple actor framework. Through this progression, we learn what we must know in order better to comprehend the politics of tax reform.

The Elementary Act of Tax Payment

We can begin by employing a framework analogous to that which is employed to analyze the behavior of consumers. We ignore, at the outset, the important feature of public goods that motivates so much of the politics of tax reform: the incentive to free ride, to shift the costs of government onto others, and so forth. We do so because focusing on the elementary act of tax payment underscores that taxpayers, in reacting to tax changes, will naturally compare the benefits from as well as the costs of tax payment. And this tells us much about what we need to know in order to comprehend the politics of taxation.

Taxes remove revenue out of the private sector. They make possible the creation of the kinds of goods provided by governments. When governments reform taxes, they alter the mix of private and public goods that people consume. For any given change in their taxes, people, behaving rationally, can be expected to compare the changes they experience in private consumption with the changes in the consumption of the public goods that the change in tax makes possible. To take an example of a rise in taxes, *and omitting for the moment consideration of the nature of public goods,* insofar as the private goods lost because of the rise in taxes exceed in value the public goods gained, people will oppose the change; insofar as the increase in public goods and services compensates for the loss in private goods, they can be expected to favor it. Governments can be expected to realize that people, behaving rationally, will react in this way.

An important implication is, as several of the authors indicate, that to understand the success of tax reform, an analyst cannot study taxes alone. Taxes represent the costs imposed by governments; the services provided by governments represent the benefits. To account for political reactions to tax reform, the analyst must therefore examine the manner in which governments package benefits with costs for specific political actors. The analyst *must* therefore know the allocation by group of the tax burden *and* the programs furnished by government.

We thus find at the outset the elementary knowledge that is required to understand political reactions to tax proposals. We can conceive of this information as two vectors. One vector would constitute the status quo. The other would constitute the allocation provided under the reformed system. An element in each vector would constitute the *net* benefit provided for each major political group in the political system and would represent that group's evaluation of the difference between the cost and benefits under each combination of taxes and expenditures by the government. How the tax reform would "play" politically would then be influenced by each group's evaluation of its welfare under the two vectors and its ability to maneuver and align in attempts politically to procure or to overturn one or the other of the two tax regimes.

It is clear that we are far from achieving the information necessary to gain this kind of insight into political reactions to tax proposals. Few of the papers provided information about government expenditures. Some noted that reforms were revenue-neutral or revenue-enhancing. But these phrases characterize total revenues and expenditures and provide little insight into the impact of changes in taxes on specific groups of taxpayers.

It is important to emphasize that it is people's evaluations that drive their political responses. And people commonly possess imperfect insight into their benefits from taxes. For example, while a candidate for the presidency, John F. Kennedy was able to convince American voters that their tax dollars were buying insufficient defense, even though the "missile gap" proved to be largely an illusion. In addition, people often will be uncertain as to what they are actually paying for the benefits they consume; professional economists, after all, find it difficult to assign the incidence of particular taxes. In light of these uncertainties, the information that is required will not necessarily be a disaggregated account of the net economic position of specific groups under different tax proposals. Rather, it may be even more important to gain insight into people's (albeit imperfect) subjective evaluation of their positions under different tax policies.

In concluding this section it should be noted that this discussion enables us better to appreciate the significance of several practices noted in the papers. It elevates them from interesting vignettes, as it were, to practices necessary to satisfy the requirements for political success, given rational behavior by taxpapers. One is the emphasis placed by Bahl, Gillis, and others on the role of data and the analysis of tax incidence. Both point to the concern of policymakers to evaluate the impact of tax reform on the economic position of key categories of taxpayers. Indeed, Bahl envisages his political sponsors as casting about, as it were, for the legendary median voters, the group whose political reaction would determine which tax reform would be politically viable.

A second practice is earmarking: the targeting of the proceeds of a particular tax for use on a particular program or kind of governmental expenditure. Viewed in the context of this discussion, we can see that such a measure makes it easier for governments to focus the attention of taxpayers on the benefits of the tax; it makes it easier for governments to assure the payers of a given tax that they will be compensated for their loss of private incomes with public services that they value.

Third, the discussion helps to explain why governments often package tax reform with other policy reform. Major tax reforms in Peru, Chile, and Colombia, Ascher's paper points out, were combined with widespread appeals for reform of the education systems, reforms that required new financing. In addition, the analysis helps to account for the support for apparently redistributive measures imposed as part of tax reforms. As noted in Ascher's paper, once again, the government in Chile imposed tax increases on the middle class in order to increase benefits for the poor. His analysis suggests that the government was able to get away with the measure by convincing the members of the middle class that they would benefit insofar as they would staff and operate the services that the government would provide. While paying the costs in terms of higher taxes, the middle class would also receive many of the benefits in the form of jobs and salaries.

Public Goods and Free-Riding: Part I

This paper has begun with a simple model of rational choice, one that underscores the significance of including in any political analysis an assessment of the benefits as well as the costs of tax payment. Severely compromising the "realism" of the discussion was that it analyzed choice as if it were made in an environment of private goods. Particularly for extracting lessons for politics, we must relax this assumption and examine the implications of rational choice in a public goods environment. In this section we therefore adopt a public, as opposed to private, choice perspective.

Public goods are characterized by nonrivalrousness in consumption and nonexcludability in supply; if the good is enjoyed by one consumer, its benefits are provided to all. One implication is that taxation inherently implies politics. Because in a world of public goods people can get a free ride, people, behaving rationally, can be expected to misrepresent their true preferences, seeking to secure the benefits of government expenditure while behaving as if they in fact placed a low value on them. In the field of taxation, political maneuvering is therefore to be expected. People can be expected to behave duplicitously.

Public goods lead to political maneuvering for another reason. Because in an environment of public goods people can expect to free-ride, they possess an incentive to seek to transfer the costs of government on to others. They possess an incentive, then, to engage in politics so as to write tax laws that enable them to consume public services while not having to pay the cost of them. This is a central lesson of Ascher's important paper in this volume, which shows that while tax reform may lead to greater efficiency, it will also be treated by rational citizens as a potentially redistributive game. For there always exists the possibility that the benefits of government can be consumed even while the costs are transferred to others; rational maximizers can be expected to exploit this possibility—and must expect that others will attempt to do so as well.

Because public goods offer rational actors the possibility of improving their welfare by misrepresenting their true preferences and by transferring the costs of public goods to others, those engaged in tax-setting face an inherently political task. This point is brought home by one of the fundamental theorems in the literature on public goods, that of Leo Hurwicz.[1] Hurwicz's theorem shows that in the absence of a dictatorship it is impossible to devise a means for efficiently allocating public goods that is robust against strategic behavior by individually rational agents. One implication is that those seeking tax reform—i.e., the efficient collection of taxes—should aspire to become dictators; put more gently, they are going to have to coerce and overcome popular protests by those "strategizing" against their proposals. Another implication is that, in the absence of perfect dictatorship, people will always find it rewarding to seek to manipulate and overturn the existing allocation of public services. Put another way, insofar as perfect dictatorship may never be achieved, the demands for tax reform will never cease.

The analysis suggests a third reason for political action in a world of public goods. In a world of public goods, governments seeking to behave efficiently should offer different tax prices to different groups. Governments find it difficult to infer the correct tax prices, however; because the incentives to free-ride are strong, taxpayers have strong incentives to misrepresent their willingness to pay for public goods. And governments, no less than the rest of us, find it difficult directly to observe tastes or preferences and therefore people's willingness to pay taxes. While some taxpayers are paying less than they should for public goods and services, given the benefits which they derive from them, others are probably paying more. A result of the inefficient spectrum of prices is that some taxpayers will feel overtaxed. All will claim to feel that way; the logic of free-riding promotes such behavior. In addition to those who grouse for strategic reasons, however, there is thus likely to be a segment of the population who are genuinely aggrieved and who feel, rightly, that they are overcharged for the services of government.

In this discussion we have examined the implications of rational choice in an environment of public goods. The most basic lesson we have learned is that taxation implies politics. Basic and elementary properties of public goods ensure that rational actors will, to put it bluntly, lie, cheat, and steal, and that governments that seek to allocate the costs of government will overtax some while undertaxing others, thereby further fueling political discontent. Applied to the central focus of this paper, this discussion gives us insight into why tax reform is demanded. Returning once again to our image of two vectors of payoffs — one that assigns net benefits to key groups in the present system and another that assigns them under a feasible new package of taxes — we can see that a majority of taxpayers will almost assuredly express a preference for the reform vector. For each taxpayer possesses an incentive to claim that under the existing system they are overtaxed. And each possesses an incentive to seek reform, hoping thereby to shift the tax burden to others while consuming the benefits of public programs.

The discussion also gives us insight into why tax reform is needed. Because rational citizens possess incentives to free-ride, governments face positive costs of tax collection. Governments therefore possess incentives to choose systems of taxation that reduce the rate of tax avoidance. Governments will tax in ways that are easiest, not in ways that are most efficient. This, of course, is the central message of Bird's important paper. Thus, we find governments taxing wages because such a tax is simple to collect from large employers; we find them collecting sales taxes because they are easy to administer; and we find them taxing imports because it is cheaper to monitor ports and terminals on the coast than roads and pathways in the interior. Given positive costs of tax collection, it is therefore understandable why governments should overemphasize taxes from such sources.

Given the incentives for consumers of public services to avoid paying taxes, we can also understand why governments choose other, seemingly inefficient forms of tax collection. Several of the papers have stressed the use of presumptive taxes.[1] An obvious advantage of such taxes is that they enable governments to measure tax liabilities in circumstances where people possess incentives to disguise their willingness—and ability—to pay taxes. Other authors have noted the popularity of taxes with some self-enforcing features. A major attraction of the VAT, they note, is that it creates incentives for one taxpayer to report the earnings of others; and a major attraction of collective levies from corporate groups is that if they are avoided by some taxpayers, they increase the burden of others, thus generating incentives for people to report tax avoidance. Given that people have incentives to misrepresent their willingness to pay for the services provided by governments and thus to free-ride, we can understand why governments would choose such forms of taxation, in spite of the distortions and inefficiencies that they might introduce into the allocation of economic resources.

Thus, we have learned two important things about tax reform: we have learned why tax reform will *always* be demanded; and we have learned why it will be needed. We have also achieved deeper insight into why it will always be political. Ironically, while giving greater insight into the inherently political nature of tax reform, we have learned more about its origins than about the factors that shape its political course and direction.

Public Goods and Free-Riding: Part II

In understanding the politics of tax reform, it is important to recognize that the logic which characterizes the production of public goods by governments applies as well to the activities of interest groups. Private groups, too, furnish public goods. And one of the most significant of these is tax relief. Understanding this point gives further insight into the need for tax reform. It helps to account for the plethora of exemptions, deductions, and special tax treatments given to particular interests and thus, as a consequence, the need for tax simplification.

In a world of public goods, providers of such goods find it difficult to determine people's true marginal valuations. As a consequence, they are likely to charge a uniform tax price. In a world of public goods, people will seek to free-ride; no matter what the tax price, they possess incentives to seek to avoid paying it. The result is that governments will set a relatively uniform tax rate and citizens will seek to exempt themselves from it.

Because of imperfections in monitoring and enforcement, the tax benefits that lobbyists secure will therefore constitute a public good; everyone bearing the attributes of that group will enjoy the favorable tax treatment for free. A lobbyist who secures an accelerated depreciation clause for commercial real estate will have provided benefits for all who invest in commercial property; favorable tax treatment for cattle herds will benefit all who own cattle; and subsidies to the makers of machine tools will tend to increase the profits and lower the costs to all who employ them.

Because interest groups provide nonexcludable benefits, they are difficult to organize; people will attempt to secure the benefits of changes in public policies while avoiding the costs of lobbying. Two implications follow. "Large" interests are therefore more likely to provide lobbyists. So too are groups for which the costs of organization have already been paid.

By "large" is meant economically concentrated. A firm is a large interest, for example, if it produces a large percentage of the value of the output in a particular industry. Because the principal problem facing the formation of interest groups is the cost of organizing in the face of incentives to free-ride, "large" interests are more likely to provide successful lobbyists.[3] For the larger the interest, the greater the portion of the benefits that it will capture from a change in the tax law; the lesser the extent to which the change in the tax law represents a public good; and the weaker, therefore, the incentives to free-ride.

In addition, given positive costs of organizing, preexisting groups—i.e., groups that have already paid the costs of organizing—possess an advantage. In such instances, the costs of organization have already been paid. It costs little to add lobbying over tax legislation to the activities of the organization—and the benefits are substantial. In the case of industrial interests, for example, firms are already in operation; contracts signed; and industrial associations formed to handle matters of common interest, be they immigration laws, licensing, freight rates, or the regulation of port facilities. It is therefore not surprising that, as noted by Ascher (chapter 12), industries, rather than economic sectors or social classes, tend to provide active lobbyists in the politics of tax reform.

This analysis helps to account for the pattern of exceptions, allowances, and special rates which characterize the tax laws of many nations. It helps to explain why these are often accorded to industries —as opposed, say, to consumers or to the poor. And it helps to explain why special treatment is given to some industries as opposed to others—to those which are highly concentrated or in which there are few firms; to the large landowners in agriculture, as opposed to the multitude of peasants.

A common thread throughout the papers of this conference is the need for tax simplification. Bureaucracies in the less-developed countries, it has been persuasively argued, are unable to cope with the plethora of special tax codes and tax treatments. Notions of horizontal equity are violated by the exemptions introduced into tax law. An additional virtue of the public choice perspective is that it helps to account for the need for tax simplification.

From Individual to Social Rationality

Thus far we have considered the implications of microlevel models of the elementary act of tax payment. The first model treated the taxpayer as if the taxpayer were a consumer of private goods; the second took into account the special incentives created by public goods. The analysis suggests why there is a demand for tax reform. It suggests as well why there is a need for it. It suggests that we should expect to see governments taxing elements of the economy simply because they can do so, multiple taxes and tax exemptions, and privileges and shelters for large interests. Even though sparse and highly stylized, these microlevel models have thus proven highly informative. Nonetheless, it is clear that they tell us more about why there is a need and demand for reform than why it takes place. In search of an explanation, we move from the level of the individual to the level of social interaction.

In switching from the individual to the social level of explanation, we switch from a perspective informed by decision theory to one informed by the theory of games. From such a viewpoint, we see that tax reform represents a collective dilemma.[3] Interpreting tax reform in this manner gives us insight into some of its key properties.

The Demand for Reform

As we have seen, behaving rationally, individuals may choose to avoid paying taxes, to pay too little by way of taxes, or to behave in ways which compel governments to tax the wrong sources or at the wrong rates. When all individuals behave rationally, however, they may find themselves worse off. They may find themselves with a government unable to pay for basic services, or compelled to finance them in ways which lead to inflation, high interest rates, and shortages of foreign exchange. Individuals, behaving rationally, may thus produce collective outcomes that are inefficient.

There is thus a collective dilemma: a disjunction between rational behavior by individuals and the rationality of collective outcomes. This disjunction leads to demands for reform; and an essential property of this reform is that it requires coercive intervention by government. In situations in which individuals find themselves, as private individuals, making choices which generate perverse collective outcomes, these individuals rationally may choose to compel themselves to behave differently. They may elect voluntarily to submit to new laws and to penalize themselves for pursuing their short-run best interests at the expense of the longer-run good.

A common element of reform in collective dilemmas is thus the introduction of means for making binding agreements. In essence, people agree to introduce coercion into social life. In order to attain higher levels of collective welfare, they may seek to transform the nature of the political economic game. Reform may require the introduction of coercion so that acting as rational individuals people can make private choices that will generate collectively beneficial outcomes.

As stressed in Ascher's paper, once coercion is introduced, however, people invest in politics so as to secure, or to defend against, economic redistribution. As Ascher states: "Tax reform is typically perceived as redistributive. After all, taxation is the direct extraction of wealth from particular individuals and firms. Prudent interest group representatives could hardly operate on any other working assumption that tax reform could redistribute wealth *from* them" (p. 2).

Tax reform thus requires introducing coercion into economic life. But once coercion enters economic life, the game becomes potentially redistributive. From the point of view of political analysis, this transformation is critical. For redistributive games are inherently unstable; they are games without a core. For each possible outcome there exists a coalition that would seek an alternative division of the spoils under which all its members would do at least as well and some would do better. On the basis of this particular theory, then, we cannot know how such games will turn out.[5]

I stressed at the beginning of this paper that it possessed methodological aspirations. I have sought to evaluate what we know, and can know, about the politics of tax reform. At the outset we found that empirical methods cannot generate prescriptive guidelines about tax reform; the data base is too thin to yield reliable inferences about what has or has not worked. When we turn to theory, moreover, we found that we could learn a lot about why tax reform is demanded and why it is needed. In addition, we gained a deep insight into and appreciation of its political nature. But we also found clearly defined limits to our knowledge. For theory suggests that in principle it will be impossible to offer prescriptive guidelines to tax reformers. For when any outcome is possible, then a best political strategy cannot exist.

Phrased more positively, a clear implication of this analysis is that if a particular tax reform package does in fact succeed, then not all coalitions were possible. For, given the redistributive nature of the tax reform game, were all coalitions possible, then some coalition would have overturned the reform measures. Should we seek guidance as to whether a reform movement will succeed or fail, then, we need to know what coalitions are possible and what ones are infeasible, as well as the interests that motivate them.

In the first instance, this leads us to a reappraisal of the political analysis offered by Harberger and Gillis. Al Harberger, the doyen of the analysts on matters of taxation, likes to speak of the importance of "great men": leaders whose backing, he feels, accounts for the success of reform movements. Malcolm Gillis, in his papers on Indonesia, likewise speaks of the significance of dedicated persons, in his case the core group of economic professionals who implemented a series of policy reforms, including those bearing on taxation, over a twenty-year period in Indonesia. In emphasizing the significance of key domestic political actors in one session of the conference, both Harberger and Gillis seemed to see themselves as offering a political interpretation of the success of reform movements. The interpretation we offer suggests that the leadership they observed is the consequence of the freedom given key political actors by the absence of decisive countervening coalitions. The great men can be great men because the political environment enables them to make proposals that will not be overturned by assemblages of other interests.

Pondered at greater length, the position offered here suggests the correct way of phrasing the central political question as to why reforms succeed or fail. The rephrased question would read: Why are coalitional possibilities constrained in some cases, thereby enabling leaders to emerge, but not in others?

Turning to the papers, we find that historical accident plays a major role, thus leaving Harberger to speak wistfully but wisely of the ripeness of opportunities for the reform-minded professional. We also find that not all accidents are of equal relevance, fortunately. Rather, the cases suggest that reforms clearly were facilitated by the comprehensive restructuring of power brought on by military occupation (Japan in the 1940s); coups (Liberia, Brazil, Indonesia, Chile, and Venezuela, among others); and massive electoral victories (Sri Lanka, Jamaica, and Peru). Decisive shifts in power help to define which interests are in and which out. By structuring power relations, such large-scale political changes severely constrain the range of possible coalitions. And they therefore make possible stable solutions to a political game which contains significant possibilities for redistribution.

There are a few other hints contained in the papers as to the political factors that made reform possible. Perhaps the most intriguing comes from Roy Bahl. What makes it intriguing is its resonance with the recent theorizing of Mancur Olson.[6] Interest groups, Olson argues, employ public power to gain private advantages while imposing costs upon others. The more encompassing the interest groups, however, the more difficult it is for them to externalize these costs. Societies which contain national peak associations—national labor federations or federations of business groups, for example—might therefore be more strongly motivated to police opportunistic behavior by special interests than would societies in which interest groups are more decentralized.

Against the background of Olson's theorizing, it is interesting to consider Bahl's analysis of the politics of tax reform in Jamaica. For, as he argues, the government in Jamaica possessed a unique advantage. It was able to bring together on one committee the leaders of major national interest groups to strike the final bargains, in which each made sacrifices in its particular short run demands for offsetting concessions from others. Such forms of concertation, in the words of the literature in political science,[7] are relatively rare in the developing world. They are far from common in the advanced industrial countries, particularly in

Europe, and they help to explain the capacity of some advanced industrial economies to evoke the compromises that are required for adjustment to shifting economic conditions.[8] Once again, then, the logic of free-riding and the strategic gamesmanship to which it gives rise offers insight into the political circumstances that make it possible for reform to succeed.

The Political Impact of Taxes

In closing, I wish to address one last issue in the politics of taxation. This is the issue of the impact of taxation upon political structures and public policies.

Taxation is a compelling phenomenon precisely because it is where the politics meets the economics. The way in which a nation taxes creates incentives that pervasively influence the way in which political and economic life become organized.

Perhaps the most vivid illustration comes from the creation of parliaments. When medieval monarchies, in need of revenues with which to pay for wars, began to tax invisibles, they found such taxable assets could be moved or hidden and that the payment of taxes had therefore to be bargained for. The owners of taxable assets exchanged tax payments for public policies; and the forum for these trades became parliaments.[9] The taxation of moveable assets thus led to the surrender of executive control over the public domain. As Quesnay and Mirabeau, illustrious members of the first generation of development economists, said of the limiting case, the taxation of commerce:

> All the possessions [of commercial society] consist . . . of scattered and secret securities, a few warehouses, and passive and active debts, whose true owners are to some extent unknown, since no one knows which of them are paid and which of them are owning. No wealth which is immaterial . . . can be got hold of by the sovereign power, and consequently will yield it nothing at all . . . the wealthy merchant, trader, banker, etc., will always be a member of the republic. In whatever place he may live, he will always enjoy the immunity which is inherent in the scattered and unknown character of his property . . . . It would be useless for the authorities to try to force him to fulfill the duties of a subject: they are obliged, in order to induce him to fit in with their plans, to treat him as master, and to make it worth his while to contribute to the public revenue.[10]

The evolution of parliaments provides one example of the impact of taxes on political organizations; the creation of collective property provides another.

Throughout the developing world, rural societies are often characterized by common property, corporate villages, and common lands; this was true in the agrarian societies of preindustrial Europe as well. The absence of individual property rights often inhibits the growth of commercial agriculture, a fact stressed not only by contemporary economists but also by the physiocrats who saw common property in France as inhibiting economic development in France by comparison with England. Many social theorists have attributed common property to the cultural preferences of peasants. But increasingly we have learned that an important source of common property rights is the state, and in particular its revenue collectors. Tax collectors find it difficult to extract taxes from individual rural households. It is far easier instead to assign tax quotas to villages, which then must organize ways of sharing the burden. The result tends to be the development of ways of sharing the means to raise revenues. Insofar as each family is liable for a share of the levy, then each family is guaranteed sufficient land to farm or access to common pastures; by this measure, each family protects itself from having to pay the share of others. No family can leave the community, as doing so would increase the tax burden on others. And, for certain, no family can transfer its lands to outsiders. Communal villages and common property thus appear to represent institutions created in response to the need for taxes.[11]

Tax systems thus create incentives which influence the institutional structure of society; as in the case of common property, these institutions themselves can affect the performance of economies, sometimes affecting their rate of development. The same can also be said of public policies. The way in which states collect their taxes affects the way in which governments make policy choices.

A vivid example is provided by two states in Africa: Uganda and Kenya. The two share a common border; both rely upon coffee exports for a major portion of their foreign earnings. In recent years, treasury officials in both countries have been counseled by international financial agencies to secure from their colleagues in cabinet policies which would strengthen incentives for their farmers. Treasury officials in Kenya readily complied; those in Uganda demurred. With the aid of local economic advisors, international financial institutions have been able to keep in place highly favorable agricultural policies in Kenya;

lacking such local allies, they have failed to influence agricultural pricing policies in Uganda. The rural economy in Kenya remains buoyant by comparison with that of her neighbor.

The revenue structure of the two countries plays a major role in the differential response of these governments toward pricing policy. Uganda taxes the goods farmers sell; the government maintains a coffee marketing board which purchases coffee at a low domestic price, sells it at the prevailing price in world markets, and pockets the difference to defray marketing costs and taxes. Through tariffs on imports and excise taxes, the government of Kenya taxes the goods farmers buy. It also collects income taxes from the more prosperous farmers.

International financial institutions have advised the economic technocrats in both Uganda and Kenya to adopt policies which would raise the prices to farmers, particularly for coffee. The technocrats are lodged in the treasury offices. From the point of view of the technocrats in Uganda, such advice was abhorrent; a rise in the price of coffee would yield lower revenues for the government—and they had colonels to pay! From the point of view of the technocrats in Kenya, the advice was welcome; for the tax system in Kenya induces a systematic preference for policies which will make farmers more prosperous.

The ways in which governments collect taxes thus affects their preferences with respect to public policies. And, as the performance of the economies of Africa shows, such policies—particularly policies toward agriculture—can have a major impact on the rate of economic growth.

Conclusion

This paper represents an attempt to extract general insights from the papers offered at the conference. It has focused on the political factors that shape the success of efforts at tax reform. Noting the limitations upon political inference imposed by the data, the paper has instead approached the problem quasi-deductively, examining the implications of decision theoretic and game-theoretic analyses of the elementary act of tax payment. From these efforts, we have discovered what data would be required to understand the politics of taxation: studies of the benefits of public expenditures as well as the costs of taxation. We also discovered that tax reform always will be demanded and that it will in all likelihood be needed. For given positive costs of tax collection created by the incentive to free-ride, governments will be compelled to tax in less than optimal ways and large interests may secure special tax treatment. Lastly, we found that theory tells us more about why tax reform is needed than why it is likely to succeed. Indeed, our analysis suggested that in principle no general formulas for success can be valid. Rather, what is needed is highly specific political knowledge, and of a specific kind: of the groups in society, their interests, and the ways in which they can—and cannot—combine.

Notes

1 See the classic exposition in Leo Hurwicz, "Informationally Decentralized Systems," in *Decisions and Organizations*, ed. C. B. McGuire and Roy Radner, 2d ed. (Minneapolis: University of Minnesota Press, 1986).

2 See, for example, the papers by Bird (chapter 9) and Ascher (chapter 12) in this volume.

3 Mancur Olson, *The Logic of Collective Action* (Cambridge, Mass.: Harvard University Press, 1965).

4 For a discussion of some of the classic forms of collective dilemmas, see Dennis C. Mueller, *Public Choice* (Cambridge: Cambridge University Press, 1979).

5 One of the best discussions is contained in William H. Riker and Peter C. Ordeshook, *An Introduction to Positive Political Theory* (Englewood Cliffs, N.J.: Prentice-Hall, 1973). For a more recent treatment, consult Peter C. Ordeshook, *Game Theory and Political Theory: An Introduction* (Cambridge: Cambridge University Press, 1986). For an interesting game theoretic treatment of the taxation policies of governments seeking political support, see Walter Hettich and Stanley L. Winer, "Economic and Political Foundations of Tax Structure," forthcoming in the *American Economic Review*.

6 Mancur Olson, *The Rise and Decline of Nations* (New Haven, Conn., and London: Yale University Press, 1982).

7 See the review by Peter Lange, "The Institutionalization of Concertation," Duke University Program in International Political Economy, Working Paper No. 26, September 1987.

8 See, for example, Geoffrey Garett and Peter Lange, "Performance in a Hostile World: Domestic and International Determinants of Growth in the Advanced Industrial Democracies, 1974–1982," Duke University Program in International Political Economy, Working Paper No. 3, November 1986.

9 For a review of the relevant literature and analysis, see Robert H. Bates and Da-Hsiang Donald Lien, "A Note on Taxation, Development, and Representative Government," *Politics and Society* 141 (1985): 53–70.

10 Quoted in Albert O. Hirschman, *The Passion and the Interests* (Princeton, N.J.: Princeton University Press, 1977), pp. 94–95.

11 See, for example, for France: Hilton Root, *Peasants and King in Burgundy* (Berkeley and Los Angeles: University of California Press, 1987); for Russia: Jerome Blum,

Lord and Peasant in Russia (Princeton, N.J.: Princeton University Press, 1961); for Central America and Indonesia: Eric R. Wolf, "Closed Corporate Peasant Communities in Mesoamerica and Central Java," *Southwestern Journal of Anthropology* 13 (1957): 1–18; and for Vietnam: Samuel L. Popkin, *The Rational Peasant* (Berkeley and Los Angeles: University of California Press, 1979).

14

....

Tax Reform: Lessons from Postwar
Experience in Developing Nations

....

Malcolm Gillis

I. Introduction: Assessing Tax Reform

Preceding chapters of this volume attest to the rich variety of experiences with tax reform, both among developing countries as well as in the same countries at different times. In this final chapter, an attempt is made to glean instructive lessons from these experiences. This task, however, is complicated by the lack of widely accepted measures of "success" or "failure" for tax reform programs. On one hand, the label "successful" might be reserved only for those reform proposals or packages that were in large measure actually enacted into law. But on this measure, reforms that became legislation but which failed to fulfill objectives of the adopting governments would qualify as successful. On the other hand, a reform program that contained the "right" elements might be viewed as successful even if the reform as such were never adopted. For example, the Kaldor reform proposals for expenditure taxes in India and Sri Lanka were tours de force in the abstract, but in terms of implementation, were classic failures. Finally, both in developing and developed countries, reforms that were never adopted might still be regarded as successful because they forever changed the national agenda for tax policy discussions. This was as true for the landmark Carter Commission 1966 proposals for Canadian tax reform[1] as for the Musgrave Commission Colombia proposals in 1968, which formed the basis of comprehensive reform six years later.

In any case, it is apparent that widely acceptable criteria for measuring success or lack of success in tax reform programs have yet to be developed. Lacking widely acceptable criteria, resort has here been made to one criterion that at least has the virtue of being readily understandable: the extent to which a particular reform achieved announced revenue and nonrevenue objectives. Typical non-revenue objectives sought for tax reform have been redistribution, promotion of growth, simplification, and improved resource allocation, not all of which have been goals common to all efforts surveyed herein.

Governments commonly have indicated the revenue objectives of reform with some specificity, and in one form or another, revenue objectives have been, as noted below, common to all tax reforms. Nonrevenue objectives, particularly those pertaining to income redistribution and resource allocation, are not so easily quantified. Accordingly, governments have typically not identified these objectives with any specificity, even in cases where nonrevenue considerations have been important factors motivating reform.

The impact of reform upon the revenue-generating capacity of the tax system is therefore the most serviceable, if not the most advisable, measure of the reform's success. But this does not mean that the only successful reforms are those that result in marked increases in tax collections. In previous chapters we have seen that while in several cases short-term fiscal crisis has been the principal factor precipitating tax reform, there also have been several instances in which governments have sought fundamental tax reform in the absence of crisis. But even in many of these cases, governments have initiated preparations for reform in order to prepare the tax system to meet *possible* future fiscal crises (Venezuela, 1959; Liberia, 1969; Indonesia, 1983–84). In still other instances, governments have turned to tax reform not to cope with imminent financial collapse, but to alleviate chronic deficits leading to chronically high rates of inflation (Chile, 1974–75). Finally, tax reform has been sought as a means of financing incremental expenditures in key sectors, such as education, as in the ambitious Colombian proposals of 1968.

All of the above examples have had, however, one element in common: the desire to improve the revenue-generating capacity of the tax system, either in the short term, when fiscal crisis requires immediate revenue enhancement, or in the medium to long term, in which cases short-run revenue neutrality may be deemed acceptable.

The expectation that reform would increase or restore tax ratios, quickly or ultimately, has been characteristic of many experiences examined in this paper. This objective has been not only ubiquitous, but typically the most ardently pursued by policymakers. Other non-revenue goals have also widely been sought. But with the possible exception of the abortive Liberian reform proposals of 1969–70 and the 1986 reforms in Colombia[2] none of the nonrevenue motives has ever precipitated, singly or jointly, the launching of tax reform programs. To be sure, the Indian, Sri Lankan, and Venezuelan reforms of the 1950s and the Colombian reform proposals of the late 1960s (and the reforms as implemented in 1974) were all infused with varying degrees of redistributive intent. Also, tax reform for promotion of economic growth was a prominent objective in early postwar reforms and recently has again become a widely discussed, if not effectively pursued, objective. Tax simplification, formerly viewed as essentially a means to other ends of tax reform, has itself been an important objective of reform programs of the eighties, including those of Chile (1974), Indonesia (1983–84), Jamaica (1986–87), and Colombia (1986), as governments sought to reduce needless costs of tax administration for governments and costs of tax compliance for taxpayers. Tax simplification, particularly where the tax system has gone unreformed for decades, has also come to be increasingly seen as supportive of the goal of reducing tax-induced barriers to improved resource allocation, a prominent goal of the Indonesian, Jamaican, and Colombian reforms of the mid-1980s.

II. Announced Objectives and Actual Performance

(A) Revenues

Tax reform programs have been undertaken in the last four decades in a very wide variety of middle-income but few very low-income developing countries. If judged only by revenue implications, these efforts appear to have been marked with some success. For developing countries as a group, the typical share of taxes in GDP (the tax ratio) hovered at about 11 percent in the 1950s. For the period 1972–76, the average tax ratio had risen to 16 percent, and in more recent years (1977–81) the average ratio had increased still further, to 17.5 percent.[3] In some countries, the tax ratio nearly doubled over the twenty-five years prior to 1985. To be sure, many of these were nations such as Indonesia with a high share of exports in raw materials, wherein the tax base is readily accessible to the tax administration. But sizeable natural resource exports are not always behind sharp increases in tax ratios: in India the tax ratio rose from 10 percent in 1960 to 20 percent in 1984.[4] More generally, tax ratios rose in virtually all developing nations when there was a material decline in the share of agriculture in GDP, and a rise in the share of more easily taxed sectors dominated by large enterprises such as industry and mining.

In several cases where tax reform episodes have been identified with very sharp increases in tax ratios, these gains have proven sustainable. In other cases, the increase proved temporary. For example, South Korea, relying more strongly on improvements in reform of tax administration than on tax structure in its reform programs of 1965–66, sought to increase tax collections by 40 percent through more effective enforcement alone. This ambitious target was not met, but within five years the Korean Revenue Service was able to reduce underreporting of personal income by one third.[5] Also, the Colombian tax reform of 1974 resulted in a 17 percent increase in the tax ratio for the first year after the reform, from 9.0 percent to 10.5 percent.[6] This relatively large gain, however, proved transitory, for reasons discussed below. The Indonesian reforms of 1983–84, initially designed to be revenue neutral, caused the share of nonoil taxes in GDP to rise by 50 percent by 1987, from 6 to 9 percent, even as tax rates were generally reduced. Most of the increase in revenues arose from a new value-added tax installed in 1985. Indeed, successful revenue results from tax reform have been strongly associated with implementation of value-added taxes in a very high proportion of cases. In the forty-odd developing countries that have adopted the VAT in tax reform programs since 1968, one of the variants of the VAT has tended to be something of a "money machine," in the sense that it has not been uncommon for the ratio of VAT revenues to GDP to exceed by at least 50 percent the ratio of the indirect taxes replaced by the VAT, within three years of implementation.[7] Moreover, by 1984 the VAT had come to account for more than 20 percent of total tax revenues in nine LDCs,[8] including (in declining order of revenue importance of the VAT) Chile (37 percent), Peru, Brazil, Colombia, Korea, Madagascar, Guatemala, Uruguay, and Turkey.

The VAT has shown strong staying power as well; both in Brazil (1968 adoption) and Chile (1974 adoption) VAT revenues in 1983 were more than 6 percent of GDP. More generally, the bulk of increased revenues from tax reform have come not from direct taxes on income, personal expenditure, and wealth emphasized by advocates of reform in the fifties and sixties, but from indirect taxes, including the VAT. This has been true not only for nations where redistributive goals have not been recently stressed in tax reform (Indonesia, Uruguay), but for those nations such as India and Nicaragua, where they have been emphasized.[9] Examples of success in securing revenue objectives of tax reform have been rare where the value-added tax has not been an element in reform.[10] Wartimé Vietnam aside, the Japanese reform of 1950 and Bolivian partial reform of 1973[11] are the only clear examples of revenue failure in reforms involving the VAT, although the Argentine VAT (adopted in 1975) did not, in its first decade, display great revenue productivity and the VAT in Morocco has been severely hamstrung by excessive numbers of rates and exemptions. But the Japanese VAT was never introduced following its enactment; and Bolivia did ultimately install a revenue-productive flat-rate VAT in 1985–86.

Reforms geared to revenue neutrality might be judged successful if actually revenue-enhancing, but not if revenue-sacrificing. The Japanese reforms, as noted, sought tax reduction at the national level (particularly for personal income taxes) and stronger tax sources for subnational governments (prefectures), implying rough revenue neutrality for the package as a whole.[12] In the event, the former was achieved, as total net tax revenue fell by 10 percent, with personal income tax revenues falling by 21 percent in 1950–51, the first year of the reform.[13] However, the failure to implement the VAT for the prefectures meant that overall revenue neutrality was not achieved. The postreform Japanese personal income tax presents an interesting phenomenon: over the next fifteen years following the cut in rates in 1950, personal income tax revenues grew at such a rapid pace that the government resorted to five separate rate reductions,[14] most notably in 1954 and 1955. It is left to future research to determine whether Japanese tax reform experience in the two decades after 1949 constitutes an object lesson supporting the less restrained claims of the supply-side school of economics or those who argue that the better part of tax reform is sustained commitment to improved tax administration.

The revenue yardstick indicates the clearest failures in cases of those reform packages that were either stillborn, partially implemented, or unduly delayed. Stillborn reforms include those in Liberia (1969), Bolivia (1976–77), and Ghana (1969–71). The Venezuelan reform package was implemented only in very small part in 1958. Tax reform languished for the next fifteen years, at which time many of the principal elements of the 1957 proposals were in fact adopted.[15] The Colombian package of 1968–69 experienced a similar fate: bits and pieces were enacted (and some rescinded) from 1968 to 1972, but the core of the original proposals was finally implemented in 1974. Both episodes suggest that delayed reform is not always lost reform.

Revenue performance has, in any case, been one of the principal criteria employed in judging the success or failure of tax reform programs. Nevertheless, it is important to note that a revenue-successful tax reform could be a failure, when seen from a wider, and arguably more appropriate, economic perspective. The "Please effect" cannot be ignored,[16] nor can it be assumed that, where present, greater public savings made possible by tax reform will be used for expenditures helpful for development.

B. Redistribution: Leveling Down and Leveling Up

Previous sections identified a number of early reforms involving some significant stress upon income redistribution. Criteria for success in this arena would differ according to whatever the emphasis is upon rectifying problems of relative impoverishment (highly skewed income distribution) or absolute impoverishment (a large share of the population at or below minimal subsistence levels of income).

Tax reforms designed to ameliorate relative impoverishment tend to place heavier stress upon increasing progressivity at the upper tail of the income distribution, usually through steeply progressive rates in the personal income tax and/or by sharp increases in taxes on "luxury" consumption. Tax reform designed to amend relative impoverishment then, is concerned with *leveling down* after-tax incomes. By contrast, a reform geared to reduction of absolute impoverishment is concerned with *leveling up*, by making the very poor better off, or by insuring that tax reform itself does not make them worse off while at the same time channeling expanded tax revenues into pro-poor expenditures. Income tax reform can, as in Indonesia and Jamaica, contribute to leveling up by enactment of personal exemptions high enough to insure that the poor fall outside the tax net.

Examples of reform focused essentially upon "leveling down" include both the Indian and Sri Lankan expenditure taxes of the mid- to late fifties. In both nations the expenditure tax affected only the uppermost ends of the income distribution. Neither attempt was notably successful; the work of Bird and DeWulf suggest that tax policy designed with this redistributive goal in mind has generally been unsuccessful across developing countries;[17] examples of successful reforms focused primarily on leveling down are difficult to find.

Rather, most reform programs have been hybrids, where redistributive goals are concerned. Examples include the Colombian reform proposal of 1968–69, as well as the 1974 reform that incorporated many elements of the 1968 proposals. In both, stress on heavier taxation of capital income, particularly capital gains and income from wealth, was due largely to a desire to reduce relative impoverishment. But the reform package as proposed also called for higher taxation of alcohol and tobacco. However desirable on social grounds, heavier taxes on these items tend to increase tax burdens on low-income families, given low income elasticities of spending on both. At the same time, the Colombian reform program, as initially designed in 1968 and as implemented in 1974, also contained measures to level up the tax burden, by expanding exemptions of food under indirect taxes, and by reducing taxes on smaller rural land parcels.

The Colombian reform of 1974 was moderately successful in leveling down for a short time: the initial impact of the reform may have shifted between 1.4 and 1.5 percent of GDP away from the top quintile of the income distribution in 1975–76.[18] Most of this gain, however, was dissipated after two years, for reasons identified earlier.

Two of the most recent comprehensive reforms of tax systems, those of Indonesia and Jamaica, stressed leveling up rather than leveling down. Both eschewed steeply progressive rates, both for income and consumption taxes, instead concentrating on tax rate reduction and upon base-broadening. Both involved adoption of personal exemptions high enough to exclude the poorest 75 to 80 percent of families from the income tax base. The Indonesian income tax rate structure calls for a maximum rate of 35 percent, with two lower rates of 15 percent and 25 percent; the Jamaican tax is imposed at a flat rate of 33⅓ percent. The only feature in the entire Indonesian package expressly concerned with "leveling down" was a special tax on such "luxury" items as autos and VCRs to complement the flat-rate VAT. Not surprisingly, the luxury tax, even at rates double those of the VAT, has accounted for less than 3 percent of total indirect tax collections since the reform was implemented. In Indonesia, as in most developing countries, the share of "luxuries" in total consumption has been so small as to preclude substantial collections from such taxes.

C. Promotion of Economic Growth

A recurring theme of tax reform over the past four decades has been that of fostering growth through tax policy. But the reform-growth nexus as seen by many advocates of reform in the late eighties is very different from that commonly perceived in the fifties and early 1960s. Growth-promoting tax reform was earlier widely thought to require manipulation of tax rates and tax bases to provide differential incentives for seizure of opportunities for saving, investment, and industrial location identified by governments. Most of the reform programs fashioned for the fifties and sixties specified a variety of special reliefs or tax preferences for this or that industry or occupation or region. A notable exception, however, was the Japanese package of 1949–50, which was criticized at that time for the absence of such provisions.[19] The principal architect of that reform, Carl Shoup, viewed such preferences as "having no place in the income tax law."[20]

By the 1980s, many fiscal economists had come around to a similar conclusion on the efficacy of using tax preferences for promoting growth in this view that the tax system may best facilitate growth by focusing upon the task for which tax systems are best suited: raising revenues to finance expenditures in noninflationary fashion. But an influential group of advocates of tax policy for active promotion of growth did emerge in the eighties. According to this group, tax policy should focus upon tax rate reduction as a means of increasing growth.

In recent years, some fragmentary evidence has appeared that points to an association between lower tax rates and high growth in some settings.[21] And Chile (1975–79) and India (three occasions since 1974) have experienced spurts in growth following reductions in the top marginal rate of income tax. But beyond that, not much evidence indicating a clear positive nexus between economic growth and tax rate reduction in LDCs has yet been published.

Attitudes toward the implications of tax policy for economic growth will in any case depend heavily upon one's views as to the international mobility of capital. For much of the postwar period, economists as well as policymakers tended to view capital as essentially immobile across international borders. Immobility of capital was thought to be particularly characteristic for developing countries, where explicit controls on movement of capital tended to be far more pervasive than in developed countries. But quite apart from both the porosity of such controls (arising from ineffective administration) and the fact that some developing countries such as Indonesia and Singapore impose little or no explicit limits on movements of foreign exchange, there is a growing body of evidence indicating a fairly high degree of international mobility of capital, both for the world in general[22] and for developing countries in particular.[23]

The greater the international mobility of capital, the greater are the constraints on taxation of capital by any one country. Tax reform in any given country that reduces the domestic after-tax rate of return to capital much below that available elsewhere increases the likelihood of out-ward migration of capital, to locales where after-tax returns have not been so curtailed. Seen this way, the connection between capital taxa-tion and growth is therefore relatively straightforward. Although mod-ern growth theory no longer gives pride of place to the factor capital, no one has yet figured out how a country may sustain growth without steady growth in its capital stock. To the extent that capital is required for growth, and to the extent that capital is mobile internationally, the lighter is the indicated taxation of income from capital, particularly in times when major capital exporting countries such as the United States and Britain have reduced taxes on capital. Recent readings of the evi-dence on both the role of capital in growth and its mobility suggests that relatively high rates of capital taxation are consistent with growth in LDCs only when they are easily avoided or evaded by capital owners large and small.

D. Tax Simplification

The tax systems of most developing countries have, more often than not, been designed to conform to assumptions prevailing in very few of them: low rates of inflation, a plentitude of skilled administrators avail-able to operate inherently complex income taxes, easy-to-follow "paper trails" in the conduct of business by the private sector, and presumed immobility of capital across national borders.

In many cases, interactions among these assumptions, together with widespread utilization of tax preferences for promotion of growth, has yielded tax systems of such complexity as to defy the intentions of the most earnest and best-provisioned tax administrators. Sustained rates of inflation, even when as low as 6 or 7 percent, engender very serious problems in defining taxable income equitably, through the effects of inflation in distorting depreciation allowances and interest income and expenses. The presence of progressive tax rates compounds these prob-lems, particularly in environments of double-digit (and increasingly, triple-digit) inflation that became all too common among developing countries in the 1980s. Inevitably, governments must provide taxpayers relief from the combined ravages of inflation and progressive rates, or else acquiesce in the eventual collapse of the system. Granting of relief, whether in the form of complicated provisions for tax indexation, inev-itably results in greater complexity in tax laws and tax administration alike.

The lack of reliable "paper trails" in the conduct of business leads to increased reliance upon crude rules of thumb in assessment of taxes, such as the much vaunted and little proven forms of "presumptive taxation." Many of the above factors unite to complicate efforts to tax what is essentially untaxable for most LDCs: the overseas investment income of the entrepreneurial and rentier class, whether businesspersons or civil servants.

Over several decades, attempts have typically been to cope with such income tax difficulties on an essentially piecemeal basis, through layers of special provisions and decrees enacted with little reference to one another, only the vexing problems of immediate concern. Consequently, taxes that typically affect no more than 2 percent of the population and account for less than a sixth of revenues come to require upwards of 90 percent of administrative resources. Ultimately, revenues may be sustained only through further increases in tax rates on steadily shrinking bases.

When this point is reached, as in Indonesia (1983), Jamaica (1986), and Bolivia (1986), tax simplification becomes attractive not only as a means of reducing needless costs of tax administration and compliance, but because the risk of revenue loss from reforms so motivated are low, and the possibility of efficiency gains high.

E. Reform and Resource Allocation

Tax systems impinge upon efficiency in resource allocation primarily through the effects of taxes upon incentives to save, invest, supply labor effort, and undertake risks. For developed countries, particularly the United States, evidence has been mounting that the adverse effects of taxes on these key incentives has given rise to welfare costs (excess burdens) that are not at all trivial.[24] Optimal tax theory provides rules for the design of tax *structures* that would allow these welfare costs to be minimized given sufficient information on demand and supply elasticities. But because optimal tax theory to date has assumed that costs of tax administration and compliance are nil, the theory furnishes few workable guidelines for reform of tax *systems*. For these and other reasons provided below (including income tax distribution considerations), optimal tax theory has yet to have much influence in shaping actual tax policy, notwithstanding its significant impact upon the way economists view tax issues.[25]

Since "optimality" in real-world tax systems is at present unattainable at any cost, tax reform directed toward more efficient resource allocation is generally measured against conditions required for greater *neutrality* in taxation,[26] particularly since optimal tax theory has provided, to date, little assistance in identifying optimal departures from neutrality in taxation. This is generally taken to imply greater *uniformity* in tax rates and *generality* in not only the *tax rules* prescribed in tax structures but in mechanisms of tax administration. Greater generality, then, requires both the broadening of *tax bases* to the extent possible, as well as more evenhandedness in tax administration.

Movement toward greater uniformity and generality also reduces the scope for horizontal inequities in taxation, with implications for resource allocation that have not been widely appreciated even among those who have stressed the potential gains that may accrue from greater neutrality in taxation. Particularly in the taxation of capital income, *apparent* horizontal inequities in tax law, e.g., lower rates of tax on one type of investment income relative to others, should result *not* in greater horizontal inequities, but in distortion in resource allocation (McLure, chapter 10). This is because investors can be expected, à la King and Fullerton (1984), to reallocate savings between investments until they earn the same after-tax rate of return in each.

Until the 1970s neutrality was not prominent among the explicit goals cited for tax reform programs in developing nations. Where present, neutrality as an objective of reform was typically implicit rather than explicit, serving to condition rather than define the shape of reform proposals. Except for such notable exceptions as the Indian and Sri Lankan reforms of the late 1950s, most published reform proposals, however, did call for greater uniformity (less dispersion) in tax rates. Similarly, arguments for reform generally evinced strong preferences for base-broadening and aversion to exemptions and tax preferences, except those deemed essential on grounds of income distribution. Emphasis on neutrality was most marked in the more recent reforms enacted in Indonesia, Jamaica, and Bolivia, but pursuit of greater neutrality in taxation also undergirded such reform packages as those enacted in Japan (1949–50) and Colombia (1986), and those proposed in Venezuela (1957), Colombia (1968–69, and again in 1986), Liberia (1969), and Bolivia (1976–77).

III. Critical Factors Underlying Success and Failure

The three subsequent sections examine factors that have been associated with some success in tax reform programs, those that may have contributed to failures in others, as well as those that have played a major role in a limited number of cases. By the standards outlined in foregoing sections, few comprehensive reforms would qualify as successful, even in the short term. There are, however, perhaps two dozen examples of partial reforms that have encountered more than just a modicum of success. Most of the latter, moreover, have been instances in which a VAT was adopted to replace other indirect taxes. As noted later in this chapter, the decision to move to a VAT, in the LDC context, has been itself a factor in successful reforms, both comprehensive and partial.

(A) Short- and Longer-Term Successes

Reforms that met or exceeded revenue objectives have also tended to be reforms that have gone further in satisfying redistributive, growth, simplification, and resource allocation goals, where these last four goals have also been sought. This statement applies both to reform packages geared to revenue enhancement as well as revenue neutrality. However, there are exceptions: the Japanese reforms of 1949–50 were successful in revenue terms for the central government tax system, but not that of the prefectures. Still, this reform episode could be classed as successful, if for no other reason than the fact that so much of what was implemented remained intact through 1987.

Other comprehensive reforms that may qualify as successful in the short term include those in Colombia and Chile in 1974, Indonesia in 1984–85, and the personal income tax component of the phased Jamaican reforms of 1986–87. Notable examples of the many successful partial reforms include the introduction of the VAT in Uruguay (1968) and Brazil (1969). Factors underlying success were different in different cases, but six may be particularly significant.

First and foremost, tax reform tends to be most successful when it has been needed least. That is, the chances for successful comprehensive reform tend to be greatest when reform is *not* a response to severe short-term fiscal crisis. Introduction of tax reform in response to acute fiscal crisis increases the likelihood that the reform will be hurried and probably poorly designed and certainly poorly implemented; it virtually guarantees that reform will emphasize *tax structure* rather than needed changes in the broader tax system, and that major implementation issues will be overlooked.

Acute fiscal crisis was absent in Japan as well as in Indonesia, 1983–84; large infusions of foreign aid meant that Jamaica faced chronic but not acute fiscal stress in the mid-1980s. In the latter two instances, preparations for reform began more than two years before the effective date of the first reform legislation. Without the pressures of acute fiscal crisis, the architects of reform had in both cases sufficient time to devise and vet major changes in tax structure suitable for each setting, to consider parallel improvements in tax administration, and to plan measures for smoothing implementation of the reforms. The success of the Japanese reforms is all the more notable because of the very tight time constraints on the reform effort: most studies of reform options were completed within four months in 1949; by April of 1950 much of the reform program was in place.

Second, except for postwar Japan, the chances for successful reform appear to be greater when a VAT is involved. This was true for the 1974 Chilean reforms, the 1984 Indonesian reform, and for all but one of the nearly 40 developing countries that have adopted one of the two most common forms of VAT since 1967.

Two factors seem responsible for the relatively high success rate for reforms involving the VAT. To begin with, the VAT has generally replaced archaic and essentially inadministrable forms of sales tax, such as multiple-stage turnover taxes and single-stage manufacturers' taxes. In addition, while the benefits of the self-enforcing features of the VAT are often overstated, the tax credit method of collection used in virtually all VAT countries not only makes evasion somewhat more difficult in practice, but helps preserve the integrity of the VAT against those interests seeking exemptions from the tax (chapter 4). This is because nonretail firms derive little or no benefit from exemptions, and as a practical matter, little or no benefit from zero-rating (the alternative to exemption) under the VAT.[27]

Third, the chances for successful tax reform are considerably enhanced when reform efforts go well beyond mere changes in tax structure, to fundamental reform of the broader tax system that also involves measures to simplify tax administration and compliance. Tax systems generally do not break down only because of the presence of defects in tax structure, but because long-standing flaws in tax structure aggravate underlying weaknesses in the machinery of tax administration.

The Japanese reforms of 1949–50 were notable for a strong focus on tax administration. The early success of the Colombian reforms of 1974 was due in significant part to major changes in the procedural and legal frameworks governing assessment, collection, and audit; judicial revocation of these changes in 1975–76 was the most significant factor in the undoing of the reform. The Indonesian and Jamaican reforms in the

mid-1980s involved unusually high stress on simplification of administration and procedural changes and also improvements in tax information systems, although the Indonesian reform as enacted delivered less
than promised on all but the latter.

Fourth, substantial attention to implementation issues seemed to
augur well for successful tax reform, if the experiences from the small
number of successful comprehensive reforms are any indication. Implementation measures conducive to success include provision of expert
legal advice in drafting of actual reform legislation from the decision of
policymakers, training of tax administration officials to operate the
reformed system, and even careful attention to the fashioning of new
forms for filing of taxes. Both the recent Indonesian and Jamaican
reform efforts placed very heavy stress upon insuring that draft legislation reflected the intentions of policymakers and upon preparation of
tax officials and taxpayers for the new tax regime; the Japanese and
Indonesian reforms were very heavily publicized prior to enactment.

Fifth, the few examples of successful comprehensive reform are associated with a relatively high degree of continuity among decisionmakers
responsible for economic policy in general and tax policy in particular.
Successful reforms in early postwar Japan, Indonesia in 1983–84, and
Jamaica in 1986–87 were designed and implemented under the same
chief executives, with no abrupt changes in the orientation of ministers of finance, the cabinet officials most crucial for success in tax
reform. Finally, the 1974 Colombian reforms were designed and implemented essentially by the same team of Colombian economists that
had participated in preparation of the 1968 package that was the precur-
sor of the 1974 reform. Continuity in decisionmaking for tax policy
seems essential not only to insure adoption of sensible reform, but to
provide for the type of active follow-up that seems, increasingly, essential for defending reform once it has been adopted. No tax reform programs can anticipate all possible problems. Once enacted, obvious gaps
in legislation and in administrative resources tend to emerge in short
order. Effective follow-up has often required the appointment of a watchdog group committed to the success of the reform. Provision for such
watchdog activity was made in Indonesia and Jamaica and, to a certain
extent, in Colombia in 1974–75, but not in Venezuela, Liberia, or Brazil (chapter 8).

Sixth, successful reforms tend to place little or no reliance on "tax
gadgets" or other "quick fixes" for fiscal problems. Such "gimmicks"
include sales tax lotteries for receipts given by firms, most forms of

presumptive taxes, including those upon agriculture, and so-called self-assessment systems for taxes on property (chapter 9).

Finally, the half-lives of successful tax reforms tend to be the longer, the larger the number of the foregoing six factors were initially present, and the longer they remained present. For example, the undoing of the Colombian reform of 1974 coincided with an interruption of continuity in decisionmaking and the overturning of key procedural and administrative provisions.

(B) Failures

Not many developing countries have consistently failed in implementing tax reform in the postwar period. Tax reforms that were stalled in Venezuela (1959), Colombia (1968), and Bolivia (1977) were followed by fairly successful reforms within a decade. The postwar history of a few developing countries is, however, studded with episodes involving failed attempts at tax reform. This has been particularly true for Peru, where there has been no fundamental tax reform for three decades[28] in spite of major reform initiatives in 1968 and 1971–75. And virtually all attempts at tax reform in Ghana and Pakistan from 1966 through 1986 ended in failure.

In general, economic factors responsible for failure of reforms actually implemented, or for stillborn reforms, tend to be the obverse of the six factors that have tended to underlay success. Reforms have usually failed when enacted in response to acute fiscal crisis; reforms not involving a VAT have been predisposed to failure; reforms involving excessive focus on tax structure at the expense of attention to administration issues tend to founder. Many reforms have failed because of inattention to implementation issues, lack of continuity in decisionmaking, and overreliance on tax gimmicks and "quick fixes" in tax administration.

In addition, two other factors may have played a role in some instances of failure: excessive reliance upon personal income taxes in reform programs; and vigorous opposition from the press.

Successful reforms have tended to be those that have implemented tax systems designed to work with poor administration. Income taxes are, by several orders of magnitude, more difficult to administer than most forms of indirect consumption taxes, including the VAT. Moreover, there are very few examples of personal income taxes in LDCs that involve more than three or four percent of the population. For both reasons, reform programs relying heavily upon personal income taxes for revenue enhancement are not likely to be successful.

The press has played a notable role in predisposing certain elements of reform packages to failure. The Japanese press sustained a barrage of criticism against the enactment of the prefectural VAT in 1949–50,[29] arguing that it was discriminatory against them. Much of the press in Colombia reacted negatively to the announcement of initiation of reform studies in 1968, so the torrent of press complaints after release of the proposals in 1969 was not surprising, but nevertheless effective in helping to throttle plans for immediate implementation.

(C) Indeterminate Factors

Some conditions have been important in affecting the outcomes of tax reform programs in certain countries, but have played minor roles elsewhere. In this sense only, these factors may be seen as indeterminant. Previous chapters identified three particularly interesting, if inconclusive factors: the place of tax reform in a sequence of broad policy reform, the extent of involvement of foreign aid donors in financing and shaping reform, and the ability of governments to maintain a tolerable level of risk for potential opponents of tax reform.

Recent literature in economic policy suggests that sequencing of major policy changes can matter greatly for the success of the set of measures in question. Too few tax reform programs have been enacted as part of any clearly definable sequence to allow any conclusive lessons to be drawn on this score. Three experiences, however, do indicate that sequencing of reforms can matter, and that the place of tax reform in the sequence may be critical: the cases of Japan (1949–50), Korea (1962–65), and Indonesia (1983–84). The Turkish tax reform of 1985 was also adopted as part of a broader sequence of policy reforms, and did encounter at least initial success.[30]

The Japanese tax reform was the last in a sequence of major policy changes imposed by General MacArthur, the Supreme Commander for the Allied Powers (SCAP) occupying Japan. In this case, lateness was a problem: postmortems on the Shoup Mission that prepared the tax reforms invariably conclude that had the Shoup reforms been submitted in 1946 or even as late as 1948, a greater proportion of the plan would have endured.[31] As it turns out, the first element in the sequence was an attempt, in 1946, to overhaul the Japanese tax administration, which quickly foundered on basic deficiencies in tax structure and on a premature attempt to introduce "self assessment under the income tax." The second was the implementation of Draconian economic stabilization anti-inflation measures of the Dodge Mission in early 1949 (before the arrival of Shoup), which, it has been argued, limited the revenue options that the Shoup Mission could have proposed.[32]

Tax reform was also late in the sequence of policy reforms in Korea in the early 1960s, but in this case lateness was not a hindrance. Successful reforms in financial policies and trade policies in 1963–65[33] preceded tax reform in 1966. The earlier reforms in the sequence smoothed the way for tax reform, by bringing stability and growth. These earlier successes may also have meant that the credibility of government economic policy was well established by the time tax reform was introduced.

The Indonesian tax reform of 1983–84 was also the last in a sequence of major policy adjustments to restructure the economy in the face of falling prices or natural resource exports. Earlier in 1983, five major changes were adopted in domestic energy policy, government consumption and investment policy, exchange rate policy, and financial policy.[34] In each case, the five previous reforms in the sequence were perceived to have been successful. The package as a whole therefore gained a measure of public acceptance: the tax reform could then be presented as the last of six major belt-tightening policy adjustments required to gear the economy to an era of lower oil prices.

Three cases, however, are insufficient for drawing generalizations about the best position for tax reform in any broader sequence of policy reforms.

It is difficult to assess the role of aid donors, both bilateral and multilateral, in the success or failure of tax reform initiatives. To begin with, the role of donors in tax reform has varied greatly from country to country. In any case, much depends on the nature of the involvement by the donor. Where the donor has been involved in long-term training and assistance in tax policy and/or tax administration in a particular country (USAID in Jamaica and Korea, the IMF in Indonesia) donor involvement has often been associated with successful tax reform either because it has helped to build up the domestic stock of specialized talent required to implement tax reform or because it has yielded a stock of studies of critical tax issues.

On the other hand, when aid donors become involved in tax reform programs that are themselves responses to fiscal crisis, donor involvement may be associated with failed tax reform. The reason has little to do with the competence of donor agencies, and not usually very much to do with local politics. Rather, because those reforms crafted to meet acute fiscal crisis are most likely to fail, donor involvement in such reforms is not likely to yield successful results.

Several donor-sponsored reform initiatives have been stillborn. These include those for Liberia, El Salvador, an early effort in Colombia in 1950, an early Chilean example (1967), and Panama in the 1970s. But a goodly number of efforts where donors have *not* been involved have suffered a similar fate, notably in Ghana (1969–71) and Bolivia (1976). Neither the Colombian reform proposals of 1968 nor the reform package actually adopted in 1974 had any donor involvement, but the first met with little initial success, while the second did. Two recent, and apparently successful, reforms cloud the picture even further. The Indonesian tax reforms of 1983–84 (and indeed the whole sequence of six major policy adjustments in that period) were undertaken without donor involvement of any kind. On the other hand, aid donors did help to initiate successful tax reform in Korea in the sixties primarily by withdrawing foreign aid, thereby increasing the need for reliance on domestic resource mobilization. Donors also played a significant role in the recent Jamaican tax reform, the costs of which were largely borne by USAID.

Finally, in some Latin American countries in particular, successful tax reform has depended upon the ability of incumbent governments to maintain a tolerable level of risk for the potential opponents of tax reform. This has been the case most notably in Colombia and Chile, where some tax reform programs have been successful, but not in Peru, where postwar history shows no instances of successful tax reform. Ascher (chapter 11) concludes that effective political management of reform depends strongly upon whether groups threatened by the reform, e.g., landowners, *rentiers*, shopkeepers, or unions, perceive the risks of tax reform as limited or as open-ended. Successful reform has been associated with tax measures that limit the risks of reform to affected groups. Under such circumstances, such groups have proven willing to bear some additional—but predictably constrained—risks associated with tax reform. This is an important consideration inasmuch as no reform involves zero costs and risks for all groups in society.

IV. Lessons from Experience

At least seventeen principal lessons can be drawn from postwar experience with tax reform in LDCs. Ten of these are somewhat conclusive; the others are, while perhaps instructive, applicable to political and economic contexts of particular countries at particular times.

A. Conclusive Lessons

Hurried Reforms Are Generally Failed Reforms. Few successful reforms, whether comprehensive or partial in character, have been undertaken in response to acute revenue crisis. With the notable exceptions of occupied Japan and possibly the recent Turkish reforms (1985),[35] there are almost no examples of successful comprehensive reforms that were designed and implemented within months. The appropriate time horizon for successful tax reform is thus best expressed in years, not months.

Time is required not only to make a convincing case for reform, but to evaluate competing reform proposals and to scrutinize and vet data prepared in support of reform. Above all, time is required to take steps to insure that new tax structures will work well with poor administration. Sufficient time was not available in the reform programs for Venezuela (1957–58), Colombia (1968–69), Liberia (1969), Ghana (1969–70), or Bolivia (1976–77). Reform was aborted or long-delayed in all these cases.

On the other hand, the recent, and apparently successful, tax reforms in Indonesia and Jamaica were developed over a period of years: four in Indonesia (counting a year devoted to implementation after enactment in 1983) and three in Jamaica, also counting a year of work on implementation.

But years of preparation do not guarantee successful reform; neither does speed in implementation necessarily always lead to failure. The Bolivian reforms of 1986 were enacted after less than three months of preparation, in response to severe fiscal crisis, wherein the tax ratio had fallen from 10 percent to 2 percent in the two preceding years. The short-term revenue results were very favorable.

Delayed Reform Is Not Necessarily Lost Reform. Reform programs meeting with initial failure do not always represent wasted effort, provided they are "placed on the shelf," ready to be implemented at a more propitious time. We have seen that reform proposals in Venezuela (1957) and Colombia (1968–69) formed the basis for actual reforms implemented years later. On the other hand, the radical Bolivian reforms of 1986 bore virtually no resemblance to comprehensive reform proposals crafted by expatriates in 1976–77.

Reform Must Focus on Tax Systems Including Tax Administration. One of the clearest lessons emerging from the postwar history of tax reform in LDCs is that while reform of tax structure ordinarily must precede administrative reform (chapter 5), comprehensive reform efforts confined to tax *structures* are unlikely to succeed. This conclusion applies with almost equal force to programs of partial reform, including the many examples of successful switchovers to the VAT.

Successful reform seems to require that tax administration be a central rather than peripheral focus of reform. This does not always require that tax reform result in sharp and immediate improvements in tax administration and dramatic declines in tax evasion. But at a minimum experience indicates that structural reform must be explicitly designed to function well with weak administration. Moreover, experience in some countries (chapters 2, 3, and 12) indicates that tax reform packages emphasizing anti-evasion measures can have strong political appeal, particularly when such measures reduce perceived horizontal and vertical inequities. This is particularly important for LDCs, where evasion may rival or surpass poor tax structure as a source of inequities (chapter 10).

While reform packages giving short shrift to administration have generally not been successful, there has been at least one case (Korea 1966) where a series of reforms focused primarily upon administrative rather than structural issues has been fairly successful, although not to the extent sought by the architects of reform.

Simplification and Rate Reduction Are Mutually Reinforcing. A worldwide movement in taxation has been discernible in the past decade: a palpable drift away from high marginal rates of tax (including marginal rates under income taxes and differentiated rates of sales tax), and away from fine-tuned tax structures, toward lower and more uniform rates and simpler structures. Both simplification and rate reduction have worked best where the other is present. Growing recognition of the extent of mobility of capital across international boundaries has contributed to downward pressure on high marginal tax rates in country after country, including Indonesia, Jamaica, Pakistan, India, Sri Lanka, and most recently Bolivia. Lower rates have contributed to simplification in several respects, not least of which is the role of lower tax rates in undermining arguments for complicated and difficult to administer tax incentives for the benefit of particular special interest groups. Enactment of generally lower rates reduces the reward for rent-seeking that accrue to those who seek and receive tax preferences. Also, reduction in height and dispersion of tax rates makes avoidance and evasion less attractive, and less feasible, for taxpayers.

Revenue Shortfalls Doom Reform. Tax reforms that fall short of revenue objectives, whether that goal is revenue enhancement or revenue neutrality, are unlikely to be successful in achieving nonrevenue objectives of reform. There are no examples of reforms involving revenue shortfalls wherein goals of either income redistribution or growth promotion were served. There may be examples wherein revenue goals of reform were badly unfulfilled and resource allocation goals realized, but such examples were not uncovered in this survey.

Indirect Tax Reform Has Been a Major Focus of Successful Reform. Successful tax reforms have tended to be those emphasizing sales taxation, and in particular the value-added tax. Except for Japan, where the VAT, first proposed in 1949, remained unimplemented through 1987, this has been a discernible pattern associated with successful comprehensive reforms, although the initially successful 1974 Colombian reforms did involve heavy emphasis upon income taxation. Partial reforms, particularly those since 1965, that have encountered success have been overwhelmingly indirect tax reforms, involving adoption of a VAT in virtually all cases. Among the family of value-added taxes, LDCs have tended strongly to adopt the type of tax pioneered in Latin America in the late 1960s and now utilized in all European Community (EC) countries: the consumption-type value-added tax, using the tax-credit method of collection and imposed on the destination principle. Moreover, developing countries have increasingly turned to the retail form of the VAT, as employed in the EC.

Implementation Is Crucial. It is not enough to ensure that reform in tax structures dovetails with administrative capacities. Successful tax reform requires detailed attention to implementation issues. Poorly drafted reform legislation jeopardizes chances for successful reform. More than one reform has foundered because of inadequate preparation of tax collectors to administer the reform and/or unintelligible instructions to taxpayers, or because new tax forms for new tax laws were unavailable or unsuitable.

Tax Reform, Income Redistribution, and Growth. The implications of tax reform for income redistribution and economic growth remain to be verified. However, the record does suggest that some income redistribution goals of tax reform have been easier to secure than others. Tax reforms that have sought to exclude the very poor from the tax net have generally been successful in doing so. On the other hand, reforms designed to bring about substantial permanent increases in the share of taxes paid by the top quartile of the income distribution have consistently failed in this respect. Tax reforms geared to "leveling up" the income distribution have had a much better record of success than those geared to "leveling down."

The nexus between economic growth and tax policy in LDCs has not yet been well established. Nevertheless, certain tax reform programs are clearly more conducive to growth than others. Tax reform packages that ignore the realities of international mobility of capital are however likely to be inimical to economic growth. Deliberate use of the tax structure to actively encourage aggregate savings, and therefore capital formation, has tended to bring mixed blessings where such measures have been effective. On the other hand, even reforms that remove strong tax incentives for investment in marginal, inefficient economic sectors are clearly supportive of economic growth, as are reform measures that reduce needless disincentives for household and business saving.

Effects of Developed Country Tax Policy on LDCs. It has never been clearer that LDC capacity to change tax systems and enact tax reform is significantly constrained by policies and events in capital-exporting countries. For example, changes in the tax law in the United States under the 1986 tax act had a profound effect on the ability of LDCs to collect income taxes on interest, since foreign depositors were exempted from U.S. withholding taxes on interest. The interaction of the foreign credit systems of capital exporting countries, as McLure has shown, has also had notable effects in limiting tax reform options for LDCs.[36]

Tax "Gadgets" Rarely Succeed. The realities of weak tax administration and low standards of taxpayer compliance have caused many governments to resort to cleverly conceived but poorly implemented tax "gadgets" in attempts to bypass these problems. Bird (chapter 9, this volume) has identified five of the most commonly used "gadgets": lotteries connected with sales taxes (Chile, Ecuador), excessive reliance upon the "self-checking" features of the VAT (Korea), other types of "self-enforcing" methods of tax administration involving interlocking taxes (the Kaldor reforms in India and Sri Lanka), tax amnesties, and moves to computerize tax systems not accompanied by other fundamental changes in tax administration.

In spite of the fact that such shopworn gadgets have proven ineffective in virtually all developing countries that have adopted them, many of them continue to surface in tax reform programs with disturbing regularity, as in Indonesia (amnesties offered in 1985–86), Pakistan (premature computerization in the reforms of 1987), and Korea (full cross-checking of all VAT returns through 1987).

Withholding Systems Are Vital for Success in Income Taxation. Several chapters in this volume (McLure, chapter 3; Bahl, chapter 5; and Bird, chapter 9) stress the centrality of comprehensive withholding systems in the successful functioning of income taxes in LDCs. Income tax reforms that have failed to extend tax withholding much beyond the incomes of civil servants and the very largest business firms have generally led to disappointing results.

(B) Nonconclusive Lessons

Comprehensive vs. Partial Reforms. Experience does not allow any firm judgments as to the relative merits of comprehensive versus partial reform; the fact that a greater proportion of partial reforms have been successful may be due not so much to the noncomprehensiveness of the reform effort, but to the fact that many such reforms involved implementation of value-added tax.

Comprehensive reform has worked best, however, when it has been undertaken in the absence of impending fiscal crisis, and when it has focused on the entire tax system, rather than merely upon tax structures.

Contemporaneous vs. Phased Reform. There have been few examples of wholly contemporaneous tax reforms. The Colombian reform of 1974 was the closest to a fully contemporaneous reform, but this reform ran afoul of judicial review shortly after implementation. A few successful reforms, including that of Indonesia in 1983–84, were *essentially* contemporaneous, but nevertheless involved some phasing in of reform measures over a two-year period.

Phased reform has been attempted most recently in Jamaica; the ultimate success of this reform will depend in very large part upon effective implementation of a planned new VAT, scheduled for 1987–88.

Sequencing of Reform. While the sequencing of policy adjustments may be extremely important for implementation of trade, exchange rate, and financial policies, there is no clear evidence that prospects for successful tax reform are dependent upon the existence of a sequence of reforms, nor of the place of tax reform in that sequence. Nonetheless, the experience of Korea (1966) and Indonesia (1983–84) does suggest that when a series of policy reforms are installed in sequence, chances of successful tax reform are *not* jeopardized by having tax reform *last* in the sequence.

Aid Donors and Reform. It is difficult to generalize about the implications of involvement by aid donors in reform. Aid donors can play both an intrusive and a nonintrusive role in encouraging tax reform.

Examples of an intrusive role include "conditionality" attached to aid programs: where aid flows are made conditional on adoption of revenue-enhancing tax reform. The record of success here is unclear. But it *is* clear that *non*intrusive involvement, such as the financing of whatever foreign skills are needed for tax reform, has proven important in several cases, as have long-term programs of assistance in tax administration sponsored by the IMF and USAID. It is also clear that a number of activities of aid donors over the long term have often been critical in setting the stage for tax reform. To illustrate, aid donors have financed cadastral surveys of agricultural and urban land in numerous LDCs. Completion of these surveys has removed the principal bottleneck to land tax reform in several instances. Further, training programs mounted by donor agencies have in many cases produced the very analysts that have been responsible for design and implementation of later reform. And although a number of successful reforms have been implemented with no involvement by donors, it is also true that many reform programs have failed without donor assistance. In any case, LDC governments in the 1980s seem no less inclined to seek donor help in tax reform than was the case a quarter century earlier.

Optimal Tax Theory and Tax Reform. The impact of optimal tax theory upon tax reform programs in LDCs has to date been small and indirect. It has been small largely because the literature on optimal taxation has not yet produced rules and criteria readily understandable by framers of tax policy, because the theory assumes frictionless tax administration and compliance and because it assumes knowledge about elasticities that is not yet available. There has been an important indirect effect of optimal tax theory, however, in that it has affected the way many policy economists view tax reform. In particular, it has caused them to sharpen as well as qualify many of the arguments long used to support shifts toward greater "neutrality" in taxation. It is now more widely recognized that "neutral" taxes are not necessarily "efficient" taxes or "optimal" taxes. While not nearly as intellectually satisfying a guide to tax policy as "optimal taxation," neutral taxation is to be preferred as a benchmark until such time as analysts are able to identify optimal departures from neutrality in real world policy settings, and until such time as administrative capacities are equal to the task of operating necessarily complicated optimal tax structures. In both developed and developing countries that time will not likely arrive before the twenty-first century.

Transferability of Lessons. The tax reform experience surveyed in this paper suggests that lessons tend to be transferred from country to country frequently and with some rapidity. In the first two decades of postwar history, the direction of transfer of lessons was largely from developed to developing countries. This may account for the strong emphasis upon income taxes in most early LDC reform episodes. Arguably, some wrong lessons were transferred, as advisers from developed countries—and LDC officials returning from study abroad—often tended to prescribe familiar tax policy changes more suitable to highly industrialized societies than to low-income nations with low levels of literacy and even more lowly paid tax collectors.

Beginning in the early 1960s, significant lessons learned in developing countries began to be transplanted to other LDCs. Some of these lessons proved instructive; particularly those learned about the VAT in Brazil and Uruguay beginning in 1968. Within two decades, more than forty LDCs had adopted one or another form of VAT, and several others were considering the tax in 1987. As noted earlier, the tax has enjoyed a remarkable degree of revenue success in all but two or three instances where it had been adopted.

Political Mileage From Tax Reform. To the extent that political factors are considered in the economic literature on tax reform, they are viewed primarily as constraints to be broken or evaded. But chapter 12 suggests that—contrary to conventional wisdom—there may be political mileage to be gained from implementation, or attempts to implement, tax reform. This must have been so for Colombia (chapters 3, 12) and Uruguay (chapter 2), considering how many times governments there have undertaken tax reform.

V. Conclusion

This distillation of lessons from the variegated, rich experience in postwar tax reform in LDCs has doubtless been strongly conditioned by the cases selected for intensive review, and may also unduly reflect undue personal involvement by the authors in many reform episodes. Both factors argue for great care in deciding which lessons derived herein might be germane to situations in other nations that may contemplate fundamental tax reform over the next decade or so. It does seem clear that healthy skepticism is justified regarding exaggerated claims made for this or that tax innovation or this or that reform strategy. Tax rate reductions may promote growth in some settings; they may predispose a country to ruinous inflation and consequently low growth in others.

Marked shifts toward heavier reliance upon indirect taxes may be advisable in some countries but unnecessary in others, particularly those with rent-generating export sectors that are easily accessible to the tax administration.

The differences, after all, between the over one hundred developing countries are at least as striking as any similarities between them. Even so, three lessons appear to be generally valid. First, tax systems are best suited to the task of raising revenues, and have not proven well suited as means for achieving other objectives. Second, successful tax policy requires that tax administration be everywhere treated not as a peripheral, but a central question in tax reform. Finally, the record of experience in taxation in LDCs over the postwar period, particularly the last two decades, provides little justification for cynicism about tax reform. Successful tax reform has not been all that uncommon in the middle-income developing countries featured in this volume. It remains to be seen whether lessons gained from the experience of these countries will prove helpful in reform of tax systems in the nearly forty African and South Asian Nations classified as low-income in the World Bank system of classification.

Notes

1   *Report of the Royal Commission on Taxation*, volumes I through V, 1966 (Ottawa).
2   McLure, chapter 3 in this volume.
3   Gillis, Perkins, Roemer, and Snodgrass (1987), pp. 263–64.
4   Bird, chapter 9 in this volume.
5   Gillis, Perkins, Roemer, and Snodgrass (1987), p. 265.
6   Gillis and McLure (1978), pp. 253–55.
7   Gillis, Shoup, and Sicat (forthcoming), p. 7.
8   International Monetary Fund (1986).
9   Bird, chapter 9 in this volume.
10   Colombia already had a crude VAT in 1974.
11   The VAT as a percentage of GDP was significantly lower in 1983 than in 1974.
12   Shoup, chapter 6 in this volume.
13   Bronfenbrenner and Kogiku (1957a), p. 242.
14   Tanzi (1969).
15   Shoup, chapter 8 in this volume.
16   The "Please effect" argues that tax increases ostensibly intended to increase public savings may, and often do, result in less, not more total domestic savings, because the government's marginal propensity to consume (MPC) out of higher tax revenues may exceed the private sector's MPC out of income extracted by taxes (Please, 1967).
17   Bird and Dewulf (1975).
18   Gillis and McLure (1978), pp. 233–58.

19 Bronfenbrenner and Kogiku (1957a) (appendix 1A).
20 Shoup, chapter 6 in this volume.
21 Marsden (1983).
22 Harberger (1980).
23 Hartman (1983); Summers (1985).
24 See for example, Ballard, Shoven, and Whalley (1985).
25 For a survey of modern theories of optimal taxation, see Auerbach (1985).
26 But neutral taxes are not necessarily "efficient" or "optimal" taxes.
27 This is because under a tax-credit type of VAT, taxes paid by firms on purchase are deductible from taxes due on sales. Except for sales to the final consumer, exemption from the VAT is generally detrimental to the firm's interests. This is because while an exempt firm pays no taxes on its sales, it still pays taxes on its purchase. Any firm purchasing from an exempt firm will have, on that account, no taxes to credit against its sales, and products made by the exempt firm will ultimately bear not less but more VAT than would be the case without the exemption.
28 Ascher, chapter 12 in this volume.
29 Bronfenbrenner (1986).
30 Information graciously supplied by Anne O. Krueger.
31 Bronfenbrenner and Kogiku (1957b), pp. 357−58; James (1987), pp. 3, 26.
32 James (1987), pp. 3−5.
33 Cf. McKinnon (1973) and Shaw (1973).
34 Gillis (1985), pp. 251−52.
35 Information graciously supplied by Anne O. Krueger.
36 McLure (1987).

References

Ahmad, E., and N. H. Stern. "Taxation for Developing Countries." In Hollis B. Chenery and T. N. Srinivasan, eds., *Handbook of Development Economics* (forthcoming).

American Chamber of Commerce of Bolivia (1986). "Tax Reform Law: An Explanation of its Contents." May.

Auerbach, Alan (1985). "The Theory of Excess Burden and Optimal Taxation." In Auerbach and Feldstein, eds., *Handbook of Public Economics* (North-Holland).

Bahl, Roy, (1987). "Tax Reform in Jamaica: Executive Summary." Syracuse University, Sept. (draft).

Bahl, Roy W., Chuk Kyo Kim, and Chong Kee Park (1986), *Public Finances During the Korean Modernization Process*. Cambridge, Mass.: Harvard University Council on East Asian Studies.

Ballard, C. V., J. B. Shoven, and J. Whalley (1985). "General Equilibrium Computations of the Marginal Welfare Costs of Taxes in the United States." *American Economic Review* 75, no. 1 (March) pp. 128−39.

Bird, Richard, and Henry Dewulf (1975). "Taxation and Income Distribution in Latin America: A Critical View of Empirical Studies." *IMF Staff Papers* 20, November.

Bronfenbrenner, Martin (1986). "Confessions of a VAT Man" Aoyama Gakiun University, Japan (unpublished).

Bronfenbrenner, Martin, and Kiichiro Kogiku (1957a). "The Aftermath of the Shoup Tax Reforms, Part I." *National Tax Journal* 10, pp. 236−54.

Bronfenbrenner, Martin, and Kiichiro Kogiku (1957b). "The Aftermath of the Shoup Tax Reforms, Part II." *National Tax Journal* 10, pp. 345–60.

Gillis, Malcolm (1985). "Micro and Macroeconomics of Tax Reform: Indonesia." *Journal of Development Economics* 19, pp. 221–54.

—— (1986). "Worldwide Experience in Sales Taxation: Lessons for North America Policy Sciences." *Policy Sciences* 19 (1986), pp. 125–42.

—— (forthcoming). "The VAT and Financial Services." In Malcolm Gillis, Carl Shoup, and Gerardo Sicat, *The Value-Added Tax in Developing Countries*. World Bank.

Gillis, Malcolm, and Charles E. McLure, Jr. (1978). "Taxation and Income Distribution: The Colombian Tax Reform of 1974." *Journal of Development Economics* 5, pp. 233–50.

Gillis, Malcolm, Dwight Perkins, Michael Roemer, and Donald Snodgrass (1987) *Economics of Development* (New York: Norton).

Gillis, Malcolm, Carl Shoup, and Gerardo Sicat (forthcoming). *The Value-Added Tax in Developing Countries*. World Bank.

Harberger, Arnold C. (1980). "Vignettes on the World Capital Market." *American Economic Review, Papers and Proceedings* (May), pp. 331–37.

Hartman, David, and Daniel Frisch (1983). "Taxation and the Location of U.S. Investments Abroad." Working Paper No. 1241. Cambridge, Mass.: National Bureau of Economic Research.

Hirschman, Albert (1963). *Journeys Toward Progress*. Baltimore: Johns Hopkins University Press.

International Monetary Fund (1986). *Government Finance Statistics, 1985*. Washington: International Monetary Fund.

James, J. C. (1987). "Japanese Tax Policy in the Wake of the Shoup Mission." Dissertation for Part Two of the Tripos in Oriental Studies, Cambridge University, Kings College.

King, Mervyn, and Don Fullerton, eds. (1984). *The Taxation of Income From Capital*. Chicago: University of Chicago Press.

McKinnon, Ronald I. (1973). *Money and Capital in Economic Development*. New York: Oxford University Press.

McLure, Charles E., Jr. (1988). "U.S. Tax Law and Capital Flight from Latin America." Palo Alto: Hoover Institution Working Paper E-88-21, April.

Marsden, Keith (1983). "Taxes and Growth." *Finance and Development* 12, pp. 6–10.

—— (1985). "Why Asia Boomed and Africa Busted." *Wall Street Journal* (June 3).

Musgrave, Richard, and Malcolm Gillis (1971). *Fiscal Reform for Colombia*. Cambridge: International Tax Program.

Musgrave, Richard, et al. (1981). *Fiscal Reform in Bolivia*. Cambridge, International Tax Program.

National Tax Reform Commission of Pakistan (1986). *Final Report*. Islamabad, December 31.

Please, Stanley (1967). "Savings Through Taxation: Reality or Mirage," *Finance and Development* 4, no. 1 (March).

Shoup, Carl S. (1959). *The Fiscal System of Venezuela*. Baltimore: Johns Hopkins University Press.

—— (1965). *The Tax System of Brazil*. Rio de Janeiro: Fundacao Getulio Vargas.

—— (1969). *Public Finance*. Chicago: Aldine Publishing.

—— (1970). *The Tax System of Liberia*. New York: Columbia University Press.

Shoup, Carl S., et al. (1949). *Report on Japanese Taxation by the Shoup Mission.* 4 vols. Tokyo, Supreme Commander for the Allied Powers.

Summers, Larry (1985). "Tax Policy and International Competitiveness." Cambridge, Mass.: Harvard University. Manuscript.

Tanzi, Vito (1969). *The Individual Income Tax and Economic Growth: An International Comparison.* Baltimore: Johns Hopkins University Press.

Appendix 1

·······

The Conference on Lessons from Fundamental Tax Reform in Developing Countries, April 22–23, 1988

·······

April 22 (Friday)

First Session   Malcolm Gillis, Moderator

Opening Remarks
The Honorable Alan Woods, Administrator, U.S. Agency for International Development

Towards a Taxonomy of Tax Reform: Malcolm Gillis, Professor of Public Policy Studies and of Economics, Duke University

The Adminstrative Dimensions of Tax Reform in Developing Countries: Richard M. Bird, Professor of Economics, University of Toronto
Presenter: Milka Casanegra, International Monetary Fund
Commentator: Carl S. Shoup, Columbia University

On Using Computable General Equilibrium Models to Facilitate Tax and Other Policy Reform in LDCs: Edward Tower, Professor of Economics, Duke University
Presenter: Glenn P. Jenkins, Harvard University
Commentator: Arnold Harberger, University of Chicago, University of California at Los Angeles

Second Session   William Ascher, Moderator

The Tax Mission to Japan: Carl S. Shoup, Professor Emeritus, Columbia University
Presenter: Hiroshi Kaneko, University of Tokyo
Commentator: Joseph Pechman, Brookings Institution

Tax Reform Initiatives in Sri Lanka: Glenn P. Jenkins, Lecturer of Economics, Harvard University
Presenter: Robert Conrad, Emory University
Commentator: Edward Tower, Duke University

Third Session   Roy Bahl, Jr., Moderator

The Indonesian Experience with Tax Reform, 1981–88: Malcolm Gillis, Duke University
Presenter: Edward Tower, Duke University
Commentator: Alan Tait, International Monetary Fund

Lessons From Four Fundamental Tax Reforms: Chile, Uruguay, Mexico and Indonesia: Arnold C. Harberger, Swift Distinguished Professor of Economics, University of Chicago, University of Los Angeles
Presenter: Charles E. McLure, Jr., Hoover Institution
Commentator: Robert Conrad, Emory University

Fourth Session   Edward Tower, Moderator

Analysis and Reform of the Colombian Tax System: Charles E. McLure, Jr., Senior Fellow, Hoover Institution
Presenter: Wayne Thirsk, World Bank
Commentator: William Ascher, Duke University

The Shoup Report of the Tax System of Brazil, 1964, and the Tax Mission to Venezuela, 1958–59: Carl S. Shoup, Columbia University
Presenter: Malcolm Gillis, Duke University
Commentator: Harvey Galper, Peat Marwick Main & Co.

April 23 (Saturday)

Fifth Session   William Ascher, Moderator

The Jamaican Tax Reform of 1986: Roy W. Bahl, Jr., Maxwell Professor of Political Economy, Syracuse University
Presenter: Vito Tanzi, International Monetary Fund
Commentator: Robert Bates, Duke University

Lessons for LDCs of U.S. Income Tax Reform: Charles E. McLure, Jr., Hoover Institution
Presenter: Emil Sunley, Deloitte, Haskins and Sells
Commentator: Zmarak Shalizi, World Bank

Sixth Session   Malcolm Gillis, Moderator

Risk, Politics, and Tax Reform: Lessons From Some Latin American Experiences: William Ascher, Professor of Public Policy Studies and Political Science, Duke University
Presenter: William Ascher, Duke University
Commentator: Richard Bird, University of Toronto

Political Economy of Tax Reform: A Political Scientist Looks at the Handiwork of Economists
Robert Bates, Professor of Political Science, Duke University
Presenter: Robert Bates, Duke University
Commentator: Roy Bahl, Syracuse University

Summary and Questions

Appendix 2

....

Biographical Data

....

William Ascher is professor of Public Policy and Political Science and codirector of the Center for International Development Research at Duke University. He is presently serving as project director for the International Commission for Central American Recovery and Development. He has also authored several books and numerous articles on comparative public policy, political development, and Latin American politics and has taught at the University of Pennsylvania and Johns Hopkins University.

Roy Bahl is Maxwell Professor of Political Economy at Syracuse University. He is a past president of the National Tax Association and is director of Jamaica's Comprehensive Tax Reform Research Project. He has served as an adviser to governments in many developing countries as well as to the World Bank, IMF, and USAID, and has written extensively in the area of public finance.

Robert Bates is Luce Professor of Political Economy and director of the Center in Political Economy at Duke University. The author of numerous books and articles on political and economic development, he served as consultant to USAID, the World Bank, and the State Department and has taught at California Institute of Technology. He has conducted extensive field research in Zambia, Uganda, and Kenya.

Richard Bird, professor of economics at the University of Toronto, presently holds the Tinbergen Chair at Erasmus University in Rotterdam. He has served as an adviser to the Colombian Ministry of Finance and as Chief of the Tax Policy Division of the International Monetary Fund. In addition, he has acted as a consultant to numerous developing countries and has published several books and a number of articles on taxation in developing countries. He has also taught at Harvard University.

Malcolm Gillis is professor of Public Policy Studies and Economics at Duke University. He is also dean of the Graduate School, vice-provost for Academic Affairs, and codirector of the Center for International Development Research. Professor Gillis works on tax policy, public sector management, and natural resource economics. He has overseen the design and adoption of new tax systems in several countries, including Indonesia and Colombia. He recently coauthored a leading text on developing countries and with a coauthor has recently finished a major study of public policies toward forest endowments around the world.

Arnold Harberger is Gustavus F. and Ann M. Swift Distinguished Service Professor of Economics at the University of Chicago and professor of economics at UCLA. He has written widely in the field of public finance and has consulted on tax policy issues with the governments of Argentina, Canada, Chile, Colombia, El Salvador, Indonesia, India, Mexico, Panama, and the United States, as well as with the International Monetary Fund, the Organization of American States, and the World Bank.

Glenn Jenkins is an Institute Fellow of the Harvard Institute for International Development as well as a lecturer on economics at Harvard. He has served as Assistant Deputy Minister Tax Policy, Department of Finance, Canada, and as a research consultant for the Economic Council of Canada. He has worked for the Ford Foundation on energy policy, and for the World Bank on taxation and pricing issues. Overseas assignments have included work with the governments of Malaysia, Indonesia, Sri Lanka, and Bolivia. Dr. Jenkins has published widely in the fields of economic development, public finance, resource economics, and investment appraisal.

Charles McLure is a senior fellow at the Hoover Institution at Stanford University. He served as deputy assistant secretary of the Treasury for Tax Analysis from 1983 to 1985 and as senior economist on the staff of the President's Council of Economic Advisers from 1969–70. McLure has written extensively on federal tax reform, the value-added tax, relief from double taxation of dividends, state taxation of natural resources, state corporation income taxes, and taxation in developing countries.

Carl Shoup is professor emeritus, Columbia University, where he was on the faculty from 1928 to 1971. He has served as an interregional adviser on tax reform planning for the United Nations and has directed tax reform missions to Japan, Venezuela, and Liberia. He has authored a study of the tax system of Brazil for the Ministry of Finance and coauthored two tax studies requested by the prerevolutionary Cuban government.

Ed Tower is a professor of economics at Duke University. He has consulted for the U.S. Treasury, the World Bank, the U.S. Agency for International Development and the Harvard Institute for International Development and has worked on projects in Indonesia, Malawi, Malaysia, and Sudan. His publications have focused on international development economics, tax and trade policy, and recently on protectionism and modeling techniques for project and policy analysis in less developed countries.

Index

....